CW00767555

CONVICTS AND THE COLONIES

by the same author

★

THE STORY OF AUSTRALIA

CONVICTS
AND THE COLONIES

A Study of Penal Transportation
from Great Britain and Ireland
to Australia and other parts
of the British Empire

A. G. L. SHAW

Professor of History
Monash University, Victoria
formerly Senior Lecturer in History
University of Sydney

MELBOURNE UNIVERSITY PRESS

First published 1966 by
Faber & Faber Ltd, London
First Melbourne University Press edition, in paperback, 1977
Reprinted 1978, 1981

Printed in Hong Kong by
Silex Enterprise and Printing Co., for
Melbourne University Press, Carlton, Victoria 3053
U.S.A. and Canada: International Scholarly Book Services, Inc.,
P.O. Box 1632, Beaverton, OR 97075
Great Britain, Europe, the Middle East, Africa and the Caribbean:
Eurospan Limited, 3 Henrietta Street, London WC2E 8LU

National Library of Australia Cataloguing in Publication data

Shaw, Alan George Lewers, 1916— .
    Convicts and the colonies.
    Index.
    First published, London: Faber and Faber, 1966.
    Bibliography.
    ISBN 0 522 84114 7.
    1. Penal Colonies, British. 2. Convicts — Australia — History.
    3. Australia — Exiles. I. Title.
365.30994

Contents

Tables

Every portrait that is painted with feeling is a portrait of the artist, not of the sitter. The sitter is merely the accident, the occasion. It is not he who is revealed by the painter; it is rather the painter who . . . reveals himself.

OSCAR WILDE

Preface

The working of the system of convict transportation to Australia has proved a subject far more complex and more extensive than it appeared when I began to study it in 1950. Even though it had to be laid aside for five years owing to my illness and other pressing work, it has taken longer than I expected and is even yet incomplete. Although I have reached a number of conclusions they need to be confirmed (or perhaps refuted) by detailed investigations both of the districts from which the convicts came, and of those they were sent to; for it is only from such studies that the whole truth can emerge, and at the moment these are extremely rare. Three works of research have nonetheless been of great value to me. First that of Mr. Brian Fletcher, of the University of New South Wales, on small-scale agriculture in the early days of New South Wales throws the light of careful scholarship on the activities of the first emancipist farmers in the colony. Secondly, the study by Miss Anne McKay (now Mrs. Rand) of the University of Tasmania of the assignment system in Van Diemen's Land under Lieutenant-Governor Arthur provides an important examination of his policy and its administration, even though its 'generality', like that of this work, demands the further local studies of the type of which I have been speaking. Last, is the examination of convict origins by Dr. L. L. Robson of the Australian National University, Canberra, made from a sample of one in twenty of all those transported. I was extremely gratified to find Dr. Robson's conclusions, reached by a statistical study of information on the convict indents, were very similar to my own. Nonetheless it is no criticism of this to say that once again further detailed studies of particular areas and groups are needed to fill out the picture sketched by both of us, and I hope some of the next generation of Ph.D. students may be persuaded to tackle them, and also to investigate in more detail some of the economic implications of the transportation system.

I am indebted to the Nuffield Foundation for enabling me to begin this work by the grant of a Fellowship in 1950-1. Since then many others, both officials and friends, have given me most valuable assistance. To librarians and archivists, I have been most troublesome in London in the Public Record Office and British Museum, in Dublin in the State Paper Office, in Sydney in the Mitchell Library and in Hobart in the State Archives where Mr. Peter Eldershaw's advice and assistance were invaluable; and there are many others. Mr. Brian Dickie helped me in my searches among the convict indents and others whose advice has enabled me to improve the manuscript are innumerable; but I should like especially to thank Dr. Robson and Mr. Fletcher for their ready help, the late Mr. John Forsyth of Avalon, New South Wales, for his valuable criticism, and of my colleagues at the University of Sydney, Jules Ginswick, Dr. Hazel King, Marlay Stephen and Professor John Ward for their wise counsels. To all these, and many others, I am most grateful, and especially to my wife, who if not a professional critic, fulfilled what is an even more important function in sustaining morale by encouragement in times of stress.

Sydney
1964

A. G. L. SHAW

Note on References

In addition to a list of manuscript sources, parliamentary papers and newspapers, a select bibliography will be found on p. 369. This includes books, articles and unpublished theses, and gives full publication details. For any work which is listed there, in the footnotes there is reference only to the author's name, or to a short identifying title where it is needed. The titles of works on peripheral subjects which are not listed in the bibliography are given in full in the footnotes.

The despatches between the secretaries and under-secretaries of state and the colonial governors will all be found in their respective series in the Colonial Office papers. Most of those referred to here have been printed, either in the *Historical Records of Australia*, series i for New South Wales to 1847, and series iii for Tasmania to 1827, or in *Parliamentary Papers*. To save what overall amounts to very considerable space, I have not except in special circumstances referred to the printed collections, where the despatches may easily be found by reference to the date of writing.

The following abbreviations have been used:

AHR:	American Historical Review.
ANU:	Australian National University, Canberra.
APC:	Acts of the Privy Council of England.
BM, Add. MSS.:	Additional Manuscripts, British Museum.
Cal. HO:	Calendar, Home Office Papers.
Cal. SP Col.:	Calendar of State Papers, Colonial.
CJ:	House of Commons' Journals.
CO:	Colonial Office Records, Public Record Office, London.
Col. Sec.:	Colonial Secretary.
Nat. Lib. Dub.:	National Library, Dublin.

Ed.R.:	Edinburgh Review.
Enc.:	Encyclopaedia.
G and GO:	Government and General Order.
HL:	House of Lords.
HMC:	Historical Manuscripts Commission.
HO:	Home Office Records, Public Record Office.
HRA:	Historical Records of Australia (Ser. I, unless otherwise stated).
HRNSW:	Historical Records of New South Wales.
Hist. Stud.	Historical Studies, Australia and New Zealand.
JRAHS:	Journal of the Royal Australian Historical Society.
LQR:	Law Quarterly Review.
ML:	Mitchell Library, Sydney.
NSW:	New South Wales.
NY:	New York.
P. Debs.:	Parliamentary Debates.
P. Hist.:	Parliamentary History.
PP:	Parliamentary Papers.
P.Reg.:	Parliamentary Register.
PRO:	Public Record Office, London.
PLV:	Public Library of Victoria.
QR:	Quarterly Review.
Roy.Ir.Acad.:	Royal Irish Academy.
SC:	Select Committee.
SPO:	State Paper Office, Dublin.
T:	Treasury.
Tas. Arch.:	Archives Division, Public Library of Tasmania.
Tas. Hist. Assoc.:	Tasmanian Historical Research Association, Papers and Proceedings.
V & P:	Votes and Proceedings.
VDL:	Van Diemen's Land.

Introduction

For eighty years after the foundation of Australia, the transportation of British criminals was integrally bound up with her national development, both political and economic; but transportation was not only important to Australia, it had long been both an element in British colonial policy and a statutory punishment for certain types of crime. As a method of punishment, to British ministers it seemed to have many advantages. It was cheap. The fear of it would deter potential malefactors. It would remove from the country the criminals it had failed to deter, while at the same time it would assist their 'reformation' by providing them with an opportunity to turn over a new leaf in a different environment, where they could readily find employment and so earn their livelihood by honest work. To the colonies, it would provide a sorely needed labour force, and so aid their economic progress.

Such was the theory; but in practice it seemed to work differently. First, the steady increase in crime, which accompanied the development of industry and commerce and the growth of the towns, showed that transportation did not effectively deter felons from their misdeeds. At first it was said to be administered too leniently and the cry for increased severity was continually to be heard. In the early days, conditions in the colonies were so primitive that merely sending men there was a severe punishment; but this was not enough when ordered communities had emerged, so colonial governors were told to make the discipline more rigorous. If only they would do so, this would put an end to crime in the mother country, it was said, in the same way that our enlightened contemporaries are convinced that severer punishments will speedily put an end to murder, rape, juvenile delinquency and motoring offences in modern society. Secretaries of State issued their instructions and the governors strove to implement them; in one way or another the system was tightened up, until it reached the height of its severity on the very eve of its abolition. After 1839, all prisoners, whatever their crime, on their arrival in the colony, were to be 'coerced' for a period in gangs, where there would be none of the favouritism or laxity which was so often found in private service; but this procedure soon proved objectionable to the colonists, while those who disliked it as a punishment continued their search for some alternative which would be a more effective deterrent, such as imprisonment in the new model penitentiaries that were just coming into fashion.

Though one support for transportation was thus removed, others remained. To build the penitentiaries, which did not exist, would be costly. The prison hulks and many of the old gaols would have to be replaced and the whole prison system remodelled. This was an expense which for years no British government was prepared to countenance; until it did so, transportation had to remain. It was defended as a cheap punishment. For half a century, bitter protagonists had been hurling figures at one another, giving conflicting estimates of costs; but gradually it began to appear that transportation would never be as cheap as some hoped. Colonial governors were as repeatedly ordered to economize as they were told to be rigorous, and the British government continually looked forward to expenditure falling as more settlers became ready to take prisoners off its hands, to act, in other words, as private gaolers, for nothing. But when they did so, they were accused of being too lenient, while, when the governors kept men in the penal gangs, for punishment and discipline, they were told that they were retaining too many at public expense. The convict that would cost little or nothing was the well-behaved convict; but not all convicts were well behaved. True they could generally be employed on public works; but these, though useful, benefited the colony and not the British government; to the latter they seemed only a needless drain on the Treasury, a drain made all the greater when all prisoners were ordered to be 'coerced' on their arrival.

One possible solution to this problem of expense was to make the colonists pay; and so Great Britain made repeated efforts to transfer the responsibility for expenditure to the colonial treasuries. They could pay for the police and gaols needed to control the prisoners; they could pay for the public works the prisoners carried out; colonial employers could be asked to pay for the private services of the convicts. These proposals at once aroused colonial opposition. If the boon of free, or at least cheap, labour were removed, why should they accept British criminals at all? As their objections grew more vociferous, appeals to their Imperial patriotism or to their humanitarian feelings fell on deaf ears.

But if transportation was not cheap, would it not be simpler for Britain to pay for the punishment of her criminals at home? This would be more effective in penitentiaries there. Moreover the object of punishment was not only to *deter* future criminals, but to *reform* past offenders; in the new penitentiaries, solitary confinement, separation from evil associates, silent meditation and the reading of the Bible would produce a lasting reformation. There would be none of the abuses of the old overcrowded and often filthy prisons. Prisoners would be properly fed, and kept clean and healthy, while at the same time undergoing the hard labour which both deterred and inculcated those 'habits of industry', which were also a necessary part of reformation. Humanitarianism demanded a penitentiary system.

True, it had long been thought that criminals would reform themselves 'naturally' in the colonies; but did they? Of this no one was quite sure. Certainly some convicts committed fresh crimes there, duly noted by the opponents of transportation; on the other hand, its supporters observed that the crime rate was very much lower than might have been expected in such communities. Apparently for many, conditions were conducive to reform; they found, said Herman Merivale in his lectures on colonization in 1841, 'space for exertion, reward for industry and a comparative oblivion for the past';[1] but critics pointed to the 'association' and contamination of the criminals and the lack of facilities for their training. Could the penitentiary training of the separate system be combined with the advantages of emigration, by being followed by 'exile' to colonies where the prisoners could readily find honest employment?

Such a policy had the advantage of removing criminals from the United Kingdom, but it struck opposition in the colonies. Deprived of their free labour, the colonists began to notice the unfortunate moral effects of this criminal influx. Free migrants and native-born children were beginning to supply the labour for development for which convicts had once been so necessary. Colonial workmen observed that English convicts were competing with them in the labour market. Others noticed that the necessary restrictions on a convict population interfered with their own political rights, such as the freedom of the press, freedom from arbitrary arrest, trial by jury and, ultimately, the granting of local self-government through popularly elected assemblies. For one reason or another colonial protests grew, to add their weight to the arguments that were making British ministers reconsider their

[1] Merivale, ii, 18. He was Drummond Professor of Political Economy at Oxford, 1837-42.

whole policy of penal transportation. And so ultimately it was abandoned, not because it was too severe, but because it was not severe enough, and neither reformatory enough nor cheap enough to justify overriding colonial wishes, once these wishes had been clearly expressed.

But the policy had done much for the colonies, and for most of its history was not unpopular there. It provided a labour force both for public works and private employment when labour was urgently needed, and in the case of Australia provided a substitute for coolies and slaves. The prisoners and their guards provided a market for local produce, and the commissariat an invaluable stimulus to the local economy, at a time when it was impossible to export foodstuffs. Even the large official establishment which the presence of the convicts made necessary may be said to have promoted not only the economic development of the community, but its social, intellectual and cultural life as well.

When in 1840 the British government stopped the transportation of criminals to New South Wales and their assignment in Van Diemen's Land, the changes were widely criticized in the former and universally condemned in the latter; only Britain's complete disregard, in the following decade, of the economic conditions on which the system was founded and of the necessary relation between the supply of convict labour and the demand for it caused the growth of widespread criticism of transportation as a whole. Thus colonial protests against the reception of convicts came to coincide with British misgivings about the penal effectiveness of the system; and if special circumstances caused it to be allowed to linger on a little longer in Western Australia, its end was clearly in sight; but if obstinacy at the Colonial Office made it the cause of bitter disputes in the 1840s, overall it had played a most important and valuable role in both British penology and Australian development.

'As a means of making men outwardly honest, of converting vagabonds, the most useless men in one country into active citizens of another and thus giving birth to a new and splendid centre of civilization, it has succeeded to a degree unequalled in history,' said Herman Merivale, just as the assignment system was being stopped. Though this was then yet another 'lost cause', it had achieved great things in the past.

I

Crime and Transportation Before the American Revolution

'Of sloth cometh pleasure, of pleasure cometh ryot, of ryot comes whoring, of whoring comes spending, of spending comes want, of want comes theft, of theft comes hanging.'

Eastward Hoe (1605), Act IV, sc. ii

Execution is a simple punishment, quick, effective, economical, but not merciful. Hence perhaps the resort to what seemed to many to be the next best thing–banishment. This at least satisfied the society from which the criminals were expelled, if no one else. There was no need to worry about their behaviour in future; the process was cheap; the receiving society could usually be ignored, though Hume suggested that the custom of banishment in Scotland arose from the chronic hostility which the Scots felt towards the English.[1] Whether or not from respect for the foreigner, in England the king had no right to compel a subject to leave the country, despite the famous case of Richard II and Henry Bolingbroke which Shakespeare has made memorable; in this, as in several other matters, Richard seems to have overridden the common law, 'deprived men of their property and inheritances and driven them into exile by arbitrary act'.[2]

Medieval banishment might follow a legal verdict, as Magna Carta had laid down; but it was usually a voluntary 'abjuration of the realm ... backed up by the intervention of the spiritual power', after an accused had taken sanctuary.[3] The prisoner chose the punishment himself, and

---

[1] Hume, *Commentaries*, ii, 369. The lower courts in Scotland could banish an offender merely from a burgh or county, leaving him free to reside elsewhere in the kingdom (*Enc. of Laws of Scotland* (1928), v, art. on 'Criminal Law', sec. 742).

[2] May McKisack, *The Fourteenth Century, 1307–1399* (OUP, 1959), 487 and 496.

[3] Craies, *LQR*, vi, 388, 393–5; cf. Holdsworth, xi, 568 ff.

he went into exile on the understanding that this would modify any other penalty (usually death) that he would otherwise have suffered. Elizabethan statutes substituted banishment for martyrdom for Jesuit priests in 1585 and for both Popish recusants and nonconformist sectaries in 1593, 'to the end that the realm be not pestered and over-charged with the multitude of such seditious and dangerous people . . . who having little or no ability to answer or satisfy any competent penalty for their . . . disobedience . . . and being committed to prison do live for the most part in better case there than they could do if they were abroad . . . '.[1] In 1667, the House of Lords refused to commit the Earl of Clarendon for trial for treason, though after he had fled, it assented to an act for his perpetual exile;[2] but by this time, parliament was pre-scribing transportation (rather than semi-voluntary exile) as the normal punishment for an increasing variety of offences.

This was probably the result of combining two vague ideas of primi-tive justice – that a society should get rid of its troublesome members (just as it had banished them in the past), who, at the same time, might be asked to carry out arduous, dangerous or unpleasant tasks for the common good. Here lay an obvious connection with colonization. Portu-gal, Spain and France had used criminals and vagrants as colonizers in the fifteenth and sixteenth centuries, and England was ready to follow suit. In 1584, Richard Hakluyt, in his *Discourse of Western Planting*, included among the advantages of colonization the value of colonies as outlets for those seeking work, or for 'sturdy vagabonds', so that 'the fry of the wandering beggars of England that grow up idly, and . . . burdenous to this realm, may there be unladen, better bred up and may people waste countries.' He assumed there was surplus labour in the mother-country, and thought it might be employed in the colonies; in fact the surplus hardly existed, so if colonies were wanted for com-mercial reasons, at least some of the labour needed for them would have to be forced.[3]

In England a Vagrancy Act in 1547 had authorized magistrates to hand

---

[1] An Act against Jesuits and Seminary Priests, 1585 (27 Eliz. c. 2), an Act against Popish Recusants, 1593 (35 Eliz. c.2) and an Act against Seditious Sectaries, 1593 (35 Eliz. c.1), J. R. Tanner, *Tudor Constitutional Documents* (CUP, 1930), 154–63 and 197–200; Craies, *op. cit.*, 395–6; Conyers Read, *Lord Burghley and Queen Elizabeth* (Cape, 1960), 489.
[2] For Clarendon, D. Ogg, *England in the Reign of Charles II* (1934), 315–7, and Douglas, *Documents*, viii, 1660–1714, 193–8.
[3] Taylor (ed.), *Writings of the Hakluyts*, ii, 211 and 319; Douglas, *Documents*, ix, 103–6; cf. Sir George Peckham, *Discourse of the Necessitie and Commoditie of Planting English Colonies upon the North Partes of America* (1583), R. H. Tawney and E. Power, *Tudor Economic Documents* (1924), iii, 257; E. E. Rich, *New Cambridge Modern History*, i (CUP, 1957), 456.

over idle persons who refused to work to masters who would compel them to, thus making them virtually slaves; though this Act was repealed in 1550, Parliament revived the principle in 1598 when it enacted that any rogues appearing 'dangerous to the inferior sort of people' or 'such as will not be reformed of their roguish kind of life' were to be 'banished out of this realm . . . and conveyed unto such parts beyond the seas as shall be at any time hereafter assyned for that purpose by the Privy Council . . . or otherwise be judged perpetually to the galleys of this realm'. In 1601, the Privy Council ordered some 'able vagrants' to be offered the choice of military service in the Netherlands instead of being 'whipped and corrected as they ought to be', but the local magistrates seem to have ignored a proclamation two years later that incorrigible rogues could be sent to Newfoundland, the East or West Indies, Spain, the Netherlands, France or Germany.[1]

However, if local authorities were unwilling to transport vagrants, the Privy Council was more ready to transport criminals. In 1577, some 'condemned men' had been recruited for Frobisher's second voyage in search of the north-west passage; though all had had to be dismissed before the expedition started, despite this unfortunate experience, more were sent to Virginia after its foundation in 1607, as well as 'unruly youths . . . (of most leaud and bad condition) . . . lascivious sonnes . . . bad servants and ill husbands', who combined to 'clogge the business' and aroused Bacon's famous protest,

'It is a shameful and unblessed thing to take the scum of the people and wicked and condemned men, to be the people with whom you plant; and not only so, but it spoileth the plantation; for they will ever live like rogues and not fall to work but be lazy and do mischief ...'[2]

Though some adventurers might go to seek their fortunes, without the political or religious persecution which stimulated emigration, who else but convicts and vagabonds could supply the need for common labourers? Sir Thomas Dale asked for 'offenders out of the common gaols' for Virginia in 1611, and to James I and his Council, increasing crime at home and the colonies' need for labour overrode any objections like those of Bacon. In the hope that prisoners 'might be rather

---

[1] Tanner, *op. cit.*, 470–1 (1 Ed. vi, c.3 and 3 and 4 Ed. vi, c.16) and 485–8 (39 Eliz. c.4); Simpson, *LQR*, xv, 37–9.

[2] Richard Hakluyt, 'A true report of such things as happened in the second voyage of captaine Frobisher, pretended for the discovery of a new passage to Cataya, China and the East India, by the Northwest. Ann. Dom. 1577', in Hakluyt, *Voyages and Documents*, 157; 'A Broadside by the Council of Virginia' (1610), in Alexander Brown, *Genesis of the United States* (London, 1890), 354–5; Francis Bacon, 'Of Plantations', *Essays* (Everyman Edn.), 104.

corrected than destroyed and that in their punishmentes some may live and yeald a profitable service to the commonwealthe in partes abroad', in 1615 the Council ordered that those found guilty of 'anie robberie or fellonie (wilfull murther, rape, witchcraft or burglarie only excepted)' might be used for service in the East Indies or the American plantations. It also argued that the punishment would be a deterrent, for when it renewed the 'commission for reprieving' in July 1622, and added the alternative of working the men in chains in England, it remarked that the service would be 'usefull and beneficiall to the commonwealth' and 'a greater terror than death itself'. For all that, transportation was only 'a desultory process', and between 1615 and 1640, only 123 reprieved felons seem to have been sent out.[1]

During the English civil wars transportation practically ceased, but neither the Commonwealth government nor Oliver Cromwell forgot it afterwards. Many Irish war prisoners were sent to Virginia, Barbados and Jamaica, and in 1655 the practice of transporting convicts with conditional pardons under the Great Seal began; though a bill drafted in 1653 for the transporting of vagrants to the plantations seems to have got lost after Cromwell became Protector, in 1656 the Council of State ordered the 'apprehending of lewd and dangerous persons . . . who have no way of livelihood . . . and treating with merchants for transporting them to the English plantations in America'.[2]

After the Restoration, transported political offenders included religious recusants, Scottish Covenanters and in 1685 supporters of Monmouth's rebellion. One of the motives for introducing, in 1670, the bill which ultimately became the famous Habeas Corpus Act of 1679 was to forbid transportation without trial, 'a necessary remedy in these times of transportation to Jamaica and Tangier'; although the bill, if passed, would, it was said, 'leave to the King no power for orderly government', passed it was, if only by a trick.[3] This Act also legalized the practice of pardoning criminals on the condition that they agreed to be transported to the colonies for a term of years, though it had then been regularly going on since 1655. Between then and 1699, about 4,500 criminals were transported in this way; others were sentenced to

---

[1] Sir Thomas Dale to Salisbury, 17 Aug. 1611, *Cal. SP Col.*, 1574–1660, 11–12; *APC*, 1615–1616, 23–5 and 248; vol. 35 (new ser.), 1616–1617, 201 and 301; vol. 36 (new ser.), 1617–1619, 82, 170, 232, 259, 285, 327, 369, 418; 1621–23, 206, 294, 310, 356.

[2] Smith, *AHR*, xxxix, 233–6; *Cal. SP Col.*, *loc. cit.*, 360, 412, 447 and 461; Craies, *op. cit.*, 401–2.

[3] Holdsworth, ix, 117; Helen Nutting, *AHR*, lxv, 527 and 532. The trick was the miscounting of the votes in the House of Lords, Douglas, *Documents*, viii, 96; the Act was 31 Car. II c.2.

transportation as the regular punishment now prescribed for their offences, such as a third conviction under the Acts against Quakers who refused to take oaths, or the Conventicle Act against dissenters, for border brigandage, stealing cloth from racks, embezzling the King's stores, or burning ricks or barns at night.[1]

During the eighteenth century, the transportation system developed so that by 1775 it had become a major ingredient of English criminal law. The preamble to the Transportation Act of 1718 declared that its purpose was both to deter criminals and to supply the colonies with labour. Since 'in many of His Majesty's colonies and plantations in America there is a great want of servants', persons convicted of 'grand or petit larceny or any felonious stealing or taking of money or goods and chattels, either from the person, or the house of any other', might be sentenced to seven years transportation to America, if they were entitled to the benefit of clergy, which, in 1705, had been extended to all first offenders, provided their crime had not been made 'non-clergyable' by statute, and so capital even for a first offence. Thus transportation might be a useful and merciful substitute for execution, by an act of royal mercy, as a reprieve or commutation of punishment; it might be a lesser penalty awarded by statute; and it might be the punishment prescribed for a first offender, who could claim 'his clergy', for, as Blackstone wrote, the 'wisdom of the English legislature' had 'extracted by a noble alchemy rich medicine out of poisonous ingredients, and converted what was at first an unreasonable exemption of particular popish ecclesiastics into a merciful mitigation of the general law with regard to capital punishment'.[2]

In 1688, there were about fifty capital offences, but between 1660 and 1819, 187 more 'capital statutes' were passed. According to the law, death was the *only* punishment for all these very different offences; to avoid uncertainty, the courts, in passing sentence, had no power to notice any extenuating circumstances or to discriminate between offenders (except those entitled to benefit of clergy, where it had not been specifically removed by statute). But if the sentence was certain for prescribed crimes, the laws were completely unsystematic, extremely confused, inconsistent and ill-coordinated. For example, in 1766 a

---

[1] Holdsworth, xi, 570–1; Smith, *loc. cit.*, 238; Ogg, *op. cit.*, 120–1, 206–7 and 489; 13 and 14 Car. II, c.1; 16 Car. II, c.4; 18 Car. II, c.3; 22 Car. II, c.5 and 22; 23 Car. II, c.7; *Cal. SP Col., America and the West Indies, 1661–1668*, nos. 101, 122, 371, 378, 523, 701, 1430 and 1431.

[2] Douglas, *Documents*, ix, 460 ff. (4 Geo. I, c.11); 6 Anne, c.9; Blackstone, bk, iv, ch. 28, p. 364, and cf. ch. 29. On benefit of clergy, Cross, *AHR*, xxii, 556. See Radzinowicz, i, Appendix 1, Capital Statutes of the Eighteenth Century, 611–59.

statute imposed a fine of £20 for an offence which a few months previously had been made a capital felony, and without making any reference to the previous act, which was therefore not repealed. Many acts were passed to meet some passing 'emergency', such as the 'Waltham Black Act' in 1722 'for the more effectual punishing wicked and evil disposed Persons going armed in disguise'. Many quite serious crimes were lightly punished; attempted murder, for example, was only a misdemeanour until 1803, unless the injured party was maimed. But during the eighteenth century, Parliament steadily tightened up the definitions of larceny and house-breaking. It made into felonies 'without benefit of clergy', that is punishable by death for a first offence, the stealing or injuring of more and more different types of property–lead, iron bars, gates, fruits, trees, ponds, canal-banks, hop-binds, timber, deer, fish, dogs, goods in shipwrecks, bonds, bank notes, promissory notes and bills of exchange, as well as food, furniture, livestock and clothing. It reduced the minimum value of the goods stolen necessary for the death penalty and added new places where the crime could be committed. It removed the necessity for 'putting-in-fear' or 'breaking in'.[1]

In 1797, according to Colquhoun, crimes punishable by death included treason and petty treason, counterfeiting gold and silver coin, murder, arson, rape, stealing an heiress, sodomy, forgery of deeds, bonds, bills, notes, public securities, the embezzling of notes or altering of dividend warrants by Bank of England clerks, piracy, destroying ships, or setting them on fire, the concealment of effects by bankrupts, burglary, house-breaking by day or night, highway robbery, privately stealing (i.e. by picking pockets) more than one shilling, shoplifting goods worth more than five shillings, stealing bonds, bills, or bank notes, stealing articles worth more than £2 in any house or on a river, stealing linen from bleaching grounds, or destroying it there, maiming or killing cattle maliciously, stealing horses, cattle or sheep, shooting at a revenue officer, pulling down houses or churches, breaking down the head of a fish-pond, 'whereby fish may be lost', cutting down trees in an avenue or garden, cutting down river or sea banks, cutting hop-binds, setting fire to coal mines, taking reward for helping another to stolen goods, returning from transportation or being at large in the kingdom

---

[1] Radzinowicz, 4–5, 23 and 49–79. Blackstone said there were 160 capital felonies in England, bk. iv, ch. 1, p. 18; Romilly in his *Memoirs* claimed there were 222. According to J. Lawrence (*History of Capital Punishment in Great Britain*, 12–15, quoted O'Brien, 52, note), 190 capital offences were abolished between 1820 and 1860. The Waltham Black Act was 9 Geo. I, c. 27; several times extended it was made perpetual by 31 Geo. II, c. 42. See Blackstone on the law of larceny, *op. cit.*, ch. 17, and his criticism of this severity, *ib.*, p. 4.

after sentence, stabbing a person unarmed or not having a weapon drawn, if he die in six months, concealing the death of a bastard child, maliciously maiming or disfiguring any person, or lying in wait for the purpose, sending threatening letters, not dispersing in an hour after the reading of the Riot Act, being accessories to felonies deemed capital, stealing woollen cloth from tenter grounds, stealing from a ship in distress, or from government stores, embezzling, burning or destroying in dockyards, challenging more than twenty jurors in capital felonies, selling cottons with forged stamps, deer-stealing, second offence, uttering counterfeit money, third offence, destroying silk or velvet in the loom, or the tools for manufacturing it, or destroying woollen goods, racks or tools, or entering a house for that purpose, the purloining by servants of their masters' goods worth 40 shillings, personating bail, or acknowledging fines or judgments in another's name, breaking prison, attempting to kill Privy Councillors, sacrilege, smuggling by persons armed, or assembling armed for that purpose, robbery of the mail, destroying turnpikes or bridges, gates, weighing engines, locks, sluices, engines for draining marshes, soldiers or sailors committing mutiny, deserting or enlisting into foreign service.

In addition to this heterogeneous list of capital offences, crimes punishable by transportation, whipping, imprisonment, the pillory, or hard labour in houses of correction included: grand larceny, which comprehended 'every species of theft above the value of One shilling, not otherwise distinguished', receiving or buying stolen goods, jewels and plate, ripping and stealing lead, iron, copper, or buying or receiving it, stealing (or receiving when stolen) ore from black lead mines, stealing from furnished lodgings, setting fire to underwood, stealing letters, or destroying a letter or packet, advancing the postage and secreting the money, embezzling naval stores, petty larcenies, or thefts under one shilling, assaulting with intent to rob, stealing fish from a pond or river, fishing in enclosed ponds, or buying stolen fish, stealing roots, trees, or plants of the value of 5 shillings or destroying them, stealing children with their apparel, bigamy, manslaughter, assaulting and cutting or burning clothes, counterfeiting the copper coin, solemnizing marriage clandestinely, cutting or stealing timber trees or stealing a shroud out of a grave; even a Thames waterman might be transported if he was carrying too many passengers and any were drowned, and so might an alien who returned after being ordered out of the kingdom. On the other hand, though the distinction is difficult to see, perjury, fraud, conspiracy to defraud, assaults, stealing dead bodies, cabbages or turnips growing, deer or dogs, robbing orchards, cutting or stealing wood and trees, setting fire to a house to defraud the insurance, selling fireworks or throwing them about the streets, uttering base money, defrauding the customs and excise, conspiring to raise wages, and keeping bawdy houses were all only misdemeanours, and *not* punishable either by death or transportation.[1]

'No man of common humanity or common sense can think the Life of a Man and a few shillings to be of equal Consideration, or that the Law in punishing Theft with Death proceeds with any view to vengeance,' insisted Henry Fielding; but 'the Terror of Example is the thing proposed, and one man is sacrificed for the Preservation of Thousands.' 'Nothing sanctions the punishment of death but the terror of example as a prevention of crime,' declared Colquhoun fifty years later. This was at least logical, for as Radzinowicz points out, 'Once the death penalty is established as the most effective instrument of crime prevention, there can be no valid reason for invoking it to suppress one offence and not another.'[2]

On the Home Circuit, between 1688 and 1718, and between 1754 and 1794, about one in eight of those *committed* for trial (i.e. including those acquitted) was sentenced to death, but of course many of these death sentences were not carried out. Between 1761 and 1765, few more than half of those sentenced in London were executed, and two-thirds on the Norfolk and Midland circuits were reprieved. In all, 566 death sentences were commuted; of these felons, of whom 490 were convicted of some form of theft, sixty-one were transported for life, 415 for fourteen years and twenty-seven for various other periods; forty-four were granted a free pardon and twelve were pardoned on condition that they enlisted in the armed forces.[3]

Since the practice of reprieving prisoners from execution on condition that they agreed to be transported to the plantations had only become common after the Restoration, although the population was increasing and more offences were made 'capital', the numbers executed actually fell. In Devon in 1598 seventy-four criminals were sentenced to death; in London and Middlesex, on the average there were about 140 executions a year between 1607 and 1616. Both these figures suggest

---

[1] Colquhoun, *Treatise* (4th edn.), 437–442.
[2] Henry Fielding, *Inquiry*, 118–120; Colquhoun, *op. cit.* (7th edn.), 453; Radzinowicz, 49 and 149–50; Holdsworth, xi, 530–536.
[3] Radzinowicz, 119–120, 146 ff. and 325. Howard, *Prisons* (1784), tables 9 and 10, 482–3, shows that more than half of those sentenced to death in London between 1749 and 1772 were executed; by 1797, Colquhoun (5th edn, 297) estimated that four-fifths were reprieved; between 1800 and 1810, according to Romilly (*Speeches*, i, 108 ff.) only between 10 and 15 per cent were executed.

that over the whole country about two thousand people were executed every year—equivalent to nearly three thousand a year in the mid-eighteenth century—or nearly three times as many as were sentenced to death, let alone actually hanged.[1] Between 1749 and 1799 in London and Middlesex, despite the excitements of the eight 'hanging days' at Tyburn each year, when the journeymen took a holiday to see the fun, the average number executed was only thirty-four; London now comprised about one-eighth of England's population, but the 'execution rate' in the country was very much less than that of the metropolis, so probably less than two hundred were hanged each year.[2] Since about a thousand a year were transported, this very bloodthirsty-looking criminal code punished only about twelve hundred a year severely, which is very much less than might have been expected.

But this quality of mercy, even if 'twice blessed', reduced the felon's fear of punishment, the deterrence so much relied upon by contemporary legislators. 'To show mankind that crimes are sometimes pardoned, and that punishment is not the necessary consequence, is to nourish the flattering hope of impunity, and is the cause of their considering every punishment inflicted as an act of injustice and oppression,' wrote Beccaria, the great apostle of criminal law reform, in 1764; but the traditional view was that, since the circumstances of crime varied, the executive must have power to vary the punishment, though why this discretion should not have been left to the courts, when they sentenced the guilty, was not convincingly shown.[3]

George III always attended to reprieves himself. He was personally severe on forgers, but generally, in exercising the prerogative of mercy, followed the advice of the trial judge—as did his son. Unfortunately the judges' recommendations were both variable and unpredictable. Sometimes reprieves would be granted because of the youth of the culprit; but in 1814, according to Romilly, the Prince Regent determined 'in

[1] Radzinowicz, 139 ff.; A. L. Rowse, *England of Elizabeth* (Macmillan, 1950), 348, quoting A. H. A. Hamilton, *Quarter Sessions from Queen Elizabeth to Queen Anne* (1878), 30–32, and cf. 71; Jeaffreson, i, p. xx, and cf. iii, pp. xxi and xxxix. Cf. D. Hume, *History of England*, iv, 726, John Strype, *Annals*, iv, 290. For population estimates, Rowse, *loc. cit.*, H. C. Darby, *Historical Geography of England before A.D. 1800* (CUP, 1951), 435; P. Hughes, *Reformation in England* (Hollis and Carter, 1952), i, 32–4; W. K. Jordan, *Philanthropy in England, 1480–1660* (Allen and Unwin, 1958), 26–7; G. N. Clark, *Wealth of England* (OUP, 1946), 41–3.

[2] Radzinowicz, 146 ff., 166 ff. and tables vi, vii and ix; George, 208; *Criminal Laws Report*, PP 1819 (585), 125 ff. and app.

[3] Beccaria, ch. 46, and Blackstone, both quoted, Holdsworth, xi, 577–8. On Beccaria generally, see Phillipson.

consequence of the number of boys who have lately been detected in committing felonies, to make an example of the next offender of this description who shall be convicted, in order to give an effectual check to the numerous instances of youthful depravity'; this was partly to deter parents teaching their children to steal and hoping they would escape punishment because of their age.[1] A first offence was usually a reason for reprieve from execution, but first offenders were sometimes sent to transportation rather than to prison, especially if the criminal were young or previously of good character, so that they might be removed from evil associates and be given a fresh opportunity in life–a curious mixture of beliefs regarding the purpose of the punishment. In one case Lord Eldon admitted having 'left for execution' a man whom a jury had found guilty of stealing a very miserable horse, worth only seven shillings and sixpence. 'The punishment of death for this offence only might appear extremely harsh,' he said, 'but, my Lords, . . . it appeared that on the prisoner were found skeleton keys of all the turnpike-gates within twenty miles of London, which he had manifestly procured for carrying on the business of a horse-stealer.' However villainous the culprit was, he had not in fact been tried for the offence for which he was actually executed.[2]

Transportation to the American colonies and plantations was in many ways like the later Australian system. It was economical to the government. The prisoner had to work for the public good; his services were 'assigned'–in America to a settler, later, in Australia, to the governor. His master had a 'property and interest' in his services for the term of his sentence, and had to be compensated if the convict were pardoned earlier, though the latter could buy his freedom if he could afford it. This process was supposed to be a punishment; even so, any persons over fifteen, including minors who normally had 'no power to contract for themselves', were specifically allowed to make a contract for their transportation for any period up to eight years, since 'many idle persons, lurking in divers parts of London and elsewhere who want employment . . . may be inclined to be transported and enter into services in some of His Majesty's colonies and plantations in America.' Thus in

---

[1] Radzinowicz, 121–2, and 523, n. 4; *Cal. HO*, ii, 1766–9, no. 841 and iii, 1769–1772, nos. 907 and 909; Fortescue (ed.), *Correspondence of George III*, i, 395 and 507, and ii, 375 and 379–81; A. Aspinall (ed.), *Later Correspondence of George III*, i (CUP, 1962), nos. 159, 564, 584, 612, 618, 655; Romilly, *Memoirs*, iii, 233–4; Douglas, *Documents*, xi, 393; *P. Debs.*, 1816, xxxiii, 374. Cf., for George IV, A. Aspinall (ed.), *Diary of Henry Hobhouse* (1947), 87 and 104.

[2] John Campbell, 1st Baron Campbell, *Lives of the Lord Chancellors* (1845–69), vii, 238–9.

some ways convict transportation was only a particular type of indentured labour.[1]

The trade in servants, whether convict or indentured, cost the government little, because merchants, looking forward to selling their services, would transport them cheaply, sometimes for nothing. Though a poor man might not be able to afford to go out at his own expense he could readily find work when he reached the plantations; by indentured servitude, he could get to the colonies, learn about the country and its way of life and so give himself a good chance of eventually gaining a decent independence, while providing the planters with labour; and, of course, the convict could do the same. The merchant found the trade in white servants cheaper than that in African slaves, and the employers found their labour better. Probably more than half of the total white emigrants to the thirteen British colonies in America originally crossed the Atlantic as indentured servants, who were bound for terms between two and seven years; while in service their masters could sell them, hire them out, even whip them in some of the colonies.[2]

Some of the servants were kidnapped or 'spirited away'; some of the convicts themselves were transported illegally. At Bristol, after 1660, 'where all people ... trade to the American plantations', the justices 'not being content to take such felons as were convicts at their assizes and sessions', often put 'small rogues and pilferers ... under terror of being hanged' unless, in their ignorance of the law, they should 'pray transportation'. To check this, in 1682 the Privy Council ordered all indentures to be signed before a magistrate, but at the end of the century there were 'kidnappers who walk the Change in order to seduce people who want services and young fools crost in love and under an uneasiness of mind to go beyond the seas, getting so much a head ... for every wretch they trepan into this misery', and in Scotland kidnapping was rife during the next century too. Perhaps those illegally despatched could console themselves by reflecting on Defoe's opinion that 'the meanest and most despicable creature, after his time of servitude is expired, if he will but apply himself to the business of the country, is sure (life and health supposed) both of living well and growing rich. A transported felon is, in my opinion, a much happier man than the most

---

[1] Douglas, *Documents*, ix, 460–1; Simpson, *loc. cit.*, 41–2; Craies, *loc. cit.*, 403. Offenders were 'made over' to the use of any person who should contract for their transportation and to his assigns (usually colonists) who were thus given a property and interest in the convict's services.

[2] Douglas, *Documents*, ix, 481–91; R. B. Morris, 313, 328, 409, 412, 468; McCormac, 71 ff.; P. A. Bruce, *Economic History of Virginia in the Seventeenth Century* (NY, 1896), i, ch. 9, espec. 603 and 608.

prosperous untaken thief; nor are those poor, young people so much in the wrong that go voluntarily over to these countries, and in order to get themselves carried over, freely bind themselves there . . . From this little beginning have some of the most considerable planters . . . raised themselves to estates of 40 or 50,000 pound.'[1]

Unfortunately this was not the whole story. 'What we unfortunat English People suffer here is beyond the probibility of you in England to Conceive,' lamented one girl to her father; 'let it suffice that I . . . am toiling almost Day and Night, . . . and then tied up and whipp'd to that Degree that you'd not serve an Annimal, scarce any thing but Indian Corn and Salt to eat and that even begrudged . . . almost naked no shoes nor stockings to wear, and . . . slaving during Masters pleasure . . . '[2] However, despite these 'economies', most masters preferred convicts to indentured servants; though their control over both was similar, the convicts' term of service was usually longer.

All the American colonies except those of New England received some convicts at some time, but most went to Maryland and Virginia. There agriculture was more 'labour intensive' than in the north, and the planters who wanted cheap labour found the prisoners a welcome addition to the still far from numerous slaves. Other colonists objected. 'Emptying their jails into our settlements is an insult and contempt, the cruellest that ever one people offered to another,' said Benjamin Franklin. Even some of the colonial governors disapproved of them, and in 1725 the Governor of Maryland 'could heartily wish they were sent to any other of His Majesty's plantations'; but, he added, 'while we purchase them, they will send them'; however in 1740 the Virginians got their own back, for when the English government asked for troops for the Spanish war, it enlisted ex-convicts![3]

Colonial legislatures tried to prohibit this transportation. In 1670, 'great danger and disrepute' was said to be brought upon Virginia, 'by the frequent sending thither of ffellons and other Condemned Persons', and the English Council confirmed a colonial order against them. Maryland banned them in 1676. Facing the almost inevitable labour shortage

[1] *Cal. SP Col.*, *1574–1660*, I, 457, 458; *Cal. SP Col.–Am. and W.I.*, *1661–1668*, introdn., pp. xxviii and xxix, and nos. 769, 770, 791; *APC, Col. Ser.*, ii, no. 99; Holdsworth, xi, 572–3; Craies, *op. cit.*, 397–9; George, 142 ff.; Jeaffreson, iv, p. li; H. G. Graham, *Social Life of Scotland in the eighteenth century* (Black, 1901), 498–500; Defoe, *Life of Colonel Jack* (Bohn edn.), 418, quoted, D. Ogg, *England in the Reigns of James II and William III* (OUP), 1955), 25; Defoe, *Moll Flanders*, quoted George, *loc. cit.*

[2] Letter from Elizabeth Sprigs to her father, from Maryland, 22 Sept. 1756, Douglas, *Documents*, ix, 488–9.

[3] Oldham, 2; Fairfax Harrison, *Virginia Mag.* xxx, 256. For New England, *Cal. SP Col.*, *Am. & W.I.*, *1696–7*, no. 1195; for New York and Pennsylvania, Butler, *AHR*, ii, 23.

in fast developing or new established communities, New York petitioned for prisoners from Newgate in 1693, and even those taking part
in the 'holy experiment' in Pennsylvania accepted some; but in 1697,
the Council of Trade was told that 'several governments . . . have passed
a law against the importation of convicts', and for a time the main
stream was diverted to the West Indies. Then in 1718 the Transportation Act revived the mainland trade, which indeed had never stopped
altogether. In 1722 Pennsylvania and next year Virginia prohibited
them again; Maryland in 1723 and again in 1755 tried to make those
who bought convict servants give a bond of £30 for their good
behaviour; but the British government regularly vetoed such acts, and
the trade went merrily and profitably on.[1] Of course, had the opposition
been serious, the colonists could have boycotted the arrivals; but this
was too much to expect, as was to be seen once more in Van Diemen's
Land in 1850.

For most of the seventeenth century, merchants trading with the
plantations were willing, and often anxious, to carry out the relatively
few convicts who were sent; but as time went on they found some,
particularly women or bad characters, who were difficult to dispose of,
and they became reluctant to take them. Criminals awaiting transportation began to accumulate at home (just as they would do before the
foundation of New South Wales), and in 1697, fifty women had to be
transported 'at the King's charge', for £8 each, for it was thought 'better
the government pay for their transportation than they be let loose.'
After the act of 1718 the Treasury let regular contracts for the job, first
for £3 a head from London and £5 from 'other parts' but after 1727, for
£5 for all; when added to the sale price this allowed a good profit, even
taking into account losses through sickness or death on the voyage.[2]

The 'trade' grew as the years went by. Between 1729 and 1745 the
two contractors for London and the Home Counties sent out an average
of 280 a year, which suggests that about 500 a year were sent from all

[1] APC, Col., 21 Oct. 1670, i, no. 903; Cal. SP Col., 1669–1674, nos. 175 and 590; McCormac,
97; Butler, loc. cit.; Harrison, loc. cit., 250; Cal. SP Col., Am. & W.I., 1696–7, no. 1557;
Douglas, Documents, ix, 461–4; APC, Col., iii, 54–5; Proceedings of the Council of Maryland, 1698–1731, Archives of Maryland, xxv (1905), re Jonathan Forward and a claim for
sureties, 435–8; Jernegan, 49 and ch. 3.
[2] Cal. SP Col.–Am. & W.I., 1696–7, nos. 535, 1134; Cal. SP Dom., 1697, 160, 221; Cal.
SP, Treasury, 1714–19, 389, 445; ib., 1720–8, 56, subseq. vols., passim; Smith, Colonists in
Bondage, 104–6. The Treasury made direct contracts only for prisoners from the Home
Counties; in other counties the justices made their own, and sent a copy to London. When
the receipt for their persons from the master of the ship in which they were to travel and, in
due course, the certificate of their arrival in America given by the colonial Governor or
customs officer reached London, the Treasury repaid the subsidy to the Justices.

England. In 1753 there were nearly 800. During the Seven Years War, 1756–1763, fewer were transported, for many convicts were sent to the army, the navy and the dockyards. For example, out of 154 who were sentenced to death or transportation at the Old Bailey between November 1760 and January 1762, while twelve were pardoned unconditionally and thirty-four on condition of transportation, five were pardoned on condition of serving in the navy, and sixty-three in the army. Other somewhat curious reasons for reprieve were that a criminal submit to have a limb amputated 'to test the styptic medicines discovered by Mr. Thomas Price', and because it would help a member's electioneering in the boroughs of Launceston and Newport.[1]

Between 1770 and 1772 a number of convicts were pardoned on condition that they joined the navy, though the Admiralty was very doubtful if they were suitable recruits. 'The Lords of the Admiralty will order [the convicts] to be taken from prison and disposed of on board some of His Majesty's ships; but they hope proper directions will be given for washing and purifying the men and furnishing them with new and wholesome clothing proper for seamen before they are discharged from prison. Their Lordships express their wishes that no more Convicts may ordinarily be ordered on board H.M.'s ships, as such persons may not only bring distempers and immoralities among their companions, but may discourage men of irreproachable characters from entering H.M.'s service seeing they are to be ranked with common malefactors'; none the less, more were respited on these terms during the American Revolutionary War.[2] Perhaps service in the navy was thought a deterrent to crime. 'No man will be a sailor who has contrivance enough to get himself into a jail,' declared Dr. Johnson, 'for being in a ship is being in jail, with the chance of being drowned.' After 1763 transportation to America increased again, and between 1769 and 1776 about 960 convicts a year were sent out. The demand for convict labour in the plantations was so high that in 1772 the Treasury was able to stop paying its £5 subsidy, though contractors were for a time still able to persuade local authorities to pay. 'The terms I take them on is £5 each,' wrote one to the Kent magistrates in December 1773.[3]

---

[1] Oldham, 15; Newcastle Papers, BM, Add. MSS, 33053, f. 45; *Cal. HO, 1760–65*, nos. 62, 430, 749, 1157; *ib., 1766–9*, nos. 510 and 548. An earlier petition for reprieve to undergo other medical experiments had been rejected on the ground that they could be tried on persons in hospitals (*ib., 1760–5*, 16 May 1763, nos. 907, 909).

[2] *Ib., 1770–2*, no. 604; HO 13/1.

[3] Howard, *Lazarettos*, table iv, 246–7; Oldham, *op. cit.*; *CJ*, xxxvi, 932 ff., xxxvii, 904–910; Duncan Campbell to John Watson of Sandwich, 6 Dec. 1773, to Evan Nepean, 29 Jan. 1787, *Letter Books*, 1 and 5 (ML).

Between 1719 and 1772, the years of the subsidy payments, 17,742 were sent from London and the Home Counties, and perhaps 30,000 from the whole of England. At least two-thirds went to Virginia and Maryland, and very probably more.[1]

Was it an effective punishment? Sir John Fielding, magistrate and penal reformer, thought it was, though in 1766 Mr. Justice Perrott declared that for common offenders it was no punishment at all, and in Scotland, in 1773, Lord Justice Clerk, lamenting the wish of the lower orders to migrate, thought the same. Both John Howard and Fielding hoped transportation might reform the criminals. It would provide work, said Howard; it would separate them from criminal connections, said Fielding; but whether it was reformatory or whether it was a deterrent were both questions on which the evidence (and opinions) were conflicting.[2]

The sea passage was unpleasant, unhealthy and dangerous, as all eighteenth-century sea voyages were. During the eight to twelve weeks' voyage, there was 'on board these ships terrible misery, stench, fumes, horror, vomiting, many kinds of sea-sickness, fever, dysentery, headache, heat, constipation, boils, scurvy, cancer, mouth rot and the like, . . . and . . . add to this want of provisions, hunger, thirst, frost, heat, dampness, anxiety, want, afflictions, lamentations.' Conditions on board were probably no worse than in many contemporary gaols, where the felons lay 'worse than dogs or swine and are kept much more uncleanly than those animals are . . . the stench and nastiness are so nauseous that no person enters without the risk of his life and health'; yet they were overcrowded with prisoners lodged in irons between decks. Many were sick when they came on board and infection spread; in the 1770s the average death-rate on the voyage was about one in seven; it had been more than one in five between 1726 and 1736.[3]

After the voyage a wealthy convict might be able to buy his freedom in America, even though this would not allow him to return to England; but since healthy convicts might sell for £10 if unskilled and even £25 if artificers, few could afford to do this, for the contractors always wanted the full market price. Duncan Campbell, in 1772, told one

[1] Smith, 116–7 and 329.

[2] Cal. HO, 1766–9, no. 376; 1773–5, nos. 39 and 324; Howard, Prisons (1780), 13.

[3] Gottlieb Mittelberger, Journey to Pennsylvania in the Year 1750 . . . (Philadelphia, 1898), quoted, Douglas, Documents, ix, 464–6; Gentleman's Mag., July 1767; cf. Howard, Prisons (1784), Wm. Smith, State of the Gaols in London (1776) and many other accounts. Howard noted that he had to travel on horseback because 'his cloathes were so offensive' that in a post-chaise he 'could not bear the windows drawn up'; CJ, xxxvii, 311; Oldham, op. cit., 61, quoting Guildhall MSS, 58, 8a.

convict's friend that 'the sum you mention is too small to free him from service in America,' although it might help him, for 'any money you pay into my hands shall be remitted to him through my agent in Virginia'; on the other hand, the *Gentleman's Magazine* reported in 1736 that five lawyers, sentenced for stealing books from the library of Trinity College, Cambridge, went down to their ship in two hackney coaches, and were accommodated 'with the Captain's Cabbin, which they stored with *Plenty of Provisions*, etc. for their Voyage and Travels'.[1]

Transportation from Ireland was very much the same. In the seventeenth century rebels and political offenders were sent out; even Massachusetts took some of these. Then the Lord Lieutenant began to pardon ordinary criminals on the condition that they went to the plantations, and in 1704 the judges were authorized to 'respite' the executions of some types of criminals and to order their transportation instead. By 1795 the Irish Parliament had passed seventy-five 'capital statutes' creating felonies 'without benefit of clergy', ranging from rape, attempted murder and buggery to witchcraft and cutting down a tree at night; but several of these were connected with rural terrorism and by and large the Irish criminal code was less bloodthirsty than the English, though that is not saying much. Since there was no Poor Law in Ireland in 1736, 'all vagabonds who wander about demanding victuals' were made liable to be transported for seven years, and indentured servants were numerous too.[2]

The system was regulated in much the same way as in England by an act passed in 1719, and after 1726 the government paid subsidies to shipmasters for the convicts and vagabonds they took out. In seven years between 1737 and 1743, they shipped 1,890 people, but less than half were convicts—only 428 out of 930 whose description is certainly known; if the total increased roughly as it did as from England, probably about 7,500 Irish convicts were transported during the century before the American Revolution.[3]

In Scotland, where simple banishment was a common punishment, the English system regulating transportation was not introduced until

---

[1] Morris, 336; Duncan Campbell, 6 May 1772, *Letter Book*, i, 25 (ML); *Gentleman's Mag.*, vi (1736), 290.

[2] *HMC, 10th Report* (1885), pt. v, 91–2 and 94–5; *Irish Statutes*, vol. viii, index; acts against rural crime and terrorism, 9 Anne c.11, 17 Geo. II c.5, and Whiteboy Act, 15–16 Geo. III c.21. 'Vagabond Act' was 9 Geo. II c.6; benefit of clergy was regulated as in England by 9 Anne c.6.

[3] See 6 Geo. I c.12, 12 Geo. I c.8 and 3 Geo. II c.4. Butler, 24; Smith, *Colonists*, 134; *Report*, 9 Feb. 1743 (O.S.), *Journals of the House of Commons of the Kingdom of Ireland*, iv, part ii, pp. cciii ff. Smith's estimate of a total of 10,000 seems much too large.

1766. The Scottish penal code never contained as many capital offences as the English, for it allowed the accused to plead mitigating circumstances for his crime and provided only moderate punishment for theft until the third offence. Only 134 Scots were sentenced to death and 97 executed between 1768 and 1788, compared with 1,910 sentenced and 890 executed in London and Middlesex at the same time from a population about half the size; hence few were reprieved on condition of transportation, and records for a slightly later period suggest that few were sentenced directly to transportation either.[1]

[1] Hume, *Commentaries*, ii, 365 ff.; *Enc. of Laws of Scotland*, v, Criminal Law, sec. 742; Smith, 133. The Transportation Act for Scotland was 6 Geo. III c.32. There are no full records in Edinburgh for 18th-century Scotland, but the *Books of Adjournal of the High Court of Judiciary* report some cases and the *Reports of Criminal Proceedings, 1818–21*, though later, give some idea of earlier events, and show only seventeen transported in 1819. The figures for executions, etc., for London and Middlesex are from *Criminal Laws, Report*, 1819, for Scotland from Howard, *Lazarettos*, tables v and vi, 248–9.

2

The Beginning of Transportation to Australia

'All social problems of all countries can be got rid of
by extirpating the inhabitants.'

GEORGE BERNARD SHAW

In 1775, the American colonies revolted. For the time being at least,
England could not send her convicts there. Those sentenced to transportation perforce had to remain at home, unless the government could
find some other destination for them; but perhaps they could be
punished in some other way.

Most contemporaries thought that crime was increasing, as contemporaries are prone to do, since, knowing little of the past, they
believe that an extremely low crime level is 'normal'. A few might have
denied it, and perhaps they were right; it is really impossible to say.
Even if convictions were increasing, this may have meant only that
detection was better and that Fielding's reforms in the police, at Bow
Street, were bearing some fruit. On the other hand, it was easier to
commit crime in a thickly populated metropolis, like London, or in the
growing provincial towns, than it had been in a small country village,
where every man was known to his neighbours. 'The tide of luxury has
swept all the inhabitants from the open country,' lamented Smollett's
Matthew Bramble in 1771. 'London, being an immense wilderness, in
which there is neither watch nor ward of any signification, nor any order
or police, affords them lurking places as well as prey.' 'Commerce itself
is the fruitful mother of the crimes of theft in all their varieties, as it
pours in wealth in a shape the most convenient for plunder,' remarked
the *Quarterly Review* a generation later. 'The rural opulence of our
forefathers was not completely safe; still their oaken tables and their
wheat ricks could not be carried off without some trouble, and men were

38

honest because property was immovable. . . . To be ready to be sold, it [property] must be ready to be stolen.'[1]

By modern standards, begging, drunkenness, gambling and prostitution were common, and they often led to crime. England's lack of police was notorious, and even a matter of pride, so it was no wonder that a pickpocket like Barrington could boast—though without giving evidence or having had any 'foreign' experience—that 'in and about London more pickpockets succeed in making a comfortable living than in the whole of the rest of Europe.' In 1797, Patrick Colquhoun, the metropolitan police magistrate, argued that there were 105,000 criminals in the metropolis (nearly one-eighth of the inhabitants), though his estimate seems a guess, even if an inspired one; though he counted 2,000 professed thieves, 10,500 thieves and pilferers, 3,000 coiners, 4,000 receivers of stolen goods and 12,000 recently released from gaol, the remainder included 50,000 prostitutes, 3,000 spendthrifts, 'profligate, loose and dissolute characters', 7,500 swindlers and cheats, 3,000 beggars and 10,000 servants 'out of place from ill-behaviour and loss of character', who were surely not all necessarily felons.[2]

In 1751, Henry Fielding, novelist and magistrate, had demanded 'a due provision for Education and the Relief of the Poor in a way of industry', fewer pardons and reprieves, and a better police in order to reduce crime. How strange it was, he thought:

'that a nation so jealous of her liberties, that from the lightest cause . . . we are always murmuring at our superiors, should tamely and quietly support the Invasion of Properties by the lowest and vilest among us. Doth not this situation in reality level us with the most enslaved countries? If I am to be assaulted and pillaged and plundered; if I can neither sleep in my own House nor walk in the Streets nor travel in Safety, is not my condition almost equally bad whether a licensed or unlicensed Rogue, a Dragoon or a Robber, be the person who assaults and plunders me?'[3]

But he was a voice crying in the wilderness. Even sixty years later the prevailing opinion was that expressed by a visitor to France: 'They have an admirable police in Paris, but they pay for it dear enough. I should rather half-a-dozen people's throats be cut in Ratcliffe Highway every three or four years than be subject to domiciliary visits, spies and the rest of Fouché's contrivances.' According to the *Morning Chronicle*, 'the police in Paris is most dexterously contrived for the purposes of

[1] Smollett, *Humphrey Clinker* (Signet-Classic edn., 1960), 95; *QR*, vii (1812), 179.
[2] Quoted in Lambert, 28; Colquhoun, *Treatise* (5th edn., 1797), vii ff.
[3] *Inquiry*, 2 and 67–8.

tyranny, but that it is so very efficacious in preventing the blackest crimes that deform and afflict human nature, we much question.'[1]

Sentiments like these prevented the establishment of an efficient police; so the usual constables were like those of Westminster, unpaid and chosen by rote, or their deputies, watchmen hired by the parish authorities for less than a shilling a night, often as a substitute for poor relief, corrupt, 'aids not hindrances to crime', sometimes pensioners, 'poor, old decrepit people who are from their want of bodily strength incapable of getting a living by work. These men . . . are to secure the persons and houses of His Majesty's subjects from attacks of young, bold, stout and desperate and well-armed villains. . . . If the poor old fellows should run away . . . no one . . . can wonder, unless he should wonder that they are able even to make their escape.'[2]

Sir John Fielding, Henry's half-brother and successor, had been able to make some improvements in the 1750s, but he could do little in the face of popular prejudice against 'thief-takers' and the refusal of the authorities, either national or local, to help him do more; the 'new plan' he proposed in 1772, involving the appointment of stipendiary magistrates, a better watch, a light horse patrol as 'sentinels or pursuers' and better street lighting, was turned down.[3]

In 1790 visitors to London were warned 'never to stop in a crowd or look at the windows of a print-shop, if you would not have your pocket picked. It would be prudent to have your coat pockets to open in the lining within; this will often prevent them from being picked'; ten years later, Patrick Colquhoun was still lamenting that it was useless for Englishmen to boast 'of liberties which are our birth-right, if the vilest and most depraved part of the Community are suffered to deprive us of the privilege of travelling on the Highways, or approaching the Capital after dark, without the risk of being assaulted and robbed, and perhaps even wounded or murdered . . . or if we cannot lie down to rest in our habitations, without the dread of a burglary being committed, our property invaded, and our lives exposed to immense danger before morning.'[4]

---

[1] Both quoted by E. Halevy, *History of the English People in 1815* (London, 1924), 44; cf. Armitage, ch. 2.
[2] Henry Fielding, *Amelia* (1752), ch. ii.
[3] Improvements were made between 1750 and 1752 by 23 Geo. II c.26, 24 Geo. II c.55 and 25 Geo. II c.36; for Fielding's plan, Melville, 137–9, *Cal. HO, 1770–2*, no. 1501, and his own books; cf. Fielding to Jenkinson, 28 June 1764, Edmund Burke, House of Commons, 8 March 1769, Douglas, *Documents*, x, 279, 275–6.
[4] Trusler, 163; Colquhoun, 2,

The government relied on the traditional policy of trying to keep down crime by punishments that would deter the criminal, keeping the military to restore order 'as a final and desperate resource'. But many people insisted that existing punishments did not deter enough. Was not the criminals' contempt of death shown not only by the prevalence of crime in general, but even by its being so widely practised among the crowds drawn to the executions themselves at Tyburn, 'not to take a lesson in morality, not to be deterred from crime, but to enjoy themselves, to have a holiday, to attend a fair', according to Francis Place? There, said Colquhoun, 'hardy offenders are engaged in new acts of theft, at the very moment when their companions in iniquity are launching, in their very presence, into eternity'. Frequent pardons and inefficient police together removed the fear of punishment, and so the 'design of the Law' was 'ineffective'; no advantage was gained by transportation other than 'getting rid of one thief, whose place was speedily supplied by another.'[1] But during the American War even this advantage had been lost; the government had to consider something else.

What alternatives were there to execution and transportation? The usual suggestions involved some form of hard labour, either on public works or in a penitentiary. Sir William Eden (later Lord Auckland) deplored the frequency of the death penalty and opposed transportation as 'often beneficial to the criminal, and always injurious to the community. The Kingdom is deprived of a subject, and renounces all the emoluments of his future existence. He is merely transferred to a new country, distant indeed, but as fertile, as happy, as civilized, and in general as healthy, as that which he had offended. It would not be incredible then, if this punishment should be asserted in some instances to have operated even as a temptation to the offence; in many instances hath its insufficiency been a fatal argument for multiplication of capital penalties'. Eden wanted 'a strict employment of a limited number of convict felons in each of the dockyards, stannaries, salt-works, mines and public buildings of the Kingdom', though, like Mandeville fifty years earlier, he thought that 'the more enormous offenders' might be sent to 'Tunis or Algiers for the redemption of Christian slaves . . . or to establish new colonies, factories or settlements on the coasts of Africa and on small islands for the benefit of navigation'. In Russia, he pointed out, even banishment was made 'subservient to public utility'; those who had 'lost all claim to the indulgence of their fellow-countrymen',

[1] Place MSS., BM 27826; Colquhoun, 366 and 453. For Tyburn crowds, Radzinowicz, 168–88.

and not law-abiding citizens, had to 'undergo . . . the rigours of a horrible climate, and the unhealthiness of the mines'.[1]

As early as 1750, a House of Commons Committee inquiring into the criminal law had recommended, among other things, that 'it would be reasonable to exchange the Punishment of death which is now inflicted for some sorts of offences into some other adequate punishments'.[2] Two years later the Duke of Newcastle wondered whether hard labour in England would not 'deter the Common People from committing those Crimes which are now punished by Transportation'. This would surely seem a 'most heavy Punishment to those who commit the greatest crimes . . . merely because they will not work'; after all in Béarn in Switzerland, where 'felons were employed as Scavengers in the streats, with marks of Ignominy', there were fewer crimes than in other countries, because of the 'Constant example which the Common people have before their Eyes'. He suggested trying an experiment with five hundred men, and if it was successful it could be extended; but a bill giving power to change the punishment for felony into confinement with hard labour in the dockyards, after passing the Commons, was rejected by the Lords.[3] 'I apprehend that such a punishment is not calculated for this *meridian of liberty*,' wrote Jonas Hanway, the philanthropist and umbrella-inventor. 'It would be displeasing to our humanity; and the evil it might do, and the terror such malefactors might create, would militate against the peace and satisfaction of the people.' As Lecky was later to observe, 'English opinion in the eighteenth century allowed the execution of criminals to be treated as a popular amusement, but at the same time revolted against the continental custom of compelling chained prisoners to work in public, as utterly inconsistent with English liberty.'[4]

So when the American war broke out, England was still heavily relying on transportation to the plantations to punish her criminals. The government had not even seriously considered a suggestion made in 1770 that some might be sent to Africa or the East Indies. After all, as was pointed out when the House of Commons debated the matter, in

[1] Eden, 12, 22, 27–9, 33; Mandeville, 48–52, thought that exchange would 'rid the country, without slaughter or the probability of Return, of the Vermin of Society'. Cf. *Proposals for Preventing the Frequent Execution and Exportation of Convicts* by a Student of Politics (1754).

[2] *CJ*, xxvi, 1750–4, 190; Radzinowicz, 416–9.

[3] *Newcastle Papers*, BM, Add. Mss. 33053, f. 45 *et seq.*, Mem. re employing convicts in dockyards.

[4] Radzinowicz, 422–3, quoting Jonas Hanway, *Defects . . .* (1775); W. E. H. Lecky, *History of England* (pop. edn., 1920), vii, 322.

India there was no demand for labour and the East India Company would have to be paid to take convicts out. In Africa they might be dangerous, and help the negroes to destroy the English forts; the sending of a few to Cape Coast Castle in modern Ghana had been the 'occasion of perpetual commotion'. But now that America was cut off it had to do something. Assuming that the need was only temporary, it decided to moor hulks on the Thames, put convicts in them and work them at hard labour. Parliament agreed, and in 1776 the hulks were authorized for two years, though they lasted eighty-two.[1]

In 1778, Lord North, then First Lord of the Treasury, claimed that 'the experiment' had 'answered beyond all expectations'; though others were more critical, a House of Commons Committee of inquiry agreed that great improvements since 1776 had made the hulks 'convenient, airy and healthy'. However they were far too small, and like the rest of the gaols, were overcrowded, as Duncan Campbell, their contractor complained. They were supposed to hold only 380, but before the war nearly a thousand felons had been shipped to the plantations every year. Some members pressed for transportation to the East or West Indies, to Canada or Nova Scotia, to Florida or the Falkland Islands; but the government had objections to all these places and was content simply to continue with the hulks.[2]

Next year, the system was examined again. This time a Commons Committee reported that 'transportation to unhealthy places, in place of sending better citizens, may be advisable', and that a 'plan of a distant colony' was 'agreeable to the dictates of Humanity and sound policy and might prove in the Result advantageous to both Navigation and Commerce'. However it did not suggest any site. It considered the possibilities of Gibraltar, or the Gambia and Senegal Rivers in Africa; Sir Joseph Banks, companion of Cook on his famous voyage of discovery, informed it that Botany Bay might be suitable. From there, escape would be difficult; it had a mild climate, neither wild animals

---

[1] *CJ*, xxxii, 882; *P. Hist.*, xvi, 930 ff.; *Transportation Report, CJ*, xi, 959; O'Brien, 114. Hulks Act was 16 Geo. III c.43.

[2] North, 6 March 1778, *P. Reg.*, ix, 4; debates on the hulks, 1 April 1776, *P. Reg.*, iii, 473 and *CJ*, xxxv, 694; 9 May 1776, *P. Reg.*, iv, 106, 23 March 1778, ix, 83–4; Hulks Report, 1778, *CJ*, xxxvi, 926–32. For the early years of the hulks, Howard, *Prisons* (1784), 465–6, *Lazarettos*, 246; *Penitentiary Houses, Report*, PP 1812 (306); O'Brien, 88–98; Duncan Campbell, *Letter Books* (ML), ii, *passim*. On 4 March 1786, Campbell claimed that his 'ships at Woolwich are as sweet as any parlour in the kingdom'; on 3 April 1787, telling his Captain at Portsmouth of a projected visit by Howard, he wrote, 'If the hospital is as clean and sweet as when I last saw it, I think the gentleman will be much pleased' (*Letter Books*, v). The hulks were extended by 18 Geo. III c.62 and 19 Geo. III c.54.

nor hostile natives, and without doubt would be able to 'furnish matter of advantageous return'.[1] But neither the Commons nor the government followed up the suggestion. After all in his *Journal* on Cook's voyage, Banks had reported New South Wales 'barren . . . in a very high degree, so far as we saw'; it 'could not be supposed to yield much to the support of man', and there is no hint in Banks's papers that he pressed the idea of establishing a new colony here.[2] In any case, for the moment the government had other things on its mind.

As well as transportation to 'any part of the globe that may be found expedient', the Committee favoured penitentiaries, where the prisoners should be kept in solitary confinement with hard labour, and with these recommendations Parliament agreed. Finding transportation to America 'attended with many Difficulties', it empowered the government for the next five years to send prisoners 'to any Parts beyond the Seas' or to keep them in the hulks; in addition it authorized the building of 'two plain, strong, and substantial . . . Penitentiary Houses', where convicts could be 'ordered to Imprisonment and hard Labour', under close supervision, and where 'during their Hours of Rest', they would be kept 'entirely separate and apart from each other'. The penal reformers were jubilant. 'If the plan be properly executed,' wrote Blackstone, 'there is reason to hope that such a reformation may be effected in the lower classes of mankind, and such a gradual scale of punishment be affixed to all gradations of guilt, as may in time supersede the necessity of capital punishment, except for very atrocious crimes.' But far from being properly executed, it was not executed at all. Disputes about sites and cost delayed the penitentiaries' building. 'The multitude of things depending has made the Penitentiary House long in deciding on,' wrote Pitt to Wilberforce in 1786; by then the government had decided to begin transportation again.[3]

It had to do something about the overcrowded gaols, for crime had

[1] *CJ*, 1 April 1779, xxxvii, 310–3.

[2] J. C. Beaglehole (ed.), *Endeavour Journal of Joseph Banks, 1768–71* (Sydney, 1962), ii, 112–3; cf. Mackaness, *Sir Joseph Banks*, 21; J. H. Rose, *Life of William Pitt* (1923), i, 436.

[3] Felons Report, *CJ*, xxxvii, 306 ff.; penitentiaries act (19 Geo. III c.74), *ib.*, 416; cf. Blackstone, iv, 371, quoted Holdsworth, x, 183; Report of Committee on Building a Penitentiary at Battersea, 1733, *Chatham Papers*, PRO, 30/8/311; O'Brien, 105–6; Pitt to Wilberforce, 28 Sept. 1786, A. M. Wilberforce, *Private Papers of William Wilberforce* (1897), 16. Apart from its dislike of the expense, the government was unwilling to *order* local justices to act; the general permissive authority given in 1784 and 1791 (24 Geo. III c.54 and 31 Geo. III c.46) was rarely acted on (Holdsworth, *loc. cit.*; Webb, *Prisons*, 39–41 and 51; Howard, *Lazarettos*, 220–6).

increased (as it usually did after the end of a war) and twice as many people were capitally convicted in London and Middlesex in 1783–5 as in 1777–9.[1] At first it had tried to send convicts to America again, hoping that the planters, though now independent, would still welcome this cheap labour. In July 1783 Lord North told the King that a Mr. Moore was 'willing to take immediately on board his ships 150 healthy and able-bodied convicts for Virginia and Maryland, at no other expense than the fees to the Clerks of the Assizes and the Keepers of the Gaols'. George was delighted. 'Undoubtedly the Americans cannot expect nor ever will receive any favour from Me, but the permitting them to obtain men unworthy to remain in this Island, I shall certainly consent to.' Unfortunately the Americans thought this 'a Fradulent Plan', and would not take them, nor would the settlers at Honduras in 1785, where Moore tried next. 'The more I consider the matter, the greater difficulty I see in disposing of these people,' wrote Lord Sydney.[2] In 1784, Parliament had replaced the Penitentiary Act of 1779 with an act 'for the effectual transportation of felons and other offenders'. This continued the provisions about penitentiaries, which were still ignored; it authorized the hulks to continue, but made imprisonment in them a preliminary to transportation, as well as a substitution for it; it revived the former transportation system, but said nothing about a destination for the convicts.[3]

By April 1785, though Pitt, the Prime Minister, denied it, the government seems to have decided on an African scheme. When the Commons heard rumours of this plan and demanded information, two orders-in-council for the transportation of convicts to Africa were presented to it. The result was a violent parliamentary attack, led by Edmund Burke,

---

[1] Radzinowicz, 147; Howard, *Prisons* (1777–80), 205, and *ib.* (1784), 492, and *Lazarettos*, 220 and 242–5. Howard gave the total number of all prisoners as 4,379 in 1779, 4,439 in 1782, 7,482 in 1788; of felons, 798 in 1779, 991 in 1782, 1,273 in 1787, 2,052 in 1788; he estimated 526 on the hulks in 1779, 1,937 in 1788; Nepean said there were 600 on the hulks in 1785, HO 7/1. For orders to send convicts to the hulks in 1783, HO 13/1.

[2] Fortescue (ed.), *Correspondence of George III*, vi, nos. 4413–4, 4419–20, 12 and 18 July 1783; Wm. Paca, Annapolis, to General Assembly, 2 Dec. 1783, Journal and Correspondence of State Council of Maryland, 1781–4, *Archives of Maryland*, xlviii (1931), 484; Rose to Nepean, 3 Jan. 1783, HO 35/4, 12 Aug., HO 13/1, 233 and 273, 20 Nov. 1784, HO 13/2; J. A. Burdon, *Archives of British Honduras* (1931), i, 146, 153, 169–70; Sydney to Governor Clarke, 5 Oct. 1784, *ib.*, 149.

[3] A temporary act was passed in March 1784 (24 Geo. III c.12, *CJ*, xxxix, 963, 968, *P. Hist.*, xxiv, 755), the renewed transportation act in July (24 Geo. III c.56, *CJ*, xxxix, 1040, Colquhoun [1795] 283). The hulk establishment was extended at Portsmouth in 1787 and at Woolwich in 1788 because of the demand for labour in the dockyards, HO 28/5 and 29/2.

and the appointment of another Commons Committee to investigate.[1] In evidence to it, Evan Nepean, the Under-Secretary, said that though the River Gambia plan 'was under the contemplation of government and preferred to every other', it had not been 'finally resolved on'; Lord Sydney declared that though 'different ideas had been suggested . . . [they] were either made in conversation . . . or appeared unworthy of attention'; but a draft letter from the Home Office to the Treasury, dated 9 February 1785, describes the proposal in detail. It said that the area abounded with timber for building, that the land was 'extremely fertile . . . and plentifully stocked with Cattle, Goats and Sheep', that the Natives were hospitable, and that tropical fruits and food would grow readily. When taken there, the convicts could be left to themselves; 'they cannot get away for there is not any person who would harbour them.' The only cost would be £8 per head for the journey out, and the hiring 'of an armed vessel on the river as a guard ship during the trading season'. Admittedly 'upon the first settlement a great many of the Convicts would die'; but after the first year, the island would be better cultivated and would 'consequently grow more healthy', so 'a regular succession of convicts could be sent out annually'.[2]

In its reports the Committee unhesitatingly condemned the proposed settlement at Lemaine, up the Gambia. It also objected to the hulks (though admitting they were temporarily necessary); they were overcrowded, and since the convicts were not 'reformed' on them, released prisoners rejoined their criminal acquaintances and resumed their nefarious activities. These 'mischiefs' were 'in great measure due to the want of a proper place for the transportation of criminals'; transportation, though not a good punishment from the point of view of example to others, was cheap, scattered the criminals and broke up their gangs; since it made honest labour possible for them, it was also reformatory. Therefore, it concluded, transportation should be revived on a considerable scale.

Having ruled out the Gambia site as too unhealthy, it remarked that there was a 'vast tract of country on the West Coast of Africa between Twenty and Thirty Degrees of South Latitude . . . seldom visited by Europeans', near the mouth of the River Das Voltas (Orange River),

---

[1] 3 Feb. 1785, an address for a statement on what steps had been taken with regard to the Transportation Act passed in 1784, *CJ*, xl, 479; 16 March, Burke's attack, *P. Hist.*, xxv, 391, *P. Reg.*, xvii, 430; 12 April, orders presented, 20 April, committee appointed, *ib.*, 838, 870; *P. Hist.*, xxv, 430; cf. HO 42/7, and 35/1, to the Treasury, 9 Feb. 1785, setting out detailed plans for sending convicts to Gambia, and 'entreating Your Lordships to take this matter into your early consideration'.
[2] *CJ*, xl, 954–60 and 1161; HO to Treasury, 9 Feb., HO 35/1.

where there were said to be copper deposits; this would be 'an excellent Place for Homewardbound Indiamen' to call, and a settlement there 'might also promote the Purposes of future Commerce or of future Hostility in the South Seas'. The convicts could go out 'in Slave ships which could then proceed up the coast in pursuit of their usual traffic'; the many American families who were still anxious to live under British rule would 'readily resort to the Coast in question' and would discipline and employ the convicts. The result would be to relieve the English gaols and 'divert the Spirit of Emigration . . . to Countries which are still subject to the Crown of Great Britain'; but, warned the Committee, since 'it will not answer the purpose of annual transportations unless it becomes a numerous and flourishing colony', it should be adopted 'so far only as the Commercial and Political Benefits of a Settlement on the south-west Coast of Africa may be deemed of sufficient consequence to warrant the Expence inseparable from such an undertaking'. After this report, the government sent the sloop *Nautilus*, in August 1785, to survey the Atlantic coast of Africa up to about the modern Angola, but it was found barren, waterless and unsuitable.[1]

In October, Pitt was looking at another scheme. This was for a settlement on the Caffre Coast, which might 'answer in some respects the purposes of the Cape, and to serve also as a receptacle for convicts'. It had its attractions for South Africa was obviously important for the route to India where the great expansion of English interests was beginning. The Cape itself produced no shipbuilding materials, but a good base nearby for repairs, victualling and water, would be a great asset; 'the Power possessing the Cape of Good Hope has the key to and from the East Indies'.[2] Though any new settlement would incur 'great losses' in its early days, and even 'total Ruin' to some, this one would have 'great advantages' in the long run. Its labour force could be provided by transported criminals. The surrounding savage Kaffirs would prevent their escape, but they would be spared the horrors of the fever-stricken West African coasts, and England would avoid 'those dayly Executions so shocking to Humanity'. If established, 'a Settlement on the Caffree Coast would be of the most important consequence to Britain and the India Company . . . We shou'd in a few Years derive every advantage from a Settlement here that the Dutch have from the Cape . . . We have lost America, and a halfway house wou'd secure us India, and an

[1] *Second Report, CJ*, xl, 1162–4; Admiralty Orders, 22 Aug. 1785, HO 28/5; J. H. Rose, *op. cit.*, 435.
[2] Pitt to Grenville, 2 Oct. 1785, HMC, *13th Rept.*, i, 257; Harlow, 122, quoting Minutes of Secret Committee of East India Co., 18 Oct. 1781; cf. Admiral Sir H. Richmond, *The Navy in India 1763–1783* (1931), 124–6.

Empire to Britain.' However, the government did not wish to annoy the Dutch, so the matter was dropped.[1]

Various other suggestions were in the air, including Madagascar, Tristan da Cunha, Algiers, employment in the North Sea herring industry, in English coal mines 'where one man at the mouth of the pit can command 10,000', or in the 'very pernicious' lead manufacture; meanwhile the criminal problem was growing worse. In March 1786, when Londoners petitioned against dangers of the hulks, Pitt told the House of Commons that 'though several new modes of disposing of the convicts had been pointed out every one was attended with difficulty and expense'. In June, the cabinet was reported to be considering plans which included transportation to Canada and the West Indies. In August it fixed on New South Wales.[2]

This does not seem to have been officially considered after the report of 1779, but it had had its unofficial apologists, who were ready to inspire rumours of plans for a settlement. James Mario Matra, like Banks, had been with Cook. In August 1783, he wrote to the government suggesting the foundation of a colony in New South Wales. He wanted to provide a new home for American loyalists, to extend British trade with Spice Islands, China and Japan, to establish a naval base to obtain naval stores, and incidentally to get a job for himself; as he had told Banks the previous month, 'I would prefer embarking in such [an enterprise] to anything that I am likely to get in this hemisphere.' This proposal had nothing to do with convicts and the government showed little interest in it.[3] Shortly afterwards an anonymous suggestion for a settlement in New South Wales, New Zealand, New Caledonia or Norfolk Island, pointed out that it would provide for the disposal of convicts as well as having commercial advantages; so did another plan for a settlement in New South Wales, submitted in January 1785 by Captain (later Admiral) Sir George Young, R.N. It would lead to 'establishing a very Extensive Commerce, . . . and greatly increase our

[1] Memorials by Lieutenant Henry Pemberton and Colonel William Dalrymple, Harlow, 127–9, quoting Pemberton's *Narrative* (India Office–Factory Records–Cape of Good Hope, vol. i); Dalrymple's Proposal, 17 Sept. 1785; to Pitt, 1787, Chatham Papers, PRO, 30/8/128.

[2] Rose, *op. cit.*, i, 438, quoting Pulteney to Pitt, 14 Sept. 1786; Oldham, 287–97, quoting, *inter alia*, proposals to Pitt in Chatham Papers; *P. Reg.*, xix, 330; *Edinburgh Mag.*, iii, March 1786 and 475; *Gentleman's Mag.*, lvi, 168; Sydney to Treasury, 18 Aug. 1786, to Admiralty, 31 Aug., *HRNSW*, i, part 2, 14–20.

[3] *HRNSW*, i, part ii, 1; CO 201/1 and HO 7/1; Matra to Banks, 28 July 1783, BM, Add. MSS. 33977, 206, and Dawson (ed.), *Banks Letters*, 593. O. Rutter, *First Fleet* (1937), 14, suggests the Government was not blind to the advantages of the plan, but confesses he has 'no evidence to . . . support . . . this fascinating theory'.

Shipping,' he wrote; it would also provide an 'Asylum' which would reduce 'the very heavy Expence Government is annually put to for Transporting and otherwise punishing the felons.'[1] This scheme appealed to Pepper-Arden, the Attorney-General, who told Lord Sydney, Home Secretary, in January 1785, that it seemed 'the most likely method of effectually disposing of convicts, the number of which requires the immediate interference of Government'.[2] The idea was dropped while the government looked elsewhere; but its failure to find an alternative and the great danger of 'infectious distemper' in the hulks decided it to found a penal settlement at Botany Bay, where seven hundred and fifty convicts should be sent immediately. In October, Phillip received his first Commission as Governor. Orders-in-Council in December replaced Africa and America, where sentences could not 'conveniently be carried out', by the eastern coast of New South Wales as the place of transportation under the Act of 1784.[3] The whole scheme was announced to Parliament in January 1787, 'to remove the inconvenience which arose from the crowded state of the gaols in the different parts of the Kingdom'. During the year an act was passed to establish a criminal court in New South Wales, and in 1788 the Transportation Act was extended to embrace the projected settlement there, though in the same years, the hulk establishments at Portsmouth and Woolwich were expanded because of the demand for labour in the dockyards.[4]

Was the decision to found the settlement at Botany Bay taken entirely for penal reasons? There was certainly a long-term interest in *terra australis incognita*; but, with one exception, all the colonial schemes submitted to the Home Office after 1783 included as one of their principal aims that of ridding England of her undesirables. This seems to have been the government's principal concern, stimulated as it was by the loss of American plantations.[5] As long ago as 1756, the Frenchman, Charles de Brosses, had suggested the establishment of a French penal colony in New Britain, for 'the political body, like the human body, has vicious humours which should be often evacuated'. This proposal was taken up by his translator, John Callander, who remarked that as well as extending his commerce, England would greatly gain by 'sending annually abroad certain people who only hurt society at home', for 'the

[1] *HRNSW*, ii, 359; i, part ii, 12 ff.
[2] Pepper Arden to Sydney, 13 Jan. 1785, *ib.*, 10; Sir George Young, *Young of Formosa* (n.d., ? 1928), 28–9; cf. Matra to Nepean, 6 April 1784, Rutter, *op. cit.*, 28–30.
[3] *HRNSW*, i, part ii, 14–20, 24, 30–1.
[4] *P. Hist.*, xxvi, 211; 27 Geo. III c.2; 28 Geo. III c.24; HO 28/5, 29/2.
[5] HO, 42/1, 7, 8 and 10 and 47/3; cf. O'Brien, 126; Melbourne, 5–7; Rose, *op. cit.*, 437–42; *Cambridge History of the British Empire*, ii, 28; Clark, *History*, 66 ff.

proper use of banishment is to send the criminal from the country he
has infested into another, where, by its dependence on the mother
country, his labour may be useful to the state'.[1]

There were objections to New South Wales. Admiral Lord Howe, in
1784, had not been enthusiastic about Matra's first, non-convict plan,
arguing that 'the length of the navigation' did not encourage the hope
'of the many Advantages in Commerce and war which Mr. Matra has
in contemplation'. Later criticism of the venture was concerned with its
being an efficient and expensive punishment, and ignored any possible
commercial value it might have. In October 1786, the *Gentleman's
Magazine* declared it 'a most extravagant scheme'; no place could be
'more improper' for felons than Botany Bay. 'The expense will be equal
to that of an expedition to the South Sea against an enemy.'[2] Alexander
Dalrymple, though interested in Pacific colonization, argued that a
settlement would violate the chartered monopoly of the East India
Company and would upset its trade with Canton. 'The project of a
settlement has appeared in many Proteus-like forms, sometimes as a
half-way house to China, again as a check on the Spaniards . . . sometimes as a receptacle for transported convicts, then as a plan of asylum
for American refugees, and sometimes as an emporium for supplying
our marine yards with hemp and cordage or for carrying on the fur
trade to the North-West of America.' But this was merely an attempt
to carry on an illicit trade. As far as a punishment was concerned it
would encourage rather than deter felons. 'For what is the Punishment
intended to be inflicted? *Not* to make the felons undergo *servitude* for
the *benefit* of *others* as was the Case in America; but to place them as
their own masters in a temperate climate, where they have *every object*
of comfort for *Ambition* before them! and although it might be going
too far to suppose *this* will *incite* men to become Convicts . . . surely it
cannot *deter* men inclined to commit theft or Robbery to know that in
case they are detected and convicted, *all* that will *happen* to them is that
they will be sent at Public Expense to a Good Country and temperate
Climate.'[3] As the rhymester in the *Whitehall Evening Post* wrote:

> *Of those precious souls who for nobody care,*
> *It seems a large cargo the Kingdom can spare;*
> *To ship off a gross or two may not delay,*
> *They cannot too soon go to Botany Bay.*

---

[1] Charles de Brosses, *Histoire des Navigations aux Terres Australes* (1756), quoted, Mackaness, *Phillip* 37; John Callander, *Terra Australis Cognita* or *Voyages to the Terra Australis*
(1766-8), quoted, Mackaness (ed.), *Proposals*, 35 *et seq.*
[2] *HRNSW*, i, part ii, 10; *Gentleman's Mag.*, lvi (2), 903, but cf. *ib.*, 915.
[3] Dalrymple, *Serious Admonition*, 22-5.

They go to an island to take special charge
Much warmer than Britain, and ten times as large;
No custom-house duty, no freightage to pay,
And tax-free they'll live when at Botany Bay.[1]

Dalrymple suggested that the convicts could be sent more cheaply to Tristan da Cunha, which was nearer England and therefore would be more easily supplied, or they could be used for 'military recruits abroad'. In 1787, as the expedition was setting out, Sir Nathaniel Wraxall poured contempt on this 'new colony of thieves and ruffians'. It was something 'beneath the disquisition of reason and below the efforts of ridicule', he said, and arguing that England would have to 'relinquish all hope or expectation of deriving any benefit . . . either immediate or remote' from the convicts' labour, he urged that they be sent not to the Antipodes but to Newfoundland or the African Gold Coast. Sir Joseph Banks and many others were showing more interest in North-West Canada than Australia; but it was to Australia that the convicts were sent.[2]

Later statements in the Colonial Office unhesitatingly assert that New South Wales was founded as a penal colony. In 1797, when criticizing the costs of Governor Hunter's administration in New South Wales, the Duke of Portland complained that 'the expence of maintaining the convicts in New South Wales, without including that of the civil and military establishments of the colony or the supplies sent from hence, is more than two-thirds of what they would have been kept for in this country'. The 'greatest part' of this arose 'from not adverting to the original purpose for which the colony was established', and considering the promotion of agriculture rather than the minimum costs of maintaining convicts.[3]

The distance of Botany Bay from England, the expense of the penal establishment, which gaol reformers disliked so much, the later progress of the settlement and the national pride of its citizens have caused some to wonder whether imperial or commercial considerations did not really underlie the project. In the draft of a letter to the Irish Government written in October 1786, explaining the convict plan in some detail, one paragraph runs:

[1] 19 Dec. 1786, quoted, Clark, *Sources*, 75–7.
[2] Wraxall, *Short Review*, 78–83; R. Cadman Etches to Banks, 17 and 20 July 1788, *Banks Papers*, Sutro Collection, National Library, Canberra (microfilm); cf. Margaret A. Ormsby, *British Columbia*; *A History* (Vancouver, 1958), ch. i; H. H. Bancroft, *History of the North-West Coast* (New York, n.d.), i, chs. 6–8; B. O. S. Scholefield, *British Columbia from earliest times to the Present* (Vancouver 1914), i, ch. 6.
[3] Portland to Hunter, 31 Aug. 1797.

'Besides the removal of a dreadful Banditti from this Country, many advantages are likely to be derived from this intended Settlement. Some of the timber is reported to be fit for Naval purposes, particularly masts, which the Fleet employed occasionally in the East Indies frequently stand in need of . . . But above all the cultivation of the Flax Plant seems to be the most considerable object . . .'
A marginal comment reads 'This clause left out in the letter written to Mr. Hamilton', which would suggest that the convict plan was thought to be the only matter of interest to the Irish government; but the interest in flax appears not only here but in the 'Heads of the Plan' sent to the Treasury and in the instructions given to Governor Phillip. Young would have agreed. 'To what end are all the Discoveries of our great Forefathers and lately those of the wonderful Cook?' he demanded, emphasizing New South Wales' value on the route to China and the extent of the market in the Pacific, and like Matra stressing the 'imperial' advantages of the establishment. 'If we entertain a wish to support and increase our Maritime Power we must extend our settlements.'[1]

Growing British interest in the Pacific during the eighteenth century had led the Admiralty to send out the expeditions of Anson, Byron, Wallis, Carteret and Cook. Constant propaganda kept up popular interest. Alexander Dalrymple insisted that a great southern continent existed in the Pacific, and that its discovery would bring a great 'accession of commerce and power'. The secret instructions given to Cook in 1768 mentioned that any discoveries might 'tend greatly to the advancement of the trade and navigation' of Great Britain.[2] Matra and Young also stressed that an Australian colony would help trade to the Philippines and South America and would be a valuable naval base in the case of war with Spain. Certainly when it was reported in 1786 that the Spaniards were proposing to constitute free ports on the western coast of South America, British trading circles showed interest (though negotiations for a commercial agreement between the East India Company and the Royal Philippine Company were abortive), and in 1790

---

[1] Copy of draft to Sackville Hamilton, Under-Sec. to Lord-Lieutenant, 24 Oct. 1786, CO 202/5, *Tas. Hist. Assoc.*, 1952, No. 4, 19; Home Office to Treasury, 18 Aug. 1786, HO 35/1, *HRNSW*, i, part ii, 14–19; Young, 29–30.
[2] Harlow, 32; J. C. Beaglehole (ed.), *Journals of Captain James Cook* (CUP for Hakluyt Soc.), i (1955), general introduction and instructions to Cook; Dalrymple, *Account of the Discoveries in the Pacific Ocean previous to 1764* (1767) and *Historical Collection of the Several voyages and discoveries in the South Pacific Ocean* (1770), i, xxvi and xxx; in *A Plan for extending the commerce of this kingdom* (1769) Dalrymple demanded an establishment at Balambangan, near Borneo, and ignored the South Pacific.

there were suggestions that a convict settlement on 'one of the Sandwich Islands' or Chatham Island would benefit British trade in the Pacific.[1]

But this agitation, like the despatch of Captain George Vancouver, R.N., in 1791, and Captain James Colnett, R.N., in 1793, and like the *later* development of seal and whale fisheries from Port Jackson, is not evidence of government motives for the *establishment* of Botany Bay. For the moment it seemed useless for trade. Neither Cook nor Banks in their *Journals* had spoken well of New South Wales. The officers on the first fleet agreed. 'If only a receptacle for convicts be intended,' wrote Watkin Tench, Captain of Marines, 'this place stands unequalled . . . When viewed in a commercial light, I fear its insignificance will appear very striking.' To Surgeon John White, it seemed 'so much out of the world and track of commerce that it could never answer'.[2]

Australia's unfortunate position, the discovery that it was sparsely inhabited, the monopoly which the East India Company possessed over all trade east of South Africa, and the absence of 'teeming peoples' in the South-Pacific to trade with (not to mention the outbreak of the French Revolutionary Wars), all caused commercial interest in the new colony to wane. Apart from references to flax, no emphasis on trade or shipping appears in the official papers, and Phillip's desire to 'render a very essential service' by establishing a colony 'which from its situation must hereafter be a valuable acquisition to Great Britain' is not evidence of government motives.[3]

In its preparations for the expedition, the government paid little heed to any commercial possibilities. No farmers were sent out, no skilled craftsmen or mechanics, no person 'knowledgable in flax-dressing' (despite the special instructions to cultivate it), no men with any knowledge of the natural sciences (botany, geology, numerology) who might discover the resources of the country; but since other preparations were equally defective (for there were no instructions about the relationship of the marines to the governor, no overseers or superintendents for the convicts, not enough clothing, no anti-scorbutics,

[1] Atkins, *Hist. Stud.*, viii, 315–8, citing *Annual Register*, 1786, xxviii, 35; Blair to Dundas, 6 Aug. 1790, HMC, *13th Report*, i, 604–5.

[2] Tench, *Narrative*, ch. xvii, 138; Surgeon John White, in *Gentleman's Mag.*, Jan. 1791, xli, 79–80, quoted Atkins, *loc. cit.* On the question of the motives for the settlement, Dallas, *Tas. Hist. Assoc.*, iii, 3, Roe, *Hist. Stud.*, viii, 202, Reese, *Aust. Journal of Politics and History*, vii, 186. Cook thought the discoveries made on his first voyage 'not great', *op. cit.*, 501 and 505 and cf. 392–7; Mackaness, *Banks*, 21.

[3] Phillip to Sydney, July 1788, *HRA*, I, i, 67; cf. 'The Influence of the East India Company on the Colonisation of New South Wales' (anon. typescript, 1936, ML, Sydney).

insufficient surgical supplies, even for the marines, and overcrowding on the ships), perhaps no more can be deduced from this than that the government was rather inefficient and did not seriously consider the needs of a new settlement, penal or otherwise. Pitt paid no more heed to the plea of his colleague, the Duke of Richmond, not to send felons among the first settlers of the new colony, than to that of Phillip, who 'would not wish convicts to lay the foundations of an Empire'. There was no question of keeping the prisoners separate from either the garrison or settlers, and as far as future settlement was concerned, Phillip was merely instructed to report on its possibilities.[1]

Though Lord Hawkesbury (later the first Earl of Liverpool), President of the Committee for Trade and Plantations, showed an interest in Britain's whale fishery, which was ably exploited by the firm of Enderby and Sons, the connection between this and the penal settlement at Botany Bay can be exaggerated. In 1789 Enderby urged that the whalers be granted an unlimited right of fishing in all seas, and arranged in 1791 that five of the convict-transports going out should be whalers; but the governors of New South Wales were repeatedly instructed to respect the East India Company's monopoly, which the whalers would inevitably interfere with, and when Phillip reported favourably on the possibilities of whaling in Australian waters, the only comment evoked was that it might 'eventually' be important to the settlement and 'be a means of extending the communication betwixt it and this country'. At the same time, British whaling interests succeeded in persuading the government to impose a duty on oil imports, in order to stifle the Australian industry, and this was still a severe handicap to it in 1820.[2]

King tried to help the whalers at Norfolk Island in 1791, and he gave them further aid after he became Governor in 1800. In 1801 three whalers, on their outward voyage, brought provisions for the colony; but this can hardly be regarded as a cause for its establishment in 1788. The British government refused to modify the East India Company's charter, and the Company impounded a cargo of seal skins and oil sent

[1] Phillip to Nepean, 4 and 11 Jan. 1787, *HRNSW*, i, part ii, 45–6; White to Phillip, 7 Feb., *ib.*, 48; Richmond to Pitt, 2 Dec. 1786, Chatham Papers, PRO, 30/8/171; Phillip's views, Feb. 1787, Phillip to Sydney, 12 March, to Nepean, 18 March, *HRNSW*, *loc. cit.*, 50–9; Phillip's Instructions, *ib.*, 89 and 91.

[2] Harlow and Madden, sec. iii, docs. 60 and 62, Charles Enderby, *Proposals for re-establishing the British Southern Whale Fishery* (1847), discussed by Roe, *loc. cit.*; Phillip to Stephens, 16 and 18 Nov., 1791, *HRA*, I, i, 303 and 312; Phillip to Nepean, 18 Nov. 1791, 29 March 1792, *ib.*, 307, 347; Phillip to Dundas, 11 Oct. 1792, *ib.*, 397; Dundas to Phillip, 17 May 1792, *ib.*, 354; Hunter to Portland, 4 July 1799; Greenwood, 79–80; Ward, *British Policy*, 10 ff.; W. J. Dakin, *Whaleman Adventurers* (Sydney, 1934); Bigge, *Agriculture*, PP 1823 (136), 56–7; O'Brien, App. G., 294–5.

to England in the *Lady Barlow* by Robert Campbell in 1805. Until 1812, any British vessel trading with New South Wales was an 'interloper'. All intercourse with India, Malaya, China or the Asian Islands was forbidden, and no ships could be built in the colony.[1] So much for the government's anxiety to encourage trade!

On the convict side, the critics complained that transportation to Botany Bay would be very expensive and totally inadequate as a punishment. Putting forward his 'plan', Sydney had told the Treasury that 'the difference of expense that this mode of disposing of them [the convicts] and that of the usual more ineffectual one is too trivial to be a consideration with Government . . . especially now the Evil is increased to such an alarming degree from the inadequacy of all other expedients that have hitherto been tried or suggested'. Though Pitt, according to Wilberforce, at one time had had ideas of criminal law reform, he had abandoned them (like many other of his reform projects) after becoming Prime Minister. In 1787 he opposed an inquiry into the penal laws, for 'it would be extremely dangerous to take any step which might have the smallest tendency to discrediting the present existing system'. That system, as modified by the foundation of Botany Bay, he stoutly defended against its critics. 'No cheaper mode of disposing of the convicts could be found,' he declared in 1791, though Major Ross of the marines thought it would be more economical to 'feed them on turtle and venison at the London Tavern'; that it was 'necessary . . . to send some of the most incorrigible criminals out of the kingdom,' insisted Pitt, 'no man could doubt.'[2]

But quite a number did doubt. Even if the convicts were too numerous to be employed in dockyards and on the Thames hulks, 'would it not in every respect be more advisable to employ them in carrying on public works and other improvements in remote and uncultivated districts in our own country ?' asked Sir John Sinclair. Why could they not build canals in Scotland ? 'Landholders would not feel easy to have great numbers of convicts quartered in their neighbourhood,'

[1] King to Portland, 28 Sept. 1800; King to Hobart, 14 Aug. and 20 Dec. 1804; cf. Portland to King, 19 June 1801; instructions to Phillip and Hunter, *HRA*, i, 15 and 524, to King, iii, 395; cf. Greenwood, 83 and 120, East India Co. to George Tierney, 5 Feb. 1807, *HRNSW*, vi, 240 ff.; Liverpool to Macquarie, 10 March 1812; Bathurst to Macquarie, 11 Dec. 1815. Banks showed renewed interest in a Pacific colony in seeking help for the London Missionary Society in 1802, but the government remained unconcerned, CO 201/24, f.39. King was officially only Lieut. Governor until 1802, but he was in charge of the colony after Hunter left in September 1800.

[2] 'Heads of a Plan', *HRNSW*, i, part ii, 14-19; W. Wilberforce, *P. Debs.*, 1811, xix, pp. lxxiv-lxxvii, *P. Hist.*, xxv, 888-913; Pitt, *ib.*, xxvi, 1056-9, xxviii, 1224; Ross to Nepean, 10 July 1788, *HRNSW*, i, part ii, 176.

Dundas had replied to this suggestion in 1789. 'You will find nothing as good as transportation . . . Death, transportation and the Bride-well are, in my judgment, the only varieties of punishment that the manners of our country will admit of.'[1] The convict transport con-tractor, William Richards, proposed 'better hulks' at Milford Haven – 'a kind of short transportation.'[2] In July 1795, Sir George Elliott suggested sending out convicts to Corsica to work on the fortifications there; but though this would have been cheaper than sending them to New South Wales, it might have produced a bad effect on the minds of the Corsi-cans; besides, absconders could have easily returned to England. In the end fifty were sent as an experiment, but the evacuation of the island in 1796 closed the question.[3]

In 1785, the provisions of the act of 1784 were applied to Scotland, and the Irish, too, soon came into the scheme. In 1778, the Irish Parliament had declared that 'until some other more effectual provisions in place of transportation . . . to America can be framed', they might be employed 'with benefit to the public' at hard labour on the Liffey, while living in hulks. Though this provision was intended to be temporary, the act was regularly renewed until a permanent system was established in 1786. The clerks of the various courts were to send lists of the persons sentenced to transportation to the Lord-Lieutenant; then he would supervise their transport to a port-town, their confinement there, and contract for a ship for their transportation overseas, the expense being paid by the Treasury.[4]

The question of their destination was at first as unsettled as in England, and a shipload despatched to Nova Scotia in 1789 were sent back home; but in 1790, naturally enough, New South Wales was fixed on. The convicts were normally collected and the ships sailed from Cork, though the Irish administration, despite frequent reminders from London, did not bother for eight years to send out copies of the indents recording the names and sentences of the convicts to the authorities at Botany Bay.[5] In 1792, the alternative of imprisonment in a penitentiary

---

[1] Sir John Sinclair, *History of the Public Law of the British Empire* (1803), 102–3 and 191–2; Dundas to Grenville, 17 Dec. 1789, *HMC*, 13th report, iii, 555–6.
[2] Proposal to Banks, 8 Aug., 1791, *HRNSW*, i, part ii, 509 ff.
[3] CO 65/2 34, 63, 67, précis of despatches from Sir George Elliott, 13 July and 27 Nov., 1795, Portland to Elliott, 3 April 1796.
[4] For the Scottish Transportation Act, 1785, *CJ*, xl, 1122, 25 Geo. III c.46; for the Irish 17–18 Geo. III c.9, 26 Geo. III c.24, HO 100/29, O'Brien, 130 ff.
[5] *HMC*, 13th rept., i, 540–555; *HRNSW*, i, part ii, 752–4; Irish Act, 30 Geo. III c.32; Hunter to Portland, 27 June 1797; Portland to Hunter, and encl., 18 Sept. 1798. The list of convicts sent out in the *Queen* in September 1791 did not reach New South Wales until May 1799, *HRA*, ii, 366 and 709.

was provided for, since it 'might tend to reform and to render useful members of society persons sentenced to transportation' if they were 'compelled to work at useful trades'; but, warned Chief Baron Hamilton, many of the local grand juries 'were much afraid of the expense'.[1]

Ministers were not as convinced as their critics that penitentiaries would provide an effective and reformatory punishment. They wanted to shift the burden of the cost of punishment, and transportation seemed likely to make it possible for them to do this, irrespective of other possible imperialist or mercantilist considerations. They were committed to transportation to Botany Bay, and they preferred the imaginary sentence which Jeremy Bentham put in the mouth of his judge: 'I sentence you, but to what I know not; perhaps to storm and shipwreck, perhaps to infectious disorders, perhaps to famine, perhaps to be massacred by savages, perhaps to be devoured by wild beasts. Away–take your chance; perish or prosper, suffer or enjoy; I rid myself of the sight of you.'[2]

---

[1] Irish Act, 32 Geo. III c.27; Hamilton to Chief Secretary, 20 May 1790, Irish State Papers, 508/17/4.
[2] Bentham, *Penal Law*, book v, ch. 2, *Panopticon* (1791), *Works* i, 490 ff., iv, 37.

3

Early Years in New South Wales

'The mind of man is more cheered and refreshed by
profiting in small things than by standing at a stay in
great . . . but in the great frame of kingdoms and
commonwealths, it is in the power of princes or estates
to add amplitude and greatness to their kingdoms.'
BACON: *Of Empire and the True Greatness*
of Kingdoms and Estates

Transportation to Botany Bay was to be a cheap punishment which
would deter criminals in Britain; if it reformed those who were sent
there, so much the better; but at least they would find it hard to come
back. For two or three years, the magazines reported news from the
settlement; in 1791 and 1793 the House of Commons discussed its
progress; after that events in Europe pushed Botany Bay into the back-
ground for a generation.[1] The 'Rum Rebellion' perforce attracted
notice in 1808, and in 1812 a Select Committee of the House of Commons considered the whole question of transportation; until then the
reluctant attention of the Secretary of State for War and the Colonies
was most easily attracted by complaints of extravagance and his desire
to keep down costs.

In 1798 the House of Commons Select Committee on Finance,
alarmed by the sudden presentation at the Treasury of bills amounting
to nearly £80,000, investigated its expenditure. It reported that the
annual average cost of victualling, clothing and transporting the
convicts, together with the cost of the civil, military and marine establishments at New South Wales, was £27.14 per head; in 1789 Secretary
Grenville had estimated only £14 'plus the cost of victuals for a year or

[1] Fitzhardinge, *Hist. Stud.*, ix, 85 ff.; cf. the publication of Phillip's *Voyage* (1789), Tench's
Narrative (1789) and *Complete Account* (1793), White's *Journal* (1790), Hunter's *Journal*
(1793), Barrington's *Voyage* (1795). Official correspondence was published by Parliament in
1792; debates, 9 Feb. 1791, 31 May 1793, *P. Hist.*, xxviii, 1221–5, xxx, 956 ff.

two at furthest'; but the cost of victuals was showing no signs of decreasing. The committee thought the hulks unsatisfactory as prisons, but found them cheap; taking into account the value of their labour, each convict in them cost only about £10 per year. On the whole it preferred the penitentiaries which Bentham and Colquhoun had been advocating, which had been authorized in 1779, but had never been built.[1]

In fact the convicts at Botany Bay at first had cost even more than the Committee thought. It assumed that during the first six years, from 1786 to 1791, an equal number were shipped each year, that none died and none were emancipated, and so deduced an average cost of £26 per man per year. In actual fact, more than half (2,443) only embarked in 1791, so the average cost per man per year was much greater, and between 1789 and 1791 it was £44 a head (Table 1). For the next six years, the Committee reckoned the cost at £33.10.0 per head; but in this account it seems to have assumed that after a man was set free he cost nothing and that the whole expenses of government should be debited to the convict establishment–assumptions which show what motives had prompted the settlement.[2] But by this time there was a small free population in the settlement, and it had begun the long process of becoming a free colony. As such, was it worthless? And was the convicts' labour valueless when they were not growing food for themselves but employed on other colonial works? Was the establishment useless as a naval base or a commercial centre? All these were matters of opinion, but there were men ready to assert that colonies were of no use to the mother-country, and certainly when Phillip forecast that the 'country will prove the most valuable acquisition Great Britain has ever made' even Grenville, the Secretary of State, merely expressed his regret that the 'principal settlement had not been placed on Norfolk Island'. If the Finance Committee agreed that at 'some distant day' Australia's trade would be profitable, it was afraid that this would benefit only private individuals, and not the government; meanwhile unfortunately the more it throve as a colony, the easier it would be to return from; transportation would become an 'emigration' without

---

[1] SC on Finance, *28th Report*, 1798, on Police including Convict Establishments. Many bills drawn in 1793, 1795 and 1796 were presented at the Treasury in 1797. Interest in New South Wales was also stimulated by the appearance of Collins' *Account* (1798). In 1789 the hulks cost £23.3.0 per head; in 1797, £23.19.0 per head. The value of labour there in 1797 was variously estimated at £14.17.9 per head and £12.13.8 per head (*Report*, 16 and appendix N). Grenville to Buckingham, 9 July 1789, HMC, 13th rept., i, 482. Cf. *HRNSW*, ii, 38–44, for the colony's expenses to 1793, *ib*., 427, for cost of hulks in 1789; for penitentiaries, above, pp. 44 and 57.

[2] *Report*, 22–5.

'terror', or just 'an adventure'; if its general progress interfered with its effectiveness as a place of punishment, the latter was the more important.[1]

Up to 1800, the total cost of New South Wales, including the naval expenditure connected with it, was £1,306,380. Even if half the costs of the civil and military establishments and all the expenditure on the navy and marines are looked on as charges for Imperial development rather than convict administration, the remainder comes to about £1,000,000 or nearly £36 per convict per year. This was more than three times the cost of prisoners in the hulks, so even if something should be deducted for the long-term value of the works on which the convicts were engaged–and they were not very valuable–it is no wonder the government kept harping on the need for economy; but by 1800 its general expenditure was higher than ever, for though the number of convicts was still comparatively few, its 'establishments' were costly and many of its free population were still 'on the stores'.[2]

New South Wales was more than a penal settlement, though the British government was unwilling to recognize it. 'When it is considered in a political point of view,' wrote Hunter in December 1801, after he had returned home, 'it will be thought to merit a better fate than that of becoming a public forrign [sic] gaol'; but the Secretary of State was not interested; he was chiefly concerned with improving the system of transportation, even if he was also anxious to find a cargo for the convict ships on their return voyage.[3]

Before the First Fleet sailed, the British Government had hoped that the settlement would be self-sufficient in two years. Phillip quickly realized this was vain. 'No country offers less assistance to the first settlers than this does,' he wrote; 'nor do I think that any country could be more disadvantageously placed with respect to support from the mother country, on which for a few years we must entirely depend.' Certainly the cost of food fell, as more was grown in the colony, from

[1] Phillip to Sydney, 9 July 1788; Grenville to Phillip, 19 June 1789; Bentham, *Pan-opticon versus New South Wales, Works*, iv, 206; cf. 'the Economists' referred to by H. Brougham, *Inquiry into the Colonial Policy of the European Powers* (Edinburgh, 1803), i, 7; K. E. Knorr, *British Colonial Theories, 1570–1850* (Toronto, 1944), chs. 7 and 8; *Finance Report*, 20, 27. Norfolk Island became self-sufficient fairly quickly; King to Grose, 20 July 1794, King to Nepean, 5 Nov. 1794, King's report, 18 Oct. 1796, *HRNSW*, ii, 240–1, 260–1, iii, 145 ff.

[2] *Gaols Report*, PP 1819 (579), app. Q and R; O'Brien. app. E (note that there is a misprint in the addition which should read £1,165,760). Hunter seems to have found it particularly difficult to keep down expenditure; he drew Treasury Bills at about twice the rate of his successor, King, twice that of the preceding 'interregnum' (1793–5) and about four times the rate of Phillip. (Communication from Mr. G. Abbott, Univ. of New South Wales.)

[3] Hunter to Pelham, 22 Dec. 1801, to Under-Sec. King, 22 March 1802, *HRNSW*, iv, 642, 728.

CONVICT COSTS IN NEW SOUTH WALES 1786–1800

Year	*A* Approx. nos. maintained	*B* Cost excluding naval expenditure	*C* Cost excluding naval, marine and half military and civil expenditure		Approx. net cost per head p.a. (C ÷ A)	Cost according to 1797 report
1786	–	£28,346	£28,339			
1787	668	29,242	25,917			
1788	720	18,008	13,820	1786–91	£45	£26
1789	680	88,058	79,327			
1790	1,550	44,774	34,854			
1791	3,060	129,020	119,057			
1792	3,311	104,588	92,895			
1793	3,120	69,962	60,275			
1794	2,900	79,382	71,871	1792–7	£29	£33.10
1795	2,500	75,281	67,546			
1796	2,400	83,855	74,520			
1797	2,000	120,372	108,937			
1798	1,800	111,514	95,041			
1799	2,050	80,274	69,024	1797–1800	£42	
1800	2,300	110,985	96,247			

The average cost per head p.a. over the whole period is £35.13. The numbers maintained are approximate only, and are based on date of embarkation, and a rough average date for death or emancipation; they include convicts on transports coming out. From the accounts up to June 1793, the cost per head, making the same deductions, was £32 per year.

(Sources: *Gaols Report*, 1819, app. Q and R; Bigge appendix, CO 201/130, N1.)

£11 a head per year, between 1793 and 1796, to less than £5 between 1797 and 1800; but the 'dead weight' of the civil and military establishments was a handicap, for their need for barracks and houses made it impossible to 'direct the labour of the convicts to the principal object [of] . . . supporting ourselves', and both these establishments were larger (and therefore more expensive) than if there had been no convicts. How much larger? Any settlement would have needed *some* protection and *some* administration. The Finance Committee

complained that their costs were increasing more than was proportionate
to the increase in the number of convicts, and suggested the common
defect in eighteenth-century government, the 'multiplication of posts',
something 'always to be looked at with jealousy'; but this was due,
principally, to the arrival of the New South Wales Corps. From July
1790 to September 1800, the 'establishment' almost doubled, while the
convicts increased by little more than a third; but after the bulk of the
Corps had arrived, at the end of 1791, it increased by only nine per cent
and then after 1795, slightly decreased; and though the number of
convicts fell by about a third between 1792 and 1800, the total population increased by more than sixty per cent.[1]

As Botany Bay became more than a mere gaol, its benefits and its
drawbacks should have been put down to the accounts of Imperial
expansion, not of convict administration; after all, its military expenditure was due as much to fear of the French as to fear of a convict rising.
But that did not make it any cheaper. Any saving in expenditure
depended on what was obviously thought to be unlikely–'the probity
zeal and intelligence of Bailiffs in husbandry, acting without personal
interest in the concern at an immense distance'; whatever other advantages the settlement might eventually bring, the Finance Committee
thought that 'a reduction in the rate of expense per head does not
appear an event either so near or so certain as to form an ingredient in
the composition of that advantage'.[2]

If it was expensive, would it reform the convicts, as contemporary
criminologists so optimistically expected that a good penal discipline
should? It was agreed that the hulks were bad, and when prisoners
were released from them, they were 'more expert in fraud' and 'more
hardened in guilt' than before. In so far as the convicts were thieves
because they had no other occupation, regular work in New South
Wales might make them honest; but regular work depended on the
commercial progress of the settlement; its 'improvement in wealth and
the means of properly employing and reforming the convicts are
essential to the progress of each other'. Reformation was more probable
for convicts who lived with a family, 'out of town, . . . removed from
their former companions, and forced into habits of industry and
regularity', than for those living with each other and working in the

---

[1] Heads of a Plan, *HRNSW*, i, part ii, 18; Phillip to Sydney, 15 May and 9 July 1788, to
Grenville, 17 June 1790; *Finance Report*, app. O; returns for the settlement, *HRA*, i, 203,
298, 399, 437, 492, 501; ii, 385, 679; Norfolk Island, *HRNSW*, iv, 252.

[2] *Finance Report, loc. cit.*, 20 and 27; cf. *Transportation Report*, PP, 1812 (341), *evid.* Commissary Palmer, 63, Robert Campbell, 70; *Gaols Report*, PP, 1816 (431), and 1819 (579),
appendix and *evid.* Riley, 25, 47.

public gangs. In the service of settlers they might 'acquire some know-ledge of farming, and if from convicts they become well-behaved and industrious servants, a further possibility is opened to them of becoming prosperous and respectable settlers'.[1] But all this depended on there being industrious and respectable settlers for them to be servants to; of these, there were few.

Phillip was more worried about keeping his charges alive than with reforming them, though his repeated requests for free settlers, if attended to, would have helped to do both. 'Farmers and people used to the cultivation of lands' would need government support for two or three years, he thought; then, probably, they would 'be able to support themselves and to take the convicts', and after five years, could pay a 'yearly fine for the lands granted . . . The sending out settlers who will be interested in the labour of the convicts and the cultivation of the country appears to me to be absolutely necessary', both for employing the convicts and growing food. At the same time, he wanted carpenters and bricklayers as overseers for the public works.[2]

The British government had other ideas. Certainly, wrote Grenville, twenty-five artificers would be sent; but they would be convicts, chosen from the hulks. Unfortunately five were lost when the *Guardian* struck an iceberg off the Cape of Good Hope in December 1789, and fourteen of the survivors were pardoned in December 1791; though compelled to remain in the colony, their services were not necessarily available to the government. Nine free superintendents had been appointed, but only five arrived after the wreck, and of these only one was a farmer. Phillip could not establish a settlement on the Hawkesbury, apart from the difficulties of communication with it, because there were 'no proper people to conduct it', and when it was established in 1794 it was often the scene of trouble.[3]

The government did not show much interest in free settlers either. When in 1790, Banks suggested sending out free families, giving them a grant of land, for which eventually they would pay rent, and supplying them with up to ten convict servants, to be victualled for four years, it did nothing; nor did it follow up, in 1792, either a proposal that fifteen

[1] *Finance Report, loc. cit.*, 14–20; *Transportation Report*, 1812, 9–11.

[2] Phillip to Sydney, 10 July and 28 Sept. 1788.

[3] *HRNSW*, i, part ii, 310, 414 and 542; Collins, *Account*, i, 193; Sydney to Treasury, 29 April 1789, *HRNSW, loc. cit.*, 230–1; Grenville to Phillip, 24 Aug. 1789, Phillip to Nepean, 9 July 1788, Phillip to Grenville, 17 June 1790; cf. King's interview with Grenville, 29 Dec. 1790, *NSW from the Records*, i, 195–6. For conditions on the Hawkesbury, Fletcher, *Small Scale Farming, passim*, a study which is of very great value for the expirees' farming activities.

Quaker families might emigrate and be given grants of land and convict servants 'supported by the rations of government' or another, that free families be sent out to work a large grant of ten thousand acres or more. Perhaps all these schemes were too 'visionary' or too expensive, or possibly 'reputable' free settlers did not want to migrate. In 1789, the government had promised settlers only such encouragement that 'can be given . . . without subjecting the public to expense'; this meant small grants of land but no tools or provisions, and convict-servants only if they were fed and clothed by the settler; later the government agreed to provide more help—tools, seed, eighteen months' provisions and convicts 'on the store'; but even then only seven offered themselves in 1792 (and of these only five sailed) and two more in 1794.[1]

In 1789, Phillip was told to offer grants of 130 acres to non-commissioned officers of the marines and eighty acres to privates, plus seed, tools and provisions for a year, to induce them to stay in the colony. They would get extra for their wife and children, and double after another five years' military service in the settlement. That they would know little or nothing about farming did not seem to matter. They might grow some food, and they would strengthen the respectable element in New South Wales. The government was more worried about its security than its economic development, and more concerned with 'the crowded state of the hulks' at home than with either. Despite Phillip's hope that few convicts would be sent for at least a year, 1,257 were despatched between July 1789 and January 1790, 'in order that [the] gaols in this may be . . . quite cleared'. What use then was there of Grenville flattering himself that 'very little further aid will be wanted from this country'?[2]

The arrival of the second fleet, in June 1790, added to Phillip's problems. Many were sick. 'The sending out of the disordered and helpless clears the gaols, and may ease the parishes from which they are sent,' he wrote; but 'it is obvious that this settlement, instead of being a colony which is to support itself will, if the practice be continued, remain for years a burden on the mother-country.' And how could the convicts be 'reformed' if all had to be kept on the public works and government farms, 'inadequately supervised' with the 'vicious and idle

[1] Banks' proposals, *HRNSW*, *loc. cit.*, 424; John Sutton to Dundas and to King, 1791, *ib.*, 580–5; additional instructions to Phillip, 20 Aug. 1789, *HRA*, i, 125 ff.; Dundas to Phillip, 10 Jan. 1792, *ib.*, 332, but see *HRNSW*, *loc. cit.*, 648 n; G. Matcham to A. Davison, 21 Jan. 1792, to M. Nelson, 11 April, *ib.*, 591, 615; Dundas to Phillip, 14 July 1792, to Grose, 15 Feb. 1794, Grose to Dundas, 16 Feb. 1793, and 30 May, encl. return of land grants.
[2] *Gentleman's Mag.*, March 1789, lix, 274; Grenville to Phillip, 19 June and 24 Dec. 1789; Grenville to Marquis of Stafford, 29 Sept., HMC, 13th rept., i, 524.

incorporated in one body', or working for officers, a practice 'attended with unavoidable inconveniences'.[1]

Nor were they much better off on their own farms. The British government instructed the governors to grant thirty acres to expirees, with an extra twenty for their wife and ten for each living child; after Hunter's arrival, if 'peculiarly meritorious or well deserving', they could get more.[2] But free land alone did not turn ex-convicts into prosperous settlers, and the grants, made on much the same terms as those to migrants and soldiers in Canada, were not necessarily suited to conditions in New South Wales. They were not intended to establish any particular type of farm, but to encourage settlement generally, to produce a revenue if possible, to reward government servants, both civil and military, and to stop large areas being seized by speculators.[3]

The first ex-convict to receive a grant was James Ruse, at Parramatta. His success—he took himself 'off the store' in little more than a year—has made some under-estimate the difficulties of emancipist farming. Ruse was a farmer by training, as few convicts were. He was industrious, and while food was short, he could profitably dispose of any surplus produce. For all that he lost his independence, though twice more granted land, and finished up working for wages. In 1791 there were eighty-six settlers near Port Jackson and at Norfolk Island—thirty-one ex-marines, eleven seamen, forty-four emancipists and Philip Schaffer, who had originally embarked in the *Guardian* as a superintendent. Fifty of these, including nine of the seamen and all the marines, were on Norfolk Island where farming was easier than on the mainland; but very few of the eligible expirees had taken up farms. By October 1792, fifty-five of them were cultivating an average of six and a half acres each, but 'apart from Ruse, all continued to act as a drain on available resources'.[4] Unless they took up land, expirees were left to fend for themselves, to work, steal or starve, or to try to procure a passage home. This was what most wanted to do, though the British Government fondly hoped it

[1] Phillip to Grenville, 13 Feb. and 17 July 1790, 5 Nov. 1791.
[2] Instructions to Phillip, 25 April 1787, *HRA*, i, 14, to Hunter, 1794, *ib.*, 525.
[3] R. G. Riddell, 'A Study in the Land Policy of the Colonial Office, 1763–1855', *Canadian Hist. Rev.*, xviii (1937), 387; N. Macdonald, *Canada, Immigration and Settlement 1763–1841* (London, 1939), 39 and ch. 3; Fletcher, ch. i, 20.
[4] Fletcher, 43; Phillip to Grenville, 17 June 1790, 5 Nov. 1791; return of land grants, *HRA*, i, 279–82; Collins, i, 158, 169, 212. On Norfolk Island, Phillip to Sydney, 13 Feb. 1790, to Grenville, 5 Nov. 1791, to Dundas, 4 Oct. 1792, encl. King to Phillip, 19 Sept.; Grenville to Phillip, 19 Feb. 1791; Dundas to Phillip, 10 Jan. 1792; cf. P. G. King *Papers* (ML) and *HRNSW*, ii, 555 ff. For expirees' condition in December 1791, Tench, *Complete Account* (ed. Fitzhardinge), 250 ff.; for their cultivation 1792, *Return*, 16 Oct., *HRA*, i, 401–2. Shaw, Missing Land Grants', *Hist. Stud.*, v, 278 ff.; Collins, i, 212–6.

would be difficult; it could not 'legally be prevented', but 'it should be distinctly understood that no steps are likely to be taken by Government for facilitating their return.'[1]

Out of 1,284 convicts whose sentences expired between 1791 and 1800, 284 received grants on the mainland, ninety-five on Norfolk Island, and a few bought or leased land from others.[2] But many of them were not suited to become settlers. As well as land, an 'adventurer' needed capital, a 'persevering character and competent knowledge', declared Tench; then after ten years, he might make himself 'comfortable and independent'. Collins, too, thought a settler must be 'a man of some property', and as such not to be looked for 'among discharged soldiers, ship-wrecked seamen or quondam convicts'. As well as capital, they needed knowledge; and even then they faced natural difficulties in farming near Sydney. Some gained an initial success near the Hawkesbury River, where conditions were easier, when that district was opened to settlement in 1794; but floods, droughts and crop diseases struck them, and by the time of the muster in 1800, of the fifty-four ex-convicts who were there in 1795, only eight remained on their farms.[3] Petitioners from Parramatta and the Hawkesbury in 1800 stressed the difficulties they were labouring under. The Rev. Samuel Marsden and Surgeon Arndell, who investigated the settlers' condition in 1798, concluded that though some were 'idle worthless characters', many of the farmers were 'sober, industrious men'; despite this, around Parramatta, of seventy-three grantees, including sixty ex-convicts settled by Phillip by 1792, only twenty-one remained in 1798, and in all, of 274 settlers on the mainland in 1795, including 251 ex-convicts, only eighty-nine remained in 1800, though as a class, they would fare better under King.[4]

The emancipists were certainly exploited by profit-seeking traders from both within and without the colony; but they were not ruined simply by extortionate rum-traders or unscrupulous officials, as a popular tradition has it. Their debts, said Hunter in 1796 'are chiefly, altho' not wholly, owing to a disposition to indulge in drunkenness ... It has been known that the produce of a whole year has been thrown away for a few gallons of bad spirit'–though whether or not they

---

[1] Grenville to Phillip, 19 Feb. 1791; Collins, i, 169.
[2] Grants: 1791–2, *Hist. Stud.*, v, 278 ff.; 1792–3, *HRA*, i, 438; 1793–4, *ib.*, 472–3; 1794–6, *Hist. Stud.*, v, 59 ff.; 1796–1800, *HRA*, ii, 454–64; 1800, *Hist. Stud.*, v, 76–8; for expirees, *Return*, 18 Sept. 1800, *HRA*, ii, 564.
[3] Tench, *Complete Account*, ch. xvii; Collins, *Account* (2nd edn. 1804), 181; cf. Lambert, 187, 213; Bigge Appendix, CO 201/123; Fletcher, 60, 68, 100 ff., 197.
[4] For Parramatta, Report of Marsden and Arndell, 1798, *HRA*, ii, 144–6; King to Portland, 1 March 1802; Fletcher, *loc. cit.*; Roe, 'Colonial Society', *Hist. Stud.*, vii, 157.

consumed more liquor than the 'free' colonist is impossible to say. Sometimes they found the government store–the best market in the colony–closed to their grain, especially between 1796 and 1800, when Williamson was acting commissary, during Palmer's leave of absence.[1] They had to compete against officer-farmers, whom the British government had authorized to receive land grants in 1793, and who were more efficient and better equipped than the emancipists. Both groups had to pay high wages, but the officers were more adept at obtaining convicts as farm servants, as well as for personal service. Both Grose and Hunter thought fit to allow the officers ten convicts at public expense, although the government had to pay for the officers' grain, unlike that from the public farms. They improved the colony's agriculture, but the English government was much more interested in saving its money, so in 1797 it sent peremptory orders to Hunter that convicts be assigned only to employers who would feed and maintain them. If no one was willing or able to do this, if other agricultural costs were too high for the settlers to support their labourers, then the government should work the convicts itself on public farms; it would then support them, but at least it would get farm produce without having to buy it. The Duke of Portland insisted that 'the individual should pay . . . for the provisions and cloathing . . . which he receives from the public store for the convicts he employs'. This would help to reduce the costs that arose 'from not adverting to the original purpose for which this colony was established'.[2]

The need for concern about the colony's agriculture was brought home by the crop failure of 1800, which made it necessary to reduce the ration again; but this hardly justified Hunter *both* supplying free labour to the farmers *and* paying them a high price for their crops. Macarthur, in 1796, offered to supply his convict labourers with bread, and only asked government for tools, clothing, nails, ironwork for buildings and the usual ration of salt meet for eighteen months. 'If my example be followed,' he said, 'government will be instantly relieved from the expense of purchasing grain . . . and after eighteen months, the grain returned to the stores in exchange for tools, cloaths etc. will be more than sufficient to answer all the demands of the settlement for bread.'

[1] Hunter to Portland, 20 Aug. 1796; King to Portland, 28 Sept. 1800; Fletcher, ch. v, sec. vi.
[2] Dundas to Phillip, 14 July 1792, to Grose, 31 June 1793; Grose to Dundas, 29 April 1794; Portland to Hunter, 10 June 1795; Hunter to Portland, 25 Oct. 1795, 28 April and 27 Aug. 1796; Portland to Hunter, 31 Aug. 1797; Hunter's Orders, 20 May and 15 Aug. 1798, *HRA*, ii, 215 and 219; cf. Hunter to Under-Sec. King, 1 June 1797; Phillip to Dundas, 4 Oct. 1792, warns that granting convicts to officers or settlers 'will increase the number of those who do not labour for the public, and lessen those who are to furnish the colony with the necessaries of life'.

Hunter did not think others could emulate this offer, and he was probably right; he was also short of convicts, for only 2,245 arrived in the years from 1792 to 1798 inclusive, compared with 3,581 from 1788 to 1791, and like Grose before him, he would have welcomed more; but though they would have been useful in the settlement, since 'our repeated demands for tools and implements of husbandry have not been answered', nor any competent farm superintendents sent out, it is doubtful if they would have reduced the cost of growing food.[1]

If many of the officers got cheap labour, they benefited in other ways too. The shortage of supplies created a sellers' market, especially for rum, whether sought as a 'solace', needed as an incentive payment for labour, or forced on the settler in return for his crops; and sometimes the officers were sellers themselves. The prices of imports were certainly kept high by the captains of the visiting ships, as Mrs. Macarthur, Collins and Hunter all reported, and they might be justified in part as the reward for a risky speculation.[2] But they were kept up by local traders, too, and though some officers, like Collins, Hunter and Patterson, kept strictly to their official duty, others, both civilian and military, like Balmain, D'Arcy Wentworth, Williamson, Johnston, Fenn Kemp and John Macarthur, either were openly criticized for indulging in the rum trade, or quickly made substantial fortunes, by fair means or foul. In this traffic, a number of ex-convicts shared and profited–Simeon Lord, James Larra, Isaac Nichols, Henry Kable, George Barrington and others; in fact, considering the settlers' complaints that 'the colony is infested with dealers, pedlars and extortioners', the 'officers' have often been too much blamed for the activities of their ex-convict competitors.[3] Whether such financial success connoted moral reform is perhaps dubious (though on some valuations it would); later it was to worry British ministers who were anxious for transportation to be made a more deterrent punishment; meanwhile it certainly handicapped the success and reform of those placed on the land.

[1] Macarthur to Hunter, 15 Aug. 1796, *HRNSW*, iii, 68 ff.; Hunter to Macarthur, 18 Aug. 1796, *ib.*, 70–1; Hunter to Portland, 25 July 1798; Grose to Dundas, 16 Feb. 1793; Hunter to Portland, 25 Oct. 1795, 10 and 20 June 1797, 10 Jan. 1798; Collins, i, 496.

[2] For prices, Marsden and Arndell's report, *loc. cit.*, petitions in 1798 from Kissing Point and Northern Boundaries, Bonwick Transcripts (ML), Box 12, from Field of Mars, *HRA*, ii, 137; Atkins' Journal, Jan. 1799; letter from T. F. Palmer, quoted K. M. Bowden, *George Bass* (OUP 1952), 54; Elizabeth Macarthur to Miss Kingdon, 1 Sept. 1798 (misdated 1795), *HRNSW*, ii, 512; Hunter's G. and G.O., 25 June 1798, *HRA*, ii, 216–7; Collins, i, 262 (Jan. 1793), 500 (Sept. 1796). For rum as an incentive payment, Hunter to Portland, 20 Aug. 1796, Collins, i, 435, and a letter attributed to Marsden, 14 Sept. 1798, *HRNSW*, iii, 486.

[3] Field of Mars' petition, *loc. cit.*; Fletcher, ch. vi, sec. 1.

A government store would have made the settlers' lot easier. King, from Norfolk Island, Hunter, and later Collins, all suggested it, but though Portland approved, and sent out goods in two ships for public sale in 1798, he could not send much, for Hunter never reported what was most wanted in the settlement. When King returned to Sydney in 1800, he found, like Paterson the year before, the 'hitherto existing monopolies and extortionate demands of usurious dealers and their dependent retailers virtually unchecked', and during the next two years, he bought or ordered several cargoes to sell to the public.[1] At the same time, private trading was increasing, so that in 1801-2, as Bass lamented to his partner, the market was 'glutted with goods, . . . and . . . our wings are clipped with a vengeance'. So many ships had arrived everything was 'wonderfully cheap'.[2]

By this time the emancipist settlers were doing better, thanks to a good season and the fall in prices. King offered premiums to 'stimulate their industry', and by 1803 most were out of debt and improving their farms and their homes. In that year, 464 convicts, or about a quarter of those in New South Wales, were cultivating farms, which suggests they were having some success; but in six years, King granted land to only seventy-one expirees, of whom forty-seven became successful farmers, and this was only about one in thirty of those released. Those who did not take land seemed to be 'idle and worthless', according to both Hunter and King; their labour only tended 'to keep them in a constant state of intoxication'.[3]

When King took over in 1800, he carried on the system much as he found it. Since London was demanding 'a material diminution' of the expenses paid by Britain, he reduced the number of servants assigned to

[1] King, Report on Norfolk Island, 18 Oct. 1796, *HRNSW*, iii, 156; Collins, i, 540; Hunter to Portland, 10 June 1797, 25 May 1798, 10 July 1799; Portland to Hunter, 31 Aug. 1797, 6 Feb. and 3 Dec. 1798, 5 Nov. 1799; King to Portland, 28 Sept. 1800, 21 Aug. 1801; Hobart to King, 30 Jan. 1802; King to Portland, 1 March 1802, to Hobart, 30 Oct. King bought the cargo of *John Jay*, *Britannia* and *Greenwich* (*HRA*, ii, 681-5 and iii, 111); stores for sale despatched by government were sent in *Walker*, *Royal Admiral*, *Earl Cornwallis* and *Porpoise*, Under-Sec. King to King, 23 Sept. 1800, Portland to King, 19 June 1801, to Treasury 29 May, *ib.*, ii, 551, iii, 99-103; cf. Under-Sec. King's comments on Enderby and Champion to Liverpool, 1 Aug. 1800, *HRNSW*, iv, 117-8.

[2] Bass to Waterhouse, 4 Oct. 1801, Rowley to Waterhouse, 14 May 1802, *HRNSW*, iv, 587 and 753; Peron's Report, 11 Dec. 1802, in E. Scott, *Life of Matthew Flinders* (Sydney, 1914), 449-50; Bowden, *op. cit.*, chs. x and xvii.

[3] King to Hobart, 30 Oct. 1802, 9 May and 7 Aug. 1803; cf. to Portland, 1 March 1802; Hobart to King, 24 Feb. 1803; Musters, 1800, 1801 and 1802; Walsh, *New Zealand Geographer*, xviii, 149 ff., using 1803 Muster; Fletcher, 245-6, and table 21; Roe, *Hist. Stud.*, vii, 157-9, and 'Administration of P. G. King', 33 and 44, using the 1814 Muster and 1828 Census; Hunter to Portland, 1 May 1799; King to Portland, 28 Sept. 1800. Cf., below, pp. 85-6.

both civil and military officers from 356 to ninety-four, as Portland had
told Hunter to do. In the hope of lowering the cost of food, with some
of the 1,409 male convicts who arrived between November 1800 and the
end of 1802 he was able to expand the public farming, which though
reduced had never been abandoned; but much of the area cultivated in
Phillip's time had 'very improperly been leased to individuals', so he
had to rent land, and since he still lacked competent overseers, the
results were mixed. In 1803, 'the 710 acres sowed on the Public Account
this Year' had 'every present appearance of yielding a plentiful return';
between 350 and 400 convicts were employed at 'public cultivation',
and by 1804 he had a good reserve of grain in store, though 'the produce
of grain raised by those at public labour' was 'very short of the expense
of their provisions and cloathing'. He did not want to stop assigning
convicts to deserving settlers, which he thought 'a saving to the
Crown', though this would depend on the price he had to pay for their
grain, compared with the cost of growing it himself; but it certainly
helped the settlers, whom he wanted to encourage. The British government's attitude fluctuated, and though Portland had told Hunter to
increase the public farms, Hobart told King, in 1803, to reduce them.
As the number of new arrivals fell off after 1802, and the sentences
of the old hands expired, he had to do so, and by 1806 he was employing on them only 177 men, most of whom he regarded as 'bad
characters'.[1]

From 1793 to September 1800, only 1,234 male and 564 female
convicts landed at Sydney; during King's rule, for the next six years,
2,363 males and 706 females disembarked, or a yearly average of more
than twice as many. But 1,393 of the men had arrived by October 1802,
so although about 2,000 were in servitude then, they dwindled as time
went on. Out of a total population of 8,593 in 1806, there were 1,114,
including women and children, on the store books of the civil and
military departments; there were 1,000 'settlers and landholders', including women. To work for these and for the government, there were
about 1,900 male convicts; 648 were assigned and the government
employed all the others who were fit. To supplement this labour force
there were about 650 female convicts and 4,000 other free persons; but
since more than half of these were women and children, and many of
the men had leased land from settlers, who, complained King, had thus

---

[1] Portland to Hunter, 10 June 1795; King to Portland, 21 Aug. 1801; King to Hobart,
7 Aug. 1803, 1 March 1804; Hobart to King, 29 and 30 Aug. 1802, 24 Feb. 1803; King's
report, 12 Aug. 1806, *HRNSW*, vi, 149 and 153. For the public farms, cf. E. Dunsdorfs,
Australian Wheat Growing Industry, 1788–1948 (MUP, 1956), 19–21.

'in great measure done away with the labouring class', it was no wonder that even with the convicts, labour was scarce and dear.[1]

King had criticized Hunter's administration, and he succeeded in cutting the average Treasury Bill expenditure from £36,000 in 1796–1800 to £20,000 in 1801–6, but other costs remained high. Between 1801 and 1809 the total expenditure on the colony, including that for the voyages to it, was £1,043,000, or just on £900,000 if we deduct (as before) half the cost of the civil and military establishments, as being due to 'imperial development' rather than convict administration. During the six years that King was governor, the average number of convicts in the colony was 2,250, so the average annual cost per head was £43; this sum was kept down in 1804 and 1805 by the extremely low expenditure on shipping when only two vessels sailed, but after that it tended upward, and from 1807 to 1809 it was more than twice as much. With fewer arrivals the numbers 'on strength' declined, and each man had to 'carry' a larger share of the general burden of the establishment, increased as it was by new settlements at Newcastle and in Van Diemen's Land. As an offset was the value of the convicts' labour on public works. Under both Hunter and King, they built houses, prisons, stores, wharves, granaries, windmills, government offices and barracks, including a government house at Parramatta, and a clock tower and Fort Phillip in Sydney, as well as making carts, roads, bricks, boats and other things; but these seemed of little consequence to ministers in London.[2] There was as yet no 'staple' (not even flax at Norfolk Island) for convict labour to produce at a profit, either directly for the government, or indirectly for private employers who might take them off the government's hands. Since food was costly to grow and imported supplies were dear, the convicts were expensive to maintain, and little could be done about it.

Most of the men on 'public labour' were on 'task-work' and usually finished their task soon after midday; but the others had short hours too, for they had to have enough 'free time' to earn wages to pay rent for lodgings which the government did not provide. This certainly allowed them to meet the demand for their labour, if they felt like it; but in the

---

[1] Convict indents, ML; Muster, 1806, *HRA*, v, 778–9; King to Camden, 15 March 1806; King's report, 12 Aug. 1806, *HRNSW*, vi, 152–5; Surgeon Luttrell to Under-Sec. O'Sullivan, *ib.*, 292.

[2] For costs, King to Portland, 28 Sept. 1800, *ib.*, iv, 203, report, 31 Dec. 1801, *ib.*, 664; *Gaols Report*, 1819, app. Q and R, for more comprehensive figures than King's estimate to Castlereagh, 11 Dec. 1807, *HRA*, v, 789, and below, p. 99. For public works, *Returns*, 25 Sept. 1800, 30 June 1803, 12 Aug. 1806, *HRNSW*, iv, 151–6, v, 163, vi, 163; Clark, *History*, 240 ff. I am again indebted to Mr. G. Abbott here; see above, p. 60.

afternoons and at night they were under little supervision, and might work, idle, drink or get into mischief more or less as they pleased. Orders in 1792 and 1795 had prescribed labour until sunset, but in 1801 for only nine hours, and in winter 'the bell' was rung at 2.30 p.m.[1] Wages, though fixed by government order, were high, because of the high cost of living; but since labour was so short, something more was needed, like rum 'without which the disspirited indolent convict cannot be excited to exertions', lamented Chaplain Marsden, or sugar or tea, 'the necessaries and the comforts of the infant society'. The trouble was, said King in 1806, 'when spirits can be procured, few will work . . . for any other mode of payment.' This was usually thought an obstacle to reformation, though Phillip had spoken of a 'moderate distribution', amounting to half a gallon per head a year, as a 'bounty many of these people well deserve', and in 1803, Hobart had recommended a 'pint of grog' to be given every Sunday to each convict who had behaved well the week before; in fact a pint a week was about the average consumption of the adult male.[2]

Outside their work, the men had little to solace them but drink. They took to the new world the love of alcohol they had in the old, where drunkenness was rife in the cities, and where, and per head of population, about half a gallon of spirits and one and a half gallons of beer were consumed every year. But in New South Wales, men were better off financially, and had little else to spend their money on. They had little or no family life, which some thought might check their bibulousness, or at least provide an alternative source of interest and affection. They mixed, perforce, with men whose tastes were like their own. Per head of population they drank more than three gallons of spirits a year, six times as much as in England, though compared with it there was little beer, and the proportion of adult males in the population was larger.[3]

By this time the masters were maintaining nearly all the convicts who were assigned, and the spread of private farming increased their numbers. If idle, they could be ordered up to 500 lashes and be kept in double irons, but any punishment had to be ordered by a magistrate, not inflicted by an employer or overseer. For idleness or

---

[1] King's report, 12 Aug. 1806, *HRNSW*, vi, 149–53; Phillip to Nepean, 29 March 1792; G. and G.O., 9 Oct. and 17 Nov. 1795, 21 July 1796, 10 March 1797, 15 May, 19 July and 30 Oct. 1798, 11 June 1799, 15 May and 23 Oct. 1801, 19 Oct. 1802, 7 Aug. 1803.
[2] King to Under-Sec. King, 3 May 1800, *HRNSW*, iv, 84; Marsden's letter, 14 Sept. 1798, *ib.*, iii, 486; Phillip to Dundas, 2 Oct. 1792; Hobart to King, 24 Feb. 1803.
[3] Alcoholic consumption in UK, Report of Commissioners of Inland Revenue, PP 1870 (c-82), xx, 377 ff.; in NSW, 1800–1802, King to Hobart, 30 Oct. 1802, and introdn., *HRA*, iii, p. xv.

misbehaviour the usual punishment was flogging, a contemporary service tradition, which was to set a standard in Australia for years to come; the gaol gang or a penal settlement were also available, but to send a man there was to deprive his employer, whether public or private, of labour.[1] Some private employers, like John Macarthur, Robert Campbell and a few others, were honourable men; most, whether small settlers, wealthy emancipists, or even officials, were not. The result was that, despite a few exceptions in 'respectable families', labour, whether in public or private service, was not likely to 'reform' the convicts in the way that some argued that it would in a penitentiary, though whether that panacea would, in fact, have been any better is another matter.

In New South Wales, the major incentive to reform was the 'pass', a certificate which excused men from compulsory labour, and allowed them to work all their time on their own. Later known as the 'ticket of leave', this was an innovation of King's. The governor granted it at his discretion, usually as a reward for good conduct; but since the ticket-of-leave men cost the government nothing, in order to reduce expenditure he, and his successors, sometimes gave tickets to convicts whether or not they were reformed or meritorious, if they were able to earn their own living and take themselves 'off the stores'.[2]

Apart from the convicts, the other principal group in the population were the soldiers of the New South Wales Corps. But the army at that time was rather 'a midden fit only for outcasts' and the 'red coat was a badge less of honour than of shame', and since it has been estimated that the *average* battalion contained fifty drunkards, plunderers, stragglers, and would-be deserters and criminals, and since the Corps included both ex-convicts and military prisoners from the Savoy, and was worse than most other British or Irish regiments, it was hardly a reforming influence.[3] But other developments were taking place in the

[1] G. and G.O., 2 and 31 Oct. 1800, 6 Feb. 1802 and 8 March 1803; indenture for assigned servants, 6 Jan. 1804, *HRA*, v, 73; King's report, 1806, *HRNSW*, vi, 153; *Transportation Report*, 1812, 11.
[2] Ticket-of-leave regulations, 10 Oct. 1801, 28 Oct. 1802, *HRA*, iii, 48, iv, 326; *Transportation Report*, 1812, evid. Hunter, 47–8. For form of ticket in 1806, *HRNSW*, vi, 47.
[3] On the army, Howard, 'Wellington and the British Army', in M. Howard (ed.), *Wellingtonian Studies* (1959), 78; C. W. C. Oman, *Wellington's Army* (London, 1912), 211–2; H. de Watteville, *The British Soldier* (London 1954), ch. 8. On NSW Corps, Collins, i, 395 (Sept. 1794); Hunter to Portland, 10 Aug. 1796; Portland to Hunter, 22 Feb. 1797; George Suttor to Bligh, 10 Feb. 1809, *HRNSW*, vii, 23; Under-Sec. King to Col. Brownrigg, 24 March 1799, *ib.*, iii, 649, King to Portland, 10 March 1801, 1 March 1802, *ib.*, iv, 320, 726; *Transportation Report*, 1812, Bligh's evid., 46; Shaw, 'NSW Corps', *JRAHS*, xlvii, 128; T. G. Parsons, 'NSW Corps', *ib.*, 1 (1964), 297; Abbott to King, 13 Feb. 1808, forwarded to Sam. Whitbread, *Whitbread Papers*, 4985, Bedford.

colony which in time would change its character completely. King was encouraging the wool industry. Its growth would eventually provide a limitless economic basis for convict labour, and so reduce the cost of transportation to the government. 'There can be no doubt of the excellence of the finest wool produced from the sheep in this colony,' he wrote. For the moment high transport costs and English competition prevented exports, but there was a local demand for blankets and clothing, as well as for meat. Marsden was showing an interest in his animal flock as well as his human one; John Macarthur was granted 5,000 acres of land and a 'reasonable number' of convicts (not less than thirty) to enable him to develop his flocks, and land and convicts were likewise promised to Gregory Blaxland.[1] There were other economic activities too. Expirees could obtain work as carpenters, tailors and shoemakers, in making cloth and hats, in potteries, tanneries, breweries, shipping and fisheries. 'The exertions of the whole colony are not now, as formerly, solely directed to agriculture,' reported Paterson in 1809. 'We have now adventurers in shipping, traders, shopkeepers and mechanics of every description.'[2]

But if the 'expirees' could get work, were they reformed? Bligh did not think so. 'By far the greater part of the Prisoners retain, after their servitude, the same characters as by their vicious habits they have maintained in their career of life, notwithstanding rewards and blessings offered to them if they do well,' he wrote in 1807. 'This melancholy truth has been proved by many of the Emancipations and Free Pardons which have been given; even those who have been raised to some degree of wealth, . . . if happily they leave off thieving, their habits of cheating and knavery seem to be increased; . . . fair and honourable principle they cannot admit . . . Not until the next or after Generations can be expected any considerable advance to morality and virtue.'[3] Perhaps the Governor was liverish when he wrote this despatch; his comments on free settlers—'in general a thoughtless set of men . . . many . . . addicted to liquor . . . and in debt'—were not much more flattering. William Richardson, once an assigned servant, told the 1812 Committee that 'notorious villains' became 'good members of society', and King had reported some years before that while not wanting to

[1] King to Hobart, 14 Aug. 1804, enclosing Marsden's Report on Sheep Farming, 11 Aug.; King to Camden, 2 Oct. 1805. On Macarthur, Camden to King, 31 Oct. 1804, King to Camden, 20 July 1805, Macarthur-Onslow, ch. iv; on Blaxland, Castlereagh to King, 13 July 1805, King to Castlereagh, 27 July 1806.

[2] Evid. Bligh, *Transportation Report*, 1812, 45; Paterson to Castlereagh, 23 March 1809, *HRNSW*, vii, 83.

[3] Bligh to Windham, 31 Oct. 1807.

suggest that 'the morals of the community are very exemplary', they 'certainly are not so generally depraved as may be imagined'.[1] There seems no way of verifying the sweeping statements of observers, except to say that doubtless there were some of all sorts, and one should not expect too much.

Bligh told the Transportation Committee in 1812 that 'a man who had been a Convict was always remembered by others as having been such'; but it was inevitable that convicts, officials and free men should be thrown together a great deal. It was very obvious that some were ready enough to cohabit with convict women, and 'appear in public as though they were their lawful wives'; Macquarie was told to stop this practice, but meanwhile it 'brought on a connection with the other class of convicts . . . and made the interest of the convicts and the officers inseparable'.[2] Some emancipists joined the rebels in deposing Bligh in 1808. Ex-convicts had been recruited to the New South Wales Corps ever since 1793, even though Collins had lamented that it 'was not improved by the introduction of people of this description'; in 1802, they joined with the free settlers in the loyal associations which King raised to guard against a threatened uprising by Irish prisoners. True Major Johnston had protested against this, but King had firmly laid down the principle that 'the King and the Legislature's Humanity in giving the Governor power to Emancipate did not consign the Offender to the Laws of his Country to Oblivion and disgrace for ever. I will aver and support that the Objects of that Mercy become as Free and Susceptible of every Right as Free Born Britons as any Soul in this Territory' – an anticipation of Macquarie's later policy.[3] So in the Sydney Association, between 1802 and 1811, four convicts and twenty ex-convicts were enrolled, and at Parramatta, six convicts and seventeen ex-convicts. Only seven were definitely without convict taint, but there are no data for the remaining fifty-four.[4]

King, like Macquarie later, was at times criticized for his leniency. Letting men off the stores might be an economy, or an inducement to reform; but though 'the meaning of this may be good,' the botanist, Caley, told Sir Joseph Banks, 'yet it is the origin of some evils, for it

[1] Evid. Richardson, *Transportation Report*, 1812, 56; King to Hobart, 1 March 1804.
[2] Evid. Bligh, *op. cit.*, 36; George Suttor to Bligh, 10 Feb. 1809, *HRNSW*, vii, 23; Castlereagh to Macquarie, 14 May 1809, *ib.*, 146–7.
[3] Collins, i, 260 (Jan. 1793), 391 (Sept. 1794), 455 (Feb. 1796); King to Johnston, 18 Feb. 1803, Johnston to King, 17 Feb., *HRA*, iv, 213–6; Macquarie to Castlereagh, 30 April 1810, quoted with approval, *Transportation Report*, 1812, 13.
[4] Duncan MacCallum, 'Early Volunteer Associations in New South Wales', *JRAHS*, xlvii, 352 ff., and 'A Study of the Defence of New South Wales' (thesis for the degree of M.A., University of Sydney, 1961), 112.

gives hopes to all for to gain such permission . . .; it also gives more room for thieving.' Banks agreed that King granted 'too many reprieves'. Phillip had emancipated twenty-six altogether, Grose an average of forty-three a year, Hunter thirty-six a year; King pardoned seventy-eight a year, though he had about fifty per cent more to deal with, including many Irish rebels.[1] Did these emancipations destroy the deterrence of transportation or encourage reformation? It is difficult to say. Certainly the British criminal did not seem deterred by the fear of 'Botany Bay', though in the early days conditions there had certainly been severe. Perhaps he did not know about this, or perhaps severe punishments do *not* deter men from crime; but if there was little deterrence, English critics were not slow to point out that many were not reformed either.

'Punishment,' said Tench, 'when not directed to promote reformation is arbitrary and unauthorized.' How could it be directed to reformation? The latter was hindered by the social struggles that soon appeared in the colony. In many places labour was poorly supervised. The Government made no provision for education, and little even for religious instruction. No schoolmaster was sent out, and there was no school in the settlement until 1800. The Government ignored the offer of a Roman Catholic priest to go, voluntarily, to New South Wales, in 1787, despite the number of Catholics among the convicts; even the official Anglican Chaplain, the Reverend Richard Johnson, complained that often less than half, sometimes only a quarter, of the convicts attended Sunday service, and there was no place of worship, not exposed to rain, to wind and sun.[2]

In Phillip's additional instructions, he was told to reserve land in every township for a church and school; but these were only reservations, not buildings. The first building planned for a church at Parramatta finished up as a granary; for a long time services in Sydney were held in a boathouse 'not fit or safe for a stable', yet Grose only put obstacles in the way of Johnson building a church. A second chaplain was sent out in the *Guardian*, but he returned to England when it was wrecked, so Johnson remained without help, in a colony of 4,000, spread over Sydney, Parramatta and Toongabbie, until Marsden arrived

[1] Caley to Banks, c. 1803, *HRNSW*, v, 296; Banks to King, 29 Aug. 1804, *ib.*, 460; cf. *HRA*, I, iv, introdn., p. xi; for the Irish, below, ch. 7.
[2] Tench, *Complete Account*, 208; Johnson to S.P.G., 1 Dec. 1796, *HRNSW*, iii, 184; the Rev. T. Walshe to Sydney, 1787, *ib.*, i, pt. ii, 119–20; Johnson to Phillip, 29 Feb. 1792, *ib.*, 594. Though Wilberforce was responsible for recommending Johnson, Pitt told him that he was not ignoring the question (Pitt to Wilberforce, 23 Sept. 1786, Wilberforce [ed.], *op. cit.*, 16–17).

in 1794. Two years before Wilberforce had suggested to Dundas that three or four clergy and a few salaried schoolmasters should be sent out; but Dundas was not interested. After Johnson left in 1800, King again had to complain that 'we have only one', though the Reverend Henry Fulton, transported for complicity in the Irish Rebellion, officiated at Norfolk Island after 1800, and missionaries on the way to and from the Pacific Islands were able sometimes to take services in the colony.[1]

In 1805, apparently on Marsden's prompting, Wilberforce wrote to Castlereagh, then Secretary of State, deploring the lack of teachers and clergy. Marsden pressed the matter further when he went to England in 1807, when Bligh was still lamenting their absence. The only school, he said, was the Orphan School with about fifty-four girls, and a small school kept by a missionary driven to New South Wales by stress of weather; thus out of 'nearly two thousand children' (actually 1,747) not a hundred received any education. Only when Marsden was at home was he able to stir the government into action.[2]

In the early days, Collins had recorded 'proofs of the incorrigible depravity of the convicts'; they were 'wretched, worthless, dissipated, indolent, presuming' and any 'hope of their amendment seemed every day to lessen'. 'A more wicked, abandoned and irreligious set of people have never been brought together in any part of the world,' lamented Hunter, after reporting the burning of the Church and Schoolhouse in 1798. 'My support of the clergy . . . has not been much relish'd by the colony at large because order and morality is not the wish of its inhabitants.' Sydney Smith, reviewing Collins's book, agreed with all this. To his mind transportation was an expensive punishment, and far from being a deterrent was exactly the opposite. When the story of the colony 'had been attentively perused in the parish of St. Giles,' he wrote, 'the ancient avocation of picking pockets will certainly not become more discredited from the knowledge that it may eventually lead to the possession of a farm of a thousand acres on the River Hawkesbury. Since the benevolent Howard attacked our prisons, incarceration had become not only healthy but elegant, and a county-jail precisely the place to which any pauper might wish to retire . . . Upon the same principle there is some risk that transportation may be considered as one

[1] HRNSW, i, pt. ii, 260 n., 602–3; Grose and Johnson to Dundas, 4 and 3 Sept. 1793, HRA, i, 451–2; Wilberforce to Dundas, 7 Aug. 1792, HRNSW, i, pt. ii, 634; King to Under-Sec. King, 21 Aug. 1801.

[2] Wilberforce to Castlereagh, 9 Nov. 1805, HRNSW, v, 727–8; Bligh to Windham, 7 Feb. 1807; Castlereagh to Archbishop of Canterbury, 1807, Correspondence, Despatches and other papers of Viscount Castlereagh, Second Marquis of Londonderry (ed. Marquis of Londonderry, 1851), 2nd Ser., military and miscellaneous, viii, 127–8.

of the surest roads to honour and wealth, and that no felon will hear the verdict of "Not Guilty" without considering himself as cut off in the fairest prospect of his career.'[1]

But the British government did not agree, and was determined to carry on. It still spoke as if deterrence and reform were both easy to achieve by transportation, just as its critics seemed to think them certain in a penitentiary system. It still dreamed of economy, ignoring the inevitable costs of development, the high expenditure per head until numbers grew large, and until colonial employers could take the men off the government's hands. It still left the governor an autocrat. This was perhaps necessary in a gaol, but it aroused the settlers' irritation, and this could readily be ventilated by malicious letters to officials and highly-placed friends at home, pulling strings, retailing scandals and spreading rumours which were so often untrue, and making the most of what were possibly legitimate grievances. So it is not surprising that the well-meaning, but elderly and rather ineffective Hunter, the somewhat tetchy King, growing old and gouty, and the vituperative Bligh all fell foul of many of their officers and settlers, whose activities they tried too closely and autocratically to control, while at the same time they failed to satisfy the British government's desire for a severity and an economy which was impossible to achieve.

---

[1] Collins, i, 230, 265; Hunter to Portland, 1 Nov. 1798; *Ed. R.*, ii (1803), 36, cf. Bentham *Panopticon versus NSW*, *Works*, iv, 178, 212.

4

Governor Macquarie

'In a fatherly kind of way
I govern each tribe and sect.'
W. S. GILBERT: *The Mikado*

On 8 May 1809 Colonel Lachlan Macquarie was appointed Captain-General and Governor-in-Chief in and over the territory of New South Wales. He was to restore a legitimate government, and that done, to try 'to improve the Morals of the Colonists, to encourage Marriage, to provide for Education, to prohibit the Use of Spirituous Liquors, to increase the Agriculture'; as to the convicts, his instructions were less explicit, but the question of assignment would 'require your consideration', while the females should be encouraged to marry.[1]

The new governor landed in Sydney on 31 December 1809, a month before his forty-ninth birthday. Industrious, courageous, honest, 'conscious of the rectitude' of his purposes, enlightened and intelligent, it seemed possible that he might be able to put an end to the incessant quarrels that racked the little settlement of which he had been put in charge; but the disputes and the conflicts of interest which they reflected were deeply based, and many of the settlers, both free and bond, were so malicious and self-seeking that it was soon apparent that his path would not be 'roses, roses all the way'. To his task, Macquarie brought a strong sense of duty, but it was coupled with firm ideas of hierarchy, degree and subordination, nourished in his childhood, as the nephew on his mother's side of the Highland Laird, Maclaine of Lochbay, and in the army where he had served with much distinction; these ideas in turn produced an intolerance of opposition, so often seen as disobedience, which, as time went on, added to the difficulties he had to contend with. None the less it was with high hopes that he

---

[1] Macquarie's Instructions, May 1809, *HRA*, vii, 190 ff.; Castlereagh to Macquarie, 14 May 1809.

addressed the citizens of Sydney, on New Year's Day, 1810, promising to promote the welfare and prosperity of the colony.[1]

In a penal settlement, convict policy was all important. In this, Macquarie strove for three things—first, which is often forgotten, improved discipline in servitude; secondly, fair treatment and the encouragement of religion; this would encourage reform, but even more striking was his third proposal: as 'the greatest Inducement that Can be held out to the Reformation of the Manners of the Inhabitants, . . . Emancipation, when United with Rectitude and long tried good Conduct, should lead a man back to that Rank in Society which he had forfeited and do away, in as far as the Case will admit, All Retrospect of former bad Conduct.'[2] He wanted more convicts to ease the labour shortage. 'The Situation of the Colony requires that as many Male Convicts as possible should be sent out, the prosperity of the Country depending on their numbers,' he wrote. He abandoned the government farms, and assigned the prisoners working on them, for the settlers were 'all in distress for people to carry on their Agricultural pursuits'; but he forecast a demand for men for 'essentially necessary Public Buildings'—barracks, a new hospital, granaries and other public stores—even though many thought that reformation was more likely in private service. Later, for its own reasons, the British Government would send out plenty of men; for the moment it took no notice.[3]

For discipline, Macquarie tried to enforce the regulation that convicts and emancipists should always carry with them a pass from either a magistrate or their master, or their ticket-of-leave, or their certificate of emancipation. Though it was impossible to prevent some employers improperly giving their servants passes, or even selling them, so long as there were so few 'respectable' masters in the colony, he kept a closer control over the prisoners than his predecessors.[4] He increased the night patrols in Sydney in 1810, and next year reorganized the police. Unfortunately most of the constables were ex-convicts—there was no one else—so the 'force' was not very efficient, and there were not enough 'active and vigilant magistrates' to keep them up to the mark. Crimes were frequent, though in proportion to the population they gradually

---

[1] Macquarie to Castlereagh, 30 April 1810; *Sydney Gazette*, 7 Jan. 1810. For Macquarie's youth and army career, Ellis, *Macquarie*.
[2] To Castlereagh, 30 April 1810. Wilberforce agreed with Macquarie in this.
[3] To Castlereagh, 8 March 1810, to Liverpool, 18 Oct. 1811; cf. Blaxland to Liverpool, 27 Nov. 1809, *HRNSW*, vii, 232, A. Fenn Kemp to J. T. Campbell, 8 Jan. 1810, Col. Sec's In Letters, Bundle 4, ML, and Macquarie's refusal to allow Kemp to keep four servants owing to the government's great need for convict labour for itself.
[4] G. and G.O., 2 Oct. 1795, 30 Nov. 1796, 20 March 1797, 30 Dec. 1800, 12 Jan. 1803, 28 July 1804, 28 July and 18 Aug. 1810.

decreased. They were not more common among 'government' convicts than those in private service, but they were most common in Sydney, because of the large numbers there, and Macquarie's building policy kept them in town, rather than getting them away into the country.[1] Convicts could not be properly controlled when not actually at work, so long as they had to find their own lodgings. While the colonial gaols were small, this was inevitable; but it is extraordinary that no convict barracks were completed until 1819. When Macquarie first proposed such a building, in April 1814, 'to enable the executive Authority to keep a due Control' over the convicts, and 'by that Means to lay the Foundation for their more Speedy Reformation', Bathurst, for all his later criticism of laxity in New South Wales, thought that although desirable 'if the funds of the Colony could meet the Expence', yet they were not so necessary as to justify a grant from England.[2] Three years later, Macquarie began the building without authority, and told Bathurst that it would 'be productive of many Good Consequences, as to the personal Comfort and Improvement of the Morals of the Male Convicts, in the immediate Service of Government at Sydney'. The Secretary of State objected no longer, but now even copied Macquarie's use of Capitals in his Enthusiasm. 'If the object of the Establishment in New South Wales be the Reform of the Population, I am aware that it must altogether fail, unless means are provided for Lodging under proper Superintendence and Control those who may be sent there.'[3]

The 'handsome brick structure', as Bigge described it, was opened on the King's Birthday, 4 June 1819, though he found that the roof leaked and the drainage was defective, and thought the walls were 'too ornamental, . . . the leading object of security being sacrificed to that of exhibiting with advantage and effect the regular proportions of the building they enclose'. At first it housed 688 of the prisoners in Sydney, leaving about 1,200 outside; but in 1820 it was taking 800, another smaller barrack 250, and another at Parramatta 150; another was building at Windsor, and there was another at Sydney for 150 juveniles. All this permitted closer discipline and longer working hours, for the men no longer had to have their 'own time' to earn wages to pay for their lodgings, and the desire to gain permission to sleep out of barracks was an incentive to good behaviour. 'Not a tenth part of the former Night Robberies and Burglaries being now committed, since the Convicts

[1] G. and G.O., 11 June 1810 and 1 Jan. 1811; evid. Druitt and Hutchinson, Bigge Appendix, CO 201/120; *Gaols Report*, 1819, evid. Riley, 64; Bigge, *Judicial Establishments*, 63, PP 1823 (33).
[2] Macquarie to Bathurst, 28 April 1814; Bathurst to Macquarie, 4 Dec. 1815.
[3] Macquarie to Bathurst, 12 Dec. 1817; Bathurst to Macquarie, 24 Aug. 1818.

6

have been lodged in the New Barracks,' reported Macquarie jubilantly.[1] Certainly the crime rate in Sydney in 1820 was only half that in Parramatta; but unfortunately, neither the governor nor Greenway, the architect, was aware of the latest theories of prison reformers, so there was 'an entire absence of classification' and 'nothing appeared of the nature of an organized system of morality'.[2]

However Bathurst did not appreciate this, and he was pleased. 'The Effect is exactly what every person acquainted with the Subject must have anticipated,' he wrote, forgetting his opposition to spending the money five years before. Even if more convicts arrived and the barracks should become overcrowded, that 'evil' would be far less than that of having the men 'without Superintendence and Control to provide a Lodging for themselves by their Crimes and Depredations'. Bathurst's only concern was that the Governor's regulations had 'overlooked the great Consideration that the Prisoners are Persons subject to Punishment for grave Offences, and as such ought to undergo more than ordinary restraints'. Should they have both Saturdays and Sundays free, as they did, even if partly occupied by washing and mending their clothes and going to church? Were not their rations larger than necessary? Not really, for he could rest assured that the convicts looked on living in Barracks as a punishment, and it prevented them earning £4 or £5 a week outside.[3]

As incentives to reform, Macquarie continued his predecessors' practice of granting pardons or other indulgences, which made up the official road to rehabilitation. The governors had been empowered, since 1790, 'to remit, either absolutely or conditionally, whole or any part' of the term of a prisoner's sentence of transportation, though in 1812 the Select Committee on Transportation thought that they had granted pardons too freely and suggested limiting their power.[4] Macquarie urged that he should still be allowed to grant conditional (but not absolute) pardons, chiefly because of the delay caused by referring cases to England, but in any case, for the moment, no more was said.

[1] Bigge, *New South Wales*, 22–3, PP 1822 (448); Macquarie to Bathurst, 24 March and 20 July 1819, 1 Sept. 1820; Bigge Appendix, evid. Wentworth and Hutchinson, CO 201/118; Reid, 273.
[2] Bigge, *NSW*, 99–100; Macquarie, *Letter to Sidmouth*, 16; Macquarie to Bathurst, 10 Oct., 1823, PP 1828 (477), 30 and CO 201/145.
[3] Bathurst to Macquarie, 27 March 1820, but cf. Bathurst to Sidmouth, 23 April 1817, *HRA*, I, x, 808, for his reluctance to sanction expenditure on such buildings; evid. Druitt, Bigge Appendix, CO 201/120.
[4] 30 Geo. III c.47; Grenville to Phillip, 13 Nov. 1790, G. and G.O., 10 Feb. 1801, 7 Aug, 1803, 28 July and 4 Aug. 1804; *Transportation Report*, 1812, 13; Bathurst to Macquarie. 23 Nov. 1812.

In 1819 the question was revived, when Macquarie was criticized for being too lenient. More important as a spur to action was the legal decision that these 'colonial' pardons were not valid, since they had not been issued under the Great Seal in England. In 1823 all past pardons were confirmed, but the New South Wales Act limited the governor's powers for the future; he was not to grant, but only to recommend, pardons for deserving convicts.[1]

At first Macquarie had remitted comparatively few, and was praised by Bathurst for his discretion; but there was sometimes a conflict between granting rewards for good behaviour and granting them for hard work, as for example in the case of pardons to men employed on making the road to Bathurst. Between 1810 and 1820 he granted 366 free pardons and 1,365 conditional ones, or about 160 a year, compared with Hunter's 36 and King's 78; but Macquarie was dealing with about three times as many convicts as King and four times as many as Hunter, so that proportionately he pardoned fewer than the one and not many more than the other, although out of 1,075 pardons which he granted after 1813, in 320 cases he broke the rules he had laid down himself.[2]

The power to issue tickets-of-leave was never questioned, though Macquarie was criticized for being too generous and too ready to grant them to anyone who could support themselves, irrespective of their behaviour. His regulations laid down that they would be granted only 'to such persons as have by a long and uninterrupted period of good conduct, and sincere contrition for past offences, evinced themselves worthy of such favour and indulgence', and only after at least three years' service and at least half their sentence.[3] But in practice he did not obey his own rules in this matter either. In 1819 Riley told the Select Committee on Gaols that though tickets were not given simply to persons who could maintain themselves, there were cases when they had been given unworthily, and Macquarie himself admitted to Bathurst in 1821, when defending himself for having given a ticket to the convict schoolmaster, Halloran, that since the ticket was revocable and was 'no remission of the Sentence of the Court', he customarily granted them

---

[1] Macquarie to Bathurst, 28 June 1813, 1 Sept. 1820 with enclosures, espec. Wylde's report; emancipists' petition, Oct. 1821, encl. in Macquarie to Bathurst, 22 Oct. 1821; mems. by F. Forbes, re New South Wales Bill, 1 Jan. 1823, and James Stephen, 10 May 1823, *HRA*, IV, i, 417, 476 ff.; Bullock v. Dodd, 1819, Eagar v. Field, 1820; Bigge, *NSW*, 132–40; NSW Act, 1823, 4 Geo. IV c.96 secs. 34 and 35.
[2] Bathurst to Macquarie, 23 Nov. 1812; Macquarie to Bathurst, 28 June 1813, encl. G. and G.O., 4 Dec. 1817, 1 Sept. 1820; Bigge, *NSW*, 120–122.
[3] G. and G.O., 8 June 1811.

'to such Gentlemen Convicts as can by their Industry or finances maintain themselves without being Burdensome to the Crown'.[1]

In all, between 1810 and 1820 he granted tickets to 2,319 convicts, or between a fifth and a quarter of those who arrived at Port Jackson. This was not an unreasonable proportion, though 'revocations' for misconduct were rare (only 37 at Sydney between 1817 and 1820), and out of 1,655 tickets granted between 1813 and 1820, 450 were given to prisoners who had not been the prescribed three years in the colony. In 1820, 1,422 convicts had tickets, compared with 9,451 still in servitude; since nearly half the prisoners had arrived since 1817, this meant that about one-third of those who were eligible, as well as a few who were not, had received them. But criticism (or the presence of Bigge) had some effect, and although Macquarie granted 570 tickets in 1819–20, about a quarter of the total he gave altogether, proportionately to the number of convicts in New South Wales they were much fewer than his grants between 1810 and 1812, when his chief anxiety had been to get men off the stores. All the same, he sometimes ignored the magistrates' recommendations and granted personal applications for tickets without consulting them and his alleged 'leniency' was one reason for the appointment of Commissioner Bigge to inquire into the affairs of the colony.[2]

Masters did not always co-operate by recommending their servants as they were expected to do, and the magistrates did not always properly check the applications and recommendations that were submitted. John Macarthur told Bigge that he never recommended anyone, for none were worthy, though he also said that the convicts made good servants if well treated, and added that he knew of no servants granted indulgences unworthily. Bigge certainly thought the tickets desirable, with all their defects, especially if not given too soon; to the British government perhaps their greatest advantage was that they reduced expenditure.[3]

In granting indulgences, Macquarie did not worry about the recipients' crimes or characters at home. He had no information about their past, other than the bare record of their sentence and a vague and untrustworthy character report from the hulks, as both Bligh and the

[1] Bigge, *NSW*, 120–31; evid. Riley, *Gaols Report*, 1819, 68–70; Macquarie to Bathurst, 20 March 1821.

[2] Bigge Appendix, Population etc., No. 3, CO 201/130; Bigge, *NSW*, 122; Bennet, *Letter to Sidmouth* and *Letter to Bathurst*; Bathurst to Sidmouth, 23 April 1817, *HRA*, x, 807–8; Bathurst to Bigge, 6 Jan. 1819, *ib.*, 4–7.

[3] Evid. Macarthur, Bigge Appendix, CO 201/120, f.127–140; Macquarie to Bathurst, commenting on Bigge's Report, 10 Oct. 1823, CO 201/145, f.82; Bigge, *NSW*, 124.

Transportation Committee of 1812 had complained. Macquarie argued that no more information was necessary. In New South Wales the men could make a fresh start, the errors of their past lives would be overlooked, and rewards and punishment would be based solely on current behaviour. This was certainly much easier for immediate discipline, but made transportation a less effective deterrent to English criminals.[1]

After the convict's sentence had expired, or he was emancipated, if he had behaved well Macquarie wanted to see him restored to 'that rank in Society which he had forfeited'. This would be a great inducement to reform. In 1812, the Committee on Transportation agreed with this idea, and with this benevolent purpose the Governor looked on emancipists sympathetically, and declared himself 'the Patron and Champion of all Meritorious Persons who have been Convicts'. But one should not forget the qualification; not all emancipists were saints in his eyes. When criticized for ordering three men to be flogged for trespassing on the Sydney Domain, he declared they were 'depraved, low, vicious Characters'; the fact that two were ex-convicts and the third had a convict wife was, to him, evidence of their worthlessness, not the reverse.[2]

Since he thought emancipists made better farmers than many of the free settlers, he was ready to carry on his predecessors' policy (and the British Government's instructions) of granting them land; but difficult as it was for them to make good, despite his sympathy he did little directly to help them. He gave them provisions and one servant, but only for six months, instead of the former eighteen, though he was certainly anxious to establish a distillery to provide a market for surplus grain in years of abundance.[3] During his administration agricultural progress was slow, especially after 1815, and Macquarie was ready enough on occasions to lambast the emancipist farmers for their inefficiency, for the 'wretched mean appearance' of their farmhouses, for their farms being 'totally devoid of fences', for there being 'a great neglect of manuring' and for their 'inattention to personal cleanliness'.

[1] Evid. Bligh, *Transportation Report*, 1812, 33; *Report*, 11; evid. Hutchinson and Druitt, 15 Nov. 1819, Bigge Appendix, CO 201/120; Macquarie, *Letter to Sidmouth*, 57.
[2] Macquarie to Castlereagh, 30 April 1810, to Liverpool, 17 Nov. 1812, to Bathurst, 28 June 1813, 24 Feb. and 22 June 1815; to the Duke of York, 25 July 1817, to Goulburn, 15 Dec. 1817, *HRA*, ix, 442–3, 735; depositions, 22 April 1816, *ib.*, IV, i, 200–11.
[3] Macquarie to Liverpool, 17 Nov. 1812, to Bathurst, 31 March 1817, 16 May 1818. Macquarie also wanted to reserve some of the land near Bathurst for 'small settlers who may have obtained their freedom' (to Bathurst 24 June 1815), Bigge, *NSW*, 142 ff., evid. Wm. Cox and John Oxley, Bigge Appendix, CO 201/120. For the distillery, Macquarie to Liverpool, 17 Nov. 1812, to Bathurst, 22 March 1817.

But despite these shortcomings, the 1819 muster described 808 land-holders and settlers as emancipists out of about four thousand male ex-convicts in the colony, and another forty-nine were ticket-of-leave holders. Macquarie reported that they were cultivating 34,840 acres (out of 192,060 acres held), and owned 2,262 horses, 24,761 horned cattle and 36,053 sheep; including those with tickets this was an average of forty-six acres cultivated, twenty-eight cattle and forty-five sheep each, compared with the 213 free settlers' *average* holding of 900 acres, with sixty cultivated, six horses, eighty-four cattle and 184 sheep. Though averages can be misleading, and some holdings were very small, these emancipist farmers comprised one-sixth of the male ex-convicts; though the total of the latter had risen by one and a half times since 1802, the emancipist farmers had not even doubled in number, but there was now far more alternative work available. Despite the Governor's strictures on them, their achievement was by no means a bad one; if only five hundred were ultimately successful, this was one-eighth of their number and suggests no mean degree of rehabilitation, and perhaps of reform.[1]

But Macquarie was concerned not only with the ordinary ex-convict, who, if not poor but honest, was still poor, but also with those who came from the higher ranks of society, or who managed to make their fortune in the colony. Though their numbers were few, they were men of notoriety, if not of importance, and in relation to them the Governor has often been misjudged. 'Mixing' with them was a part, though often an exaggerated part, of Macquarie's policy. Bligh had told the Transportation Committee in 1812 that an ex-convict was always remembered as having been such, was never invited to Government House, and 'ought not to be allowed to hold places of trust and confidence'. All the same, he had had to employ the convict attorney, George Crossley, and the emancipist farmer, Andrew Thompson, was his man of affairs at the Hawkesbury. In 1810, Macquarie admitted Thompson and Surgeon Redfern to his table, as well as the Reverend Henry Fulton, who was accepted by all, and D'Arcy Wentworth, whose past was somewhat ambiguous. He appointed Thompson, Wentworth, Lord and Fulton magistrates. Later he invited Robinson the 'poet laureate', Meehan the Surveyor, Greenway the Architect, Simon Lord, the emancipist merchant, and Richard Fitzgerald, the Agricultural Superintendent, as officials to levies and receptions at Government House, and he wanted to appoint Redfern to the Bench.[1] He employed some emancipists on government service, partly because of the shortage of educated men in the colony, and partly because he found them loyal and conscientious servants. Since there were no free lawyers, except Deputy Judge Advocate Ellis Bent, he had to allow convict attorneys like Crossley, Eagar, Robinson and Chartres to appear in the Courts. He had to use ex-convict surveyors, like the Irish rebel Meehan, who was fully as honest and honourable as the 'gentleman' Dangar was later on, and was praised even by Bigge. Since no free architect had been sent out, Macquarie had to employ the convict Greenway – and so on. Most of the superintendents and overseers, including Richard Fitzgerald, who earned Bigge's commendation, and the Principal Superintendent, Hutchinson, who did not, were emancipists.[2]

A few of the convicts were political offenders rather than felons, like Redfern, who had been involved in the naval mutiny at the Nore, or Fulton and Meehan in the Irish rebellion; a few like Andrew Thompson (who probably suffered from a miscarriage of justice), Simeon Lord or D'Arcy Wentworth (who was technically not a convict), might be considered as having committed only juvenile misdemeanours, which they had since outgrown. 'Some of the most meritorious men of the few to be found who were the most capable and the most willing to exert themselves in the Public Service were men who had been Convicts', Macquarie told Bigge; he claimed the 'necessity and justice' of recognizing 'their merits and situation in life' as if they 'had never been under the sentence of the Law'.[3]

The justification was not always adequate, but it existed. Many free settlers were 'perturbators'; they had rebelled against Bligh, and were now critical, quarrelsome and unhelpful, like Marsden, Nicholas Bayly, the Blaxlands, Oxley, Dr. Townson, William Howe and others; but despite this, and despite Macarthur's admission that the number of ex-convicts admitted by Macquarie to society was 'very few', and his own later support of that unpleasing forger, Dr. Halloran, and despite Marsden's support of his sanctimonious, hymn-singing but worthless servant Ring, Macquarie's alleged 'patronage' of emancipists, wildly exaggerated as it was, formed one of the major criticisms of his

[1] Macquarie to Castlereagh, 30 April 1810; evid. Bligh, *Transportation Report*, 1812, 36; Bigge, *NSW*, 144 ff.; Bigge to Bathurst, 19 Oct. 1819, CO 201/141.
[2] Macquarie, *Letter to Sidmouth*, 63; Bent to Bathurst, 1 July 1815, *HRA*, IV, i, 137; Bigge, *NSW*, 146 ff.
[3] Macquarie to Bigge, 6 Oct. 1819, CO 201/142; Bigge, *NSW*, 144 ff.; J. V. Byrnes, 'Andrew Thompson, the Outcast Goat', and *JRAHS*, xlvii, 105 ff.

administration. Though in the few cases where it was carried far this patronage was almost certainly justified, it annoyed the officers' mess in the same way that association with 'Socialists' or alleged 'Fellow-Travellers' would annoy these conservatively-minded people today, just as it annoyed the narrow-minded Marsden to see the Governor hob-nobbing with publicans and sinners. Macquarie could well paint the great merits of Redfern, 'holding as he already did a Commission in His Majesty's Service and being a Gentleman of Unimpeachable Good Character'; yet appointing him a magistrate was rather different from appointing Thompson and Lord when suitable men were so scarce in 1810. Though concerned with the conflict caused in colonial society by 'welcoming' the educated convicts, Bigge found no objection to Fulton; perhaps he was saved by his cloth. But he could point to the shortcomings of Lord and Thompson; and though Macquarie claimed that their promotion had had a 'good effect on the minds of sensible and reformed convicts', Riley had affirmed that it 'unquestionably lessened the respect of the inheritants towards the magistracy'. As for Redfern, to Bigge and Bathurst he was a rebel, who had taken part in 'the most foul and Unnatural Conspiracy that ever disgraced the Page of English History'; this could never be forgotten. Bathurst was soon prepared to accept the appointment of John Macarthur; but apparently rebellion meant (as it still does) different things on different occasions.[1]

Bathurst and Bigge wanted to 'tighten up' the transportation system, and make the punishment more of a deterrent; Macquarie regarded New South Wales as a place for 'the Reformation, as well as the Punish-ment, of the Convicts', who, with the expirees, comprised the bulk of the population and possessed the bulk of the wealth. They should not be cast out into utter darkness by narrow-minded, prejudiced, capri-cious and often disloyal men, especially since, at least in Macquarie's early years, some seemed settlers preferable to the rather dissolute free men then coming out from England. 'My successor,' wrote Macquarie in his final apologia, 'will find a very tractable and useful part of the population in the emancipated Convicts, inferior to none of their neighbours in loyalty.' As for social mixing, Macquarie argued that

[1] Macquarie to Bathurst, 22 Feb. 1820, and enclosures, including Bigge to Macquarie, 10 Nov. 1819; cf. *HRA*, x, 819, n. 56, and CO 201/142; Macquarie, *Letter to Sidmouth*, 50; Bigge, *NSW*, 89 and 150; evid. Riley, *Gaols Report*, 1819, 55. On Halloran, Darling to Hay, 1 May 1826, *HRA*, xii, 255, M. H. Ellis, *John Macarthur* (Sydney 1955), 508. On Macarthur, Brisbane to Bathurst, 27 Feb. 1822 (encl. Wylde and Field to Brisbane, 19 Jan.), 6 Sept. 1822, 1 Nov. 1824; Bathurst to Brisbane, 26 March 1823, and mem., *HRA*, xi, 908–9 n. 11. On Marsden and Ring, Brisbane, Forbes and Archdeacon Scott to Bathurst, 10 Aug. 1825, *ib.*, 717 ff.

free settlers coming to a penal colony ought to know what to expect; they never objected to mixing with convicts and emancipists in trade.[1]

Another less controversial incentive to good conduct and reform was for the government to send out a convict's wife and family. At first *allowing* wives to go out was an 'indulgence'; it could only be 'considered as not inappropriate' for prisoners who 'should by their industry be placed . . . in such a situation in New South Wales as to leave little doubt of their being enabled to maintain their families'. A number promised to support themselves, and were permitted to go; but they often became a burden on the colony, so for a time they were 'discouraged'.[2] In 1816 the government allowed them to go again, for the Home Office was in favour of the 'indulgence'. It asked the Governor to send home lists of 'deserving' convicts, who could support their families; their going was a reward for good behaviour and an encouragement to stay out of England, and they were sent in female convict ships at public expense.[3]

A more important 'encouragement' to 'reform' was the prospect of magisterial punishment for misconduct. Unfortunately the benches varied widely in their standards and in their efficiency, though Macquarie tried to supervise the sentences imposed on the prisoners and in 1814 ordered quarterly returns to be sent to him. In Sydney he could keep a fairly close watch on them, but it was not so easy in other districts. He did not always receive returns regularly, and he could not, as he said, interfere directly with sentences passed by the courts 'unless I should interpose what would be justly termed an Illegal and Tyrannical

---

[1] Emancipists' petition, 1821, encl. in Macquarie to Bathurst, 22 Oct. 1821; Macquarie to Bathurst, 27 July 1822; Bigge, *NSW*, 147–50; Macquarie to Bathurst, 28 June 1813.

[2] Bathurst to Macquarie, 23 May 1817. A number went out in *Broxbornebury*, female convict ship, in Feb. 1814, M'Leay to Goulburn, 4 Jan., CO 201/74. Macquarie to Bathurst, 7 Oct. 1814, 1 April 1817; Bathurst to Macquarie, 10 Nov. 1812; Bunbury to Macquarie, 4 Dec. 1814, *HRA*, viii, 385.

[3] Bathurst to Macquarie, 11 May 1816, is somewhat ambiguous, but a party of wives was sent in *Lord Melville* in July, after Becket, at the Home Office, had reminded Goulburn on 9 May that the Transportation Committee of 1812 had strongly recommended 'this indulgence' to persons who appeared likely *not* to become 'burthensome' on their arrival, and suggesting the Governor send home lists (CO 201/82, and cf. 4 July, *ib.*). Goulburn to the Rev. A. Wood (10 Feb. 1817 CO 324/138, f.83), passed on this information, but Bathurst's despatch, 23 May 1817, per *Friendship*, which did not sail for another month, arrived only on 15 Jan. 1818, and was not acknowledged by Macquarie until 3 March 1818; it therefore had not been received when he sent his list for *free passages* on 9 Dec. 1817, wherein he refers to 'instructions' (undated); but on 25 March 1819, he refers to instructions 'some time since received'. Outward despatches, CO 202/8, f. 97 and 200; Macquarie to Bathurst, 9 Dec. 1817 and 25 March 1819.

Exercise of the Powers vested in me'; but his check was better than nothing. By 'the Mingling of Mercy with Justice' he was able to mitigate the excessive sentences of some Benches, though normally he would be too late to modify sentences of flogging, and this brutalizing punishment was the one most commonly imposed.[1]

Many government officers, including such lowly persons as superintendents and overseers, were assigned convicts 'on the store' as part of their salary. This was worth about £25 per man per year; but it often led to misbehaviour. If the officials kept the men in their service they were often idle; and if they allowed the men, as they sometimes did in return for a money payment, to work for themselves, this removed them from all control. Because of his other public expenditure and Bathurst's reiterated demands for economy, Macquarie hesitated to abolish this practice, though in 1817 he asked for authority to do so 'as soon as the Increase of the Colonial Funds will admit of a Pecuniary Compensation being made'; but he did try to control it, and in 1814 he forbade everyone, whether officials or ordinary masters, to allow their servants to work for themselves. Unfortunately he could not strictly enforce these orders, and the system remained, to be condemned by Bigge; not until 1823, did Brisbane report that 'Convict clerks and overseers are remunerated without the appropriation to them of working convicts'.[2]

The Principal Superintendent was in charge of the general distribution of assigned servants, and kept a record of every convict's movements and conduct; but the magistrates supervised their local employment. A settler was not obliged to retain a convict assigned to him; when he dismissed a convict servant he did not necessarily even inform the Principal Superintendent, but only the local magistrates; however, even this formality was sometimes neglected, and at Parramatta convicts were often assigned (and received back) by Rouse, the Superintendent of Public Works there, without word to anyone. There was, of course, then, as later, much argument about the value of the assigned convicts, but Macquarie insisted that most of the settlers had only themselves to blame for many of the shortcomings of their servants, 'whose original callings were not suited to the Employment they are required for', and he thought that 'many convicts who might have been rendered useful

---

[1] G. and G.O., 10 Sept. 1814; Acting-Judge Garling to Macquarie, 2 Dec. 1817, encl. in Macquarie to Bathurst, 4 Dec.; for irregularity of returns, Report of Inquiry by Council, 27 Sept. 1825, *HRA*, xi, 854 ff., and below, p. 202.

[2] Bathurst to Macquarie, 3 Feb. 1814; Macquarie to Bathurst, 7 Oct.; G. and G.O., 10 Sept. 1814; Macquarie to Bathurst, 1 April 1817; Bigge, *NSW*, 54 ff.; Brisbane to Bathurst, 28 April 1823, and below, p. 191.

and good men, had they been treated with humane and reasonable control, have sunk into despondence by unfeeling treatment'. Many convicts, echoed Dr. Reid, 'potentially improvable' were set back by 'harshness . . . in the situations to which they were assigned'; but as ex-convicts were allowed servants, some of the 'potentially improvable' were led back into temptation by unreformed masters, and the result was 'wrong-doing by the convicts and settlers together'.[1]

Although there was not enough demand by private employers for all the 'ordinary' convicts who arrived after 1818, the services of 'mechanics' were always much sought after. In distributing them, Hutchinson, the Principal Superintendent, was accused of being 'moved by caprice if not motives more unworthy'; though Bigge thought this unfounded, the control over convict distribution, like that of granting land, added to the governor's powers of patronage, and inevitably aroused criticism. Bigge objected to so many men being kept for government works. In 1818, Macquarie told Druitt that 'all artificers and mechanics' in the *Morley* were 'of course exclusively reserved for government work'. This was the normal policy, though its effects have been exaggerated. Bigge in his report argued that two-thirds of the 'government convicts' were mechanics whom the settlers would gladly have received, but Hutchinson's evidence was that there were only 120 mechanics in government service who could have been assigned, less than a quarter of the 'useful tradesmen' the settlers were demanding. Marsden suggested sending blacksmiths and wheelwrights to the country to help the farmers; but unless a type of loan gang were established, they were not easy to dispose of and keep occupied. Only about two dozen 'superior settlers' could employ mechanics full-time, and had applied for them. Marsden had ten, Macarthur was 'reasonably satisfied', and so were Cox and D'Arcy Wentworth, though Jamison, Bayly, Blaxland, Howe, and Dr. Townson had been aggrieved. Between 1814 and 1820, the government took 1,587 out of 2,418 mechanics when they arrived, leaving only 731 immediately available for private individuals; but in 1821, only 517, or less than a third of those who had arrived in the past three years, were still in government service. These were enough to arouse the lamentations of those who did not get them; more justified would have been the lamentations of the convicts themselves, since Macquarie thought 'the situation of a well-behaved Convict in the service of a good Master must at all times

[1] Evid. Druitt, Hutchinson, William Cox and Richard Rouse, Bigge Appendix, CO 201/120, f.14, 66, 109 and 183; Macquarie to Bathurst, 10 Oct. 1823, CO 201/145, 89–90; Reid, 273 ff.

be preferable to the service of Government when confined to Barracks'.[1]

MALE CONVICT DISTRIBUTION 1814–1820

| Year | Total Number Arrived | Mechanics | | Labourers to Govt. | Total Govt. | Total non-Govt. |
		Number Mechanics	To Govt.			
1814	819	194	122	186	308	511
1815	909	226	143	203	346	563
1816	1,257	211	120	142	262	995
1817	1,653	263	157	243	400	1,253
1818	2,748	577	390	531	921	1,827
1819	2,376	477	385	865	1,250	1,126
1820	2,003	470	270	830	1,100	903
Total	11,765	2,418	1,587	3,000	4,587	7,178

(Bigge Appendix)

If Macquarie was unable to control the employment of assigned servants as well as he would have wished, at least he insisted on a weekly muster, on Sundays, and attendance at church. Marsden, it is true, claimed that the musters provided opportunity for thieving, drunkenness and debauchery; but by 1817 Marsden disapproved of everything Macquarie did, and Macquarie's opinion that they were 'productive of the most beneficial Effects on the Morals and general Conduct of the Convicts' was supported by all the other magistrates except Hannibal Macarthur.[2]

Proper control of assigned servants depended on the arrival in the colony of enough 'Respectable *Married Men*', who would be fit and proper persons to be masters, and could take 'Six or Eight Male Convict Servants off the Store'. For the next twenty-five years, such men would provide the basis of the convict system. Economical for government, who would not have to maintain the prisoners, allegedly reformatory by removing them from the temptations of the city and association with

[1] Macquarie to Druitt, 13 Nov. 1818, evid. Druitt and Hutchinson, Bigge Appendix, CO 201/118, f.142–200, 201/119, f.49 and 104, 201/120, 66 and 72; evid. Marsden, *ib.*, CO 201/118, 387 ff.; Reid, 251–4; Bigge to Macquarie, 14 June 1820, CO 201/141; Bigge, *NSW*, 52; Macquarie to Bathurst, 10 Oct. 1823, CO 201/145.
[2] Macquarie to Bathurst, 4 Dec. 1817; G. and G.O., 10 Sept. 1814; reports from magistrates, Nov. 1817, *HRA*, ix, 522–41, including Marsden to J. T. Campbell, 28 Nov., *ib.*, 535–7; Bigge Appendix, CO 201/119, f.249.

their fellows, assignment to these employers would keep the convicts under magisterial discipline, teach them the benefits of hard work and how subsequently to earn an honest living and at the same time would develop the colonial economy. After 1816 the government eased the restrictions on emigration and more prosperous settlers began to go to New South Wales. Macquarie might regret that in the past the 'encouragement' of free persons with land, labour and victualling at government expense had been expensive. These settlers had often been idle and ignorant, and had 'not contributed to the advancement of Agriculture; so far from showing a disposition to be grateful', they were 'the most discontented unreasonable and troublesome persons in the whole country.'[1] But now the British government insisted that settlers should possess capital. As investors, they were usually industrious and intelligent, and they wanted to acquire estates by grant or purchase, for agriculture, grazing or timber-working. Macquarie retained his dislike of emigrants *without* resources. They were only a nuisance and an expense. But respectable men with '*at least Five Hundred Pounds*' were another matter, so long as they did not 'Expect or receive any further Assistance or Indulgence . . . after their Arrival here, excepting Grants of Land in proportion to their respective Capitals, with as many Male Convicts off the Store as they Can Afford to Maintain'.[2] 'Is there no way for a man to get to New South Wales but by stealing?' demanded a Treasury official in 1820. 'Can you not tempt some of our superabundant population to go to New South Wales?' Becket, the Under-Secretary at the Home Office, asked Goulburn. But despite the lack of 'temptation', many more did go after 1819.[3]

Men with capital were attracted by the increasing wealth to be won by grazing cattle and sheep, pioneered by John Macarthur, the Rileys, Marsden and others. In 1810 there were 26,000 sheep and 12,500 cattle in New South Wales and Van Diemen's Land; in 1821, there were 290,000 sheep and 103,000 cattle.[4] John Macarthur told Bigge that 'no occupation, except agriculture, is to be found at this period in New

[1] Macquarie to Liverpool, 17 Nov. 1812, to Bathurst, 7 Oct. 1814; cf. Bathurst to Macquarie, 3 Feb. 1814.

[2] Macquarie to Bathurst, 31 March 1817, 16 May 1818.

[3] Goulburn to Baynes, 21 May 1817, to W. Johnson, 31 May, CO 324/138, f.191; cf. Goulburn to Capt. Laycock, refusing assistance, Aug. 1816, CO 201/82; Treasury to Goulburn, Becket to Goulburn, 1820, quoted Phillips, 114-5, 118; cf. *Gentleman's Mag.*, lxxxix (1819), 175; Madgwick, chs. 1 and 2; Wentworth, ii, 59 ff., 99 ff., 117 ff.

[4] Bigge, *Agriculture*, 15-17, *NSW*, 161 ff.; Wentworth, i, 441 and 464, ii, 67 ff.; Marsden to Miss Stokes, 26 Nov. 1811, 25 June 1813 and 8 Oct. 1814. G. Mackaness (ed.), *Some Private Correspondence of the Rev. Samuel Marsden* (Sydney, 1942) 43-5, 51-2; cf. 'Emigration', *Westminster Review*, iii (1825), 448 ff.

South Wales for any considerable number of convicts which would make a return to defray the cost of their provisions'; but they could cultivate 'land enough to furnish bread for ten times their number', and 'the labours which are connected with the tillage of the earth and the rearing and care of sheep and cattle are best calculated to lead to the correction of vicious habits. When men are engaged in rural occupations their days are chiefly spent in solitude—they have much time for reflection and self-examination and they are less tempted to the perpetration of crimes than when they are herded together in towns . . .' Growing wool, 'as fine as Saxon and superior to Spanish', was even better. It would 'provide employment . . . for a great many Convicts, and afford the Proprietors a sufficient income to support their families respectably'. It would be necessary 'to induce a large body of respectable persons . . . to settle in the colony', persons who could be entrusted with authority to punish their convict servants, to compel them to work and to determine their rewards according to their industry and good behaviour. Though this might lead to abuse, 'that portion of evil must be submitted to'; if the colony were to continue as a penal one, the convicts should be kept under control by 'confiding to intelligent and honest men great powers, subject to the inspection and control of a vigilant government'.[1]

Macarthur said he did not like constantly sending his servants to the magistrates for punishment. 'The method I adopt is to feed them well clothe them comfortably and sometimes give them extra rewards . . . I cannot however boast of my success'. He gave rations and clothing to the value of £15 a year, unless the convicts were 'idle and worthless', when the allowance was cut to £10—the rate of wages, established by government; 'to those who behave well' he gave gratuities up to £5. He thought the convicts more difficult to manage than in the past, but he admitted this was due to their increased numbers; 'when their past lives are considered, it is a matter of surprise to me that they behave so well'. He thought that the 'indiscriminate granting of land to convicts' (presumably he meant ex-convicts) should be stopped, and they should not be allowed 'to roam through the colony' tempting servants 'to commit depredation upon any property within their reach'.[2]

Bigge agreed with Macquarie that there might be danger in 'placing so many convict labourers in remote situations, under no better control than that of the individual superintendent of the establishment'; this

---

[1]Bigge Appendix, A.49, 'Opinions of individuals on the management and discipline of convicts'; John Macarthur to Bigge, 7 Feb. 1821, CO 201/118 f.362.
[2] Evid. Macarthur, Bigge Appendix, CO 201/120, f.127-140,.

was an 'essential objection to the extension of settlements in which convicts are employed'. He shared the fears of the Transportation Committee, in 1812, that too many servants given to one master would mean 'association' and destroy the benefits of assignment; but was not this association, limited as it was, better than the congregation of men in Sydney, often idle and ill-disciplined, and engaged in extravagant public works which the colony could well do without? 'Shepherding' would at least take convicts off the stores.[1]

Some of Macquarie's greatest difficulties arose from his lack of dependable man-power. For a long time he had argued that ex-soldiers and persons 'who had become free' and who were granted small farms made the best settlers; but was it likely that 'a class of men of abandoned and profligate habits' would 'by their example or conversation mend those who are committed to their care?' asked William Howe. Small emancipist farmers should not have convict servants. Marsden, who like Howe favoured helping the free farmer, and wanted the convicts scattered in agricultural employment, suggested abolishing the town gangs and replacing them with 'farm gangs' from the idle; they would help settlers with their clearing and could progress from these to private assignment as a reward for good conduct—a policy which several witnesses recommended.[2]

Bigge had sought such suggestions. 'With a view to stimulating the inhabitants to the suggestion . . . of new modes of successfully employing the Convicts,' he told Bathurst, 'I have rather encouraged a belief that in case no new system could be devised that His Majesty's Government would be compelled to abandon the present one, . . . and as the prosperity, nay the existence of the Settlers depends upon the continuance of the Convicts in it, I have found a strong disposition among them to suggest and concur in new schemes of employment more efficient and less expensive than the present.'[3] He agreed that if all the convicts were employed in cutting wood or clearing trees, things which even London thieves could do, it would increase cultivation, improve the colony and get the convicts out of Sydney. But could they all be employed in this way?

Macquarie doubted it. 'The influx of male convicts in the past five years has been so great . . . that the settlers had not employment for one-eighth of the number that annually arrived in the colony,' he wrote,

[1] *Transportation Report*, 1812, 11–12; Bigge, *NSW*, 30–1, 48.
[2] Evid. Howe, Cox, Marsden, Bell, Bigge Appendix, CO 201/118, f.367 ff.; cf. Jamison, Rouse, Blaxland, the Rev. R. Cartwright, Hannibal Macarthur, CO 201/120, f.142 ff.
[3] Bigge to Bathurst, 19 Dec. 1819, 24 Aug. 1820, CO 201/141.

with some exaggeration, in 1822. While 3,239 male prisoners and 949
females landed at Port Jackson between the arrival of Macquarie and
the end of 1815, three times as many, 11,385 males and 899 females,
arrived in the second half of his administration, so perhaps his public
works expenditure was not so unnecessarily excessive as Bathurst and
Bigge suggested. In 1819, out of 9,064 male prisoners, 200 were at
Newcastle and 6,388 were in private service, apart from those with
tickets of leave; but of the 2,476 in government service (or ill), 2,368
were in Sydney; they were a nuisance to its citizens, even after the
barracks had removed about half from the streets–though the 1,940
in private service in Sydney were a nuisance too.[1]

For those in government employ there were many occupations–
road-making, timber-cutting, lime-burning, brick-making, quarrying,
as well as work on transport, at the docks, in the lumber-yards, or even
as superintendents or police. The numbers were increased by Macquarie's building programme, but he claimed that its cost was only that
of feeding and clothing the convicts employed on them, and 'as such a
vast Number of Male Convicts at present Unavoidably remain on the
Hands of Government, who must be fed and Clothed at all Events, the
Expence of Erecting Public Edifices are Comparatively small, whilst
they Afford very Useful Employment for those persons who would
otherwise be Altogether Unemployed, whilst . . . Necessarily Supported
by the Crown'. This depended on whether or not they could be
assigned. In 1819 they could not be; but if they could, the 'Clothing
and Victualling' of the large numbers employed on public works was a
'Principal Article in the Expence of the Colony', as he had admitted in
1814. When the works were finished, he said, he hoped to be able to
discharge half of the men, 'Which will be a very Considerable Saving';
but they were never finished. Despite repeated promises, he never
reduced the employment of convicts or the expenditure on his building
programme, though from 1818 onwards, of course expensive government works were needed to keep the men occupied.[2]

As early as December 1817, worried both by the 'growing scarcity of
Disposable Lands' and the influx of prisoners for whom neither government nor settlers could then possibly find employment, Macquarie had
proposed forming a new settlement at Jervis Bay; but his lack of military force and the unfavourable report on the area which Oxley made in

---

[1] Macquarie to Bathurst, 27 July 1822; cf. 16 May 1818; Bigge, NSW, 60–1; Bigge Appendix, Population, etc., no. 3, CO 201/130.
[2] Macquarie to Bathurst, 9 Nov. 1812, 28 June 1813, 28 April and 7 Oct. 1814, 12 Dec.
1817, 16 May 1818, 24 March 1819.

1819 deterred him from carrying out this plan, and he eventually decided on expansion at the Hunter and at the newly discovered Port Macquarie instead.[1] In the meantime, to deal with the problem caused by unassigned men on his hands, he decided, reluctantly, to employ some of them on growing their own food, and to reopen 'a Government Agricultural Establishment'. Though he insisted then that 'nothing but Necessity could have Induced me to resort to this Mode of Employing Convicts as I am aware that there is No Great Economy . . . in Cultivating Lands on Account of the Crown', next year he was congratulating himself for having restarted an institution which he had abolished on his arrival. 'It will induce habits of Sobriety and Industry amongst the Convicts employed there and after first Year will more than reimburse Government the Expense of Victualling and Clothing Them.' When he got back to England, Macquarie described the Emu Plains farm as 'one of the most useful that has ever been resorted to for the Improvement of Convicts by bringing them into those regular habits of useful industry . . . and one of the few methods by which great savings in the Expense of the Colony to the Government could be effected.' Three hundred convicts were 'most usefully employed there in productive labour'.[2]

What the convicts cost is hard to say. Many bills were not presented at the Treasury for two or three years after they were incurred, and of course not all ought to be debited to the convict account. Some of the costs of the civil administration and of the military establishment should again be put against 'imperial development', and in 1816, out of civil estimates for £12,423, only £2,565 was directly for the convict establishment; but other expenditure could only be sorted out in 1827 by completely changing the system of accounts.[3]

The works and buildings produced by the convicts were not worthless, however much the British Treasury might dislike paying for them, though they naturally seemed more important to Macquarie in Sydney than to Bathurst in London. But what value should be placed on the Lighthouse on South Head, the Turnpike Road to Parramatta, the Fort, the Stables, the Factories, Barracks and Churches, the Obelisk and the Fountain in Sydney and all the other works Macquarie under-

---

[1] Macquarie to Bathurst, 12 Dec. 1817, 16 May 1818, 20 July 1819; Oxley to Macquarie, 10 Jan. 1820, *HRA*, x, 254 ff. For Newcastle and Port Macquarie, below, p. 189.
[2] Macquarie's Instructions to Fitzgerald, the first superintendent at Emu Plains, 15 Sept. 1819, CO 201/119, 353–60; Macquarie to Bathurst, 28 Feb. and 1 Sept. 1820, 27 July 1822; *ib.*, 10 Oct. 1823, CO 201/145, 82 ff. For his objections to government farms, Macquarie to Liverpool, 18 Oct. 1811, to Bathurst, 20 July 1819.
[3] Darling to Goderich, 9 Feb. 1827, 8 Jan. 1828; Goderich to Darling, 30 July 1827.

7

took? What set-off should be allowed against the convicts' maintenance, as was done when the government estimated the costs of the hulks and Millbank Penitentiary? Was Wentworth right in asserting, flatly, that works in New South Wales were 'much more valuable' than those in either the dockyards or the penitentiary 'could possibly be', and leaving them all out of account altogether? Whether right or not, all three should certainly be treated on the same basis.[1]

In 1810, the population of New South Wales was 10,452. There were 1,283 convicts and 1,416 soldiers; with the civil officers, dependants and new arrivals, who were supported from the store, about two-fifths of the inhabitants were still 'wholly or in greater part' victualled at the public expense. Since a convict labourer then cost the government £30 a year to maintain, and the 'establishment' had to be paid for as well, Botany Bay was certainly an expensive resting-place for convicts. Between 1810 and 1821, the total expenditure on the settlement was nearly £3,000,000 even if we take off half the cost of the civil and military establishments; but although the total rose steadily every year, the average cost, per head, fell tremendously. Between 1810 and 1812, when there were less than 1,500 convicts in the colony this *average* cost exceeded £100 per man. Between 1813 and 1815 the number doubled; the cost per head was halved, helped by the fact that so few were on the government's hands—only about 600 out of 3,250 in 1814 for example. Between 1816 and 1821, despite the much larger proportion which the government was supporting, administrative expenses were more widely spread, freight rates had fallen after the war, so the cost per convict came down to less than £30.[2]

Treasury Bill expenditure tells the same story. After King's administration, when it averaged only £9 per year per convict, it rose rapidly to more than £60 a year between 1810 and 1812 when Macquarie had to make good the running down of the stores and the losses due to the floods in the preceding years. Thereafter he steadily reduced it to less than £25 a year in 1813–16, and to less than £15 a year in 1817–20, though of course the *total* grew steadily after 1813.[3] These figures help to explain both the British government's agitation and Macquarie's assertions that he was not being extravagant. Perhaps he *could* have

---

[1] Wentworth, ii, 159–164, compares costs in NSW, hulks and penitentiary, but his figures are incorrect. For Macquarie's public works, *HRA*, x, 368 ff., 684 ff., Ellis, *Macquarie*, 416–9.

[2] Macquarie to Bathurst, 28 June 1813; *Returns*, 1810, 1812, 1819, *HRA*, vii, 281, 638, x, 286; PP 1812 (341), app. 37; 1816 (324), xii, 285; 1818 (334), xvi, 175; 1819 (579), app. R, (191), xvii, 331; 1821 (557), xiv, 199; 1823 (531), xiv, 631; Bigge, *NSW*, 163.

[3] Bigge Appendix, Bonwick Transcripts, Box 15, 1511–13 (ML); Commissariat Accounts (ML); communication by Mr. G. Abbott.

COST OF CONVICTS, NEW SOUTH WALES AND VAN DIEMEN'S LAND, 1801–1821

Years	Total Expenditure	Expenditure less half Civil and Military Costs	Average p.a.	Average approx. no. of convicts in the colony in each year	Average Cost per convict p.a.
	£	£	£		£
1801–3	390,000	354,000	118,000	2,250	53
1804–6	269,000	229,000	76,000	2,250	34
1807–9	374,000	314,000	104,000	1,000	104
1810–12	579,000	521,000	174,000	1,400	120
1813–15	625,000	566,000	189,000	3,500	54
1816–18	717,000	661,000	220,000	7,200	30
1819–21	1,125,000	1,053,000	351,000	14,022	25

The governors reported the number of convicts in 1800, 1804 and 1805, 1819, 1820 and 1821; the muster for 1814 gives a count of 3,247. For other years, one can make an estimate from the number arriving and the approximate number who may have died or been emancipated. The figure for 1819, arrived at in this way, was within five per cent of that given in the return for that year. The low expenditure in 1804–6 is due to the low transport costs in those years, when few were sent out.

been more economical; but the cost of each convict during his term of office was much less than it had been during those of his predecessors, even though the *total* expenditure naturally increased. In comparison, the *gross* cost of a convict in the hulks was about £40 per man per year; in the Millbank penitentiary a prisoner cost over £50 if we include interest on the cost of the building. The *net* cost depends on the value of the prisoners' labour. In the hulks it was about £20 per man per year; but between 1816 and 1821 the *gross* cost in New South Wales was only about £26.10, so it seems likely that the *net* cost there was then much less than it was in the hulks.[1]

Female prisoners had always been a problem. In his first despatch, Phillip had asked for more, because 'to send for women from the

[1] For hulks, *Returns*, PP 1814–15 (326), xi, 211; 1816 (319), xviii, 301; 1819 (32), xvii, 321; 1821 (18), xxi, 449; *Millbank Report*, PP 1819 (80); *Penitentiary Houses Report*, PP, 1812 (306).

Islands . . . would answer no other purpose than that of bringing them to pine away in misery'. When they arrived it was hoped they would find a 'matrimonial connexion', but many remained prostitutes, as was perhaps inevitable. 'Be she ever so despicable in person or in manners,' wrote convict Thomas Watling, 'here she may depend that she will dress and live better and easier than ever she did in the prior part of her prostitution.'[1]

'Female Convicts', reported the Transportation Committee in 1812, had formerly been 'indiscriminately given to such of the inhabitants as demanded them, and were in general received rather as prostitutes than as servants; and so far from being induced to reform themselves, the disgraceful manner in which they were disposed of operated as an encouragement to general depravity of manners'. Castlereagh twice gave orders for them to be more closely controlled, but this was easier said than done. Certainly they were no expense; in 1806, 1,216 out of 1,412 women in the settlements were either married or living with free people, but 'those who behaved well bear but a small proportion to the many . . . thoroughly depraved and abandoned'. Only 360 couples in the colony were married; of 1,808 children under nineteen, 908 were illegitimate. King insisted that 'every proper precaution is taken by putting the females on their arrival into the manufactory under the inspection of the resident magistrate at Parramatta'; from there, 'the well-behaved are selected and applied for by settlers and others to become their house-keepers or servants, and the incorrigible are left confined'. But assignment usually meant prostitution, owing to the 'general loose and dissolute character of the settlers and their servants'.[2]

When he arrived, Macquarie thought that 'these unfortunate Females have been in general very improperly disposed of heretofore, which has led to great Depravity of Manners and Vicious Habits'. He enjoined marriage and promised to keep the women separate until they could be properly distributed. He thought female convicts a 'great drawback', but in 1812 the Transportation Committee felt they were necessary; though 'the women sent out are of the most abandoned description, yet . . . let it be remembered how much misery and vice are likely to prevail in a society in which the women bear no proportion to the men . . . To this, in great measure, the prevalence of prostitution is

---

[1] Phillip to Sydney, 15 May 1788; Grenville to Phillip, 19 June 1789; Watling, *Letters*, 35.
[2] *Report*, 12; Castlereagh to Bligh, 31 Dec. 1807, to Macquarie, 14 May 1809; King to Windham, 12 Aug. 1806, *HRNSW*, vi, 150-1; Spencer Percival, 27 Dec. 1807, *ib.*, 393; Foveaux to Castlereagh, 6 Sept. 1808, *ib.*, 741.

reasonably to be attributed'. Macquarie assigned 'as Many of them to Married Settlers, as Servants, as Can be disposed of in that Way; but great Numbers still remain on the Hands of Government; the only Mode of Advantageously employing that Description of Persons that I know of at present, is in the Government Factory at Parramatta'; this would have to be enlarged and enclosed, with 'a high Stone Wall' and a 'proper and well qualified respectable Person as a Superintendant–a *Married Man* of good Moral Character'.[1] Bathurst wondered if it would be possible to suspend sending female convicts to New South Wales; he would not sanction Macquarie's proposed factory at Parramatta if they could be kept in England. Though this was impossible, the number was reduced, but the delay gave Marsden an opportunity in 1815 suddenly to discover that the lack of proper accommodation for the women was a great cause of crime at Parramatta, for their male companions resorted to plunder in order to meet their wants. Certainly crime was more frequent in Parramatta than in Sydney, and Bigge agreed that the factory's defects gave the women 'an early inducement, if not an excuse, for resorting to indiscriminate prostitution'.[2]

Macquarie said that he had delayed rebuilding it only because he was waiting for Bathurst's authority to do so, though he did not always wait for such authority before spending money on public works; in the end, though still without approval, he announced in April 1817, that as soon as the churches at Sydney, Windsor and Liverpool were finished, he would build a new factory at Parramatta for the women. It was, he said, 'particularly Necessary for keeping those Depraved Females at Work within Walls, so as in some Degree to be a Check upon their Immoralities and disorderly Vicious Habits'. Begun in July 1818, it was not finished until 1821.[3]

By 1817, Macquarie was coming under fire at home. The government thought him extravagant and that his leniency was destroying the effect of transportation as a punishment. His colonial critics, like Marsden, Nicholas Bayly, the Bents and others combined with English opponents of transportation to increase Bathurst's doubts. In 1817, he discussed with Sidmouth, the Home Secretary, the expediency of sending a

---

[1] Macquarie to Castlereagh, 30 April 1810; *Transportation Report*, 12; Macquarie to Liverpool, 17 Nov. 1812.

[2] Goulburn to Becket, 18 Jan. 1814, HO 30/3; Marsden to Macquarie, 19 July 1815, quoted, Bennet, *Letter to Sidmouth*, Appendix, 126 ff.; Ellis, *Macquarie*, book iv, ch. iv; Hassall Corr., ii, ML A1677, 136, 210–7; Bigge, *NSW*, 69–70, 101.

[3] Bigge, *NSW*, 69–70, 101; Macquarie to Bathurst, 7 Oct. 1814, 4 April and 4 Dec. 1817; Ellis, *Francis Greenway* (Sydney, 1953), 98 and 100; *Macquarie's Journal*, 9 July 1818, ML A774.

commissioner to inquire whether the 'System of Transportation to New South Wales' should be reformed or abandoned. Sidmouth had no objection, but it was not until 1819 that the Commissioner, J. T. Bigge, sailed, and not until 1822 that he reported; in the meantime, the controversy continued, fired by evidence before the Select Committee on the state of the gaols in England in 1819 and the vitriolic writings of Henry Grey Bennet, M.P., an ardent advocate of penitentiaries.[1]

Basing his opinion on Collins's *Account*, then nearly twenty years out of date, Bennet insisted that transportation as a punishment was neither 'equal, exemplary nor reformatory; it deters no man from crime, restores few to virtue', and the judge's sentence condemned the criminal 'to the society of felons' for the rest of his life. 'Pursue the career of crime abroad which you have begun so well at home . . . We see not your misery and we shall soon forget you ever existed.' In this he reflected an increasing opinion in England, though contemporaries seemed too ready to associate the increase in crime with inadequate punishments (as some do today), and to forget the effects of the growth of towns, the changes in industry and the end of the war. In this view New South Wales was a failure. 'As a mere colony it is too distant and too expensive,' declared the *Edinburgh Review* in 1819. 'If considered as a place of reformation for criminals, its distance, expense and the society to which it dooms the objects of the experiment are insuperable objections to it.'[2]

In his instructions to Commissioner Bigge, in January 1819, Bathurst emphasized that 'the Settlements in New Holland had not been established . . . with any view to Territorial or Commercial Advantages', but 'as Receptacles for Offenders in which Crimes may be expiated at a distance from home by punishments sufficiently severe to deter others'. Their 'Growth as Colonies' was a 'Secondary Consideration'; the 'leading Duty' of their administration was to 'render Transportation an Object of serious Apprehension'. At first this had been the case, but latterly the 'Apprehension' had been diminished; therefore 'the first Object of your Enquiry should be to ascertain whether any and what Alteration in the existing system of the Colony can render it available to the Purpose of its original Institution and adequate for its more

[1] Bathurst to Sidmouth, 23 April 1817, *HRA*, x, 807; Sidmouth to Bathurst, 25 April, CO 201/87; Bennet, *Letter to Sidmouth, Letter to Bathurst* . . .; Wentworth, *op. cit.*, John Slater, *A Description of Sydney, Parramatta, Newcastle, etc.*, Settlements in New South Wales (Nottingham, 1819); Holford, *Substance of a Speech* . . .; *P. Debs.*, xxxv, 920 ff., xxxix, 464–509, 1124 ff.; *Gaols Report*, 1819; *Police Report*, PP 1818 (423), 32.
[2] Bennet, *Letter to Sidmouth*, 26 ff., 34, 44, 52 ff., 76 ff., 126 ff.; *Letter to Bathurst*, 114; *Ed. R.*, xxxii, 47.

extended application'. Bathurst seemed already convinced that the system was not working; Bigge was to say what changes were necessary –tighter discipline, more barracks, more regular employment, new settlements, better classification or anything else, and he was to consider the cost 'as compared with other systems of Punishment'. He was to report on many other topics–officials, the courts, agriculture, land prices, distillation, colonial revenue, and especially the 'Propriety of admitting into Society Persons who originally came to the Settlement as Convicts'; but the 'most important and therefore the main Objects of your Investigation' was the Convict system. 'Transportation to New South Wales is intended as a severe Punishment . . . and must be rendered an Object of real Terror'.[1]

Probably the real trouble lay in irregularities. The system was complex, its administration difficult and the government's manpower insufficient and unreliable. Special cases were regarded in England as normal, and rumour exaggerated, as it always does, the unusual and the striking. Macquarie insisted that he had improved convict discipline; he obtained reports from the magistrates to support him and he was certainly right; but he forgot that improvement was not perfection, and he forgot that on English government standards he had been spending too much money. He assured his brother that Bigge's report '*must* be favourable to my administration . . . and highly honourable to my character; . . . it will place my Conduct on an Eminence beyond the reach of Faction, Malevolence and Gross and envious Misrepresentation'. He admitted the convicts' lot was a good one, for 'no People in the World live better or have less to Complain of than the Convicts both Male and Female in New South Wales so long as they Conduct themselves with Common Propriety', thus partly justifying some of his critics; all the same, he insisted that 'with every indulgence . . . transportation is far from being a light sentence. It is at best a state of slavery; and the fate of the Convict, as to misery or comparative comfort depending on the will of his Master, the constant sense of degradation and loss of liberty is a severe punishment which has no remission while he is in that state of bondage'. Many convicts were 'reclaimed' by transportation, he said later; though certainly others were not, he did not think vice and crime prevailed to the extent which a reasonable person would expect. And Bathurst should have been pleased that between 1810 and 1820, only 389 ex-convicts left New South Wales, and in 1820 there were 4,376 emancipists in the colony,

---

[1] *HRA*, x, 4 ff.; cf. to Sidmouth, *ib.*, 807.

who would otherwise have been troubling the government at home, while between 250 and 300 left the hulks every year.[1]

While Bigge was in the colony, a Select Committee on Gaols was taking evidence in London on conditions in New South Wales. Alexander Riley thought that 'unquestionably there are many instances of men and women transported having become useful inhabitants, acquiring property and bringing up families; ... numbers, who are now free, are contented, industrious and orderly and well situated, ... who ... if again exposed to the influence of their former connexions in England would have again become burdens to the society of which they are now useful members'. But this reformation, however desirable, was not the deterrence so much wanted by the British government, and Riley warned the committee that the numbers arriving since 1817 had 'very materially retarded' the former improvement. Jeffrey Hart Bent, remembering his quarrel with Macquarie, naturally thought everything bad; according to him, there was neither punishment nor reformation.[2]

The evidence given to Bigge was equally conflicting. His report is often said to have been unfair, partial, based on biased evidence, and hostile to Macquarie whom he was determined to find fault with. It was certainly a disappointment to the Governor, so anxious for praise, so conscious of his difficulties, his good intentions and the malice of some of his critics. Bigge's 'nauseous trash ... polluted with private scandal ... collected from the very dregs and refuse of the people – from the whores and vagabonds of Sydney' greatly upset the young W. C. Wentworth; furious at having the characters of his parents impugned, he was not very complimentary to the leading colonists who had given evidence to the Commissioner. But though incorrect in some details, and unnecessarily critical of some of Macquarie's activities, Bigge praised others, and while his criticisms reflected the wish of the British government to economize and to tighten up the convict administration, his recommendations, which were in general acted upon, laid the basis of great development in New South Wales in the next twenty years.[3]

Bigge wanted to get the convicts out of Sydney. There, in 1820, there was one crime for every three convicts, compared with one in eight, at

---

[1] Macquarie, Letters to his brother Charles, 7 and 19 Oct. 1819 (Nat. Lib., Canberra); Macquarie to Bathurst, 28 June 1813, 4 Dec. 1817, and report to Bathurst, 10 Oct. 1823, CO 201/145, 82 ff.; Macquarie, Letter to Sidmouth, 49, 65, 70, 79; Bigge, Agriculture, 80–1; Bigge, Appendix, Population etc., no. 7, CO 201/130 f.52; numbers discharged from the hulks, Returns, PP 1814–15 (355), xi, 217.

[2] Evid. Ridley and Bent, Gaols Report, 1819, 64, 88–9, 123.

[3] Wentworth, i, 388 ff.; Bigge to Bathurst, 29 July and 3 Aug. 1822, Bigge Appendix, (ML) Box 28, 66, 94. For the implementation of Bigge's recommendations, below, chap. 9.

Windsor, for example; but offences were even more numerous at Parramatta, and perhaps the Commissioner was more worried by the fact that half the 4,308 prisoners in Sydney were in government service. This he disliked because public works were expensive and employed too many mechanics; depreciating the value of Macquarie's buildings, and ignoring the number of recent arrivals who could not at once find other employment, he urged that the public works be reduced; however he praised the barracks and the government farms, and recommended that until 'a more enlarged System of Employment can be brought into operation', other government farms should be founded and the convicts be employed on clearing. To assign more prisoners to the 'more opulent settlers' with not less than fifty acres, would be both cheap and reformatory; on the other hand, 'the worst classes' should be withdrawn from farmers and returned to government. Convicts' 'good conduct should fairly entitle them to the advantages of a favourable location with Individual settlers' and in due course to a ticket-of-leave; but this should be granted only for good behaviour; a 'conviction before the Magistrate should form an impediment to a remission of sentence'; there should be a closer liaison with the country benches and a better registration of the convicts. Bigge supported wool-growing, which would spread convict labour and increase the assignment of the well-behaved; for the worst convicts, he recommended more Penal Settlements, 'by which an entire separation may be effected of the Convicts who are in a state of Punishment from a Participation in those comforts and advantages which seem to be inseparably connected with the Progress of Colonisation'.[1] He assumed that prisoners would prefer private to government employment and that assignment should be regarded as an 'indulgence'; but if return to government was to be thought a punishment, discipline in government service would have to be tightened up. Men in the road-parties should not be idle, or think they would not be worked hard in a government gang; 'task work' should cease, so that the prisoners would not finish early and have leisure for dissipation, if not robbery.[2]

After the old governor had returned home and written a spirited defence of his administration, Bathurst admitted that in general he had governed the colony well. 'If as a place of punishment, it has not answered all the purposes for which it was intended,' this was 'mainly

---

[1] Bigge Appendix, Population etc., CO 201/130; Bigge, *NSW*, 17–24, 53–4, 98, 101, 159–163; Bigge to Bathurst, 19 Dec. 1819, CO 201/141; Bathurst to Brisbane, 9 Sept. 1822.

[2] Charles Throsby, J.P., and Thomas Moore, J.P., to Macquarie, 2 Oct. 1821, Col. Sec's In-Letters, 1821, Bundle 15, No. 62 (ML).

to be attributed to the many difficulties, with which the rapid and unprecedented succession of Convicts transported of late Years to New South Wales, appear to have embarrassed your Government'; though a 'Change of System' was needed, its necessity had increased 'by such slow and imperceptible degrees, as not necessarily to force itself upon your attention'.[1]

This, perhaps, was damnation by faint praise, and to an ex-Governor seeking justification, Bigge's reports seemed worse. Macquarie received a pension—his due; he was refused any 'honour', though he deserved one far more than most recipients then and since; not until 1828 would the Colonial Office publish his *Apologia*, and his answer to the 'vile and insidious' report.[2] Its attitude was ungenerous, but like most attitudes, comprehensible. To it, New South Wales was still primarily a place of punishment; to Macquarie it was a growing colony. Though, in his view, the lot of the convicts was a hard one, while they could contribute to colonial progress their punishment was not the overriding consideration of his rule; so long as the British government thought it should be, it could not feel satisfied with the administration of a man who, all the same, was one of Australia's greatest governors.

---

[1] Bathurst to Macquarie, 10 Sept. 1822.
[2] Macquarie to Bathurst, 27 July 1822, 10 October 1823, PP 1828 (477).

5

The Voyage

'One of the pleasantest things in the world is going a
journey; but . . . the soul of a journey is liberty,
perfect liberty, to think, feel, do just as one pleases.'
WILLIAM HAZLITT

The critics of transportation strongly objected to the voyage to Australia. It was very expensive. The convicts were said to suffer from disease and ill-treatment on the way out. On the transports, they were inevitably 'associated', and the worse characters 'contaminated' less vicious offenders; gambling was rife; with women, there was prostitution.

The Admiralty chartered and provisioned the ships of the first fleet. Naturally by modern standards they were small, varying from about 320 to 450 tons, about 100 feet long and 30 broad, and so, inevitably, crowded with men, women, provisions, stores, sheep, hogs, goats and poultry, not to mention rats, cockroaches and vermin between decks. Like all contemporary ships, they were difficult to ventilate, especially when the hatches had to be closed.

The government's initial preparations did them little credit. 'The garrison and convicts are sent to the extremity of the globe as they would be to America, a six weeks passage', wrote Phillip tersely; but thanks to his reiterated complaints (which should not, of course, have been necessary), his thorough overhaul of the arrangements and the surgeons' care at sea, on that first voyage only twenty-four convicts died out of 759 who sailed – a death-rate of about three per cent. The provisions, supplied by contract, were good – in Tench's opinion, 'much superior' to those usually provided – and Phillip had successfully, though with difficulty, insisted on a proper supply of anti-scorbutics. 'Frequent explosions of gunpowder, lighting fires between decks, and a liberal use of that admirable antiseptic, oil of tar, were the preventives we made use of against impure air,' said Tench. 'It is pretty extraordinary,' wrote Surgeon Bowes, 'how very healthy the convicts... have been during so long a passage and where there was a necessity of stowing them thick together.'[1]

The second fleet had a very different experience. Out of 1,095 convicts who sailed, 267 died on the voyage and nearly 450 needed medical treatment when they reached Sydney. 'Great numbers were not able to walk nor to move a hand or foot'; they were filthy, and 'covered, almost, with their own nastiness', according to Chaplain Johnson who saw the disembarkation. 'The slave trade is merciful compared with what I have seen in this fleet,' wrote Captain Hill of the New South Wales Corps, who had travelled out in the *Surprize*.[2]

Phillip explained that the ships had been over-crowded, that the convicts had been 'too much confined' on board, heavily ironed and rarely allowed on deck. 'I believe, Sir,' he went on, 'while the masters of the transports think their own safety depends on admitting a few convicts on deck at a time, and most of them with irons on, which prevent any kind of exercise, numbers must always perish on so long a voyage.' Many were improperly and inadequately fed, deprived of their rations by the ships' masters, who, on their arrival in Sydney 'immediately opened stores and exposed large quantities of goods to sale . . . at most extortionate prices'. In the first fleet, the officers of the troops had to inspect the quality of the provisions and 'to order that every one received his just proportion'; in the second, their 'distribution rested entirely with the masters of the merchantmen, and the officers were expressly forbidden to interfere'.[3]

The ships, like almost all those that followed, were provided and equipped by private firms, who of course expected to earn a profit from the transaction. Sir Charles Middleton, at the Admiralty, had reminded the Home Office, in 1786, that the merchants who had taken convicts to America had 'an interest in them after they were embarked', while on the voyage to Australia they had 'no other advantage but the freight and the victualling, and take the risk of their Ships (which, by the bye, is no small one) upon themselves'; but this warning for the moment went

[1] Phillip to Nepean, 4 and 11 Jan., 1 and 18 March 1787, to Sydney, 28 Feb., 12 March, *HRNSW*, i, part ii, 45 ff.; Secretary Stephens to Phillip, 23 Feb., Nepean to Sir Charles Middleton, 18 April, Middleton to Nepean, n.d., Sydney to Phillip, 28 April, *ib.*, 48, 79, 93; Tench, *Narrative*, 19, 46–7; Surgeon A. Bowes Smyth, Journal, quoted, Bateson, 100–101; O'Brien, part ii, ch. ii, and app. B. For full details of the ships, Mr. Bateson's work is invaluable.

[2] Convict Indents, ML; Phillip to Grenville, 13 July 1790; Captain W. Hill to Wathen, 26 July 1790, Johnson to Thornton, *HRNSW*, i, part ii, 367 and 387.

[3] Phillip to Grenville, 13 July 1790; Tench, *Complete Account*, 51; Collins, 121, 127; *HRNSW*, ii, 791.

unheeded. The contractors for the second fleet, Camden, Calvert and King, had told Traill, the master of the *Neptune*, to dispose of unexpended provisions 'to the best advantage for our account'; Traill was to 'be very careful and see the expenditure does not exceed it' (the contract for provisioning), and 'at all events there must not be a greater consumption than we have agreed for'.[1]

Despite the outcry that this affair provoked, and Dundas's assurance of 'the strictest inquiry . . . in order to the bringing to punishment the persons who have been the cause of that shocking calamity', the contractors were neither prosecuted nor sued. In fact, the *Neptune* had been fitted up properly, but after the news reached England, Camden, Calvert and King were not again employed in the convict service. What was more serious was that Surgeon Beyer, from the *Scarborough*, was employed twice more; successfully in the *Boddingtons* in 1793, when he was under the eye of the naval surgeon, Kent, but again with disastrous results in the *Britannia* in 1797.[2]

Traill was charged with the wilful murder of three men. He said that he feared a mutiny by the convicts; but even so, this would seem no reason for using irons described as 'barbarous', and Traill's explanation is weakened by the fact that he did not dare to remain in England to answer the charges against him. He did not attempt to explain the huge death-roll, except to blame the Government Agent, Lieutenant Shapcote, who conveniently for him, had died soon after the fleet left Cape Town. Shapcote may have been weak in not standing up to the captain; but it is easy to blame the dead, and he can hardly be held responsible for the deaths of convicts that occurred after his own. For all that, Traill was appointed Master-Attendant at the Cape in 1795.[3]

When the third fleet arrived in 1791, Phillip reported that 198 convicts died out of 1863 embarked, and 576 came under medical treatment after they disembarked. Some were sick when they went on board, but again there were frauds in the issue of rations, for a short weight was used in the *Queen*, and this time the contractors, still Camden, Calvert and King, had not supplied what was stipulated. Phillip doubted if he had 'the power of inflicting a punishment adequate to the crime . . . although the convicts landed from these ships were not so sickly as

[1] Middleton to Nepean, 11 Dec. 1786, quoted, Rutter, 73–4; Contractors' Instructions, 19 Dec. 1789, *HRNSW*, ii, 750–2.
[2] Under-Sec. King to Phillip, 10 Jan. 1792, Thos. Evans to King, 20 Jan., *HRNSW*, ii, 590, 460–4; Bateson, 115, 129, 143 ff.; Hunter to Portland, 6 July 1797, report of inquiry, *HRA*, ii, 33–68.
[3] Evans to King, *loc. cit.*; Traill's reply, *Woodfall's Register*, 4 Aug. 1792, *HRNSW*, ii, 802–6; *New South Wales from the Records*, ii, 61–2; Bateson, 114; Hill to Wathen, *loc. cit.*

those brought out last year, the greatest part of them are so emaciated, so worn away by long confinement, or want of food, or from both these causes, that it will be long before they will recover their strength, and which many of them will never recover'. But again no one responsible was prosecuted; perhaps the government was afraid that the critics of the system would cry out all the louder if its abuses were openly revealed in court.[1]

The contracts which the government made stipulated that the ships be sea-worthy, properly manned and fitted out, with the convicts' quarters clean and ventilated. The contractors were to provide a surgeon. The prisoners were to be allowed on deck 'as much as possible consistent with safety'. Log-books were to be kept 'of all remarkable observations, particularly respecting the convicts', and given to the governor at Sydney. The surgeon was to keep a diary, relating to the sick, the number admitted on deck, the fumigating and cleaning of the prison and 'all other circumstances which may immediately or remotely affect the health of the said convicts'.[2] But often in the early voyages masters took little notice of all this after the ships had lost contact with the authorities on shore, although a bond of £1,000 was lodged with the government as security for their performance. Supervision at sea rested in the hands of the Naval Agent and the Surgeons; the colonial government and the Admiralty could check afterwards, by hearing complaints and by examining the ships' logs and surgeons' journals; but this examination could not prevent a disaster that had already occurred, and the powers of the agent, the surgeons and the ships' masters were so ill-defined, that the master could usually flout the others if he wanted to.

When several ships sailed with only one Agent, he could not see to anything except on the vessel on which he was actually sailing. 'It therefore highly concerns Government to lodge in future a controlling power in each ship over these low-lifed barbarous masters, to keep them honest', urged Captain Hill, after his voyage with the second fleet. Partly as a result of its experience, in 1792 a naval surgeon was appointed to every vessel, but his position was not an easy one.[3]

Surgeon Kent, engaged for the *Boddingtons* in December 1792, was told to assist the contractors' surgeon (who was the incompetent Beyer from the *Scarborough*) in attending the sick, to 'enforce a compliance

---

[1] Grenville to Phillip, 19 Feb. 1791, encl. 6; Phillip to Grenville, 6 Nov., encl. report of Examination of Master and Second Mate of *Queen*; Bateson, 120.

[2] For a typical charter-party, *HRA*, iii, 358–63.

[3] Hill to Wathen, *loc. cit.*; Dundas to Phillip, 10 Jan. 1792; Commissioners of the Navy to Phillip, 17 May 1792, *HRA*, i, 356; Under-Sec., Home Office, to Surgn.-Supt. Kent, 12 Dec. 1792, *HRNSW*, ii, 486.

with the several stipulations made with the contractor' and to report both to the Governor of New South Wales on his arrival and to the Home Office on his return to England. But on other vessels, the naval surgeons were volunteers on leave of absence, not on naval service, which did not help them when the master, as almost inevitably happened, contested their authority. 'In justice to the Contractor,' reported Kent, 'I must say his provisions were of the very best kind . . . but I must say it would be right to bind down the captains of ships carrying convicts under the direction of an agent, that he might comply with the orders given him for the preservation of the lives and health of the convicts . . . for my orders respecting them were never attended to and Captain Chalmers told me he only came in the ship to navigate her.'[1]

'I am sorry I cannot say much for the health of those come out in the last ship [the *Britannia*],' Hunter told Portland in 1797, reporting an inquiry conducted by the acting Judge-Advocate, Richard Atkins, the Principal Surgeon, Balmain, and the Chaplain, the Reverend Richard Johnson, into the conduct of the ship's master, Thomas Dennott. The surgeon on board, Beyer again, had offered no serious protest against the other's brutality. When exercising on deck the convicts were often ironed; in this case, they were 'kept in irons the whole voyage in consequence of some conjecture that they meant to seize the ship,' said Hunter. 'They look most wretchedly from the long confinement.' More than that, several had been brutally ill-treated, and six virtually flogged to death. Dennott's conduct was censured as 'imprudent and ill-judged' and 'bordering on too great a degree of severity', and Beyer was held 'culpable' in not protesting; whether or not the former could have been convicted of manslaughter, if prosecuted, is open to question, but at least neither was employed in the convict service again.[2]

After the frightful death-roll in the second fleet, the Home Office attended to Middleton's advice of 1786; the shipping contractors were given 'an interest' in the convicts' welfare, by being paid so much for every convict who reached Sydney; for example, the owners of the *Hillsborough* in 1798, were to receive £18 per convict embarked and £4.10.6 extra for every convict landed, instead of the approximate £23 per head, paid according to the early agreements; all the same it did not prevent a heavy death-roll from pestilential fever in that ship, where the 'loathsomeness' of the convicts' situation, in 'perfect darkness', was 'beyond description', according to some missionaries on board. The prison, said Dr. Vanderkamp, with its 'dreary darkness . . . heat and

---

[1] Kent's instructions, *ib.*; Kent to Naval Board, 2 Sept. 1793, *ib.*, 61–2; Bateson, 41.
[2] Hunter to Portland, 25 June and 6 July 1797, encl. report of inquiry; Bateson, 142–7.

putrid effluvia . . . with the clank of the chains affords the strongest idea of Hell and of the damned which can be conceived'.[1] Apart from this, the men's clothing was sometimes found unsuitable when the cold weather set in. In 1799, Hunter had to complain again, 'much against my inclination', about 'the want of cloathing and blankets. These people have been put on board . . . with a miserable mattrass and one blanket, and the cloaths only in which they embark'd.'[2]

These complaints were not acknowledged; but they were not entirely ineffective. In June 1801, the Transport Commissioners issued new instructions for convict ships. They were to be kept properly 'sweet and clean', a proportion of the convicts were to be brought on deck every day 'when the weather permit of it', and their berths were to be 'properly cleansed and ventilated'. These particulars were to be noted alike in the master's log and the surgeon's diary, both of which were to be produced to the Governor of New South Wales 'upon Oath' if required. The Governor was ordered to 'cause particular inquiry' after the voyage, and 'either grant . . . Certificates of Good Conduct, if it shall appear to you that they have been deserving of encouragement, or, on the contrary apprize us of any neglect or misbehaviour that proper notice may be taken of the same . . .' Making regular a practice adopted spasmodically since the sailing of the *Surprize* in 1794, the government promised to pay a gratuity to masters and surgeons for 'their Assiduity and Humanity', when they produced their certificates. Neglect would also be 'properly noticed'. The following year the Governor was told that he would receive a copy of the health return drawn up by the Medical Inspector when the convicts embarked, which would help him in any inquiries which he was told 'most earnestly . . . on no account to fail to make'. At the same time the government decided to withhold two-thirds of the contractors' charges until the Governor's certificate arrived.[3]

Certainly the convicts were sometimes sick when they embarked, and after 1796, ships calling at Portsmouth were inspected on behalf of the Home Department, but neither the *Ganges* nor the *Britannia* in 1796–7

[1] Collins, i, 304–5; Richards to Nepean, 16 Oct. 1792, *HRNSW*, i, part ii, 670; Navy Board to Grose, 5 March 1794, *HRA*, i, 466–7; contract for *Hillsborough*, 1798, Transport Commissioners to Portland, 11 June 1800, *HRNSW*, iv, 92; Thomas Haweis to Sir Joseph Banks, 18 July 1799, *Banks Papers*, Sutro Collection, Australian National Library, Canberra; R. Lovett, *History of the London Missionary Society* (London, 1899), i, 485–6; *Transactions of the Missionary Society*, i (1795–1802), 360–2.
[2] Hunter to Portland, 27 July 1799, to Under-Sec. King, 28 July.
[3] Transport Commissioners to Masters and Surgeons and to Acting-Governor King, 8 June 1801, *HRA*, iii, 97–8; Pelham's Instructions, 10 June, *HRNSW*, iv, 399 ff. and CO 201/20 f.239; Hobart to King, 30 Jan. 1802; Instructions to Masters and Surgeons of Convict Ships, *Transportation Report*, 1812, App., 24, 26 and 27.

nor the *Hillsborough* in 1798 were improved as the inspector recommended, and in 1800 both the *Hillsborough* and the *Royal Admiral* took
on board prisoners already suffering from fever. The hulk authorities in
England and at Cork were repeatedly ordered not to send out anyone
unfit, but they occasionally did so, particularly from Ireland. Almost
forty years later, sickness in the *Prince George* in 1837 was blamed on
the ill-health of the convicts when they embarked, but by this time the
death of six out of 250 was considered both to be unusual, which it was,
and a matter serious enough to demand investigation.[1]

In 1802, Lord Pelham, then Home Secretary, proposed using naval
vessels to carry the convicts. H.M.S. *Glatton* sailed with 275 males and
126 females in October, and the following April, H.M.S. *Calcutta* took
out 307 males, under David Collins, to found a new settlement at Port
Phillip, though they soon moved on to the site of Hobart. Unfortunately
this plan was abandoned when the Napoleonic wars began again in
May 1803, but King had warmly welcomed it, for he had had to report
the 'great debility' of those from the *Royal Admiral*, in November 1800,
and further disasters in two ships from Ireland, the *Hercules* and *Atlas*,
which arrived in June–July 1802 with 'the whole of their convicts in
either a dead or dying state'. They were both filthy and overcrowded,
thanks to the 'great quantity of spirits and other private trade belonging
to the master of the *Atlas*', which 'evidently deprived the convicts of
air and the means of being kept clean'.[2]

This private trading was not forbidden until 1817; and when it was,
Macquarie protested against the shutting down of the supply of goods
to the colony; not until the monopoly of the East India Company was
removed in 1819, did the need for bringing goods by convict ships disappear. As for Brooks, the master of the *Atlas* in 1802, he may have

---

[1] James Fitzpatrick to Under-Sec. King, 23 Oct. 1796, *HRNSW*, iii, 161–3; for *Hillsborough*,
Hunter to Portland, 28 July 1799, and correspondence with Transport Office, June 1800,
ib., iv, 89–93; Fitzpatrick to Hobart, 30 Jan. 1802, to Portland, June 1802, *ib.*, 683 and 787;
King to Portland and to Transport Commissioners, 10 March 1801, *HRA*, iii, 5 and 83;
cf. the favourable report on *Perseus* and *Coromandel* in Jan. 1802, Fitzpatrick to Graham,
Graham to Under-Sec. King, CO 201/23; Irish convicts in *Three Bees*, 1814, *HRA*, viii,
278, cf. Register of State Papers, Ireland, 1818–31. On *Prince George*, Bourke to Glenelg,
27 June 1837, encl. rept. of Surgeon Bell, *HRA*, xviii, 799, Glenelg to Gipps, 30 Dec.,
encl. report of the Physician-General, *ib.*, xix, 223.

[2] Pelham to Admiralty, 9 March, Admiralty to Pelham, 4 April 1802, CO 201/23, f.150,
171; Hobart to King, and encl., 29 Aug. 1802, cf. *HRNSW*, iv, 635 ff.; Transportation Act,
1802, 43 Geo. III c.15; King to Hobart, 9 May 1803; King to Portland and to Transport
Commissioners, 10 March 1801, *HRA*, iii, 5, 83; King to Hobart and Commissioners,
9 Aug. 1802, *ib.*, 535, 552 ff.; King to Hobart, 30 Oct.; Surgeon Jamison to Hobart, 8 Nov.,
ib., 701 ff.; King to Transport Commissioners, 9 Nov., *ib.*, 718 ff.; Convict Indents, ML,
4/4004.

been mulcted for failure to comply with the terms of the charter-party, and the Transport Commissioners said he would be prosecuted; but they seem to have done nothing, and in 1806 he was again in command of a convict ship – the *Alexander* carrying forty female convicts – though on this voyage there were no complaints. Betts, master of the *Hercules*, was found guilty of manslaughter in the Vice-Admiralty Court at Sydney, for shooting down a convict in cold blood; but the British law officers at home declared that a suit could not be brought in the colony, and he seems to have escaped punishment.[1]

Since those who committed any offences on the voyage could only be prosecuted in England, offenders could avoid legal action by flight, as in the case of Donald Traill, master of the *Neptune*, of the Second Fleet, or rely on being acquitted through lack of evidence, for that taken in the colony was not admissible. Witnesses were sent home only once – in the case of the *Chapman* in 1817. Then the master, the surgeon and some of the guard were prosecuted for killing three and wounding twenty-two by wild and excessive shooting, which they indulged in after hearing vague reports of a convict plot, and for the excessive punishments, irons, short rations and privations which they imposed afterwards. Macquarie, seeking a chance of punishing men responsible for inflicting three months' misery on two hundred helpless prisoners, and causing twelve deaths, had hoped that even if 'effectual justice' were not done, 'sufficient may be effected at least to protect the persons of Convicts in future on their passage from the Cruelties and violence to which they have heretofore been exposed'. But thirteen convicts had to be pardoned and returned to England to give evidence as witnesses; when the accused were acquitted, the governor was reprimanded for the 'inconvenience' and expense he had caused. The government was as unwilling to give the colonial court jurisdiction to try offenders in New South Wales as it was indifferent whether prosecution in England succeeded or not, so long as convicts were not pardoned and sent back to England and public money was not spent on a trial.[2]

Rations, based on those in the navy, were ample if they were properly distributed, as they nearly always were after the scandals on the Second and Third Fleets. Brooks gave out short weight in the *Atlas* (1802), and the prisoners were short served in the *Adamant* (1821); less serious

[1] On masters' trading, Bathurst to Macquarie, 12 Dec. 1817 and 4 Aug. 1819; Macquarie to Bathurst, 1 March 1819; cf. Goulburn to Riley and Jones, 12 Dec. 1817, CO 202/8, 54; King to Transport Commissioners, 9 Aug. 1802, *loc. cit.*; Edward Bray to Commissioners, 9 June 1803, Commissioners to King, 14 Nov., *HRA*, iv, 425–7; Bateson, 167.
[2] Macquarie to Bathurst, 12 Dec. 1817; Bathurst to Macquarie, 12 April 1819, encl. Hobhouse to Goulburn, 29 Jan.

complaints were made about the *Harmony* (1827), *Southworth* (1830), and *Emperor Alexander* (1833); but these were certainly unusual. The prisoners were divided into 'messes' of six, each with cooking and eating utensils. In 1802, each mess was receiving, weekly, 20 pounds of bread, 12 pounds of flour, 16 pounds of beef, 6 pounds of pork, 12 pints of pease, 2 pounds of rice, 1½ pounds of butter, 1½ pounds of suet, 3 pounds of raisins and 6 pints of oatmeal. These were little altered, but later sugar, vinegar and lime-juice were added. The daily wine allowance was three or four gills; the water ration three quarts. 'The rations are good and abundant,' wrote Surgeon Cunningham in 1825. 'The common diet of the convicts is certainly *more* than is requisite to keep them in health, as they have no work to do.'[1]

The ships were certainly seaworthy. H.M.S. *Guardian*, a naval store-ship and not primarily a convict transport, struck an iceberg off the Cape of Good Hope in 1789, to cause a disastrous shortage of supplies at Botany Bay; five of the twenty-five convicts on board her were lost. In 1797 a mutinous guard carried off the *Lady Shore*, with sixty-six female convicts, to South America; in 1812 the *Emu* was captured by an American privateer. But no ship ever foundered on the voyage, and no convict ship was wrecked before 1833, when the *Amphitrite* went ashore near Boulogne in a gale and 106 female prisoners were drowned. In 1835 the *George III* had a disastrous voyage. A fire destroyed much of the food. The prisoners were put on short rations; some contracted scurvy; all were weakened. Then, nearing Hobart, the ship struck a rock in D'Entrecasteaux Channel. Many of the convicts were too sick to struggle to safety; the death-roll was increased because the prisons were tardily opened and 127 were drowned. Soon afterwards the *Neva* ran aground on King Island in Bass Strait, and 138 convicts were drowned, but when the *Hive* ran ashore on the coast of New South Wales, owing to faulty navigation, all the prisoners were saved. In 1842 the *Waterloo* was driven ashore when at anchor in Table Bay, at the Cape, and 143 convicts were lost. All told, out of more than 160,000 convicts transported, only 519 lost their lives because of shipwreck, and of the wrecks, only that of the *Waterloo* could be even remotely ascribed to unseaworthiness.[2]

[1] For naval rations, Michael Lewis, *Social History of the Navy, 1793–1815* (1960), 404; rations in *Coromandel*, 1802, *HRNSW*, iv, 693; in 1812, *Transportation Report*, app. 25; in 1816, Haslem, 5–7; in 1823, Cunningham, ii, 213–4. Cf. Jamison to Hobart, 9 Nov. 1802, *HRA*, iii, 702; Bateson, 207, 209, 246.
[2] For reports on *Neva* and *George III*, Barrow to Stephen, 30 Oct. 1835, Wood to Maule, 29 Dec. 1835, CO 280/62 and 70; for the results, Hay to Phillipps, 1 Feb. 1836, CO 408/11; Bateson, 108 ff., 172–3, 226 ff.; Ingleton, 156–9.

CONVICT SHIPS: DISASTERS AND MISADVENTURES

Date	Ship	Mishap
1789	Guardian	wrecked, 5 convicts drowned
1797	Lady Shore	carried off by guard, with 2 male and 66 female convicts
1812	Emu	captured by U.S. privateer with 40 females
1817	Chapman	mutiny, 12 convicts shot
1833	Amphitrite	wrecked, 106 female convicts drowned
1835	George III	wrecked, 127 male convicts drowned
	Neva	wrecked, 138 female convicts drowned; 6 subsequent deaths
	Hive	wrecked, no lives lost
1842	Waterloo	wrecked, 143 males drowned

Apart from these wrecks, the overall death-rate from disease on the convict ships was one for every sixty-eight men and eighty-four women carried; but this showed a marked improvement over the years—for men, from one in nine before 1800, to one in twenty-four between 1801 and 1815 and one in 113 thereafter, and for women, from one in thirty, to one in sixty-seven and ninety-four respectively. All long journeys in

CONVICT SHIPS, VOYAGE STATISTICS

Date of departure	No. of ships	Average tonnage	Av. no. of days on voyage	Av. no. of convicts per ship	Death rate: no. landed per no. died	
					M	F
1787	6	350	258	126	27	63
1787–91	17	480	180	217	6	18
1792–5	8	485	175	145	49	60
1796–1800	10	565	184	194	8	40
1801–1805	15	480	178	172	14	50
1806–10	13	420	165	137	43	95
1811–15	27	540	165	175	30	72
1816–20	79	480	134	169	161	122
1821–5	79	450	125	157	122	284
1826–30	126	445	123	164	103	82
1831–5	133	440	124	209	109	77
1836–40	106	470	120	220	94	183
1841–5	88	550	106	216	148	62
1846–50	55	590	106	221	85	88
1851–2	22	700	108	270	120	103
1850–68(W.A.)	37	810	88	263	183	

Deaths exclude those drowned in wrecked ships.

sailing ships were at this time uncomfortable, dangerous and often
deadly. In the Royal Navy, between 1778 and 1806, one-sixth of the
men every year were sick; from 1793 to 1815 the *disease* mortality rate
in the navy each year was about one in thirty, while the 'national' rate
for men aged between twenty and forty was only one in eighty. Twenty
years later, in some ships carrying Irish emigrants to Quebec, a fraction
of the distance to Australia, a tenth of the passengers died at sea, and in
all emigrant ships from Liverpool to North America in 1849, the
average death-rate was three per cent. In some migrant ships single
berths were reported to be eighteen inches wide and two feet high in
1791; in 1835 sometimes four adults slept in a berth six feet by four feet
six inches. This was less than what the convicts had had since 1790—
four to a berth six feet square, in dormitories, which meant an average
of about fifty cubic feet per person; though in 1842 the Passenger Act
prescribed for emigrants a minimum of nine square feet, bringing them
up to the convicts' standard, the House of Commons Committee on
Emigrant Ships found as late as 1854 that 'few emigrant ships would
have satisfied the Admiralty specifications for Convict Ships'.[1]

Surgeon Reid asserted that 'many persons who emigrated to distant
countries would consider themselves exceedingly at ease were they as
well circumstanced' as the convicts, for 'though with an honourable
name ... they were yet supplied with accommodation infinitely short of
those necessary in providing for the transmission of the idle, dissolute
and criminal'. Bigge agreed. 'As the voyage is now conducted, it produces no greater degree of bodily inconvenience to ordinary men than
many are exposed to who are not in a state of punishment,' he said.[2] By
1825, the ships were faster and the voyage was therefore shorter than it
had been, and the prisoners were more regularly brought up on deck.
But all ships pitched and rolled. They were often 'wet'. They were
cramped. At least in the beginning of the voyage many were seasick.
The dormitories could not be well ventilated, even at the best of times;
in bad weather when the hatches were battened down, and when
passing through the tropics, the stench of perspiring humanity and
stale bilge-water must have been horrible.

[1] Lewis, *op. cit.*, 413, 441; C. Lloyd and J. L. S. Coulter, *Medicine and the Navy, 1200–1900*,
iii, 1714–1815 (Edinburgh, 1961), app. B; for emigrants, O. Macdonagh, *Pattern of Government Growth 1800–1860, Passenger Acts and their Enforcement* (London, 1961), 50, 129, 187,
219, 276; *Emigrant Ships Reports*, PP 1854 (163, 349, 429), xiii and xiv; specifications for
convict ships, *HRNSW*, ii, 793, Cunningham, ii, 212.

[2] Reid, 20; Bigge, *NSW*, 9; for contemporary ship conditions, C. N. Parkinson, *Trade in the
Eastern Seas, 1793–1813* (CUP, 1937), Kathleen A. Walpole, 'Emigration to North America
under the Early Passenger Acts', summary of thesis, *Bull. Inst. of Hist. Research*, vii (1930),
187–9.

When the charter-parties laid down that convicts were to be allowed on deck as far as was consistent with their security and the safety of the ship, who was to decide when they should come up, and how many at a time – the master, the officer commanding the guard or the surgeon? Some were more nervous of mutiny than others, but though there was always some risk, in fact outbreaks were rare, especially after 1800. If we exclude the *Lady Shore*, a *female* convict ship which was seized by its own guard, convict disturbances occurred in the *Scarborough* and *Albemarle* in the second fleet, the *Marquis Cornwallis* in 1795, the *Britannia* (1797), the *Barwell* (1798), the *Anne* (1800), the *Hercules* (1802), the *Chapman* (1817), the *Ocean* (1823) and the *Somersetshire* (1842); but rumours of plots were frequent and the fear of an outbreak often caused the convicts to be heavily ironed or kept below. Then sickness would often follow, but ships' masters were likely to look on this as a lesser evil than the loss of their ship; they were responsible for the security of the prisoners, and they had the decisive word.

Whether or not masters were 'low lifed and barbarous', as Hill had described them, they were usually, Redfern suggested later, men with little claim to education, refined feelings or even common decency. In 1797 the magistrates, inquiring into the *Britannia*, had declared that 'all ships . . . should have on board an officer of the Crown, who should be invested with proper power and authority, as well for the conducting of the ship as for the particular inspection and direction of the management of the convicts on board', thus echoing Kent's recommendation to Nepean in September 1793. Hunter agreed. 'It is much to be regretted . . . that one of the King's naval officers, or some person properly qualified, is not sent out in the ships. The convict has no person to complain to whatever cause he may have'; but though Portland agreed too, in September 1798, nothing was done.[1]

By this time, the naval surgeons, first appointed in 1792, were no longer on board. Between the sailing of the *Marquis Cornwallis* in August 1795 and the *Northampton* in January 1815, only one privately owned convict ship carried a naval officer – Lieutenant James Marshall in the *Earl Cornwallis* in 1800. During the French wars, the navy had no men to spare for convict service, so the contractors' surgeons were left unsupervised and unassisted. It is not surprising that for such a long and disagreeable voyage, the men offering were not the leading lights of their profession; while they looked after the prisoners' health,

---

[1] Hunter to Portland, 6 July 1797, encl. magistrates' report; Kent's report, 1793, *HRNSW*, ii, 61; Portland to Hunter, 18 Sept. 1798; cf. Redfern's *Report*, 1814, *HRA*, viii, 275; *Transportation Report*, 1812, App., 24, 26, 27; Bigge, *NSW*, 7–8.

and the master controlled the convicts' general treatment, their admission on deck and the cleaning and ventilation of their berths, it is not
surprising that there were a number of scandals.

On 10 February 1814, the *General Hewitt* arrived in Sydney with
'266 Male Convicts . . . in a very Weak and sickly State'; thirty-four
had died on the way out. Macquarie thought that 'proper Attention had
not been paid by the Master and Surgeon . . . to the Health and Comforts of the Convicts on board'. He appointed a Court of Enquiry,
which found that 'the Conduct of the Commander has been highly
Culpable in some Instances', even though 'several of the Convicts were
received on board in a state of debility' and the 'primary and chief cause
of the Sickness . . . is to be attributed to a continuance of wet weather,
to the Bedding having been wetted . . . and the necessity of the Convicts remaining so long confined below, not being able on account of the
Rain to have access to the Deck'. When they received this report,
Sidmouth and Bathurst refused to pay the usual gratuity to the surgeon,
and Bathurst told the Governor in future to hold a 'full and minute
Investigation into the Conduct of Surgeons entrusted with the Care
of the Convicts during the Voyage'.[1]

On 6 May, the *Three Bees* came in. She had lost nine dead, and fifty-
five had to be sent to hospital. Twelve weeks later the *Surrey* arrived,
in which fifty people had died, including the Captain, the Surgeon, two
mates and thirty-six convicts; Surgeon Redfern, in his report to
Macquarie, hoped that this might 'operate as an Awfull and useful
lesson in future on the minds of the Officers of Transports'. These
disasters were a blow to complacency. Even if the death-rate on the
voyage had fallen from one in ten between 1795 and 1801, to one in
forty-six in the ten years thereafter, the Transportation Committee had
perhaps been over-optimistic when it had reported in 1812 that 'however bad the treatment of the convicts on board the vessels had formerly
been, the present system appears to be unobjectionable'.[2]

Redfern now recommended that the convicts should have more warm
clothing and an additional blanket; they should be forbidden to sell any
of their food; they should receive (and use) more soap; they should
pay more attention to cleanliness and ventilation, which would prevent
the generation of 'a most subtle poison', which often caused disease,
and which 'diffused its Malignant influence through every part of the

---

[1] Macquarie to Bathurst, 28 April 1814; report by Wentworth, Redfern and Luttrell, *HRA*,
viii, 244; Bathurst to Macquarie, 21 Dec. 1815.

[2] Macquarie to Bathurst, 24 May 1814; Macquarie to Transport Commissioners, 1 Oct.,
encl. Redfern to Macquarie, 30 Sept. 1814, *HRA*, viii, 274 and 281; *Transportation Report*,
1812, 10–11.

Ship and Spared none, who came within the sphere of its Action. . . . To effect a Complete renovation of Air in the Prison', he urged that all the convicts should be allowed on deck at least once every day, as of course was always permitted on the females' ships, where there was no security problem. Most important of all, 'with a view of providing Skilful and Approved Medical Men for this Service', he pressed for the appointment of naval surgeons, 'Men of Abilities who have been Accustomed to Sea practice, who know what is due to themselves as Men, and as Officers with full power to exercise their Judgment, without being liable to the Controul of the Masters of the Transports'; they could, in fact, combine 'the Offices of principal Medical Officer and . . . Agent for Transports'.[1]

This report has been described as 'one of the major Australian contributions to public health'. Redfern's suggestions, unlike those of Kent and Hunter nearly twenty years before, were promptly adopted. The Transport Commissioners at once began to appoint Surgeon Superintendents, and the first, Dr. Joseph Arnold, sailed in the *Northampton* in January 1815. 'The good and beneficial Effects' of the new system of 'Appointing respectable and Skilful Surgeons of the Navy to be Surgeons and Agents of the Convict Ships' were 'eminently Conspicuous', reported Macquarie next year. Convicts arrived 'in Excellent Health and Without any Complaints against the Commanders. Whereas, previous to this Arrangement, Very few Ships Arrived without a Long List of Grievances . . . for bad Treatment and Short Provisions . . . Many Lives of Convicts' were saved, and 'the Difference of Expense' was 'Nothing in Comparison of the great Advantages obtained'.[2]

The major difficulty remaining was the constant bickering over the 'Relative Powers and Duties' of the ships' masters, the commanders of the guard and the surgeon superintendens. Unfortunately, complained Macquarie, there was 'a Mistaken Notion' of what was expected of to be done by each, and this 'Jealousy of Authority' was embittered by interservice rivalry. Could not these 'Powers and Duties' be 'properly Explained' before the ships sailed? 'Specific instructions . . . would be of very great Benefit to the Public Service,' he urged, though the rules he suggested and his proposal to give deciding power to a majority of the three officials would not have overcome all the difficulties. Bigge's solution of the problem of divided authority was to give more powers to surgeon-superintendent, including the responsibility of punishing the

---

[1] Redfern to Macquarie, *loc. cit.*, 275 ff.
[2] Ford, 21–4; Redfern's report, *loc. cit.*; Bathurst to Macquarie, 4 Dec. 1815; Macquarie to Bathurst, 18 March 1816, 4 April 1817.

convicts, and to provide 'penal consequences' against the captain and the owner for 'unwarrantable opposition' to the surgeon's requirements. What was unwarrantable he did not say; but instructions to both surgeon and master showed greater weight being given to the former.[1]

In 1818, the surgeon was still neither 'the naval agent for transports nor authorized in any way to interfere with the management of the ship'; but he was ordered to *compel* the master to keep to the terms of the charter-party, to examine the health of the convicts coming on board and to reject the unfit and to supervise the quality and distribution of rations. He was now to see that the convicts' cabins were kept clean and properly ventilated, and not only the hospital as formerly; he was to note in his journal how many were allowed on deck each day and when their quarters were fumigated. He was to inspect all the convicts daily and was responsible for their conduct and punishment. In 1832 the masters were formally ordered 'to comply with such Requests as the Surgeon-Superintendent may consider necessary, regarding the Management and Treatment of the Convicts' and to admit the prisoners on deck, 'weather permitting and the Surgeon Superintendent requiring it'.[2]

During the wars, the calibre of the naval surgeon had greatly improved. In the eighteenth century, he was a craftsman rather than 'an officer and gentleman'. His duties were to act as physician, surgeon and apothecary on board a ship of war. His examination by the Surgeons' Company was by no means testing. If he ranked with the master in pay, he was below him in status. Styled 'warrant officers of wardroom rank', the surgeons were not 'commissioned officers of quarter-deck rank'; they had no uniform before 1805 and did not appear in the Official List of Sea Officers until 1814. No wonder it was 'perennially difficult to recruit the right sort of man' for a service whose 'prestige was so low'. But the pressures of the French wars, and the agitation of men like Dr. Thomas Trotter and Sir Gilbert Blane led to reforms in 1805 which almost revolutionized the service, even though the surgeons were appointed by warrant, and not by commission, until 1843. Blane could record that the mortality rate among the sick in the navy had fallen from one in eight in 1780 to one in thirty in 1812. 'No longer did thousands perish from scurvy, typhus and smallpox. Ships were better ventilated . . . hygiene had been improved . . . a more efficient medical department

[1] *Ib.*, 18 and 24 March 1819; Bigge, *NSW*, 8.

[2] Instructions to Masters and Surgeons, *Transportation Report*, 1812, app., 24, 26, 27; *Gaols Report*, 1819, app. S; HL, SC on Gaols, *4th and 5th Reports*, PP 1835 (441), app. 26, 27.

established . . . and above all a better type of man attracted to the service by the prospect of improved pay, status and conditions.'[1]

Such were the surgeons who came to work in the convict service after the war. Some of them made a number of voyages and showed great interest in the convicts' welfare. They were told to try to reform them. A copy of the New Testament, two Books of Common Prayer and two Psalters were to be provided for every eight prisoners, and a Bible for every sixteen. 'It being highly desirable to keep the minds of the people on board convict ships as constantly and usefully employed as possible, you are to use your best endeavours to establish Schools, under such regulations as circumstances will permit . . . You are to read Church Service to the Convicts every Sunday and also a Sermon, or some well selected parts from the religious tracts which are supplied to you. You are to use every possible means to promote a religious and moral disposition in the Convicts . . . and on arrival in New South Wales to report the names of such . . . as have been exemplary in their conduct during the voyage and who from the proper use of the Books may deserve to have them as presents.'[2]

Was this 'reformation' successful? That depended on one's standard. 'Nancy Reid, a convict of notorious character,' wrote Dr. Reid, the surgeon in *Morley* in 1820, 'gave satisfactory evidence of reform by reciting a hymn which I had given her to commit to memory a few days before'; on the other hand, another surgeon, Dr. J. Haslem, was so impressed by the convicts' hypocrisy and degradation that he thought any reformation hopeless.[3]

Reid argued that reform was always possible and said that he saw signs of moral improvement on the voyage, even if employment on board was a problem and idleness produced evils; though he thought the majority were not reformed, he found to his pleasure that from his first ship (the *Neptune* in 1818) only nine out of 170 had been called before the magistrates after two and a half years in the colony. John Dunmore Lang claimed that the convicts landed 'with better feelings and dispositions' than when they embarked, though Molesworth found two surgeons who thought the opposite to testify in 1837. Dr. Colin Browning thought that throughout the voyage 'the prisoners breathe a

---

[1] Lloyd and Coulter, *op. cit.*, ch. 2, espec. pp. 10, 13 and 32–7, and cf. vol. iv (1963); Gilbert Blane, *Statements on the Comparative Health of the Navy* (1815), *Med.-chir. Trans.*, vi, 490–573, quoted, Lloyd and Coulter; Lewis, *op. cit.*, 235–6, 243–6, 303–4, 402–14.
[2] Surgeon's *regulations*, Navy Commissioners to Home Office, 29 May 1823, CO 201/144, f. 141 ff.; Surgeon's *instructions*, Bigge Appendix, CO 201/118; evid. Surgeon Bromley, *Gaols Report*, 1819, 101–5.
[3] Reid's *Journal* for *Morley*, CO 201/119, f.378; Haslem, 14–16.

moral and spiritual atmosphere' during a period 'most favourable to the reformation of the guilty'. To judge from his books, Browning was a strange man, but Arthur praised his system. Others, like Cunningham, found the prisoners gambling constantly, and did not much mind. In 1819 one of the colonial chaplains coming out in the *Hibernia* complained that the surgeon, Dr. Carter, had 'obstructed' him in visiting the sick, 'ridiculed' his 'Plans for the Moral improvement and instruction of the Prisoners' and refused to interfere even when 'Bibles, Testaments, Prayer Books . . . *were destroyed to make Cards*' for gambling. Carter replied that he did not believe it, though 'I confess I never did suppress Card Playing . . . from a thorough conviction that during a long voyage the minds of most men require now and then the solace of some light amusement'. Macquarie disapproved of this conduct despite the good health of the convicts on their arrival; but apparently the latter consideration weighed more with the naval authorities, for Carter made four more journeys as surgeon-superintendent before being suspended from the 'convict service' in 1826, on Darling's recommendation, after another 'misunderstanding' with a clergyman passenger on board the *Henry Poucher*.[1]

By this time ships were faster. Fewer goods had to be taken for the colony on government account and masters were forbidden to carry cargo for trade. This meant that more could be carried for use on board and the lengthy stops at Rio, the Cape or elsewhere for provisions became unnecessary. Overall the average time *en route* fell from about six to about four months – to the great benefit of the 'passengers'. The musters held when the ships arrived gave the prisoners an opportunity to make complaints; though some may have kept silent in fear of the consequences of speaking out, there do not seem to have been any successful or systematic efforts to stifle criticism. Sometimes the condition of the convicts on landing was enough to cause inquiries to be made; these colonial investigations were thorough, and the reports sent to England in the long run were not without effect.

After 1820, the few troubles that occurred, including two of the wrecks, were often the fault of incompetent or tactless individuals, but

[1] Reid, 76–9 and 301; John Dunmore Lang, *Journal*, 1825, and *History* (1834), quoted, Gilchrist, i, 76–7; evid. Drs. T. Galloway, Morgan Price, *Transportation Report*, PP 1837 (518), q. 2825, 4139–40; Browning, 11, 23, and chs. 1–3; Arthur to Le Fevre, 1 Sept. 1834, CO 280/49, cf. Surg. J. Sterel to Col. Sec., Hobart, 3 Oct. 1834, encl., Arthur to Stanley, 14 Oct., CO 280/50; Cunningham, ii, chs. 10 and 11; Sorell to Macquarie, 21 May 1819, HRA, III, ii, 399; Macquarie to Bathurst, 17 July 1819, encl. the Rev. Richard Hill to Macquarie 8 July, Surgeon Carter to Secretary Campbell, 13 July; Darling to Bathurst, 4 Feb. 1826; Bathurst to Darling, 12 July.

out of 440 ships, there were only two cases in which the convicts'
provisions were served 'short', four 'scurvy ships' (the *Minerva* in 1821,
Ocean in 1823, *George III* in 1835 and *Lord Lyndoch* in 1838), one outbreak of 'Hooping Cough', one of smallpox and two of cholera. Dysentery remained a perennial problem but was less fatal. By 1838 the
Select Committee on Transportation, bitterly hostile to the system as it
was, had to admit that 'the physical evils of the long voyage to Australia'
had been effectually remedied; however, it thought that 'moral evils'
remained, the 'necessary consequences of the . . . communication
between so many criminals, both during the period of confinement previous to embarkation and during the weariness of a long
voyage'.[1]

By this time, then, the two major problems on board were 'employment' and 'contamination'. The activities of Satan among the idle are
proverbial; and despite schools and the best of intentions, there was
much idleness on board ship. As for the 'uninterrupted association and
habitual indolence' of the convicts, this was regrettable; but what could
be done? The illiterate could be taught; the women might make straw
hats, so long as this did not 'encourage a passion for dress'. 'Contamination' in crowded quarters was inevitable, for the convicts could not be
kept apart. Boys were shipped with the men until as late as 1833. In
1817 the prison was divided into three parts by 'open iron railings',
which did not impede the current of air, and might make it possible to
separate the 'more or less hardened offenders'. Macquarie was delighted,
but as a 'classification' it was primitive. Any effective division of the
prison would have impeded ventilation and Bigge agreed that it was
impossible; all that could be done was to make the voyage direct and as
short as possible.[2]

As late as 1866, a letter describing the voyage of one of the last ships
to Western Australia shows little change. The rations were 'sound and
good'. In the evening, singing in the hatchway and 'step-dancing, an
exhibition which gives great delight'. Cards were even more popular,
'maintaining their ascendancy to the close of the voyage. By day there
are faint attempts . . . to carry on a school, but they come to nothing'.
There are 'a few fights . . . seldom interfered with, it being thought best
to let the men settle their quarrels in their own way'. Below, at night,
'foul conversation . . . no savageness or brutality; but filthiness beyond

[1] Bateson, ch. 10; Darling to Huskisson, 28 Aug. 1828; *Transportation Report*, PP 1837-8
(669), v.
[2] Bigge, *NSW*, 6, 11; Macquarie to Bathurst, 16 and 30 May 1818; Navy Commissioners to
Goulburn, 22 Dec. 1818, *HRA*, x, 143.

belief. The god of the professional thief is . . . not the god of hate and pride, but of lewdness and dirt'.[1]

On the female ships, prostitution was a never-ending source of trouble. 'In some of the ships,' wrote Surgeon White, of the First Fleet, 'the desire of the women to be with the men was so uncontrollable that neither shame nor the fear of punishment could deter them from making their way . . . to the apartments assigned to the seamen'.[2] This desire remained as long as women were transported, though after 1806, the females were sent in separate ships, except for the *Providence* in 1811; even so, the sailors, and sometimes their officers, caused trouble.

The *Lady Juliana* carried no male convicts in 1790, but 'every man on board took a wife from among the convicts, they nothing loath', according to John Nicol, her steward, in his sometimes exaggerated reminiscences; and much the same situation existed a generation later. Nicholas Bayly complained in 1816 that it was 'customary when the Female Convicts embark for this Country that every Sailor be allowed to live with a Woman during the Passage'. Next year, Mr. Justice Field agreed, but was not upset. The women 'were certainly permitted to cohabit with the Officers and Seamen . . . but to prevent connexion . . . would (I am convinced) be quite impossible, even if the hatches had been battened down every night. Upon the whole, however, I believe there was as little immorality on board the *Lord Melville*, as it is possible should prevail among a Ship's company of different sexes, so brought into contact. Of this I am sure, that a decent exterior was preserved'. Promiscuity was worse in the *Friendship* the same year, 1817, but Macquarie could do nothing about it; 'there was no power vested in the authority of New South Wales to Punish the Offenders'. The British government would have to give this if it really wanted reform. Another bad case was the *Janus* in 1820, but despite this, and other frequent accusations of prostitution made concerning the female convict ships, all that Bigge could recommend in his report were stronger stanchions and more padlocks, and the loss of wages as a punishment for intercourse. Cohabitation in the *Providence* in 1826 showed that the problem was not solved.[3]

Though the voyage was inevitably costly, freights came down after

[1] *Cornhill*, xiii, 500–1, quoted, Hasluck, 23.
[2] John White, *Journal of a Voyage . . .* (1790), 31.
[3] Nicol, 119; Nicholas Bayly to H. E. Bunbury, 13 Mar. 1816, encl. in Bathurst to Macquarie, 24 Jan. 1817; Mr. Justice Field to Macquarie, 1 Dec. 1817, encl. in Macquarie to Bathurst, 4 Dec.; Surg. Cosgreave to Macquarie, 14 Jan. 1818, encl. in Macquarie to Bathurst, 3 March; for *Janus*, report of inquiry, encl. in Macquarie to Bathurst, 19 July 1820; Bigge, *NSW*, 11–12; re *Providence*, Arthur to Hay, 20 June 1826, *HRA*, III, v. 285–7.

the war. Ships were cheaper and quicker trips reduced the cost of food and the time when the convicts could do little profitable work. Although the average freight was about £40 per man between 1791 and 1800, it rose to £50 in the next ten years. Between 1811 and 1815, it fell to about £40, to £36 between 1816 and 1820, to little over £30 in the 1820s and less than £20 per man in the 1830s.[1]

FREIGHTS OF CONVICT SHIPS FROM U.K.

Dates	No. of Ships	Total Tonnage	Freight	Per ton
			£	£
1791–1800	31	–	212,000	
1801–10	26	11,046	222,000	20
1811–15	27	18,726	169,000	9.18
1816–20	79	38,171	486,000	12.15
1821–25	80	37,560	464,000	12.8
1826–30	128	58,547	623,000	10.11
1831–1835–6	129	57,476	372,000	6.10

Even for a 'seven-year man' this last figure worked out at an average of under £3 a year, and for a 'lifer' of course it was far less. This was extremely cheap if the convict could then be assigned and cost the government little more; unfortunately there were too few who could be so easily disposed of, though the British government kept hoping for the best. But eventually it came to feel that assignment was no punishment and did not deter criminals; its cheapness was not enough.

[1] *Returns: Transportation Report*, 1812, app. 37; PP 1818 (334), xvi, 175, 1819 (191), xvii, 331; *Gaols Report*, 1819, app. Q and R; PP 1821 (557), xiv, 199 (439), xxi, 465, 1822 (136), xxii, 335; Bigge Appendix, CO 201/130, N.i.; *Transportation Report*, 1837–8, app. I, no. 58, 320.

6

Controversy in England, 1810–1830

'As one reads history, . . . one is absolutely sickened
not by the crimes the wicked have committed, but
by the punishments the good have inflicted.'
OSCAR WILDE: *Soul of Man under Socialism*

During the Napoleonic wars, despite periodic distress in years of bad
harvest, crime did not seem to be such an urgent problem as it had
been, or as it was subsequently to become. Convict labour was 'of great
utility' in the dockyards, and at the same time, the 'Establishments of
the Hulks' were 'constantly decreased from the great number of Convicts of a better description that have been selected for the Army and
Navy'. True the Admiralty was sometimes reluctant to take men from
the yards 'from the great want of useful convicts' there; they objected,
for example, to having a man who 'has not been to sea, nor is stated to
be otherwise useful on board a ship of war than by playing on the Fife'.
Even so, the hulks in 1805 were 'more than sufficient for the number of
convicts sent from the different Gaols', and three years later they were
still 'considerably deficient in their proper complement'.[1] Fewer than
2,000 males and 800 females were convicted each year up to 1808; of
these only about 300 and 40 respectively were sentenced to death, and
about 600 and 150 to transportation, either directly or as a condition of
their reprieve from execution; as they could be kept in the hulks instead, it is not surprising that few were sent to Australia, an average of
less than 350 between 1802 and 1809, and none at all in 1804.[2]

After 1810 the crime rate seemed to rise. A few denied it. Francis
Place, for example, insisted that in the past there had not been 'the
same disposition to pry into the state of society . . . It would appear to

[1] Entry Book, Home Office to Admiralty, 17 April and 11 July 1804, 15 Feb. and 20 Oct.
1805, 7 June 1808, HO 29/5.
[2] *Criminal Returns*, 1805–8, PP 1810 (47 and 55), xiv.

a cursory reader . . . that there has been an increase of crimes . . . That this is not the case is fully proved by the unqualified testimony of every person examined who was qualified to judge of the state of the metropolis thirty years ago'. But whatever Place's impressions, the steadily rising number of convictions posed a problem for British ministers.[1]

What could be done? Many and varied were the reforms that were claimed would be a panacea for society's ills. Democrats, spurred on by the ideas of 1789, wanted a more popular government and an end to the exploitation that was such a powerful cause of crime. Political economists wanted less government spending and freer trade. Others put their faith in better education.[2] Evangelicals wanted a sterner moral code. William Wilberforce thought that 'great crimes' could be prevented 'by endeavouring to repress that general spirit of licentiousness, which is the parent of every species of vice', though later Sydney Smith, with justice, referred to Wilberforce's Society for the Suppression of Vice as one only for 'suppressing the vices of persons whose income does not exceed £500 per *annum*'.[3] Humanitarians and utilitarians alike wanted punishments made less severe. They were combining to reform the prisons; this done, they would claim to have found a more efficacious punishment than transportation. The utilitarians, led by Jeremy Bentham, long advocated, with little success, a better police; but the conversion of the pragmatic, efficient Peel led to a force being established in London in 1828, which was copied, though slowly, in other parts of Great Britain. Police reform meant the prevention of crime; the greater likelihood of detection made punishment more certain, and certainty could replace severity as a deterrent.[4]

Change and reform came in the criminal law, but only after 1830, more than sixty years after Beccaria's epoch-making work on *Crimes and Punishments* had been first published in English translation and

---

[1] *Place MSS.*, BM, Add. MSS. 27826, f.192–3; Returns,| PP, 1813–4, 1814–5, 1818, 1831–2; *Criminal Laws Report*, PP 1819 (585), appendix, 125 ff.

[2] R. Owen, *New View of Society* (1813), Joseph Lancaster, *Improvements in Education* (1803), Henry Brougham, *Practical Observations on the Education of the People* (1825); *Ed. R:* xvii (1810), 58; xxx (1818), 486; xlii (1825), 206; xlvi (1827), 228; xlviii (1828), 258; i (1829), 181; cf. Chester New, *Life of Henry Brougham to 1830* (OUP 1961), chs. 17 and 18; R. K. Webb, *British Working Class Reader, 1790–1848: Literacy and Social Tension* (1955); Douglas, *Documents*, xi, 706 ff.

[3] Wilberforce, *Diary*, 12 June 1787, quoted Halevy, 455; Sydney Smith, *Ed. R.*, xiii (1809), 333, 342. Cf. R. Coupland, *Wilberforce, a Narrative* (OUP, 1923), chs. 2 and 7, M. G. Jones, *Hannah More* (CUP, 1952), part 3, Radzinowicz, iii, part iii.

[4] Bentham, *Constitutional Code*; E. Chadwick, 'Preventive Police', *London Review*, 1829, no. 1, 252 ff., *Police Report*, PP 1828 (533); *P. Debs.*, 1829, n.s., xxi, 867; Radzinowicz, iii, part vi; Gash 487 ff.

after Romilly and Macintosh had toiled for years in vain effort to persuade Parliament to mitigate the 'barbarous laws which were more fit
for a nation of savages'. Between 1779 and 1786 the criminal law in
Austria, Prussia, Sweden and Tuscany was codified; but if the scope
of the death penalty was restricted, many cruel punishments remained
and the Austrian code of 1787 prescribed flogging, branding, the
galleys and imprisonment with heavy chains. European criminal law
had made little progress since the Middle Ages, and punishments were
unequal, cruel and barbarous. Basic reform only followed the French
Revolution–in France in 1791 and 1810, Prussia in 1794, the Cisalpine
Republic in 1797, Austria in 1803, the Netherlands in 1808, Sardinia,
Modena and Bavaria in 1813, the Two Sicilies in 1817, Parma in 1820
and Spain in 1822 for example; if by modern standards punishments
were still severe, they were no longer cruel, and no longer irrational.[1]

Codification, though Bentham might urge it, did not attract either
the English government or English lawyers.[2] Even when liberals or
philanthropists, like Holland, Grey, Lansdowne, Canning, Charles
James Fox, Wilberforce, Fowell Buxton, Clarkson, Henry Thornton,
Shelley, Byron, Southey, Thomas Paine, Godwin, Hazlitt, Brougham
and many others, urged that capital punishment be reduced, public
opinion was indifferent, and conservatives were strong and hostile.

That so many of the reformers sympathized with some aspects of the
French Revolution delayed their progress and made their task harder;
for, as Wilberforce remarked in 1819, he 'remembered once to have
heard opinions against alterations of sanguinary laws, urged with as
much apparent fear as if the person proposing them were about to
introduce the horrors of the French Revolution'. When the *Quarterly
Review* could describe Romilly as 'our professor of humanity like
Robespierre, who wrote a treatise against the punishment of death',
was it any wonder that he might give up hope? 'If any person be
desirous of having an adequate idea of the mischievous effects which
have been produced in this country by the French Revolution and all
its attendant horrors, he should attempt some reforms on humane and
liberal principles,' he wrote. 'He will then find not only what a stupid
spirit of conservatism, but what a savage spirit, it has infused into the
minds of his countrymen.'[3]

[1] Mackintosh, speech on Criminal Law, 1819, *P. Debs.*, xxxix, 777. For Europe, von Bar,
248–57, 315–38, 343, 365; M. Birnbaum, 'De la tendance de notre siècle à la reforme du
droit criminel', *Themis* (Brussels), ix (1828), 180. Cf. Radzinowicz, i, 286–300, 313–96;
Morning Chronicle, 10 April 1823.
[2] Bentham, *Morals and Legislation, Penal Law*; *Bentham Papers*, BM, Add. MSS. 33546.
[3] Wilberforce, *P. Debs.*, xxxix, 828; *Q.R.*, xv (1816), 574; Romilly, *Memoirs*, ii, 90.

Nor were the revolting Americans a much better example. Their criminal laws, inherited from Britain, were severe. They came to vary from state to state, as reforms were introduced, but the amelioration was 'slow and sporadic'. If by 1816 Pennsylvania, New York, Kentucky, Massachusetts, Maryland and Ohio had greatly modified their laws, North and South Carolina were homes of 'legal conservation'; there as in other states, flogging, branding and public executions continued. The Legislature of Louisiana might ask Edward Livingston to prepare a model code in 1822; but when he did so on Benthamite principles, it did not adopt it. If the New Jersey code of 1796 was better than that of 1668, 'many of the vestiges of barbarism' were allowed to remain; as de Tocqueville remarked in 1831, in many states penal laws remained 'with all the rigour of a code of Draco'. The modification of punishments depended on improved prisons, and in 1834, William Crawford, when investigating for the British government, found a milder code in states which had new model penitentiaries; but this was a development of the future, and in any case Great Britain could hardly be expected to model her laws on those of radical, republican, revolutionary, trans-Atlantic states.[1]

English Parliamentary opinion, particularly that of the House of Lords, was very reluctant to reduce the number of capital offences. Lord Ellenborough, the Lord Chief Justice, as conservative in his criminology as many of his successors, declared flatly, in 1810, that he and his colleagues were 'unanimously of the opinion that the expediency of justice and public security requires that there should not be a revision of capital punishment' as the penalty for stealing privately in a shop goods to the value of five shillings; after all, he said, the alternative – transportation – was 'a summer's excursion, an easy migration to a happier and a better climate'. This argument was repeated in 1819 by Sidmouth, then Home Secretary, who agreed with Lord Chancellor Eldon that any mitigation of the criminal law would lead to an increase in crime, even though the death penalty was rarely enforced. 'It is not the circumstances of the severity of the law being put into execution to the fullest extent, so much as the imaginary terrors of it on the mind

[1] Edward Channing, *History of the United States* (Macmillan, N.Y., 1921), v, 184; J. B. McMaster, *History of the People of the United States from the Revolution to the Civil War* (N.Y., 1895), iv, 541; C. Eaton, *History of the Old South* (Macmillan, N.Y., 1954), 497–8 and *Growth of Southern Civilisation 1790–1860* (London, 1961), 272–4; Barnes, *Penology in Pennsylvania*, 72–114, *New Jersey*, 57; E. Livingston, *Complete Works of Edward Livingston on Criminal Jurisprudence* (N.Y., 1873), introdn. by Salmon P. Chase, i, p. vi; *Dictionary of American Biography* (London 1933), xi, 311; Beaumont and Tocqueville, 15; William Crawford, *Report on Penitentiaries in the U.S.*, 5–6, and app., PP 1834 (593).

that produces the abhorrence of crime,' Eldon had declared in 1811, despite the evidence that the fear of execution was no deterrent at all. So when Romilly introduced bills to abolish the death penalty for stealing goods of the value of five shillings privately in shops (shop-lifting) or of the value of forty shillings in dwelling-houses, the Lords rejected them; though he succeeded between 1808 and 1812 with bills to abolish the death penalty for soldiers begging without a pass, and to punish picking pockets and stealing from bleaching-grounds by trans-portation for life instead of by execution, Parliament also responded with alacrity in 1812 to the suggestion that destroying stocking frames should be made a capital felony.[1]

In 1819, the reformers, now led by Sir James Mackintosh and Fowell Buxton, succeeded in persuading the House of Commons to appoint a Select Committee to inquire into the Criminal Laws. The evidence given to it was valuable propaganda, but its recommendations were not heeded; fortunately, remarked the *Quarterly Review*, the House of Lords was 'a floodgate against the tide of legislation which is now rolling so impetuously through the House of Commons'.[2]

The reconstruction of the Tory government after the death of Castle-reagh changed little. Peel, the new Home Secretary, accomplished minor reforms; he admitted that the existing law was not 'some criminal code which must be maintained in all its integrity'; he persuaded Parliament to replace the death penalty by transportation as the punish-ment for larceny unaccompanied by breaking in, larceny in shops, on board vessels, in a church or chapel, in open booths and tents, mali-ciously shooting at a person or sending threatening letters, cutting down the banks of a river, stealing naval stores or assaulting revenue officers. He raised the 'limit' for 'petit larceny' from one to five shillings, but argued that 'grand larceny' could then be punished by transportation for *fourteen* years, instead of *only* seven; stealing from a dwelling-house was to be capital only if the value of the goods stolen exceeded £5, instead of £2; but this was partly because it was 'so desirable' to retain the death penalty for the offence. Further than this he would not go. 'Willing as he felt to reduce the amount of capital convictions, he

---

[1] Ellenborough, Eldon and Sidmouth, *P. Debs.*, 1811, xix, app., 1821, n.s., v, 1233; Romilly, *Speeches*, i, 106 ff., *Memoirs*, ii, 90, 93, 132–3, 142–4, 150–4, 196–8, 201–2, 243; Douglas, *Documents*, xi, 389–94; Radzinowicz, i, 497 ff.; Larceny Act, 48 Geo. III c.129; Stealing from Bleaching Grounds Act, 51 Geo. III c.41; Vagabonds Amendment Act, 52 Geo. III c.31; Destruction of Stocking Frames Act, 52 Geo. III c.16.

[2] *P. Debs.*, 1819, xxxix, 777, 1820, n.s., ii, 491, 524; *Criminal Laws Report*, 1819 (585), extracts in Douglas, *Documents*, xi, 394–9; *Q.R.*, xxiv (1820), 195 ff., though cf. *Ed. R.*, xxxv (1821), 314 ff., *Times*, 8 July 1819; Radzinowicz, i, 532 ff.

advised the house not to be led away too far by mistaken feelings.'[1]

Crime in the 1820s seemed to be steadily increasing; Peel was a member of a government still Tory, even if it was less reactionary than it had been. As consolidations, Peel's Acts did much to make the law easier to discover and interpret, but he never tried, or wanted, to codify it. 'A servant of necessity and common sense,' inspired by an orderly mind and his experience in Ireland, his acts did not greatly mitigate the severity of the law or restrict capital punishment.[2] The *Quarterly* confessed, with pleasure, that the alterations were 'little more than an assimilation of the law to the gradual habit of mitigation which had influenced the executive for so many years . . . long before the laws themselves were altered'; in the *Edinburgh*, in 1831, Brougham declared, with truth, even if spiced with political prejudice, that Peel must be moved 'from the silly pedestal which flattery and imbecility subscribed to raise for him . . . as the great law reformer of his age'. It was not until after the advent of the Whigs in 1830 that really extensive amendments (as opposed to consolidations) were made, though Peel had taken the first small step, which is often the hardest, and he had established a police force in London.[3]

Some reformers had great faith in imprisonment with hard labour as a punishment, if only a sojourn in prison were made thoroughly unpleasant, possibly with a treadmill, though it certainly should not be made harmful to health, or be the subject of extortion or ill-treatment by gaolers which it had so often been in the past. Others agreed, but stressed the need for religious education and moral training as well, so as to turn the gaols from 'nurseries of crime' into agencies of reformation. But the Prisons Act of 1791 was only permissive, and its suggestions for penitentiaries had rarely been carried out. In 1811 the Select Committee on Penitentiary Houses had praised the new prison in Gloucester, for it was 'not confined to the safe custody of the person' but extended 'to reform and to the improvement of the mind, and operated by seclusion, employment and religious instruction'; but the

---

[1] Peel to Liverpool, 12 Dec. 1822, *Liverpool Papers*, BM, Add. MSS. 38195, 121–5; *P. Debs.*, 21 May 1823, 9 March 1826, 22 Feb. and 13 March 1827, n.s., ix, 421, xiv, 1214, xvi, 632, 1155; Peel to Eldon, 14 March 1826, *Peel Papers*, BM, Add. MSS. 40315, 252; Gash, 329, 335–41.

[2] *Criminal Commitments and Convictions Report*, PP 1828 (545); Gulland, 230–6, and *Bull. Inst. Hist. Research*, viii, 182–5. Peel's Acts were 7 and 8 Geo. IV c.27, 28, 29, 30; 9 Geo. IV c.31; 11 Geo. IV and 1 Will. IV c.66.

[3] *Q.R.*, xlvii (1832), 170 ff.; *Ed. R.*, liv (1831), 185 ff.; cf. Radzinowicz, i, 574–80, 598–9, n. 24, 26. E. Halevy's admiration for Peel has led him to exaggerate a little when he wrote 'as far as the penal code was concerned his successors had very little to do' (*History*, ii, 192).

committee recognized how expensive penitentiaries were, and it concluded that 'the extent of any general plan for the imprisonment of transportable convicts in Penitentiary Houses must very much depend on opinion . . . relative to the expediency of pursuing, on a more contracted or a more enlarged scale, the practice of confining offenders of that description on board the Hulks, or of sending them to Botany Bay'. It did, however, recommend building a male and female penitentiary for convicts sentenced to seven years' transportation from London and Middlesex.[1]

This the government began to do, at Millbank; unfortunately this new penitentiary, when it was at last finished in 1821, had cost over half a million pounds and turned out to be unhealthy. Since many of the older prisons were still overcrowded, ill-regulated and defective, the reformers, led by Neild, Sir George Paul, Holford, H. G. Bennet, Sam Hoare and 'that stately, fascinating and emotional moral genius', Elizabeth Fry, had plenty to agitate about. After 1816, the Society for the Improvement of Prison Discipline, a product of humanitarian philanthropy, carried on unceasing missionary work, and Ladies Prison Committees in many provincial towns paid particular attention to the welfare of women prisoners.[2] By the Gaol Act of 1823, visiting justices were ordered to inspect the prisons; more important, quarterly returns were now to be made to the Home Office, which led to further reforms in the future. But the Act prescribed 'classification' just as reformers were beginning to distrust this principle; it was too hard to distinguish enough 'classes', and within each the danger of 'moral contamination' remained. Unfortunately, too, the Act applied only to county prisons, and to those of London, Westminster and seventeen provincial towns; inspection was by local magistrates and not by government inspectors, and there was no provision for compelling negligent local authorities to obey it, so it by no means either ensured that proper prisons should be provided, or solved the problem of punishing criminals. The unreformed gaol was 'rather an asylum than a place of punishment', declared the recorder of Liverpool; so until the prisons were made more satisfactory, they were unlikely to replace transportation.[3]

Healthier gaols meant (or were thought to mean) that they must be

---

[1] *Penitentiary Houses Report*, PP 1810–11 (199 and 207); Webb, *Prisons*, chs. 4, 6, 7. Cf. Neild, *Prisons; Gaols of London Report*, PP 1813–14 (157); *King's Bench, Fleet and Marshalsea Prisons Report*, PP 1814–15 (152); Douglas *Documents*, xi, 377–84.

[2] Millbank Act, 52 Geo. III c.44; *Millbank Report*, PP 1823 (533); Webb, chs. 5, 8, and pp. 71–5; *Gaols Report*, 1819.

[3] HL, *Gaols Reports*, PP 1835 (438–441); *Liverpool Mercury*, 4 May 1827; Gaol Act, 4 Geo. IV c.64; for Ireland, 3 Geo. IV c.64, 7 Geo. IV c.74.

made in some other way unpleasant. The great John Howard, when he began his prison reform campaign, had had to face the objection that 'the dread of confinement was in great measure taken off and the lower classes of people find them more comfortable places of residences than their homes'. How could they be made 'sufficiently irksome and disagreeable, especially to the idle and profligate?' The prison authorities were confronted with the same dilemma which faced the Poor Law Commissioners after 1833 – how could they make prison (or workhouse) conditions worse than those outside, when so many were ill-fed, badly clothed and badly housed? Controversies were continuous over the employment of prisoners, their possible profitability, the use of the tread-wheel and the crank, 'association', 'solitary confinement', 'classification' and education both religious and secular with the (often contradictory) objectives of safe custody, health, economy, deterrence and reform.

The tread-wheel sometimes caused serious injury, but was defended as being a deterrent. Was it profitable? Possibly, if leased out, like water-power, to millers; but was it reformatory? Almost certainly not. Many reformers advocated the teaching of handicrafts, and virtually turning gaols into factories. This might be profitable; it might even reform by the teaching of a trade; but would it deter, when employment was often scarce? Would it not bring into 'association' the hardened and the first offenders, types who ought to be kept separated? And might it not lead to differential treatment according to skill, and not according to character and conduct? As C. C. Western put it, 'If prisons are to be made into places in which persons of both sexes and all ages may be well fed, clothed, lodged, educated and taught a trade; where they may find pleasant society . . . the present inhabitants should be turned out and the most deserving and industrious should be invited.'[1]

Imprisonment was not solely to inflict pain, argued the Prison Discipline Society in the 1820s, but some punishment was necessary; since 'the personal suffering of the offender must be the first consideration, as well for his own interest as for the sake of example', the society 'decidedly and unequivocally' was the advocate of 'hard labour such as is calculated to alarm the criminal'. Although 'excess application' of the tread-wheel might make it 'the instrument of unjust rigour', the wheel 'was not inconsistent with human feeling and interferes in no way with the inculcation of moral and religious impressions'. 'If coercive labour and restraint is calculated to reform or deter from crime, no system of discipline can be better calculated for this purpose than the tread-mill,' it reported in 1827. This was in line with Sydney

[1] *Remarks on Prison Discipline* (1821), 16.

Smith's demand for toil, 'as monotonous irksome and dull as possible – pulling and pushing instead of reading and writing . . . no tea and sugar, no assemblage of female felons round the wash-tub . . . no public schools, maintained at the expense of the county, for the encouragement of profligacy and vice'. He wanted the gaols made disagreeable, with periods of solitary confinement on bread and water, 'if it were not thought proper to render their confinement entirely solitary during the whole period of their imprisonment. The first object should be the discomfort and discontent of the prisoners, . . . that they should feel unhappy . . . A prison must be a place of sorrow and wailing. The Prison Discipline Society should be more stern and spartan in their discipline . . . Mrs. Fry is an amiable and excellent woman . . . but hers are not the methods to stop crimes'; what was needed was 'coarse food, a dress of shame, hard, incessant, irksome and eternal labour, a planned and unrelenting exclusion of happiness and comforts', although in order 'not to excite compassion for the sufferer', he would 'not recommend torture or the amputation of limbs'.[1]

Smith's principal object was deterrence; but others were more sanguine in their hopes for the prisoners' reform. 'There is something so impressive in the calm perusal of the New Testament that obdurate indeed must be the heart that can reflect upon the doctrines and practices it inculcates without feeling the mind softened and improved thereby,' wrote J. C. Lettson in *Gentleman's Magazine* in 1804; according to Neild, 'proper places of seclusion dispose the mind to penitence and produce lasting alterations in the principles of the prisoner'; but most of the politicians were more cynical, or more realistic.[2]

If penitentiaries were certainly expensive and doubtfully reformatory, the alternatives to building them, or to overcrowding the existing unsatisfactory gaols, were more hulks or more transportation. Like the prisons, the hulks were a source of much complaint. Originally 'temporary', they had become a regular part of the penal system. They were intended for prisoners awaiting transportation and for those unfit to go, but many of those so sentenced never proceeded any further. Government officers had taken over their control from the contractors, partially in 1802 and completely in 1815; for as a Select Committee had reported in 1812, although 'the arrangements under which offenders are now confined . . . cannot reasonably be objected to, as either insufficient for

[1] Society for Improvement of Prison Discipline, *4th Report*, 1822, 14; *5th Report*, 1823, 35; *6th Report*, 1824, 49; *7th Report*, 1827, App., 348–9; Clay, 92; Smith, *Ed. R.*, xxxv (1821), 286 ff., xxxvi (1822), 354 ff.

[2] *Gentleman's Mag.*, lxxiv (1804), 799, 1089; cf. Clay, 81, 98, 112.

the safe custody of the prisoner, or unfavourable to his health . . . in regard to his moral amendment . . . they are by no means satisfactory'. The decks were separated to prevent 'communication', but this was only a first step towards 'classification'; there was no close supervision at night, and it was 'doubtful whether an officer could go down among the prisoners at night without the risk of personal injury'; there was no schoolmaster and only limited opportunity for religious instruction by the chaplains; if there was no 'atrocious vice', there was some violence, much gambling and 'vicious conversation'.[1]

That same year, one Thomas Holden, who spent nearly a year in the hulks after being convicted of administering unlawful oaths at Great Bolton – one of the relatively small number of persons transported for political or trade union offences – was describing conditions from the other side. 'Dear wife,' he wrote, 'I would try and content myself, but to be sent from my native country perhaps never to see it again distresses me beyond comprehension and will terminate with my life . . . and to part with my Dear Wife and Child Parents and friends [and] to be cut off in the Bloom of my youth without doing the least wrong to any person on Earth.' He was able to get some money from home, which, on the hulks was 'of the greatest service . . . for people Newly Coming here must of course be ill treated or if they have not some Trifle of money to help them'; the Captain looked after it and allowed three shillings weekly 'which supplies us with what necessaries we want . . . I will stand much in need of 3s. every week here [at Langston] for we have not the smallest way of making one penny here and the ship allowance is too Scanty to support Nature . . . We are not debarred from having any Necessary food if we have a little money to provide it' – good eighteenth-century prison practice, but not necessarily conducive to discipline, deterrence or reform. He reported that all the officers seemed 'very humane' and there was a three-monthly report on conduct – though this was of little use, though he did not know it, for nearly all were recorded 'good' in the absence of flagrant disorderliness, and minor variations seemed to have little influence in determining either transportation or early release.[2]

[1] *Penitentiary Houses Report*, 1812, 135–47; cf. evid. Capper, *Gaols Report*, 1819, 298–300, *Transportation Report*, 1812, 77, *Secondary Punishment Report*, 44 ff., PP 1831 (276); Holford, *Hulks*, 38–46, 82–5; cf. letters to Sam. Whitbread, M.P., 1811, Bedford Records, nos. 4995, 5002. For improvements in fitting out hulks, corr. between HO and Admiralty, HO 29/5, 29/6, 29/7, *passim;* cf. the Act in 1802, 42 Geo. III c.28, s.2.

[2] Correspondence, Lancashire County Record Office, June, July 1812. He found conditions in New South Wales more comfortable, though living costs were very high. 'I have £20 a year in current money' – only equivalent to £12 in English coin – 'so my dear Brother I hope you will stay at home . . . and be contented in the state you are in' (June 1815).

Further reforms followed the amending act of 1815 and the appointment of a Home Office official, John Henry Capper, as Superintendent. Overseers were to reside on each ship and they were to keep a 'character book'. There was to be no alcohol, dice or cards. All convicts were to work on shore every day, except those needed for duty on board. The hulks were divided into more compartments, 'which greatly eased the problem of discipline'; prisoners were locked in cells of ten to twelve men, which officers on duty could inspect at night (though, as critics were in future to complain, this 'separation' was not enough).[1]

The Chaplains regularly reported 'contrition', even if the sincerity of the penitents may well be doubted. The prisoners' 'conduct during Divine Service is truly exemplary', wrote the Reverend Edward Edwards, from the *Bellerophon* in 1818. 'Where the Rubric directs, the kneeling posture is strictly observed; and that of standing during the Psalmody which is now performed in an excelling and devotional manner'. Since 125 could say the Catechism and twenty-five repeat the Thirty-nine Articles by heart, when 'restored to Society they will not so easily be led astray by every wind of doctrine', which was doubtless highly desirable. Schools for reading and writing were started and proved very popular, and Capper prided himself on encouraging the learning of trades to provide a livelihood to the prisoner after discharge; though the number of prisoners 'exceeded all former times', there had been a 'great improvement in the past two years', leading to 'the greatest order and decorum', he reported in 1819.[2]

Hitherto about a third had been sent off to New South Wales, the 'bad characters', second offenders, and those sentenced for life or fourteen years, but this was not enough, and overcrowding made the proper classification of prisoners impossible. Capper decided who should be transported and who kept on board, though it seems strange that this decision should rest not with the Secretary of State, but with the Superintendent, who was consequently the man to ask for favours. For example, in 1817, William Lamb (later Lord Melbourne) asked Capper for favour towards the *brother* of one of his servants; since the latter was a 'most meritorious character', perhaps the former, who was a first offender, might 'merit indulgence'. Capper reported that the culprit's conduct was good and agreed to 'recommend him for release at the end of the year when half his sentence has expired'. Since the conduct of

[1] 55 Geo. III c.156; *Instructions*, re Convict Establishment at Portsmouth, Sheerness and Woolwich, PP 1816 (10 and 19), xviii, 319.
[2] The Rev. S. Watson (Woolwich), 26 June 1816, the Rev. T. Price (Sheerness), 2 July, in Capper's *Report*, 1816, 4–5, PP 1817 (37), xvi, 141; cf. *Report*, 1817, 10, PP 1818 (15), xvi, 207 ff.; evid. Capper, *Police Report*, 1816, 218–9; *Gaols Report*, 1819, 298–300.

nearly everyone was reported good, it paid to have friends in high places.[1]

In 1832 the Select Committee on Secondary Punishments expressed their 'unqualified disapprobation' of the whole hulk establishment; its redeeming feature was that it was then costing only about £6.10.0 a year per man. For those who could be given work, this was very cheap; but as Peel had admitted in 1826, 'without regular employment' in the dockyards, keeping prisoners in the hulks was 'worse than transportation'. Since the available work was limited, and since building penitentiaries was expensive, he had been forced to resort to transportation and it had been increased in the 1820s. In 1823 an act permitted convicts to be employed in hard labour in *any* colony which the King might determine; between three and four hundred were then sent to Bermuda, to work in the dockyards there, and that establishment was increased by another two hundred in 1827; but transportation still meant essentially transportation to New South Wales or Van Diemen's Land.[2]

On reformation there, the reviews in the 1820s wrote quite favourably. 'There really does take place a moral renovation of a very decided nature,' declared the *Edinburgh* in 1828. The *Quarterly*, in 1825 and 1828, though regretting that a convict labourer in New South Wales was often better off than an agricultural labourer in England, thought transportation satisfactory. It relieved the English labour market and poor rates, and meant that the ex-convict did not return to crime; convicts there were then well-managed and reformed, and at least one could say that if they wanted to they could earn an honest living when their sentence expired.[3]

Was it satisfactory as a deterrent? Most contemporaries assumed that the fear of punishment would deter men and women from committing crime if the right type of punishment was inflicted. Execution was no good, argued one reformer in 1833. Men did not leave the army or navy because some were killed; neither would they stop crime because a few were executed. 'The only punishment they dread is transportation,' he

---

[1] Capper's *reports:* 1817, 15; 1818, 8; 1819, 12 ff., 321, and annually thereafter; cf. his evidence, *Transportation Report*, 1812, 77, *Secondary Punishments Report*, 1831, 44 ff.; Sidmouth, 25 Feb. 1819, *P. Debs.*, xxxiv, 647; Holford, 86, 93–5, 120 n., 124; Lamb to Capper, 28 March 1817, Capper to Lamb, 3 May, *Hatton Papers*, PRO 30/45/1.

[2] *Secondary Punishments Report*, 1831–2, 12; Peel to Sydney Smith, 24 March 1826, Peel Papers, Douglas, *Documents*, xi, 388; mem. by Hobhouse, 23 May 1822, HO 29/6; 4 Geo. IV c.47; Hay to Dawson, 3 and 4 Jan. 1827, CO 202/18, 293–9.

[3] *Ed. R.* (reviewing Wentworth, *Statistical Account* . . . and Cunningham, *Two Years* . . .), xlvii (1828), 92–3; *Q.R.*, xxxii (1825), 313–40, xxxvii (1828), 19 and 24–5; cf. *Letters to Sir Robert Peel* . . . (1824), by a late resident (E. Eagar).

asserted; but its value was weakened by its uncertainty since only one in four of those sentenced to transportation were actually sent out of the country.[1] Perhaps by this time it had become less popular among some criminals, but in the past, plenty of observers thought they liked it. Dr. Bromley, on his third trip to New South Wales as Surgeon-Superintendent, had told Bigge in 1820, that most of his 'passengers' were 'happy to leave'; about the same time, officials at Newgate insisted that many prisoners courted transportation, for it was 'not conceived of as a punishment', but 'was received as a reward'.[2]

Supported by his experience in Newgate, Edward Gibbon Wakefield agreed, and his Imperial theories benefited. In 1831, the Keeper there told the Select Committee on Secondary Punishments that transportation *could* be made a severe punishment and would be a deterrent if it were known that convicts would have to work in gangs for two years. Surgeon Rutherford insisted that it aroused 'great apprehension', the Governor of Cold Bath Fields prison that it was a severe punishment, though 'no punishment would deter a confirmed thief'. Capper and one of the mates on the *Retribution* hulk thought confinement there was a severer punishment than being sent overseas; a discharged convict affirmed the opposite. Only one witness mentioned the hardship of being separated from his family; perhaps this was not thought a hardship! Four years later, four witnesses told a House of Lords Committee on Gaols that transportation excited 'great dread'; four others said prisoners were 'anxious' to be sent away.[3]

Unfortunately the great difference between the felon's real and apparent suffering was only too true, owing to exaggerated stories of the success of one or two transports in the past. 'The community in this country sees the convict sent on a long voyage to a fertile country lying in a fine climate,' the *Edinburgh* had written as long ago as 1813. 'The reality is that the miserable wretch, after rotting in hulks for a year or two is crammed with some hundreds of his fellows into a floating prison, or maybe a pest-house, in which, if he survives the risk of famine, pestilence, mutiny, fire, ship-wreck and explosion, he is conveyed . . . to a life of alternating slavery and rebellion, . . . [with]

[1] A Barrister, *Old Bailey Experience* (1833), 6, 42.
[2] Bromley to Bigge, 1820, CO 201/119 f.15; *Police Report*, 1816, 53-4, 101; *ib.*, 1818, 171, 178-84.
[3] *Secondary Punishment Report*, PP 1831 (276), evid. John Wontner, Newgate, 359, 399-401, G. L. Chesterton, Cold Bath Fields, 517-8, T. G. B. Estcourt, 571-3, J. H. Capper, 743-8, E. G. Wakefield, 1436 ff.; *ib.*, 1831-2, (547), evid., A.B., 671-6, T. Hawkins, of *Retribution*, 834-5; Wakefield, *Facts*, 186, 194; HL, *Gaols Report*, PP 1835 (438), evid. Crawford, 14, Orridge, 236, Capper, 238, Bruton, 244, Newman, 315; *ib.* (439), Russell, 60-1, Cope, 304, Dexter, 320-1.

exquisite suffering [and] uniform misery . . . All this passes at the opposite extremity of the earth, from whence it operates no more upon the inhabitants of England than if it were passing in the moon.' Also it was uncertain, and affected some more severely than others, though this might have been said of any form of punishment.[1]

Some, like James Mill, Sydney Smith or Archbishop Whately, falling into the rationalistic error of so many reformers, had no doubts on the matter, and fortunate were those who were so sure they were right. Mill followed his master, Bentham, in thinking neither the 'pain' of transportation an adequate deterrent, because it was unappreciated and uncertain, nor its discipline reformatory, because insufficiently graduated; a Panopticon penitentiary was the solution. He magnificently ignored details, for which he had 'no room'. There was 'no occasion for proof; the fact is notorious'. Transportation had 'not even the appearance of punishment' (what a pity he was not sent to Norfolk Island), and 'of all places in the world', Australia was the one 'where there was the least chance of reform' (except of course in an unreformed British prison!). Smith had assured Peel that a 'sentence of transportation to Botany Bay, translated into common sense, is this. Because you have committed this offence . . . you shall no longer be burdened with the support of your wife and family. You shall immediately be removed from a very bad climate and a country overburdened with people to one of the finest regions of the earth, where the demand for human labour is every hour increasing'. That was why migrants should be sent to New South Wales, where the 'lower orders' instead of 'perishing for lack of bread' were 'waxing fat', and where 'the heart-broken pauper and the abandoned profligate shall be converted into . . . a jolly-faced yeoman'; but Smith, like many others, ignored what were to many, free or bond, the considerable hardships of leaving one's home and family, and apart from this, as Cobbett pointed out, 'even if you are a single man, a sea voyage and the necessary hard treatment on board of ship are not things to be thought little of'.[2]

In 1788 and for some years after, conditions at Botany Bay were undoubtedly far worse than those in England; many respited criminals accepted their conditional pardon 'with great hesitation', and one at least declared she would 'rather die than go out of my own country to be devoured by Savages'. But for some at least, after 1815 the reverse was

---

[1] Ed.R., xxii (1813), 17–18; Romilly, Speeches, i, 268.
[2] Mill, 'Government and Jurisprudence', sec. v, punishments; Sydney Smith to Peel, 13 March 1826, Parker, Peel, i, 400; William Cobbett, Twopenny Trash, 1 March 1831; cf. Whately, and replies by Lieutenant-Governor Arthur.

true. In 1824 the Prison Discipline Society at least favoured the transportation of juveniles, after they had been imprisoned in a penitentiary in England 'for a period sufficiently long to derive a moral benefit' from it; but by 1832 it had decided that transportation was 'essentially defective in those qualities which should attach to judicial punishment'. What was needed was a 'well regulated system of penitentiary discipline, . . . which shall inspire dread . . . by unremitting occupation, seclusion and restraint . . . with hard labour, strict silence and judicious solitary confinement'. Clay insisted that although transportation might seem 'an alarming bugbear' to 'men of strong home ties and large families', to 'adventurous rogues without encumbrances' it seemed a rather 'pleasing contingency'; though generally he thought the transported convicts' fate 'wretched', still 'the exceptional cases of better fortune were sufficiently numerous to mitigate considerably its terror'. He put his faith in the separate system, rather than 'the specious crotchets' of 'classification' and religious instruction on which Mrs. Fry and her school relied; but Mrs. Fry in turn was dubious about reform in penitentiaries, and others were sceptical of all systems. They would have agreed with Surgeon Cunningham that 'the volleys of curses that assailed the ears, and the showers of mouldy crusts and well-picked bones that rattled about the heads of a . . . coterie of lady visitors' to Millbank showed 'how unprofitably the public money had been expended in the building'. Like the *Morning Chronicle*, they had 'little faith in that reform in the character of a criminal which can be effected in a prison by means of its discipline'.[1]

Transportation was cheaper than gaol building; if it did not prevent crime by deterrence, at least it got rid of criminals. From the first the government had decided that while no prisoner whose sentence had expired should be hindered from leaving the colony none should be assisted either. Males might work their passage and females gain a free trip by their charms. Some saved enough to pay their fare, either by hard work, by dishonesty or by selling the land they were granted. How many left in the first twenty years is uncertain. Up to the end of 1795, judging from Collins's account, nearly a hundred expirees legally departed, or about 10 per cent of those entitled to do. Almost as many had successfully absconded while still under sentence.

From 30 July 1803 to 12 July 1804, 126 free persons were 'discharged

[1] *HRNSW*, ii, 749–50; Sarah Mills, Guildhall Sessions Papers, 1789, 483; Prison Discipline Society, *6th Report*, 1824, 49, *Eighth Report*, 1832, 5–7; Clay, 100, 155 and 166; Rev. P. Hunt, *Criminal Commitments Report*, PP 1826–7 (534); *Secondary Punishments Report*, 1831–1832, Mrs. Fry, 1894; Cunningham, ii, 273; *Morning Chronicle*, 23 July 1827.

from the colony', apart from those who left for its dependent settlements or in coasting vessels. How many were ex-convicts we do not
know, but judging from the general composition of the population, we
might guess that at least half were; if so, and if the departure rate was
steady, this would suggest about fifteen per cent of the prisoners
returned when their sentence expired–though since for part of this
time the colonists thought that the French wars were over, possibly the
number returning was slightly greater than before. Macquarie recorded
that only 389 former convicts left the colony between 1810 and 1820 or
about ten per cent of those free to do so. How many succeeded in
absconding is uncertain, but it could have been as many as another three
hundred. Concerned by the females' resort to prostitution to get home,
the 1812 Transportation Committee had urged the government to
provide some facilities for the women's return, but this seems to have
been done only once. When Macquarie sent the *Kangaroo* back to
England in 1817, he gave free passages to nine male and twelve female
emancipists, including two who accompanied their husbands from the
46th regiment. In 1821, the muster recorded 6,257 emancipists in the
colony. About a thousand had only 'conditional' pardons and so could
not leave, but more than five thousand were legally free to do so. At that
time there would have been nearly 7,000 convicts alive who had been
transported to Australia and had either become free by servitude or
been pardoned; therefore, of those who were free to leave, about three-
quarters had not done so.[1] From the British point of view, the situation
looked better. She had got rid permanently of those sentenced for life
or who died as well as of those who could but did not go back; since
only about ten per cent of those transported returned home it mattered
less whether they had been reformed or not.

As time went on, the proportion of expirees who returned became
smaller. In 1826 only seventy-two former convicts left New South
Wales, or about seven per cent of those becoming free to do so that
year. Once again others must have departed unrecorded. Eleven were
reported to have absconded. Some of the 1,200 who became free may
have needed time to earn and save money for their passage, for the
restriction of land grants to emancipists which followed Bigge's report
deprived many of them of funds; but as the colony was becoming a more
desirable place to live in, and conditions there better than in post-war

[1] Grenville to Phillip, 19 Feb. 1791; O'Brien, 216; King to Hobart, 14 Aug. 1804, encl. 8;
Bigge Appendix, Population, no. 7, CO 201/130; Bonwick Transcripts, Box 12, 327, ML;
Transportation Report, 1812, 16; Macquarie to Bathurst, 4 April 1817, and encl. 8; Muster,
1821, encl., *ib.*, 30 Nov.

England or Ireland, fewer wanted to return. Those who obtained their ticket, that is the best behaved who were the most likely to be able to save enough for their fare, often planted roots in the colony which they did not wish to pull up when their sentence expired. Of the agricultural rioters transported in 1831, apparently only one returned home when pardoned.[1] A quarter of all the prisoners were transported for life and could never return. Overall it seems probable that only about five per cent of the convicts who came to Australia returned to the United Kingdom, though the proportion was higher before 1820. To the British government, this was a strong argument for transportation.

If the convicts were 'the refuse of the trading towns' and so 'unsuitable for colonial employment', as the *Quarterly* had declared in 1820, did it matter much? 'Do you wish criminals to labour?' 'Britannicus' had asked the previous year. 'Transport them. Do you wish to reform them? Transport them. Do you wish to decrease your criminal population? Transport it. Do you wish to provide an honest living for criminals after punishment? Transport them. Do you want empty jails? Transport the criminals. Do you wish to preserve a Civil Police? Adopt transportation on an enlarged scale . . . to embrace every crime and misdemeanour to which it can possibly be applied . . . extending it to sturdy beggars, vagabonds and the most depraved of street prostitutes'. In fact, the government did rely chiefly on transportation, and it had plenty of defenders. In a charge to the Wiltshire Grand Jury in 1827, Lord Chief Justice Best welcomed its recent extension, by Peel's acts of 1827, not only to 'many offences which under the old law were capital, but [to] some offences that . . . were not liable to transportation for life before the passing of the late statutes'. There was in the prisons 'a vicious population, the removal of whom from the country was a measure of absolute necessity', declared the Recorder of Liverpool. Next year, the *Quarterly* agreed that the 'entire removal of the individual to a new scene of life affords at once the only security to society against his future crimes and the contagion of his habits, and the only chance left for himself of regaining decency and respectability'.[2] Parliament was satisfied, and if the reformers were not voices crying in the wilderness, they were crying out with little apparent effect.

In 1832, the Select Committee on Secondary Punishment, lacking the courage, or self-opinionatedness, of its successor on Transportation

[1] Darling to Hay, 9 Feb. 1827; Rudé, 'Capt. Swing', *Tas. Hist. Assoc.*, xii, 18.
[2] 'Britannicus', 33; Best, J., *Charge*; *Liverpool Mercury*, 4 May 1827; *Q.R.*, xxvii (1828), 172; *Gentleman's Mag.*, xcviii (1828), 212.

in 1838, condemned all existing punishments, while rather hedging in its recommendations. Transportation by itself, it thought an 'inadequate punishment'; it was not severe enough unless all the prisoners were sent to road gangs, and this would cause 'increased depravity and expense'; however it tentatively suggested an 'improved system' in the dockyards as a *preliminary* to being sent overseas – an idea of Samuel Hoare's, pressed by the *Edinburgh Review* in 1834 and the *Quarterly* in 1838, and the first semi-official suggestion of the 'exile' system, which was adopted with various modifications in the 1840s.[1] But this demanded accommodation for over 7,000 convicts at home and the government could not, or would not, yet accommodate so many in England, either in the dockyards or in other public works; 'improved systems', like penitentiaries, were too expensive. Driven, *faute de mieux*, to rely on transportation, it could only try to make it more severe, as Bathurst, Brisbane, Wilmot Horton, Peel, Darling, Arthur, Melbourne and Stanley all tried to do in turn.

Peel had told the Commons in 1823 that he would like to see transportation made a more effective punishment, if it were to replace the death penalty widely. 'It should be known that it was intended to make transportation a much more severe mode of punishment than it had generally been hitherto', he declared next year. The Transportation Acts were amended and consolidated. In 1824, the Superintendent of convicts was empowered to set convicts at 'special labour'; the governors' power to pardon was restricted; 'internal secondary punishment' and the penal 'dependencies' for the worst class of convicts were made harsher. Even so, Peel was not satisfied. Writing to Sydney Smith in March 1826, he said that the government was again occupied in devising the means of giving to transportation some degree of salutary terror as a punishment.

'I admit the inefficiency of transportation to Botany Bay, but the whole subject of what is called secondary punishment is full of difficulty . . . arising mainly . . . from the vast harvest of transportable crime that is reaped in every assize . . .

'I can hardly devise anything as a secondary punishment in addition to what we have at present. We have the convict ships, which at this moment hold four or five thousand convicts employed in public works. There is a limit to this, for without regular employment . . . it is worse even than transportation.

'Solitary imprisonment sounds well in theory, but it has in a peculiar

---

[1] *Secondary Punishments Report*, 1831–2, 14–20; *ib.*, evid. Hoare, 1601–5, 1780–90; HL, *Gaols Report*, 1835, 27; *Ed.R.*, lviii (1834), 351 ff.; *Q.R.*, lxii (1838), 502 ff.

degree the evil that is common to all punishment, it varies in severity according to the disposition of the culprit . . .

'Public exposure by labour on the highways . . . would revolt public opinion in this country . . .

'As for long terms of imprisonment without hard labour, we have them at present, for we have the Penitentiary (Millbank) with room for 800 penitents. When they lived well, their lot in the winter season was thought by people outside to be rather an enviable one. We reduced their food, and from the combined effect of low but ample diet, and . . . depression of spirits . . . there arose a malignant and contagious disorder, which emptied the prison, either through the death or removal of its inmates.

'The present occupants are therefore again living too comfortably, I fear . . .

'The real truth is the number of convicts is too overwhelming for the means of proper and effectual punishment.'[1]

Three years later, he was just as perplexed. There was 'no sufficient demand' in the colonies for convict labour under proper regulation. New South Wales was 'gradually exchanging for the character of a prosperous colony its original one as a penal settlement', and it was 'no easy matter' to form new ones. Transportation had not deterred criminals, and crime continued to increase. The evidence given to the Select Committee on Secondary Punishment converted the *Quarterly*, which argued in 1832, that 'the condition of the generality of convicts in New South Wales was anything rather than severe endurance and penal suffering . . . This mischievous system *may* possibly be altered by making all the convicts work in gangs on the roads, and by stricter police', but as it was, transportation possessed 'few effective terrors for those classes of persons against whom it is the business of the law to secure property and society'. Parliament and government agreed, and tried to tighten up the system still further; but neither the Act of 1832 restricting the Governors' power to grant tickets-of-leave, and depriving the ticket-holder of the right to own property, nor the increased rigour which Stanley ordered in 1833 seemed to make it a more effective deterrent to crime.[2]

---

[1] Peel and Wilmot Horton, *P. Debs.*, 4 June 1824, xi, 1091–3, 18 April 1828, xviii, 1567; Transportation Acts, 4 Geo. IV c.47, 5 Geo. IV c.84; Peel to Smith, 24 March 1826, Douglas, *Documents*, xi, 388.
[2] Peel to Reginald Carew, Devonport, 24 Sept. 1829, HO 84/2; *Q.R.*, xlvii (1832), 210; Lord Wynford, *P.Debs.*, 1832, 3rd ser., xiv, 168; 2 and 3 Will. IV c.62; Stanley to Bourke, 21 Aug. 1833; see below, chs. 9 and 11.

7

Who were the Convicts? - Great Britain

'What a fool Honesty is! . . . If I had a mind to be
honest . . . Fortune would not suffer me.'
                                        The Winter's Tale

More than thirty years ago, Sir Keith Hancock remarked that 'the tendency of a folk to idealize its origins is universal among mankind and may be observed even in Australia'. Hence the popular legend, similar to that held by some Americans about those transported to Virginia and Maryland, that most of the convicts were more sinned against than sinning, victims of a harsh criminal law, driven by want to some petty crime in times of economic depression or social stress, caused by the enclosing of the commons or the 'industrial revolution'. As the balladist put it:

> *The law locks up the man or woman*
> *Who steals the goose from off the common,*
> *But leaves the greater villain loose*
> *Who steals the common from the goose.*

In addition to these, there were others considered to be political martyrs, exiled for heroic protests against tyranny in the causes of political democracy or infant trade-unionism; or they might be oppressed Irish, like other nationalities 'struggling to be free', even if, in their case, the adverb 'rightly' were denied them, since they were Papists, and opposition to the English was obviously something very different from any struggle for political and national liberty against foreign despots. The most outspoken academic exponent of these views was probably Professor George Arnold Wood; but though the myth is now firmly embedded in the national ethos, where it will doubtless remain for generations, historians have come to doubt it more and more.[1]

As in so many other things, no *simple* description can do justice to the manifold variety of the prisoners who were sent out; since transportation to some part of Australia went on for about eighty years, its character was very different at different times. At first it was simply a rather unorganized and slipshod method of relieving the overcrowded gaols, when between May 1787 and March 1792, 4,077 males and 769 females were sent off, including one shipload of 155 from Ireland; of these about a third of the English and more than half the Irish were from London, Middlesex and Dublin. But after the wars against France began, convict labour was urgently needed in the dockyards in England, and sometimes even in the services themselves; the number transported fell, but felons were then mixed with Irish rebels and the handful of naval mutineers and of English and Scottish radicals and democrats thought guilty of sedition or conspiracy. From 1793 to 1810, only 5,263 males and 1,810 females sailed from England and Ireland, a larger proportion of women than at any other period up to 1846, but giving an annual average of only 292 men and 100 women; this meant that in what was more than one-third of the period of transportation to eastern Australia, only a twelfth of all the convicts transported were sent out.[2]

From 1811 to 1815, transportation increased considerably and the number sent out each year rose steadily from about seven hundred to more than a thousand; but it was after the end of the Napoleonic Wars in 1815 that the great movement began, for this seemed to ministers the best way to deal with the post-war increase in crime, aggravated as it was by contemporary economic changes, despite the complaints that the punishment was not sufficiently severe to deter the criminals. Fewer criminals were executed, but more and more were sent out of the country. From 1816 to 1825, the average number was 2,600 a year; in the next ten years, it was 4,900. Peel's reforms in 1827 almost doubled the numbers sentenced to be transported – from an annual average of 2,149 between 1824 and 1826 to an average of 4,160 between 1828 and 1830. Police reform meant that more criminals were caught, and Home

---

[1] W. K. Hancock, *Australia* (Benn, 1930), 33; Clark, *History*, ch. 6; cf. Thomas Jefferson, *Works*, ix, 254, quoted *N.S.W. from the Records*, i, 19, P. A. Bruce, *Economic History of Virginia . . .*, i, 603 and 608; Morris, 323–347 gives a more dispassionate appraisal; Wood, *JRAHS*, viii, 177 ff.

[2] For figures, see Appendix below; HO 11/1–16, CO 207/1, Convict Indents, Sydney and Hobart; Bateson, ch. 8 and appendices; *Commitments Reports*, PP 1826–7 (584); returns, 1831–2 (282), and annually. All figures vary slightly, according to whether they are based on numbers sailing or arriving, the date of sailing or arrival, and whether or not they include Irish.

Office policy was now to send more away; but as administration improved, even fewer than before were transported for trivial crime.[1]

It is perhaps the magic of the First Fleet that makes so many writers emphasize eighteenth-century sentences, but three-fifths of all the convicts were transported after 1830, so the later criminal law is more important. Between 1832 and 1837, the Whig Government at last set about genuinely reforming it. It abolished the death penalty for almost all offences and after 1835 it provided for imprisonment as a clear alternative to transportation. At much the same time, by the Prison Acts of 1835 and 1839, it began to create a national prison system which would in time provide a satisfactory 'secondary punishment' at home. This meant that proportionately fewer were even sentenced to transportation, and from this time onwards the crimes of those who were so sentenced were increasingly serious, even if by modern standards their punishment was very severe.[2] Between 1831 and 1840, 43,000 males and 7,750 females set sail from Great Britain and Ireland as convicts for Australia—an average of more than 5,000 a year, though the numbers began to decline in the latter half of the decade; between 1841 and 1845 the average was 4,000; since nearly all went to Van Diemen's Land, even this number was more than enough. Colonial opposition was by then becoming serious, aroused not only by the growing free labouring class, but by the 'lower standard' of the felons shipped out; it was supplemented by increasing criticism in England of transportation as a punishment. Grey's reforms in the system, based on sending out convicts only *after* imprisonment at home, reduced the number to fewer than 3,000 a year between 1846 and 1852; and since 1840, one-fifth had been women, compared with only one-eighth in the preceding twenty-five years. Then in the last stage of the system, Western Australia remained the site of a penal establishment for major criminals until 1868, and took about 500 men each year to bring the grand total to nearly 162,000.[3]

Between 1787 and 1852, nearly 25,000 convict women arrived in Australia, transported under the same laws as the men. They were the mothers of most of the first generation of native-born Australians, the 'currency' as they were called, whom contemporaries, rather to their

---

[1] For effect of Peel's reforms, *Returns*, PP 1840 (252), xxxiii.
[2] The Whigs' reforms were, in 1832, 2 and 3 Will. IV c.34, 62, 123; in 1833, 3 and 4 Will. IV c.44; in 1835, 5 and 6 Will. IV c.81; in 1837, 7 Will. IV and 1 Vic. c.84–91. The Prison Act, 1835, 5 and 6 Will. IV c.38, provided for the appointment of Home Office Prison Inspectors whose powers were increased in 1839 by 2 and 3 Vic. c.56; (cf. Factory inspectors, first appointed 1833, 3 and 4 Will. IV c. 103).
[3] For a further discussion of the numbers transported, see Appendix.

surprise, found to be law-abiding and resourceful, unlike their parents. For this there were good reasons. They could obtain 'honest' employment, for which they were well paid; in the Australian environment there were fewer temptations to crime than in the crowded, commercially active cities of the mother-country. All the same they carried 'convict blood', of which, until recently, many of their descendants have appeared unduly sensitive. In New South Wales, in 1848, there were then living 17,000 persons one of whose parents was a convict; to this must be added the small number of convicts' grandchildren, and those still to be born of emancipist parentage. In Van Diemen's Land, there were fewer children; but the 9,000 female convicts who arrived after 1840 cannot be expected to have been barren, so we might guess that in 1850 out of a population of 400,000, there were about 50,000 Australians of whose forbears at least one had been a convict. This figure seems reasonable if we assume that *on the average* each of the female prisoners had two children who grew up and remained in Australia, and that owing to the great surplus of males in the community, not many of the male prisoners were able to marry free immigrants or their daughters; it would suggest that about a century later there might be rather more than half a million Australians with some trace of convict blood imported from the United Kingdom, though this figure is an answer to speculative curiosity rather than a matter of practical utility.[1]

The most popular sentence, which applied to more than half those transported, was for seven years. A quarter were sentenced for life, but the proportion of lifers slowly declined as time went on. Nearly all the remainder received fourteen years until 1840; after that ten-year sentences became fairly common.

At the Old Bailey, between December 1788 and October 1789, 838 were tried and 543 convicted; of these, 376 were sentenced to death or transportation, and only 167 (*thirty per cent*) to lesser punishment. In April 1816, of 154 persons convicted, twenty-four were sentenced to death (of whom two were executed and the rest transported), fifty were sentenced directly to transportation and seventy-nine, or *half the total*, were sentenced only to be imprisoned, fined or whipped. As far as the Old Bailey was concerned, this figure remained fairly constant, at least until after the law reforms of the 1830s; though by then the number

---

[1] For the first generation of convict children, Coghlan, i, 561–2; Ward and Macnab, *Hist. Stud.*, 289 ff. From their figures (*loc. cit.* 294–6, 299), avoiding double counting, I deduce the average of two; it might be slightly greater. Thereafter, I assume their descendants increased approximately in geometric progression.

tried had more than doubled, about half those convicted were still sent
to transportation. Over all England, before 1834, about *one-third* of
those convicted in the higher criminal courts were sentenced to transportation; thereafter the proportion steadily declined, to 27 per cent
between 1835 and 1837 to less than 14 per cent in 1847–8.[1]

Of those sentenced to transportation, or whose execution was respited
on condition of transportation, before 1818, less than a third were
actually sent away; the remainder got no further than the hulks. In the
1820s, at least two-thirds were actually transported, about three-
quarters in the early 1830s, about two-thirds between 1835 and 1840,
three-quarters again from 1841 to 1843, and then the proportion
steadily declined. 'Lifers' were usually sent, and most prisoners in their
twenties; the elderly and sick were not; for teenagers it seems to have
been a toss-up. Theoretically 'character' was a consideration; but
though some reports from the local gaols were informative, others were
not, and behaviour on board the hulks was almost invariably recorded
as 'good' or 'very good'.[2]

Date	Per cent of all those convicted at assizes and sessions who were sentenced to transportation or respited for it	Per cent sentenced who were actually transported (*Approx.*)
1811–17	31	30
1818–24	34	60
1825–31	34	70
1832–4	35	75
1835–7	27	66
1838–40	22	66
1841–3	19	75
1844–6	17	66
1847–8	14	40

Of those transported from Britain, out of a sample of 4,331 males,
783 had no previous conviction; 1,665 had one or more, and in the
remaining 1,885 cases in the sample, chiefly in the early years, no information is available. If these were nearly all 'old lags', which is

[1] Old Bailey, Sessions Papers, HO 16/1–6; *Criminal Returns*, PP listed in bibliography.
[2] Prison Inspectors, *14th Report*, PP 1850 (1173), table 16; Quarterly Hulk *Reports*, HO
8/1–41; Capper's reports on the Hulks, PP. For the table, *Criminal Returns*, PP.

unlikely, about a fifth of the total would be first offenders; if they were *all* first offenders, which is also unlikely, then three-fifths of the total were not convicted before being transported; but if the unknowns were fairly typical, as they probably were, then about two-thirds would have been previously convicted for some offence.[1]

Before 1840, most of the first offenders were sent to New South Wales, and those with worse records, or guilty of more serious crimes, went to Van Diemen's Land. Overall, the proportion of *recorded* first offenders there was less than one-eighth of that in New South Wales. Among two batches of convicts who arrived at Hobart in 1825–6 and 1836, not only did seventy per cent of them have 'bad' records before they were transported, but the crimes of the remainder were 'serious' in every case but three, who may, of course, have been 'known' at home, without having actually been convicted; on the other hand, from a sample of over four thousand who arrived in New South Wales between 1830 and 1840, only forty-five per cent had previous convictions.[2]

The majority of English convicts sent to Australia came from the cities, especially from London and Middlesex, and as time went on, from the growing industrial towns of Lancashire. The population of the London metropolis was little more than ten per cent of that of England and Wales, but it supplied about twenty-two per cent of those committed for trial between 1813 and 1819, and nineteen per cent between 1827 and 1833; Lancashire, with about a twelfth of England's population, supplied about one-eighth of her crime; in these two centres, with less than a fifth of the English population, more than a third of the crime was committed. Although in 1840 the whole of Lancashire was not one huge urban mass, most Lancastrians were townsmen; and considering all the other English cities in Yorkshire and the Midlands, the market towns in agricultural counties and the ports like Bristol and Southampton, it seems certain that even though, as Sir John Clapham has rightly insisted, the 'man of the crowded countryside was still the typical Englishman', he was not the typical convict. More than half of these came from the cities. As late as 1835, when one Englishman in 619 was

[1] Robson, 'Origin and Character'. Dr. Robson, took a random sample of 1 in 20 of the convicts transported. Generally I was gratified to find that his conclusions tallied closely with those I had reached from the criminal statistics and other records in the United Kingdom. I have used a few of his conclusions to supplement my own, particularly where they deal with categories on which the U.K. records are silent. Since this manuscript went to press Dr. Robson has published his results in *The Convict Settlers of Australia* (MUP, 1965).

[2] Convict Record Books (Tas. Arch.), convict indents, ML. 'Serious' crimes include manslaughter, horse-stealing and major robberies; the others were lesser thefts.

committed for trial for a criminal offence, one in 290 was committed in
Bristol, one in 336 in London and Middlesex, one in 464 in Surrey and
one in 481 in Lancashire—the four 'wickedest' areas in the country;
though the manufacturing districts 'improved' a little in the years that
followed, they relapsed badly in the depressed years from 1839 to 1842,
like London and Middlesex in the 1840s.[1]

Of those actually transported from England, about a third came from
the London metropolis until 1819, about a quarter in the 1820s and
1830s, about a fifth after 1840 and about a quarter over-all. The worst
areas were around St. Giles, Seven Dials, Drury Lane and in Maryle-
bone; the most common crime, by far exceeding even the rate for the
country as a whole, was larceny. Of the perpetrators who were transported, more than the national proportion were juveniles, first offenders,
transport workers or personal servants; half were migrants to London.
Lancashire's share steadily increased from about one-fourteenth up to
1820 to about an eighth after 1835, though the crime rate went up a little
in the depression of 1827–8, 'when moral restraint must have been
dissolved among those on the point of being starved to death', and again
between 1837 and 1841. Over the whole period, more than one-third of
the English convicts came from these two mainly urban areas, and the
government showed its concern by transporting from them a disproportionate share of first offenders.[2]

Considerably fewer than one thousand were political prisoners rather
than criminals. Among them, the most numerous were the 464 agricultural labourers, including 256 from Hampshire and Wiltshire, who
were transported after the riots in the winter of 1830–1. They were
older than the average convict, and more were married. Although 105
had previous convictions, these were chiefly for minor offences, including thirty-two for poaching, and this was less than half the usual
proportion of old offenders. More than two-thirds were sent to Van
Diemen's Land, which was a little surprising for usually that colony
received more serious offenders. Perhaps the British government
thought them very dangerous in the excitements of the time; after
all, their leaders were politically strong radicals and, socially, either
a 'superior' class of artisans or 'hard-working' peasants, whose

[1] J. H. Clapham, *Economic History of Modern Britain* (CUP, 1930), i. 66–7; on the depression, A. D. Gayer, W. W. Rostow and Anna Schwartz, *Growth and Fluctuation of the British
Economy, 1790–1850* (OUP, 1953), i, ch. 5. *Criminal Commitments, 2nd Report*, 4, PP 1828
(545); *Constabulary Report*, PP 1839 (169), annual returns of Criminal Offenders.
[2] These proportions are based on the 'place of conviction' given in the lists of convicts
transported, HO 11/1–16; cf. Robson, 'Origin and Character', 43, 49, 73, 90–1, app. 6 (b,)
8(d) and (g).

transportation might deter others like themselves.[1] The directors of the
Van Diemen's Land Company, who, as local gentry, knew them at home
were interested too; they argued that if the men were assigned to the
Company they would be well-treated, reformed and kept away from the
other criminals on the island, and at the same time, of course, their
labour would be valuable. Whether or not this would have been the
case, Arthur was unwilling to co-operate and only assigned it twenty-
five; but like most political prisoners they were in any case well-behaved,
and all but a few had been pardoned by 1837.[2]

Other 'politicals' included the five 'Scottish martyrs' in 1794, about
fifty Luddites in 1812, eleven Derbyshire rioters in 1817, five lesser
lights among the Cato Street conspirators in 1819 and fifteen others
guilty of high treason who arrived in 1820.[3] Trade unionists were
very few, for all summary convictions under the so-called Combination
Acts, 1799 and 1800, carried only a sentence of three months' imprisonment, not transportation. Unionists could be indicted for conspiracy
under the Treasonable and Seditious Practices Act, 1799, and the Act
against Illegal Oaths, 1797, and this applied to the six Tolpuddle
Martyrs, 'victims of Whiggery', in 1834. Seventy-two unionists and
Chartists were transported between 1839 and 1842, and eight in 1848.
In 1840, 148 rebels were sent from Canada, with about fifty soldiers
guilty of desertion there.[4]

Throughout the period, more than nine-tenths of those transported
from England (and four-fifths from the whole United Kingdom) committed some form of theft, ranging from burglary, breaking and entering,
highway robbery with violence, and in the country, horse, cattle and
sheep stealing, to shoplifting or picking pockets. But it is difficult to find
out exactly what the criminals had actually done, for until 1835 the

[1] Colson, 'Hampshire Agricultural Labourers', 143 and 280 ff.; Rudé, 'Popular Disturbances', *Hist. Stud.*, x, 464; cf. J. L. and B. Hammond, *Village Labourer* (1912), chs. 11 and
12, B. Newman, *Lord Melbourne* (1930), 92 ff.
[2] Bischoff to Goderich, 8 and 14 Jan. 1831, Goderich to Bischoff, 22 Jan., CO 280/32;
Bischoff to John Kerr, Directors to Curr, 13, 14 and 27 Jan., 2 Feb. 1831, Curr to Arthur,
1 Feb., Arthur to Curr, 4 Feb., Curr to Directors, 22 July, V.D.L. Co., *Letter Books* (Tas.
Arch.), despatches, no. 1, 503 ff., Foreign, no. 3, 154. For pardons, Glenelg to Arthur,
7 Aug. 1835, Arthur to Glenelg, 28 Jan. 1836.
[3] Darvall, 88, 104, 129; Goulburn to Macquarie, 22 May 1820; mem. in Gipps to Glenelg,
24 Nov. 1838.
[4] Combination Acts, 39 Geo. III c.81, and 39 and 40 Geo. III c.106; Treasonable and
Seditious Practices Act, 1799, 39 Geo. III c.79; Act against Illegal Oaths, 1797, 37 Geo. III
c.123. George, *Economic Journal, Supplement*, 1927, 214–28; *ib.*, *Economic His. Rev.*, vi,
172; A. Aspinall (ed.), *Early English Trade Unions – Select Documents* (Batchworth, 1949);
Times, 18 and 20 March 1834; *P. Debs.*, 3rd Ser., xxii (1834), 725, 860, 938, xxiii, 114; G. B.
Hurst, 'Dorchester Labourers, 1834', EHR, xl (1925); Convict Records, Tas.; Indents, ML.

crime charged often had little relation to the offences which were thought to have been committed; since any offence earned the same punishment, why bother to prove more than one?

The burglar, pickpocket or highway robber was practically never executed (though he could be), but nearly half of them were transported. According to the indictments, the sums or goods alleged to be stolen were often, though not always, small; but this can be misleading. In 1817, when an unskilled labourer was fortunate to earn ten shillings a week, men convicted at the Old Bailey were sentenced to transportation for stealing goods worth £29, £40, £55 and £191 at one extreme and from ten shillings down to two shillings at the other. But from 1835 onwards, only a minority of those convicted of theft of some kind even at assizes were sentenced to transportation – one in five in 1843; since the greater numbers tried at quarter sessions received lesser punishments too, by this time transportation was reserved for serious offenders.[1]

Earlier, though plenty of criminals received other punishments, their fate seems to have depended more on reputation and hearsay. One man, charged in 1819 with 'stealing from the person' a watch worth £1.12.0 was transported partly because he was said to be 'a noted character'. Another, a boy, convicted for stealing a handkerchief worth three shillings, was said to have 'tried several gentlemen's pockets . . . under the direction of another boy' before his 'success'; he seemed one of a pickpockets' gang, so he, too, was transported. Another, who 'bit my finger and made it bleed freely', was at first charged only with assault; but this was changed when it was 'heard' that the accused 'was a bad character' and was one of a gang. At Cambridge in 1827, a youth was sentenced to transportation for seven years for stealing a hat and a handkerchief, because he was said to be 'the leader of a well-trained gang of young thieves, long in the habit of plundering the rooms of students of the University'. The record of another transported shortly afterwards for stealing a bridle was more definite; he had been three or four times previously in gaol, and it was 'necessary to give the gaolers some relief'.[2]

On the other hand, sometimes men 'escaped' for very technical reasons. A man charged with being at large during his sentence of transportation was acquitted because the indictment did not state the 'nature of the felony for which he had originally been sentenced';

---

[1] Old Bailey *Sessions Papers*, 1817; Criminal returns, 1843.
[2] Old Bailey *Sessions Papers*, 1819; *Cam. and Herts. Independent Press and Hunts. Beds. and Peterboro' Gazette*, 3 Aug. 1827, 15 March 1828.

another charged with attempted poisoning was acquitted because, although all was admitted, the intended victim did not eat any of the poisoned cake offered, and under the statute the poison 'must not only be given to the victim but actually swallowed by him'. A man convicted of sheep-stealing was pardoned because the animal was a 'ewe', and since the relevant act specified 'horse, mare, gelding, colt, filly, bull, cow, ox, heifer, calf, ram, ewe, sheep or lamb', sheep was not a general term. Another indicted for stealing a 'leather horse back-band' and other property of John and Peter Calvert, Jeremiah Murrell and Thomas Cole was acquitted because the name of another partner in the firm was left out of the indictment. Not until 1827 was this legal hair-splitting abolished – by Peel.[1]

'Capital respites' were usually ordered to be transported for life, but the reasons for 'mercy' are inconsistent. One girl, convicted of 'uttering', was 'not an abandoned character', but there seemed 'no effectual security but her removal from the country'; on the other hand, two young men, both said to be bad cases, were recommended short prison terms because of 'strong representations' in their favour. In 1830 in Ely, a male 'utterer' was recommended to be transported, not executed, the 'present state of the Isle being so favourable as not to require examples of extreme severity', and a sheep stealer was to serve only a short prison sentence because his wife was 'near being confined', his five children were 'suffering under severe privation' and he was an 'industrious sober man of good character driven to . . . crime from the pressing feeling of distress'. Two other thieves were recommended to be sent out of the country to give to one an 'opportunity of considering the most probable method of enabling him to regain his character' and to get the other away from the 'bad company' he was keeping.[2]

The Game Laws were blamed for a great deal of 'rural crime', and they were, of course, a favourite target for anyone critical of the landed gentry. Poaching led to 'affrays'; it was said to create a 'ferocious spirit'; certainly the laws helped to fill the country prisons, and if it was true, as was widely believed, that men learned 'criminal habits' there, they may have started off some on a career of crime. In Bedfordshire, for example, between 1820 and 1827 nearly a quarter of those committed were in prison for poaching offences, and between 1839 and 1848, summary

[1] Mr. Justice Bailey to Sidmouth, 21 Nov. 1821, HO 6/5; Abbott to Lord Chancellor, 28 Nov. 1825, re Somerset Assizes, HO 6/10; Mr. Justice Parks to Peel, 19 Feb. 1830, HO 6/15; Old Bailey *Sessions Papers* 1788, no. 32; 7 and 8 Geo. IV c.28, sec. 14.

[2] Recommendations for Royal Mercy, Mr. Justice Bayley to Sidmouth, 10 Oct. 1820, Mr. Justice Christian to Sidmouth, 30 March 1820, W. Bailey to Bayley, 30 March 1830, Mr. Justice Gaselee to Peel, 19 April 1830, HO 6/5 and 15.

convictions against the game laws numbered about 3,000 each year; they made up more than a quarter of all summary convictions in rural counties like Bedford, Rutland, Buckingham and Wiltshire, and about six per cent of all the summary convictions in England.[1] It was 'difficult to make an uneducated man appreciate the sanctity of private property in game' when 'the produce of a single night's poaching was often more than the wages for several weeks' work', lamented a journalist in 1826; on the other hand, it was argued that the Game Laws helped to persuade the English gentry to live on their estates, which was most desirable. 'This most useful and valuable class' was 'entitled to properly regulated . . . amusement and relaxation after the performance of their public duties'; their residence had saved the country from anything like the horrors of the French Revolution and it contributed to the 'virtue and civilization of the English peasant'.[2]

Broadly speaking, until 1831 only the owners of very large estates and their heirs could legally kill game; no one could buy or sell it. But since many wealthy and otherwise respectable citizens like to have it for their dinner, they were willing to break the law to get it. Poulterers pandered to their demand, and bought from poachers; but these were not merely hungry labourers looking for their dinner; in 1818 a gang captured in Bedfordshire was reported to earn between £50 and £70 a week in wages.[3] Even after the sale of game was made legal, in 1831, and men could take out licences to kill it, unlicensed taking continued; it was difficult to stop it, and poachers still found it easy to sell. But it was rare for men to poach from distress, the Chief Constable of Staffordshire, an opponent of the laws, told the Select Committee inquiring into them in 1846; the poor could not afford 'the beautiful description of nets that were used'. Poachers formed part of a highly organized and profitable trade; after all, pheasants and hares were easy to steal, and the 'loot' was easy to dispose of.[4]

In the eighteenth century, penalties for poaching were moderate –

[1] *Criminal Commitments Report*, PP 1826–7 (584), 4–6, evid. Rev. P. Hunt, 31, Gaoler at Bury St. Edmunds, 41, Sir James Graham, 56; Prison Discipline Society, *7th Report*, 1827, 31–2; Hunt to Peel, 19 Feb. 1827, HO 52/4; *P. Debs.*, 11 May 1827, 6 May 1828, n.s. xvii, 733 ff., xix, 360 ff.; *Game Law Returns*, PP 1819, 1820, 1826–7; *Game Laws Report*, PP 1846 (463), Table, 265–6; Prison Inspectors, *14th Report*, 1850.
[2] *Hunts., Northants., Beds., and Cam. Weekly Journal*, 18 March 1826; *P. Hist.*, xxxii (1796), 821–854; *Morning Chronicle*, 10 May 1826; Best, J., in Ilot v. Wilkes, *Manchester Guardian*, 26 May 1821, and charge at Somerset Assizes, *Morning Chronicle*, 19 Aug. 1827.
[3] Stephen, iii, 281; Holdsworth, xi, 543–5; *Game Laws Report*, PP 1823 (260); *Hunts., Beds., Cam. and Peterborough Gazette and General Advertiser*, 26 Dec. 1818.
[4] *Ed. R.*, xlix (1829), 55, liv (1831), 277; 1 and 2 Will. IV c.32; *Game Laws Report*, 1846, Bright's draft, xxxiii ff., evid. Hatton, i, 503.

usually a £5 fine, though this might lead to imprisonment if it was not paid. In 1803 it was made a capital offence 'to shoot, stab or cut a person with intent to kill, rob or maim or prevent an arrest'; though this act covered all attacks on persons, and was not specially intended as a 'game law', its effect was that participants in a 'poaching affray' might be executed. If they were, they inevitably became 'the objects of pity', wrote Cobbett, in his *Rural Rides*; 'the common feeling of the community' was in their favour; those who caused the punishment became 'objects of abhorrence'.[1] In 1816 any persons found within any game preserve at night, with the intent of illegally taking game, might be transported for seven years; though next year they had to be 'armed' to incur this penalty, this might be only with a bludgeon! After 1828, transportation was the penalty only for a *third* offence of this kind, unless three or more persons were involved, or a gamekeeper was resisted with violence. The accused were to be prosecuted at the assizes and not in quarter sessions, which made prosecutions more expensive and so discouraged game preservers from bringing them; they preferred to take summary proceedings against poachers for taking game without permission. For this, the usual penalty was '£5 or three months', but it caused great ill-feeling in the country, where poaching was rarely looked on as a moral offence.[2] In 1769, the conservative Blackstone had said that 'the only rational footing upon which we can consider it a crime is that in low and indigent persons it promotes idleness and takes them away from their proper employments and callings . . . which is an offence against the economy of the commonwealth'; certainly its punishment by country justices tended to lower the rural benches in popular esteem.[3]

Popular opinion credits many poachers with being transported, but if they were sent off, they were usually guilty of violence or thought to have committed some other crime as well. For example, in Bedford, in a case of 'great violence', one of a captured gang was only sentenced to prison and not to transportation because he 'did not strike or injure any keeper'; but another group were transported, for they had 'long been a great pest to the neighbourhood, not confining themselves to poaching

---

[1] Holdsworth, xiii, 390, for 43 Geo. III c.58; William Cobbett, *Rural Rides* (Everyman, 1912), ii, 151–6.

[2] 56 Geo. III c.130 (1816) against 'being in enclosed land at night with the intent of taking game', modified by 57 Geo. III c.90 (1817) making it necessary to be 'armed' to be transported, and by Night Poaching Act, 9 Geo. IV c.69; *P. Debs.*, xxxv (1817), 338 ff., 837, xxxvi, 127.

[3] Blackstone, ch. 4, ch. 13, sec. 9, 175; Brougham on local justices, *P. Debs.*, n.s., xviii (1828), 162, 166.

but making free with their neighbours property'. On the other hand, when Thomas Lee, allegedly 'a prosperous farmer', was sentenced to seven years' transportation for stealing a fishing net, his *real* offence was that he was *suspected* of poaching, and 'opened his house as a *rendezvous* for poachers'.[1]

Juries often refused to convict poachers. For example, a man charged with being found armed with a gun in the night was acquitted because his air-gun was 'in parts' and would only have been 'an instrument of death' if put together; and another was acquitted because though he had a gun, which had just been fired, and was holding a 'warm pheasant', there was no proof that he had actually fired the gun. There were also cases of gamekeepers being successfully prosecuted for shooting at and wounding poachers; it was 'illegal and dangerous', declared Bayley J., for a keeper to use fire-arms.[2]

Between 1817 and 1826, 1,221 poachers—120 a year—were convicted under the acts of 1816 and 1817; between 1825 and 1831, 160 a year were convicted, with 518 in 1827 and 1828; between 1839 and 1843, 464 were convicted—93 a year. But though all were *liable* to transportation, relatively few—only an average of fourteen a year—were sentenced to it; and remembering the proportion of those sentenced who were actually sent off, we may estimate that about three hundred at the most came to Australia—or less than one in four hundred of all the male convicts.[3]

Gangs of professional horse and cattle stealers, organized between England and the continent, were long active, just like the gangs of professional poachers. They were greatly helped by the lack of any efficient police, though their existence encouraged the demand for severe punishment *in terrorem*.[4] And not only were there no police, thanks to popular prejudice, but there were no public prosecutors either. Prosecution was normally left to the individual who had suffered

---

[1] *Hunts., Beds., Cam. and Peterborough Gaz.*, 17 Jan. 1818; Chairman of Bedfordshire Quarter Sessions to Sidmouth, 23 Feb. 1818, Mr. Justice Warren to Sidmouth, 1 April 1820, HO 6/1 and 15; *Manchester Guardian*, 3 Aug. 1822.

[2] *Cam. and Herts. Indep. Press*, 15 Jan. 1825, 30 March 1827; *Colchester Gaz.*, 22 Jan. 1825.

[3] *Returns*, 1819, 1820, 1826, 1826–7; *Criminal Commitments Report*, 1827, Tables 67 and 70; *Returns*, 1825–31, PP 1831–2; *Game Laws Report*, 1846, 265, 290. In 1845, 95 were tried at Assizes for breach of the Night Poaching Act, 67 found guilty, 6 sentenced to transportation, *Return*, PP 1846 (712). In Essex, 13 were indicted 'for entering enclosed ground at night armed' between 1817 and 1821, while 226 were convicted summarily (Essex Quarter Sessions Q/CR/9/3).

[4] *Hunts., Beds., Cam. and Peterborough Gaz. and General Advertiser*, 9 Jan. 1819; *Hunts., Beds. and Cam. Weekly Journal*, 3 Sept. 1826; cf. *Chelmsford Gaz.*, 16 April and 17 Dec. 1824, 4 Feb. 1825; *Colchester Gaz.*, 8 Jan. 1825; *Police Report*, PP 1822 (440), 11.

ᴌoss; but he had to collect his own witnesses, and could not recover his costs until 1818, and then only in cases of felony; not until 1826 was he allowed 'reasonable recompense' in cases of misdemeanour, by Peel's act for improving the administration of justice; but this did not make good the loss of his time. 'No one in petty cases has an interest to convict,' lamented the *Taunton Courier* in 1828, after reporting rather as a matter of surprise that there were 'only' four robberies at the Bath races; it was 'vain to expect . . . either vindictive feelings or a sense of public duty strong enough to make one sacrifice their time to pursue a petty thief'. In theory, a hundred where a crime had been committed and the offender not brought to justice might be fined. In 1696–7 at Romney Marsh some gentry had given up their estates, when so punished for not capturing smugglers, but such action was rare! As a rule there was 'no separate body of men whose interest it was to suppress crime'.[1]

To fill the gap, men of substance sometimes formed societies for the Protection of Property or for the Prosecution of Felons; but like many other 'self-help' associations, they were not well suited for their work. At West Ham, for example, a Society was founded in 1817. Its subscription was £3.3.0 for the first year and £1.1.0 a year thereafter. It offered rewards for the capture of felons, or for information leading to it; they were payable even to accomplices. The scale was £10 for burglary or highway robbery on a subscriber, and £5 on a nonsubscriber, while murder was worth £5 and £2 respectively; but after 1823 it could not afford to pay for offences against non-members. It paid for prosecutions, at an average cost of about £15; but on the average it paid only one a year. Its subscriptions were 'wholly inadequate', and after 1839 its Minutes cease – presumably by then the police had taken over; but until they did, detection, capture and prosecution were inevitably such matters of chance as to encourage both the 'enterprising burglar' and the humble pickpocket.[2]

Overall crime in the country, as in the city, may have been increased

---

[1] 58 Geo. III c 70; 7 Geo. IV c.64; D. Ogg, *England in the Reigns of James II and William III*, 57–8, 104; *Taunton Courier*, 9 July and 10 Sept. 1828.
[2] West Ham Society for Prosecution of Felons, *Minute Book*, West Ham Library, London; cf. Olney, Turvey and Harrold Assoc. for Prosecution of Criminal Offenders, *Minute Book*, Bedfordshire Records, Black Rock Assocn., Dublin, for 'apprehending, prosecuting and convicting all persons guilty of house-breaking, highway robbery, felony or trespass' (1782), *Minute Book*, Nat. Lib., Dublin. The Hunts. Assoc. for the Apprehension and Effectual Prosecution of Horse and Sheep Stealers, Felons and Thieves was established in 1787, Biggleswade Assoc., 1803, Cambridge Assoc., 1813, Bedford Assoc., 1826. See *Cam. and Herts. Indep. Press*, 14 Oct. 1825, Webb, *Statutory Authorities*, 440, Radzinowicz, ii, 122–6.

by poverty, low wages and distress, but this was certainly not its only cause. That a third of those transported from rural counties were not born in the county where they were tried suggests that many were 'wanderers', and much crime was the work of vagabonds around provincial markets; but in Bedfordshire at least, village crime seems to have no connection whatever with the enclosures of various parishes, even if there, as elsewhere, poverty was increased by the decline of domestic industry, in this case straw-plaiting.[1] Up to 1819, from seven rural counties, Bedford, Cambridge, Dorset, Hertford, Oxford, Salop and Wiltshire, with about nine per cent of the population, there came only about six per cent of those transported to Australia. Thereafter the position grew worse. In the 1820s about ten per cent came from these counties, more in 1830–1 and about eight per cent in the ten years that followed, though they now held only about seven and a half per cent of the population. This may have been the result of agricultural depression, a defective poor law and the slow decline of 'domestic industry'; it may have been due to the weakening of village life, the growth of towns and the development of commerce even in these rural districts; but as their 'crime rate' was increasing, their proportion of the whole population was declining; agricultural labourers, though comprising nearly a third of the English occupied population, remained scarce among the convicts, amounting to less than a fifth of those transported, to the great regret of the settlers in Australia.[2]

Most of this crime was committed by young, unmarried men. Between 1835 and 1839, nine per cent of those convicted were under sixteen, nearly half under twenty-one and two-thirds under twenty-five. Only one-fifth of the population was then aged between sixteen and twenty-five, but these committed fifty-five per cent of the crime. Earlier figures are more difficult to discover; but, to take one example, of those in Bedfordshire Gaol in 1821, a quarter were under twenty and over three-quarters under thirty; in 1827, thirty per cent were under twenty and over eighty per cent under thirty; more than half were unmarried. In Ilchester Gaol, Somerset, in 1828–9, two-thirds were unmarried. From the sample of those transported, the records specifically show that

---

[1] Clapham, *op. cit.*, i, 66, 114; Robson, 'Origin and Character', 66 and app. 8; *2nd and 3rd Emigration Reports*, evid. PP 1826–7 (237 and 550); Lydia M. Marshall, *Rural Population of Bedfordshire, 1671–1921*, Bedford Hist. Record Soc., xvi (1934); F. G. Emmerson, *Relief of the Poor at Eaton Socon 1706–1834*, *ib.*, xv (1933); cf. T. Batchelor, *General View of the Agriculture of Bedfordshire* (1808); Bedfordshire Gaol Book, Bedfordshire Records, QGG 10/1.

[2] *Gaols Report*, 1819; *Criminal Commitments Reports*, 1826–7 and 1828; *P. Debs.*, 6 March 1828, n.s. xviii, 985; Robson, app. 4(f).

half were single, half were aged between fifteen and twenty-four, with nearly one-third between twenty and twenty-four; about one-fifth said they were married; the remainder gave no report.[1]

Juveniles were perhaps the greatest problem of all. Since imprisonment as often as not made them worse, and transportation sometimes seemed very severe, how could they be at once deterred, punished and reformed? In a manner suggestive of recent controversy, in 1827 Sir John Eardley-Wilmot, later to be Governor of Van Diemen's Land, urged that they be summarily whipped; he thought there was 'great advantage' in corporal punishment. Next year, rather more constructively, the Select Committee on the Police of the Metropolis, which was gravely worried by juvenile crime suggested that the boys be sent to the navy or at least trained for the sea.[2]

Of course many juveniles were professionals. Apart from Fagin and the artful dodger, we read in 1821 of a boy, arrested for a petty felony and found with several articles of stolen property in his possession, who offered to show where others were. He took the beadles to a cellar, and there they found a man aged fifty, superintending three boys breaking up stolen metal and 'cooking' (i.e. disfiguring) a large brass cock in the fire, to make it look like old brass. All were arrested, but though the 'master' was sentenced to transportation for fourteen years, of the four boys, two with previous convictions were sentenced to two years in prison, the other two to six and three months. This may not have been very constructive, but it was a considerable advance on the death sentence imposed in 1791 on two boys aged fourteen who had robbed another aged twelve; 'though of tender age', they were 'old and daring depredators', who had belonged to a gang of pickpockets and footpads; their execution was 'necessary for the public safety . . . so that other boys would learn that their tender age would not save them from an ignominious fate'.[3]

Many of these juveniles were orphans, or were neglected by their parents. They had learned no trade, but Henry Mayhew, that 'pioneer special correspondent' in his account of London life, did not think their crime was due to 'unavoidable want'; it arose from the temptation of obtaining property with 'less labour than by regular industry', especially

[1] Crim. Returns, PP 1840 (252); xxxiii, 355; Bedfordshire Gaol Book, Q GV 11/1; Ilchester Gaol, *Description Book*, Somerset Records, Taunton; Robson, app. 9(g).

[2] Eardley-Wilmot, 13; *Police Report*, 1828, 8, 32, and evidence; *Criminal Commitments Report*, 1828, evid. Samuel Hoare, app. by Members of Prison Discipline Society; of. *Report of a Committee Investigating the causes of the alarming increase of Juvenile Delinquency in the Metropolis* (1816).

[3] *Manchester Guardian*, 26 May 1821; Rayner and Crook, iv, 187, v. 89.

if only casual unskilled work was available, sometimes irksome and always uncertain.[1] As the balladist sang:

> My mother she dwelt in Dyot's Isle,   (a)
>   One of the canting crews, sirs;   (b)
> And if you'd know my father's style,
>   He was the Lord Knows-who, sirs!
> I first held horses in the street,
>   But being found defaulter,
> Turned rumbler's flunky for my meat,   (c)
>   So was brought up to the halter.
> Frisk the cly, and fork the rag,   (d)
>   Draw the foggles plummy,   (e)
> Speak to the tattler, bag the swag,   (f)
>   And finely hunt the dummy.   (g)
>
> My name they say is Young Birdlime,
>   My fingers are fish-hooks, sirs;
> And I my reading learnt betime,
>   From studying pocket-books, sirs.
> I have a sweet eye for a plant,
>   And graceful as I amble,
> Fine draw a coat-tail sure I can't,
>   So kiddy is my famble.   (h)
> Frisk the cly, and fork the rag,
>   Draw the foggles plummy,
> Speak to the tattler, bag the swag,
>   And finely hunt the dummy.[2]

(a) Dyot Street, St. Giles.
(b) Canting crews, beggars.
(c) Flunky, one who held horses, or 'assisted' passengers from hackney coaches, etc.
(d) Pick a pocket and take money.
(e) Draw handkerchiefs skilfully.
(f) Steal a watch and pocket-chain and seals.
(g) Search for a pocket-book.
(h) Skilful is my hand.

Disposing of the 'loot' was no problem, for most costermongers would buy anything without asking questions, and the ubiquitous 'low

[1] Mayhew, i, 46, 251 ff., 408–22, iii, 369; cf. selections from Mayhew, ed. Quennell. Mayhew and a number of collaborators made similar observations on crime in provincial areas, *inter alia*, in a series of articles in *Morning Chronicle*, 1851.
[2] Reprinted by permission of Angus and Robertson, Ltd., Sydney, from G. C. Ingleton, *True Patriots All* (1959), 86, originally in Hindley, *Life and Times of James Catnach* (1878).

lodging houses' were haunts of receivers. Though the boys might have aroused 'pity rather than blame', the latter was the more common; but in any event they were a great nuisance and a profound social problem. Most of them, unmoved by whipping or prison, were almost certain to be transported sooner or later, especially if operating in London and Lancashire.[1]

In 1826, the Recorder of Liverpool regretted that more than seventy in the Calendar were under twenty. 'The reclaiming of young criminals,' he said, was 'not being achieved by prison discipline'. There was, until it was broken up in 1834, a juvenile hulk, but its inmates were 'often the worst of all', and its closing marked its shortcomings; as Capper told Melbourne in 1831, the boys were kept at work, but most of them had 'led a vicious course of life, and are without friends to take proper charge of them if discharged in this country', so it was advisable 'as they grew up' to send them to Australia.[2]

In 1818 a small county asylum had been opened in Warwick; in 1838, a small House of Refuge, built by voluntary subscription, opened in Glasgow; more important was the national penitentiary for juveniles at Parkhurst on the Isle of Wight, which opened the same year. This was a prison, not a reformatory, and it was not for first offenders; but it was something.[3] Soon afterwards, the Recorder of Exeter told the Home Secretary that he was sentencing some boys to transportation 'not of course intending that they should go abroad', but 'with the hope of procuring their admission to the Penitentiary'; if this was impossible, their 'punishment should be commuted to imprisonment for one month', which seems an extraordinary alternative. But juveniles on the whole had to await the Reformatory Schools Act of 1854 for special treatment.[4]

Unfortunately there tended to be one law for the rich and another for the poor. Eldon's confession in the House of Lords in 1827 that as a boy he had been a 'great poacher' was greeted with laughter. When two boys were accused of stealing fruit at Cambridge, in 1824, it was asked, 'What is the crime of a boy stealing a hatful of apples? This was committed daily by the most high-born youths of the country'; but, it was

---

[1] Mayhew, *loc. cit.*; *Police Report*, 1816 and *ib.*, PP 1817 (233 and 484), 1818 (423).

[2] *Liverpool Mercury*, 14 April 1826; Capper's annual reports on juvenile hulks; Phillipps to Le Fevre, 2 July 1834, CO 201/243.

[3] Juvenile Delinquency (1842) (reprinted from the *Christian Teacher*, July 1842), 23–5; Report on proposed Juvenile Prison, 3 Sept. 1836, PP 1837 (80); *Criminal Law (Juveniles) Report*, *ib.* (79); Parkhurst Prison, Annual Reports, from 1840.

[4] Rogers, Recorder of Exeter, to Normanby, 5 Sept. 1840, Mr. Justice Coleridge to Phillipps, 6 Nov., and Thomas Coltman (Lancs.) to Normanby, 15 Aug., HO 6/25; *Criminal Juveniles Report*, PP 1852 (515); Reformatory Schools Acts, 17 and 18 Vic. c.86, 19 and 20 Vic. c.109.

said from the bench, 'garden plunderers are of a very different description and it is indispensably necessary to restrain a species of crime, which like Sabbath-breaking, may be considered a prelude to other and deeper transgressions'. True this referred to two 'old offenders . . . perfectly adept in the commission of petty crimes', who had been more than once expelled from school. But was transportation good treatment for them? This is, perhaps, hard to say, though another boy on a similar charge was only sent to the House of Correction for a month, and three more prosecuted for stealing apples were acquitted, though caught red-handed, for 'the jury felt the execution of their duty productive of grievous cruelty'.[1]

Of the females less need be said, for they comprised only about one-sixth of the total. On the average three years older than the men, they were predominantly single, from the cities, especially from London and Lancashire, and two-thirds were guilty of larceny or stealing wearing apparel. Though how many were prostitutes will never be known, almost all contemporaries regarded them as particularly 'abandoned'; and even if these contemporaries exaggerated, the picture they presented is a singularly unattractive one.[2]

Overall most of the convicts were not the 'atrocious villains' so often spoken of, though some of them were; but most were ne'er-do-wells, stimulated to crime by low wages, a bad poor law, bad living conditions, periodical unemployment, lack of education and non-existent family life, though often 'polished, artful and vicious', said Surgeon A. Osborne after six voyages. 'Should I be asked whether the whole, or at least the greater portion, of the convicts on board the hulks, really merited the punishment inflicted on them, truth would compel me to answer in the affirmative,' wrote the famous Jorgen Jorgenson after his sojourn there in 1822.[3] Though the increase in crime in years of economic depression suggests that some offenders, at least, were moved by distress, offenders of this type were not often transported. Some were, of course, for with a harsh law, even if mitigated in practice, injustices were bound to occur; but they were relatively few, and became all the rarer in England after 1835.

The only bright spot in Great Britain seems to have been Scotland. There, in 1832, 1,758 criminals were tried in the superior courts and

---

[1] *P. Debs.*, 11 May 1827, n.s. xvii, 738; *Huntingdon, Bedford and Cambridge Weekly Journal,* 8 Oct., 1825; *Cam. and Herts. Indep. Press,* 5 Nov. 1825.
[2] Robson, 'Women Convicts', *Hist. Stud.*, xi, 43 ff.
[3] Journal, Surg. Alexander Osborne, 1833, CO 201/234; Jorgenson, quoted A. J. Villiers, *Vanished Fleets* (1931), 59, was a Danish seaman of considerable talent who none the less finished up in Van Diemen's Land. For his career, J. F. Hogan, *The Convict King* (1891).

1,577 convicted; this was less than ten per cent of the number convicted in England and Wales, though the Scottish population was about fifteen per cent of that of all Great Britain. Sentences were milder too. Despite the manifold deficiencies of Scottish prisons, only six were sentenced to death and 322 to transportation, or about one-fifth of those found guilty, whereas in England and Wales, over 5,000 prisoners, or more than a third of those found guilty, were sentenced to transportation. Ten years later, in the economically depressed year of 1842, 3,177 were found guilty of crimes, but only 284 – less than one-tenth – were sentenced to transportation, of whom more than half were from Edinburgh and Glasgow; in England, of 22,726 found guilty, nearly a fifth were sentenced to transportation. Per head of population, the Scottish rate of transportation was less than a quarter that of England between 1810 and 1821, and only about two-fifths after 1830; as a result Scottish criminals were far less common in Australia than English or Irish; as in England, nearly all (eighty-five per cent) were sentenced for some form of theft, but they were, on the whole, more serious offenders.[1] All sailed out together, the Scots being sent, in the first instance, like the English, to the hulks at Portsmouth or Woolwich.

In 1853, the Constabulary Commissioners' Report spoke of 16,000 criminals in London who were known to the police – one in 140 of its population; and like London, were Manchester, Glasgow and other great cities. Here was the personnel from which the convicts were recruited – a distinct body of people, according to Mayhew. They were professional and habitual criminals, the majority aged between fifteen and twenty-five. Many grew out of 'their habits', if they were not transported, though others never changed their ways. Of the pickpockets, the majority sprang 'from the dregs of society', commonly trained from the cradle; the common thieves, lacking the 'manual dexterity' of the pickpocket, or the skill of the burglar, were ragged, squalid and unwashed, pilfering from shops, fruit stalls, children, drunks, carts, or drying clothes. Some were servants, 'attic thieves'. All in all they were a disreputable lot.[2]

[1] Returns of Criminal Offenders, PP 1812 (45), 1814–15 (163), 1833 (45), 1835 (34), 1837 (109), and annually thereafter. Scottish prisons Inspectors' *Report*, PP 1836 (117); annual returns from 1837. Census, 1841, with comparative tables from 1801, PP 1841, sess. 2 (52), ii, 275. Scottish population was 15 per cent in 1801; the proportion very slowly declined between 1807 and 1841. For proportion of Scottish convicts, HO 11/1–16.
[2] Mayhew and Binney, 43–5, 89.

8

Who were the Convicts? - Ireland

'So there have been divers good plots devised and
wise counsels cast already about the reformation of
that realm, but . . . it is the fatal destiny of that land,
that no purposes whatsoever which are meant for her
good will prosper or take good effect.'

SPENSER

About a quarter of the convicts transported to Australia, nearly 30,000
men and 9,000 women, came directly from Ireland. Six thousand other
Irishmen had crossed St. George's Channel to seek work and got caught
up in the criminal life of Great Britain, especially in London and
Lancashire; they made up about four per cent of all the convicts, and
their offences and character are hardly distinguishable from those of the
ordinary British offenders. The men who were tried and sentenced in
their own country on the average were two years older than the British
convicts. More were married. Juveniles were fewer. Far more were
countrymen, even though a fifth came from Dublin. From here and
Cork, half had previous convictions; otherwise far more were first
offenders–nearly three-quarters of those whose previous record is
known.[1] All this was due to the presence among them of men who were
not felons, but were guilty of crime only in a technical sense, nationalists
fighting British domination and social rebels protesting against a harsh
and unjust land law which condemned them to poverty and starvation.
How many were of this type ? Probably nearly one-fifth, as we shall see.

After the end of the Napoleonic Wars, more than three-quarters of
the Irish sentenced to transportation were actually sent out of the
country. Only the unfit were left behind, for the prisons were bad, the
hulks were used only for temporary accommodation, and it was repeatedly argued that 'immediate removal' was an effective deterrent to

[1] Robson, app. 6(b) and 8, tables I, i and vi; convict indents, ML and Tas. Arch.

crime and outrage in the country. Since the Irish population during the first half of the nineteenth century comprised about a third of that of the whole United Kingdom, and the proportion of transports was only a quarter, relatively more were transported from England, and very many more were sentenced there. This might mean that the Irish were more law-abiding than their Protestant Anglo-Saxon neighbours; but it might only mean that their criminals escaped conviction or that their criminal code was less severe. Although most of the criminal and transportation records were destroyed in the Four Courts in 1922, and the Irish statistical returns presented to Parliament cannot be compared with the British in detail because they were drawn up on different bases, enough remains to suggest strongly that 'ordinary' crime was less common in Ireland than in Great Britain. Of course, except in Dublin there was no urban population, which in England provided so many of the criminals; but most visitors and officials testified both in their writings and to successive committees of inquiry that in general the country people were surprisingly honest.[1]

Of the political prisoners proper, the most important, apart from the sixty Fenians sent to Western Australia in 1867, were the rebels of 1798 who had demanded a more democratic and independent government for Ireland, and the seven famous leaders of the 1848 fiasco – Smith O'Brien, John Mitchel, Thomas Meagher, Patrick O'Donohoe, Terence McManus, Kevin O'Doherty and John Martin. After their abortive rebellion and transportation, their writings of protest in their exile won them much sympathy; but in truth they do not seem to have been harshly treated by the power against whom they had rebelled, whether compared with contemporary Poles, Italians or Hungarians, with Spaniards or anti-Nazis between the wars or present-day anti-Communists in eastern Europe – provided, of course, one admits that any government possesses a right to punish those of its subjects who refuse to recognize its authority.[2]

The earlier rebels were more numerous, worse treated in Ireland and caused far more trouble in Australia than did Smith O'Brien and his associates with all their complaints fifty years later. In March 1800,

[1] Inspector-General of Prisons, *Report on State of the Gaols*, PP 1823 (311); Prison Discipline Society, *Report*, 1823, Appendix, 194; *Observations on Penitentiaries in Ireland* (1821); Irish Prisons reports and Irish Criminal Returns, PP annually. Contemporary observations are innumerable.

[2] W. S. O'Brien, Journal kept at Maria Is., Smith O'Brien Papers, 3400, Dub. Nat. Lib., MSS. 449', Mitchel, *Jail Journal*; John Martin, Diary (PRO Belfast); Irish Political Prisoners' Letters, National Library, Canberra. Cf. Cullen, *Young Ireland*, Kiernan, *Irish Exiles*.

after the arrival of the *Minerva* and the *Friendship*, Hunter had complained that among the Irish were too many 'bred up in genteel life or to professions unaccustomed to hard labour'; they included the Reverend Henry Fulton, three priests, James Meehan, the surveyor, Captains Alcock and St. Leger, Joseph Holt, two schoolmasters and twenty weavers. By September King was worried by the 'number of seditious people' sent 'since the late disturbances'. He said there were 235, apart from the 'Defenders sent out in 1794'; but as none had come then, he was probably including some 'Defenders' and other 'rebels' from the *Marquis Cornwallis* in 1796 and *Britannia* in 1797, as well as the recent 'politicals', who, according to the indents, would have numbered far less than two hundred. He thought that the 'whole numbers' of the rest of the Irish in New South Wales were about 450, which tallies with the August muster when one remembers how many of the convicts died or left the colony at this period of its history; but he surely exaggerated when he complained that the 127 on the *Luz St. Anna* (or Anne) were '137 [*sic*] of the most desperate and diabolical characters that could be selected throughout that Kingdom, together with a Catholic priest of the most notorious, seditious and rebellious principles', and that they raised to six hundred the people 'avowing a determination never to lose sight of the oath by which they are bound as United Irishmen . . . and only waiting an opportunity to put their diabolical plans into execution.' If we distinguish between Irish and United Irish, which King as a rule did not do, there would have been less than 350, out of 3,035 adult males mustered in New South Wales in 1800. Though these included 476 officials and military personnel, the Governor was nervous, and hoped that no more of these 'violent Republican characters' would be sent out for some time, 'particularly the priests'; if they were, 'I do not know what will be the consequences.'[1]

In fact they could easily be guessed. A few were sent from Sydney to Norfolk Island, and soon King's agitation calmed down. 'The conduct of many who were sent here from Ireland during the late rebellion . . . has been uniformly good and highly deserving,' he reported in August. Father O'Neil had been sent out by mistake; perhaps his principles were not seditious after all. Certainly the United Irish had no wish to destroy society, and before long the Governor had granted many of them conditional pardons. He would have liked to let them return

[1] Hunter to Portland, 20 March 1800; King to Portland, 28 Sept. 1800, 10 March 1801; to Under-Secretary King, *ib.*, *HRA*, iii, 74. *Anne* carried 127 male and 24 female convicts (*Return, ib.*, 18). Cf. Kiernan, *Transportation from Ireland*, espec. app. 1, 6, 7, 8, and my comments, *Hist. Stud.*, vii, 83–8. 1800 Musters, *HRA*, ii, 617; there were 519 adult males at Norfolk Is., including 104 officials and military (return, *HRNSW*, iv, 252–3).

home, but this he was not allowed to do. They must not leave the colony, wrote Lord Hobart, for in Ireland the Lord-Lieutenant did not know what their crimes or their sentences were and he could not discriminate between them. They had been convicted 'mostly by Courts-Martial prior to the time when the proceedings of such Courts were sanctioned by law', or summarily, 'before magistrates who exercised their powers under the Insurrection Acts, and whose proceedings were, in the disturbed state of the country, not recorded'.[1]

The nature of their 'trials' makes their good conduct all the more surprising, for Father O'Neil was not the only man improperly sent off. Another transported without trial, after having been released on bail, was John Temple; his wife sent a petition setting out his case, but it reached Dublin Castle only after his ship had sailed from Cork. 'It is apprehended there must be several cases of this description, if it were possible to ascertain them', minuted the Secretary. It was not much consolation for such men to reflect that they were lucky to have been transported and not shot out of hand or tortured, at a time when 'the enormities committed by the partisans of Government were such as must disgrace our annals', and when the Commander-in-Chief could describe his army as being 'in a state of licentiousness which must render it formidable to everyone but the enemy'.[2]

The disturbances, even before the Rebellion, had been suppressed with little regard for legal niceties. In 1796, when the Whig, Ponsonby, told the Irish House of Commons that 'certain magistrates had privately conferred together, and without any information on oath or good evidence of any kind, at their own pleasure and without any Form of Law did lay hands on several of their fellow subjects and transport them', and asked 'would any man justify this conduct?', a number of members answered 'yes' – a fair enough indication of the prevailing temper. The Insurrection Acts of 1796 and 1799 authorized the Lord-Lieutenant to proclaim disturbed counties, in which a night curfew was imposed, to ban meetings, to execute persons convicted of administering an illegal oath and to transport for life those who took one, and empowered any two magistrates to transport without trial by jury persons out at night or thought guilty of offences. Military courts-martial also wielded extensive and summary powers, not always according to law; they were

---

[1] King to Portland, 21 Aug. and 14 Nov. 1801; to Under-Secretary King, 21 Aug., CO 201/20, f.64; Hobart to King, 29 Aug. 1802, encl. Lord-Lieut. of Ireland to Pelham, 21 May.
[2] Prisoners' Petitions, 1800, SPO, Dublin, vi–16–2–784; E. Wakefield (1812) and Sir Ralph Abercrombie (1798), quoted in Locker-Lampson, *State of Ireland*, 49, 52–3.

'trying offences committed before the proclamation, and even procuring capital sentences', John Ogle, J.P., of Newry, told Castlereagh in 1798.[1] Even if not tried by martial law, the accused faced difficulties. In 1797, Sir G. F. Hill had advised Under-Secretary Cooke that 'a light punishment will excite revenge, not terror; . . . you should transport all prisoners in the gaols and give full powers to the generals.' To a large extent this was done. 'All the United Irish who were in on treasonable practices are only indicted for a lesser offence, so as to come under transportation; for that reason no objection lay against Jurors' (as it might have done for capital offences), wrote E. Newton, a magistrate of Omagh. Castlereagh later admitted that 418 prisoners had been 'banished or transported by sentence of court-martial', and as late as 1809, a Waterford magistrate confessed, 'I am aware that the strict letter of the law will not perhaps justify my conduct; but experience has taught me that the magistrate who never steps in critical times beyond that letter will render but feeble services to King and Country . . . I feel confident that His Grace [the Lord-Lieutenant] will not deem my conduct deserving of censure.' He did not.[2] Clearly many United Irishmen were illegally, harshly and sometimes barbarously punished, though whether they were rightly protesting against monstrous misgovernment, or endangering the security of Great Britain in a perilous situation by making common cause with her enemy is a matter of opinion.

In 1802, in the *Hercules* and the two *Atlases*, King said there were another '400 Irish convicts (mostly Rebels)'; more had sailed, and nearly all were rebels, but after 127 deaths in the first two, only 369 males and 51 females landed. Early in 1804, the governor reported again that there were more than six hundred Irish in the colony ready to revolt; but most of these may be better classed as 'social' than 'political' prisoners. If we count a hundred of the 1802 arrivals among the latter, and add them to the 350 who had come earlier, plus fifteen on the *Minorca*, in 1801, who had been tried by court-martial at Portsmouth, and the eight supporters of Robert Emmet on the *Tellicherry* in 1806, it would seem that less than five hundred political rebels were transported from Ireland at this period, and less than six hundred

---

[1] *P. Reg.*, Ireland, xvi, 50, 128, 150 ff.; W. E. H. Lecky, *History of Ireland in the Eighteenth Century* (London, 1892), iii; Ogle to Castlereagh, 14 July 1798, SPO, State of the Country Papers, 2nd ser., 30/207.
[2] Hill and Newton to Cooke, 12 March and 4 April 1797, SPO, Rebellion Papers, 620/29/58 and 196; cf. W. H. Maxwell, *History of the Irish Rebellion in 1798* (London, 1845), espec. chs. 18, 24, 28, 37; Irish State Papers, SPO, vi, 16/2/784, 22 May 1802, 18/1/1239, 7 Nov. 1809.

during all the years that the transportation system was in operation.[1]
But if 'political' rebels were relatively few, 'social rebels' were many.
Driven to despair by poverty, they were always ready to attack their
landlords and all who seemed to be supporting them. They 'cared not a
jot' for any plans for 'an ideal republic', according to the historian of the
United Irish. 'They might be induced to take arms, for they were
almost constantly on the verge of insurrection . . . but their revolt was
sure to be nothing better than a *Jacquerie*'.[2] White-Boys, Oak Boys,
Peep-of-Day Boys, Right Boys, Thrashers, Defenders, Shanavats,
Caravats, Lady Clares, Terry Alts, Rockites and Ribbonmen—one after
another tried by force and by terror to redress the grievances of the
peasant which arose from agricultural distress. Just as constantly, the
government felt compelled to resort to strong measures to 'preserve law
and order', to protect life and property and stop the constant agrarian
outrages.

There were sixty from the 'disturbed districts' in the *Boddingtons* in
1793, though not all were necessarily 'agrarian offenders'. About one
hundred 'Defenders' came in the *Marquis Cornwallis* in 1795 and the
Britannia in 1797, described by both Hunter and King as 'turbulent',
'discontented' and 'worthless'; their ranks were augmented by many of
the arrivals in the *Hercules* and the two *Atlases* in 1802. Their outlook
was improved neither by their treatment on the voyage out, which on
several of these ships was scandalous, nor by the failure of the Irish
government to send out details of their sentences, which meant that
many were kept too long in servitude. Many tried to escape, and since
they were always on the look-out for a chance to recover their freedom,
if need be by the forceful methods they had used at home, their
suspected plots in 1800, their rising at Castle Hill in March 1804, and
their subsequent unrest at Newcastle are hardly to be wondered at; but
the United Irish in the true sense were probably less responsible than
men like the Scottish 'martyr' Margarot, and the Irish 'gentleman', Sir
Henry Grant Brown Hayes.[3]

[1] King to Hobart, 23 July and 9 Nov. 1802; Kiernan, *Transportation from Ireland*, app. 13
and 14. For *Minorca*, Portland to King, 18 June 1801, encl. 6; *Tellicherry*, Secretary
Marsden to King, 17 Aug. 1805, *HRA*, v, 551–2. For numbers in 1804, King to Hobart,
12 March 1804.
[2] R. R. Madden, *The United Irishmen, their Lives and Times* (London, 1842), i, 31.
[3] Hunter to Portland, 3 March and 12 Nov. 1796, 25 June 1797, 10 Jan., 15 Feb. and 1 Nov.
1798; King to Portland, 28 Sept. 1800, to Hobart, 30 Oct. 1802, 9 May 1803; King to
Under-Sec. Sullivan, 21 Aug. 1805, *HRNSW*, v, 451. There was ill-treatment in the *Queen*
(1791), *Britannia* (1797), *Hercules* and *Atlas* (1801). *Anne*'s indents did not arrive until 1820
(*HRA*, x, 203); records for *Friendship* were never made up (*HRA*, iii, 569); indents for
Queen, *Marquis Cornwallis* (1795) and *Britannia* only arrived in 1799 (*HRA*, ii, 366).

For fifty years the Irish government continued to transport 'agrarian offenders'. Irish poverty, due to a combination of excessive population, ignorance, lack of capital, relatively poor natural resources and the absence of industry which could give work to the people if they left the land, was greatly accentuated by a defective land system. The tenant, except in Ulster, received no compensation for any improvements he made; the landlord was usually unwilling or unable to make any, and his non-residence often discouraged his taking much real interest in his property. The increase in population led to holdings being more and more sub-divided; the spread of arable farming and reliance on the potato for food made this possible and encouraged rack-renting. High rents, short leases and the post-war fall in the price of corn made the peasant more than ever dependent on the landlords; efforts to 'consolidate' farms and to replace arable by grazing stopped the slight but short-lived wartime improvement in living conditions and caused many evictions.

The peasant lived on his potatoes, and, if he was lucky, his pig and a little milk. His wages, or his corn, went to pay his rent. He ate from ten to twelve pounds of potatoes daily himself, or about forty pounds with his family. This could be grown on about three-quarters of an acre; but if he were evicted from his potato ground, or if the crop failed, he was left without resource; and the potato did fail, partially in 1811, 1825, 1836, 1839 and 1844–5, in the south-west or west in 1821, 1831 and 1835–7, badly in 1816–7 and disastrously in 1846–8.[1]

On top of his other obligations, he had to pay to an alien church tithes which were collected in a most inefficient and provocative manner and from which graziers were exempt. No wonder that the Irish cottar, 'half famished, surrounded by his wretched family, clamouring for food' objected when he could not pay and saw 'his cow driven off to the pound to be sold', depriving his children of milk, to make good his default. No wonder that from time to time, especially in bad years, the peasant resorted to violence in self-protection, to resist the sometimes impossible demands of landlord and parson, and to keep his miserable little plot of land – his only safeguard against starvation, in the absence, until 1838, of any organized system of poor relief. 'Land in Ireland is the common refuge,' wrote Beaumont in 1839. 'It is not enough to say

[1] W. R. Wilde, 'On the Introduction and Period of the general use of the Potato in Ireland', *Royal Ir. Acad., Proc.*, vi (1853–7), 356 ff., 364–8; H. D. Inglis, *Journey throughout Ireland during 1834* (3rd edn., London, 1835), ii, 300–2; K. Connell, *The Population of Ireland, 1750–1845* (OUP, 1950), 61–2.

that land is desired; it is envied and coveted . . . and when it cannot be occupied by fair means, it is seized by crime.'[1] The White-Boy Associations were, in a sense, a 'vast trades' union for the protection of the Irish peasantry'; their object, Judge Jebb told the Limerick Grand Jury in 1831, was 'to deprive landowners of the power of disposing of their property as they may think fit . . . to dictate to them the terms on which their estates and property shall be dealt out to the peasants and to punish . . . such as disobey those dictates'; but while land was 'a necessity of life', men would 'struggle for it to the death', according to Sir Matthew Barrington in 1852, after thirty-six years' experience as Crown Solicitor in Munster.[2] Even in 1812, before the agricultural depression and before the population pressure increased, Wakefield thought that the Irish peasant was in a far worse condition than the Russian serf; and as time went on, his poverty grew worse. In 1823, the Select Committee on the Employment of the Poor agreed with a witness who declared that 'a large proportion of the peasantry live in a state of misery of which he could have formed no conception, not imagining that any human beings could exist in such wretchedness'. Two years later, J. G. Lockhart, journeying through this country with his father-in-law, Sir Walter Scott, noticed the latter's increasing 'melancholy' at the 'spectacles of abject misery . . . the rueful squalid poverty . . . the exhibitions of human suffering, such as it had never entered into our heads to conceive'; this, wrote Scott on his return, made up 'the extreme of human misery'. In 1842, the German traveller, Johann Georg Kohl, concluded that 'to him who has seen Ireland, no mode of life in any other part of Europe however wretched will seem pitiable'; in 1845 the Devon Commission agreed that the sufferings of the labouring classes were 'greater . . . than the people of any other country in Europe have to sustain'.[3]

In such circumstances, the wonder is, not that there were 'distur-

[1] E. Wakefield, *Account of Ireland, Statistical and Political* (1812), ii, 486; cf. Whitworth to Sidmouth, 13 June 1817. HO 100/192, Gash, 200–5, Fletcher, J., in *Saunders' News Letter*, 2 Jan. 1822; G. de Beaumont, *Ireland* (1839), i, 304–11. On rents, wages and prices, etc., cf. H. D. Inglis, *op. cit.*

[2] Lewis, *Disturbances in Ireland*, 99; *Irish Outrages Report*, PP 1852 (438), evid. Barrington, q. 4786; Richard Webb, *Charge* (1831).

[3] Wakefield, i, 244 ff., 508–10; J. G. Lockhart, *Memoirs of the Life of Sir Walter Scott, Bart.* (one vol. edn., Edinburgh, 1845), 561; *Journal of Sir Walter Scott* (Edinburgh, 1890), i, 1–2; Inglis, i, 67, 79, 98, 143; Kohl, quoted C. Maxwell, *Stranger in Ireland* (Cape, 1954), 290–1; *Employment of the Poor in Ireland Report*, PP 1823 (561), 335–6; Devon Commission *Report*, PP 1845 (605), 16; cf. *State of Ireland Report*, PP 1825 (129), *Emigration Reports*, PP 1826 (404), 1826–7 (237, 550); *State of the Poor in Ireland Report*, PP 1830 (589, 654, 665); *Poorer Classes in Ireland Reports*, PP 1836 (35–42, 269); Devon Commission, evid., PP 1845 (605–6, 616, 657, 672–3).

bances', but that there were not more; not that some agents were shot, houses burnt and cattle maimed, but that there was no general holocaust. Certainly it is not surprising that the peasantry was 'not to be terrified by the gallows . . . or the almost certain prospect of transportation', and that 'remonstrance' to them was 'utterly unavailing'. 'The law affords the Irish peasant no protection,' wrote Poulett Scrope to Melbourne in 1834. 'It is to their own White-Boy law that their allegiance is considered due . . . They do more or less obtain from the White-Boy Associations that essential protection to their existence which the established law of the country refuses to afford . . . The White-Boy system will never be put down until the legislature establish a law for . . . protecting the lives of the Irish peasantry and securing to them the means of living by their industry.'[1]

It is true that not all the White-Boys were starving peasants. They needed leaders, some of whom were 'respectable' men, farmers of some standing, and some ne'er-do-wells joined in, 'without a local habitation or a name, accidental vagabonds or natural born blackguards'.[2] But as the Lord-Lieutenant, the Marquis Wellesley, told Peel in 1822, nearly everyone would have agreed that 'the apparent union of the great body of the population in a common system of disobedience to the Law . . . may be ascribed in great degree to the common pressure of distress'.[3] 'Many of the alarming insurrectionary movements have either originated with tenants dispossessed of their farms, or have been materially aggravated in their extent . . . by the discontent and wretchedness of this class of population . . . The miserable beings dislodged from their abodes find themselves without resource or refuge,' declared the Select Committee on Emigration in 1826. Six years later, Matthew Barrington, already experienced in prosecuting terrorists, told another committee that outrages generally arose from 'attachment to or dispossession' from land; they were due to lack of alternative employment; but 'I have never known a single case of direct hostility to government'.[4]

Even so, it was in part the government which was attacked, because government was failing to preserve 'law and order' in whatever way this

[1] *Dublin Evening Post*, 1 Oct. 1822; Poulett Scrope, 29–30.
[2] HL, *Ireland Report*, PP 1839 (486), evid. Solic.-Gen. for Connaught, re 1821–2, q. 8399–8403; T. C. Foster, *Letters on the Condition of the People of Ireland* (London, 1846), 340, 347.
[3] Wellesley to Peel, 3 Jan. 1822, Wellesley Papers, Dub. Nat. Lib., 322; cf. *ib.*, 9 Feb. 1822, 27 April 1823, Wellesley's Irish Corr., BM, Add. MSS. 37298, 37301; Fletcher, J., 'the troubles . . . not . . . a conspiracy against the government', and Baron McClelland, 'there was no religious or party feeling', *Saunders' News Letter*, 2 and 11 Jan. and 26 Feb. 1822.
[4] *Emigration Report*, 1826, quoted, *State of the Poor Report*, 1830, app. R; *Disturbed Counties Report*, PP 1831–2 (677), evid. Barrington, 4–6; cf. HL, *Ireland Report*, PP 1839 (486), evid. Judge Moore, 14375 ff.; *State of the Poor Report*, 1830, evid. Bishop Doyle, 4409.

was looked at. In 1847, Lord John Russell, then Prime Minister, comparing the state of Ireland with that of England, commented that certainly 'landlords in England would not like to be shot at like hares and partridges by miscreants banded for murderous purposes; but neither does any landlord in England turn out fifty persons at once and burn their houses over their heads, giving them no provision for the future.' From the other political camp, Sir James Graham agreed. 'I have the greatest respect for the rights of property,' he wrote to the Lord-Lieutenant, in 1845, when Home Secretary, 'but British feelings are outraged by these sweeping ejectments.'[1]

But outraged or not, nothing was done to stop them. Much as the government might deplore the behaviour of some landlords, only between 1836 and 1841, when terrorism significantly declined, did it act on the principle that 'property has its duties as well as its rights', and it was to 'the neglect of those duties' that most outrages were due. Parliament preferred Lord Palmerston's dictum that 'tenant right is landlord wrong'. It refused to legislate to protect the tenant, and in its inexcusable ignorance sheltered behind a plea of *laissez-faire*, although it was said that in no other country in Europe did the landlords possess 'more unlimited power over their tenants than in Ireland', and Lord John Russell admitted, when Home Secretary, that they exercised their rights 'with the utmost rigour'. Of course, governments at this time did not approve of public works; and their attitude was influenced by the fact that some landlords who were politically important were also proprietors who behaved very differently from the majority, and who were themselves beyond criticism, like Stanley, Devonshire, Lansdowne and Palmerston. 'I hope,' said the last in 1843, that 'the landlords will abstain from exercising that power which the law gives them, and by showing a little more consideration to the peasants whom they find on their estates they will seek to do away with that grievance which is expressed by that somewhat absurd term "fixity of tenure".'[2] Such a hope resembled that of Canute's courtiers or Mrs Partington, but it helps to explain government inertia.

The Irish were 'taught by their circumstances to hate society', and it became difficult for either the moral teachings of the church or the physical force of the state to check the spread of rural 'outrage'. 'The

[1] Russell to Clarendon, 12 Nov. 1847, Clar., Irish Dep. Bodleian, Box 43; Graham to Heytesbury, 3 April 1845, C. S. Parker, *Life and Letters of Sir James Graham* (1907), ii, 35; cf. *Times*, 7 Dec. 1842, 1 Nov. 1843.
[2] W. R. Anketel, *Conduct of the Resident Landlords of Ireland* (1844), quoted K. Connell, 61–2; Lord John Russell, *P. Debs.*, 15 April 1839, 3rd ser., xlvii, 34; Inglis, i, 121, 167, 209, 311, ii, 126; Foster, 165, 174, 337–8, 397, 540; *P. Debs.*, 23 June 1843, lxx, 281–3.

great majority of a people never . . . become rebels without sufficient reason,' wrote Wakefield. 'It is not in human nature that a whole nation, or any considerable portion of one, should reject the comforts and protections of a civilized life for preference,' declared the *Manchester Guardian* a decade later; all the same, some held that the Irish rural terrorist was 'uncivilized', just as others believed that he was a heroic defender of his rights.[1]

As early as 1776 Arthur Young, on his visit to Ireland, had noticed White-Boys 'set up to be the general redressers of grievances. They punished all obnoxious persons who advanced the value of lands, or hired farms over their heads'. Unfortunately 'having taken the administration of justice into their hand, they were not very exact in the distribution of it . . . They sometimes committed considerable robberies . . . and destroyed the whole substance of men who were obnoxious to them'. Such activities naturally enough led to an act making it punishable by death to assemble with offensive weapons, to send a threatening letter, to persuade others or compel them by force or threats to leave their employment or farms, or at night maliciously to injure a house, property or livestock. Those condemned for these offences were usually reprieved, and transported instead, and after 1831, transportation was the maximum penalty; but suspected 'Ribbonmen' were often acquitted at their trials.[2] Arguing that juries were terrorized or sympathetic, and in either event not to be relied on, the government would then resort to special 'coercive' powers, to make it easier to obtain convictions; as time went on 'coercion' became the rule rather than the exception, though certainly after the Union in 1800 it was administered more carefully than before it.

'Coercion' covered many things. The extreme powers of the Suppression of the Rebellion Acts (1801-4) and the suspension of Habeas Corpus Acts (1802-5, 1822, 1847-9) were rarely called for. Restrictions on the import, manufacture and possession of arms were almost continuous, and to possess unlicensed weapons might mean transportation. The various acts against insurrection, disturbances, crime and outrage had the common feature of enabling the Lord-Lieutenant to 'proclaim' disturbed districts, where the government might use 'special powers'. Persons accused of any offences against the White-Boy or the Arms Acts might be tried by special courts, usually without juries; in

[1] A. MacNevin, *Letter to Lord Roden on the Causes of Irish Crime* (1837), 28; cf. Foster, 20 ff., 338 ff.; Wakefield, ii, 837-8; *Manchester Guardian*, 10 Nov. 1821; cf. Gash, 174.
[2] Arthur Young, *Tour in Ireland 1776-9* (ed. Hutton, London, 1892), i, 82 ff.; cf. Lewis, ch. 1, W. Lecky, *History of Ireland* (cab. edn., 1892), ii, 1-40. Irish Whiteboy Act, 15-16 Geo. III c.21, was amended by 1 and 2 Will. IV c.44.

addition, magistrates were authorized to make 'domiciliary searches'. To make convictions easier, a curfew was imposed; between 1814 and 1818 and between 1822 and 1825 persons out at night could be transported.[1] Under all this legislation, many were transported; but how many? Although some 'White-Boy' offences can be easily recognized, such as the taking of illegal oaths, or being out at night in a proclaimed district, others – house-breaking, cattle-stealing, assault or manslaughter, for example – may or may not be connected with the struggle for the land.

Between 1807 and 1814 there was no 'coercion' in Ireland. No areas were 'proclaimed' under the Insurrection Act of 1807, which lapsed in 1810. War-time prosperity decreased the crime rate; the potato crop was usually adequate, though its partial failure in 1811 coincided with a series of outrages in Tipperary which resulted in six being sentenced to death and twenty-seven to transportation. But most of the 700 male and 200 female Irish convicts transported in these years were ordinary criminals. About a third of all those convicted were sentenced to transportation, but less than a tenth were sent off; three-quarters were guilty of some form of house-breaking or theft and about twelve per cent of stealing cattle, sheep or horses; there were not many 'White-Boy' offences except for the Tipperary cases.[2]

In 1814 disorder revived. In August an Insurrection Act was passed, and the counties of Limerick and Tipperary were soon proclaimed. In the winter of 1815–16 ninety-nine were convicted and sentenced to be transported for 'White-Boyism' and nothing else; in the *Guildford* and the *Surry*, 108 out of 368 were guilty of 'agrarian offences'.[3] But, as in England, post-war crime filled up the gaols and the Inspector of Prisons complained that the number there 'exceeds by a vast proportion . . . all similar accumulations during twenty-three years of my official experience'. More transportation was necessary to relieve them, and from 1817 onwards, this became, in fact as well as in law, a common punishment for larceny, receiving, embezzlement, forgery, coining, horse-stealing, highway robbery, burglary, house-breaking and stealing sheep and

---

[1] For typical 'coercion' acts, 54 Geo. III c.180, 4 Geo. IV c.58, 3 and 4 Will. IV c.4, and the Arms Act, 1 and 2 Will. IV c. 47. On obtaining convictions, Torrens to Wellesley, from Limerick, 9 April 1822, *Wellesley's Irish Corr.*, BM, Add. MSS. 37299, f.40, Blacker at Fermoy, *Southern Reporter*, 8 July 1823.
[2] Richmond to Wellesley, 17 Nov. 1808, *Richmond MSS.*, 92, Nat. Lib., Dublin; Cal. of Prisoners' Petitions, SPO, 1a–17a–4; *Irish Prisons Reports*, PP 1808 (239), 1809 (265), 1814 (264).
[3] Gash, 167 ff.; Lord-Lieut. to Sidmouth, *Disturbances in Ireland*, PP 1816 (479), app. 13; Convict indents, ML.

cattle. Between 1817 and 1821, only about six per cent of those transported had been found guilty of specifically White-Boy offences, or had been convicted of assaults and robberies connected with Ribbonism.[1]

From 1822 to 1825 Insurrection Acts were in force again. Under them, 298 men were sentenced by Special Commissions between 1822 and 1824, though this was less than twelve per cent of all those sent away. The Commissions tried men for ordinary crimes as well as for White-Boyism and for the minor offences which made them 'idle and disorderly persons'; in Cork, ordinary crimes comprised half the cases, and though this was exceptional, probably those convicted in this way roughly equalled those found guilty of White-Boy offences by the ordinary courts in the undisturbed and unproclaimed counties. This would mean that there were about three hundred White-Boys transported while the acts were fully in force, and a few more after they had been relaxed, but less than four hundred altogether.[2]

How guilty were the alleged White-Boys when convicted under the drastic 'coercion laws', when even being out at night in a 'proclaimed' district was a transportable offence? Magistrates and Commissions seem to have tried hard to use with great discrimination the very extensive powers given to them; their moderation was praised by the press and by a House of Commons committee, but rumour and suspicion rather than proof were often the deciding factors. One Michael Carroll, tried at Limerick in 1822 for being out after curfew, was convicted because he was 'one of those persons suspected as being connected with the disturbances'; the court having 'heard that he was a conspirator' left it to the accused to prove his innocence. He was transported, declared the *Manchester Guardian*, on the strength of 'rumours, suspicions and underhand swearing'; on the other hand, his companions, who were equally guilty of the nominal offence, were discharged.[3]

In 1822 the *Dublin Evening Post* thought that of the 172 sentenced to transportation by the Special Commissions at Cork, Clare, Limerick, Carlow, Tipperary and Mayo, half the men 'deserved a better fate'; but during the operation of the Acts, more than a fifth of those found guilty had their sentences mitigated. In determining guilt, the courts

[1] Lord Norbury, Aug. 1817, Cal. Prisoners' Petitions, *loc. cit.*; Archer, Inspector of Prisons, 9 Sept., SPO 569/488/43; Returns, PP 1821 (620), 1835 (535).
[2] *Returns*, PP 1822 (433, 489, 552), 1823 (311), 1824 (280, 174); Peel Papers, 19 July 1825, BM, Add. MSS. 40331, f.106; cf. Assize reports, *Belfast News Letter*, Jan.–March 1823; special commission at Cork, *Freeman's Journal*, 19 Feb. 1822; Convict indents ML.
[3] Disturbances in Ireland, and Ireland under Insurrection Act, *Reports*, PP1824 (372), 1825 (20 and 200); *Manchester Guardian*, 16 March 1822.

relied heavily on a man's character, which was tremendously important 'when doubts existed as to the facts'; but this could be oppressive. The Insurrection Act suspended a 'beautiful part of the constitution', admitted Judge Blacker, when it made a man's absence from his house at night *prima facie* evidence of his guilt. One's house was not one's castle, for magistrates could enter it; a man could not go where he pleased at night and he could be transported for riot, unlawful assembly, concealing arms and delivering threatening notices.[1]

But the discrimination which the Commissions used, despite the 'severity absolutely necessary' and 'the terror of the law', is shown by the numbers they acquitted – 571 out of 702 tried in 1822, 1,324 out of 1,582 in 1823 and 1,317 out of 1,593 in 1824, or nearly four-fifths of those tried. The Commissions by no means blindly accepted evidence given by the police. In Tipperary the latter exhibited 'unnecessary severity', and were reprimanded by the Commission. At Fermoy, far more of those accused were acquitted because of 'good characters' than condemned because of 'bad'. Apparently the Commissioners were satisfied to have suspects 'picked up' for a short period, and men were only transported when the suspicion that they had committed an 'outrage' was extremely strong.[2]

From 1817 to 1829, more than a fifth of the 9,500 male Irish convicts transported came from Dublin and nearly a quarter from Ulster; there were few White-Boys here, or from the cities of Cork, Limerick and others. On the other hand, nearly forty per cent came from the impoverished provinces of Munster and Connaught, including about twenty-five per cent from the particularly 'disturbed' counties of Cork, Limerick and Tipperary. In 1824 Sergeant Blackburn discovered that 'with the means of paying rents appears to have returned the disposition to do so'; there was a 'great lull' in agrarian crime between 1825 and 1830, when neither the *Cork Advertiser* nor the *Limerick Chronicle* could find outrages to report.[3] 'Ordinary' crime never stopped, especially in the towns. Convictions for larceny rose from about 1,500 to nearly

---

[1] *Dublin Evening Post*, 1 Oct. 1822; *Southern Reporter*, 8 July 1823; cf. these papers and *Saunders' News Letter*, *Belfast News Letter*, 1822–23.

[2] Goulburn to Wellesley, 28 Feb. 1822, BM, Add. MSS. 37298; Wellesley to Peel, R. R. Pearce, *Memoirs and Correspondence of the Most Noble Richard Marquess Wellesley* (1846), iii, 348 ff. Returns show that, of those convicted, between a fifth and a quarter were soon pardoned. Cf. *Dublin Evening Post*, 7 Sept. 1822; *Southern Reporter*, 8, 10, 12, 15 July, 16, 21, 30 Oct., 13, 16, 18 Dec. 1823; *Freeman's Journal*, 10, 27 July, 5, 17 Sept. 1822.

[3] Blackburn, encl. in Wellesley to Peel, 28 Jan. 1824, *Wellesley Papers*, BM, Add. MSS. 37302; *Cork Advertiser*, 28 March 1826; *Limerick Chronicle*, 1826, 1827; cf. Goulburn to Peel, 22 July 1825, 25 July 1826, *Peel Papers*, BM, Add. MSS. 40331 f.111, 40332 f.65; R. B. O'Brien, *Fifty Years Concessions to Ireland* (1883–5), ii, 88.

2,000 a year between the early and late 1820s. Horse, cattle and sheep stealing more than doubled. Between 1826 and 1830, when offences are given in the convict indents, just under two hundred men were transported for specifically White-Boy crimes, and roughly an equal number are probables, making up, together, less than eight per cent of the Irish males transported. Of these only fifteen came on ships from Dublin; most came from Tipperary, Limerick, Sligo and Longford on ships from Cork. Overall between 1815 and 1830, less than 1,200 men, including probables, seem to have been agrarian offenders, or under twelve per cent of the total.[1]

After 1830, crime increased as the 'tithe war' was added to the perennial conflict with the landlords, and spread disturbance from Munster to Leinster. During the next decade, proportionately rather fewer came from Dublin, but a larger number from Cork City kept up the urban contingent. After the Coercion Act of 1833, setting up special courts in disturbed districts, convictions there rose by two-thirds, but under this act, unlike its predecessors, men were only transported for proven offences, whether White-Boy or other, and not simply for breaking curfew. Convictions for 'Ribbonism' or for other crimes clearly connected with agrarian agitation rose from thirteen per cent in 1831 to just on twenty per cent in 1833; thereafter they fell again steadily, to eight per cent in 1835. In these five years there were at least seven hundred guilty of Ribbon offences, or of assaults connected with them, and possibly a few more for the latter are difficult to distinguish.[2]

In 1835, of 965 sentenced to be transported, about half were guilty of larceny, and a fifth of offences which had nothing to do with the land; only forty-nine were clearly 'White-Boys'. What of the 143 guilty of burglary, house-breaking, manslaughter or assault? Contemporaries testified to the bitterness of Irish factions throughout the country; personal feuds and religious differences, added to a readiness to resort to violence, which became proverbial, produced a 'perfect contempt for human suffering and utter disregard for the value of human life'. From January to May 1834, when the 'tithe war' was at its height, 7,869 outrages were reported. Only about a quarter (1,953) were connected with Ribbonism, according to the returns, though of the nearly nine hundred 'serious' assaults, the White-Boys were responsible for more

---

[1] *Returns*, PP 1829 (256); *State of Poor Report*, PP 1830 (667), 19 ff., and app. K, 137–9; indents, ML.
[2] For figures in following paragraphs, convict indents, ML, annual *Returns*, PP 1831–2 to 1841; cf. *Disturbed Counties of Ireland Report*, PP 1831–2 (677), app. 75 ff.; HL, *Ireland Report*, PP 1839 (486), evid. Drummond, 14024 ff.; Locker-Lampson, 167; Lord Mulgrave, 27 Nov. 1837, *P. Debs.*, 3rd ser., xxxix, 230–4.

than half. But as the rural agitation died down, the proportion of 'Ribbon' assaults to others would have declined too, so it seems reasonable to ascribe to them forty per cent in 1835 (instead of fifty-five per cent in early 1834); this would mean about a hundred Ribbonmen were sentenced to transportation in that year, and slightly fewer sent out. This accords with the estimates suggested by the ships' indents in Sydney and by the proportions who came from the 'disturbed' counties, though there had been more among the larger numbers sentenced to be transported in 1833 and 1834 and who came out in 1835.

Returns from the convict hulks at Dublin and Cork in 1835 give further details of the crimes which had earned transportation since 1820. Unfortunately of the 5,968 who sailed from Cork, 1,564 are 'not particularized', and the same applies to 1,199 out of 4,795 from Dublin. Of those that are recorded, from Cork, twenty-seven per cent were guilty of stealing sheep, cattle or horses, twenty-three per cent of larceny or picking pockets, seventeen per cent of burglary or robbery, thirteen per cent of White-Boy offences, nine per cent of murder, manslaughter or assault, and eleven per cent of other crimes. Since some of those guilty of assaults, house-breaking and burglary were certain to have been White-Boys, these may have comprised between a fifth and a quarter of those who sailed from Cork. From Dublin a third were guilty of larceny, a quarter stole livestock, a fifth were burglars or robbers; White-Boy offences were only six per cent of the total, manslaughter, murder and assaults five per cent. With fewer White-Boys in the north, their share of the robberies and assaults would be smaller; but if we assume that White-Boys were responsible for about half the robberies and assaults in the south and about a quarter in the north, and add their number to those convicted of specific White-Boy offences, these figures suggest again that about fourteen per cent of those transported at this time were White-Boys.

After 1835, White-Boy offences decreased and were confined to fewer counties. During the next five years, just under five per cent of the 3,700 males transported were clearly White-Boys; another nine per cent were guilty of offences which may have been connected with them, but even if we put them down for half of these less than ten per cent of those transported between 1836 and 1840 could be described as White-Boys. In 1838, of 167 from Limerick and Tipperary, probably two-thirds were Ribbonmen, while from the rest of Ireland came thirty-six certain and more than fifty probable, or nearly 200 altogether. In 1839, when 1,161 were *sentenced*, 183 were Dubliners and 82 came from Cork city; of these 228 had committed larceny. By this time only about three-quarters of those sentenced were shipped to Australia, and less than five hundred White-Boys were sent out in these years.

From 1841 to 1846 inclusive, when 3,000 men were transported, the annual flow fell by more than forty per cent. The penal code was now less harsh, though about half the Irish were still first offenders. Belfast was beginning to rival Dublin (it far surpassed Cork city) as a base for larceny. Rural crime went on; but though house-breaking increased and more livestock was stolen (a third were transported for stealing animals), assaults and rioting were less – except, as always, in Tipperary. There, according to the Devon Commission, in 1844 a quarter of all the 'outrages' in Ireland were committed, but now only a sixth were agrarian, instead of a quarter ten years before. In 1845, more than a quarter of those transported were guilty of attacking either persons or property maliciously or with violence, and probably a half of those transported for such attacks were agrarian offenders. Adding the three per cent directly guilty of Ribbonism, this would mean again about fifteen per cent of the male Irish convicts were White-Boys. Since the Tipperary figures confirm this estimate, between 1840 and 1846 about five hundred might be described as agrarian offenders.[1]

After November 1846, no convicts were sent from Ireland to Australia for nearly two years; then between September 1848 and November 1852 came a final batch of 4,000 or about twice as many each year as in the earlier 1840s. Of these, most were driven to steal by the famine. There were more than twice as many convictions of all sorts, per head of population, between 1848 and 1851, as before 1847 and after 1853; more than three times as many were sentenced to transportation, though few more than half could be sent away, despite Grey's efforts to find some destination for them somewhere in the British Empire. For the first time proportionately more Irish than English were transported to Australia. How many were guilty of 'outrage' is uncertain; from the offences given in the Van Diemen's Land records, they would seem to be a smaller proportion than before; certainly few of the 'famine-offenders' should be described as criminals.[2]

Altogether, of the 30,000 males transported from Ireland, less than six hundred were specifically political prisoners. Of 'social rebels', however they be described, there were probably about five hundred in the early period and another hundred before the end of the wars; about

[1] Devon Commission, *Report*, iii, app. 35, PP 1845 (657); *Returns*, PP 1842–46, 1851; Robson, 'Male Convicts', *Tas. Hist. Assoc.*, ix, 44, 47, 54.
[2] Wilson, *Statistics of Crime*, 8–10; Redington to Sir G. C. Lewis, 15 Jan. 1849, Convict Letter Book, 1845–57, SPO; annual returns, PP; Robson, *loc. cit.*

1,200 between 1815 and 1830 and slightly less in the next ten years; with under five hundred between 1840 and 1846 and another five hundred between 1848 and 1853 the total would be under four thousand. About four per cent of the 9,000 Irish females transported were guilty of arson, compared with only one per cent in England, so apparently some women took part in agrarian agitation too.[1] If we add another three hundred on this account, that would suggest that nearly five thousand of the Irish prisoners of both sexes were either political or 'social' offenders.

Of the rest, most were guilty of minor thefts, about half from Dublin and other Irish towns; the remainder were divided between those guilty of more serious crimes, forgery, coining, embezzling, fraud, receiving, highway robbery and house-breaking and assaults from 'ordinary', not 'White-Boy', motives. Save that they were more often driven to crime by desperate poverty, they were very like the English convicts, but since prison accommodation was so short, far more of those sentenced to transportation were actually sent away.

A quarter of all the Irish transported were women, or twice the proportion of the British convicts; consequently three-eighths of all the female prisoners in Australia were Irish, but only about a quarter of the men were. In the final period in Van Diemen's Land, forty-two per cent of the women were Irish, largely as a result of the famine. Most of these were illiterate country-dwellers whose conduct in the colony was far better than that of the average convict.

Until December 1840 no ship sailed directly from Ireland to Van Diemen's Land, though Macquarie sent down the *Minerva* from Sydney in 1818 and the *Castle Forbes* in 1820. In 1835 the *Lady Kennaway* arrived from Woolwich, with thirty-one military prisoners she had picked up at Cork, but as their assignments were made out to New South Wales, Arthur sent them on. As a result thirty per cent of the male and nearly forty per cent of the female convicts sent to New South Wales were Irish. This increased the relative number of both Roman Catholics and first offenders there, compared with Van Diemen's Land. On the average they were better labourers than the more common urban thief from England; and those who were 'White-Boys', and had rejected the social order which seemed to them unjust at home, showed themselves ready enough to accept the different one which prevailed in Australia.

---

[1] Robson, 'Women Convicts', *Hist. Stud.*, xi, 51; Payne, 'Female Convicts . . . 1843-53', *Tas. Hist. Assoc.*, ix, 57-9.

9

Increasing Severity

Speak roughly to your little boy,
And beat him when he sneezes;
He only does it to annoy,
Because he knows it teases.

LEWIS CARROLL

When between 1822 and 1824 the British government was considering Bigge's reports and the changes thought necessary in the transportation system and in the administration of New South Wales, it had not only the settlements around Port Jackson to think of. By this time, they had begun to spread in a process which was eventually to lead to the occupation of the whole Australian continent; but all were still penal establishments even if some had been originally founded for other reasons and their administration was bound up with penal policy.

The first 'out-settlement' to be occupied was Norfolk Island, which Phillip had been told 'to secure' before the first fleet sailed. It had quickly proved its value, for during the famine years that followed, its grain and pigs helped to feed hungry mouths from Port Jackson; but Phillip discovered to his cost its major drawback, 'the lack of a good harbour or roadstead', when H.M.S. *Sirius* was wrecked there in March 1790; as Surgeon White said, it was 'only a place for angels and eagles to reside in'.[1]

Though King praised its fertility, and in 1801 found it a useful place to send discontented Irish to, Grose, Hunter and Foveaux had been critical; mindful of its 'great expense' and the difficulties of communication, in June 1803 Lord Hobart ordered part of the establishment there to be removed to Van Diemen's Land. King did this, but strongly opposed the complete evacuation of the island when it was mooted;

[1] Phillip to Grenville, 11 April, 17 June and 14 July 1790; White to Skill, *HRNSW*, I, ii, 332–3.

thanks to his advocacy, the reluctance of the settlers to move and the conflicting views of successive Secretaries of State, though the settlement was steadily reduced, it was not abandoned until February 1814.[1] Meanwhile settlements had been founded to the south. The British government, like Governor King, wanted to anticipate the French, who seemed to be thinking of 'establishing themselves in . . . Basses Straits' after the end of the first round of the revolutionary wars. King was also interested in the seal fisheries, and as well as this, nervous of the Irish rebels and fearing an influx of convicts after the Peace of Amiens, he wanted to divide his charges; the Colonial Office added that if 'an interval of some years were to be given for moral improvement' without more convicts arriving, the settlement at Port Jackson would benefit.[2]

The first site selected was on Port Phillip, whither Lieutenant-Colonel David Collins, late Judge-Advocate of New South Wales, set sail on 24 April 1803, with 300 male convicts, sixteen married women, officials, a guard of marines and eighteen settlers – 466 in all. To prevent them escaping, Collins was 'to take particular care that all clandestine communications with the possessions of the East India Company, as well as the coasts of China and the islands . . . should be prevented'; this suggests that, as in 1786–7, the government was more concerned with prisons and bases than with commerce. But Collins did not like Port Phillip, and decided to move; on 15 February 1804, he arrived in the Derwent, in Van Diemen's Land.[3]

The previous year, King had sent down Lieutenant Bowen, from H.M.S. Glatton, to prevent 'the French gaining a footing on the East side of these Islands; To divide the Convicts; To secure another place for procuring Timber, with any other production that may be discovered and found useful: The advantage that may be expected by raising Grain; and to promote the Seal Fishery'. Bowen had settled at

[1] King's report, 18 Oct. 1796, HRNSW, iii, 145; Grose to Dundas, 5 July 1794; Hunter to Portland, 25 May 1798; Foveaux to Portland, 19 Sept. 1801, CO 201/29, 20–2; Hobart to King, 24 June 1803; King to Camden, 30 April 1805, encl. King to Piper, and 15 March 1806; to Under-Sec. King, 5 June 1802; to Banks, 14 Aug. 1804, HRNSW, v, 448; Foveaux' observations, 26 March 1805, ib., 581–5; Windham to Bligh, 30 Dec., 1806; Bligh to Windham, 31 Oct. 1807; Castlereagh to Bligh, 31 Dec. 1807; Bligh to Castlereagh 31 Aug. 1808; Foveaux to Castlereagh, 6 Sept. 1808; Foveaux to Macquarie, 17 Jan. 1810, HRNSW, vii, 273; Macquarie to Castlereagh, 8 March 1810; Liverpool to Macquarie, 26 July 1811; Macquarie to Bathurst, 28 April 1814.

[2] CO Mem., 1802, HRA, III, i, 1–3; King to Portland, 21 May 18c2; King to Paterson, Paterson to King, 18 Nov. 1802, King to Baudin, to Hobart, 23 Nov., Baudin to King, 23 Dec., HRNSW, iv, 1006–9.

[3] Hobart to King, 14 Feb. 1803, encl. Collins Instructions (7 Feb.); Collins to King, 5 Nov. and 16 Dec. 1803, HRA, III, i, 28–9 and 783, n. 8; Sullivan to Collins, 5 April 1803, ib., 18, to King, I, iv, 66; Collins to King, 16 Dec. 1803, to Hobart, 28 Feb. 1804,III, i, 46, 61

Risdon in September; but Collins now chose a site on Sullivan Cove, lower down the river.[1]

During the next few years, very few convicts arrived. The British government was taking no interest in the new settlement and the Sydney authorities very little. They were just as negligent in sending details of the convicts' sentences as those in England had been twenty-five years before, and Collins had repeatedly to ask for more provisions, clothing and medicines.[2] It was all very like Port Jackson over again, though like it, in time the Derwent settlement prospered.

The 279 male convicts in 1804 dwindled to less than two hundred in the next four years, but by October 1808 554 people had arrived from Norfolk Island. In 1810 Macquarie sent sixty more servants, and in 1812, 199 arrived in the *Indefatigable* direct from England; but Macquarie found the demands in New South Wales 'too pressing' for him to spare more. He preached to Collins's successors, Davey and Sorell, in Van Diemen's Land, the economy he was not able to practise in New South Wales. 'You must not employ so many *for the use of the Crown*,' he told Sorell in 1818. 'His Majesty's Ministers find great fault with so many Convicts being employed on the Govt. Works . . . and have desired the numbers so employed now to be very considerably reduced. I am doing so here accordingly all I can, and must enjoin you to do the same . . . the more Convicts you can get the Settlers to take *off the Store* the better.'[3] Davey, finding it futile to ask for more men from Sydney, in 1816 sought them direct from England, a request which Macquarie supported next year; but by then he was receiving more convicts than he could handle himself, and in 1818 he was glad to send down a number to Hobart.[4]

After Sorell succeeded Davey as Lieutenant-Governor in April 1817, Van Diemen's Land had an honest and efficient administrator at its head. He immediately formed a 'system of perpetual reference and control' over the convicts, recording the arrival, employment and

[1] King to Hobart, 9 May 1803, encl. instructions to Bowen; to Nepean, 9 May, *HRA*, I, iv, 249; Collins to King, 28 and 29 Feb., to Hobart, 4 March 1804, *ib.*, III, i, 218 ff.

[2] Collins to Hobart, 3 Aug. 1804, to Castlereagh, 17 June 1806, 10 May 1809, to King, 20 April 1806, *HRA*, III, i, 359. There are no despatches from CO to VDL and only one reference to it in despatches to Sydney between 1804 and 1810.

[3] Returns, 3 Aug. 1804, 23 Oct. 1808, 10 May 1809, *ib.*, 258, 409, 421; Collins to Castlereagh, 20 April 1808, 10 May 1809; Oxley's *Report*, 1810, *ib.*, 576; Macquarie to Sorell, 7 April 1818, *ib.*, III, ii, 314; cf. to Geils, 1 June 1812, i, 481, to Davey, 18 July and 30 Oct. 1815, 30 Sept. 1816, ii, 112, 136, 164.

[4] Davey to Bathurst, 13 April 1816; Macquarie to Bathurst, 5 June 1817, to Sorell, 26 June 1817, *HRA*, III, ii, 260; Sorell to Macquarie, 23 May 1818, *ib.*, 319; Macquarie to Sorell, 31 May 1818, 8 March 1819, *ib.*, 324, 384. On Macquarie's surplus, cf. above, p. 97, Macquarie to Bathurst, 16 May 1818.

assignment of all prisoners in a series of registers, holding weekly musters of assigned servants and ticket-of-leave holders, and instituting a strict system of passes. But he faced two difficulties. The island lacked a supreme court, and so, as from Norfolk Island later, persons charged with serious crimes had to be sent to Sydney if they were to be tried. He had no penal settlement, and when he proposed establishing one at Macquarie Harbour, though Macquarie favoured the idea he felt it necessary to refer the matter to England, so nothing was done until 1821.[1] Bigge's inquiries revealed in general the same system as in New South Wales. Inspection on board ship, selection for public work and private assignment, Sunday musters, the ticket-of-leave system, the keeping of registers, the granting of passes and the sending out of convicts' wives and families were the same in both colonies. The defects were the same too—incompetent overseers, lack of barracks (the first in Hobart were not occupied until 1822), the comparative freedom of the prisoners, their ability to work for themselves, their frequent misconduct and occasionally the too speedy granting of tickets.[2] Unfortunately, Sorell, like the early Governors in New South Wales, frequently had subordinates (and even superiors!) less conscientious than himself. The New South Wales authorities often did not send particulars of the convicts' sentences, the prisoners often arrived without proper clothing and the Tasmanian settlements seemed to be chronically short of stores. In 1820 Sorell told Cimitière, Commandant of the settlement on Bass Strait, also founded to anticipate the French, in 1804, that though he might regard the inspection and distribution of convicts as 'an unpleasant duty, ... I look upon it as equally connected with Justice to the Settlers, the success of the Colony and the reform and order of the Prisoners'; but at Launceston there was no gaol, the assigned convicts were under little control, the constables were unreliable, and the Superintendent of Convicts was often drunk. Here were a large proportion of 'the most depraved and unprincipled people in the universe', he said in 1821; few could be less fitted to help the convicts' reform.[3]

[1] Evid., Humphrey to Bigge, 11 March 1820, ib., III, iii, 274 ff.; cf. Sorell to Cimitière, 7 Aug. 1819, to Loane, 28 Dec. 1818, ib., ii, 522, 692. Sorell's remarks on judicial establishment, 19 Nov. 1819, ib., iii, 517; Sorell to Horton, 30 Nov. 1824, ib., iv, 584. On Macquarie Harbour, Macquarie to Bathurst, 16 May 1818; Sorell to Goulburn, 12 May 1820.
[2] Examination of Major Bell, 26 Feb. 1820, of Humphrey, Supt. of Police, 11 March, ib., iii, 231 ff., 271 ff.; cf. forms and registers, ib., 513 ff., 542 ff.; Sorell to Bigge, 26 May 1820, ib., 656–8, to Goulburn, 26 April 1822.
[3] Sorell to Macquarie, 15 May 1820, ib., iii, 23; Sorell to Cimitière, 3 and 4 Dec. 1819, 22 Jan., 11 March and 12 April 1820, ib., ii, 540 ff., iii, 82, 92, 97–8; Bigge's examination of Lieut. Van der Meulen, J. B. Boothman and Cimitière, April 1820, ib., 374–85; Sorell to Goulburn, 10 Dec. 1821.

For all that, when he handed over to Arthur in May 1824, Sorell had successfully laid the foundations of the system his successor was to develop so carefully. The recent arrival of 'a better class of people' as the masters of assigned servants had led to 'a state of more rigid servitude', which the men had often escaped in the past when the settlers needed servants whatever their conduct, and 'the penal discipline of the Convicts and the application and concession of their services to the Settlers' were 'in a continual state of collision'. True policy was 'to stimulate the settler . . . so that it may be his interest to employ numerous convicts'; then, when convict labour was 'a boon', the demand for it 'in its natural course will sufficiently relieve the Government'—as was soon in fact to be the case. The worst characters should always be kept under 'restraint, coercion and privation', and not assigned; though this was only possible, without danger, if actual accommodation existed, now to a limited extent it did.[1]

Meanwhile, penal settlements had been founded on the mainland. In 1801 King sent sixteen convicts under guard to mine coal on the present site of Newcastle. They did not remain long, but in 1804 the governor remembered the spot as 'an eligible situation for the most turbulent and refractory characters to be kept at the coal works', so he sent up some 'deluded Irish' after their insurrection, instead of transporting them to Norfolk Island, which the British government was planning to evacuate. Newcastle was more accessible, yet still quite isolated. The work there, mining and cedar cutting, was arduous, so the settlement became primarily a place of punishment, and it gave 'constant employment to our most disaffected characters'.[2]

As time went on, an overland route was opened and free settlers appeared in the neighbourhood. They were often sympathetic to absconders, and sometimes even encouraged the men to 'run', so they could employ them on their farms. Two runaways, who were 'out' for nine months, were kept with food and given a musket in return for skins. Though Bigge admired 'the strictness of its discipline and the beauty of the regularity then established among the convicts', the Commandant, Morisset, complained in 1820 that 'the conduct of many of the settlers

[1] Sorell to Arthur, 22 May 1824, encl. in Arthur to Bathurst, 9 June 1824; Sorell to Horton, 19 Nov. 1824.
[2] King to Portland, 21 Aug. 1801; G. and G.O., 24 March 1804, *HRNSW*, v, 363–4; King's instructions to Menzies, *HRA*, iv, 619 ff.; Menzies to King, 19 April 1804, *ib.*, v, 407–20; King to Hobart, 16 April and 14 Aug. 1804; King to Banks, — Dec., *HRNSW*, v, 528; Throsby's General Orders, 1805–6, *ib.*, vi, 836 ff.; Macquarie's instructions to Purcell, Oct. 1810, *ib.*, vii, 421.

is so bad that I cannot get any work done by the Parties sent in their neighbourhood'. Macquarie thought it would soon become a 'most eligible and desirable Settlement to send Free Settlers to'; but its value as a penal settlement had been destroyed by the extension of trade, especially in timber, and by the exploration of the overland route from Windsor. If a place 'were discovered to the Northward . . . with a safe Harbour, where Prisoners could be transported to and secured against Desertion by Distance and Natural Barriers . . . it would be highly expedient to remove the convicts . . . from Newcastle', he wrote, so he was delighted to be able to report soon afterwards that Oxley had discovered about 220 miles up the coast 'a safe and capacious Harbour, . . . most happily situated on a large river and surrounded by a country of great fertility of soil'. Here, at Port Macquarie, in 1821 he ordered a new settlement 'to secure a secondary Place of Punishment for the worst description of Convicts . . . and to find suitable Labour for them', and this establishment and the opening of Newcastle replaced the plan he had formerly projected of forming a settlement at Jervis Bay.[1]

Bathurst approved, but Bigge favoured even more remote establishments, at Moreton Bay, Port Bowen or Port Curtis. There the hot climate would make labour 'more oppressive and more effectual in subduing the refractory or turbulent spirits', he said. 'The great charm of New South Wales is the beauty of the climate; if transportation there is in future to be held as a punishment, the Charm must be dispelled by approaching those Latitudes in which the Heat of the Sun renders even light labour oppressive.'[2] Bathurst told Macquarie's successor, Brisbane, to investigate the possibilities, and in 1824, the Governor decided to found a settlement at Moreton Bay; but by then Bathurst had come to fear that even 'that part of the Country, by reason of its fitness for general Colonisation, no longer appears . . . calculated to fulfil the objects in view, when I directed your attention to the formation of a Convict Establishment at that Station for the worst Class of Offenders', so he ordered Brisbane to reoccupy Norfolk Island. This would be 'far preferable to . . . any of those Places pointed out by Commissioner Bigge on the coast of New South Wales', for there 'secondary punishment'

[1] Col. Sec.'s. In-Letters, Newcastle, ML, 20 June, 6 July, 4 Aug., 15 Dec. 1810, 4 April 1811, 24 July 1815, 3 April 1816, 14 Nov. 1817, 8 July 1820; Macquarie to Bathurst, 15 Feb. and 8 March 1819; Brisbane to Bathurst, 6 Nov. 1824; Bigge, NSW, 114–8; Morrisset to Goulburn, Col. Sec.'s In-Letters, 7 Sept. 1821; Macquarie to Bathurst, 19 July 1819, 21 March 1821. On Jervis Bay, above, p. 97.

[2] Bathurst to Macquarie, 18 May 1820; Bigge to Horton, 2 Dec. 1822, CO 201/142; Bigge, NSW, 164 ff.; Hobhouse to Horton, 28 July 1823, CO 201/144, 150.

would avoid the 'mitigation' common 'when the Convict has been placed in the midst of a thriving and prosperous colony'. Forgetting former difficulties, he hoped it would be economical. The prisoners could 'produce a great part, if not the whole of their food, and even perhaps to supply exports'.[1]

Brisbane obeyed, and in 1825 Norfolk Island was reoccupied, to be the '*ne plus ultra* of Convict degradation'. He would have liked 'permanent martial law' to be made 'part of the punishment' to 'save the complicated machinery of Civil Courts', for there was 'nothing so effectual with Convicts as Summary Proceedings'. He decided to form a station at Moreton Bay too, since Norfolk Island could not take all the minor offenders it was 'necessary to remove to remote parts of the colony', and since Port Macquarie had become so easy to escape from that it was 'almost useless as a penal settlement'. As the example of Port Macquarie showed, it would pave the way for free settlers who 'would never venture so far amongst savage tribes until Government preceded them'; in the meantime, it would be difficult to escape from. He also fitted up the *Phoenix* hulk in Port Jackson to relieve the gaol; as the prisoners on it would be worked in irons, it would have 'a very salutary effect in repressing crime'.[2]

If Moreton Bay would ultimately help the settlers, the clearing gangs, which Brisbane had formed in 1822, would do so immediately. 'The idea occurred to Me of clearing the Country for the Settlers by Convict Labor,' he wrote, 'not more from the immediate consideration of rendering that Labor most productive, but, viewing its effects prospectively, [from] the beneficial consequences which would ultimately result to the Colony in bringing extensive tracts of Lands into a State for Cultivation by the Settler.' In 1824, 1,150 men were employed in fifty parties. Though they had to be 'associated' in the gangs, this was a defect of all public employment, and if one magistrate complained of the men's misconduct in terms as bitter as had been used against Macquarie's road gangs, Brisbane was convinced that 'the Moral condition of the unhappy Convict' improved in them, and the men gained a valuable training for country work. Their receipts paid their expenses, but even if they had not, they were of greater immediate benefit and more economical than Macquarie's public works, however much posterity might prefer the latter, and from them the

---

[1] Bathurst to Brisbane, 9 Sept. 1822; Brisbane to Bathurst, 3 Feb. 1824; Bathurst to Brisbane, 22 July.

[2] Brisbane to Horton, 24 March 1825; Brisbane to Bathurst, 21 May, 1 Aug. and 7 Sept 1825; cf. Hay's minute, CO 201/161, 227, deprecating 'hulks'.

convicts could be directly assigned to settlers all over the colony.[1] Brisbane recognized that there was a strong demand for convict labour as well as for free land, so he ordered those given land grants to maintain one prisoner for every hundred acres they received, thus anticipating the idea which Wakefield later claimed as his, that cultivation should be encouraged and 'dispersion' prevented. Despite Bathurst's fears that such a condition would deter settlers, grantees willingly agreed to it; they wanted servants, and the need to superintend them encouraged settlers to reside on their estates.[2] Brisbane made mechanics available to settlers too, which reduced their accumulation in government service in Sydney. Up to November 1824, 408 tradesmen had been hired out at 5s. 6d. per week, and the return was more than enough to give money payments to the convict clerks and overseers who had previously been rewarded by having other prisoners assigned to them as servants. In March 1825, there were only 1,851 convicts in government service, compared with 4,051 in December 1821, when Macquarie had left; in the meantime though 5,000 convicts had arrived in Sydney, there was an outstanding demand for 389 mechanics and 249 farming men and labourers.[3]

All this had followed the British government's decision, after it had considered Bigge's report, that it would continue transportation, but try to tighten up the system. Brisbane had been told to employ 'government' convicts on public farms instead of works in town, to cut out task work, to increase magisterial supervision, to take away all the prisoners' property when they arrived so that they could not use it for trade, as men like Solomon Levey or Daniel Cooper had done, and to make sure that the prisoners received neither preferential treatment because they happened to be skilled workmen nor tickets-of-leave except as reward for good conduct.[4] He assured Bathurst that this was what he was doing. He was retaining in government service 'only those whose character is the worst'; they were employed in the clearing gangs and public farms,

[1] Brisbane to Bathurst, 30 Aug. 1822, 29 Nov. 1823, 23 July 1824; returns, encl. 7, in *ib.*, 3 June 1825; Atkinson, 87–9. On the gangs, Charles Throsby, J.P., and T. Moore, J.P., Liverpool, to Macquarie, 2 Oct. 1821, Col. Sec.'s In-Letters, 1821, bundle 15, no. 62; the Rev. Thomas Riddell, J.P., to Goulburn, *ib.*, 1822, bundle 17, no. 4.
[2] Brisbane to Bathurst, 10 April 1822, 29 Nov. 1823; Macquarie's land regulations, Macquarie to Bathurst, 28 Nov. 1821; Bathurst to Brisbane, 20 and 31 May 1823, 13 July 1824, 1 Jan., 17 April, 18 May 1825; instructions to Darling, July 1825, *HRA*, xii, 121. I have found only one complaint against Brisbane's regulation, from Mr. P. Wood in Van Diemen's Land, 24 July 1822, Col. Sec.'s In-Letters, bundle 16, no. 56.
[3] Brisbane to G. Harrison, 11 Oct. 1825, T 64/83; Brisbane to Bathurst, 29 Oct. 1824, 17 Jan., 18 March 1825. For assignment as part payment of salaries, above, p. 90.
[4] Bathurst to Brisbane, 9 Sept. 1822; cf. Bigge to Macquarie, 6 June 1820, CO 201/141.

on 'labour more irksome and more fatiguing' than work for the settlers. As the demand for assigned servants increased, he was able to cut down the gangs, but he kept up Emu Plains to employ convicts turned in by the settlers; it was 'by far the best School of Reform in the Colony'. He reduced the public works, which he thought expensive and badly supervised, though there were so few free contractors that he had to keep up one establishment in Sydney; but he got rid of the 'educated convicts', who might be politically dangerous or do too well for themselves, by sending them off first to Bathurst, and later to Wellington Valley, where they were 'out of temptation'.[1]

The assigned men were entrusted only to 'the more opulent settlers', who could support them and keep them hard at work. Early in 1823 he transferred control of the convicts from the emancipist superintendent, Hutchinson, to the Colonial Secretary, Frederick Goulburn, hoping to improve the keeping of the registers and the records of conduct and punishments, in the past so 'inefficiently performed'. But 'effectual correspondence' with the magistrates was not easy, and despite Macquarie's orders, their records were not always properly kept either. Hutchinson had justly complained that he could not be expected to know 'when individuals have been up the country some years, what course of conduct they have pursued, unless the same is forwarded . . . which is seldom or ever the case'. The returns of ticket-holders 'formerly made to this office' had been discontinued, and he was not even told for which districts men had obtained their tickets. At the same time, the magistrates complained of their limited power. They could not help a respectable and deserving convict to obtain his ticket if his master objected, protested those on the Minto Bench; they needed to be able 'to investigate the claims of convict servants'.[2] When the new free superintendent, F. A. Hely, arrived from England, things might have been expected to improve; but by 1824 the quarrel between the Colonial Secretary and the Governor was paralysing the administration.

Brisbane increased the number of magistrates, as Bigge had recommended, with the assent of the Legislative Council increased the power of single magistrates to punish convicts summarily, despite his Attorney-General's doubts of its legality, and asked for 'stipendiaries' to be

---

[1] Brisbane to Bathurst, 23 April 1823, 29 Oct. 1824, 14 May, 24 Sept. 1825; Brisbane to Horton, 16 June 1825, encl. Ovens' report, *HRA*, xi, 648 ff.

[2] Bathurst to Brisbane, 30 May 1823; Hobhouse to Horton, 21 Feb., CO 201/144; Brisbane to Bathurst, 28 April 1823; Macquarie to Bathurst, 4 Dec. 1817; report of inquiry by the Council, 27 Sept. 1825, *HRA*, xi, 854 ff.; opinion of Archdeacon Scott, 17 June, 1828, *ib.*, xiv, 236; Hutchinson to Goulburn, 6 and 13 Feb. 1823, Col. Sec.'s In-Letters, bundle 20, nos. 3–9; Minto magistrates to Brisbane, *ib.*, no. 18.

appointed at Parramatta, Windsor and Liverpool, as well as at Sydney.[1] Though he was recalled before all these matters were resolved, his proposals foreshadowed reforms carried out by his successor; that they were necessary, two cases brought clearly to light.

In 1823, old Sam Marsden was prosecuted for permitting his servant, James Ring, to work for himself. He said he was rewarding industry, and that this was a 'frequent practice'. Certainly Richard Rouse, the former Superintendent of Public Works, and D'Arcy Wentworth said they knew of many others 'out' similarly; but since it was contrary to the regulations proclaimed to 'prevent an assigned servant . . . from deriving property from his labour', which was equivalent to a private master granting him a ticket-of-leave, Ring's assignment to Marsden was cancelled and he was put in the Parramatta Barracks. Whether or not the regulation forbidding this 'private work' was 'nearly obsolete' (though Brisbane had repeated it in 1822, as Macquarie had in 1820), such a practice did not well become Marsden, who had been one of the principal critics of the ex-governor's alleged favours to the convicts; perhaps the fact that Ring sang in his choir affected his judgment, but the Parramatta 'gentry' had always been rather a law unto themselves.[2]

This affair, like the Ann Rumsby case the previous year, when Dr. Henry Grattan Douglass was accused of immorality,[3] formed part of an attack on the government by a Parramatta group led by Marsden and Hannibal Macarthur; but this personal feud brought to light actions by the magistrates which were 'equally illegal and injudicious' and 'repugnant to the clearest maxims both of Law and moral Justice', namely the practice of sentencing convicts to punishment extended over a period, with the possibility of mitigating it, if the culprit gave the magistrates some information that they wanted. This was not, it was said, to extort a confession of crime, but to induce a *convicted* culprit to restore stolen property or to betray his accomplices; none the less it was improper and illegal, and illustrates the rough-and-ready attitude to the administration of justice prevalent in the penal settlement and

---

[1] Brisbane to Bathurst, 28 Jan., 24 May, 25 and 29 June 1825.
[2] Brisbane, Chief Justice Forbes, Archdeacon Scott to Bathurst, 10 Aug. 1825, *HRA*, xi, 717 ff.; cf. Marsden to Peel, 28 Jan. 1824, Bathurst to Governor, 2 Sept., *ib.*, 307 ff., 351 ff.; G. and G.O. 25 July 1822, *ib.*, 765; Forbes to Horton, 30 Oct. 1825, *ib.*, 950 ff.; Macquarie's regulations, 20 April 1820, *HRA*, IV, i, 337 (even if King's of 1801 and 1804 were forgotten) On the Parramatta magistrates, cf. Macquarie to Hannibal Macarthur, 21 Nov. 1820, Col. Sec.'s In-Letters, 1820, bundle 14, no. 97.
[3] Brisbane to Bathurst, 6 Sept. 1822; Stephen to Horton, 2 Sept. 1824, *HRA*, IV, i, 556 ff. and 563-4.

the callousness and brutality of many of its officials and magistrates.[1] Despite these magisterial eccentricities, Brisbane and Sorell had done much to tighten up the administration of the convict system, and they had founded penal settlements where Bathurst expected that 'the legitimate terrors, which orginally attached to a state of transportation cannot fail to revive and to resume their power of checking the inroads of Crime by the certainty of effectual punishment'. But the British government remained dissatisfied, and when Darling and Arthur succeeded them, in its eyes one of their most important tasks was to revive among the criminal classes that 'dread of transportation' whose absence was so disturbing.[2]

As was customary, both the new governors were military officers. Both had served in the Napoleonic Wars. Both were strict disciplinarians; both were inclined to regard all opposition as disobedience, to be punished. Each, while governing Mauritius and Honduras respectively, had found that his attempts to suppress slavery had aroused the anger of his civilian subjects.[3] Each proved an efficient administrator. Each was criticized for favouring his relatives and other members of a small official clique, understandable though such a preference was considering the quality of most of the other settlers.

Soon after his appointment, James Stephen told Arthur that Darling was a 'very honourable man, . . . but with little reach of thought or variety of knowledge, stiff in his manners', having 'a great formality in business' and being 'a perfect martinet in military discipline'. Young John Macarthur thought him 'limited, cold, formal' and forecast he would be unpopular.[4] He was quite right. Unlike Arthur, Darling lost the confidence of his superiors, largely because of the colonial ferment which his illiberalism aroused. He was recalled five years before his colleague in the south, who went from strength to strength in the good books of Downing Street. 'Of all the Governors whom this department has employed in my time,' Stephen told him in 1835, 'you have enjoyed the most uninterrupted Reputation for all the qualities which a Governor ought to possess and the strongest hold upon the favourable

---

[1] Brisbane and others to Bathurst, with enclosures, 11 Aug. 1825; Brisbane to Bathurst, 28 Sept., encl. Report of Enquiry by Council, 21 Sept.; returns, encl. Brisbane to Bathurst, 10 Oct.; Forbes to Horton, 30 Oct., *HRA*, xi, 950–7.
[2] Bathurst to Darling, 24 Sept. 1826.
[3] N. Leon, 'Social and Administrative Developments in British Honduras, 1798–1843' (B.Litt. Thesis, Oxford, 1958); Anon., *Defence of the Settlers of Honduras* (1824); John Armstrong, *Candid Examination of the Defence of the Settlers of Honduras* (London, 1824); Arthur Papers, Royal Commonwealth Soc., London, letter books, espec. 6 and 7. Darling in Mauritius, *HRA*, xi, introdn., p. xii.
[4] Stephen to Arthur, 9 Oct. 1826, Arthur Papers, iv, ML; John Macarthur, Junior, to his father, 12 June 1825, Macarthur Papers, xv, ML.

opinion of your official superiors'.[1] His recall in 1836 was due to the effluxion of time, after twice the usual term in office, but the removal of this autocratic, puritanical, high-minded but vindictive ruler, like that of Darling, was a step in the direction of giving the colonists a more liberal administration.

Their two successors, Sir Richard Bourke in Sydney and Sir John Franklin in Hobart, though personally less rigid than their predecessors, were both hampered by their conservative officials. In penal matters, Bourke put a stop to some malpractice. He leaned towards the gradual stopping of transportation, and especially of assignment, which he believed the Colonial Office had decided on. He 'could not see how parents could send a child to be taught by a convict'. He wanted, like his much underrated supporter, the ex-Secretary of State Sir George Murray, to reduce cruel and unnecessary punishments, though he believed that severity was necessary so long as convicts were being sent out, and neither he nor Franklin advocated sudden or drastic changes; but in time Franklin had a new system imposed on him from London, and both in fact adopted policies intended to increase the severity of convict discipline.[2]

Darling was the first governor not to be instructed to settle deserving ex-convicts on the land, in order to seek their rehabilitation as small farmers. His first thoughts were not of reformation but to make transportation more severe. 'Previously to my coming out,' he told Bathurst in 1827, 'I had formed a Plan, with a view to the prevention of Crime at Home, of working all Convicts in Irons on the public works for a certain period after their arrival; at the expiration of which, I had purposed to assign them to Settlers, and, in the event of misconduct, of replacing them in the Road Gangs. Their employment on the Roads in Irons, in the first instance, would have rendered their assignment to the Settlers a desirable release from a painful and degraded situation; and in proportion to their dread of being so employed, they would have behaved to their Masters so as to avoid being returned to Government. But as the demand for labour was so urgent, at the time of my arrival, I was obliged to relinquish the intention of disposing of them in the manner above mentioned, and to assign them at once to the Settlers . . .'[3]

With these views about the convicts who would be under his control,

---

[1] Stephen to Arthur, 8 July 1835, Arthur Papers, *loc. cit.*

[2] Hazel King, 'Bourke', *JRAHS*, xlix, 360 ff.; Parry's Diary, 15 April 1833, ML; Murray to Bourke, 15 May 1832, Bourke Papers, xi, ML; Murray to Darling, 10 Sept. and 27 Nov. 1828; minutes on Darling to Goderich, 31 Dec. 1827, and Darling to Huskisson, 17 March 1828, CO 201/183 and 192; Bourke's minute of instructions, June 1831, CO 202/27.

[3] Darling's Instructions, 1825, *HRA*, xii, 107 ff.; Brisbane's instructions, 1821, *ib.*, x, 599; Darling to Bathurst, 1 March 1827.

the new governor assumed office on 19 December 1825, assisted by a new Colonial Secretary, Alexander M'Leay, and the free Principal Superintendent, F. A. Hely, who had been appointed to replace Hutchinson in 1823 as a result of Bigge's criticisms. Darling transferred control of convict administration from the Colonial Secretary back to this department. It was to be responsible for supervising and checking the preparation of certificates of freedom and of recommendations for tickets-of-leave, for the returns and musters of ticket-of-leave men, the applications of convicts to marry, the mustering and inspection of prisoners on their arrival, the communications with local benches and the records of their punishments, for the convicts in Sydney, for records of runaways, of the quarterly musters of ticket holders, of applications for servants and of their assignment, of issues of clothing, of victualling men out of barracks, of rations issued to gangs, as well as an overall register of all the convicts in the colony with a 'black book' of punishments and a book of merit. Hely was also given direct charge of the Hyde Park barracks and general supervision over all government convicts. Though Darling was not able to stop all assignment in town, as he wanted, and though the convict department was too small to keep all the records the governor desired, a board of inquiry in March 1827 reported great improvements in control. It was not as efficient as in Van Diemen's Land, where with about half the population and a smaller territory, Arthur was able to keep a far closer watch on his subjects; but it was far better than it had been in the past, and Darling was proud of his first achievements. He had established a Board for the distribution of convict servants to replace the 'caprice' of the Civil Engineer; he had taken in hand the reform of the female factory at Parramatta, and the Carters' Barracks in Sydney; he had improved the ticket-of-leave system, the magistracy, the police and the penal settlements; though the 2,919 he had in the immediate service of government were more numerous than he wanted, he was hoping to reduce them.[1]

Control of the convicts was enforced by the local magistrates; but

[1] Govs. *Mems.*, ML, 8, 17 and 20 April, 4 and 25 May; *Minutes*, ML, 1826, Nos. 39, 57, 59, 61, 16 Feb., 15 and 16 March, 10 Sept.; M'Leay to Hely, 11 Sept., Col. Sec.'s Out-Letters, 1826, No. 785; Govt. order, 16 March 1827, *HRA*, xiii, 166, cf. M'Leay to Land Board, 27 Nov. 1830, instructing them to assign convicts in Sydney; Darling to Bathurst, 8 April 1827, encl. report of Board, 6 March, CO 201/182, 70–90; Darling to Goderich, 2 Oct. 1827, encl. mem. of duties of Principal Supt. of Convicts and report by Board on his business, 25 Aug., CO 201/183, 327 ff.; Darling to Huskisson, 24 and 28 March 1828, forwarding application by Hely, 7 March, for increase in salary and statement of his duties; Darling to Murray, 4 Oct. 1830, encl. Hely to M'Leay, 26 July and 12 Aug. 1830, requesting extra clerks; Harrington to Hely, 26 and 27 Nov., 1 and 3 Dec. 1830, Col. Sec.'s Out-Letters, 30/996, 1004, 1006, 1020–1, 1027; Darling to Hay, 23 March.

their powers were sometimes irksome to the free population. Before he retired, Brisbane had reported that 'the Police of the Colony has been thought to be necessary in a Convict country upon a different principle from that which governs the Mother Country. A System of requiring Passes to be carried by persons who at Home would not be objects of suspicion nor under restraint was till lately held to be lawful under the orders of the Governors from the foundation of the Colony,' though whether this was still necessary in 1825 was 'a subject . . . much thought of'. Though Bathurst had queried it as early as 1812, Bigge found it accepted with little question; but wide as the magistrates' powers were, they were often exceeded and illegal sentences were common. Despite Macquarie's orders to the contrary, it was 'the established practice' to punish *all* convicts summarily, and often to send them to the penal settlements 'without reference to headquarters', Edward Close, J.P., told the Colonial Secretary in 1823. When Darling arrived he had to free five hundred men who had been improperly sent to Port Macquarie.[1]

This did not foreshadow any reduction of magisterial power. Bathurst told Darling that the local act passed in 1825 giving special powers over convicts to single justices had been annulled by a British act which insisted on two; but to maintain discipline and 'to overcome the difficulty of bringing two Magistrates together', he authorized him, as both Bigge and Brisbane had recommended, to appoint 'stipendiaries' in 'two or three of the most important Townships', as well as suggesting, at the instigation of the younger John Macarthur in London, that the Legislative Council be asked to pass a local act giving these benches the power to sentence convict delinquents, after summary trial, either to the penal settlements or to work in chains. It did so in 1826, and two more acts, in 1830, extended the magistrates' powers still further; but like his predecessors Darling seemed unwilling or unable to see that the law was obeyed. Irregular punishments continued, and Bourke had to reverse a number after he arrived in December 1831.[2]

[1] Brisbane to Bathurst, 8 Feb. 1825; G. and G.O., 28 July, 18 Aug. 1810, *HRNSW*, vii, 398, 405; Bathurst to Macquarie, 23 Nov. 1812; Macquarie to Bathurst, 28 June 1813; Bigge, *Judicial Establishments*, 89, 160–2; Close to Goulburn, 6 Dec. 1823, Col. Sec.'s In-Letters, Newcastle, 1823; Macquarie's Instructions to Magistrates, 20 April 1820, *HRA*, IV, i, 337; Darling to Bathurst, 25 May 1826; report of inquiry, Exec. Council Mins., 28 April 1826, CO 204/1.

[2] Brisbane to Bathurst, 24 May and 25 June 1825, reporting 6 Geo. IV, no. 5 (NSW), passed 8 Feb.; Bathurst to Darling, 11 Sept. 1825, reporting 6 Geo. IV c.69; John Macarthur, Junior, to Elizabeth Macarthur, 9 May 1825, to his father, 12 June 1825, Macarthur Papers, xv, 263, 297; Darling to Bathurst, 31 Aug. 1826, encl. Act for Transportation to the Penal Settlements, 7 Geo. IV no. 5; 11 Geo. IV nos. 12 and 13; Bourke to Goderich 30 Oct. 1832; Governor's Minutes, 11 June 1832.

The previous year, the Council had passed the Bushranging Act, authorizing arrest on suspicion, and casting on any person accused of being a convict at large the onus of proving his innocence. This was a source of great grievance to free labourers travelling about the colony seeking work, and it often led to unjust arrests; all the same it was renewed in 1832 and again in 1834. Judge Burton thought it repugnant to the law of England and Bourke agreed it was contrary to its spirit; but, he wrote, 'I believe . . . [its] necessity is very generally admitted and it would occasion very great dissatisfaction amongst the free People of the Colony to deprive them of the protection which this law affords'. Gipps agreed with this in 1838, and argued that it had caused 'very little inconvenience to persons of good repute', though by then the Governor had ordered that persons arrested under it were 'not to be treated with undue severity' and were to be allowed every practicable means of proving their freedom.[1]

The presence of emancipists, expirees and sometimes even of serving prisoners in the police made these wide powers all the more irritating. In New South Wales convicts had been enrolled as constables since Phillip had organized the first 'night-watch' in 1789, and when Mac-quarie put the Sydney force under civilian control in 1811 the new superintendent, D'Arcy Wentworth, selected his men from free men, emancipists and convicts alike. Gradually the last disappeared, but inevitably emancipists remained, and in 1826 both Darling and Went-worth's successor, Rossi, lamented the poor quality of many in the force.[2]

In the rural police there were many ex-convicts too—twelve out of thirty-four at Windsor in 1830, for example. Over them, there was no central control, as in Sydney. Supervision was in the hands of the local magistrates and there was little co-operation between the benches. In 1824 and again in 1825 Brisbane urged that a mounted force be formed, on the lines of the Horse Patrol which Bigge had recommended, and in due course the British government approved. At first many of its members were 'drunken and disorderly . . . in general unequal to exposure and fatigue', but when Darling enrolled sixty volunteers from the garrison in 1827, and raised the strength to one hundred in 1830, he created a force whose efficiency made it possible to cut down the

---

[1] 'Bushranging Act' (11 Geo. IV no. 10) passed in 1830 for 2 years, re-enacted 1832 (2 Will. IV no. 9), and with minor amendments in 1834 (4 Will. IV no. 9); Bourke to Goderich, 19 March 1832, to Stanley, 15 Sept. 1834, encl. judges' opinions; NSW Legs. Council, *V & P*, 1824–37, ii, 146 ff., 1838, 2; Harris, 226–8; Deas Thomson to Principal Supt., 21 July 1837, Col. Sec.'s Out-Letters, 37/592.
[2] Phillip to Sydney, 1 Feb. 1790; Hazel King, *Police*, 168, quoting Wentworth's evid. to Bigge; Rossi's report, 7 Oct. 1826, *HRA*, xii, 679 ff.

ordinary police. This was just as well, for he had begun to employ convicts as constables again in order to economize. They were given inducements to good conduct but Bourke found he could not trust them. It was 'difficult under any arrangement to procure good Constables in the colony', he wrote. 'I have little hopes of seeing for many years a decent Constabulary Force in New South Wales.'[1] This was part of the price the colony had to pay for its convict labour.

In Van Diemen's Land, Arthur had organized a mounted police force in 1826, during 'the heat of bushranging'. He deliberately filled it from 'the best conducted prisoners', who were 'stimulated to exertion by the hope of a mitigation of their sentence'. He thought this provided a motive for their reformation and created 'distrust and disunion among the Prisoner population', though their presence, like that of emancipists among the ordinary constables, lowered its standing. But the governor exercised closer control than in New South Wales, and in 1828 reorganized the whole force. He now divided the colony into nine police districts – previously five – and put a stipendiary magistrate, with a force of convict mounted police, in charge of each.[2]

Even the governor's critics admitted that this police system was an 'excellent piece of policy', and Arthur regarded the magisterial surveillance associated with it as 'the pivot on which the whole system is turned'. Assisted by unpaid justices, the 'stipendiaries' supervised everything – the conduct of ticket-of-leave holders, assigned servants and their masters, the issue of passes and recommendations for indulgences, the holdings of musters and the prosecution of offenders of every sort, and when the magistrates' summary jurisdiction was questioned, the Quarter Sessions Act of 1830 put it beyond dispute. Reflecting his military training, Arthur had told Bathurst that 'every convict should be regularly and strictly accounted for, as Soldiers are in their respective Regiments'. He wanted to keep a full record of their conduct, their services, their good conduct and their offences 'from their day of their landing until . . . their emancipation or death', so he ordered the compilation of the series of 'Black Books' (as valuable to the historian of today as to himself!) and appointed a special officer to keep them. Thus

---

[1] H. King, 174–5, 271 ff.; Bigge, *NSW*, 106, *Judicial Establishments*, 60; *Police and Gaols Report*, NSW Legs. Council, *V & P*, 1835, 335 ff.; Brisbane to Bathurst, 18 June 1824, 14 May and 8 Nov. 1825; Bathurst to Darling, 4 June 1826; Darling to Hay, 8 Feb. 1827, to Bathurst, 5 May 1827, to Murray, 5 Oct. 1830, 3 Feb. 1831, to Goderich, 6 June 1831; Goderich to Bourke, 14 Dec. 1831; Bourke to Goderich, 3 Nov. 1832, to Stanley, 15 Jan. 1834.
[2] Arthur to Bathurst, 16 and 24 March 1827; West, i, 105; Mins., Exec. Council, 8 June 1829, CO 280/21.

as well as the police magistrates, and a Principal Superintendent who had general oversight over all the convicts plus particular supervision over those in government service and those near Hobart, the Governor was aided by his muster-master, who was also assistant police magistrate in Hobart. He relieved the Principal Superintendent by examining the convicts when they arrived, recording their history from the papers sent from England, from the Surgeon's report and from his own inquiries; since he also kept the registers Arthur found so useful, his existence on the Van Diemen's Land establishment, as well as the greater number of paid magistrates there than in the more extensive and more populous New South Wales, helps to explain the closer check kept on the convicts in the southern colony.[1] By this time, the mainland governors had more non-penal colonial matters to think about, and, in any case, Supreme Court decisions between 1827 and 1830 had seriously hampered Darling's convict administration; but at least, in 1832, Bourke was able to follow Arthur's example and have passed a single comprehensive act to define and consolidate the magistrates' powers.[2]

Bourke's critics alleged that under this the magistrates could not control the prisoners properly; but it authorized a single justice to order up to fifty lashes, fourteen days' solitary confinement or two months' imprisonment with hard labour for drunkenness, disobedience, neglect of work or disorderly conduct; two justices could double these punishments for a second offence, and for a second absconding, or any misdemeanours or pilfering, could order similar flogging or labour in irons for up to twelve months. This reduced the maximum summary sentence imposed by a single magistrate from 150 to fifty lashes, and Bourke watched closely to see that the act was obeyed; but he was by no means opposed to corporal punishment, reported on its effectiveness and showed in his returns that it continued at a tremendous rate. No wonder that it was difficult to find enough scourgers, though the suggestion of training a 'corps of floggers' at Hyde Park seems somewhat grisly.[3]

[1] Melville (ed. Mackaness), i, 55; Arthur to Goderich, 27 Feb. 1833; VDL Acts, 10 Geo. IV no. 2, 11 Geo. IV no. 8, 6 Will. IV no. 2; Arthur to Bathurst, 3 July 1825; Arthur's Mem., 24 Feb. 1828, Col. Sec.'s Corr., 1/252/6040; Instructions to Ppl. Supt., 1/386/8728; Chief Pol. Mag. to Col. Sec., 9 Aug. 1838, 5/134/3227; *Transportation Report*, 1837, evid. Arthur 4362 ff.; Darling to Murray, 3 Feb. 1831; Hely to M'Leay, 22 Aug. 1832, encl. in Bourke to Goderich, 23 Jan. 1833. See Eldershaw, *Guide*, sec. 3, introduction.

[2] For Supreme Court decisions, below, p. 23; Arthur to Bourke, 19 Sept. 1832, Forbes to Bourke, 16 June 1832, Bourke Papers, ML, A1738; Arthur Papers, ML, A1962; Forbes' circular, Forbes Papers, ML, A1381; NSW, 3 Will. IV no. 3.

[3] Bourke to Stanley, 15 Jan. 1834; Governor's Minutes, no. 3144, 3 Aug. 1834, 3294, 2 Feb. 1835; Harington to Hely, 16 Sept. 1833, Col. Sec.'s Out-Letters, 33/640; Returns, 22 Oct. 1838, *HRA*, xix, 654; cf. *Transportation Report*, 1837, App., 238.

In Van Diemen's Land, outside the penal settlements flogging was less frequent than in New South Wales. In 1834, of those brought before a magistrate, only eleven per cent were flogged; twelve per cent were admonished, nine per cent (who were ticket-holders) fined, eight per cent sent to a road party, eight per cent to a chain gang, six per cent to solitary confinement, three per cent had their sentence extended, two per cent were put on the tread-wheel and two per cent were sent to a penal settlement; five per cent were committed for trial in higher courts, where, if found guilty, they would probably be sent to a penal settlement or chain gang or have their sentence extended; the rest were discharged or ordered to give sureties. Even so between 1830 and 1835 almost one male convict in six was flogged each year, receiving an average of thirty-five lashes. As in New South Wales, flogging decreased from 1836 onwards. In 1839, for example, magistrates in Van Diemen's Land sent a quarter of those brought before them to solitary cells; between 1835 and 1839, only one male convict in ten was flogged there each year, so that instead of his being likely, on the average, to receive one flogging during his sentence, before receiving a ticket-of-leave, the odds were now nearly two to one against it.[1]

Despite his later reputation for severity, Arthur thought that flogging 'should be resorted to as seldom as possible', just as he had in Honduras. When he heard in 1834 that in one road party thirty-three men had been punished with 100 to 150 lashes each for insubordination, he was 'shocked and much distressed to see so severe a punishment inflicted on such a body of men'. In the magistrates' report on the affair, he found 'nothing in the evidence' to show the 'combined feeling of insubordination' that was spoken of. 'I very deeply deplore' the passing of 'so severe a sentence, indiscriminately, upon all offenders', he wrote. There was nothing 'to show the absolute necessity of subjecting so many men to corporal punishment . . . I cannot avoid marking my disapprobation'. He thought corporal punishment not in the least reformatory, and he was glad when he was able to introduce alternatives.[2] For too long they were not available for minor offences – only the chain gangs and penal settlements for repeated absconding and major crime – and if one asks

[1] *Returns*, 21 March 1834, 30 July 1838, 13 June 1840, CO 280/47, 96, and 120; *Transportation Report*, 1837, App., 280.
[2] Arthur's mem. on Rept. of Supt. of Convicts, 13 Feb. 1830, minute on weekly report of offences and punishments, 28 Aug. 1833, Col. Sec.'s Corr., 1/6354, 14863; Arthur to Hay, Sept. 1836, quoting his Honduras orders, 23 March 1818, Arthur Papers, i, ML; Leon, *op. cit.*, 161-2; Arthur to Stanley, 15 Oct. 1834; report of offences, encl., *ib.*, 19 Dec. 1834; Arthur to Hay, 25 July 1835, to Glenelg, 28 Jan. 1836.

RETURNS OF CORPORAL PUNISHMENTS

New South Wales

	1830	1831	1832	1833	1834	1835	1836	1837
Absconding				1,149	1,368	827	830	750
Absenting				732	1,019	1,043	1,045	830
Disobedience				738	766	805	858	635
Drunkenness				386	414	670	878	934
Disorderly Conduct				605	577	863	648	702
Neglect, idleness				921	842	1,588	1,517	1,037
Insolence				407	438	510	392	477
Other				886	904	797	736	551
Total				5,824	6,328	7,103	6,904	5,916
No. of male convicts in the colony				23,357	25,200	27,340	29,406	32,102
Average percentage flogged				25	25	26	23	18
Average no. of lashes per flogging				41	38	46	44	45

Van Diemen's Land (excluding Penal Settlements)

	1830	1831	1832	1833	1834	1835	1836	1837
No. of male convicts in the colony	8,809	10,240	10,784	12,651	12,824	13,800	14,214	14,426
Percentage flogged	17	11	16	18	17	11	9	6
Average no. of lashes	33	33	36	37	34	34	30	30

Port Arthur

	1830	1831	1832	1833	1834	1835	1836	1837
No. of convicts	68	151	278	475	735	911	937	919
Percentage flogged	7	34	24	23	23	29	13	29
Average no. of lashes	19	38	43	50	38	29	42	26

Point Puer

	1830	1831	1832	1833	1834	1835	1836	1837
No. of boys					105	192	249	259
Percentage beaten					21	56	44	70
Average no. of strokes					16	15	15	15

'why not?', there is only the economical answer that flogging was cheap and easy to administer.

For all that, Arthur insisted that absconding be 'instantly and severely punished'. When a convict, Joseph Greenwood, who absconded from his chain gang and stabbed the constable arresting him, was flogged for the first offence and then executed for the second, the Governor was 'not prepared to say that even humanity might not in the end be best consulted by undeviating adherence to this system, for it follows . . . that the desperate convict who escapes from a chain gang or a penal settlement must commit other crimes to support his existence'; he told the magistrate that the flogging was 'undesirable', and the man should have been prosecuted for absconding only if he had been acquitted of murder, but he would not commute the death sentence, simply because the man had been flogged.[1]

All this may have been necessary to keep order, but it was often brutal and brutalizing. 'When I was living near . . . Bothwell, had a wish to see a man flogged,' wrote George Russell, in Van Diemen's Land, much as if he were interested to see a novel scientific experiment; the Journal of T. J. Lempriere, when Commissariat Officer at Port Arthur, unconsciously reveals a similar disregard of and unconcern for human values. '3 April. The preacher thundered until my head ached. My old servant, W., stabbed the constable, for which he received 75 yesterday. Mr. Moreton's and Powers' babies were christened. . . . 21 Sept. My journal again neglected. Another murder has been attempted by X on Y by knocking him on the head with the pole of his axe. Y will recover. Weather very changeable.'[2]

Short of a convict's execution for serious crime, after he had been tried and convicted in the Supreme Court, the most dreaded sentence was one of secondary transportation to one of the penal settlements— Port Macquarie, Moreton Bay or Norfolk Island in New South Wales, and Macquarie Harbour or Port Arthur in Van Diemen's Land. This could be ordered after summary trial by two or more magistrates, and both Darling and Arthur were anxious that the discipline at the settlements be most rigorous. Every man should be 'worked in irons, that the example may deter others from the commission of crime,' ordered Darling in 1827.[3] New regulations then momentarily tightened up conditions at Port Macquarie, where inquiry the previous year had

[1] Arthur to Glenelg, 3 Jan. 1836; West, ii, 250.
[2] Brown (ed.), George Russell, 52–4; Lempriere, Diary at Port Arthur, ML.
[3] Darling to Hay, 10 Feb. 1827; regulations, 16 March 1827, Govt. Order no. 13, encl., Darling to Bathurst, 17 March 1827.

shown that a 'system of relaxation, petty traffic and abuse' had become 'inveterate'; but another inquiry in 1828 revealed more irregularities, and in 1830 Darling decided to cease using the place as a penal settlement and open it to free settlers. The convict buildings would be used for invalids and 'educated' prisoners, who were thought too dangerous to assign; this made it possible to close the establishment at Wellington Valley, where they had been sent to in the past.[1]

Meantime, he had put the other penal stations 'on a more determinate footing'. Fresh regulations in July 1829 went far beyond those of 1827. As far as possible convicts were to be employed 'exclusively in Agricultural operations, . . . the use of the Hoe and the Spade shall be as much as possible adopted, . . . the Plough given up and no Working Cattle are to be employed in operations which can be effected by Men and Hand Carts'. The men were to be 'steadily and constantly employed at Hard Labour from Sun Rise to Sun Set'. Task work was prohibited. As 'a Reward of and encouragement to good conduct', the prisoners were to be divided into two classes. The higher was to have 'lighter' work and to be allowed tobacco; from it the overseers, constables, clerks and officers' servants were to be chosen and two years' diligent service as constable or overseer were to count as three years' servitude in the settlement; but men were to be admitted to this higher class only after two, four or six years at the station, according to the term of their sentence there, and capital respites only after the Governor had approved. No convict was to work on his own account; no wife of any man in the second class was permitted to go to the settlement; convicts were not to possess 'knives or sharp instruments'.[2]

The penal establishment at Moreton Bay flourished for about twelve years after Brisbane founded it in 1825. At its peak in 1830, 952 prisoners were there, under the command of Captain Patrick Logan. Discipline was always harsh. In 1827 more than a third of the men were punished in six months. Allan Cunningham thought it more severe than on Norfolk Island.[3] But it was an expensive and unhealthy station. In 1829 the crude death-rate was over eleven per cent; even between 1830

[1] Report of Inquiry, Exec. Council Mins., 28 April 1826, CO 204/1; Darling to Goderich, 26 Sept. 1827; Murray to Darling, 26 Nov. 1828; Darling to Murray, 4 and 24 May 1830 encl. report of inquiry at Port Macquarie, 4 Aug. 1828; Backhouse, 406; Darling to Goderich 22 Dec. 1827.
[2] Regulations for Penal Settlements, 1 July 1829, encl., Darling to Murray, 15 Aug. 1829; Governor's Mins., nos. 43 (26 July) 1827, nos. 7, 8, 11 (10, 11, 21 Jan.) 1828, 33 (24 March) 1829.
[3] Brisbane to Bathurst, 21 May 1825; Returns, CO 201/219; evid. Cunningham, *Secondary Punishment Report*, 1831–2, 138; Spicer Journal, Oxley Library, Brisbane. Book of Trials, 1835–6, also records very severe punishments.

and 1832, when the authorities had improved the diet, procured a purer water supply and reduced overcrowding by building new barracks, it was over two per cent; though it was falling rapidly it was about ten times what would be expected among a similarly aged population today. In 1832 both Bourke and the Colonial Office were speaking of doing away with it, and the latter became more impatient as time went on because of its cost. Between 1834 and 1836 the average number there was less than four hundred; by 1837 there were only three hundred, chiefly 'convict women . . . sentenced in the colony to transportation for a second offence'. If they were to be removed, Bourke did not know where else they could be sent without 'additional buildings and consequent expense', and he was worried by the 'propriety' and the expense of throwing it open to free settlers. However by 1838 there were only a few men to look after the government livestock and Gipps ordered a survey to be made as a preliminary to selling land. Brisbane's penal days were over.[1]

Norfolk Island, today a beautiful, almost idyllic resort, with high cliffs all around, washed by a heavy surf which makes landing by sea difficult and keeps the place peaceful in its isolation, provided the most terrible aspect of the system after it was reoccupied in 1825. Though only 211 men were there in 1829, after Port Macquarie was closed and Moreton Bay cut down the number steadily rose to 1,400 in 1838. The prisoners were nearly all among 'the most depraved and dissolute' of the convicts, and the story of the settlement is tragic and horrible. Proper supervision from Sydney was difficult, and the combination of isolation, poor buildings, the lack of all female companionship except for the families of the highest officials, the character of the prisoners, including those employed as overseers, and the summary trials for offences against discipline, all combined to make homosexual and sadistic practices almost inevitable.[2]

Despair of early release made things worse. Though prisoners might rise to the 'first class', for some years none could hope to leave until their sentence had expired. Until 1836 the government could find no clergyman willing to go there except for brief visits, so there was no

---

[1] Medical records, 1829–34, Oxley Library; Bourke to Goderich, 3 Nov. 1832; Goderich to Bourke, 25 Dec. 1832; Register of Convicts, Oxley Library; D. Gordon, 'Sickness and Death at Moreton Bay', *Aust. Med. Journal*, Sept. 1963; Glenelg to Bourke, 26 Dec. 1835; Bourke to Glenelg, 5 Nov. 1837; Gipps to Glenelg, 1 July 1839. Cf. Alison Goleby, 'Penal Administration', and Greenwood and Laverty, ch. 1.
[2] Darling to Hay, 10 Feb. 1827; Regulations, 1829, *HRA*, xv, 104 ff.; Bourke to Stanley, 15 Jan. 1834; returns, 1 Feb. 1829, 26 Aug. 1831, *HRA*, xiv, 648, xvi, 339; Bourke to Glenelg, 5 Nov. 1837; H. Maude, 'Norfolk Island' (A.N.U. thesis, ML), 110.

religious instruction, and no one to whom the prisoners could turn for comfort or sympathy. There were neither schools nor books nor any kind of relaxation – nothing but bitterness, vice, hardship, pain, toil and possibly death. 'Let a man be what he will when he comes here, he is soon as bad as the rest,' a prisoner charged with mutiny told the court trying him in 1834. 'He loses the heart of a man and gets the heart of a beast,' said Bishop Polding. The men's 'feelings were habitually outraged, and their self-respect destroyed', wrote reformer Maconochie later.[1] The secret society of the Ring terrorized the men as much as their warders. They perverted their language 'to adapt themselves to the complete subversion of the human heart', said Father Ullathorne, the future Catholic Bishop of Birmingham, in 1838. 'Blasphemy, rage, mutual hatred, and the unrestrained indulgence of unnatural lusts' greeted the prisoner, reported the visiting Anglican, the Reverend W. T. Stiles. 'This island, beautiful by nature and comparable to the Garden of Eden, is rendered not only a moral wilderness, but a place of torment to these men, not so much by the punishments of the law, as by their conduct to one another,' concluded the Quaker Backhouse, after his visit in 1835,[2] on the first Quaker mission to Australia.

That the place was vicious is indisputable; was it also the site of brutality and torture? Reports are contradictory. Doubtless conditions varied under different commandants. Lieutenant-Colonel Morisset, in charge from 1829 to 1834, whose severity at Newcastle ten years earlier had been notorious, and whose conduct on the Island has had a 'bad press', was said to have ordered floggings (apart from work in irons) at the average annual rate of one per man, or about four times the average for *all* the convicts in the colony. Horrible as this was, considering the type of men there it is less extraordinary than it sounds at first, though it must have involved terrible suffering for the worst of the prisoners; but neither Allan Cunningham, the botanist-explorer, nor that other explorer, Charles Sturt, a humane man, when commanding the troops there, nor his successor Crotty, thought the convicts' treatment at this time unduly harsh, even if the last two were inevitably influenced by the severity of contemporary military discipline.[3]

Bourke, when he arrived, was anxious to do something to improve

[1] All quoted, Barry, *Maconochie*, 96.

[2] Transportation Report, 1838, Polding and Stiles, App., 264, 267, evid. Ullathorne, q. 275; Backhouse, 267, 278; Colin Roderick in quoting this verdict (*John Knatchbull*, 211) omits the last 16 words and so distorts Backhouse's opinion. Cf. Price Warung (William Astley), *Convict Days*.

[3] *Secondary Punishments Report*, 1831-2, evid. Cunningham, 189, 235 ff.; Exec. Council Minutes, 27 Feb. and 5 March 1832.

conditions on the island. It was unfortunate that he never visited it, but he approved the regulations which Colonel Lindesay, the acting-governor, had issued as soon as Darling had left, establishing a regular system for the mitigation of sentences on the island so as to give the prisoners an incentive to good conduct and some hope of an earlier release. Even so, in the seven years from 1832 to 1838 only 429 men left the island (sixty-one a year) while 1,479 arrived (211 a year). Bourke told Morisset to remember that reform, not mere punishment, should be his aim; did he need more power to reward convicts, for example, by letting them have a garden? In January 1833 he confirmed Morisset's regulations for this 'indulgence', and next year, after appointing Major Joseph Anderson to succeed as Commandant, he advised him to issue a 'settlement order' setting out the 'relaxations and indulgences' which the regulations offered for good conduct; but the probation required was 'long and irksome' and the 'relaxation' was small, until Maconochie took over in 1839.[1]

Anderson afterwards claimed that he reduced corporal punishment by nine-tenths, after 'a partial and momentary severity to two or three individuals', as one prisoner put it. The island, wrote the latter, was not 'an earthly hell', and Anderson gave 'humanity a fair trial'. Perhaps he did, though Anderson's own statement, made long afterwards, is sweeping and vague, and is not supported by statistics. Still Backhouse, the visiting Quaker, who strongly disagreed with those ignorant English critics who asserted that transportation was not a severe punishment, said in 1835 that flogging was then 'but seldom resorted to'. He thought the men not overworked, their diet 'not unwholesome' and their health good. Anderson was praised, too, by Judge Burton, who staunchly advocated reforms on the island after his visit there in 1834, by Ulla-thorne, and by his own successor, Major T. Bunbury. The second Anglican chaplain, the Reverend T. Sharpe, quarrelled with Anderson. He criticized a great deal that he did, thought that he gave too much credence and support to the overseers, who were convicts themselves, and that he took little interest in the prisoners' reform. As one of his chief criteria was whether or not an overseer was a Papist, and he thought the Commandant too subservient to Roman Catholics and to the nefarious 'Whig-radicals' in the government in London and Sydney, his standard of judgment must be suspect; but he confirmed the improvement shown by at least some of the prisoners after clergy were

[1] Maconochie, 'Criminal Statistics', *Jour. of Stat. Soc.*, viii, 11; Bourke to Morisset, 12 March 1832, Col. Sec.'s Corr., Out-Letters, Norfolk Island; Morisset to Col. Sec., 16 Jan. 1833, *ib.*, In-Letters, 33/3; Governor's Minute, 3169, 25 Aug. 1834.

appointed and schools established in 1837, and he admitted the benefits of Anderson's earlier establishment of definite standards for mitigations and indulgences. Unfortunately however, these were made too much dependent on the men's work, and too little on their character, according to Father McEncroe, later the Roman Catholic chaplain on the island. In his desire to make the prisoners' labour productive, and so to gain the approbation of his superiors, Anderson drove them too hard, and created a 'most merciless and oppressive class of overseers', who were virtually slave-drivers, and too often both cruel and corrupt.[1]

If McEncroe thought Anderson 'over-rigid', one convict, John Knatchbull, was even more critical of the commandant's 'duplicity, villainous conduct and black heart', and another, Thomas Cook, hoped that 'for the honour of England' the soldiers on the island would 'never show such traits of savage ferocity to an enemy' as they displayed to the prisoners. The protest of the first chaplain, the Reverend T. Atkins, against the flogging, for refusal to work, of a sick convict, Castleton, who proved his illness beyond doubt by dying, has a sincerity in it which strongly suggests that the inquiry into the incident, only held after his strenuous demands, produced a piece of the all-too-common type of bureaucratic whitewashing, which reflects very badly on all concerned. Atkins' memoirs show him to be a 'difficult' man, who had quarrelled with the Commandant partly because the latter very properly would not compel Roman Catholic prisoners to attend his services. His evidence may be questioned, as for example by one author who describes his remarks about Knatchbull as 'a hotch-potch of hearsay and fiction', even while he believes what he says about Castleton. Cook was later Principal Overseer under Alexander Maconochie, and therefore had an interest in stressing the latter's improvements, while Knatchbull had a perennial grievance against authority and was mentally unstable.[2] For all that, all this evidence cannot be entirely ignored. Clearly nearly all reports were prejudiced, one way or the other, and if the evidence of men like Backhouse and Judge Burton suggests that, under Anderson, Norfolk Island was not quite as bad as it has sometimes been painted, this is saying little enough.

[1] Anderson, 159–89; Backhouse, 263–80, and app. J, no. 3, lxxix, quoting convicts' letters; cf. J. Backhouse and G. W. Walker, *Report of a Visit to Norfolk Island*, ML, B705; Burton, quoted, L. G. Young; on improvements between 1834 and Dec. 1835, *Transportation Report*, 1838, evid. Ullathorne, 276; Bunbury, ii, 313, ch. 7 *passim*; T. Sharpe, Journals, ML, B217–8, espec. i, 189, 239, 290, ii, 117 and 177, Norfolk Island, ML A1502, 179; McEncroe, *Aust. Cath. Record*, xxxvi, 285 ff.

[2] Roderick, 93, 209, 212–3; T. Cook, *Exile's Lamentation*, ML, A 1711, 136; Atkins to Bourke, 22 April 1837, Col. Sec.'s Corr., Norfolk Island, 37/3986; Deas Thomson to Atkins, 26 April, 1837, *HRA*, xviii, 768.

Bourke warned Anderson of the danger of dispensing with the prisoners' irons 'to any considerable extent', and told him that he would not 'upon any consideration authorize the use of any but manual labour on the farms', nor have any mill 'not urged by the labour of convicts' nor allow deep ploughing and manuring to replace hoeing, even though all this was inefficient and expensive, as it also was at Moreton Bay. He told Anderson to remember how extensive was 'the discretionary power of summary punishment' which he possessed under the 'Bushranging Act'–up to three hundred lashes, two years in a chain gang or three extra years on the island–and he urged him to use these powers for almost every crime short of murder, although he had persuaded the British government to have an act passed by Parliament setting up on the island a special criminal court whose procedure would be rather less abrupt.[1] On the other hand, he was concerned that he could get no clergy for the establishment; and though he refused to listen to Atkins' protest over the Castleton affair, and sharply reprimanded him for saying the man 'was murdered' (which was probably true), he warned the Commandant and Surgeon of the need to use 'the utmost caution', in refusing to treat prisoners thought to be malingering. But he had not thought it necessary to report the 'disturbance' of 1834, and when specifically asked about it a year later, seemed concerned to play it down; though he admitted in 1846 that the settlement was 'not all it might have been', he never seemed to try to follow Burton's urging to turn it from a place 'of much failure to a glorious achievement'.[2]

In his final report on it, in November 1837, he virtually admitted that he had not achieved a great deal. The island was tranquil, and Anderson's superintendence 'humane but firm and vigilant', but there was no reformation there. Its justification was that it prevented crime in the colony. If it were abolished, what could be done with the prisoners who were sent there? It was a necessary part of the system. With this Gipps agreed in 1842, when recommending that it be continued as a place of punishment, conducted as it had been under Anderson and 'still more under Major Bunbury', in 1839, when the 'far too great severity' that had once existed there had ceased.[3]

[1] Governor's Minute, 35/9940; Miller to Goulburn, 30 Sept. 1824, Bishop to M'Leay, 14 Oct. 1826, Col. Sec.'s In-Letters, Moreton Bay; M'Leay to Anderson, 3 April 1835, 14 Jan. and 31 Dec. 1836, Out-Letters, 35/5, 36/1 and 10; Bourke to Stanley, 30 Nov. 1833; Spring Rice to Bourke, 1 Aug. 1834. The act was 4 and 5 Will. iv c. 65.
[2] Bourke to Goderich, 23 Feb. 1832; Deas Thomson to Anderson, 24 April 1837, Out-Letters, 37/52, to Atkins, *loc. cit.*; Spring Rice to Bourke, 1 Aug. 1834; Bourke to Spring Rice, 15 Jan. 1835; *Criminal Law, Report*, PP 1847 (637), evid. Bourke, 4295–6; Burton to Bourke, 25 Oct. 1836, Bourke Papers, xi, ML.
[3] Bourke to Glenelg, 5 Nov. 1837; Gipps to Stanley, 15 Aug. 1842.

14

In London, James Stephen was trying to take a firmer stand, though, as was to be the case ten years later, he could achieve nothing. 'My own opinion is,' he wrote in 1834, 'that . . . if the case were once fairly made known the universal abhorrence of Society would compel the abandonment of it.' Three years later, he commented that Stiles' report was 'an addition to the many other accounts . . . which convince me . . . that let the expense, trouble or risk be what they may, the abandonment of that place as a penal settlement is a matter of the most urgent necessity and of the most sacred duty'.[1] But to the politicians, as to Bourke, some such place seemed necessary; its existence could be said to be part of the 'moral cost' of the system; and despite the insistence on hand labour, it was cheap. A prisoner there cost only £13 per year, against £17 in chain gangs on the mainland; if the labour of the latter was more useful, it benefited only the colony, not the British Treasury who paid. Perhaps the only consolation was that only 2,265 were sent there from 1825 to 1838, or six per cent of the male convicts who came to New South Wales.[2]

In Van Diemen's Land, the first penal settlement was founded by Sorell in 1822 at Macquarie Harbour on the rugged west coast of the island. Impenetrable forests and rocky mountain-tops wrapped in mist and often capped with snow cut it off from the rest of the colony; its narrow and treacherous entrance through Hell's Gates made a fitting climax to the cold and stormy voyage from Hobart. With more than three hundred rainy days a year, and in winter lashed by fierce south-westerly storms from the Antarctic, its climate, forbidding even to the visiting fisherman in midsummer, added to the horrors of its discipline for the unfortunate convicts sent there. They could hardly be expected to appreciate the giant century-old eucalyptus, over a hundred feet high, or the great beauty of the foliage on the rare days when the sun was shining; they only saw it as a place where crops would not grow and animals would not live, where the gloom of everlasting cloud and incessant rain dampened their spirits and lowered their vitality, worn by toil and hardship.

It was a 'place of the most severe punishment' for the 1,153 prisoners who were there during its ten years' existence. At first more than half were flogged each year; after Arthur sent a Wesleyan missionary to this 'moral desert', punishments fell off by two-thirds, possibly because of his ministrations. He began a school in the evenings, where many of the men were taught to read and to write and Captain Butler reported a

---

[1] Minutes on Bourke to Stanley, 30 Nov. 1833, CO 201/233, on Stiles' report, 5 Nov. 1837, CO 201/263.
[2] Bourke to Glenelg, 5 Nov. 1837; Maconochie, 'Criminal Statistics', *loc. cit.*

marked improvement in their temper. At the same time he reduced corporal punishment by ordering confinement on 'a small barren island' in the harbour instead. The men had to cut the huge trees, drag them 'by hand' along a track cut over moist or swampy ground to the water's edge, and then, often working up to their waists in water, float them to the 'ship-yards'. Here some fine vessels were built, and a few of the men became skilful craftsmen; but more often the lumbering, heavy rain and bad diet combined to bring on rheumatism, scurvy and dysentery, which despite the efforts of the Reverend Mr. Schofield were more common products than reformation of character.[1] Arthur never liked the station. It was too small and too remote. Certainly it was not easy to escape from, but the voyage to it was uncertain and dangerous, and in 1829 the brig *Cyprus* was piratically seized on its way there by the convicts on board. Next year the Governor decided to establish the famous penal station at Port Arthur, on Tasman's Peninsula; its expansion, with its greater convenience and security, allowed him to abandon first, in 1832, the settlement he had set up on Maria Island only seven years before, and next year Macquarie Harbour itself.[2]

Port Arthur could be easily reached from Hobart by boat across Storm Bay; but the whole of Tasman's Peninsula was joined to the mainland only by the narrow, easily guarded Eaglehawk Neck. Secure and easy to control, in time it became a flourishing settlement, the third largest town in the colony, with a handsome church, a well-designed hospital, attractive officers' bungalows and a fine village green and parade-ground, leading to extensive wharves and shipbuilding yards. Yet just as Rome was not built in a day, during the whole of Arthur's administration – and longer – it was much less perfect than its founder liked to suggest. Its soil was not fertile. Its buildings were for years inadequate and overcrowded. There were no means of classification or solitary imprisonment until 1835. The church was not finished until 1836; the reclamation of the bay was only begun in 1841 and the model prison in 1847. But the frequency of Arthur's visits showed his interest in it; the fact that they *could* be so frequent showed its superiority to Macquarie Harbour and Norfolk Island. He was indefatigable in his

[1] Instructions to Lieut. Wright, 16 June 1824, *HRA*, v, 630–4; report from Cmdt. Butler, 30 June 1827, Col. Sec.'s Papers, no. 264, encl. Arthur to Hay, 1 July 1827; Arthur Papers, xxix, Convicts, ML; Lempriere, *Penal Settlements*, chs. 1–4; West, ii, 214; Pretyman, *Tas. Hist. Assoc.*, i, 8–10.
[2] Ingleton, 127; West, ii, 215–9; the brig *Frederick* removing the last people from Macquarie Harbour, in January 1834, was similarly seized, Ingleton, 181, West, ii, 220–1. Arthur to Murray, 3 March 1831, to Goderich, 16 Feb. and 10 Oct. 1832; Col. Office Mem., 16 April 1831, CO 206/61. On Maria Island, Instructions to Lieuts. Butler and Murdock, 1825, *HRA*, v, 634–5, J. R. Morris, *Tas. Hist. Assoc.*, xi, 157–77; Lempriere, ch. 5.

instructions for its improvement; and certainly the Commandant, O'Hara Booth, though 'the personification of unimpassioned severity', was 'as prompt to reward as to punish'.[1] His management, according to West, who was no friend of the system, was 'compared with every other settlement of its class . . . more humane because more impartial', but Backhouse and Walker deplored the lack of 'classification' and the lack of reform. They thought that well-behaved prisoners should be allowed a garden-plot to cultivate; and they regretted the lack of small cells and the prevalence of 'immorality'. Forster found that the 'educated convicts' particularly 'appear to feel most acutely the misery and degradation to which they are exposed'. Frequently under cloud, with its surrounding hills forbidding, overpowering, it was 'a place of profound misery', said West. 'It carried the vengeance of the law to the utmost limits of human endurance'. It utterly 'debased the soul' of its inmates. To Burnett, it was 'worse than death'.[2]

Up to 1835, three thousand out of the twenty thousand convicts who had been sent to Van Diemen's Land (about fifteen per cent) had spent some of their time in one of the penal settlements, including 1,711 at Port Arthur; in that year, out of about 14,914 male convicts on the island, 1,172 (or eight per cent) were at this station; but by this time, Arthur, like his colleagues on the mainland, had developed the system of keeping men 'at hard labour in Chains in settled Districts'. This saved the expense of transporting them to a penal settlement; the labour was useful to the colony, and the chain gangs formed an 'admirable mean' between the penal settlements and the unironed road parties. When dissatisfied with Macquarie Harbour and before he developed Port Arthur, he found the gangs particularly valuable and sent off two-thirds of those sentenced to the penal settlements to work in them instead. In 1832, they held 568, compared with 182 still at Macquarie Harbour and 260 at Port Arthur, and though the latter grew rapidly after that, the governor kept up the chain gangs too; 805 men were working in them in 1835, more than five per cent of the male convicts.[3]

---

[1] Arthur's report, Feb. 1834, PP 1834 (614), xlvii, 295; Arthur to Goderich, 15 Feb. 1833, to Stanley, 4 Feb. 1834; *Transportation Report*, 1837, App., 323 ff.; Booth to Arthur, 29 March and 5 May 1834, Arthur Papers, xxiii, ML; Burnett to Booth, 8 May 1834, CO 280/48; Stanley to Arthur, 26 Aug. and 12 Oct. 1833.

[2] West, ii, 244–5; Backhouse and Walker, Reports, ML, B706–7, i, 27, 231 ff.; Forster's Report, 30 Oct. 1833, and Burnett's minute, Col. Sec.'s Corr., 1/12637.

[3] Montagu, *Statistical Returns* (1836), preface and 35; returns, 1836, CO 280/66; Arthur to Glenelg, 25 Jan. 1836, and Report of Legs. Council, 26 Jan., CO 280/64; Arthur to Goderich, 1 Dec. 1827; mem. on convict discipline, 9 May 1826, Col. Sec.'s Corr. 1/3004; Arthur to Murray, 25 Sept. 1829, to Goderich, 8 Sept. and 15 Nov. 1831, 10 Oct. 1832; Col. Sec.'s Corr., 1/4239, Tas. Arch.

The prisoners were concentrated in 'some extensive undertaking', like the wharves at Hobart or the causeway at Bridgewater, where military assistance was at hand, if the superintendent wanted it. Magistrates visited the gangs regularly to hear complaints and to punish offenders. At Bridgewater, there were small punishment cells, seven feet by three feet six inches, in which a stout man could not turn around, had to be pushed in head first and drawn out by his heels. Usually offenders were removed from them at night, and, reported the Commandant, 'the most refractory and troublesome are glad to return to their labour in one or two days . . . The use of these cells have [sic] enabled me to maintain correct discipline and to exact more than the usual labour and to dispense with corporal punishment'. Owing to them, the weekly crime list was light; without them, there would have to be 'a more frequent resort to flagellation'. The magistrates thought well of them, but Arthur did not, and in 1833 forbade their use.[1]

With such cells removed, Backhouse and Walker approved of the parties, though they thought it a pity so many were lodged in each hut, and that convicts were employed as overseers. Arthur had ordered that 'humanity should attend' the sentence to them, but punishment was more frequent than in assigned service, for the men were worse, and the superintendents and visiting magistrates could order it on the spot. 'Great attention' was supposed to be paid to classification, based to a 'minute attention to the conduct of every individual', the keeping of a register and of weekly returns and frequent inspection by visiting magistrates; but apparently, though the returns could be made and the men inspected, classification was easier to order than to put into effect. The 'better' men were given sugar and tobacco; that was simple; but it was not so easy to keep them separate from their fellows. However, the hope of assignment was thought to encourage good conduct.[2]

On such stations, the government naturally looked after those who were ill, but sometimes the sick parade had odd features. 'I was rather surprised by the extraordinary simplicity of the remedies prescribed,' wrote Boyes of that at Bridgewater. These 'in every case consisted of either cold or warm water or a dose of salts, although the latter being a costly medicine was directed in only one instance. I learnt afterwards

[1] Cheyne's report, 29 Oct. 1836, Arthur Papers, xxxiv, ML; Boyes' Diary, 16 Oct. 1831; Arthur's Private Sec. to Commandant at Bridgewater, 9 Nov. 1833, Lieut.-Gov.'s Letter Book; Mem. to Arthur from Commandant, 11 Nov., Col. Sec.'s Corr., 1/15219.
[2] Backhouse and Walker, Reports, ML, i, 110–5; Forster to Col. Sec., 25 June 1836, Col. Sec.'s Corr., 1/18380; Exec. Council Mins., 16 June 1834; Standing Instructions for Discipline of Convicts employed in Road Dept., 1827; Instructions to the Principal Supt., Jan. 1829, Col. Sec.'s Corr., 1/8728.

that the prescription was regulated . . . by the size of the medicine chest which contained neither more nor less than a few ounces of Epsom salts', though the officer of the guard thought 'a more liberal application of the cat would render the attendance of the medical officer superfluous'.[1]

In New South Wales, the chain gangs were employed on the roads. Darling had correctly argued when forming them in 1826 that they would save founding more penal settlements. They were controlled by the surveyors and regularly visited by the magistrates; but they had only convict overseers. This made them cheap to superintend, but it also led to inefficiency, favouritism and brutality. Darling, perhaps naturally, was very proud of them. That the *Gazette* should praise them was to be expected; what is more surprising is that at first the *Australian* was pleased with them too; all it wanted was double-irons and a neck-collar, instead of the 'toy-like' nine-pounds chain normally worn, though within four months it would be passionately and vituperatively screaming about Darling's severity.[2]

In time, perhaps because of the furore over the death of the ex-soldier Sudds, while he was being punished in irons, their discipline relaxed; when Bourke arrived he decided to put them 'under a stricter control'. He kept the surveyors to direct their work, but gave them power to order up to fifty lashes for inefficiency, and replaced the convict overseers by paid superintendents and free constables. By 1834, he was arranging for visiting magistrates to try more serious offences, and placing military guards at each stockade. This reduced escapes from the gangs from 265 in 1830 to thirty a year in 1833–4, but the surveyors' supervision did not improve their work much, so he began to put them under the superintendence of military officers, whom he made magistrates, after he received an extra regiment in the colony in 1835.[3] This was an effective change, and several times later he repeatedly asked for discretionary power to put in irons all who were not in assigned service. That they could then work in these chain gangs was doubtless good for discipline, but it is a reminder of the limits to his ideas of leniency.[4]

---

[1] Diary, 16 Oct. 1831.
[2] Governor's Minutes, nos. 55, 63, 121, 8 and 21 March, 8 Aug. 1826; Darling to Huskisson, 28 March 1828, to Murray, 20 Aug. 1829; Governor's Minute, no. 95, 6 July 1830; Col. Sec.'s circular to magistrates, 30/41, 30 Aug. 1830; Governor's mems., 25 Sept. 1830, 1 Feb. 1831; *Sydney Gazette*, 10 and 24 May 1826; *Australian*, 6 and 27 Sept. 1826.
[3] Bourke to Goderich, 3 Nov. 1832; Bourke to his son, 13 Oct. 1835, Bourke Papers, vi, ML; Bourke to Stanley, 15 Jan. and 10 Oct. 1834; to Spring Rice, 9 Dec. 1834; Minutes, 6 Nov. and 19 Dec. 1834; instructions for Supts., HRA, xvii, 336; 3 Will. IV, no. 3, sec. 28
[4] Bourke to Stanley, 15 Jan. 1834, to Glenelg, 26 Dec. 1835.

The men were locked up at night, in groups of about twenty-five, in 'Prisoners' Boxes', mounted on wheels, and these, according to Backhouse, did 'not afford more than eighteen inches in width for each individual to lie down in'.[1] By day they were kept hard at work, under the military guard, not allowed to talk, and 'liable to suffer flagellation for even a trifling offence, such as an exhibition of obstinacy'. Of course, conditions varied. One superintendent allowed fire and extra blankets; another forced the men to run to work at the point of the bayonet, even if their irons hurt their legs, and though the resistance of the soldiers eventually put a stop to this, in another case the rank and file were very ready to carry out 'the tortures wished for by their officer'. In 1836, Bourke reported that corporal punishment was 'not so frequent as the previous bad habits of these Criminals might be supposed necessary'. Perhaps he did not know what was going on; perhaps he supposed a great deal to be necessary; but only two months earlier Backhouse had recorded that some men in the gang at Marulan had 'received from 600 to 800 lashes within the space of eighteen months'.[2]

By this time, there were a thousand men, with sentences of from one to three years, working in sixteen gangs. From the beginning of 1837, to Surveyor-General Mitchell's satisfaction, the change begun two years before was completed and they were put entirely under the superintendence of the Commanding Royal Engineer.[3] The old, unironed road gangs, whose idleness and misbehaviour had aroused justified criticism in the past, no longer existed.[4] The 'incorrigibly idle . . . whom no prudent settler will feed and clothe', as Bourke described them, had been sentenced to labour in chains; they no longer remained 'a useless charge on the Treasury and a reproach to the laws' as in the past, even if they then cost £17 a man every year.[5]

These arrangements had their defects, despite Bourke's enthusiasm. The employment of military overseers was 'objectionable in the highest degree', minuted the Colonial Office; in any case, it was officially reported to Gipps in 1839 to be 'a complete failure'. The road parties out of irons were 'an important branch of convict discipline'; their abolition left an awkward gap between men working in irons and assigned

[1] Gipps to Glenelg, 14 July 1838; Jamison to Bourke, 7 March 1832, Bourke Papers, xi, ML; Backhouse, Report, 18 Jan. 1837, Narrative, app. O, cxxviii.
[2] Iron gang instructions, 10 Sept. 1832, HRA, xvii, 336–40; Transportation Report, 1838, app. C, no. 41, E; T. Cook, op. cit., 57 ff.; Bourke to Glenelg, 29 Dec. 1836; Backhouse, 439, re 7 Oct.
[3] Bourke to Glenelg, 29 Dec. 1836; Mitchell to M'Leay, 3 Jan. 1837, HRA, xviii, 694.
[4] Burton's 'charge', Nov. 1835, Macarthur, NSW, app. 34; Bourke to Glenelg, 18 Dec. 1835; Cook, 17–22.
[5] Bourke to his son, 21 April 1834, Bourke Papers, vi, ML; Bourke to Glenelg, 5 Nov. 1837.

servants. Bourke admitted that the convicts in the gangs were worse off than those not in irons on Norfolk Island. Arnold, of the Commissariat there, agreed; Backhouse could 'scarcely conceive a situation more miserable' than theirs; death would be preferable 'were it not for the eternal consequences that await the unprepared'. Bourke tried to provide the books, the schools and the religious instruction whose absence Backhouse had deplored, but since the gangs involved hardship, cruelty and 'association', though deterrents to misconduct, they were hardly reformatory.[1]

In 1836, about eight per cent of all male convicts in New South Wales were in the chain gangs or on Norfolk Island; but the proportion who spent *some* of their time there was naturally far larger. In the ten years that followed Darling's organization of the ironed road parties, nearly five thousand men, or about eighteen per cent of the males transported to the colony, were confined in them at some time; adding to these the men sent to the penal settlements, and allowing for those who served in both, between one-fifth and one quarter suffered one or other of these most severe punishments. In 1834, Bourke had warned Stanley that 'punishment appalling in its duration as well as its intensity . . . will induce a state of despair in the mind of the Convict which is to be found utterly at variance with reformation', a view with which Aberdeen (and Stephen) thoroughly agreed; but in his anxiety to keep order among all the prisoners in the colony, by providing an effective deterrent to misbehaviour, he seemed in danger of forgetting his own warning.[2]

For fifteen years the governors had been increasing the severity of the punishment inflicted on convicts who misconducted themselves. Perhaps this severity was necessary to make the assignment system work; if so, it could be justified if it were thought that assignment was a good form of punishment. Arthur, like most of the colonists, thought it was; many in England and a few in Australia did not. Some of its critics changed their minds when they saw the results of its abolition, but it was criticized as being a 'lottery' and likely to be too lenient; it was defended as being in fact quite a severe punishment, while being economical and reformatory. Whichever be true, it provided another aspect of transportation; but no one who knew the facts could say that the convict under punishment in Australia did not suffer a terrible fate.

---

[1] Minute on Bourke to Glenelg, 29 Dec. 1836, CO 201/255; Gipps to Glenelg, 29 March 1839, reporting Engineer's opinion; Arnold to Bourke, 27 Aug. 1837, *Transportation Report*, 1838, app. E, no. 45; Backhouse, Report, *loc. cit.*; C. Campbell to Berry, 29 July 1839, Berry Papers, xv, ML.

[2] Bourke to Stanley, 15 Jan. 1834; Aberdeen to Bourke, 4 March 1835.

10

Prisons without Bars

'The mould of a man's fortune is in his own hands'.

BACON: *Of Fortune*

The normal fate of the well-behaved convict was assignment to private service. Bigge had recommended it and the British government encouraged it, for it saved money by taking the prisoner off the government's hands; but in a sense it was a forerunner of the probationary and open prisons of today. It scattered the men throughout the colony, which broke up their 'evil associations', it taught the convicts those 'habits of labour' whose absence had so often started them on their criminal career, and it gave them experience which would make it easier for them to gain useful employment when their sentence expired. It would be especially reformatory, it was thought, if employers looked after their servants as they should, and gave them proper moral and religious instruction. For this, 'a shepherd's life' was excellent, Charles Campbell wrote in 1839. 'He who leads it has constant but not laborious employment, enjoys the light of heaven and . . . is secluded from the company of the drunken and the dissolute.'[1]

In Van Diemen's Land, Lieutenant-Governor Arthur took upon himself 'the entire management' of the convicts' assignment, as soon as he arrived in 1824, for he wanted to gain 'a perfect insight into the circumstances of their employment'. He never gave this up, nor was it challenged, as in New South Wales, by the judges. Though he set up an Assignment Board in 1832, he supervised it closely, and used it to maintain both his patronage and his power. His opponents accused him of favouritism. In 1832 one-tenth of the settlers had nearly half the 'mechanics' who were available. Ten government officials had 105;

---

[1] Bathurst to Darling, 31 March and 2 April 1827; *Transportation Report*, 1837, evid. Forbes, Breton, James Macarthur, Arthur, q. 1292, 2438–41, 3031, 4286; Campbell to Alexander Berry, 20 July 1839, Berry Papers, xv, ML.

Colonial Secretary Montagu had nineteen and Principal Superintendent Forster sixteen, when others were crying out for any at all; but
perhaps these officers were the most suitable masters. George Meredith,
'the King of Great Swan Port', complained in 1828 that he was not
receiving servants: he was told that 'no instruction' had been given to
deprive him of his servants, but 'you cannot expect any particular
interference by the Lieutenant-Governor to facilitate your wishes,
whilst many respectable settlers who have by cordial co-operation
strengthened His Excellency's hands in the furtherance of such
measures as have been deemed expedient in the administration of the
affairs of the colony . . . have been no less desirous of Convict assistance
on their farms'. Meredith rejoined that this was making assignment an
indulgence dependent 'not upon their wants, but upon the construction
the Governor may be pleased to put upon the political sentiments and
conduct of the applicant', which was true; but what if a master opposed
his governor's *convict* policy? This would surely justify his not receiving
convict servants, and then followed the question whether a line could be
drawn between convict and general policy, in a colony like Van Diemen's Land?[1] Certainly the power to revoke assignment and to grant
indulgence to the prisoners seemed to Arthur 'the mainspring by which
the movement of a mass of men can be worked with advantage here',
and the basis of his control over the men and their numerous unpaid
settler-gaolers. He refused to reward settlers for taking convicts; their
service was enough, in a community short of labour. And masters must
discipline and reform the men. They might not be reassigned, or paid
wages, or given cattle or sheep or allotments to work for themselves,
which might have encouraged thieving; they must be kept at work, kept
sober and as far as possible sent to church on Sundays.[2]

But even in a small colony the Lieutenant-Governor could not be
everywhere; much depended on the quality of the settlers and the
magistrates. Among the former, there was 'a universal propensity to
excessive drinking', and if too many servants were withdrawn, there
would be too many employed by the government, usually in the towns.
The magistrates should have enforced the regulations, but they were

[1] Arthur to Bathurst, 10 Aug. 1825, to Goderich, 10 Sept. 1832, Anne McKay, 141 ff.,
172, 256–60; *Colonist*, 16 July 1833; Arthur to Stanley, 14 Oct. 1834; Burnett to Meredith,
20 Nov. 1828, Meredith to Burnett, 30 Dec., Meredith, *Correspondence*, 3 and 8.
[2] Govt. Orders, 16 Dec. 1825, 30 Sept. 1827, 18 June 1828, 1 Jan. 1829; Mem., Ppl. Supt.
to Col. Sec., 9 May 1826, Col. Sec.'s Corr., 1/3004; Instructions to Muster Master, Col. Sec.,
42/1/4; Supt. of Convicts' Letter Book, Tas. Papers, ML, F79, 141, F80, 283; Arthur to
Bathurst, 4 April and 25 Oct. 1826, encl. G.O., 30 Sept.; Arthur to Hay, 4 June 1826;
b., 9 Oct. 1826, 10 Jan. 1828, CO 323/146, 280/16; Arthur to Murray, 7 Aug. 1829.

often interested parties, and, despite Arthur, they were, like those in New South Wales, not always trustworthy. Inn-keepers, except with permission of the local magistrate, ex-convicts, relatives, ne'er-do-wells, those without free overseers and those who broke the rules might be forbidden to receive convicts; if a man married a convict he was to lose his assigned servants; but these prohibitions left many who were unsuitable still available. The police could help with advice about which settlers were suitable; but the police were not always reliable.[1] Assignments could be revoked – legally after 1830, but previously without protest; but though such revocations might deter masters from misbehaving, their actions were sometimes unnoticed and unpunished, especially in thinly inhabited districts. Arthur could not always judge how far his rules were obeyed, for the colonists would not tell him what was going on but there can be no question of the trouble he took to supervise the enforcement of his regulations.[2]

In fact assigned servants were often paid. One, assigned to a magistrate, was found, in 1828, to be owning cattle. He had acquired them before their possession was forbidden, reported his master, and it was difficult to force him to sell when the new regulations were imposed. 'How can it be expected that the Convicts shall ever be kept under proper discipline,' minuted Burnett, 'when the Governor's express orders are not only openly violated by the Magistrates but when encouragement is held out to his Convict servant to set them at defiance?' In fact 'exceptions to the rule were nearly equal to the instances that establish it,' wrote Boyes in his diary. Servants benefited either in money, tobacco, from their gardens, or in 'clandestinely assisting their neighbours'. Still, perhaps he was prejudiced, for he disliked Arthur, and thought the British government was exploiting the colony, reducing both its liberty and its trade, and filling it with pauper migrants who were 'worse than the plagues inflicted on the Egyptian idolaters'.[3]

[1]
  Col. Sec.'s Corr., 10 Feb. 1832, 1/13104, 13584; cf. Franklin's mem., Feb. 1839, ib., 5/3990; Arthur to Col. Sec., 20 Oct. 1827, ib., 1/4150; Arthur to Ppl. Supt., 2 April 1828, 24 Oct. 1829, ib., 1/6298, 9584; cf. 1/4079, 4876, 4935, 5963, 22/1/106, 51/1; Franklin to Glenelg, 7 Oct. 1837, Encl. 1; Arthur to Goderich, 7 April 1832, Encl. 4; Arthur to Bathurst, 15 Aug. 1824; Levy, 51-2.

[2] Col. Sec.'s Corr., 1/5434, 3004, 6363, 10362 (no free overseer); 8394, 8659 (servants lent out); 13232 (convict trading in spirits); 6298 (dismissing an assigned convict); 12796 (illtreatment); 13671 (master intemperate); 13268 (Sunday work); 11858 (female left without supervision); Clyde Co. Papers (OUP, 1941), i, 72; Pedder to Arthur, 28 March 1836, Arthur Papers, x, ML; Boyes' Diary, 16 March 1837.

[3] Bathurst to Arthur, 31 March 1826; Arthur to Bathurst, 23 March 1827; Arthur's minutes, 14 Sept. 1826, 30 Oct. 1827, 4 June 1828, Col. Sec.'s Corr. 1/370, 4892, 6329; Supt. of Convicts' Letter Book, Supt. of Convicts to Principal Supt., 2 July, 1832, ML, F79, 141; Boyes' Diary, 15 March 1836, 9 Feb. and 16 March 1837.

Most servants received 'indulgences' like tea, sugar, tobacco or even spirits, as an incentive to work and a means of discipline. In New South Wales, Atkinson thought that 'kindness was more effective than severity'; the less one had to do with the magistrate the better, for 'the belly was more vulnerable and sensitive than the back'. 'For the most part', they were 'well and kindly treated', said the explorer Eyre–too well in the opinion of some people.[1] 'It is true,' wrote Curr, Superintendent of the Van Diemen's Land Company, 'that convicts are sent out here as a punishment. But it is equally true that it is not in the interests of the master to make his service a punishment, but rather to make the condition of the convict as comfortable as is consistent with economy. The interest of the master essentially counteracts the object of transportation', for his 'sole object is to obtain the most work at the least expense'.[2]

Curr found the convicts good servants. 'The Company has few men assigned to it who are not well worth their maintenance,' he told his Directors, 'five out of six I believe are here converted into useful members of society as cheap labourers.' With him, they were isolated; they could not easily obtain spirits, and it was to their interest to gain his approbation. This did not apply to servants everywhere, but Curr found them better than free indentured labourers. With 'management and temper', there was no trouble with servants, wrote T. Betts; the magistrates' extensive jurisdiction gave masters better control over them than others, and the convict servants were 'not near so stupid . . . as the ordinary country bumpkin'.[3]

Meredith, when deprived of his servants by Arthur, said he was totally ruined, because the 'emigrant farmer depends solely on his convict labour for convict servants were the only available means of carrying on their important avocation in life'. H. W. Parker thought much the same, for 'the freeman was often more insolent, more idle and more dissolute than the Convict'. That acidulous diarist, Boyes, differed. After long waiting, a convict arrives, he wrote, 'escorted by one of those disreputable characters who are paid 2/– a day . . . for lounging about the streets . . . with a short club in their jacket pocket, and twice that amount by the public house keepers for passing their doors without looking in'. Then you have not a 'manservant who can wait at table' but a boy 'who never saw a mahogany table in his life'.

[1] Atkinson, 113–9 and 140–1; E. J. Eyre, Autobiography, ML, A1806, 45.
[2] Curr to Directors, no. 162, 12 Jan. 1831, VDL Co., Foreign Letter Book, no. 3; cf. VDL Co., Annual Reports, 1832, 1833.
[3] Ib.; Betts, 47–9.

After six months, and fearful damage, just when he is beginning to be useful he is taken off to be a constable, and more months follow 'during which your family must wait upon one another if they want to be waited on at all', until 'you are exposed to new trials of pence and patience. At the end of the year, if you keep accounts, you come to the conclusion that the unpaid services of compulsory labour are not so desirable in point of economy . . . as you had been led to expect' – but this was a minority opinion.[1]

Arthur thought the convicts generally 'good and well conducted while properly managed and kindly treated', though 'expensive servants' because 'regardless of their Employers' property and much inclined to waste . . . On the whole I don't think there is much ground of complaint against them, for I believe the misconduct of convict servants proceeds generally from the faults or ill-treatment of their masters'. Though Bourke told Arthur that 'forced labour was never, and never will be, as . . . efficient as free', Alexander Harris, the emigrant mechanic, argued that a convict cost his master only about half as much as a free labourer, while he asserted that 'between the fear of being flogged and the hope of getting a little indulgence . . . their labour was nearly or quite equal'. 'By dismissing freemen employed at large wages I have lessened the Expenditure of the Estate upwards of £200 p.a.' wrote young Riley, from 'Raby', about 1831, even though growling at the quality of the government men he received. Next year, Bourke and the principal superintendent, Hely, estimated that assigned servants cost only about £14 a year; since wages for unskilled labour were about ten shillings a week, plus board, it was no wonder that the convicts were in demand, even if they were less efficient than free men – though John Hawdon told his mother they were 'quite as good as labourers in England'. Eyre found it 'quite extraordinary how well they are behaved'. Charles Campbell preferred free workmen, and another employer found they would 'steal all they can lay their hands on', but Gipps, later on, said that their employment was worth about £10 a year per man to the settler; considering the demand for their services, it seems clear enough that most employers, despite their complaints, found them satisfactory.[2]

---

[1] Melville, 88; Meredith, iv; Meredith to Glenelg, enc. in Arthur to Glenelg, 30 Dec. 1837; Parker, 39; Boyes' Diary, 9 March 1837.
[2] Report, 1828, Arthur Papers, v, ML; Bourke to Arthur, 28 Jan. 1834, *ib.*, viii; Harris, 66–7; Riley Papers, ii, 273, ML; Bourke to Goderich, 30 April 1832, with encls., CO 201/226; Coghlan, i, 233; J. Hawdon, Letters, 1821–33, ML, A1329, 43; Eyre, Autobiography, ML; Gipps to Stanley, 13 Feb. 1845; Waugh, 36–7; *Secondary Punishments Report*, 1831, evid., J. Walker, q. 797, 830–8 and 882–94; NSW Legs. Council, *V & P* 1838, Committee on Immigration, Report, 1–47.

Whether mild treatment was better than coercion was a matter much debated. 'There is reason to think X is not as considerate of his servants as might be,' wrote Arthur in one case; 'consideration is the best way to reform, and it is to the master's interests, though the men . . . are more eager to complain than it is satisfactory to observe in convict servants'; on another report, that eight servants had received 1,436 lashes in five years (average 36 per man per year), he minuted, 'I trust such a case . . . may be impossible ever again . . . It is more disturbing than I can describe.'[1]

In New South Wales, writing from Shoalhaven in 1829, Alexander Berry told his partner, Wollstonecraft, 'We must adopt other and more effectual modes of punishing our people than pinching their guts'. At first he had not been in favour of excessive flogging. 'It is silly to object to any man because he is a rogue when they all come here for their crimes. All I care about is having able-bodied men – for the rest, no matter if they have been born and bred in Hell. With quiet peaceable and humane measures, I will make the most refractory see that it is to their interest to behave well . . . To turn in men for flogging because they . . . behave ill is utterly childish and the sure way to have constant trouble . . . It is easy to contrive punishment . . . which although slight in appearance will be sufficiently disagreeable – such as digging the swamp, sticking to the government ration or locking them up every night in a dark solitary cell . . . Work them like free people by task work with indulgences'. This was the prescription in 1823; it had 'succeeded admirably' with slaves in the West Indies. But as time went on his views hardened. 'We have utterly spoilt' these 'rogues' by 'pampering', he declared in 1825. 'We have been teasing ourselves to death and injuring both our health and our property in endeavouring to render ungrateful and irreclaimable profligates more comfortable than they ever have been in their lives'. 'Strict discipline' alone could do any good with a 'set of miscreants . . . unfit to live anywhere unless loaded with heavy, permanent irons . . .' This too was the attitude adopted, on his own testimony, by Mudie, at Patricks Plains; he may have given his men proper rations, but he describes several floggings ordered for apparently little reason. A government inquiry found his servants' complaints 'for the most part unfounded', but he was told that his overseer had acted 'imprudently and unjustifiably' in striking his servants, and had been 'reprehensible' in bringing a servant to be

[1] Report, 1828, Arthur Papers, v, ML; Col. Sec.'s Corr., 1/13669 (Brodribb), 16398 (Hudspeth); cf. 1/398 where a master was warned not to overstrain the power he possessed of preventing a servant escaping.

punished twice for the same offence. Such a mild reproof speaks volumes for the general standards of the colony, and Mudie was not deprived of his servants for the future. Probably he was no worse than many, though it sometimes seems surprising that 'outrages' against overseers, masters and their property were not more frequent.[1]

Hobler's diary reveals much that went on, even under Arthur's jurisdiction. When building a cottage, the government stonemasons worked on Sundays against the rules, as they did at the harvest, thanks to 'very high encouragement in the shape of wine and tobacco'; a similar 'bribe' to a free servant was unsuccessful, Thomas 'lolling on his bed while my corn can go to the Devil . . . When rid of him, I will not again be annoyed by such vermin as free servants. Over ticket of leave men one may have some influence'. One of the servants was constantly 'out at night' hoping to get at 'our government women'; his example would 'spoil a regiment', but the 'fellow can work and therefore must not hastily be thrown up'. On another occasion a new servant was said to be a carpenter; he was not, but his father was one, and it seemed to be 'presumed the qualification is hereditary'; but, since hands were short, he had to make do, and at least the convicts were not always demanding excessive wages.[2]

When a number of the servants were taken to magistrates to be flogged, in December 1828, 'at my request' the sentence was suspended 'until further misconduct', for 'the knowledge of the strictness of the discipline he is exposed to will answer my purpose as well as the actual punishment, which as far as it can be done I wish to avoid'; but next September there was no reprieve for a man reported for refusing work, and the sentence was fifty lashes. 'I have now had sufficient experience of convict servants to be convinced of the impossibility of their being kept in any order without from time to time an example of this nature,' wrote Hobler. It was 'nearly twelve months' since the last flogging. 'I will feed them well . . . and make them . . . more comfortable than honest labourers at home, and in return I will exact a fair proportion of labour, but above all things, subordination and civility'. Three more floggings followed before the end of the year. 'I have now 15 prisoners who do the whole work of the farm without my paying 1s. in wages, but

[1] Berry to Wollstonecraft, 25 Feb. 1829, 7 June 1823, 13 Oct. 1825, 8 Dec. 1826, Berry Papers, ML, xi and xii; cf. *Sydney Gazette*, 4 Feb. and 1 April 1826, *Monitor*, 3 March 1828; Mudie, *Vindication*, vi and 50–1; Bourke to Stanley, 20 Sept. 1834, encl. M'Leay to Larnack, 13 Jan., CO 201/240, 280 ff.; another outrage, cf. Bourke to Goderich, 20 Aug. 1832, encl. W. Dun to Bourke, 16 Feb. 1832.
[2] Hobler Diary, 23–4 March, 20 Sept., 20 Dec. 1827; 13 March, 13 April, 22 Nov. 1828; 20 March, 8 Sept. 1829, ML, C422–5.

how much looking after they require . . .' Two more in February–'I do sincerely hope my firmness in these . . . will have the desired effect and do away with that sluggish and insubordinate spirit . . . It is very painful for me to be obliged to flog in this manner, but if I give way to them at all, they at once become my masters'. Unfortunately, in 1832, instead of being 'well flogged and returned to his work', one of the men was sent to the roads, 'thereby punishing me instead of him', for such work, though in irons, was 'no punishment'. The governor, complained Hobler, 'wants to abstain from the only punishment that causes harm to these trebly distilled villains', (i.e. flogging) so the magistrates deprive masters of their servants.[1]

If conditions were often hard, if the men had to live in huts with 'roofs of stringy bark laid on sapling rafters tied with cords from a kurrajong tree' and beds of 'wooden slabs covered with bark', if their food was tough and their work hard, the squatters in the 1830s were little better off themselves; or as Lord Birkenhead once remarked, 'the position of the well-behaved man was not much worse than that of a seaman in the navy or a deckhand on a clipper'. But as too often in the army or navy, punishments were brutal, and, among the convicts, haphazard; if flogging was less in assigned service than on government establishments, it was far too common; to many of the settlers a convict was just 'a slave, a machine for making money by . . . merciless over-working'. Against ill-treatment he could seek protection only from the magistrates; but, said Bourke in 1834, they were men 'directly interested in maintaining the strictest subordination and in exacting the most laborious exertion which the law permits'.[2]

Bench Books show what Eyre described as 'a natural bias' in favour of the masters' evidence. One observer even thought the magistrates *ought* to 'lean to the settler even at the expense of *legal* justice', for 'equality' only encouraged the 'refractory disposition of the Convicts'. Whether this was so or not, complaints against convict servants were rarely dismissed; though Lieutenant-Colonel Breton told Bourke that sometimes when the men properly complained and their masters struck them, they were punished for making 'vexatious' complaints when they

---

[1] *Ib.*, 8 May, 9 Nov. 1827; 26–7 Feb., 30 Sept., 1 Dec. 1828; 17 Jan., 1 April, 19 Sept., 22 Oct., 3 and 10 Nov., 23 Dec. 1829; 23–4 Feb., 23 June, 16 Aug., 6 and 16 Oct. 1830; 20 Feb. 1832; 3 March 1836.
[2] Birkenhead (ed.), *Ralph Rashleigh*, introduction, ii; Bourke to Stanley, 15 Jan. 1834; Stephen's minute on Hall to Goderich, 9 Feb. 1832, CO 201/230, f.48; to magistrates, 19 Aug. 1830, Col. Sec.'s Out-Letters, Circulars, 30/40. Harington to Hely, 27 Nov. 1830, 23 Nov. 1831, *ib.*, 30/1004, 31/1101, and many others order withdrawal of servants from unsatisfactory masters.

carried their grievance to the magistrates. That is not to say that most of the latter did not try to do their duty fairly as honourable and high-minded men in a difficult position; but they did not always succeed. 'The prisoners would behave if their masters and especially the magistrates would do them justice', was Breton's verdict.[1] Here is a case from Port Stephens:[2]

'28 Dec. John Flannelly – servant of Lieutenant W. Caswell. Accuser Lt. W. Caswell, retired R.N. Idleness and insolence. To receive 25 lashes.

'28 Dec. John Flannelly – do. do. Disturbing the peace of his master's family on Christmas Day. Reprimanded and discharged.

'29 Dec. John Flannelly – do. do. Shoving and colaring [sic] his master. To receive 50 lashes.'

So idleness rebuked led to insolence and punishment; anger at this led to assault and further punishment. All this created angry feelings on the one hand, and 'a slave-owning mentality', as Bourke put it, on the other.

Magisterial control over the assigned servants and their masters naturally varied according to the personalities on the various Benches, but the laxities and prejudices disclosed in the Ring and Rumsby cases did not disappear overnight, despite M'Leay's instructions in April 1826. The magistrates at Minto seem to have been active and efficient; on the other hand, those at Windsor had thought for six years that a convict farmer there was a free man. At Bathurst, a convict insurrection in 1831 was said to be due to masters' ill-treatment of their servants; but when, after complaints about insufficient rations to the servants of a Mr. McKenzie had *twice* been upheld by the local bench, and after the Executive Council reaffirmed its policy that 'well-grounded complaints should be redressed' and ordered McKenzie's servants to be withdrawn, only two were removed.[3]

This control was made more difficult by the need for more stipendiary magistrates and the lack of men willing and suitable to be made honorary

[1] Bench Books, Dungog, ML, A1582, Cawdor and Stonequarry Creek, ML, A1772–6; Eyre, Autobiography; John Henderson, 13; Criminal Law Report, PP 1847 (637), evid. Bourke, 4213 ff.; Breton to Bourke, 21 Feb. 1834, Bourke Papers, xi, ML; Lyndsay Gardiner, ch. 7.
[2] Port Stephens Bench Book, 1834, quoted, Young, 80.
[3] Exec. Council Minutes, iii, no. 1, 6 Jan. 1831; M'Leay to Hely, 18 Jan. 1831, Col. Sec.'s Out-Letters, Assignment Board, 31/52; Windsor Police Office, Letter Books, ML, A1398, 1 and 3 Sept. 1830; Col. Sec.'s Out-Letters, 30/614; M'Leay to Land Board, 21 Oct., 2 Nov. 1831, Col. Sec.'s Out-Letters, 31/975, 1020.

justices. In New South Wales in 1827, twenty were civil officials; there were only thirty-two 'independent gentlemen' like the justices in England; twenty-one military officers had had to be appointed to make good the deficiency. When he arrived Bourke favoured the English practice, which incidentally provided an independent check on the governor's power; but by 1834 he had come round to Darling's opinion (and Arthur's practice), that the 'stipendiaries', usually military, 'cannot with propriety be dispensed with', for he had found the 'independents' unreliable. In 1832, he had had to reprimand those concerned with the 'trial' of the servants of John Bingle, J.P., in his own house by a fellow magistrate who was a guest there; three years later he had to remove a number from the commission of the peace.[1]

How far was Arthur's system reformatory? In a study of it, Miss McKay concluded that roughly about one-fifth of the convicts' masters showed a sincere concern for rehabilitating their servants, and another two-fifths were men who encouraged their convicts for their own interests. Twenty per cent relied on punishment rather than encouragement and the remainder were almost pure slave-drivers. Certainly, as Arthur admitted, the men were 'infinitely better fed and clothed than the common field labourer in England', and could obtain high wages when set free; but this material improvement was desirable, for the convicts' condition must 'never approach the inhuman'; 'to the mass of prisoners transportation is perfect slavery and is a most severe punishment', and '*if Reformation form part of your plan*, you must be merciful and make some concessions to meritorious conduct even in a Convict'. These assigned service could provide. The prisoner was separated from 'the most depraved' and had 'an opportunity of redeeming his reputation'. Self-interest, if nothing else, made settlers take trouble in 'watching, advising and actually reforming' their servants, James Ross insisted. This was much better than the penitentiaries which Archbishop Whately and others praised so highly, but whose 'reforming' efficacy was only asserted and not proved, while at the same time, they suggested that if convicts benefited by their transportation, their 'reform' was 'proof of its inefficiency' as a punishment.[2]

Arthur's puritanism caused him to stress the importance of religious

[1] Darling to Bathurst, 31 Jan. 1827, to Murray, 3 Feb. 1831, to Goderich, 20 June; Bourke to Goderich, 3 Nov. 1832, to Stanley, 29 Sept. 1833, 24 Jan., 15 April 1834; M'Leay to Bingle, 28 May 1832, Bingle Papers, ML, A1825; Bourke to Stanley, 24 Aug. 1832, to Glenelg, 28 Feb. 1836.
[2] Anne McKay, 355; Arthur to Bathurst, 23 March 1827; to Hay, 1 May 1827, 3 April 1829, to Stephen, 23 April 1835, CO 280/14, 20, 57; Ross, *Almanack*, 1833, art. Prison Discipline, 47–8, 58–95, 99; *ib*., 1835, letter to Whately, 314–6.

teaching.[1] Unfortunately many masters preferred work to church, and the religious establishments in both New South Wales and Van Diemen's Land were too small. Backhouse and Walker were disappointed that not even so wealthy a 'master' as the Van Diemen's Land Company provided any religious teaching or educational facilities at any of its settlements. Arthur thought that the government 'should interpose in this matter much more earnestly and zealously than it has hitherto done . . . [for] securing for the Convicts the privilege of attending Divine Service at least once every Sunday'; after all, as he later told Fowell Buxton, an 'inward regulator in the heart' was ten times more effectual 'than all the fear and alarm that could be exerted from without'.[2] He wanted more clergy, especially Methodists, and men of 'the Evangelical party in the Church of England'. 'Do pray assist my views in obtaining a reinforcement of the Church and School Establishment', he asked Stephen in 1835; unfortunately this request, like similar ones from Bourke and like those for more superintendents, constables, troops, clerks and gaols weakened the argument for economy which so strongly appealed to the British government.[3]

For all that, whether the reason was better control or more reformation, as time went on major crimes (including stealing, but not including such offences as disobedience, idleness, insolence, negligence, absconding, adultery or even wife-beating) became noticeably fewer. From a random sample of a hundred convicts who arrived before 1820, the records show that thirty-six were later convicted of sixty-five major crimes, and from another equal sample who arrived between 1821 and 1824, thirty-one were so convicted; but from a sample from 1827–9 arrivals, only twenty-three per cent were found guilty of such crimes, from 1830–1 arrivals, only twenty per cent, and from 1832–3 arrivals, only fourteen per cent, despite the fact that in the last group twice as many as in the first had previous convictions before being transported. In New South Wales the situation was better. From 1831 to 1835, 2,087 persons of all types were convicted of felonies or misdemeanours in the

---

[1] Arthur to Bishop of London, 24 Dec. 1817, to his sister, Betsy, 1818, 8 Nov. 1819, Arthur Papers, Royal Commonwealth Society, London, Letter Books, 6 and 7; to Montagu, 27 Jan. 1837, Arthur Papers, v, ML.
[2] Arthur to Bathurst, 15 Aug. 1824, to Bishop of London, 10 Oct. 1826, Arthur Papers, v, ML; Col. Sec.'s Corr., 17 July 1830, 1/7891; Arthur to Fowell Buxton, 27 Jan. 1835, Lieut.-Gov.'s Letter Book (Tas.); Backhouse and Walker Reports, i, 65 ff. and 198 ff.; Backhouse, *Narrative*, app. F, xlvi, lii–liv.
[3] Arthur to Glenelg, 13 Aug. 1836, Arthur Papers, iv, ML; Arthur to Stephen, 23 April 1835, CO 280/57; Arthur to Goderich, 27 Feb. and 1 July 1833, to Stanley, 14 Oct. 1833, to Hay, 30 Jan. 1834, to Glenelg, 15 Oct. 1835; Bourke to Goderich, 28 Feb. 1832, to Stanley, 30 Sept. 1833, to Glenelg, 18 Dec. 1835.

Supreme Court and Quarter Sessions. If every person found guilty was a prisoner, this would amount to three per cent of the convict population, or the same as in Van Diemen's Land; hence if the expirees and others were not surprisingly law-abiding on the mainland, the convicts there were about twice as well-behaved as further south.[1]

Colonel Breton told the Transportation Committee that in Argyle less than a quarter of the convicts were brought before the magistrates each year for breaches of discipline, but evidence to the New South Wales Council's inquiry on Police and Gaols in 1835 would suggest that there, as in Patrick's Plains, Windsor, Bathurst, Penrith and Argyle itself, the proportion was about half, and it was higher in Sydney and the gangs. In Van Diemen's Land, between 1833 and 1836, nearly three-quarters of the prisoners were brought before the courts each year; of these about three-quarters charged with offences against convict discipline, such as insolence, negligence or disobedience, more than another ten per cent charged with drunkenness and disorderly conduct, and about the same number with other misdemeanours; less than four per cent of those charged, or three per cent of all the convicts each year, were accused of serious crimes while under discipline. Unfortunately, for those whose sentence had expired it was a different matter. Between 1831 and 1837, about a fifth of all the emancipists were convicted of 'serious' offences before the Supreme Court or Quarter Sessions; though some of them had not reaped the full benefit of Arthur's 'improvements' in discipline, perhaps he was justified in thinking about a quarter of the prisoners 'irreclaimable'. But this left three-quarters who were, and he insisted that an assigned servant had a better prospect of being reformed than a prisoner under any other system, though one might wonder that any were, if George Loveless, the 'Tolpuddle martyr', was fair when he wrote of the 'greater part' of the men being 'such monsters as I never expected to see and whose conduct I am not capable of describing'.[2]

Good character and good behaviour under discipline were not necessarily synonymous. Only eleven per cent of those who arrived between 1830 and 1833 succeeded in maintaining a 'clean sheet'; but some of the best behaved had bad English records, including previous convictions and men described as 'very bad', 'most depraved' and so on. One man, transported for fourteen years on a third conviction, having been eight

---

[1] Convict Record Books, Tas.; Macarthur, app. 4.
[2] *Transportation Report*, 1837, evid. Breton, 144–9, Arthur, 4287, 4350, 4592 ff.; Police and Gaols, Report, NSW Legs. Council, *V & P*, 1835, 329 ff.; Montagu, *Statistical Returns*; Convict Record Books; Returns, 1 Jan. 1833, 31 Dec. 1834, 31 Dec. 1835, 30 July 1838, 13 June 1840, CO 280/39, 57, 66, 96, 120; Loveless, 11.

times in prison, and regarded as a 'very bad character' in his home county of Bedfordshire, was but once drunk (fined five shillings), received his ticket-of-leave in 1838 and a conditional pardon in 1841. Of nine with 'good' English records in 1826, four 'did well' in the colony and two very badly; of thirteen 'goods' in 1836, seven were 'good' after they arrived, two bad, and the rest moderate, but Surgeon-Superintendent Browning told Montagu that it was 'not easy to speak too highly' of seventeen convicts whom the Home Office had especially recommended for hard labour because of their 'bad' past records.[1]

The agricultural rioters who were transported in 1831 were a different kettle of fish. Most were agricultural labourers and rural craftsmen. They behaved in a 'most exemplary manner' after landing, and in three months 'none . . . were convicted of the most trifling offence, a circumstance unprecedented in the history of the colony'. Just on half were punished for minor misdemeanours during the rest of their sentences, but on the average they committed only about one-third as many as the normal male convict. Only a dozen were convited of serious crimes, and nearly all were pardoned in 1836 or 1837.[2]

As in all 'open prisons', which is what New South Wales and Van Diemen's Land were for assigned convicts, discipline depended not only on punishment, but also on the existence of rewards as incentives to good conduct. The grant of a free passage to the wives and children (boys had to be under ten) of recommended prisoners, which had been begun in Macquarie's time, in the 1830s applied to an average of nearly two hundred a year; it was a small substitute for government's refusal to repatriate expirees, but since only about a quarter of the male convicts were married, and some doubtless had no wish to see their wives again, it was not insignificant, for it satisfied nearly a sixth of the prisoners who had families.[3]

Of much greater significance was the ticket-of-leave. Macquarie's regulations about tickets were tightened a little by the order of 1823; more important after that they were strictly watched. The ticket was not a *right*, and convicts had no *claim* to indulgence, but they were *eligible*, if well-behaved for four, six or eight years according to the length of their sentence. In New South Wales, the better keeping of the

[1] Convict Record Books; Bedfordshire Gaol Book, Bedford Archives, re Crouch, convicted 3 Jan. 1832; Browning to Montagu, 20 June 1836, Arthur Papers, xxix, ML.
[2] Gunn to Arthur, 9 July 1831, Col. Sec.'s Corr., 1/11376; Bischoff (VDL Co.) to Howick, 8 Jan. 1831, CO 280/32; Arthur to Goderich, 8 Feb. 1833; Glenelg to Arthur, 7 Aug. 1835; Convict Record Books; Rudé, 'Popular Disturbances', *Hist. Stud.*, x, 464, 'Captain Swing and VDL', *Tas. Hist. Assoc.*, xii, 12.
[3] Bourke to Goderich, 20 Nov. 1832; Annual returns of recommendations, CO 201 and 280.

convict registers and the more rigid adherence to the prescribed minimum periods of good behaviour cut down many of the abuses connected
with the tickets which had worried Lord Bathurst for so long. In 1826
Darling forbade ticket-holders to be assigned a convict servant or to
hold a publican's licence, and ordered the issue of tickets to convicts
who changed their master to be delayed, unless 'it shall clearly appear
that their removal from their places was not occasioned by misconduct'.
Men who 'habitually' neglected divine service, if within five miles of a
place of worship were to be reported; on the other hand, tickets might
be granted 'early' to those who assisted in capturing offenders or gave
information about them.[1]

Like the rest of the system, much depended on magisterial control,
and some benches, when making their recommendations, were occasionally misinformed or lax; but Bourke watched the applications as well as
Arthur (if less flamboyantly) and tickets were certainly not freely handed
out, as so many English critics asserted. In 1839, only 6,026 out of
38,605 convicts in the colony had tickets; between 1825 and 1836 fewer
than one-fifth of those who were qualified by time received them; in
1839, the proportion was still only about a quarter in New South Wales
compared with one-third in Van Diemen's Land.[2]

There Governor Arthur undertook 'much personal labour' in considering these claims, because of the effect the granting of each ticket
had 'upon the general efficiency of secondary punishment'. In 1833,
only ten per cent of the convicts had them, or about a sixth of those
eligible by effluxion of time; although by 1837, a quarter of all the
convicts had them, between 1834 and 1837 Arthur refused more
than half the applications that were made and granted tickets only to
about one-third of those who were eligible. Whether these men were
'reformed' is another matter, but a convict who wanted one had to
behave, though in 1827, a prisoner received his ticket because he had
been 'often useful to the police', though 'a very drunken character' who
had often been punished for misbehaviour.[3] In 1834, when settlement

---

[1] Brisbane to Bathurst, 28 April 1823, encl. G. and G.O., 7 Nov. 1822; Darling to Bathurst,
1 May 1826, 2 Jan. 1827, encl. Govt. Order, 1 Jan.; Forbes to Horton, 6 Feb. 1827, *HRA*,
IV, i, 685.
[2] Hely to Col. Sec., 17 Sept. 1830, In-Letters, 9/44 A1398; Governor's Mem., 7 March
1831; M'Leay to Land Board, 9 and 16 May 1831, Col. Sec.'s Out-Letters, 31/365, 398;
Governor's Mins., nos. 3492, 3580, 3685, 22 Dec. 1835, 7 March and 27 July 1836; returns,
tickets-of-leave, *HRA*, xii, 268, xiii, 83 and 691, xiv, 317 and 649, CO 201/216, 2 April
1830, PP 1830 (585), 1838, CO 280/96; Crowley, 183-5.
[3] Arthur to Goderich, 1 Dec. 1827, encl. mem., 19 Nov.; applications for tickets, Nov. 1832,
Transportation Report, 1837, app. 1, 20 ff.; Arthur to Glenelg, 6 June 1836; Convict Records,

across Bass Strait was mooted, the Governor suggested to London that well-behaved ticket-holders might be given a pardon 'on condition of residing in Southern Australia', to 'draft off part of our Convict population' and make room for more to be 'certainly punished and probably reformed' in Van Diemen's Land; but though pardons on condition of remaining in the colony had been granted almost since the foundation of the settlement, this idea of spreading expirees throughout Australia was not taken up until the island had become overcrowded with convicts ten years later.[1]

By this time the status of ticket-holders in both colonies had been worsened by a British act passed in 1832. This unreservedly forbade 'early' grants, which hitherto local regulations had permitted in special cases, particularly as a reward for capturing runaways, and by not allowing them to sue or be sued took away all legal protection from their property. Both Bourke and Arthur protested repeatedly that this would deprive the convicts of an incentive to reform and allow them to be swindled, and Bourke recommended more conditional pardons to evade the restrictions, but though successive Colonial Secretaries agreed with the governors and promised to amend the law, nothing was done until 1842.[2]

In New South Wales, decisions of the Supreme Court for a time had weakened the government's control over the system. The Governor insisted that through the Principal Superintendent and the local benches he must be able to restrict the movements of assigned servants, fix their place of residence, and see that they were kept at work, were properly looked after and that their masters were respectable persons. The usual sanction against masters who were said to have broken the regulations was simply to withdraw their servants, by executive order; but in 1827, this was held to be illegal, though, complained Darling, it had been 'always acquiesced in'. Such revocation of assignments, whether to give a convict servant a ticket-of-leave, or because a master was said to have broken the regulations, was a possible engine of tyranny, for it affected the value of the settlers' estates. 'Without labour, land in this Colony is useless, and the only laborers . . . are assigned Prisoners,'

Arthur Papers, xxxv, ML; Returns, 30 July 1838, CO 280/96; Col. Sec.'s Corr., 1/4811, 16110, 13/3087.
[1] Arthur to Hay, commenting on memorial of James Henty, March 1834, quoted Bassett, 288.
[2] 2 and 3 Wm. IV c.62, limited the discretion allowed by 9 Geo. IV c.83, s. 9. Bourke to Goderich, 29 Nov. 1832; Stanley to Bourke, 4 Sept. 1833; Bourke to Stanley, 18 Oct. 1834; Arthur to Goderich, 8 Feb. 1833, to Hay, 26 Feb.; cf. to Bourke, 2 Feb., ML, A1962; NSW Act, 5 and 6 Vic. c. 76

declared Chief Justice Forbes.[1] The English Law Officers supported Forbes' interpretation of the Transportation Act of 1824; but if assignments were irrevocable, the servant became no more than a slave. To this, naturally enough, the British government was opposed, so it inserted a clause in the New South Wales Act of 1828 explicitly giving the Governor power to revoke assignments and so restoring his control.[2]

The 'controverted question' thus seemed 'set at rest', but Judge Forbes and Judge Stephen, in their suspicion of Darling, suggested that the Governor's power was still limited. By this time, James Stephen was showing signs of impatience. 'The New South Wales affair has taught me that you soldiers are not more dangerous depositories of irresponsible authority than are the lawyers', he had written to Arthur, in December 1828. 'If a man be honest, and a soldier, . . . he will be imperious, but high minded and unimpeachably honourable; if he be honest and a lawyer . . . he will be most dogmatical and mulish . . . Your objections to the powers of the Chief Justice in the old act are very just'.[3] The Judges, wrote the Secretary of State, Sir George Murray, were 'blameable' for 'departing from the true intention of the law in order to give a cavilling interpretation of its meaning' and this with an 'imputation of having done so from a factious motive'; their decision was 'declared by the highest legal authorities to be destitute of even a plausible foundation'. The Transportation Act was not intended to supply the colonists with labour, but to punish criminals and to save public expense; the settler had no right of property in the labour of the convicts assigned to him; this was a 'mere indulgence: a temporary, revocable loan of services, for which he has given no consideration . . . a benefit held at the pleasure of the Crown'. Thereafter Darling removed convicts from masters who did not seem to him

[1] Circular to Magistrates, 10 April 1826, HRA, xii, 329–30; Darling to Bathurst, 1 March 1827; ib., 3 Aug., encl. Govt. notice 30 July, and Forbes to Darling, 1 Aug.; Darling to Goderich, 8 Nov. 1827, encl. Forbes to Darling, 3 Oct.; Bathurst to Darling, 19 Feb. 1827, encl. Hobhouse to Hay, 13 Feb.; Forbes' opinion, ex parte Jane New, 21 March 1829, encl. in Darling to Murray, 20 May.
[2] Transportation Act, 1824, 5 Geo. IV c.84, sec. 8. Stephen thought it a 'most extraordinary enactment, very inconsiderately framed', 8 Aug. 1827, CO 201/183, 145–54; Law Officers to Huskisson, 17 Dec. 1827, CO 201/185, 408 ff.; Hay to Darling, 14 Feb. 1828, CO 324/86; Murray to Darling, 30 Aug. 1828. In his report on Darling's Instructions, 27 March 1825, HRA, IV, i, 607 ff., Stephen had suggested that the Governor could make conditional assignments; cf. Hobhouse to Hay, 13 Feb. 1827, encl. in Bathurst to Darling, 19 Feb. NSW Act, 1828, 9 Geo. IV c.83, sec. 9.
[3] Murray to Darling, 30 Aug. 1828; Murray's minute, 24 Dec. 1829, CO 201/205; Stephen to Arthur, 3 Dec. 1828, Arthur Papers, iv, ML.

to be fulfilling their obligations, just as Arthur had always done.[1] Though the legal technicalities involved were as irritating to the non-legal mind, including that of the Governor, as they nearly always are, the ill-feeling between him and the Chief Justice embittered the controversy. In the end Forbes had been roundly told to behave himself; but the justification for his conduct lay in a not altogether unwarranted fear that Darling would use any powers given to him less to protect the convict than to harass his political opponents, and the only redress against 'a possibly vexatious exercise of this authority' seemed to be a reproof from the Secretary of State. In fact, in due course this arrived, when Darling withdrew servants from the editors of the opposition newspapers, the *Australian* and *Monitor*, whose ceaseless attacks on his administration he had for three years been vainly trying to curb. He was told to act only after consulting his Executive Council. 'Whatever your motives may have been (and I am bound to suppose they were unexceptionable), yet it would be vain to expect from the Public at large any other construction than that you were endeavouring by this use of your power to harass a political opponent,' wrote Murray. 'I deeply regret that any ground whatever should have been given for such an imputation, however well I may myself be convinced of its injustice. . . . You will distinctly understand that the benefit of the Convict is to be the principal, if not the exclusive consideration for your guidance in the exercise of this power . . . It would be a total abuse of this trust, if it were used as a resource for patronage, or as an instrument for punishing offences against your own Person.'[2]

Certainly assignment had its problems. 'There is no one subject half so embarrassing or perplexing,' Darling told Macarthur in 1831. When only about half the applications for servants could be granted, there was plenty of scope for criticism of alleged patronage. The Assignment Board, which Darling established when he arrived, was attacked for favouritism, though at least one impartial observer, Atkinson, thought the distribution perfectly fair. Regulations declared that new arrivals, settlers in the country, and 'other claims being equal, persons of moral character who pay due attention to the conduct of their servants' were to receive preference; for a time assignment in Sydney was forbidden,

[1] Murray to Darling, 30 Jan. 1830, encl. H. Twiss's report, 1 Dec. 1829; Darling to Murray, 9 Aug. 1830, encl. Forbes to Murray, 19 July. For the Judges' bias, Darling to Goderich, 16 Jan. 1828, encl. Forbes and Stephen to Darling, 31 Dec. 1827, Baxter and Foster to Darling, 29 Dec., commenting on the trial of Wardell for libel; magistrates, 19 Aug. 1830, Col. Sec.'s Out-Letters, Circulars, 30/40.

[2] Murray to Darling, 30 Aug. 1828, 30 Jan. 1830; Murray's Minute, Jan. 1830, CO 201/205, 276–7; Murray to Darling, 3 May, 8 Nov. 1830.

though in 1830 M'Leay told the Board that tradesmen in town 'must be attended to in their turn, as well as persons residing in the country'. Masters who frequently returned servants to the government, who treated them badly, who hired them out, who did not reside or have a free overseer, or who were ticket-of-leave holders themselves were not to receive servants.[1]

By regulations first issued in February 1834 and confirmed after minor amendment next year, Bourke substituted 'an intelligible qualification and a strict routine of business in lieu of discretionary power' to 'reconcile many interests that were thought incompatible . . . dispose equitably and productively of the services of the convicts' and so to put an end to accusations of favouritism. One convict was to be allotted for every 160 acres of land owned and another for every forty acres cultivated, up to a maximum of seventy men (though on a diminishing scale for cultivated farms over 160 acres). A mechanic was to count as two or three labourers, according to his trade. The Assignment Board was abolished and replaced by a single Commissioner for Assignment. All ordinary convicts were to be assigned in the country, and as far as possible mechanics too. To prevent the magistrates abusing their power, none was to be withdrawn without the Governor's order; to check his possible favouritism, the magistrates could withhold assignees; as a final safeguard, lists of servants were to be published.[2]

These regulations helped to reduce the numbers asked for, but some exclusives disliked small farmers having servants, either because this reduced the number available for themselves, or because they thought these men were unfitted to have prisoners in their charge. The small settlers were 'not much more civil . . . than the naked Savage of the Woods', old John Macarthur had told Darling in 1831. Why should men so 'bred to labour' have servants?[3] But not to have them might mean ruin, and in any case were all the large settlers above reproach? Apparently Bourke thought the small farmer could be trusted for when he had more convicts available in 1836, he allotted a labourer to settlers with as few as twenty acres. Certainly in 1838 there were

[1] Darling to Macarthur, 4 July 1831, Macarthur Papers, iv, 274, ML; Darling to Hay, 2 Feb. 1826, encl. G. and G.O., 5 Jan.; Regs. for Assignment Board, 9 March 1826, *HRA*; xii, 252-3; *Monitor*, 16 March 1827; E. S. Hall to Murray, 12 March 1829, *HRA*, xv, 56, Atkinson, 115; Darling to Bathurst, 17 March 1827; M'Leay to Land Board, 27 Nov. 1830, Col. Sec.'s Out-Letters; cf. Darling to Goderich, 21 June 1832, Misc. Papers, ML, A2146 99 ff.
[2] Bourke to the Secretary of State, 26 June 1835; *Transportation Report*, 1837, app. 8, no. 1, 203; *Monitor*, 4 Feb. 1834.
[3] Macarthur to Darling, July 1831, Macarthur Papers, i, 1334-5, ML; *Herald*, 25 May, 4 June 1835.

thousands of unsatisfied applications; but assignment was then on its last legs. Some employers were making a last effort to get convicts before it was too late, and others were ready to indulge in propaganda to encourage the government's immigration programmes.[1] Although Downing Street ordered Bourke to make a special assignment of five hundred men to the Australian Agricultural Company in 1836, Bourke's regulations in 1834 deprived the governor of his patronage in servants just as the 'Ripon regulations' had ended his patronage in land grants. Arthur had certainly found his patronage useful in Van Diemen's Land, and Bourke, perhaps depressed by the death of his wife, regretted being 'almost wholly deprived of those means of influence which in former times were exerted with effect for the support of authority'. He found governing 'the exercise of a succession of ungracious offices . . . the rejection of unreasonable claims, the resistance of encroachment on Crown property, the Collection of Rents, Debts and Taxes'.[2] But, if patronage was sometimes useful, it was a double-edged weapon. 'Every man who cannot obtain Land and Convict Servants as he wishes thinks . . . he has a right to complain of the Governor's injustice,' Darling had lamented just before he left, perhaps thinking of his refusal of both to E. S. Hall, editor of the *Monitor*; its reduction was desirable from the point of view of both government and governed, and was a step towards the constitutional ideals of a more liberal state.[3]

The extent of government patronage, like the wide powers of the magistrates and of the police, seemed all the more potentially dangerous to liberty in a colony whose citizens lacked the traditional freedoms of Englishmen, which could be used to check executive abuses. Both Darling and Arthur were accused of tyranny and nepotism, yet just as the presence of the convicts made a strong executive necessary, so it delayed the introduction of a free press, of trial by jury and of representative institutions. In 1769 Blackstone had declared that English colonists took with them to an uninhabited country only so much of English law as is applicable to their new situation, 'so the birthright of every English subject' belonged to them only with 'very many and very great restrictions'. The instructions given to Phillip and his successors made them autocrats, and Bathurst warned Macquarie in 1812 that

---

[1] Governor's Mins., 16 Dec. 1835; returns, 1835, CO 201/248; p. 272 below; NSW Legs. Council, *Immigration, Report*, and evid. Slade, *V & P*, 1838.

[2] Glenelg to Bourke, 19 Aug. 1835; Bourke to Glenelg, 6 Oct. 1835; Glenelg to Bourke. 1 Feb., 23 April 1836; Darling to Goderich, 14 July 1831; Bourke to Goderich, 24 Aug. 1832.

[3] Darling to Hay, 12 Sept. 1826, to Murray, 2 Jan. 1829, 12 April 1830.

there was a great danger in 'weakening the higher authorities in a society composed of such discordant materials'. He was mindful of the settlers' rebellion against Bligh as well as of the convicts, but later on it was the large number of former prisoners among the free population which was thought to be the major obstacle to the extension of its rights.[1] Bathurst had told Darling that complete freedom of the press in New South Wales was 'highly dangerous'. Hay thought Brisbane's removal of the censorship 'unfortunate'; 'one might as well permit a radical newspaper to be published in Newgate', wrote Field to Marsden; but though even the 'liberal' Judge Forbes in 1826 supported restrictions, Darling did nothing for a year, apparently preferring to let sleeping dogs lie.[2] Burnett's complaint from Van Diemen's Land was equally applicable to New South Wales. 'One of the greatest obstacles to the prosperity of a penal Colony . . . is . . . a licentious and unrestrained press, which unceasingly endeavours to thwart the Government by expatiating on the cruelty of . . . every regulation which is adopted for the better discipline and safe custody of the convicts.' 'Your newspapers call loudly for correction,' wrote Hay to Darling in July 1827, and by that time the Governor had convinced himself that they had 'succeeded in exciting a strong spirit of discontent among the prisoners'. Forbes disagreed, and he held illegal both Darling's proposal to make the newspaper publishers take out a 'revocable licence', though it had been suggested by Bathurst and Chief Justice Pedder made no objection in Van Diemen's Land, and also a proposed heavy stamp duty of fourpence on every copy of the papers.[3] The British government agreed with Forbes, but Darling pursued the newspaper editors with libel actions for two years, always hoping that the British Parliament would impose further restraints on them; when it did not do so, he persuaded his own legislature to tighten up the libel law. This would 'silence all except the Governor's supporters', said Stephen; this was Darling's 'real object', and the Act was 'in its whole frame and spirit repugnant to the laws of England'; though agreeing that in a convict colony severer

[1] Blackstone, i, 107; Phillip's Second Commission, *HRA*, i, 2–8; Bathurst to Macquarie, 13 Nov. 1812; *Transportation Report*, 1812, 8; Melbourne, 116–7; Campbell, *JRAHS*, l, 61.
[2] Bathurst to Darling, 12 July 1825; Stephen to Arthur, 24 Aug. 1824, Arthur Papers, iv, ML; Hay to Darling, 31 Oct. 1826, CO 324/85, cf. 26 Dec., *ib.*; Hay's minute on Darling to Hay, 23 March 1827, CO 201/181, 423; Field to Marsden, Marsden Papers, ML, i, 460; Forbes to Horton, 4 Dec. 1826, Forbes Papers, ¡ML, A1819, f.62; *ib.*, 6 Feb., 27 May 1827, *HRA*, IV, i, 681, 719 ff.; Darling to Hay, 24 May 1826, to Murray, 21 Dec. 1830.
[3] Burnett to Hay, 18 March 1827, CO 323/149; Hay to Darling, 19 July 1827, CO 324/85; Darling to Bathurst, 8, 11, 29 May 1827, encl. corr. between Darling and Forbes; 8 Geo. IV nos. 2 and 3, *HRA*, xiii, 854; Forbes to Horton, 27 May 1827, *ib.*, IV, i, 719.

restraints on the press were necessary than in England, the Whigs, now in office in London, had a very different outlook from the Governor, and they could not allow this.[1]

This dispute, like a similar one in the Cape at the same time, underlined the restrictions on Englishmen's liberties in a socially divided colony. The traditional freedom of the press was impossible; so was an elected assembly, because respectable masters could not properly leave their properties to sit in it. New South Wales was a 'police state'. 'A great mass of the Population here must consider the Government in the odious light of a *Taskmaster* and Oppressor, and this feeling is increased by Settlers holding out its service *in terrorem* to their Servants . . . Men under the influence of such impressions *cannot be supposed to feel* well affected to a Government they are taught *only to dread*', Darling told Hay in 1827. 'The Executive does not possess a particle too much power,' he declared next year. 'The Laws of England were not made for Convicts; and a Convict Population requires more coercion than those Laws sanction.' 'Our prisoners are taught to think that necessary restraints are acts of injustice and uncalled for rigour,' wrote Dumaresq three years later; but, argued Darling, 'it surely is not . . . too much to expect that Individuals who make up their minds to reside in a Convict Colony, should conform to such rules as the peculiar nature of the Community, of which their interest or inclination has induced them to become Members, may render necessary for the Public good.'[2]

Arthur also thought it necessary to control the press, and was sorry that in 1828 the British government disallowed his newspaper Licensing Act. After he returned to London, he told Glenelg that 'notwithstanding the unpopularity of the measure, I very humbly but earnestly submit to your Lordship that . . . the press of Van Diemen's Land be put under some restraint, if it is to be retained as a penal colony'; he thought its character, with a 'peculiar institution', made a free press and trial by jury impossible, and rigid pass laws necessary.[3]

If, by 1830, the colonies, thanks to Downing Street's control of the governors, had won liberty for their press, subject to a stringent law of

[1] Hay to Darling, 25 Aug. 1830, CO 324/86; Darling to Murray, 4 Feb. 1830, encl. 11 Geo. IV, no. 1; Stephen to Murray, on this Act, 14 July 1830, CO 323/47; Goderich to Darling, 6 Jan. 1831; *ib.*, 15 March, CO 202/25; Darling to Goderich, 20, 26 July 1831; Stephen's minute on the former, CO 201/220.

[2] Index, CO 201/181; Darling to Hay, 4 Feb. 1827, CO 323/149, 9 Feb., *HRA*, xiii, 96; Darling to Huskisson, 1 March 1828; Dumaresq to Hay, 15 Jan. 1830, CO 323/162; Darling to Murray, 24 July 1830.

[3] Arthur to Hay, 12 March 1827, to Bathurst, 24 Sept. 1827, to Goderich, 27 Nov. 1827; Murray to Arthur, 25, 31 July 1828; Arthur to Murray, 2 Jan. 1829, to Hay, 26 Jan., 3 April 1829, 30 Jan. 1834, to Glenelg, 26 May 1837.

libel, they still lacked trial by jury. When the settlement was established, in 1787, Lord Chief Justice Camden had suggested to Pitt that this should be granted 'as soon as it can be done with propriety', and as long ago as 1811 both Macquarie and Ellis Bent had recommended it.[1] Civilian juries were ordered for the Quarter Sessions established in November 1824, under the New South Wales Act of 1823, but the question at once arose, were ex-convicts entitled to act as jurymen? It was widely assumed they were not, but, though generally excluded from the lists, they were occasionally empanelled after the British Transportation Act of 1824 and Jury Act of 1825 had been reported in the colony.[2] Most of the magistrates, and of course the emancipists' spokesmen, spoke well of them, but their enrolment was not regular, and civilian juries were not permitted in Supreme Court trials, except in civil cases when both parties agreed. By 1828, the emancipists had come to regard them as an indispensable part of their birthright, just as the 'exclusives' had come bitterly to oppose their introduction.

The former had hoped that the amending New South Wales Act, 1828, would grant trial by jury generally; instead, it removed juries from the Sessions.[3] Certainly the Act permitted the colonial government to decide on their reintroduction there and their extension to criminal cases in the Supreme Court; but to avoid dissension in the colony, the British government refused, temporarily, to make the Order-in-Council needed to authorize the colonial legislatures to act on the matter.[4] In 1830 it did so. Darling was told to provide for juries in cases where the governor or any of his officers were involved; but most of the members of the Legislative Council, even including Forbes, opposed any further change for the moment. 'No Colony, so long as it continues to be a receptacle for Criminals, can . . . be considered eligible to the possession of the English Constitution,' declared Darling, and Goderich agreed.[5]

[1] Camden to Pitt, 29 Jan. 1787, quoted, J. H. Rose, *William Pitt*, i, 439; Macquarie and Ellis Bent to Liverpool, 18 and 19 Oct. 1811, *HRA*, vii, 393, 814.

[2] *Sydney Gazette*, 21 Oct. 1824; Bannister to Horton, 8 Feb. 1825, *HRA*, IV, i, 583; Darling to Goderich, 24 Jan. 1828, encl. Forbes to Darling, 19 Jan.; J. M. Bennett, *Sydney Law Review*, 1961, 463; 5 Geo. IV c. 84; 6 Geo. IV c. 50. The alternative to a civilian jury was one composed of military officers.

[3] Magistrates' reports, encl. in Brisbane to Bathurst, 25 Oct. 1825; address to Brisbane, 26 Oct., *HRA*, IV, i, 627 ff.; petition, Jan. 1827, encl. in Darling to Hay, 9 Feb. 1827.

[4] Eagar to Murray, 1 July 1828, CO 201/197; Stephen's mem. 1828, CO 201/195, f.336; John Macarthur, Junior, to Horton, 11 and 14 July 1826, 4 June 1827, CO 201/179 and 188; Murray to Darling, 31 July 1828; *P. Debs.*, 1 and 18 April 1828, n.s., xviii, 1430, 1559; 9 Geo. IV c. 83.

[5] Murray to Darling, 7 April, 17 July 1830; Darling to Murray, 7 Oct. 1830; Goderich to Darling, 29 March 1831. The local jury acts were 10 Geo. IV, no. 8, 11 Geo. IV, no. 11.

Bourke had a liberal political outlook, and wanted to extend the system, as he had agreed with Goderich and Howick before leaving England; but colonial conservatives were nervous, mindful that convicts and emancipists still outnumbered the adults who arrived free, and that many 'native-born' had emancipist sympathies.[1] The Jury Act of 1832 did little more than permit civilian juries in cases involving the Governor and his officials, but next year the Governor, by his influence in the Council, was able to have an act passed which effectively established 'trial by jury'. Despite bitter criticism, which intensified ill-feeling between emancipists and exclusives, New South Wales had gained at last this important constitutional privilege; but in Van Diemen's Land, the special juries established in 1834, kept alive the cry that emancipists were discriminated against.[2]

Their presence, like that of the convicts, also caused difficulties in establishing any form of representative assembly, which might control the actions of the governor. 'Had I the understanding of Jeremy Bentham himself, I should not trust my own judgment as to what is really practicable in such remote and anomalous societies,' Stephen had confessed in 1830; and six years later he advised Howick that 'a Society so strange and anomalous' could not have free institutions when the adult male expirees still outnumbered the adult males who were not ex-convicts. Not until 1840 could Lord John Russell declare that the 'danger . . . from the preponderance of the emancipist interest . . . will soon become entirely visionary'. For long it had restricted the growth of self-government and the exercise of civil liberties, though Glenelg in 1836 foreshadowed future events when he expressed his great reluctance to assent to the local act prescribing summary trial and special punishments even for ex-convicts, and by implication belittled Arthur's fear that, aided by 'a loose and disorderly press', they might join with the poor immigrant class to 'form a party of considerable strength', opposed to the government, and destructive of convict discipline. Though this might have increased 'the terrors of transportation' and tightened control still further, by discriminating against 'quondam felons', the Secretary of State felt certain that by making a man's 'former condition' a 'criterion for insidious distinctions', Arthur was 'infallibly' laying the foundation for 'Civil Discord'. Darling had been able to 'discover no just or reasonable ground for treating the

[1] Minute to Bourke, June 1831, CO 202/27; Bourke to Howick, 28 Feb., to Goderich, 19 March 1832; R. Mansfield, *Analytical view of the Census* (1841), 1.
[2] Bourke to Stanley, 12 Sept. 1833; 2 Will. IV no. 3; 4 Will. IV no. 12; Arthur to Goderich, 12 Aug. 1833, to Hay, 30 Jan. 1834; Stephen to Arthur 16 Aug. 1834, Arthur Papers, liv, ML; West, i, 172–3.

Emancipists as a Body with indiscriminate contumely . . . or making them feel that reformation is unavailing'. He would not be doing his duty if he acted as if the Emancipists were 'for ever to be regarded as under the immediate sentence of the law'.[1]

If the political status of the male emancipists sometimes caused contention, this raised no problems as far as the females were concerned; on the other hand, though up to 1840 only a sixth of the men in number, their misbehaviour was a constant subject of disapproval. More quarrelsome and more excitable than the men, they were also more difficult to control. They were not allowed to be flogged, and until cells were built wherein they could suffer solitary confinement, no punishment worried them over-much. Their 'reform' was a problem, too, for the disproportion of the sexes encouraged prostitution, and in return for services rendered, they were often able to persuade gaolers, soldiers and masters alike to waive regulations in their favour.

When they arrived, they were kept in the 'factories' at Parramatta or Hobart until they could be assigned. Unfortunately the latter was very dilapidated and both were overcrowded. Assignment of females except to their husbands or to married employers always raised the problem of prostitution, and few respectable colonists wanted to have them. They were difficult to discipline. They were likely, like one of Hobler's, to be forever 'keeping appointments with her paramour'; he determined not to notice in order not to lose her services. Although the shortage of female servants was acute, Mrs. Leake told an English acquaintance that it was 'almost impossible for those families who study the quiet and morality of their children to endure Female Convicts'. Darling found the women 'so thoroughly abandoned' that their dispersal 'is attended with much difficulty'. He tried to 'encourage matrimony', aware that this was the 'best species of reform'; but despite the inequality of the sexes in both colonies, husbands were not always forthcoming and the factories remained overcrowded.[2]

In 1822, when the Parramatta factory, only just rebuilt by Macquarie, was already too full, Brisbane sent thirty-two volunteers to the government farm at Emu Plains. Charges of scandal followed. Bathurst thought

---

[1] Stephen to Twiss, 25 Aug. 1830, CO 111/98; Stephen to Howick, 11 Jan. 1836, Grey Papers, Durham, 123–11; NSW Census, 1836; Lord John Russell, quoted, A. C. V. Melbourne, in *Cambridge History of the British Empire*, vii, pt. 1, 163; Glenelg to Arthur, 28 April 1836; West, 174–7; Darling to Hay, 10 Dec. 1825.

[2] Arthur to Goderich, 25 Oct. 1827, encl. report on the female factory, 13 Feb. 1826; Darling to Bathurst, 3 Sept. 1826; Hobler's Diary, 13 March 1828; Elizabeth Leake to Mrs. Taylor, Leake Papers, *Hist. Mss. Tas. Report* (1964), 51; Darling to Hay, 26 July 1826. In NSW, 7,341 arrived between 1820 and 1839; in VDL, 3,778.

them 'nothing less than a conspiracy against the highest officers in the colony', and a Board of Inquiry reported that the women had conducted themselves creditably and twenty-four obtained husbands, but the uproar caused the government to abandon the experiment, 'fraught with good' though it was. In August 1826 Darling appointed a new Board to supervise female assignment and to look after the factory. The inmates were to be divided into classes, the highest, composed chiefly of 'those without blame', being given 'every indulgence consistent with good order'; the hope of being promoted to this class should have been an incentive to the good behaviour of the others, but many of them were not enticed by it. He ordered additions and alterations, which were completed in 1828, but next year he suggested that female transportation be suspended.[1]

The British government thought Darling could overcome his difficulty by insisting that the masters of male servants take women too. Darling rejoined that this was 'liable to objections, which, perhaps it may not be necessary to enumerate'. They would, in any case, be quickly returned for misconduct, probably 'in a state of destitution and disease'. Instead, he proposed to increase the weaving establishment and, as an experiment, to give the women tickets-of-leave 'after short periods of Probation . . . That it will fail in most instances, I have little doubt' was his optimistic opinion. The only consolation seemed to be that owing to 'the very small Establishment' needed, the annual cost of maintenance was only £7 a head.[2] However, in 1830, despite his forebodings, he found his troubles partly solved. A Ladies' Committee was formed, which 'raised Funds for rewarding the Women Annually who continue in the same Service', and the ticket-of-leave experiment had worked well, despite his gloomy expectations. The women did want 'these indulgences'; they were better behaved than before and marriages were more common. Altogether, though the women were 'of the worst description', the system was 'tolerably effectual' and reduced the numbers in the factory from 537 to about 400.[3]

But it remained only 'tolerable'. The Ladies' Committee, like many such committees, dwindled away, especially after the departure of Mrs.

[1] Brisbane to Bathurst, 28 April 1823, 24 March, 21 May, 10 Sept. 1825, encl. report of inquiry; minute on Darling to Bathurst, 12 May 1827, CO 201/182; Darling's minutes, 123 129, 130, 12 and 21 Aug. 1826; Darling to Huskisson, 15 May 1828; to Murray, 18 Feb. 1829.
[2] Murray to Darling, 17 July and 6 Dec. 1829; Exec. Council Minute, no. 47, 17 Dec. 1829; Darling to Murray, 30 Dec. 1829.
[3] Darling to Murray, 14 July 1830, to Goderich, 11 June 1831; Glenelg to Bourke, 4 Dec. 1836.
16

Darling. Bourke was unfortunate in having no 'Governor's lady' to inspire it. Employers returned their assigned servants to the factory very quickly; as more free women arrived after their migration began to be assisted in 1831, it became more and more difficult to find positions for the prisoners, and in 1836 there were 115 women waiting whose services were not wanted. Bourke removed the weaving loom for 'reasons of economy', so those at the factory remained idle, but he did little else. By the end of 1835 there were 646 there, 'considerably exceeding' the 537 which Darling in 1829 had 'represented, apparently on very satisfactory grounds to be inconveniently large'; Glenelg complained that he had received no report, only 'most unfavourable' accounts unofficially 'from various quarters', doubtless suitably embellished by Marsden's hostility.[1] In fact Bourke had acted in August, perhaps stirred by Glenelg's reminder in February of suggestions which Elizabeth Fry had sent out in 1834. He replaced the matron with a married couple, and six convict monitresses with free turnkeys – three male and four female. He revived the Ladies' Committee. He appointed a teacher to open a school. He proposed to increase the labour of the 'most criminal and refractory', necessary enough with 273 women there under colonial sentences.[2] Glenelg approved these arrangements, but though John Dunmore Lang reported an improvement (perhaps the new régime was suitably anti-Catholic) neither Gipps nor the new matron who came out from England was impressed. All were 'in absolute idleness'. No stones were broken for the roads – the hard labour ordered – but in the dormitory windows 'scarcely a pane of glass remains'. The buildings were hopeless for separate confinement – after all, prison design had progressed since the factory had been built; but as with Norfolk Island, Bourke had shown a curious reluctance to try to reform one of the black spots of the system, and when he did try he certainly did not succeed.[3]

In Van Diemen's Land, in 1827, Arthur bought the Cascade distillery and remodelled it for 'the reception and confinement' of the women. He made provision for 'classification' (but not separation), some Spartan

---

[1] Goderich to Bourke, 28 Sept. 1831; Govt.'s Minute, 30 May 1832; Anley, 41; Backhouse, 301; Glenelg to Bourke, 4 Dec. 1836; cf. Edward Parry to Mrs. Fry, 26 Nov. 1836, replying, when in England, to queries about the factory, Parry Papers, ML, App. 6.

[2] Bourke to Glenelg, 10 Sept. 1836; Govt.'s Minutes, 21 Aug., 5 Oct. 1836; Glenelg to Bourke, 5 Feb. 1836; Howick to Bourke, 4 Sept. 1834.

[3] Glenelg to Bourke, 4 May 1837; *Transportation Report*, 1837, evid. Lang, q. 3567; *Colonist* (Lang's paper), 15 Sept. 1836; Gipps to Glenelg, 13 March 1838; cf. Elizabeth Fry to Sir George Grey, 7 Dec. 1838, to Glenelg, 19 Dec., Parramatta Female Factory Papers, ML, A1813.

amenities for those who obeyed the regulations 'as to cleanliness, extreme quietness, perfect regularity, and entire submission', religious instruction for all and punishment for the refractory; for all that, the factory and its inmates remained subjects of periodical criticism. It became grossly overcrowded. The woman learned bad habits, including drinking and smoking. Mortality was high. Among the children this was partly because the diet, though theoretically sufficient, lacked protein and vitamin C, but all the inmates suffered from being cooped up 'in a crowded unwholesome place, without necessary air and exercise'.[1]

In assignment, the women could bring up their offspring themselves, but from mothers in the factory the children were removed as soon as possible. In New South Wales, orphan schools dated back to Governor King's establishment in 1800, and Arthur founded one in Van Diemen's Land in 1827. They had a successful history, but despite the numbers of juveniles who were transported, for many years little was done for them.[2] After the Carter's Barracks had been built, Macquarie used them for boys, and Darling insisted that those who were there be taught a trade, and to read and write; but as there was room there for only about a hundred they were constantly overcrowded. Settlers did not like taking them as servants, but at the end of 1832, Bourke adopted a semi-apprenticeship system. He assigned boys directly from the ships; they were to remain in service for their full seven years' sentence, and in consideration for this long 'engagement', masters should not return them but 'exert themselves to impart such habits of industry and propriety as may render them useful and . . . respectable members of society'. This was obviously desirable, but equally obviously it depended on the master; however, under this system there were 1,322 applicants for the 991 boys who arrived during the next six years, and 881 were assigned. After December 1833 boys of sixteen were assigned in the ordinary way as labourers, and apprenticeship took care of the remainder; the Carter's Barracks were closed, and New South Wales was left without any special institution for juveniles. Gipps was to oppose their coming. 'It is much to be feared,' he wrote in 1839, in reply to a query about their possible employment and rehabilitation, 'that, though called apprentices, they will for the most part be associated with, and treated

[1] Arthur to Bathurst, 24 March 1827; to Goderich, 25 Oct.; Backhouse, 21, 204; Rules for House of Correction, 1829; *Colonial Times*, 29 May 1838; *True Colonist*, reporting an Inquest, 30 March 1838; Hutchinson, 'Female Factories', *Tas. Res. Assoc.*, xi, 51.
[2] King to Portland, 9 Sept. 1800, with encls.; Arthur to Bathurst, 24 March 1827; Backhouse, 204, 301, 418.

as Convict servants, and that . . . apprenticeship . . . will be found to differ but little from Assignment'.[1]

In Van Diemen's Land, Arthur had founded a boys' establishment at Port Puer in 1834. This was a sub-station of Port Arthur, about two miles from it across the bay, and like its 'parent', was handy, easily supervised and on the whole efficiently managed; but though the boys were sent there direct and in special ships after 1836, to avoid 'contamination' in Hobart, they were often 'corrupted' by the Port Arthur convicts who were employed as overseers, taught the boys their trades (lawful and the reverse) and whose influence inevitably percolated through the establishment. Perhaps there had not been time for this when Backhouse visited it a few months after it was opened. He was impressed, and thought the surveillance, diet, education, labour and religious instruction all likely to make the boys 'useful members' of the community; though they found the restraint to be 'irksome', they were 'pleased with being put in the way of earning a livelihood'. Certainly a third of the boys were flogged in both 1835 and 1836, and a half in 1837 and 1838; but was this very different from contemporary schools? There is no suggestion of cruelty in the minutes of the Wesleyan committee whose missionary had oversight of the schools at Point Puer. The institution shows Arthur's interest in 'reform' for boys 'thrown upon the world totally destituted . . . the agents of dextrous thieves . . . but objects of compassion'. Since they could not be at once assigned they were to be taught a trade; but they were to be kept under strict discipline, which meant they would be subject to severe corporal punishment. 'Keep in mind that the boys have been very wicked,' Arthur told the Commandant when establishing the institution. 'They are transported in order, by their punishment, that other boys may be deterred.' Not until 1838 did the British government think of special treatment for juveniles at home.[2]

Notwithstanding its difficulties and some shortcomings, the system of transportation with assignment was by no means working badly on the eve of its abolition. 'As a means of making men outwardly honest, of

---

[1] Governor's minute, 1826, no. 39, 16 Feb.; Darling to Bathurst, 7 April 1827; A. Murray to M'Leay, 3 Jan. 1831, *HRA*, xvi, 74; Hely to Col. Sec., 3 Oct. and 9 Dec. 1833, Col. Sec.'s Corr., Carter's Barracks; M'Leay to Hely, 31 Oct. 1832, Col. Sec.'s Out-Letters, 32/972, to Assignment Board, 12 Dec. 1833, *ib.*, 33/119; *Transportation Report*, 1837–8, evid. Ullathorne, q. 161 ff.; Gipps to Glenelg, 29 May 1839.

[2] Backhouse, 226–7, and Reports, i, 238–9; Franklin to Glenelg, 8 April 1837; Lempriere, chs. 9 and 10; Arthur to Turnbull, 8 Feb. 1834, Exec. Council Letter-Book, 1833–6; Phillipps to Stephen, 20 Oct. 1836, CO 280/70; Hooper, 'Point Puer', 23–4. See above, p. 163.

converting vagabonds, most useless in one country, into active citizens of another, and thus giving birth to a new and *splendid country*, it has succeeded to a degree perhaps unparalleled in history,' wrote Charles Darwin after his visit in 1836. Potter Macqueen claimed that of his servants, sixty-three had been 'reclaimed' and received their 'tickets', one 'reclaimed' had returned to England, and sixty-two, though still under sentence were 'well-conducted'; compared with these, twenty-nine were 'indifferent', seven 'depraved', eleven had been sentenced to the gangs or penal settlements, and seven, though freed, were 'worthless'. Apparently 126 were reformed, and only fifty-four were not. Bourke's opponents and the critics of transportation for their own ends misrepresented Judge Burton's critical comments on the state of society in New South Wales, but he never 'on any occasion, in public or in private, to any individual even of my own family, expressed an opinion that there had been an increase of crime in this Colony'. Forbes agreed. 'Criminals *may* endanger the principles of the community, but that it has produced increased crime cannot be proved,' he wrote. Hitherto it had not been 'destructive of morals in general'. Though the *Herald* and its supporters argued that the criminals were polluting society, such pollution as there was came to a large degree from the brutality of those in control.[1]

Bourke criticized the system early in 1834, again in 1835 and again when he returned to England. He recognized its economic value; his objection lay in what was too rarely appreciated–its effect on the character of the masters in creating a 'slave mentality'. This was what he had tried, not without success, to control. In other respects, he recognized its merits, and thought the stories of colonial immorality greatly exaggerated. He explained to Glenelg in December 1835 how every year was 'placing out of the reach of ordinary Temptations, and in the ranks of those interested in maintaining the rights of property, many who commenced life in their systematic violation', and the following August, he told his son that conditions had improved so much that 'the *Herald* is at a loss for cases to illustrate the horrors of the . . . system'. He agreed with Maconochie that assignment was uncertain both for punishment and reformation; yet 'it is undoubtedly true that

[1] Charles Darwin, *Voyage of the Beagle* (London, 1842), 531, cf. *Journey to Bathurst*, 1836, in G. Mackaness (ed.), *Fourteen Journeys over the Blue Mountains of New South Wales, 1813–1841*, Aust. Hist. Monographs, xxii (Sydney, 1950), 45; MacQueen, 13; charge, Judge Burton, 1835, printed Macarthur, app. 3; Burton to Bourke, encl. in Bourke to his son, 15 May 1836, Bourke Papers, vi, ML; cf. W. Burton, *Col. Mag.* (1840), i, 437–40; Forbes, mem. on Transportation, 1836, ML, A747.

both are in a great majority of cases obtained by this imperfect and unpromising process'.[1]

Arthur was more enthusiastic. He complained that ignorant critics in England were weakening transportation's deterrence by out-of-date comments on its leniency, which they contradicted in almost the same breath by attacking the harsh treatment which slave-driving masters meted out to their servants. He claimed that magisterial supervision ensured a 'uniformity and certainty of discipline', which checked possible 'tyranny', while the spread of settlement made assignment similar to indentured service in the American colonies. In all punishment there was a contradiction between deterrence and reform, and if deterrence alone was considered, there should be a return to 'noisome dungeons'; but transportation was 'the best secondary punishment ever yet devised, as a scheme combining Reformation and Punishment', while removing 'portion of the population from a part of the Empire in which the inducements to commit crime surpass the powers of resistance, to another part of the same Empire in which these are more nearly balanced', to the benefit of both.[2]

Economical to Great Britain, it was a remarkably successful attempt to arrange for basically a civilian population to supervise criminals, using irons and close confinement only in cases of misconduct. While Molesworth, Whately, Bischoff and other English critics denied that the convict was reformed, most, though certainly not all, local observers in both colonies affirmed the contrary. True, John Dunmore Lang wanted greater severity. Bourke and James Macarthur agreed in thinking that whatever the merits of the system, New South Wales was no longer the place for it. Bishop Ullathorne was a more outspoken critic – 'We have taken a vast portion of God's earth and made it a cesspool, . . . we have poured down scum upon scum and dregs upon dregs of the offscourings of mankind and we are building up with them a nation . . . to be . . . a curse and a plague'; but one must remember that in part he wrote, at the request of Drummond, Chief Secretary in Ireland, to oppose the idea that it was desirable to be transported.[3] With all its shortcomings, it was probably as good as any other punishment in force at the time,

---

[1] Bourke to Stanley, 15 Jan. 1834, to Glenelg, 18 Dec. 1835; Bourke's mem. to Lord John Russell, 28 Dec. 1838, *Criminal Law Report*, 1847; Bourke to Spring Rice, 19 Feb. 1835, Bourke Papers, ix, ML; Bourke to his son, 21 Aug. 1836, Richard Bourke to Bourke, 27 May 1837, *ib.*, vi and xii; Bourke on Maconochie, 1837, *ib.*, vii.
[2] Arthur, *Defence, passim*; mem. to S.C. on Criminal Law, 1847, app., 206.
[3] Lang, *Transportation and Colonisation*; Macarthur, *op. cit.*; W. Ullathorne, *Catholic Mission*, iv, cf. *Horrors*; Dom Cuthbert Butler, *Life and times of Bishop Ullathorne* (1926), 59; *Transportation Report*, 1837, evid. Lang, Macarthur, Ullathorne.

and, as Backhouse and Walker commented, 'superior to that of the Jail system in England'. Though it affected the social life of the colonies and retarded their political development, it provided a labour force before free migrants were able to do so, and as Bourke said, it was factious for men who had 'attained to wealth by the service of Convicts, who . . . are emulating each other in frequent and urgent application for more Convict Servants; who are continually travelling to their farms . . . over roads . . . wholly formed by the labor of Convicts, [to] spend their lives in cavilling at the evils by which these advantages are inevitably accompanied'.[1]

Darling, Bourke and Arthur all contributed a great deal to the working out of the system. Arthur was an outspoken, vehement and successful propagandist for this cause, and certainly had no wish to hide his success in convict management from officials and interested parties in England. Since his colony and its population was smaller, it was easier for him to be supervising 'everywhere', or at least for him to read and annotate the reports submitted to him. He was never handicapped, as Darling was, by what to the military mind were tiresome legal pedantries, and the sometimes factious opposition of the judges; but it is doubtful if his contributions to penal discipline were greater than those of his colleagues in New South Wales, even if he publicized them better, and had the advantage of ruling twice as long as either. In practice, the system, built up from the common bases of Macquarie's rule and Bigge's recommendations, was essentially the same in both colonies, and, like Arthur, Darling and Bourke, steadily and substantially improved its administration.

Darling had been hindered while Arthur had been helped by his judicial officers; though both faced bitter opposition from the radicals, these were more numerous in New South Wales, and temperamentally Darling was ill-fitted to deal with political opponents. Bourke confided to Arthur that he thought him 'not exempt from error', but 'he was persecuted when he meant well'. Bourke welcomed his predecessor's knighthood, and his vindication at the inquiry into his conduct; less magnanimously, Darling never ceased to growl at the machinations of the Whigs, which he insisted had been all that had caused his recall, and to criticize ill-temperedly both the character and policy of his successor. Goderich assured Darling that he was 'entirely free from blame' in the disputes which had been referred to the Colonial Office, but thought that 'the misunderstandings and dissensions' in New South Wales

[1] Backhouse and Walker to Maconochie, 29 April 1837, Barry, 256; Bourke to Glenelg, 18 Dec. 1835.

made a new governor desirable; however, it cannot be said that under
Bourke's rule the dissensions ceased, though the conservatives then
had less gubernatorial sympathy.[1]

Still, Darling handed over a much more efficient administrative
machine than he had inherited, and despite the Treasury's persistent
demands for economy, he had developed the chain gangs, made the
penal settlements more terrible and tightened up convict discipline
generally. These achievements, when added to the solution of the
frustrating legal problems of the past, enabled Bourke to improve the
system further, strengthening the chain gangs, reducing the possibilities
of favouritism in assignment, and, above all, controlling more effectively
the colony's magistrates; their behaviour he thought perhaps the
greatest weakness in the penal administration and the tighter rein he
imposed on them was his greatest contribution to it.

In Van Diemen's Land, when Arthur departed in 1836, opposition to
transportation was negligible, and his successor, Franklin, reported
favourably on it. In New South Wales, when Bourke departed at the
end of 1837, public opinion was generally favourable, and Gipps, like
Bourke, deprecated any sudden changes in it.[2] It was in England that
assignment was most under fire and that the growing expenses were
being criticized; the changes ordered in 1838 were dictated by considerations of English penal policy, and just as in the past the British
government had varied its policy to meet the demands of the Home
Office and the Treasury, they were then little influenced by colonial
wishes.[3]

---

[1] Bourke to Arthur, 21 June 1836, Arthur Papers, viii, ML; Darling to Arthur, 14 Feb.
1835, 27 April 1836, ib., vii; Goderich to Darling, 15 March 1831, CO 202/25.
[2] Arthur to Franklin, 29 Oct. 1836, CO 280/68; Franklin to Glenelg, 7 Oct. 1837; Gipps to
Glenelg, 1 May 1838; NSW Legs. Council, V & P, 1839, xxxiv.
[3] Glenelg to Gipps, 24 March 1838, and encl.; to Gipps and Franklin, 6 July 1838.

II

Deterrence and Economy, 1826-1837

'The wringing of the nose bringeth forth blood.'

Prov., XXX, 33

Deterrence and economy, the two watchwords of British penal policy after the Napoleonic Wars, still held sway in the 1830s. Even if transportation did not seem to deter English criminals as much as the government wished, any possible alternative seemed sure to be more expensive and by no means certain to be any more effective; but just as Peel had expressed doubts in the 1820s, when James Stephen had told Arthur 'of the strong opinion in England, especially at the Home Office, that convicts . . . have too easy a time in the Australian colonies', so did Goderich from the Colonial Office in 1832, echoing Stephen's fears that if the Governors were 'too liberal', as they sometimes were, 'the great end of transportation and the only real compensation this country expects from our costly establishments in New South Wales and Van Diemen's Land will be lost.'[1]

Unfortunately, despite its admitted ignorance, the British government showed itself ready enough to act without properly considering the consequences of its policies, and sometimes to ignore the advice of its representatives, the governors. Thus when the House of Lords interfered with the ticket-of-leave system in 1832, the Colonial Office made no protest, for it shared the widely-held belief that the governors were too lenient, though unlike the many opinionated amateur penologists in Britain, it was in a position to know how the system worked. Only after Arthur and Bourke had protested did it admit that it had not understood what the provisions would do; it promised to

[1] For Peel, see above, pp. 144-5, Stephen to Arthur, 3 Dec. 1828, Arthur Papers, iv, ML; Goderich to Arthur, 27 Jan. 1832; Stephen's minute, 29 June 1831, on Arthur to Murray, Aug. 1830, CO 280/25.

have them repealed, but allowed ten years to elapse before doing so[1].

Despite this mistake, it remained convinced that a more severe discipline was called for; so it proceeded to commit not merely an error of judgment but a breach of the law. In 1831 and 1832 Hay had noted letters from Arthur describing how 'the convicts were subject to the greatest hardship' when engaged on public works. These, the Governor had reported, constituted 'a most desirable means of punishment'; they provided 'laborious employments highly suitable to convict labour', and the 'Engineer's Department with the Road Department was the cornerstone on which Convict discipline was erected'. With these opinions in mind, Hay forgot his previous criticism of Darling for keeping too many prisoners on the government's hands, and in March 1833 commended to the Home Office the suggestion made to the Committee on Secondary Punishments that to make transportation 'a real punishment, . . . all convicts, without distinction' might be employed for 'a certain period on the public Roads'; he added the proposal, which Stanley, the new Colonial Secretary, heartily endorsed, that the judges might be given power to sentence men to different degrees of transportation according to the 'enormity' of their crimes.[2]

The idea seemed a good one, though no one bothered ever to empower them, and after a conference with the Home Office, Stanley announced the new policy in August. He admitted that life in the penal settlements might be 'of a very irksome and painful description', but assignment was the reverse. Since building prisons 'would be an undertaking far too expensive to admit of', and 'much evil' would result from the convicts being set free at home when their sentences expired, transportation should continue; indeed about a thousand more prisoners would be sent out each year, making five thousand a year altogether, and 'to remove the more practised offenders from the Metropolis' all the convicts from Middlesex and Surrey would be sent off. Though 'on grounds of economy' (and no other) all the men would not be ordered to the public works, some would be. 'His Majesty's Government have determined to adopt the principle of subjecting . . . them to different degrees of severity according to the Magnitude of their offences and

---

[1] Bourke to Goderich, 20 Nov. 1832; Stanley to Bourke, 4 Sept. 1833; Bourke to Stanley, 18 Oct. 1834, and to Glenelg, 23 and 26 Dec. 1835; Gipps to Russell, 1 Jan. 1839 and 3 April 1840; Arthur to Hay, 26 Feb. 1833; Goderich to Arthur, 22 July 1833; Arthur to Bourke, 2 Feb. 1833, Arthur Papers, ML A1962; Bourke to Arthur, 28 March, *ib.*, A2168.

[2] Arthur to Hay, 11 July 1831 and 25 July 1832, with Hay's minute; Hay to Phillipps, 22 March 1833, CO 324/87; Bathurst to Darling, 2 April 1827; *Secondary Punishment Reports*, 1831, evid. Busby, 1256–7 and app. 131, Jas. Walker, 893–4, Wm. Walker, 978, and 1831–2, 19.

the notoriety of their previous course of life.' The 'most hardened' were to be sent to the penal settlements; others 'whose crimes have been less enormous' should be given 'severe labour . . . in the Chain Gangs'; the rest were to be assigned as before.[1]

Both Arthur and Bourke were perturbed by these instructions. The former thought hard labour on the roads was 'sufficiently severe without the addition of chains'. Irons were 'an addition to sentence, not sanctioned by law', except after a magistrate's sentence, or in particular cases to prevent escapes. They would 'tend to drive the convicts to despair'. He had just written defending his system against growing British criticism, especially that of Archbishop Whately and the 1832 Select Committee on Secondary Punishment. He had arranged for far more 'classification' than ever would be possible in a penitentiary, for the prisoner might have a ticket-of-leave, or be employed in the police, as an overseer, in assigned service, in the public works, in the mechanics' loan gang, in a road gang, in a chain gang and at a penal settlement, with or without irons. He had 'long anticipated' everything recommended by the Select Committee on Secondary Punishment, except for assigning *all* convicts in country districts, and this was done as far as it possibly could be. All would be well so long as he could preserve a 'mean' between having free labour too dear, and consequently convict labour so valuable that masters would pamper their servants, and having it so cheap, as a result of too much immigration, that masters would have no incentive to employ convicts and take the trouble that was necessary to superintend them properly and try to reform them. Backhouse and Walker had assured him that 'from misrepresentation in England they had no adequate notion of the efficiency as to Punishment of . . . as to Reformation, of Transportation'. What was wanted was that the 'great privations' of the convicts be made known in England, and Arthur very justifiably criticized complaints about 'indulgences extended to Convicts . . . by persons who know nothing of the mental degradation or summary laws' to which they were subject. Such ignorant persons included English statesmen, and, he told Bourke, 'without much personal experience it is not possible to legislate . . . at such a distance. . . . I have anxiously striven to maintain a very strict discipline . . . but . . . have ever felt that the deluded creatures were far greater objects of compassion than of vengeance'; they were really 'subjects of mental delirium, seeing things through a false

[1] Phillipps to Hay, 26 Feb. 1833, CO 280/44, 20 May and 22 July 1833, CO 201/234; Hay to Phillipps, 25 June 1833, CO 202/29; Stanley to Bourke, 21 Aug. 1833, and to Arthur, 26 Aug.

medium', and their reform should be a 'prominent consideration'.[1]

Bourke, who had gone to New South Wales expecting that transportation there would gradually be stopped, likewise protested against the new 'severity' policy. He stressed the hardships which even the assigned convict already suffered and argued that the sentences in irons were 'too long', for they 'almost shut out hope, and with hope exclude reform', though despite his reputation for leniency he favoured 'imposing Irons for the period of extra punishment, as I cannot sufficiently watch the ordinary Road Parties so as to render their labour more severe than that which is their lot in private service'.[2] But Arthur was the more vehement. In six despatches written in five months, Arthur reiterated that the policy would be expensive and less reformatory than the old; 'the pernicious effect' of 'long punishment without prospect of relief' would be to increase the difficulties of discipline and encourage absconding. It demanded a larger military force. It would demoralize the community. It would reduce the settlers' interest in transportation, and so it was opposed to the real interests of the mother country. Rather than needing severer treatment, 'the great mass of the Convicts in this colony is already as truly miserable as can be desired'.[3]

To the relief of the governors, the policy was found to be illegal. It imposed an extra and unauthorized punishment on its victims; the instructions were partly countermanded, though some prisoners were still singled out for 'special treatment' without irons, and were not assigned when they arrived; but the reports on the convicts' condition prompted Stephen to reflect on 'the inherent absurdity of this system of punishment. If we could send our Convicts to another Planet from which no intelligence could ever reach us, and there consign them to miserable sufferings to deter others from Crime . . . we should be acting in the same spirit and with equal reason as in thus creating . . . unknown misery on one side of the Globe in order to prevent the perpetration of offences on the other side'.[4]

'The cause of Penitentiaries and home confinement seems to be gaining ground in the country,' Hay admitted to Arthur in 1834, 'but I

---

[1] Arthur to Bourke, 10 July 1834, Bourke Papers, ML A1962; Arthur to Goderich, 8 and 27 Feb. and 1 July 1833; Arthur, *Observations*; Arthur to Howick, 14 April 1832; Standing Instructions to Road Dept., 1827; Arthur to Stanley, 15 Oct. 1834; West, ii, 228.
[2] Bourke to Arthur, 5 Sept. 1834, Arthur Papers, ML A2168; Bourke to Stanley, 15 Jan. 1834.
[3] Arthur to Stanley, 24 Jan., 4 Feb., 1 March and 4 April 1834, to Hay, 30 Jan. and 10 May; cf. G. W. Walker to Margaret Bragg, 24 May 1834, Walker Papers, Hist. Mss. of Tas., 151.
[4] Stephen to Phillipps, 17 Nov. 1834, CO 202/31; Phillipps to Hay, 12 Feb. 1835, CO 201/249; Aberdeen to Arthur, 21 Feb. 1835, to Bourke, 4 March 1835; Stephen's minute on Bourke to Aberdeen, 24 July 1835, CO 201/246.

cannot persuade myself that it will ever be expedient to adopt such a system; I understand that the report made by Mr. Crawford [on the U.S.A.] is anything but satisfactory to the opponents of transportation ... the more the question is looked into the less chance there is of any material change in the present system.' A year later he was even more confident, and could 'not imagine the Penitentiary system ever being adopted ... to any extent', especially when the result of Crawford's inquiry became known. Eventually he would be proved wrong, but the 'grounds of economy' which Stanley had mentioned were very strong. Transportation was by no means a lost cause yet, and if the 'severity' was reduced, more men were sent off from the hulks than before.[1]

The controversy over 'special treatment' had raised another difficulty. Bourke argued that he could not usually classify prisoners when they arrived because of the vague and inadequate information given on the indent, of which the governors had repeatedly complained before. He admitted that the working of the colonial law often separated the sheep from the goats before long, but if he were told more about the men when they arrived, he could distribute them to different types of work more effectively. But the Home Office thought this impossible. They did not have very good information either. In future it would send out with each ship a list of those who were to be worked on the roads (though not in chains) instead of being assigned; but these amounted to less than ten per cent of the total, and of the rest, the governors knew no more than their crime and whether or not they had been previously convicted.[2]

'Special treatment' conflicted with economy, for with closer discipline, Bourke reminded the government, 'a considerable expense, chargeable on the British Treasury, will be incurred'. In the penal settlements, the ban on all machinery and draught animals, and on tools except the spade, mattock and hoe, imposed to make labour there more irksome, certainly increased costs. 'The grand impediment to preparing the land for ... cultivation arises from the total want of oxen and ploughs,' complained Miller from Moreton Bay in 1824; and the same was true of Norfolk Island. As a compensation, both places were very

---

[1] Hay to Arthur, 8 April 1834, CO 324/75, 194, 19 June 1835, CO 408/10; *Hulk Reports*, PP 1834 (49), 1835 (65). Cf. Crawford, *Penitentiaries of U.S.*, PP 1834, Webb, *Prisons*, ch. 8.
[2] Bourke to Stanley, 15 Jan. 1834; Phillipps to Hay, 12 Feb. 1835, *HRA*, xvii, 689. Previous complaints, Arthur to Goderich, 30 Oct. 1827; Darling to Huskisson, 5 April 1828, encl. mem. by M'Leay; Darling to Murray, 30 Dec. 1828, 8 April 1829, contradicting assurances stated by Murray to Darling, 26 June 1828, encl. Phillipps to Twiss, 18 June; Darling to Twiss, 4 Sept. 1829; Hay to Darling, with encls., 8 June 1830. For numbers to be worked on roads, in NSW, *HRA*, xvii, 309, 624, xviii, 254, 631.

fertile; but convicts there cost more than three times as much as in assignment–in 1837, £13 a year per man. The chain gangs were still more expensive–£17 a head in New South Wales, though Bourke thought them even more irksome to the men than the penal settlements, and therefore a strong deterrent, and both he and Arthur agreed that their work was of value to the colony.[1]

To save money the British government wanted to have the convicts assigned. Though it was a pity if this meant they were not sufficiently punished, at least they would be off the hands of the government, and supported by their masters. In 1828–9, in New South Wales the government paid, on the average, over £15 a year (tenpence a day), for a convict kept for punishment or for employment; in Van Diemen's Land it paid £14; but those assigned cost only £4. In 1827, Forbes had declared that a third of the demand for servants could not be satisfied; the more interested Dawson of the A.A. Co. said it was a half; Edward Barnard, the Agent for New South Wales, told Hay that the lack of convict labour would ruin the prospects of emigrants and settlers; but despite this 'scarcity of assignable convicts', Bathurst found reason to complain of 'the enormous and increasing expense with which this Country is still charged'.[2]

This scarcity continued, though fluctuating a little according to economic conditions. In the next six years, the number assigned in New South Wales nearly doubled, though still only about half the applications were fulfilled; in Van Diemen's Land, the demand grew more slowly and two-thirds were satisfied; but as time went on, free labourers, whether emancipists, migrants or colonial-born, became more numerous, and in 1835, just before the tremendous boom of pastoral expansion, nearly all applications were met in both colonies–an important portent for the future, even though 27,000 convicts were then in service.[3]

By this time the British government had begun to assist free emigrants, with the intention of relieving both distress at home and the

[1] Bourke to Aberdeen, 24 July 1835; Miller to Goulburn, 30 Sept. 1824, Col. Sec.'s In-Letters, ML, Moreton Bay; Bourke to Glenelg, 5 Nov. 1837.
[2] Returns, NSW, CO 201/214, 375, PP 1830 (64), 69; Anne McKay, 338; Forbes to Horton, 6 March 1827, Forbes Papers, ML A1819, 203; Dawson and Barnard to Horton, 13 Feb. and 23 Jan. 1827, CO 201/185; Darling to Bathurst, 1 Sept. 1826; Bathurst to Darling, 2 April 1827.
[3] NSW Legs. Council, S.C. on Immigration, V & P, 1835, 287 ff., 1838, 1 ff.; ib., S.C. on Immigration of Asiatic Coolies, V & P, 1837, 629 ff.; VDL Legs. Council, S.C. on Immigration, Report, encl. Arthur to Goderich, 3 July 1833; Returns of convict servants applied for and assigned, NSW: HRA, xiii, 676, xiv, 636, Secondary Punishment Report, 1831, app. 3, CO 201/225, 232, 248; VDL: CO 280/20, 25, 30, 42, 48, Transportation Report, 1837, app. 8.

CONVICTS IN ASSIGNED SERVICE

	New South Wales				Van Diemen's Land			
	1827	1830	1833	1835	1827	1830	1833	1835
Number of servants applied for	5,042	8,452	9,050	4,983	2,577	2,138	2,524	3,130
Number of servants assigned	2,754	3,827	4,716	4,836	1,232	1,679	1,676	2,740

shortage of labour in Australia. To finance their passages, it had suggested, when proposing its scheme in 1831, either raising a tax on convict labour or on ticket-of-leave men, or using the revenue from the sale of Crown lands.[1] While Darling disliked the proposals, Arthur was horrified. The proposed immigrants would be habitual paupers; their arrival would throw convicts on the hands of the government. Certainly 'thousands could come' in a government migration scheme, for a 'hardy peasantry' was desirable; but the colony could not afford to pay for this. Graziers could not afford to buy their properties; they needed large grants. A tax on assigned servants would fall on the 'most respectable' of the colonists (including, incidentally, Arthur's own tenants and mortgagees); it would only cause the convicts to be returned to government, and so increase expenditure. A tax on ticket-of-leave holders to repay the cost of their own forced passage would not be quite so bad. They could afford about £5 a year, for wages were too high; this might reduce their 'dissipation', and if the money were used to bring out free migrants, wages might fall.[2]

Instead of imposing a tax on convict labour, then, asked Goderich, could not the government hire out convicts to settlers instead of assigning them? In this way it would realize the value of their labour, and it could still withdraw them from their master when necessary and use its discretion regarding suitable employers. Though this cost would fall on the respectable classes, did respectability entitle great pecuniary advantage from the public? No one had a *right* to free convict labour, and the proportion of the labour of the convict (i.e. of his wages) which if he were a free man he would himself receive, should be paid to the government. The land fund would establish a peasantry, and this would end a state of affairs in which colonial prosperity was so dependent on transportation. The Legislative Council was not convinced. Its committee on immigration felt sure that though the settlers enjoyed

[1] Goderich to Darling, 9, 23 Jan., 23 March 1831, to Arthur, 28, 29, 30 Jan.
[2] Arthur to Goderich, 9 July 1831, 28 June 1832; Mins., Exec. Council, 12 Oct. 1831. For Arthur's financial affairs, Arthur Papers, v, xvi, liii, lxiii, ML.

great advantages from assigned convicts, they ought not to be charged for their labour. The servants were 'dissolute and idle' and had to serve 'a long apprenticeship' before being of any use. A general charge would alienate the affections of the settler, on whose goodwill, as Arthur so frequently insisted, the success of the whole transportation system depended.[1]

Bourke was confronted with the same proposals when he arrived in New South Wales. Darling had already expressed doubts about the tax on convict servants; if levied at the rate of ten shillings each, it would only bring in enough to pay for a hundred single labourers and sixty families, and though it might be justified 'as soon as the State of the Colony Shall permit of its being imposed', as settlers could not afford it at the moment it should be postponed for at least two years. He was more favourable to the proposed tax on ticket-of-leave men, but Bourke opposed them both, the first because of the distressed state of the colony, and the struggles of the smaller settlers to survive, and the second because it would weaken the convicts' desire for a ticket, and so would impede their reformation.[2] So the proposed taxes were abandoned; for the moment the needs of convict discipline were to override those of economy. To finance emigration, Goderich relied solely on the revenue received from the sale of Crown lands, and he hoped that the policy of sale would check 'the too great dispersion of Settlers' and make it easier to maintain order and suppress bushranging.[3] It did not stop dispersion, but immigration increased the free labouring population in New South Wales and made it easier to stop transportation there later on.

Meanwhile the Treasury's campaign for reducing the burden of convict expenditure on the British Exchequer continued. It was not so worried about severity, but insisted that the number of convicts kept by the government be reduced. When Bathurst, Hay, Huskisson and the Chancellor of the Exchequer complained that the colonial governors were keeping (and therefore paying for) too many men in government service, the latter denied it. In New South Wales, the men were not kept 'voluntarily', Darling explained in 1827, but 'from necessity, the Settlers finding it impossible from the badness of their characters to retain them'; they included those in the penal settlements, road parties,

[1] Goderich to Arthur, 27 Jan. 1832; Arthur to Goderich, 28 June, 31 July 1832, encl. Rept. of Legs. Council on Immigration, 29–30 July; Goderich to Arthur, 23 March 1833.
[2] Goderich to Darling, 23 Jan. 1831, to Bourke, 29 Sept. 1831; Darling's minute to Exec. Council, 20 Aug. 1831, encl. Darling to Goderich, 10 Sept.; Bourke to Goderich, 27 Feb. 1832, encl. Exec. Coun. minute, 22 Dec. 1831, 30 April 1832.
[3] Spring Rice to Arthur, 9 Nov. 1834; Goderich to Darling, 23 March 1831.

gaols and hospitals, as well as the agricultural establishments, the coal mines, and those employed on other public works or in government departments, and totalled about 5,000 or about thirty per cent of the prisoners in the colony. Darling had said he was trying to reduce the number, but since, in 1836, they amounted to only 5,772, or about eighteen per cent of the prisoners, perhaps there was some substance in the English complaints. The numbers then under punishment had risen by fifty per cent, but made up only twelve instead of fifteen per cent of the prisoners; the others maintained by government were no more numerous than before, and comprised only six, instead of fourteen, per cent of the total; but by this time, there were free contractors able to undertake public works, which was not the case in Van Diemen's Land.[1]

DISTRIBUTION OF CONVICTS

New South Wales

	1827	1828	1832	1835	1836
Number of convicts	17,049	17,092	21,635	29,182	31,486
Number with ticket-of-leave	1,021		3,160	3,650	4,480
Number assigned	11,533	11,953(a)	13,486	19,247	20,934
Number under punishment	2,050	2,954	2,829	4,320(b)	3,859(c)
Others maintained by government	2,445	2,185	2,160	1,919	1,913

(a) includes those with tickets.
(b) including an estimated 300 females in the factory.
(c) including an estimated 300 on Goat Island and in gaol.

Van Diemen's Land

	1828	1834
Number of convicts	7,449	15,700
Number holding tickets or assigned	5,455	11,021
Number in penal settlements, in chain and road gangs	730	2,218
Others employed by government	1,264	2,461

Sources: *HRA*, xiv, 636 and 648, and xvi, 270; CO 206/81; *Herald*, 27 May 1833; NSW Legs. Council, *V & P*, 1837, 657; CO 280/20, 48 and 52; Transportation Report, 1837, app. 8.

[1] Bathurst, Hay and Huskisson to Darling, 2 April, 7 July 1827, 12 May 1828; Herries to Horton, 24 March 1827; Darling to Goderich, 31 Dec. 1827; Report of Board of Inquiry,

17

Darling admitted that the department of works was 'a serious burden' on the government, and should be closed as soon as possible, but it was needed so long as free contractors were scarce, and the ordinary citizen wanted the services of the government mechanics who were normally allowed to perform private work on Saturdays (and on Fridays if well-conducted). In 1828 he reduced the number in government service in Sydney to ninety-three, but this was 'not equal to keep the existing Buildings in repair', and two years later there were twice as many again; despite the Governor's anxiety to get rid of them, he wanted their services too badly.[1] In December 1830, he ordered all newly arrived mechanics to be assigned; a week later their assignment was forbidden until a new wing of the Benevolent Asylum had been built; a month later this prohibition was made general—no mechanics were to be assigned until the public departments were supplied.[2]

However, the Colonial Office and the Treasury knew better than the Governor. Hay was sure that so long as the government retained so many mechanics itself for public works, 'individuals will not come forward for the purpose of undertaking them'. So, in December 1830, he ordered the Governor not to retain mechanics in government service, and to execute all public works by contract. Darling immediately called for tenders for them, but had no more success than he had had before; however, his report of this did not reach London in time to prevent Goderich repeating these instructions to Bourke.[3]

Despite his optimism when in London, the latter in turn learned by experience that contracts were not easy to let, even by assigning convicts to contractors 'whose personal interests would prompt them to exert the necessary control'. Even if the lumber yards had formerly 'exhibited a picture of idleness and petty peculation', the new system was 'trouble-some and expensive', and his experiment of roadmaking by contract was a failure; before he retired he was getting nearly all the road work

---

6 March 1827, CO 201/182, 70-90, Darling's mem., 18 Dec. 1827, minutes, 135, 144, 4 Dec. 1828; M'Leay to Hely, 30 March, 9 April 1827, Col. Sec.'s Out-Letters to Ppl. Supt.; Darling to Murray, 16 Feb. 1829, 12 July 1830; Returns: 1828, *HRA*, xiv, 637; 1836, Legs. Council, *V & P*, 1837, 657.

[1] Darling to Murray, 12 Dec. 1828, 3 Oct. 1830, 5 Jan. 1831; *Secondary Punishment Report*, 1831, evid., de la Condamine, 1129-35, Wm. Walker, 976; Darling to Bathurst, 1 March 1827; Exec. Council Mins., 15 Oct. 1828; Darling to Huskisson, 27 May 1828, to Murray, 12 July, 3 Oct. 1830, to Hay, 30 Sept. 1830.

[2] Governor's Minutes, 72, 87, 1831; M'Leay to Land Board, 23 and 28 Dec. 1830, 18 Jan. 1831, to Mitchell, 8 Oct., 4 Nov. 1830, Col. Sec.'s Out-Letters, ML.

[3] Darling to Murray, 12 July 1830; Hay to Darling, 14 Dec. 1830; Darling to Howick, 24 July 1831; Goderich to Bourke, 29 Sept. 1831; cf. minute of instructions, June 1831, encl. in Bourke to Goderich, 11 Jan. 1832, CO 201/225.

done by men under punishment in the ironed gangs, but was letting contracts for public buildings, except for trifling repairs'.[1]

Arthur had never agreed with this policy. Like Darling, he had always stressed the need for keeping men in government service for punishment; to assign them to contractors who would spoil them in order to get their work done, would be 'destructive of the end of transportation'. Backing this up with the assertion that there were in any case no competent free employers in Van Diemen's Land, he was able to persuade the Treasury to abandon its idea that the works should be performed by contract, instead of by convict labour. In 1834, as in 1828, the government was employing sixteen per cent of the convicts, and since those under punishment had increased from ten to fourteen per cent, there were thirty per cent on government hands.[2] But Arthur agreed with Bourke that the chain gangs did work that was useful to the colony; although, in 1833, they were costing £9.8 per man, and the road gangs £8.2, by this time he was getting some payment in return. This was good news to the Treasury, but it then proceeded to send in a bill which caused a great deal of friction.[3]

As early as 1825 Arthur had suggested that the local government in Van Diemen's Land could bear a larger share of the colony's expenses than it was then doing; it could pay, perhaps, for the gaols, police, schools, churches and roads, while the British government looked after the penal settlements, barracks and general convict administration. In this way 'the Mother Country should defray the Expenses of the miserable outcasts from whom she is relieved, so long as Van Diemen's Land continues a penal colony'; when transportation should cease British expenditure should cease too, and the colony could stand on its own feet.[4]

This idea bore fruit in both New South Wales and Van Diemen's Land, when the British government adopted the principle of dividing costs between the colony and the mother country. Until 1827, all colonial expenditure, civil and penal, had been added together, and Great Britain met the very substantial deficit. Under a new system, announced in 1826, the colonies were to pay all the 'civil' and judicial

---

[1] Bourke to Stanley, 15 Jan. 1834; Bourke to Arthur, 14 Nov. 1832, Arthur Papers, ML A2168; Bourke to Goderich, 3 April 1832, to Spring Rice, 13 Jan. 1835, to Glenelg, 29 Dec. 1836.

[2] Arthur to Goderich, 1 Dec. 1827, to Howick, 18 Feb. 1832; Stewart (Treasury) to Hay, 4 Sept. 1833, CO 280/44; Stanley to Arthur, 21 Sept. 1833; Spring Rice to Arthur, 9 Nov. 1834.

[3] Bourke to Stanley, 15 Jan., 8 July 1834; Arthur to Goderich, 8 Sept. 1831, to Howick, 18 Feb. 1832; Col. Sec.'s Arch., 1/16110, 16030, 13/3087.

[4] Arthur to Bathurst, 3 July 1825.

expenses, while for the moment the British government agreed to meet all convict expenditure, including stores from England, the penal settlements, the medical establishment, and the whole of the police and gaol establishments. Darling, like Arthur, had suggested the colony might pay for these, but Goderich concluded they were 'intimately connected with the Convict Branch of the Service'; however, he said, as the colonies became more prosperous and their revenue increased, they could 'expect that some portion at least of the Convict Expenses (particularly those of a mixed nature such as the Police) will eventually become chargeable on the Colonial Treasury'. They would have to pay over any surplus revenue to the Military Chest, 'as the British government directs', though in Van Diemen's Land, Bathurst admitted that this was an event which he did not expect 'for some time to come'; but since the colonies benefited indirectly from the expenditure on the Convicts, while Britain would pay the cost of controlling them, she would not repay any expenditure 'incurred by Establishments beyond those necessary for their restraint and religious instruction'.[1]

Both governors reorganized their administration to suit these arrangements. Convict work was transferred from the Colonial Secretary to the Principal Superintendent (though of course the Secretary still had to correspond with the Superintendent); from British funds in the Military Chest, the Commissariat paid the salaries of officers whose duties arose solely from the convict establishment. Although it was almost impossible to estimate accurately what the convict expenditure had been in the past, for 'many departments originally instituted for convict purposes were now incorporated in the Colonial establishment', in future, the two sets of accounts would be kept completely separate.[2]

At the Exchequer, Herries welcomed the better management of the colonies' financial affairs, but when in 1834, Howick, then Under-Secretary, tried to work out the costs in relation to that of other forms of punishment, he found that most details he wanted were not available. 'The only way in which it is practicable to obtain any estimate of the actual expense is to assume that the whole net expenditure incurred . . . should be charged to the system,' he concluded; from this amount, and

---

[1] Hay to Herries, 4 Jan. 1826, CO 202/16; Hay to Darling, 9 March 1826; Bathurst to Arthur, 23 April 1826; Darling to Hay, 16 Dec. 1826; Goderich to Darling, 30 July 1827, to Arthur, 31 July.

[2] Darling's Minutes, 43 and 44, 26 July 1827; Col. Sec. to Principal Supt., 1 Feb. 1828, Convict Papers, Misc., ML, A664; Darling to Goderich and encls., 5 Oct. 1827, 8 Jan. 1828, Colonial Office minute thereon, CO 201/191, 41; Hay to Hill (Treasury), 31 July 1827, CO 202/19; Frankland-Lewis (Treasury) to Stanley, 27 Nov., CO 201/186; Huskisson to Darling, 30 Jan. 1828; Arthur to Bathurst, 22 May 1827, encl. Exec. Council Minutes, 26 Dec. 1826; Arthur to Goderich, 31 Dec. 1827.

the number of convicts, he could average the cost. On this basis he estimated that the government was then paying £6.18.0 a year for a prisoner in New South Wales and £6.6.0 in Van Diemen's Land.[1] But there was more to it than this. First, the cost of transport had to be added. This had been falling since early in the century, had come down to £28 a head between 1825 and 1829, and in the middle thirties was only £17.9.0 for a male and £21.12.0 for a female to New South Wales, and £16.17.0 and £21.8.0 to Van Diemen's Land. Assuming that the average effective sentence for men was then eight years, for fewer died or were pardoned than in the early days, and that it was still seven years for women, the charge for each prisoner each year would be a little over £2 for a man and £3 for a woman.[2]

At this time, perhaps even more than in the early days, the military were needed chiefly to guard the convicts. With the Royal Navy supreme at sea, and neither the French nor any other power displaying great interest in the South West Pacific, defence was no great problem, either against possible foreign foes or against the Aboriginals. It was the presence of the convicts too, as the colonists vociferously complained, that made large police establishments necessary. Some police and some military contingents would have been needed anyway; but perhaps it would be fair to allot two-thirds of the police and military expenditure to the convict account. If this is done Howick's estimate will be reduced. If the cost of the voyage be then added, the average annual cost per man was about £7.10.0 during the early thirties. In comparison, prisoners in the hulks cost £6.10.0; in the gaols their food alone cost £5, and to this had to be added clothing, superintendence and the cost of building.[3]

But economical as it was, when the Treasury found surpluses in the colonial treasuries, and deficits in the military chests, what was more natural than to transfer charges from the latter to the former? It had warned, in 1827, that it would do as soon as it could; now the time seemed ripe and the colonies could pay for the Police and Gaols. The Treasury stressed the benefits that the colonists received. They had cheap assigned labour, and the local governments were able to employ

[1] E. Herries, *Memoir of the Public Life of the Rt. Hon. John Charles Herries* (1880), i, 146–7; P. Debs., 10 May 1830, xxiv, 509 ff.; Howick to Le Fevre, 3 March 1834, CO 201/243; mem. to Howick, 1834, CO 202/31, 168.
[2] Admiralty to Hay, Jan. 1831, CO 201/222, 161; Victualling Dept. to Stephen, 3 Sept. 1836, CO 201/256.
[3] Returns: 1828, CO 206/61; 1830, CO 201/220; Arthur to Goderich, and encl. 6, 31 Dec. 1827; *Transportation Report*, 1837, app. H; *Secondary Punishment Report*, 1831, 12; Phillipps to Stephen, 14 Nov. 1836, CO 201/256.

CONVICT COSTS

	Convict Expenditure £	Cost Military £	Cost Police £	Average no. of Convicts in each year	Cost per head per year— all expenditure £.s.	Yearly cost per head counting ⅔ police and mil. £.s.	Yearly cost per head, including voyage, and ⅔ mil. and police £.s.
New South Wales							
1828	121,000	65,000	17,000	17,250	12.0	10.0	13.10
1830	150,000	60,000	22,000	18,500	8.6	6.12	9.12
1827–36	682,000	522,000	225,000(b).	22,000	7.3	5.18	8.8
1831–6	394,000	292,000	110,000	24,400	6.4	5.4	7.5
Van Diemen's Land							
1827	77,000(a).		7,000	7,260	11.10		
1827–36	327,000	233,000	110,000(b).	12,000	6.1	5	7.10
1831–6	269,000	156,000	75,000	14,000	6.16	5.18	7.18

a. Total Commissariat expenditure, less Police.
b. From July 1835, Police expenditure was paid by the colonies, thus reducing the cost to Great Britain.

'refractory' prisoners on the roads.[1] New South Wales paid for tools and implements for the latter, and for their superintendence if they were not ironed, but Britain paid for their maintenance, even though they were working 'solely for the benefit of the Colony'. Forbes thought this worth £40,000 in 1834, which was almost identical with the cost of the Police and Gaols. Since 1831, Van Diemen's Land had paid for some of the work of the unironed gangs, but only about a third of what it would have cost to have employed free unskilled labourers; this gain was greater than the Police and Gaol account, but Arthur was afraid that the colony might not be able to pay both; if forced to pay for the Police, it would have to cut down on its works, and Great Britain would be the loser.[2] But this was hypothetical; for the moment the British government transferred the Police and Gaols expenditure to the colonies, and though it offered to them any *surplus* that might accrue in the land fund as a partial offset, it insisted on continuing to control this fund's appropriation, and to spend the bulk of it on migration.

In 1835 there was a surplus in New South Wales, but it would soon disappear as immigration increased, and there was no surplus in Van Diemen's Land;[3] on the other hand the Commissariat provided a great stimulus to the economy as a whole. In Van Diemen's Land, it spent £1,000,000 between 1828 and 1836 and twice as much in New South Wales, perhaps a tenth of all the expenditure, both public and private, in the colonies. It was to this 'more than any other circumstance' that Van Diemen's Land owed 'the commanding station she has reached in the scale of colonies,' wrote Henry Melville in the *Tasmanian Almanac*, in 1834. Depressed though the farmer was, he would have been worse off but for this enormous element in his market.[4] Since this money was spent, in the first place, for the benefit of Great Britain, the colonists saw no good reason why they should contribute much to it; but naturally the British Treasury did, and their payment for the Police and Gaols seemed as good a means of contribution as any.

[1] Goderich to Darling and to Arthur, 30 and 31 July 1827; VDL, Legs. Council, *Mins.*, 12 Oct. 1833; Bourke to Stewart (Treasury) 30 Jan. 1834, to Stanley, 1, 2 and 3 Sept. 1834, to Aberdeen, 18 Aug. 1835; Col. Office minute, 12 June 1834, CO 206/61; Spring Rice to Bourke, 15 Nov. 1834, encl. Baring to Sir Geo. Grey, 23 Sept.; to Arthur, 17 Nov.; Glenelg to Bourke, 10 July 1835.

[2] Min. No. 8, 1828, encl. Darling to Goderich, 12 Jan. 1828; encl. in Bourke to Goderich, 28 Oct. 1832, CO 201/227; Financial Minute to Legs. Council, 14 June 1833, CO 201/232, 224; Forbes, mem. on Transportation, Forbes Papers, ML; Arthur to Goderich, 9 July, 8 Sept. 1831, to Glenelg, 2 Oct. 1835, 20 Sept. 1836. For wages in VDL, Hartwell, 85–6.

[3] Bourke to Aberdeen, 12 Aug., to Glenelg, 18 Sept.; Arthur to Spring Rice, 21 April 1835, to Glenelg, 2 Oct.

[4] Hartwell, 95–102 and chs. 6, 8, 9; Melville, quoted, Dallas, 'Transportation and Colonial Income', *Hist. Stud.*, iii, 308–9.

In New South Wales the revenue from spirit licences had been applied to the Police since 1830; in 1833 the colony was paying nearly £9,000 and for 1834 Bourke proposed a further increase of £3,000. He admitted that since their increasing cost was 'occasioned in a great degree by measures adopted by the Colonists in a successful pursuit of wealth' in grazing, and since the free population was increasing, it was very proper 'to defray the extension from Colonial Revenue'.[1] But that naturally did not prevent either Governor, colonists, press or Legislative Council from protesting against having the whole expenditure thrown on the colony by the British government. In 1832, Bourke had stressed that the police charges had 'with great reason' been assigned to Great Britain, for the presence of the convicts greatly increased them; now he insisted that if they were to be entirely thrown on the colony, it would be 'necessary to encroach upon resources urgently required for other objects', especially Immigration and Education.[2] Glenelg suggested to the Treasury that the arrangements be 'regarded as temporary only'. Bourke asked for a grant of £20,000 from Great Britain. But the Treasury would not hear of such expedients, even though increased expenditure on emigration might leave no surplus in the Land Fund.[3]

In Van Diemen's Land public opposition was equally vociferous, while Arthur's protests were even more forceful. His colony was less prosperous than New South Wales. Its land revenue was smaller and did not nearly offset the police charge. If the local revenue were to be spent on British rather than colonial objects, this 'might well arouse a determined or general spirit of opposition' to the whole convict system, and if the police were put under local control, 'convict discipline will take its character from colonial interests'.[4] He told Bourke in 1835 that the British government should act 'not only with all the circumspection necessary in the direction of the financial affairs of every colony, but with a peculiar regard to the condition of this community, which, to render transportation a reformatory as well as an exemplary punishment, must be induced cordially to co-operate with the government in

[1] Darling to Goderich, 6 June 1831, re Act 11 Geo. IV no. 11; Bourke to Goderich, 28 Oct. 1832, 5 Feb. 1833, to Glenelg, 20 Jan. 1836; Bourke's Address to Legs. Council, 30 May 1834, Financial Minute, 24 June 1836, CO 201/239 and 247.

[2] *Australian*, 3 and 7 July, *Herald* and *Monitor*, 9 July 1835; NSW Legs. Council, *V & P*, 1835, 257-60; petition, encl. Bourke to Aberdeen, 12 July 1835; Bourke to Goderich, 3 May 1832, to Glenelg, 18 Sept. 1835; Glenelg to Bourke, 23 March 1837, encl. Stephen to Spearman, 9 Jan. 1837.

[3] Stephen to Treasury, 26 March 1836, CO 202/33; Bourke to Glenelg, 8 Sept. 1837; Glenelg to Gipps, 4 Sept. 1838, encl. Baring to Stephen, 30 Sept. 1837; cf. Stephen to Baring, 5 March 1838, CO 202/38.

[4] Arthur to Spring Rice, 21 April 1835, to Glenelg, 2 Oct.

all their dealings with the convicts in assigned service . . . The charge of the Police is certainly the very last transfer which should be thrown upon the colony'. As Boyes, the colonial auditor, had argued four years before, when urging that the colony ought not to be asked to repay a loan it had borrowed from the military chest, although the colony benefited from the convicts, this was 'not to be put in competition with the great and enduring advantages' transportation brought to England, so the mother country ought always bear 'a large proportion of the Colonial Expenditure'. In 1836, the Legislative Council approved the Police and Gaols appropriation only through the unanimous, if unwilling, vote of the official majority, while the unofficial members and the press again opposed it violently; but as with New South Wales, the Treasury refused to give way.[1]

Stephen and George Grey agreed with both Governors, but felt 'it would be futile after what has passed to express any opinion opposed to that of the Treasury'. When it reiterated its previous opinion, Stephen noted that 'this is entirely a Treasury decision formed in the face of a full caution as to its probable consequences'; but the burden remained on the colonies.[2] They bore it without further fierce protest during the three years of the land and squatting boom that followed, but it caused a great deal of bitterness against the mother country after 1840, and played no small part in the growth of the colonial opposition to transportation. This might have seemed a cheap form of punishment to the British government, even if it was not always a sufficient deterrent to crime; but the efforts made to increase its severity and reduce its cost did not make for good relations with the colonies.

[1] Arthur to Bourke, 14 Oct. 1835, Bourke Papers, ML A1962; Boyes' Diary, 26 May 1831; Arthur to Glenelg, 20 Sept. 1836; Baring to Stephen 19 Jan. 1836, CO 280/70; Glenelg to Arthur, 29 Feb. 1836.
[2] Bourke to Glenelg, 8 Sept. 1837, with Stephen's minute, CO 201/262; Stephen to Spearman, 5 March 1838, Baring to Stephen, 9 Oct. 1838, HRA, xix, 614-5, and Stephen's minute, CO 201/279, 257; Glenelg to Gipps, 15 Oct. 1838.

New Projects in Penology, 1837-1843

'It were good therefore that men in their innovations
would follow the example of time itself, which indeed
innovateth greatly, but quietly and by degrees
scarce to be perceived.'

BACON: *Of Innovations*

From the welter of inquiries into prison discipline in the 1830s, and the growing propaganda against transportation, it was obvious that changes would soon be made in the system, however vigorously Arthur might defend it. Despite the insistence of those who knew that the convicts' lot was 'not a happy one', the British government remained anxious to make its 'secondary punishment' even more deterrent by making it still more severe, and the failure of the Stanley-Melbourne experiment of 1833 only made it more anxious to consider possible alternatives at home and abroad.

In its discussion, the most powerful voices were those of Lord John Russell, Home Secretary since 1835, who was to move to the Colonial Office in September 1839, and Lord Howick, the future third Earl Grey, in the Cabinet as Secretary at War, who had been Under-Secretary for the Colonies, from November 1830 to April 1833. Both were leading members of the government; both were energetic ministers; both were reformers, and both were men of determination. Howick had been, and Russell still was, directly concerned, officially, with the problem of punishing criminals. Both were members of the Select Committee on Transportation (the Molesworth Committee), which was appointed on 7 April 1837, and both were of course aware of the evidence given to it long before it finally reported in August 1838.

In 1832, the recommendations of the Select Committee on Secondary Punishment had been somewhat inconclusive; in any case ministers were then too busy with parliamentary reform to pay much heed to them; but in 1835 a House of Lords' Committee on Gaols conducted 'the most comprehensive and searching survey' of the prisons yet made, and in five voluminous reports, disclosed their shortcomings for all to see.[1] Lord John Russell was ready to try to correct them by strengthening the control of the central government over institutions which had hitherto been managed largely by local magistrates, and their improvement naturally reduced the dependence on transportation as a punishment.

Peel's Prisons Act of 1823 and Prison Discipline Act of 1824 had laid down some rules, and compelled county justices to *report* to the Home Office; but the latter had no power to inspect the prisons or to enforce the law, and in any case the Acts applied only to county gaols. The 'classification' prescribed was crude, and had failed, even where it had been introduced; the authorities were divided between their desire to make convicts' labour profitable, and their wish either to reform or to deter their criminals. After Parliament passed the Act of 1835 'for effecting greater uniformity practice in the government of prisons and for appointing inspectors of prisons in Great Britain', the inspectors' annual reports record the gradual application of a uniform policy, even though for some time there was some dispute about what this policy should be.[2]

Gradually the 'official panacea' became 'cellular isolation', in the form of 'separate confinement', with only instructors and officials to mitigate the prisoners' solitude. Originally adopted to counteract promiscuity, when both absolute silence and 'classification' had proved unsatisfactory, it has been condemned as 'one of the great aberrations of the nineteenth century', but in their report in 1838, the Prisons' inspectors expressed their 'strong persuasion' of its 'superiority'; indeed they were so gratified by 'its practical efficacy' that Parliament was induced to approve it explicitly in the Prisons Act of 1839, despite the expensive buildings it called for. Unfortunately the benefits of its 'hard labour', bible reading, religious instruction and solitary meditation did not in the end prove as reformatory as its advocates hoped. The Select Committee on Metropolitan Police Offences in 1837 more realistically reported that no form of secondary punishment would achieve all the objects that were wanted and insisted that London crime was not merely due to the defects of transportation and that good conduct in prison might betoken hypocrisy rather than reformation; but the government

---

[1] Webb, *Prisons*, III; *Secondary Punishments Report*, 1831–2; *Gaols Reports*, 1835.
[2] 4 Geo. IV c.64; 5 Geo IV c.85; Webb, *Prisons*, 73 ff.; Holdsworth, xiii, 318–20; 5 and 6 Will. IV c.38.

ignored this caution when considering its penal policy for the Australian colonies.[1]

Its first decision, taken in April 1837 just as the Molesworth Committee was appointed, was that assignment was bad and should be stopped. It now accepted, what it had rejected four years before, that *every* convict should be subject to a fixed period of labour on the public works. 'The *certainty* of a given quantum of punishment' must replace 'the uncertain coercion which is the consequence of assignment', Sir George Grey, Under-Secretary at the Colonial Office, had told Arthur the month before. But since this change would prove expensive, it was the beginning, and not the end, of the matter. Russell agreed that fewer should be transported; Sir George Grey thought that 'the means from time to time existing for profitable Employment on Public Works' should determine their number. To discover what this was, Glenelg addressed both Bourke and Franklin; he asked the latter to consider 'the means which now exist' for subjecting 'any portion of the convicts to a more efficient system of prison discipline', and both for 'any suggestions which may occur to you with a view to the discontinuance, at the earliest practicable period, of the Assignment of Convicts to individual Settlers'.[2]

When he received this despatch, Bourke at once announced that assignment was soon to cease; he thought that so long as the stoppage were gradual, it would not cause distress. On the other hand, Franklin, who was as sympathetic to it as Arthur had been, postponed any announcement as long as he could, and hoping to persuade the government to change its mind did nothing until 1839.[3] His private secretary, Alexander Maconochie, a fellow naval officer, came to the conclusion that the Lieutenant-Governor was vain and irresolute, a man 'of childlike simplicity . . . utterly unsuited to the position in which he was placed', where he had to rule and reform a penal colony. If this is the verdict of a man who fell out with him, it is not unsupported. Certainly he faced a serious problem, for Van Diemen's Land was no longer a mere gaol, as Arthur had treated it: 'the temper of the times had changed and Colonel Arthur alone, was standing still'. But if changes were needed, Franklin was hardly the man to make them. Sir John was a 'very excellent and kind-hearted man,' wrote Surveyor Frankland,

---

[1] Prisons Inspectors, 3rd Rept., PP 1838; Webb, 127; 2 and 3 Vic. c.56; *Metropolitan Police Offences* Report, PP 1837 (451); cf. Beaumont and de Tocqueville, *Penitentiary System.*
[2] George Grey to Arthur, 23 March 1837; Phillipps to Stephen, 15 April 1837, Grey to Phillipps, 29 April, *HRA*, xviii, 764; Glenelg to Bourke, 26 May 1837, to Franklin, 30 May.
[3] NSW *Gov. Gaz.*, 18 Nov. 1837, *HRA*, xix, 800; Bourke to Glenelg, 22 Nov.; Franklin to Glenelg, 15 Feb. 1839, encl. Gazette notice, 17 Jan.

'but the sort of responsibility vested in a Governor is quite out of his way.' The Canadian exile Miller described him as 'an imbecile old man . . . a paragon of good nature, with an excellent opinion of himself and little wit to uphold it.' Curr of the Van Diemen's Land Company agreed with Mrs. Maconochie's verdict that the Lieutenant-Governor was a 'cypher', a 'puppet of certain members of his own government'; the real Governor was still Arthur, ruling through his nephews. Franklin needed the 'help of some experienced practial man of business, in whom he could put confidence', wrote Boyes, the Auditor-Diarist, in 1837. At first he found this in his Colonial Secretary, John Montagu, whom Lady Franklin described in 1839 as 'a very gentlemanly and extremely clever man'; but Montagu did not regard his chief in the same light, and long before there was any question of a quarrel between them, he told Arthur, in December 1837, that 'the high qualities which were so conspicuous in Sir John . . . at the North Pole, have not accompanied him to the South'. Later Montagu lost patience with his superior and spoke and behaved to him with great insolence; but by then 'petticoat influence' had largely replaced his own.[1]

Franklin had undertaken a full-scale investigation of the convict system stimulated by the activities of his private secretary and inquiries from the Prison Discipline Society, before he received Glenelg's inquiry about the possibility of replacing assigned service with labour on the public works. The Society's interest was commendable, if belated; but its sixty-seven questions showed its complete ignorance of the system which most of its members were so vociferous in condemning. Maconochie, whom it first asked to carry out its investigations, had no special knowledge of penal discipline; but he was an intelligent man, who had been the first secretary of the Royal Geographical Society and the first Professor of Geography in University College, London.[2]

In discussions on the voyage out, Maconochie 'uniformly supported' Arthur's views on convict discipline, and when he came to see it in

[1] Barry, 52; Maconochie to Back, 11 Jan. 1839, Maconochie to Backhouse, 14 March, quoted, in part, Barry, 28; Mary Maconochie to Backhouse, 30 April (Scott Polar Inst., Cambridge—copies kindly lent to me by Sir John Barry); Frankland to Arthur, 7 Oct. 1838, Arthur Papers, xxvii, ML; Miller, 267; Curr to Directors, VDL Co., 15 Nov. 1838 and 3 Jan. 1839, Foreign Letter Book, nos. 143 and 168; Boyes' Diary, 14 Dec. 1837; Montagu to Arthur, 9 Dec., Arthur Papers, xv, ML; Lady Franklin to Mrs. Simpkinson, 3 Jan. 1839, G. Mackaness (ed.), *Some Private Correspondence of Sir John and Lady Franklin* (Sydney, 1947), 54. This correspondence shows the very considerable extent of Lady Franklin's participation in public business, whether or not such interference was helpful or the reverse.
[2] Franklin referred Glenelg's despatch to his Exec. Council on 4 Dec. 1837; cf. West, ii, 264–6. For Maconochie's previous career, Barry, ch. 2, and R. G. Ward, Capt. Alexander Maconochie RN, 1787–1860, *Geog. Journal*, cxxvi (1960), 459.

practice in Van Diemen's Land, he continued to hold a 'strong abstract approval of transportation as a secondary punishment', if it were to be modified in its practice according to his suggestions; but his report, completed in four and a half months, wholeheartedly condemned the existing system. It was 'cruel, uncertain, prodigal; ineffectual either for reform or example; can only be maintained in some degree of rigour by extreme severity . . . It defeats . . . its own most important objects; instead of reforming, it degrades humanity'. It was the root of evil in the colony. 'Do not think it is the Prisoners that demoralise these colonies. They are bad no doubt . . . but being made Domestic Slaves they are universally made worse, and their condition even more than themselves reacts on the free Community. We are slaves and slave-holders, both of the worst character – the first not having been born in that condition but thrust down to it, and the second without any parental feeling for their own bondsmen, but on the contrary jealous, suspicious and disdainful towards them to the last degree.[1]

Maconochie's insistence that the convicts' condition was worse than that of the negro slaves contrasted with British critics who said they were too comfortable; but he was not concerned only to denounce; he also proposed reforms based on ideas which he first thought out 'in Van Diemen's Land in 1837'. He demanded the end of assignment ('domestic slavery'), a separation between 'punishment, certain and appropriate – inflicted, upon system, and in seclusion', and 'training, not less systematic, but social and probationary . . . in parties of six, joined in a common fate by mutual agreement'. He 'favoured trans-portation as a secondary punishment, even for minor offences', but sentences should be indefinite, and dependent on reformation. He wanted, which is often forgotten, a term of severe restraint, accom-panied by religious and moral instruction; but this was to be followed by a longer period of reformatory training, without corporal punish-ment or special interference by the police until by good conduct the prisoners earned their release. Their treatment should be such as to 'train them to return to society, honest, useful and trustworthy members of it'. Though accepting the right of society to punish as a means of social control, and as a deterrent, he wanted punishment to be constructive; 'its *immediate* and *direct* object *in every case* should be the

[1] Maconochie's Report; Maconochie to Washington, 21 July 1838 (Scott Polar Institute, Cambridge). Maconochie (and Franklin) arrived on 5 Jan. 1837. He gave his report to Franklin, for despatch to England, on 20 May. It was enclosed in Franklin to Glenelg, 7 Oct. 1837, and was published with the comments of the local officials in PP 1837–8 (309), xlii; his 'summary' of it was published separately, PP 1838 (687), xl, 237. See Barry, 46–50 and 243 ff.

reform of the criminal ... The object of setting a deterring example is a selfish and low one. It ... implies our willingness to commit injustice for under its guidance we even assert our right to punish with disproportionate severity in order to obtain it'. During the period of his reformatory training, the prisoner should earn 'marks' for labour and good conduct which should accumulate to redeem his sentence, while also being available for the 'purchase' of minor luxuries and indulgences. Offences should be punished by fines, also expressed in marks, which would lengthen a man's sentence or deprive him of privileges. In the final period of his detention, the convict should be associated with a small group of his fellows, who should earn (and lose) their marks jointly, each member of the party being responsible for the conduct of the others. The result of this 'social' system would be to train men for their social responsibilities; brutal punishments would not be used; the prisoner would learn to conduct himself well, and for such good conduct he would be rewarded.[1]

On 20 May 1837, Maconochie submitted his report to Franklin. The Governor at once asked the Principal Superintendent, the Chief Police Magistrate and the Director of Roads to comment on it, and in due course he forwarded to London their opinions, together with those of the members of his Executive Council and his own.

Maconochie gained strong support from the Quaker investigators, Backhouse and Walker, who were still in the colony. Cheyne, the Director of Roads, also agreed with him. He denounced assignment and wanted it replaced by working parties of two or three hundred on the roads. This would make punishment more certain and equal, transportation more formidable; it would also improve the labour on the roads, especially if accompanied by task-work and plenty of indulgences as incentives to reform, 'the more the better', with a ticket-of-leave to follow. It might mean 'association', but the gangs would be classified; this, with education and the indulgences, would ensure good behaviour, and the increased work done would offset the cost.[2]

Forster, the Chief Police Magistrate, defended assignment, but thought the convicts should be put on the roads when they arrived. He distrusted Maconochie's hopes for reform; he objected to freeing the convict from police surveillance and to the indefiniteness of his punishment under the proposed mark system as well as to the sudden

[1] Maconochie, loc. cit., and his pamphlets generally.
[2] Backhouse, Narrative, 485 ff.; Backhouse and Walker to Maconochie, 29 April, 10 Aug. and 5 Sept. 1837, printed, Barry, appendix, 256 ff.; Cheyne's observations, encl. Franklin to Glenelg, 7 Oct. 1837, and report on Roads, 28 Oct. 1836, Arthur Papers, xxxiv, ML.

change from road-work to ticket-of-leave that Cheyne suggested. The Treasurer, Gregory, also preferred assignment, for some at least, and argued that to put all indiscriminately on the roads would be as bad as the present system of indiscriminate assignment. Franklin insisted that 'transportation with assignment' was 'a punishment of considerable severity'; it was one where 'the state of the Convict is the least removed from his natural condition, is the least artificial ... and ... which seems to prepare [him] best for the restoration of his freedom'; moreover, it was the only punishment 'which can be conducted without difficulty in a new colony, where the officers necessary to the duties of a more artificial system can be obtained ... only with difficulty and at great expense'. As he was later to point out, in reply to the allegation of the Transportation Committee that assignment was slavery, all punishment was slavery, and to put all convicts in the government gangs was very harsh, though that of course was what the British government desired. Thus Franklin and his Council wished to keep assigned service, but bearing in mind that transportation was intended to deter men from crime, the Governor concluded that *before* assignment there should be coercion in government gangs for about four to six months, even though this would increase the cost of the system.[1]

Despite these opinions, assignment was by this time a lost cause, though the government had apparently taken its decision lightly, on the strength of English criticism, without considering either local conditions, or how this pillar of the transportation system could be replaced. Both Stephen and Grey were later to admit that they had acted too hastily, but only when the damage had been done; for the moment, in June 1838 Glenelg repeated his instructions to Franklin to inform the colonists that 'the early abandonment of assignment' was likely, and a few days later he ordered the Governor to stop domestic assignment at once and to arrange for all convicts to be 'coerced in groups under the immediate control of the local government' when they arrived. Franklin, who had refused to act the previous December until he had received a reply to the voluminous reports sent to London only two months before, now obeyed. He announced that domestic assignment would cease from the following July and there would be no more assignment in Hobart or Launceston. In future all convicts would be worked in gangs on their arrival.[2]

[1] Franklin to Glenelg, 7 Oct. 1837, Forster's mems., minutes by Gregory, Forster, Montagu and Franklin.
[2] Phillipps to Stephen, 3 May 1838, CO 280/100; Stephen's minute on Gipps to Stanley, 20 May 1843, CO 201/333; Glenelg to Franklin, 30 June and 5 July 1838; Franklin to Glenelg, 6 Jan. 1839; Gazette notice, 17 Jan.

In August 1838, six weeks after these instructions were despatched, the Molesworth Committee reported, criticizing all transportation and particularly condemning assignment. Its recommendations bore little relation to the evidence presented to it, and rest largely on the pre-conceptions of Molesworth and his disciples. 'I cannot help suspecting that the Committee have . . . by the help of a lively imagination meta-morphosed their own theories into supposed facts,' declared Merivale, Professor of Political Economy at Oxford, and as yet unconnected with the Colonial Office, when the report appeared. There seems no reason for the historian to change this verdict.[1]

'I am astonished at the ignorance and prejudice which prevail at home on the subject of transportation,' Lady Franklin wrote to her father in December 1838. 'I cannot believe the Ministry is yet prepared to adopt anything so vague, impracticable and dangerous as [its] recommendations,' she told Mrs. Simpkinson shortly afterwards.[2] The Governor was by this time a whole-hearted defender of the existing system. He denied that the servants were slaves, except to the extent that their labour was not their own and they were subject to summary punishment – but this applied to all prisoners, even to those in peniten-tiaries. Assignment was reformatory, cheap and easy to conduct when paid overseers were so hard to obtain. He claimed that the system was conducted more efficiently in Van Diemen's Land than in New South Wales.[3] This was probably not then true; but true or false, neither his protests nor those of the colonists could save it.

Revolutionary as Maconochie's proposals seemed, Molesworth's Transportation Committee concluded in August 1838 that they 'might in part at least be attempted with advantage'. It rejected the 'division of convicts into small parties, responsible for each other's conduct', but was 'decidedly of opinion that it would be advisable to ascertain, by experiment, the effect of establishing a system of reward and punish-ment not founded merely upon the prospect of immediate pain or immediate gratification, but relying mainly upon the effect to be pro-duced by the hope of obtaining or the fear of losing future and distant advantages'. For the rest, the committee recommended that gang labour might be adopted temporarily in some colonies (not New South Wales) while penitentiaries were built in England; it agreed with the Prison Inspectors in regarding these as the best means of punishment, and

[1] *Transportation Report*, 1837–8, 22 and 37; Merivale, 359; cf. Franklin to Glenelg, 27 Oct. 1838, 15 Feb. 1839.
[2] *Correspondence*, loc. cit., 53 and 56.
[3] Franklin to Glenelg, 15 Feb. 1839.

18

ignoring their defects and their expense, wanted them to be generally adopted.

The government thought finance an obstacle; but as Howick had argued four months before, they could be tried, and so could both Maconochie's plan and gang labour. Howick also reminded Russell that he had agreed to the committee's recommendations; it was then the 'duty of the government with as little delay as possible . . . to adopt preparatory measures'. Thus pushed, and mindful that the four thousand convicts being sentenced to transportation every year had somehow to be disposed of, Russell eventually made his proposals, rather surprisingly 'with much diffidence'. He concluded in favour of continuing transportation to Van Diemen's Land for long term men, while building an experimental penitentiary for a thousand in England; Maconochie should conduct his experiment on Norfolk Island; a few more men should be sent to Bermuda, and more kept on the hulks at home. Those transported to Van Diemen's Land should first work in gangs, as Franklin had already been told; subsequently they were to obtain private employment for wages. At this stage, they would remain under some restrictions to make their 'control' easier, but these would be lessened as a reward for good behaviour; they would not be 'slaves' like the assigned servants in the past.[1]

Russell estimated that to transport 4,000 convicts to Australia would cost £60,000 a year. Certainly in Bermuda their work earned the government £13 a year, but only a limited number could be sent there. In England, they would cost about £8 per year in the hulks and £24 in a penitentiary; so to keep the 4,000 convicts at home even for four years, instead of transporting them, would cost about £120,000 in the hulks and £360,000 in a penitentiary, that is £60,000 and £300,000 respectively more than for their transportation. In order that no more should be sent to Van Diemen's Land than could be employed there, other destinations were canvassed – Corfu, the Falkland Islands, St. Helena and Cape Town, as well as the possibility of sending juveniles elsewhere as 'apprentices', but all these proposals proved as vain as had the suggestions in 1831 to use the Cape or the Ionian Islands, or to form penal establishments at Mauritius, Trinidad or Gibraltar. So in January 1839 the government decided to send more to the hulks, Bermuda and the Millbank Penitentiary, to build a new prison and to transport about 2,000 a year to Australia, including

---

[1] Howick, *mem.*, 20 April 1838, Russell Papers, PRO, 30/22/3; Howick to Russell, 6 Aug., Grey Papers, Durham, 120–3; Howick, *mem.*, 23 Nov., Russell, *mem.*, 2 Jan. 1839, Transportation Papers, PP 1839 (582).

those to be subjected to Maconochie's experiment on Norfolk Island.[1] Next year Russell lost his earlier unusual 'diffidence' and decided, without bothering about evidence, that Maconochie's experiment had failed; it had stopped making 'the penalty of the law a punishment to evil-doers'. He seemed to think 'the object of a penal colony is to make the convicts as happy as possible', minuted Vernon Smith, reflecting the opinion already held and soon to be expressed by James Stephen that his 'speculations' were 'of little worth' for 'his mind is enveloped in a sort of fog'. No more men were sent to Norfolk Island after November 1839.[2]

Then transportation to New South Wales was stopped. New South Wales had become too well settled and too civilized to be a good penal colony; what was the punishment in being sent where so many free labourers were anxious to go? So after the government in 1839 had reduced the number sent out, it declared next year that New South Wales was to receive convicts no longer. The last convict ship for the time being arrived in Sydney harbour on 18 November 1840.[3]

The upshot of these developments was that Russell had to warn Franklin that he would receive more prisoners in Van Diemen's Land and to decide how they should be dealt with. He had already said that he thought the terms Franklin had proposed for gang work were too short; since the men were not to be assigned when they left their gangs, they should remain in them up to four years, according to their sentences; but he agreed that during this time severity should be gradually relaxed, as a reward for good conduct. How should this be done?[4]

Montagu, in England on leave, urged that they should first 'be employed in the settled Districts in any manner approved by the Government upon a rate of wages considerably below the average obtainable by free people'; then according to their behaviour they should be allowed to receive higher wages, have a wider choice of work and be less under government supervision. To Montagu, this seemed probably the next best thing to the assigned service that was now

[1] Russell, *mem.*, *ib.*; Phillipps to Stephen, 1 Sept. 1838, to George Grey, 14 Sept., CO 201/278; Stephen to Phillipps, 18 Oct., CO 202/39; circular desp., Glenelg to Governors, 20 May 1838, *HRA*, xix, 422; Navy Office to Howick, 14 Jan. 1831, CO 201/222; Howick to Phillipps, 25 March 1831, CO 202/26; Maule to Grey, 30 Jan. 1839, *HRA*, xx, 154; Normanby to Gipps, 11 May 1839, to Franklin, 17 May.
[2] Minutes on Maconochie to Glenelg, 7 June 1839, CO 280/117 and on Gipps to Russell, 1 May 1841.
[3] Bourke, mem. to Lord John Russell, 26 Oct. 1838, PP 1839 (582); Normanby to Gipps, 11 May 1839; Russell to Gipps, 6 July 1840, encl. order-in-council, 22 May.
[4] Phillipps to Stephen, 5 July 1839, CO 280/114; Normanby to Franklin, 23 Aug. 1839; Russell to Franklin, 10 Sept. 1840.

forbidden, but Russell would have none of it. He decided that after their first service in the probation gangs, they should still remain in public employment. They 'might be paid wages', but they should be 'worked in parties', making roads, clearing, fencing and putting up buildings, 'in short improving Crown property for sale'. They should in this stage begin to learn the social responsibilities which Maconochie had thought so important, but the bulk of their wages would be banked, and they would still be under close magisterial control; later they could report to the magistrates less frequently and receive more of their wages for immediate spending, and later still obtain all the rights a ticket-of-leave holder had possessed in the past. They would thus gradually progress to full freedom, and incidentally their services would benefit the colony on the way.[1]

For the last two years Franklin had been concerned with organizing the gangs for prisoners when they arrived, as he had been instructed in July 1838. These, he had planned, should contain about three hundred men. They would be kept away from the settled districts, but would work under a free superintendent and six free overseers, and be regularly visited by a clergyman and a magistrate. The men's behaviour would be closely recorded, and after good conduct for one-tenth of their whole sentence (which might be 'judicially' added to or subtracted from by the magistrates), he had hoped they should be assigned. They would be subject to summary jurisdiction, but not to flogging except in extreme cases. These gangs would be 'pioneers of the colony', declared the Lieutenant-Governor. They would 'facilitate its extension', even if they did not bring an immediate return. Since the colony was supplying the mainland in 'this season of scarcity', it might even become 'the Granary for the other colonies' if 'transportation be continued' and throughout 1841 the government was besieged by petitions for gangs for road-building.[2]

The organization of the gangs was easier said than done, and by 1840 Franklin was speaking of increasing them to five hundred, to make their superintendence and religious instruction easier. Finding free overseers scarce, he thought convicts could be used. They would be cheap, and would get more work done. Since they would not be appointed before two-thirds of their gang sentence was finished, having by then presumably achieved a speedy reformation of character they would do no

---

[1] Montagu to Vernon Smith, 12 and 31 Aug. 1840, *HRA*, xx, 809–12; Russell to Franklin, 6 and 18 July and 10 Sept. 1840.
[2] Glenelg to Franklin, 6 July 1838; Franklin to Glenelg, 15 Feb. and 11 March 1839; Montagu to Director-General of Roads, 24 Aug. 1838, Tas. Papers, xxxvi, ML A1065; Col. Sec.'s Corr., 76, 16/45/2, Tas. Arch.

harm morally; 'in any case they would be concerned with work only, and their oversight would create industrious habits.' But uniconed road gangs had long been under fire in New South Wales, and a Van Diemen's Land magistrate with no particular axe to grind, Captain Mackenzie, who supported the idea of compulsory labour, had criticized the employment of 'inferior officers', bond or free, who were 'not to be depended on'. Convict overseers might 'advance the works far better than free men', but they were 'given to dishonesty' and encouraged stealing. In the next two years complaints like these were to become more frequent, even seeing official light of day in Forster's correspondence.[1]

By the end of 1840, Franklin was becoming less enthusiastic. His orders to cease assignment made the gangs bigger than he had bargained for, and he was afraid that if the prisoners were given tickets-of-leave as soon as they left them, the 'transition from hard labour in secluded districts to comparative freedom and indulgence' would be 'too sudden'. The convict overseers were not coming up to expectations. He lamented the 'almost total absence' of persons qualified to act either in this capacity or as superintendents, and asked for free men for these positions to be sent with every convict ship. He wanted more ministers of religion. He was worried by the expense of buildings. He warned Russell that it would be some time before proper accommodation would be available for the men in the unsettled districts, or that the 'separate system' could be applied on Tasman's Peninsula.[2]

Crossing the governor's account of his difficulties came Russell's despatch of September 1840 warning Franklin that more convicts would be coming, and giving him his instructions about working the men in 'parties' not in private employment after they left the probation gangs. Perhaps Stephen was right to say that Maconochie's 'speculations' were 'the productions of a man less fitted for an active than a contemplative life'; but at least he had visited the penal colonies. Russell's views were even more the product of 'the closet'. He knew little of the local conditions, and he had spurned Montagu's advice about the employment of the men. This may have been interested, but at least it was informed.[3]

Back at Hobart, Forster and Montagu at once pointed out the 'great

[1] Franklin to Russell, 22 May 1840; Mackenzie to Normanby, 3 April 1839, CO 280/117; Forster to Montagu, 3 May 1841, Corr., PP 1843 (158); cf. Tas. Papers, xxxiii, ML A1062.
[2] Franklin to Russell, 18 Nov. 1840, 12 and 19 Jan. 1841. On the convict overseers, Gates, *Recollections*, and Miller, *Notes*.
[3] Minute by Stephen, 1 Sept. 1841, CO 201/309, 205; Russell to Franklin, 10 Sept. 1840; Montagu to Vernon-Smith, 12 and 31 Aug., *HRA*, xx, 808-11.

expenditure involved'. Costs would mount as more men moved from the gangs into the parties. Russell had forbidden their employment in the settled districts, where they could be easily controlled and perform useful work; what he suggested for them was worthless, for settlers preferred their runs 'in a state of nature' and would not pay more for them because they had been 'prepared' for sale. Writing in July 1841, Franklin did not stress these objections. He merely asked for more superintendents, reported that the Council approved the policy, and appointed Forster Director of the Probation System to make arrangements for it.[1] In the gangs, there were 1,500 men allegedly subject to 'rigorous and uncompromising' discipline; but superintendence and buildings were inadequate and many men were absconding. Franklin found that in 1841 only thirty-six per cent of the convicts were found guilty of disciplinary offences, compared with sixty-four per cent in 1838; a quarter of the prisoners were never brought before a magistrate and only a quarter were 'ill-conducted'. Did this mean that 'no system of convict discipline which I have hitherto heard of is so likely to afford lasting benefit to the criminal as well as to society as this one'? or that the reduction of assigned service had reduced the opportunities for misconduct? or merely that administration was lax?[2] The Governor does not seem to have thought of the last two possibilities.

Franklin's only apparent–though very justifiable–concern at this moment was that too many prisoners were being sent to Van Diemen's Land. Already increased by closing New South Wales, the number to be sent was doubled by the House of Commons voting in 1841 to transport the 'seven year men' whom the government had intended to keep at home. It was not surprising that the Governor should want Britain to establish another penal colony; but his suggestion of Auckland Island, far away to the south, as a site for it reflected perhaps his Polar interests rather than his wisdom or his appreciation of penal problems, even if Montagu's and Arthur's insistence that Tasman's Peninsula could take 25,000 was equally foolish. The Home Office was pressing for more to be transported as the hulks were filling steadily. At the Colonial Office, Gairdner noted that 'any number' could be sent; in October 1841 Stanley, who had replaced Russell, minuted there was 'no doubt' that

[1] Franklin to Russell, 15 April 1841, encl. Exec. Cncl. Mins., 29 March. Neither Russell nor Stanley appears to have heeded this warning about expenditure, as Franklin complained to Stanley, 1 April 1842. The minimum price of £1 per acre had not yet been fixed, and Crown land was selling at an average of 11s. 4d.

[2] Franklin to Russell, with encls., 6 July 1841; mem. on Convict Discipline for Government of India, 30 June 1841, Tas. Arch., Records Branch, i, no. 8; Legs. Council Papers, *Stat. Returns.*

Franklin could 'provide for their reception'. The disastrous influx of the next five years was on its way, though the fact that Van Diemen's Land had been able to absorb only 2,004 migrants between 1838 and 1841, inclusive, was a warning of the limitations of the labour market.[1]

Certainly in 1840 and 1841, there had been a shortage of labour, in contrast to 1838. Then convicts were still being assigned to private service and there were plenty of farm labourers. Assisted migration was suspended in 1839 and Franklin had been unable to persuade mechanics to stay in Van Diemen's Land instead of going to Port Phillip. In 1840 he wanted to promote immigration again to meet the needs caused by stopping assignment, and told Russell that the labour shortage would be felt more and more; but apparently he overlooked the fact that it soon would be cured when convicts began to emerge from the gangs. Next year several witnesses warned the Legislative Council Committee on Immigration that although there was a 'fair opening' for good farming men, they did not want 'a large indiscriminate influx of labour', convict or free.[2] Unfortunately Franklin did not stress this warning, so it was hardly surprising that the British government ignored it too, though it is doubtful whether the opinionated Stanley would have heeded this forecast of the likely effect of transporting large numbers of convicts, even if it had been pointed out to him.

In April 1842, Franklin reported that the arrangements for the 'first stage' of gang labour were complete. He had received two thousand more men for it than he had originally expected, but he had established a number of 'out stations' on Tasman's and Forestier's Peninsula – at Flinders Bay, Impression Bay (Premaydeena) and Cascade (Koonya) for timber working, and at Saltwater Creek and Wedge Bay (Nubeena) for agriculture. There, certainly, no more room was available, but most of the others were also in places 'cut off from temptation'. All he wanted was more clergy and superintendents of a 'superior class', and a greater military force.[3] By July he was ready to proceed with Russell's 'second stage'. The men would still work for the government. They would be employed on useful projects, like making roads to Macquarie Harbour

---

[1] Franklin to Russell, 6 July 1841; *P. Debs.*, 23 March 1841, 3rd ser., lvii, 522–557; on Auckland Island, Franklin to Russell, 3 Aug. 1841, encl. Minutes of Exec. Council, 19 May; Manners-Sutton to Stephen, 16 Oct. 1841, minutes by Gairdner and Stanley, 19 Oct., CO 280/139.

[2] Franklin to Russell, 22 May 1840; Franklin to Glenelg, 4 April 1838; Madgwick, 166–7; Franklin to Russell, 6 Aug. 1841, 3 Dec. 1841, encl. Report of Legs. Council on Migration, *Corr.*, Emign., PP 1842 (301); Legs. Council Minutes, 1841. Stephen suggested £30,000 p.a. be spent on emigration to Van Diemen's Land (to Emigration Commissioners, 30 Aug. 1841).

[3] Franklin to Stanley, 1 April 1842; to Russell, 12 Oct. 1841, encl. Foster's mem. 24 Sept.

and to the estates of the Van Diemen's Land Company, the latter 'one of the greatest boons' possible for it, according to its manager. Unfortunately such employment, even with Saturdays free and an allowance of tea and sugar did not offer the 'palpable marks' of being 'in advance of punishment labour', which the Principal Superintendent thought so necessary. The result was discontent and unrest, although Franklin thought the men had 'no just cause for complaint'. When this stage was completed, the men could seek private employment through government hiring stations; though he feared here the 'prospect of a well-stocked labour market', he did not stress the dangers implicit in this situation. He admitted that he had not yet had time to learn what would be the system's 'ultimate effect on character', and in a memorandum three months later, he noted ill-discipline and idleness in the gangs; but though 'the benefits which I anticipated' had not been 'so full obtained as I could have wished', he concluded, there was 'no cause for discouragement'.[1]

By November 1842, Franklin found himself having to deal with a rapidly increasing number of prisoners. Expenditure was naturally mounting, but he had received no reply to the requests which he had made more than a year before, in April and July 1841, for more information and instructions about the government's plans. Feeling compelled to make some changes on his own initiative, he proposed to unite the first two stages of probation, since the division was costly and difficult to supervise, even though delay in getting out of the gangs caused some unrest among the prisoners. If he could not work the men in settled districts, at least he would put more of them where their labour would be profitable to the community, instead of being 'wasted' in the 'sterile' Tasman's Peninsula; but, he insisted, 'whilst the convict remains in a Gang, it will be understood distinctly that the primary object of his detention there is punishment for the sake of example'. When they came out, the men should be distributed in service among the free people. This would incorporate those parts of the assignment system 'found to work well', it would add the privileges of earning wages up to £9 a year and of choosing their master, and exclude those features which resembled slavery. A board (similar to the old assignment board) would consider applications for employment, and would approve persons 'whose circumstances and character' afforded a 'genuine guarantee' for the 'discipline and moral improvement' of their

[1] Franklin to Stanley, 22 July; Govt. notices, 29 Sept. 1842, nos. 256–8; VDL Co., Gibson to Court, 24 March 1842, Foreign Letter Book, 6; Col. Sec.'s Corr., 21 July 1841, 22/57/491, and 29 June 1842, 22/59/890; Franklin's mem., 25 June, G.O. 52/7, Tas. Arch.

servants. They were not to reside in Hobart or Launceston. Every master was to superintend his men personally or maintain a free overseer; he was to send them to church if within two miles of a place of worship. The contract of service would be a fair one; but would there be enough work for all those who would soon be seeking it?[1]

While Franklin was writing this despatch, Stanley was drawing up detailed instructions for *his* probation system. This too combined the 'seclusion stage' and the 'probation gang stage' and provided that those leaving the gangs should work for wages with a 'probation pass', so he could comment, 'we seem to have anticipated his proposals as he our instructions'; but in fact it gave more privilege to the passholder than Franklin had proposed at this stage. As always ready to blame his officials, he criticized the Governor for not writing earlier (rather than himself for ignoring his previous despatches) and for making changes without the authority of the British government; but Stanley's system superseded Franklin's last proposals, and at least proposed to remedy what had been a cause of convict discontent, by making a 'definite and substantial' distinction between the gang labour and wage-working stages, and speeding up the move from the gangs. In its concoction, Montagu, back in England after Franklin had suspended him from his position of Colonial Secretary, was ready with advice. He was moved to no small extent by Stanley's desire to reduce the growing expenditure which the Colonial Office had hitherto ignored, and he was soon to write to Arthur triumphantly that Stanley had declared '*in my presence* that I had enabled Her Majesty's Government to introduce . . . an improved system of Secondary Punishment', at which the Chancellor of the Exchequer was 'much pleased'.[2] A year before, when it had appeared to the Treasury that the estimated cost of Russell's proposals would be not less than £77,000, the possible substitution of a cheaper plan had been very welcome. As late as October 1842, Stanley admitted to Peel that he found the question 'beset with difficulties'; but after 'frequent discussions' with the Home Secretary, he had decided that 'we must come as a government to the consideration and adoption of an extensive measure embracing the whole system of secondary punishment'.

[1] Franklin to Stanley and encls., 17 Nov. 1842.
[2] Stephen and Stanley, minutes on Franklin to Stanley, 17 Nov. 1842, CO 280/147; Stanley to Franklin, 25 Nov. 1842; Stephen's minutes on Manners-Sutton to Stephen, 16 Oct. 1841, and on Franklin to Stanley, 22 July 1842, CO 280/139 and 145; Forster to Col. Sec., 21, June 1842, Col. Sec., 22/59/890, Tas. Arch.; Montagu to Stanley, encl. mem. on Transportation, 11 Nov. 1842, CO 280/157; Stanley mem. on Convict discipline and notes on Montagu's mem., Nov. 1842, CO 280/149, 332 ff.; Montagu to Arthur, 26 Dec. 1842, Arthur Papers, xvi, ML A2176.

Putting aside his misgivings, he drew up his plan and sent off his instructions with confidence, and this he was to maintain during the next three years.[1]

The shorter periods in the gangs, which Franklin had wanted but Russell had forbidden, varying from one to two years, according to the prisoner's sentence, would reduce costs. As 4,000 convicts would be sent out each year, if an average were taken of eighteen months, there would be about 6,000 in the gangs at any one time. While in them, the men would be subject to the best reforming influences—religious teaching and reward for good behaviour. At least equally important, was the hope, first expressed in 1837, that working in the unsettled districts, they could support themselves; this, wrote Stanley, 'was the first and most essential object to which their labour should be directed', and by this means he looked forward to 'a considerable reduction in the charge hitherto thrown on the British Treasury'.[2]

On leaving the gangs, the men should work for wages with a 'probation pass'. This proposal was also similar to Franklin's. It cut out the 'second stage' which Russell had ordered and Franklin was implementing, but involved more government control than Franklin had envisaged over the behaviour of both the prisoners and their employers. These might be either private individuals or the colonial government; but the latter would no longer receive convict gang labour free of charge, for it, not Great Britain, should pay for works which opened up the colony. Superintendents and clergy were needed for Stanley's system as for Franklin's, but though Stephen feared they would be hard to find, Stanley ignored this warning. Nor did he consider the possibility of their not finding jobs; when unemployment developed later he would say he had not been forewarned, which was not correct, even though Franklin had not emphasized this danger as he should.

At this stage, popular opinion of the new system was not altogether unfavourable. Certainly the colonists regretted the stopping of assignment, and were outraged by the criticisms of themselves made by Maconochie and by the Transportation Committee. But after their efforts to save assignment had proved fruitless, many were prepared to make the best of a bad job. Even without assigned servants, 'we shall retain the benefit of transportation', said the *Colonial Times*. 'In a

[1] Clark (Treasury) to Stephen, 4 Oct. 1841, CO 280/140; Forster's mems., 19 May and 24 Sept. 1841, *Corr.*, PP 1843 (158); Stanley to Peel, 3 Oct. 1842, *Peel Papers*, BM, Add. MSS. 40467, 239.
[2] Stanley's mem.; Stanley to Wilmot, 24 April 1843; cf. Spearman to Stephen, 6 Feb. 1837, Glenelg to Franklin, 28 March, CO 280/87.

pecuniary point of view', the supply of convict labour was 'more advantageous than a representative assembly', argued the *True Colonist*, which was just as well, for both Russell and Stanley insisted that the two were incompatible. 'The state of distress is much less felt here than it would have been but for the large expenditure of public money which . . . is of unspeakable benefit to the community', noted *Murray's Review* early in the 1842 depression. 'Transportation was the greatest boon which Britain could bestow on Van Diemen's Land.' The colonists did not yet know the disadvantages of the probation system; but commissariat expenditure of £2,465,000 between 1840 and 1849 was no mean offset to the economy.[1]

But after the colonists lost their assigned servants, they became all the less willing to meet the Treasury's demand that they pay for the Police and the Gaols. Much of this cost arose from Britain using Van Diemen's Land as a penal colony, and Franklin, like Arthur, supported the colonial objections; but he had to carry out his instructions, and push the Police and Gaols vote through the Legislative Council. In 1837. 1838 and 1839, like Arthur in 1836, he had been able to do this, against the opposition of all the non-official members, only by the vote of all his officials and his own casting vote, but in 1840 he had to draw on the land revenue to meet the expense. This would 'not again be approved', declared the Treasury; the land fund must be kept to assist emigration. Franklin urged that a fixed amount of the land fund be appropriated for the Police, leaving only the balance for migration, 'for it was highly desirable to put an end to the struggle which annually takes place on the subject'. Stephen was afraid that the Council's financial powers might have to be reduced, Russell that they were making the colony bankrupt.[2] For a few pounds the Treasury was causing much discontent. In the end it agreed that if half the land revenue were spent on migration, fifteen per cent on the Aborigines and ten per cent on surveying, then the Legislative Council could dispose of the 'unappropriated balance', on the police if they wished; but this was not enough. In 1840 and 1841 the land revenue was buoyant and the Treasury could point to the benefit the colony gained from the cheap convict labour on colonial

---

[1] Franklin to Glenelg, 3 Jan. 1839; Franklin to Archer, 17 May 1839, Corr., PP 1846 (400); *Colonial Times*, 16 July and 17 Sept. 1839; *True Colonist*, 6 Nov. 1840; *Murray's Review*, 15 and 29 April 1842; Hartwell, 102 and 234.

[2] Arthur to Glenelg, 20 Sept. 1836; Franklin to Glenelg, 10 Aug. 1837, 17 May 1838; Franklin's financial minute to Legis. Council, 5 July 1838, encl. in Franklin to Glenelg, 24 Aug.; Franklin to Glenelg, 10 July 1839, and Stephen's minute, CO 280/109; Trevelyan to Stephen, 15 April and 23 July 1840, minutes by Russell and Stephen, CO 280/126; Russell to Franklin 25 Sept.

works; in 1842 the sale of land had stopped owing to the depression, and there was no 'unappropriated balance'. Meanwhile Stanley had made things worse by ordering Franklin to charge the Colonial Government for the maintenance of all the convicts it employed except those in chains, though Britain still paid for their superintendence, lodging and clothing.[1]

All this time, while Franklin was repeatedly expressing his general approval of the new arrangements, he seems also to have been entirely satisfied with the juvenile establishment at Point Puer. Though in 1841 he stressed the need for more separate cells (and then apparently put the matter from his mind), he found the establishment 'most gratifying in every respect . . . highly conducive to the interests of morality . . . embodying, . . . practical education and training'. There was 'excellent discipline'. 'Moral improvement' was obvious. He praised Captain O'Hara Booth, the Commandant, most highly.[2]

But was the discipline 'excellent'? Though Booth wrote in his Journal that he was 'sick at heart from the number of boys I am obliged to punish', he thought it important that 'the most trivial crime' should be dealt with, either by confinement to the muster-ground during rest periods, confinement to the cells after work, confinement on bread and water or corporal punishment. In 1840, out of 494 boys, 351 were punished for a total of 1,011 offences. Larceny and absconding were common, and there were many cases of attacks on overseers, due either to their 'inflexible discipline' or 'intolerable tyranny'. Among the boys a 'desperate and unscrupulous element', aided by a strong corporate feeling, kept up a 'general hatred of authority'.[3]

At the end of 1842, B. J. Horne, an English prison official, visited Point Puer, to advise on the 'assimilation' of the discipline there with that of the recently established juvenile prison at Parkhurst on the Isle of Wight. Neither Franklin nor Booth had noticed anything wrong, not even the 'semi-decay' of the buildings; to Horne, its defects seemed

[1] Stephen to Trevelyan, 26 Oct. 1840, Trevelyan to Stephen, 7 Nov., CO 280/121; minutes on Trevelyan to Stephen, 12 Sept., CO 201/303. The land revenue was £53,500 in 1840 and £59,400 in 1841 (CO 280/146); for its fall, Franklin to Stanley, 24 Feb. 1843. The Land Sales Act, 1842, 5 & 6 Vic. c.36, raised the price to £1 per acre, but did not come into effective operation in Van Diemen's Land until 1844 (Hartwell, 50). Stanley's orders to Franklin, 23 Aug. 1842.

[2] Franklin to Glenelg, 8 April and 4 Aug. 1837; Forster to Booth, 12 Jan., 1841, encl. in Franklin to Russell, 19 Jan. 1841.

[3] Booth, Journal, 20 Feb. 1836; report encl. in Franklin to Glenelg, 4 Aug. 1837; return of punishments, 30 July 1838, CO 280/96; Franklin to Russell, 19 Jan. 1841; Hooper, chap. 7. Col. Sec.'s Corr., 49/10, shows that in 1843 408 boys out of 706 were punished for 969 offences.

obvious. The locality was badly chosen – 'a wretched, bleak, barren spot without water, wood for fuel, or an inch of soil that is not for agricultural purposes absolutely valueless', said the new commandant, Champ, in 1844 – a description with which the visitor today will concur. For the sake of economy, it had been placed too near Port Arthur. Convicts were employed as overseers. The buildings were poor. There was no 'classification'. Nothing had been done to introduce the separate system, which Franklin had wanted 'without delay' in 1841. Though the food was good, the clothing was not. Formal trials for trivial offences, which could often have been overlooked, were far too frequent; both Franklin and Booth had ignored the misgivings of T. J. Lempriere, that 'the system of discipline' was not 'such as will lead to the reformation of the boys'. There was not much inducement to reform, for little attention was paid to 'character' in the selection of future employment. Religious instruction was 'meagre and unsatisfactory', with a great emphasis on learning passages of scripture by heart. Conditions were made worse by overcrowding, as the number increased from sixty-six in 1834 to 716 in 1842. The general moral state was low. 'It was impossible that it should be otherwise,' concluded Horne.[1]

However there was a credit side, which perhaps justifies some of Franklin's complacency. West described the place as 'an oasis in the desert of penal government'. Though agriculture was hampered by the poor soil, the boys were taught trades – to be boat-builders (introduced at Franklin's own suggestion), blacksmiths, carpenters, sawyers, stone-masons, brickmakers, coopers, bookbinders and shoemakers – 'the first attempt to provide practical vocational training for boys on a considerable scale in the Australian colonies'. In 1843 nearly half the boys, 292 out of 643, were in the trade classes, compared with only seventy-four out of 273 in 1837. After their training, they were assigned, and a special hiring depot for them was established at New Town to prevent their being 'contaminated' by association with other convicts while they were waiting for employment.[2]

This treatment for the 'incorrigible' boys sent to Van Diemen's Land supplemented the plans of the English Prison Commissioners for disposing of other juveniles. After 'reformatory discipline' at Parkhurst, they were to be sent as 'exiles', not as convicts, to places where they might fairly easily earn an honest living. Stanley agreed that even boys

[1] Franklin to Stanley, 16 July 1843, encl. Horne's report, 7 March; Forster to Booth, 12 Jan. 1841, Booth's reply, 12 Feb., Col. Sec., 5/7120; Champ to Controller-General, 3 June 1844, encl. in Wilmot to Stanley, 14 July; Lempriere, 93.
[2] West, ii, 247; Hooper, 91, 124 and ch. 13; Blue Book, 1844; Legs. Council Minutes, 18 Aug. 1842.

who had benefited by Parkhurst training 'should not be turned loose on the world in England'. He thought that the best of them could be pardoned on condition they went to the colonies, where 'to all intents and purposes they would be free settlers'; they probably would not want to return to England, but if sent to Australia rather than Canada they would find 'greater difficulties in the way of such an attempt'. A second class might be pardoned on condition of serving a term of apprenticeship; colonial legislation might be necessary to control them, but he would 'not allow their original sentence of transportation to revive'. These plans, it was hoped, would lead to 'systematic and permanent' arrangements to provide for 'the future emigration of such further number of boys as may hereafter be deemed expedient'.[1]

Parties were sent to New Zealand and Western Australia as well as to Van Diemen's Land. The first, in 1843, comprised twenty-four emigrants and nine apprentices to New Zealand and twenty-eight apprentices to Western Australia. To Van Diemen's Land went twenty-two apprentices, eleven with tickets-of-leave, seventeen for probation parties and seven for Point Puer, but when a second batch arrived the Governor complained that they were less 'reformed' than the boys at Point Puer itself. They were 'troublesome, deceitful, liars and drunken', their training an 'instrument not of good but of evil'. No more such boys were desirable.[2]

Females were not wanted either. When assigned to domestic service, their conduct was all too often such as to 'preclude their mistresses recommending them' for tickets-of-leave; but stopping assignment made it all the more difficult to decide what should be done with them. Sometimes they were allowed to marry and given a ticket; but as Lady Franklin complained there were 'no receptacles' for them except 'the home of the convicts'. It was 'next to impossible' to do anything with those in the factory, 'huddled as they all are together, and such impudent creatures'.[3]

Stanley insisted that the transportation of women must go on to prevent the disproportion between the sexes becoming even greater than it was. Six hundred would be sent out each year. Since the factory

[1] Stanley's minute on Phillipps to Stephen, 5 April 1842, CO 280/149; corr. encl. in Stanley to Gipps, 26 May 1842.

[2] Phillipps to Stephen, 13 April, 31 May 1842, CO 280/149; Stanley to Franklin, 16 May, 1 June, to Hutt (W.A.), 16 May; Stanley to Wilmot, 8 May 1843, to Hutt, 4 May, and to New Zealand, 7 May, CO 280/164; Turnbull to Wilmot, 15 Feb. 1844, encl. in Wilmot to Stanley, 30 Aug.; Hooper, 109-113.

[3] Spode's Mem., 21 Aug. 1837, encl. in Franklin to Glenelg, 31 July 1838; Lady Franklin to Mrs. Simpkinson, 4 Oct. 1838, and to Mrs. Fry, 3 Aug. 1841. Correspondence, i, 37-8 and ii, 22.

was so 'very discreditable', a new penitentiary should be built. Colonel Jebb, the English prison expert, was ordered to advise on its construction and estimated cost, though he complained, as might be expected, he had 'no very precise information on the subject of building materials and other essential points'. Franklin welcomed the belated decision of the British government to grant funds for it. He thought that many of the allegations about the old factory were exaggerated; but there was no 'classification' in it, and haphazardly built for two hundred and fifty, it usually contained about four hundred. A press critic was more outspoken. He likened the working rooms to 'the hold of a slave ship', and added that 'what the sleeping rooms must be, shut up during the whole night with the accompanying circumstances not to be particularized, must be obvious to all'. In 1834, Backhouse had regretted the lack of a women's visiting committee. In 1841 one was formed on the instigation of Lady Franklin, with a protégée of hers as secretary; but by this time Lady Franklin was not popular, and the press, who might have been expected to welcome it, joined with officials, who might not, to vilify the project, which in these circumstances soon came to grief.[1] Franklin regretted the hasty abolition of female assignment. Though 'not free from abuses', it was 'by all esteemed as a privilege and desired as a boon', and it imposed a more 'stringent control' than a ticket-of-leave. The 'penitentiary system' would 'congregate' the women instead of scattering them throughout the colony; but this was what Stanley ordered. In future, after they arrived they were to be kept for six months in the new Penitentiary, when it was built, and there, it was hoped, they would continue a 'reformation' begun on the voyage out. The 'factory' was to be reformed and used as a place of punishment, with severe discipline. Without it the Penitentiary, holding four hundred, would be too small; but whether it could be made adequate was another matter. The penitentiary was authorized and Dr. and Mrs. Bowden were sent out to take charge of it, but the English Prison Commissioners remained doubtful about both it and the new male prison to be built in Hobart. 'Distrusting as we do the means . . . of carrying into effect any beneficial system of prison discipline' in the colony, and the need to employ convict overseers, they regretted the large expenditure on building there; they preferred 'those measures

[1] Stanley to Franklin, 25 Nov. 1842; Jebb to Phillipps, 11 Jan. and 17 Feb. 1843, CO 280/164; Franklin to Stanley, 4 June 1843; Report of Inquiry into Female Convicts, 1841, Col. Sec.'s Corr., 22/50/169, Tas. Arch.; *Murray's Review*, 29 Oct. 1841; Backhouse, 204; Payne, 'Female Convicts', *Tas. Hist. Assoc.*, ix, 61; Hutchinson, 'Mrs. Hutchinson', *ib.*, xi, 63.

which are now happily in progress in this country for the salutary punishment of transports before their being sent abroad'.[1] The officials, if not the politicians, were looking forward to the end of the system. Most of these problems were more lightly felt in New South Wales. Certainly many colonists there were disappointed when they were warned first that assignment would cease, and then that there would be no more convicts at all. The Legislative Council had deplored the shortage of labour in 1837, but next year, its protests against the Report of the Transportation Committee were more concerned with the 'unfavourable impression' it produced about the colony than with any loss that stopping transportation might bring. Many witnesses to its Immigration Committee, like James Macarthur in London, emphasized the superiority of free immigrants; and although the colonists, with every justification, continued to protest against the 'reiterated misrepresentations . . . so industriously circulated in the United Kingdom', these libels, for such they were, underlined the incompatibility of continuing transportation and increasing free immigration. In October 1836, Bourke had suggested the granting of bounties for bringing migrants out. Next September Glenelg approved, and when the system got into its stride, since New South Wales had funds available, 60,000 migrants, including 18,000 assisted to the colony, greatly relieved its labour shortage; this and the depression in 1841, for the time being allayed the fears expressed in 1838.[2]

These migrants also added to the other opponents of transportation, the emancipists and their children, those who deplored what they regarded as a degrading influence on the colony and those who wanted greater political freedom, which they thought would never be granted to a penal colony. 'None are so deeply interested in the immediate discontinuance of transportation as those . . . who petition for representative government,' Buller told the Australian Patriotic Association in October 1838. 'The continuance of that system [is] the obstacle that has thwarted all my efforts to obtain what you desire. Nor do I believe that Government or Parliament will ever be induced to grant you such a self-government as a colony should have until the prospect has arisen of its being no longer used for penal purposes.' A year later, Russell told Howick the same. 'As I contemplate the introduction of free institutions

[1] Franklin to Stanley, 4 June 1843, with Stanley's minute, CO 280/157; Stanley to Wilmot, 14 June and 2 Nov. 1843; Report, Prison Commissioners, 27 Sept. 1842, encl. Phillipps to Stephen, 29 Sept., CO 280/149.
[2] NSW, Legs. Council, *V & P*, 1837, 674-6, 1838, 36 ff.; Macarthur, 56 and ch. v; Gipps to Russell, 25 Oct. 1840; Bourke to Glenelg, 14 Oct. 1835; Glenelg to Bourke, 18 Sept. 1836; Gipps to Glenelg, 1 May 1838; Madgwick, 166-7; Gipps to Russell, 13 Sept. 1841.

into New South Wales, I am anxious to rid that colony of its penal character.' When transportation was stopped no significant protest was heard, and the cessation of assignment, in July 1841, caused no difficulties.[1]

For Gipps this decision solved a number of minor problems. The British government had wanted to check convicts being sent to the Port Phillip District, but this had proved impossible. In 1838 there were 267 there, including 121 employed by the government on public works—roads, Government House, a jetty at Williamstown and a dam at Yarra Falls. Whereas in 1838 all that the Governor could do was to order that only men of 'good character' should be sent there, now he could refuse to supply them at all.[2] Nearer Sydney, he was able to abandon both Bourke's arrangements for putting the ironed gangs under military control, which had been a failure, and his own scheme for using sappers and miners to supervise them. Though he still had to deal with some under punishment, the number was becoming smaller, and most could be employed on public works.[3]

In the Female Factory, neither Bourke's reforms nor the new staff had achieved much improvement; but that institution too now became less of a problem. In 1840 Gipps reported that seventy-two cells had been built there for 'more efficacious punishment', as an alternative to transportation to Moreton Bay. With these, by the end of the year, good discipline temporarily prevailed; but it was still difficult to find suitable employment for the women.[4] The numbers rose steadily to 1,203 in July 1842, in spite of Russell's hope that the cessation of transportation would reduce them. Free immigration and the depression had caused many servants to be 'returned'; they could no longer be discharged into assigned service, but only when free or given tickets-of-leave. However, the numbers quickly fell in 1843, when Gipps started to put the women into private service for wages under government supervision, and this satisfied the women's grievance that by being kept in the Factory they were being too harshly treated for too long. Apart from the later

[1] Buller to A.P.A., 20 Oct. 1838, quoted Hanks, *Australian Patriotic Association*, 662, ML B1165–7; Russell to Grey, 15 Oct. 1839, Grey Papers, Durham, 119–1, and cf. above, p. 239; Russell to Gipps, 6 July 1840; Gipps to Russell, 21 July 1841.
[2] Glenelg to Bourke, 15 Sept. 1836; Bourke and Gipps to Glenelg, 31 May 1837, 1 Oct. 1838; Boyes, 58 ff.; Lonsdale's Returns, *Vic. Hist. Mag.*, iv, 106; Lonsdale's Letter Book, 143, 175, 254; Census, 1838, Pt. Phillip; Pol. Magistrates' Letters, PLV, 38/211; Deas Thomson to Hely, 3 Jan. 1838, 27 Jan. 1841, NSW, Col. Sec.'s Out-Letters, Convicts, 38/13, 41/27; Gipps to La Trobe, 9 May 1840, Gipps–La Trobe Corr., PLV H6991.
[3] Gipps to Glenelg, 20 Sept. 1837, 29 March 1839; Glenelg to Gipps, 23 March 1838.
[4] Gipps to Glenelg, 13 March, 12 and 19 Sept. 1838; Gipps to Russell, 10 Feb. and 1 Oct. 1840; NSW Statutes, 3 Vic., no. 22.

19

discovery of some frauds there, it gave little more trouble until it was closed in 1848.[1]

Gipps was not so worried as Franklin by the need to employ new arrivals on public works. In 1839 the building of a dam at Cook's River, 'shelter . . . for the reception of prisoners' on Cockatoo Island, and after that, 'works of a military nature, namely the New Barracks and the Fortifications of the Harbour' disposed of this problem until the last shiploads were got rid of.[2] Even the Police and Gaols dispute quietened down during these years of prosperity, though in 1840 Gipps reported that this was 'the never ceasing cause of nearly all the abuse which is heaped on Her Majesty's Government and myself'. The Legislative Council and the Governor continued to protest against the charge, and even the Colonial Office, finding the Treasury's 'dictatorial style' becoming 'daily more objectionable', and apprehensive of a lack of funds for migration, wrote what were for it strong letters to the Lords Commissioners; but the latter remained adamant, and continued to demand further economies, even though Gipps had halved the British convict expenditure between 1839 and 1842, and owing to the fall in the price of food, the cost per convict had fallen by nearly twenty per cent to less than £4 a year.[3] Soon squatting regulations and constitutional questions raised fiercer arguments, and as the number of British convicts in the colony declined, this question slowly died a natural death, but only after playing no small part in the colony's rejection of the scheme for its local government by District Councils.[4]

Gipps' chief worry came from Norfolk Island, where Maconochie had been sent to try his 'experiment' in February 1840. Gipps allowed him money for a library and for musical instruments, authorized him to remit punishments and appointed several additional officers, being determined, as he told Russell, 'to give him all the support in my power'; but the island was small and Maconochie was handicapped by the 'doubly convicted' prisoners already there, and his orders to keep these 'old hands' separate from the newcomers. Russell would not allow

[1] Russell to Gipps, 27 April 1841; Gipps to Stanley, 20 May 1843; Stanley to Gipps, 28 Dec. 1843; Gipps to Stanley, 17 March 1844; Deas Thomson, 6 Jan. 1848, Col. Sec.'s Out-Letters, Convicts, 48/11.

[2] Gipps to Glenelg, 8 July 1839, to Russell, 21 Oct. 1840, 6 Feb. 1841.

[3] Gipps to Glenelg, 12 Oct. 1838; Stephen to Spearman, 31 May and 22 Aug. 1839, CO 202/39 and 41; Gipps to Glenelg, 2 Dec. 1839; Trevelyan to Stephen, 30 May and 12 June 1840, and minutes, CO 201/303; Russell to Gipps, 28 June; Gipps to Russell, 17 July, 8 Oct. and 28 Dec. 1840, 16 Oct. 1841, to Stanley, 1 Jan. 1843; Stanley to Gipps, 3 Sept. 1843.

[4] Gipps to Stanley, 17 Nov. 1842, 28 Oct. 1843, 27 July and 30 Sept. 1844; Stanley to Gipps, 10 Aug. 1842, 29 March 1844; Melbourne, 308 ff.

Maconochie another site, as he wanted, and was soon so sceptical of the business that he sent no more men to the Island; but 'notwithstanding the objections', he wanted the experiment to be tried.[1]

Maconochie very soon 'merged' the 'old hands' with the new, and he promised his charges early release in return for good conduct marks. In the first he disobeyed his instructions. In the second, he was likely to break the law, for prisoners could not leave the island until they had served 'the full term of four, six or eight years, according as their sentences are respectively for seven or fourteen years or for life'. It was no use Maconochie saying, 'If I have done wrong in deviating from these rules, I am quite certain that in the circumstances His Excellency would have done so too', or arguing that 'though the means of earning release are apparently placed within the men's reach in comparatively short periods', they would not be likely to earn it. Gipps could not sanction this illegality; all he could do was to press the British government to decide quickly whether the law should be altered so that Maconochie's promises could be confirmed.[2]

Russell's answer was hardly satisfactory. He agreed that the government should have removed the 'old hands'; but that was poor consolation to Maconochie. As for the marks, the men could not leave the island, but might be given 'tickets' on it. Maconochie had wanted 'to place my men in circumstances of *physical freedom*, but with strong motives to *voluntary* rectitude'; the limitations imposed certainly weakened these motives. 'Much of your theory is founded on sound principles,' Gipps admitted. 'The difficulties and embarrassments . . . have arisen out of your failing to give due attention to the position in which you were placed . . . The errors which you committed have been the consequence of your too sanguine temperament and of your looking too lightly on the difficulties which were before you.'[3]

Notwithstanding these difficulties, the system was by no means a complete failure. Father McEncroe, a sensible and, in this case, unprejudiced observer, noticed the overcrowding and the expense, and thought Maconochie perhaps had too high an opinion of human nature;

[1] Normanby to Gipps, 11 May 1839; Gipps to Normanby, 23 Nov. 1839, to Russell, 24 and 25 Feb. and 1 March 1840; Russell to Gipps, 10 Sept.; McCulloch, *Hist. Stud.*, vii, 387 ff.; Barry, ch. 5; above, p. 274.

[2] Maconochie to Gipps, 26 March and 27 May 1840, Col. Sec.'s In-Letters, Norfolk Island, 1840; Deas Thomson to Maconochie, 28 April, 26 June and 15 Sept. 1840, Out-Letters, *ib.*; Gipps to Russell, 27 June and 29 Sept. 1840, with encls., CO 201/297 and 299, and 6 Feb. 1841.

[3] Russell to Gipps, 1 Aug. 1841; Gipps to Stanley, 26 May 1842; Maconochie to Gipps, 2 July 1841, encl. in Gipps to Russell, 28 Aug., CO 201/310; Deas Thomson to Maconochie, 20 Aug. 1841, encl. in Gipps to Russell, 27 Aug.

but writing to Gipps soon after he left the island, he praised the scheme and thought it should be tried elsewhere. When Gipps himself visited the place a year later, in March 1843, if not enthusiastic, he was not unfavourably impressed, and did not relish the prospect of the experience gained being 'wholly thrown away'. The system had not been so expensive as he had feared. Though both gambling and unnatural vice were too common, the convicts did not steal from each other as much as was usual, and there were 'fewer depredations on the Government Crops' than in the past. There had been some increase in crime, for the greater freedom of the men gave them more facilities to commit it, but report had grossly exaggerated it, and it was 'balanced by a diminution of other offences'. Since Maconochie had not been able to enforce fully the punitory part of his system, it was the less surprising that the plan for 'mutual responsibility' had failed; but this could be put right. Discipline in the first stages of punishment should be stricter, and marks less lavishly distributed in the second; but they would be beneficial if they were given a definite value, as they should have been. Although many tasks were less efficiently performed than formerly, this too could be corrected without great difficulty. And whatever the shortcomings of the 'experiment', of the management of the 'old hands' Gipps could speak 'with almost unqualified approbation'; he thought the relaxations of previous severity had produced great benefit, despite his earlier commendation of the 1839 régime, which had probably been based on McEncroe's earlier letters.[1]

Unfortunately, by the time this report reached London, Stanley had already decided on the strength of previous despatches to restore Norfolk Island to its former state. The Home Office had come to disbelieve in Maconochie's system as a punishment, and Gipps' forecast of a 'considerable increase in expense', made in May 1842, was to hand when Stanley, with the help of Montagu, was working out the probation system which he hoped would be so economical. In it, as he told Franklin in November, Norfolk Island would again become a place of the severest punishment. Maconochie was to be relieved. His experiment was over.[2]

He had handicapped himself by reports that were always 'lengthy and discursive', and which irritated both Gipps in Sydney and Stephen in London. He had struck two successive bad seasons. His superintendent

[1] McEncroe to Gipps, *Letters* 3 and 4, 300; Gipps to Stanley, 15 Aug. 1842, 1 April 1843; Barry, 137–46.
[2] Gipps to Stanley, 26 May 1842; Russell to Gipps, 12 Nov. 1840; Stanley to Gipps, 23 Jan. and 26 Jan. 1843 with encls.

of agriculture was incompetent, if not dishonest. All this, the poor site, and Maconochie's own exertions, Stanley admitted; but he argued that the 'relaxation of discipline' had diminished again the 'dread' of transportation, and another 'very serious evil' was the 'great and indefinite expense'. This was all important. 'The worst thing that Maconochie has done may be expressed in the word "Expense",' Gipps told Latrobe. 'This is the point on which the Home Government will, I think, throw him overboard.' He had aroused concern over his expenditure on public works. Rewarding prisoners by making them overseers or police reduced the number of working hands; giving others tickets-of-leave, issuing them with government breeding sows and making them small farmers from whom the Commissariat would have to *buy* provisions, seemed a terrible extravagance. The average cost per man rose from £10.18.0 in 1838–9 to £13.14.0 in 1840–2. Marks were used 'to purchase luxuries at the expense of the British Treasury'. The island bore 'no more resemblance to a penal settlement . . . than a playhouse to a church', lamented Deputy-Commissary Miller. 'The world will be turned upside down, and this is the beginning of it.'[1]

Before he left, Maconochie was told to send to Van Diemen's Land with tickets-of-leave his experimental prisoners and those of the 'doubly convicted' men whose conduct he thought justified it. During the preceding years, he had sent 920 of the latter back to Sydney; despite two murders, which aroused disproportionate excitement in the Legislative Council, their general good conduct bore witness to the benefits of his system. 'I found the island a turbulent, brutal hell and left it a peaceful, well-ordered community,' he wrote. Possibly exaggerated a little, this statement seems more borne out by the evidence than the equally interested verdicts of his opponents that it had proved a complete failure, though his unceasing and voluminous correspondence annoyed officialdom and helped to arouse a determination not to employ his services again. Whatever the shortcomings of the 'mark' system proper may have been, Maconochie's success with the 'old hands' was in itself an indictment of the brutality that preceded and that followed it; but success or failure, it was finished. For the moment, fewer than two hundred men remained on the island, but the arrival of nearly 1,400

[1] Gipps to Stanley, 7 Feb. 1842; Stephen's minute on Gipps to Russell, 1 May 1841, CO 201/309; Stanley to Gipps, 29 April 1843; Gipps to La Trobe, 29 March 1843, PLV, H7159; McEncroe to Gipps, letter 4; Gipps to Stanley, 15 Aug. 1842, with encls., Maconochie to Col. Sec., 20 June, Dep. Comm. Miller to Col. Sec., 16 June, 26 July and 5 Aug., Deas Thomson to Maconochie, 29 July, CO 201/322; Trevelyan to Stephen, 14 Jan. 1843, with encls., *HRA*, xxii, 509 ff.; Gipps to Stanley, 1 April 1843, with encls., CO 201/332; Trevelyan to Stephen, 28 June 1843, encl. Miller to Treasury, 20 Jan., CO 280/163.

'bad' characters from England and Van Diemen's Land during the next two years crowded it once more. In February, the new Superintendent, Captain Childs, of the Royal Marines, took up his command. On 29 September, its management was transferred to Van Diemen's Land.[1] Coercion returned there in full blast, to breed brutality and mutiny.

Stanley had devised his system almost entirely with British interests in mind, following the Whigs' over-hasty condemnation of assigned service. This alone had made transportation workable in a colony which was more than simply a penal establishment. Accepting the ill-informed opinion that a great deal of assignment was too lenient, first Russell and then Stanley, seeking a more uniform and a more deterrent punishment, had insisted on replacing it by a system of gang labour, in defiance of official advice from Van Diemen's Land; for if Franklin underrated the difficulties his instructions were placing on him, he had pleaded strongly that assigned service should not be stopped. Russell had condemned Maconochie's system without even hearing how it was working, and Stanley ignored Gipps' last report on it, belated though it was. The majority in Parliament still wanted to get British criminals out of the country. Stanley and the Treasury wanted punishment to be cheap. Montagu helped to delude the government that what they wanted was possible, though it is doubtful if, except on details, his voice was as decisive as he claimed, for by 1842 Franklin was reporting optimistically on the gang system. The result was a disastrous breakdown in convict administration, and increasing antagonism between the colonies and the mother-country.

[1] Stanley to Gipps, 22 March, 6 April, 30 Oct., 10 Nov. 1843; 6 and 7 Vic. c.35; Gipps to Stanley, 31 Jan. and 28 Nov. 1844, with minutes by Hope and Gairdner, CO 201/350; letters from Maconochie, 1845, CO 280/240, *passim*; Barry, 149 and 167 ff.; Maconochie, *Norfolk Island*, 13. One of the murderers was the psychopath, Knatchbull, though he had left the island the year before Maconochie arrived there.

13

Break-down in Van Diemen's Land

'I never thought of thinking for myself at all.'
W. S. GILBERT: *H.M.S. Pinafore*

When he first assumed office as Secretary of State for the Colonies, Stanley was ready–and apparently anxious–to 'leave to the Home Department the management of all questions of convict discipline'. Next year he changed his mind. The Home Secretary, he declared, could not 'attempt to control the conduct of officers . . . who were not subject to his authority'. In the past, 'the subject of Convict Discipline was left almost entirely to the discretion of the Governor', because the Colonial Secretary had not directed measures which were 'foreign' to his department, even though they affected 'British rather than colonial interests'. To stop this 'local control of an Imperial interest', Stanley decided to superintend the convict establishment himself, though he would refer pardons and other matters concerning individual prisoners to the Home Office. He concocted the 'probation system' and undertook to supervise its administration, in order to impose 'a much more careful . . . control than hitherto over convict expenditure' and prevent the 'great waste' of the past, when the colonial government incurred heavy expenditure 'without informing the Home government until months afterwards'.[1]

Economy was a major objective. Religious instruction was needed in the gangs, and it would have to be paid for; but after the men obtained their 'probation pass', like the assigned servants of the past they would cost no more. They would work for wages, either for private settlers or

---

[1] Stephen's minutes, 1 April 1842, on Gipps to Russell, 27 Aug. 1841, CO 201/310, 3 Dec. 1842, CO 280/149, 306; Stephen to Phillipps, 5 Jan. 1843, Phillipps to Stephen, 6 Jan., Stephen to Trevelyan, 16 Jan., Trevelyan to Stephen, 23 Jan., *Corr.*, PP 1843 (159), CO 280/164; Stanley to Wilmot, 23 June 1843; Treasury to Commissariat, 26 Aug. 1843, Col. Sec. Tas. 22/98/2058.

for the local government, and the latter would henceforth pay for any convict labour that it employed. The men would cost about 1s. 6d. a day for maintenance, and the 'establishment' of each gang, containing between 250 and 300 men, would cost about £1,000 a year; so if the average 'gang term' were eighteen months and four thousand men were sent out each year, only twenty gangs would be needed; since some of the gangs would grow their own food, a panacea which Stephen and the Treasury had long been urging, the annual expense should not be more than about £175,000. Judging from past figures, about 750 of the worst long-term prisoners would be sent from England to Norfolk Island each year. This would mean there would normally be about 2,700 men there, before they were 'promoted' to gang labour in Van Diemen's Land; they should cost about £13 each or £35,000 a year. If the passage cost about £18 a head, or £72,000 altogether, and overheads about £10,000, the total expenditure (apart from the colonial contribution to the Police and Gaols) would be less than £300,000 a year for more than 35,000 men under sentence—and if Stanley ignored the extra cost of those under punishment in the colony, presumably under this system few would be so misguided as to deserve it! Imprisonment in the hulks would certainly cost little more than half as much; but the hulks were almost universally condemned. An equivalent term in a house of correction would cost about the same as seven years' transportation, but this would not get the convict out of the country, and houses of correction had many faults. A new penitentiary would be a different matter, but imprisonment in it would be twice as expensive.[1]

Having despatched his instructions for the new probation system, in November 1842, Stanley had to choose officials to carry it out. Both his nominees turned out incompetent. That he should recall Franklin after his six years in office was natural enough; but it was surprising that he should choose as his successor Sir John Eardley-Wilmot, a sixty-year-old M.P., whom he had recently described to Peel as a 'muddle-brained blockhead'.[2] Possibly he was influenced by considerations of English politics, or even personal friendship. Wilmot, like both Stanley and Peel, had been at Oxford; he had followed Stanley from the Whigs to the Conservatives in 1834, and he was a neighbour of Peel's. He had studied law at Oxford and in 1822 had published an abridgement of Blackstone. He had been in a position to see the working of the Warwick

---

[1] Stanley to Franklin, 25 Nov. 1842; Montagu to Stanley, 11 Oct., 11 Nov. 1842, encl. also mem., 10 Oct. 1839, CO 280/151; Stanley's mem., Nov. 1842, CO 280/149, 332 ff. For cost of passage, p. 261 above.
[2] Stanley to Peel (n.d.—? 1842), Peel Papers, BM, add. MSS. 40467.

County Asylum for juvenile offenders, which had been opened in 1818; but neither his *Letter to the Magistrates on the Increase of Crime* in 1827 advocating the summary whipping of juveniles, nor the bill he introduced into the House of Commons in 1840 to authorize such a procedure indicated very progressive views on the problems raised by young delinquents, even if they showed his interest in them. Like most of his class, he was a county magistrate, but he had had no other administrative experience and had no knowledge of colonial affairs. Boyes' verdict was that 'there had been no government here since the arrival of Sir Eardley' in August 1843. West was more charitable, and ascribed his failure to the 'precision of his instructions', which left him 'no alternative but to obey', and to the 'interested reports of his subordinates'; but this hardly acquits him of failing to find out and report home more about the weaknesses of the system, even if he did not, like his much younger and more forceful contemporary, Sir George Grey, in New Zealand, regard it as his duty if necessary 'to disregard, or act contrary to orders issued from the other side of the globe'.[1]

Under Wilmot, Stanley appointed Captain Matthew Forster as Controller-General of Convicts, instead of Franklin's nominee, the chief police magistrate, Milligan. Forster had been Principal Superintendent of Convicts in Van Diemen's Land, had married a niece of Arthur's and had been an official under him. But though competent enough in the past, he was not a good choice either. Trained in the Arthur system, he had little sympathy with one based far more on 'indulgence' than 'coercion'. According to Maconochie, he 'did not value the moral influence'; certainly his remarks in the 1837 discussions show no great interest in the principles of convict discipline, and in 1842, Franklin became dissatisfied with the way he dealt with unrest in the probation gangs. On top of all this, his health was beginning to fail. He asked for leave in April 1845, after only a year and a half in office, and died the following January before receiving an answer to this request.[2]

As in 1841, Forster was greatly concerned by the amount he expected the new system to cost. To reduce the expenses on buildings and superintendence, he increased the size of the gangs from 300 to 400 men; that this would reduce their efficiency seemed irrelevant. The convicts would now be accommodated at twenty instead of twenty-seven

---

[1] Boyes, Diary, 21 Jan. 1847; West, i, 259–60; J. Rutherford, *Sir George Grey, KCB, 1812–1898, a study in colonial government* (OUP, 1955), 168.
[2] Franklin to Stanley, 17 Nov. 1842; Stanley to Franklin, 23 March 1843; Forster to Wilmot, April 1845, Tas. Arch.; *Observer* (Hobart), 13 Jan. 1846.

stations, and fifteen of these were made 'milder', with a reduced scale of superintendence; unfortunately, the work of the superintendent, who was 'responsible for the discipline and management of the gang', was an important feature of the system. So was classification, but this was impossible without many new buildings; so was regular employment for the men, but this would soon be lacking. For all that, in December 1843, after four months' experience, Wilmot reported that he had 'no doubt of the moral and religious improvement' of the prisoners, a comment all the more surprising since only the month before he had written a private letter on 'unnatural vice' in the gangs. Perhaps he had been excited by the sending out of a schoolmaster in 1843, with books for the convict library, a contribution to reformation apparently easier to supply than overseers and clergy; although the first list of titles had contained 'a remarkable predominance of the theology of the Old Puritans', another list had eventually been chosen which Stephen thought 'more calculated to allure Prisoners to read'.[1]

To the question of unnatural vice, the Lieutenant-Governor never returned. Both he and Forster insisted that all was well. The first stage of probation had fully answered its object, declared the Controller in January 1845; the religious and moral instruction of the convicts was 'strictly attended to' (despite Wilmot's complaints of a shortage of clergy); the convicts' conduct in private service was better than it had been under assignment, and the system as a whole was 'vastly superior' to any that had preceded it. Port Arthur, he thought, was 'an effective place of punishment', and conditions at Point Puer, had been improved. However the Prison Inspectors were concerned at the overcrowding, the lack of separation, classification, supervision and religious instruction everywhere, and the 'filthy and sordid practices' which accompanied male convicts sleeping in dormitories; they wanted separate compartments, lighting and inspection at night, and 'ample' means of solitary confinement at every station.[2]

This was provoking because it would involve increasing further expenses which were already greater than had been estimated. These had grown to £320,000, *plus* the cost of Norfolk Island, and Stanley foresaw a further increase for religious superintendence. Between 1837 and 1843 commissariat expenditure had increased by sixty per cent, the

[1] Wilmot to Stanley, 3 Oct., 5 Oct. encl. Forster's Report, 28 Sept., 2 Nov., 2 Dec. 1843; Stanley to Wilmot, 20 Sept. 1842; Stephen's minutes on Phillipps to Hope, 1 Jan., 26 Feb. 1843, CO 280/149.
[2] Forster's report, Jan. 1845, encl. in Wilmot to Stanley, 31 Jan.; cf. Wilmot to Gladstone 26 Sept. 1846; Prison Inspectors' Report, 24 July 1843, encl. in Phillipps to Stephen. 27 July 1843, CO 280/164.

number of convicts by only about twenty per cent. Stephen thought there was a 'waste of public money' due to a 'want of system', an excessive establishment and too large an outlay on rations (£164,500) 'in a Country where the Crown possesses in the most ample abundance all the Resources for raising the necessary provisions'; having abandoned assignment, the government must compel the convicts to maintain themselves; this was possible and should be seen to, so that 'the great part' of the cost of food should be saved.[1] Franklin had planned to employ the convicts for the benefit of the colony, but to Stanley, this was a 'secondary consideration'. The primary object, he told Wilmot, was 'diminishing the charge entailed on the mother country'; the 'first and most essential object' of the convicts' labour should be their own maintenance.[2] But the gang sites had been chosen for the purposes of road-making and cutting timber rather than for growing food. Since Stanley had forbidden the employment of convicts on colonial works, except for full wages, which the colony could not afford to pay, these sites were now more or less useless, though they were kept up because of the existence of the buildings. In time, the men would be removed to the unsettled districts to grow their food, but they could not go while there were no stations with barracks for them to be moved to.[3]

By 1844, the economic depression had destroyed more hopes for economy. Though the fall in food prices reduced expenditure, when the pass-holders emerged from the probation gangs, they could not find work. Since neither the settlers nor the colonial government could afford to employ them on the terms Stanley laid down, Wilmot explained that he had had to keep many in Government service to keep them at work and maintain discipline. Stanley approved this 'deviation' from his instructions, for he had assumed there would be a sufficient demand for labour; but the Governor's suggestion that the men be made available to the colonial government for colonial works, in return for its paying the cost of superintendence (about a quarter of the total), leaving Great Britain to pay for the men's maintenance, was abhorrent. Though Stephen minuted that 'the alternative seems to be, for the present at least, between taking £4,000 a year which may still be had for the

---

[1] Trevelyan to Stephen, 28 Jan. 1843, Stephen's minute, 11 Feb., Stephen to Trevelyan, 28 Feb., Trevelyan to Stephen, 18 March, CO 280/163.

[2] Forster to Montagu, 15 May 1841, Montagu to Forster, 17 May, Col. Sec. 76/1; Gibson to Directors, VDL Co., 24 March 1842, Foreign Letter Book, no. 6; Stanley to Wilmot, 24 April and 23 June 1843, 26 March 1844; cf. Treasury to Commissariat, 28 Aug., Col. Sec. Tas., 22/98/2058, and Hartwell, 102.

[3] Trevelyan to Stephen, 22 Jan. 1844, encl. McLean to Trevelyan, 12 Sept. 1843, CO 280/176; Stephen's minute on Wilmot to Stanley, 14 July 1845.

superintendence of Convict labour or having that labour thrown back on the government as a commodity too dear to purchase', Stanley insisted that to pay £4,000 for the equivalent of £16,000 would be 'to carry the delusion that such services are worth nothing to anybody' (and neither they were!). If the British government paid for colonial works, it would lead to 'improvidence and waste'. Van Diemen's Land was first and foremost a penal settlement. The convicts were 'not intruders' there and the free population could claim no indemnity, such as cheap labour, for their presence. If the colony 'cannot purchase the labour we have to sell at the price it is worth our while to accept', they could not have it, and the British government would consider 'other advantageous employment'. He forgot that there was none.[1]

CONVICTS IN VAN DIEMEN'S LAND

	Number Arriving		Passholders awaiting hire (Dec.)
	Male	Female	
1838	2,166	284	
1839	1,376	302	
1840	1,181	184	
1841	2,682	626	
1842	4,819	681	
1843	3,048	684	
1844	3,959	644	3,179
1845	2,263	607	3,268
1846	786	340	2,025

The avalanche of prisoners arriving since 1841, which increased the convict population of the colony by over forty per cent in four years might have caused some confusion at any time; but coming under a new system, under which more than before were to be worked by the government in the new probation gangs, arriving in the middle of an acute economic depression, when employers were asked to pay wages which they could not afford, when the colony was ruled by an elderly, inexperienced governor, who received scant sympathy or help from his superiors in London, they might even have been expected to cause more. In May 1844, there were 16,000 requiring work, 4,000 with conditional pardons, 5,000 with tickets-of-leave and 7,000 with passes, and another

[1] Wilmot to Stanley, 2 Dec. 1843, with minutes by Stephen, Hope and Stanley, CO 280/161, and 8 March 1844, encl. Forster's report, 27 Feb.; Stanley to Wilmot, 31 Aug.

2,000 would be gaining their passes soon. More than 1,000 of these were unemployed then; next year more than 3,000 were, or nearly a third of the pass-holders. Unless government did something, the men could only 'starve or steal'; yet Stanley's instructions prevented it offering them work. So too did *laissez-faire* prejudices. In January 1845, for example, the Controller-General recommended undertaking ship-building at Port Arthur, which, he said, would help communications with the new penal stations on the Peninsula, and provide at the same time a 'hiring establishment' on the coast; it was difficult to find employment at Port Arthur and this would give the men a trade. But to the Commissary-General, this project was merely 'an unprofitable speculation to Government', and as such undesirable. In July 1844, Wilmot suggested employing some men on irrigation works, but that was vetoed in London; it would mean, minuted Stephen, that they would be 'employed in the most costly works merely to keep them from idleness and crime'. Stanley agreed that they should be employed in growing food and building hospitals and schools for themselves, for the colonists must not think that the British Treasury depended on them for employing the convicts (though in fact it did!); but the result of forbidding them to do anything else was of course to increase unemployment. The Commissariat expenditure of more than £250,000 might have 'saved Van Diemen's Land from the degree of misery that the other colonies suffered', but the 'inundation' of ex-convicts seeking work was a cause of much distress.[1]

To relieve it, Wilmot suggested, as well as the vetoed 'works', that emigrants with capital be *granted* land again; they might employ some men. Alternatively, the pass-holders themselves might be given allotments. Stanley objected to creating 'cottier' tenants; but in 1844 he agreed that if unemployment increased further he might consider authorizing the Governor to lease land to ticket-holders. He also agreed to repeal the Australian Waste Lands Act of 1842 insofar as it applied to Van Diemen's Land, so that settlers could buy Crown land for less than £1 per acre; this fitted in with the theory of the 'sufficient price' for land, which in the conditions of Van Diemen's Land was then obviously too high. Next year, to afford further relief there, he agreed that conditionally pardoned convicts should be allowed to go anywhere on the Australian mainland to seek work, and the only result of violent protests from the other colonies was to have this privilege extended, in

---

[1] Committee on Convict Expenditure in VDL, Minutes, 1843–7 (Tas. Arch., E), 4 March 1844, 25 Jan. 1845; Wilmot to Stanley, 29 May, 25 June, 18 July 1844, with Stephen's minute, CO 280/170, 31 Jan. 1845, encl. Controller-Gen's. Report, and 5 Aug. 1845.

1846, to permit the prisoner to go to any part of the Empire, except to the place where he had originally been convicted.[1]

Apart from unemployment, a 'nameless crime' was also beginning to cause concern. Wilmot had referred to this in a private letter to Stanley, written soon after he had arrived. His Lordship had ignored this, as he ignored so many other displeasing things, but in August 1844, Hope sapiently observed that the 'congregation of convicts in large gangs' was likely to aggravate homosexuality, 'the existence of which, unluckily, was well known before'; he did nothing, however, and Wilmot's report, written in September, suggested that everything was satisfactory. 'The present system of convict management was well calculated to forward the interests of both the mother country and the colony', he declared. It required 'no alteration'. Not perhaps without justification, Under-Secretary Hope minuted on this that 'though nothing is said by the Governor directly of the system . . . the inference is that he considers it to be working well'; and this conclusion seemed confirmed by an even more enthusiastic report from Wilmot, written in January 1845. Offences in the gangs were 'trivial and few', and had not increased as much as the numbers of convicts. The system was 'vastly superior' to any that had preceded it, declared Forster, in his next half-yearly report. Of 24,824 convicts, only 1,209 were at Port Arthur under punishment – certainly a smaller proportion than ten years before under the old system. In four years from July 1841, while 5,500 men had committed offences in the gangs, 4,555 had earned their passes without fault. It was a pity that two-thirds of the men then showed they had not been properly reformed in the gangs by committing offences as pass-holders, and by being convicted in the Supreme Court and Quarter Sessions.[2]

Hope and Stephen by this time were regretting the abolition of assignment, a system the latter thought, as early as December 1843, to have been abandoned 'inadvisedly' and a year later, 'rashly, hastily and ignorantly. Every fresh report seems to me more and more strongly to show how little the Transportation Committee understood the subject,

[1] Wilmot to Stanley, 29 May, 25 June and 20 Aug. 1844; Stanley to Wilmot, 31 Aug. 1844, 5 Feb. 1845; Wilmot to Stanley, 7 July 1845, with minutes by Hope, Stanley and Gladstone, CO 280/183; *South Australian*, 5 Sept. 1845; Sir George Grey (S.A.) to Stanley, 6 Sept. 1845, Crowther and M'Laren (S.A. Co.) to Gladstone, 17 Feb., 2 March 1846, Gladstone to Robe, 13 May, Lyttleton to M'Laren, 16 May, *Corr.*, PP, 1846 (692); Gipps to Stanley, 13 Dec. 1844, 13 Aug., 20 Oct. 1845; Gladstone to Fitz Roy, 13 May 1846.

[2] Hope's minute on Maconochie to Stanley, 4 Aug. 1844, CO 280/178; Wilmot to Stanley, priv. and confidential, 2 Nov. 1843, CO 280/163, 5 Sept., 1844, with Hope's minute, CO 280/171; *ib.*, encl. Controller-General's Reports, 1 Jan., 5 Aug. 1845; Convict Record Books, Tas. Arch., and below, p. 343.

and how inevitable a return to it is', he wrote. This was impossible; its critics had done their work too well. But this very impossibility made the working of the new system all the more important, and yet, as Stephen justly complained, 'it was impossible to derive any distinct impression of what is passing . . . Nothing can be less satisfactory than the manner in which the Lieutenant-Governor and the Controller exercise their duty of reporting'; in fact their reports could 'not be credited in the face of the testimony we possess'. Certainly there was a stream of reports complaining of idleness, homosexuality and crime. 'It only requires a moderate allowance of gin and tobacco to make the life that was intended to be a formidable punishment one of the most pleasant and desirable in the colony,' commented Boyes of the first, in December 1844. The second would be reduced when new huts on the separate system were built; but, as Stephen complained, neither Wilmot nor Forster seemed in any hurry about them, apart from vague references 'in the future tense'.[1]

In May 1845, Dr. J. S. Hampton, a surgeon-superintendent, and his assistant, Boyd, an ex-Pentonville instructor appointed to Maria Island, declared roundly that the system provided 'punishment with no reformation'. Convicts were employed as overseers. Conduct was bad, criminal habits unbroken, religious instruction and secular education both inadequate. Soon after this, there arrived from Wilmot a 'not very conclusive answer' to complaints of mismanagement at the Brickfields' hiring depot, which had been made ten months before. This showed 'no very earnest desire to ascertain the facts or to elicit the truth', thought Stephen. No wonder he was becoming more and more worried.[2]

Next January, the Deputy-Commissary-General wrote a strong condemnation of seven of the convict stations, and in April, the first report by the new Controller-General, Champ, appointed in January on the death of Forster, was far more critical than any of those of his predecessor. True, many of the establishments were satisfactory, including two on Maria Island which had aroused Boyd's ire, and all the men at Port Arthur were employed on useful works; but of the twenty-three regular stations, six, he said, were defective, and at Brown's River, near Hobart, 650 men were in a 'state of utter idleness'. Perhaps the bad

---

[1] Minutes on Gipps to Stanley, 20 May 1843, CO 201/333, on Wilmot to Stanley, 8 March, 18 July, 13 Aug. 1844, CO 280/168, 170 and 171; Boyes' Diary, 21 Dec. 1844; West, ii, 310–4.
[2] Hampton's Reports, 1 March, 7 May 1845, Boyd's report, 31 Dec., Boyd to the Rev. W. Russell, 29 April 1845, Hampton to the Pentonville Commissioners, 9 Aug., *Corr.*, PP 1846 (402); Wilmot to Stanley, 24 July 1845, encl. magistrates' report, 30 Sept. 1844, and Stephen's minute, CO 280/184, 158 ff.

conditions here, so close to the capital, helped to swell the criticism of the whole system; certainly this station illustrated the difficulty of working the men at hard and useful labour while keeping them accessible to potential employers; but in the light of these reports, it is surprising to find Wilmot, in January 1846, making the extraordinary assertion that 'the moral, and religious improvement' brought about 'by the new system cannot be doubted by unprejudiced persons'.[1]

Meanwhile Wilmot had been quite inactive about building the new women's penitentiary which had been authorized. In 1844, he wrote about it 'with his usual indistinctness and vagueness', sent home no estimates or plans, said it would be expensive, and suggested keeping up instead the hulk *Anson* which Dr. Bowden was using 'temporarily' as a female establishment. When Bowden sent a full report in 1845, the Governor made no comment. Stephen thought it 'strange that on a matter of such importance the Lieutenant Governor would have nothing to say', but that appeared to be his way. All that could be done was to ask for plans again, and keep the hulk for the time being. 'You do not show that you have given any attention to the establishment,' Gladstone told him. The factory remained 'a scene of feasting, complete idleness, vicious indulgence . . . and every evil communication', without reformatory discipline or religious instruction, with little classification and few separate cells. Its 'vices' might have originated in economy, but nothing was done to correct them, no penitentiary was built and the women remained as neglected as in the past.[2]

Norfolk Island was another cause of trouble. When its control was transferred from New South Wales to Van Diemen's Land, in September 1844, Wilmot's report on its problems was described in London as 'singularly jejune and meagre'. He agreed that it should be used for the worst convicts, but not until July 1845, after a reprimand for his taciturnity, did he endorse Gipps' suggestions about the new penitentiary which was needed there, though the lack of it was a major cause of the appalling conditions on the island. As in other cases, he seems to have been too nervous of recommending expenditure and too reluctant to interfere with incompetent subordinates, in this case Major Childs, another of Stanley's nominees, despite Gipps' warning of the dangers

---

[1] Mem. on the probation stations, Maclean to Trevelyan, 6 Jan. 1846, encl. in Wilmot to Stanley, 24 Jan., with minutes by Stephen and Gladstone, CO 280/191; Champ's report, 30 April 1846, encl. in Wilmot to Stanley, 13 May; Wilmot to Stanley, 9 and 12 Jan. 1846.
[2] See above, p. 287. Wilmot to Stanley, 13 Sept. 1844, and Stephen's minute, CO 280/171; *ib.*, 22 Nov. 1845, encl. Bowden's report, 25 Oct., and Stephen's minute, CO 280/185; Stephen's minute for Lyttleton, 7 Feb. 1846, CO 280/184, 36 ff.; Gladstone to Wilmot, 27 and 30 April 1846; Fry, 192.

likely to arise from the lack of supervision of such a distant establishment. Certainly he sounded a more urgent note in December 1845, and
the following April, spurred on by more and more critical accounts from
the settlement, he sent a magistrate from Hobart to investigate its
affairs. This seemed to presage action, but in the meantime, the
rumours from the island had increased the colonial criticism of the
whole convict administration, his unwillingness (or inability) to discuss
its problems had annoyed the Colonial Office, and eventually the report
on it in June 1846 disclosed another breakdown in Stanley's plans.[1]

By then Wilmot certainly had begun to realize the need for reporting
home more fully, but he continued stoutly to defend the system. Its
difficulties, he assured Gladstone in July 1846, were due only to the
financial difficulties of the colony. Even though Stanley had cavalierly
rejected his suggestion that the local government should not have to pay
for convict labour on colonial works, Wilmot insisted that there would
be no surplus labour if prosperity continued to revive, if the holders of
conditional pardons continued to go to the mainland, if the colonial
revenue improved and if the settlers increased their demand for labour
–a somewhat formidable list of conditions! Certainly Bishop Nixon had
refused to ordain the religious instructors sent out for the gangs; but
this matter would soon be corrected. To the complaint that he 'had for
so long a time left [Stanley] uninformed altogether about the real state
of the convicts and about the progress of his Lordship's experiment for
improving their discipline and management', he replied that up to the
end of 1844 he had not had enough time to see how the system would
work. He claimed that it was working well except for the unemployment, and it was infinitely preferable to the old. The extent of 'unnatural
vice' was exaggerated. The convicts were improving physically, and
their conduct was satisfactory. Of 9,000 pass-holders, only 400 had been
guilty of offences against 'morality', that is, more than mere breaches of
convict discipline, though the critic might observe that such a crime
rate was by no means negligible and was double that of five years
before.[2]

If Wilmot in this apologia was ready to ignore again the defects

---

[1] Gipps to Stanley, 20 July and 20 Aug. 1844; Wilmot to Stanley, 21 Sept. 1844, and
Stephen's minute, CO 280/171; Gipps to Stanley, 9 Feb. 1845, encl. Deas Thomson to
Col. Sec. VDL, 30 Oct. 1844, and Forster to Deas Thomson, 30 Nov.; Stanley to Wilmot,
6 March 1845; Wilmot to Stanley, 21 July 1845, 19 Dec. 1845, encl. Childs' report, 1 Oct.;
Wilmot to Gladstone, 6 July, 1846, encl. Stewart's rept., 20 June; West, ii, 296–8.

[2] Wilmot to Stanley, 16 March 1846, and Stephen's minute, CO 280/193; Wilmot to
Gladstone, 10 July and 28 Aug. 1846, and Stephen's minutes, CO 280/194 and 199;
Nixon, CO 280/222; Champ's report, 30 April 1846, encl. in Wilmot to Stanley, 13 May,
CO 280/194, 132 ff. For crime, below, p. 343.

noticed in Champ's report only three months earlier, local opinion, press, clergy and Legislative Council were unwilling to follow his example. They were becoming increasingly hostile to the gangs and to the ex-convicts who were said to be overrunning the country. When hired by private employers, men with probation passes did less work than the former assigned servants. They had 'merely been trained in Gangs on the roads', and neither taught to be 'a very useful handy man', nor encouraged in a 'spirit of Industry', complained John Leake. In their leisure they were 'often roaming abroad without permission and sometimes committing depredations on their Master's property or that of his neighbours . . . A greater inveteracy of bad habits and evil practices' resulted from their being herded together in the gangs when they arrived, instead of being dispersed, as before, among the free people. The only independent testimony apparently favourable to the system by 1846 was from the Reverend Mr. Fry, whose comments Wilmot quoted with relish; but even they were ambiguous, and Stephen remarked that 'the few sentences which have sustained some of [the governor's] general opinions are immediately connected with statements . . . which, one would have supposed, would have been most unwelcome to him'. The previous year a petition had asked that transportation be gradually abolished. Wilmot asserted that its allegations were 'erroneous and exaggerated' and that it bore only 1,750 signatures out of a free male population of over 20,000; though he was probably right to suggest that the majority still wanted convict labour, it was a sign how the wind was blowing.[1]

This opposition was whetted by the parsimony of the British Treasury. The colonists argued that in return for their taking prisoners they now received nothing, neither convict labour to settlers or government, nor police protection, nor cheap land nor a market for their produce. This was an exaggeration. Government expenditure had not only mitigated the depression in 1842, but it made recovery easier. But Wilmot's economies, imposed on orders from home, reduced its benefits; the governor agreed that the colony had suffered economically by being 'deprived of unpaid labour', and the commercial distress encouraged hard feelings towards the mother country.[2]

From 1841 to 1846 revenue had fallen by a third. Land sales dropped

[1] West, ii, 313–5; Bishop Nixon to Gladstone, and private letters, 1846, CO 280/203, espec. from P. Murdoch, 21 March, and Dr. Motherwell, 19 June; Leake to Wilmot, 31 Sept. 1846, *Hist. MSS. Tas.*, 68; Stephen's minute on Wilmot to Gladstone, Sept. 1846, CO 280/196, encl. a letter from Fry, *Corr.*, PP 1847 (262); Wilmot to Stanley, 7 Aug. 1845, encl. letter from Pitcairn; *ib.*, 6 Feb., 16 March 1846.
[2] Wilmot to Stanley, 9 Jan., 14 May 1846.

to nothing. Retrenchment was the order of the day, and yet the colony was asked to pay for the convict labour employed on public works, for the swollen Police and Gaols expenditure and for a 'disproportionate' charge for religious instruction. In 1843, the Treasury had even objected to paying for half the Hobart Water Police. Told by Stanley in September 1843 that he could 'dismiss from his mind' any hope that Great Britain would pay the colony for convict labour, censured and told to repay £39,000 which he had borrowed to meet his deficit in 1844, Wilmot faced mounting opposition in the Legislative Council. In the 1845 session, he met outspoken protests against 'taxation without representation', and in October, six unofficial members, 'the patriotic six', resigned, leaving the Council without a quorum, rather than see the estimates carried by the votes of officials, who with the governor's casting vote made a majority. Though after some difficulty Wilmot managed to replace them, and held a successful council session in the spring of 1846, a first-class political crisis had arisen.[1]

The previous year, when it was almost too late, even Stanley had agreed to 'the necessity of affording relief to Van Diemen's Land' by taking over 'a considerable part' of the Police and Gaols expenditure; in March 1846, Gladstone told Wilmot that Britain would pay two-thirds of their cost, as 'an earnest of its anxiety to act in a spirit of liberal justice towards Van Diemen's Land'. Stephen hoped that 'the concession at last made by the Treasury . . . after many years of fruitless solicitation from this office' might allay colonial 'excitement'; but the excitement was considerable. Stephen thought the unofficial members 'quite right' for the Treasury had 'persisted from year to year, in defiance as I cannot but think of reason and justice, in throwing on the Colony the whole expense of the Police and Gaols'. The real blame for the crisis lay with the British Government–'with the Treasury for unreasonable parsimony; with the Home Office for throwing the whole current of convicts into Van Diemen's Land by an ill-advised and unconsidered pledge to abandon transportation to New South Wales, with this office for acquiescing, without monstrance, in these . . . decisions, with this office, for substituting probation gangs for assigned service, and with the Committee of the House of Commons for drawing

[1] Wilmot to Stanley, 25 June 1844, encl. Blue Book; Wilmot's Finance minute to Legs. Council, 1844; Wilmot to Stanley, 13 and 26 Aug.; Trevelyan to Stephen, 4 Sept. 1843, CO 280/163; Stanley to Wilmot, 22 Sept. 1843, 8 July 1844, 8 Feb. 1845; Mins. of Exec. Council, 1 and 4 July; Finance minute to Legs. Council, 30 July 1845; Wilmot to Stanley, 26 Aug.; Legs. Council, *V & P*, 31 Oct. 1845; Wilmot to Stanley, 5 Nov. 1845, 11 Feb. 1846; cf. *Hobart Town Courier, Hobart Town Advertiser, The Colonial Times*, 1844–5, Townsley, 68–89, Hartwell, ch. 13, West, i, 233–52.

up impractical rules regarding transportation which had the effect of destroying one evil–assignment–and producing another and much greater evil which now exists'. Even so the Treasury's attitude persisted. Should Great Britain pay for the cost of prosecuting convicts in Van Diemen's Land? 'No,' said the Treasury. Their judgment 'in their own cause is partial and unfair', minuted Stephen. 'The request should be allowed.' It was.[1]

The Colonial Office at last was prepared to take a stronger line, and at the eleventh hour it forced the Treasury to give way over the Police and Gaols whose cost had risen from £14,000 in 1836 to £36,763 in 1845. Certainly the colony had to surrender the land revenue in return, but at the moment this was zero, owing to the depression and the expansion of the mainland colonies. Stanley hoped that leasing allotments to ticket-holders and paying for the police would make it possible for the government to avoid a potentially hostile Commons' committee of inquiry and to provide sufficient immediate relief to Van Diemen's Land for it still to be used as 'a great reformatory prison'; but though the former aim was achieved, the latter was not, and in March 1846, Gladstone, who had replaced Stanley at the Colonial Office, told Wilmot that transportation to the colony would be suspended for two years.[2]

By then the Colonial Office had wearied of Wilmot's administration. It had commented on twenty-seven of his despatches in two years in 'terms of disapprobation'. Notwithstanding the shortcomings of the probation system, the exaggerated hopes of reform based on it, the difficulties created by the British government's insistence on economy, the general economic depression, the unsuitable land policy imposed on Van Diemen's Land and Stanley's general arrogance and lack of sympathy, Wilmot too had been found wanting. Whether owing to personal weakness or to lack of experience, he was too hesitant either to disobey his instructions, or to protest emphatically and insistently against them, or to support the mild protests he did make with chapter and verse pointing out the system's shortcomings. As Gladstone told him, in April 1846, 'You assumed the government of Van Diemen's Land at a period when a new system of convict discipline had been adopted and was in course of establishment . . . for the purpose of affording a

---

[1] Stanley's minute on Wilmot to Stanley, 21 Jan. 1845, CO 280/179; Stephen to Trevelyan, 27 Nov. 1845 and 9 Jan. 1846, Trevelyan to Stephen, 2 Feb. 1846, Gladstone to Wilmot, 14 March, *Corr.*, PP 1846 (402); Stephen's minutes on Wilmot to Stanley, 5 Nov. 1845, reporting the resignation of the 'Patriotic Six', and on Wilmot to Stanley, 19 Nov., 15 and 17 Dec., CO 280/185 and 186.

[2] Drafts, Stephen to Trevelyan, on Police and Gaols, Stanley for the Cabinet on the Land Act, Nov. 1845 and Jan. 1846, CO 280/201, 331 ff.; Gladstone to Wilmot, 14 March 1846.

solution to one of the most difficult social problems . . . with a view not
to economy but to moral purposes . . . This was a method of management in which the transported prisoners . . . should be separated from
the free population at least during the earlier portion of their terms, and
associated together in probation parties'. In the 'very arduous task' of
organizing these parties, of maintaining their severity and yet
'neutralizing by discipline and by religious and humanitarian influences
all those dangers which arise from . . . the constant intercourse of
criminals among themselves', Wilmot would not have been blamed 'for
partial failure'; but he had not given his 'mind and time to the pressing
exigencies of convict discipline'. He had shown no interest in the moral
problems involved; he had even seemed unaware of their existence;
therefore there was 'no hope through your instrumentality of bringing
the character and results of transportation to a fair issue, of being
enabled either to achieve success or even to ascertain failure'.[1]

So Gladstone recalled Eardley-Wilmot, and entrusted the administration of Van Diemen's Land to La Trobe, the Superintendent at Port
Phillip, until a new Lieutenant-Governor could be sent from England.
But he felt that the probation system, as 'an experiment on a very
momentous and very difficult subject matter . . . must still be regarded
as untried'; and since the 'information received from the Cape of Good
Hope, where the Colonial convicts are managed under the immediate
supervision of its chief projector, [Mr. Montagu] . . . appears to indicate
complete success', the system 'ought not to be abandoned' in Australia,
but 'improved in its management'. What was wanting was 'a Governor
of large capacity and energy', minuted Stephen. 'To such a person
could be committed almost unlimited powers to correct, on the spot, the
whole of the convict system. I have long since abandoned the hope that
anyone at this distance can either devise or enforce the execution of any
wise or practicable schemes for this purpose.'[2]

Next year La Trobe sent home a full report on the situation as he
found it. He thought the superintendents and the overseers were
inadequate, and commented on the 'insufficiency in all the sub-

---

[1] Stephen's minutes on Wilmot to Stanley, 7 and 26 Aug. 1845, CO 280/184; Gladstone to
Wilmot, draft, Gladstone Papers, BM, Add. MSS. 44364, 47; Gladstone to Wilmot, 30
April 1846, Corr., PP 1847 (262). Cf. Stafford Northcote, *The Case of Sir Eardley-Wilmot . . .*,
(1847).
[2] Stephen's minute on Wilmot to Stanley, 23 Jan. 1846, CO 280/199. For the success at
the Cape, Napier to Stanley, 27 Oct. 1843, encl. mem. by Montagu, 16 Aug., and report of
Board of Inquiry, 9 Sept., Corr., PP, 1847 (742); Napier to Stanley, 23 Jan. 1844, CO
48/238; Maitland to Stanley, 2 Dec. 1844, 3 March 1845, 26 Feb. 1846, with minutes by
Stephen and Lyttleton, CO 48/251 and 260; Stephen to Phillipps, 13 May 1846, Corr.
PP 1847 (262).

divisions of subordinate agency', of discipline, medical attention and religious instruction. But, he said, the system had not had a fair trial. Too many convicts had been sent before proper arrangements to receive them had been made; there had been many 'makeshifts', and a reluctance to incur necessary expenditure. Probably proper classification was impossible; but idleness, variation in punishment, petty insubordination, vice and the evils of 'aggregation' were certainly prevalent. Of the stations, he thought eight were satisfactory or good, and the notorious Brown's River was much improved; but six were bad, and the road parties were unsatisfactory. At the Bridgewater depot the buildings were old and dilapidated. The prisoners' barracks at Hobart and Launceston, equally old and also overcrowded, needed to be completely rebuilt. Point Puer was 'decayed'. Port Arthur, with its old wooden buildings, offered no opportunity for proper classification, so irregularities there were inevitable. As a settlement for timber-getting, Macquarie Harbour was a complete failure, and so was the female establishment in the *Anson* hulk, despite Bowden's satisfaction with it. In all, La Trobe concluded that the 'heavier portion' of the criminals' punishment should be incurred in England, not 'in this distant colony'.[1]

Wilmot protested against the injustice of his recall, which Gladstone most foolishly had associated with quite unjustified reflections on his private life. Gladstone's successor at the Colonial Office, Earl Grey, agreed with the verdict on the Lieutenant-Governor's inefficiency, and refused to re-employ him. Though later Grey admitted that reports from La Trobe and the new Lieutenant-Governor, Sir William Denison, had proved 'conclusively that the failure [of probation] cannot justly be attributed to the fault of the individuals who were charged with the duty of carrying it into execution, but . . . to inherent defects in the system itself', this verdict offers no explanation why those individuals should have claimed it was working well instead of drawing attention to its defects.[2]

That in practice the probation system was a failure is indubitable, but why? Montagu naturally insisted that it was not ill-conceived. Certainly it was not well-administered by Wilmot and Forster, though both justly complained of the lack of clergy and reliable superintendents. Many, wrote West, were 'qualified to control, but utterly unable to instruct', and since the government wanted peace and quiet, 'it was understood by the lower officers that the shorter their black lists, the more agreeable

[1] La Trobe to Grey, 31 May 1847, encl. Controller-General's Report, 6 May.
[2] Gladstone to Wilmot, 9 March 1847; Grey to Wilmot, 30 March and 13 April 1847, to Denison, 27 April 1848, replying to Denison to Grey, 10 July 1847, CO 280/210.

their periodical reports'.[1] But the principal reason for its failure was surely that too many men were sent to Van Diemen's Land. They could not be properly disciplined in the gangs; when they obtained a pass they could not find work, and unemployment inevitably led to idleness, vice and crime. Stanley might have foreseen this. Even though not expecting the depression, Franklin had hinted at possible unemployment, and if Wilmot is blameworthy in not stressing the troubles more strongly than he did, Stanley is at least equally culpable for not heeding the remarks which both the Lieutenant-Governors did make.

It was clear that stopping assignment had been expensive. During Franklin's administration, while the number of convicts had increased by a third, commissariat expenditure increased by two-thirds. By 1846, compared with 1837, the number of convicts had increased by seventy-five per cent, but commissariat expenditure had doubled, so the cost per man had increased by a fifth, notwithstanding that prices, especially of food, had fallen heavily, perhaps by about a quarter. It was equally clear that transportation without assignment was unpopular in Van Diemen's Land. Since the British government remained opposed to assignment, the breakdown in Van Diemen's Land strengthened the case for penitentiaries at home; but since they could not be built overnight and the government was still reluctant to resort to them exclusively, it remained for it to continue the search for an alternative.

[1] West. ii 307.

14

Earl Grey's Exiles

'That celebrated,
cultivated,
underrated
nobleman.'

W. S. GILBERT

When three years' experience proved the failure of the probation system which Stanley had planned so confidently in November 1842, the British government had to examine its penal policy again; but it was seeking only an alternative *mode* of transportation, for parliamentary, official and judicial opinion agreed in desiring to keep it as a standard form of punishment. To the 1847 Select Committee on Criminal Law prison officials and magistrates testified in its favour; few of them doubted that it was the punishment most dreaded by the convicts. M. D. Hill, the penal reformer, and the Roman Catholic Bishop Willson from Hobart agreed that if it were properly carried out its benefits outweighed its defects. The Anglican Bishop Nixon, though concerned by its effects on colonial society, admitted its benefits to the mother country. Sir Richard Bourke, though opposing it to New South Wales, did not object to it elsewhere. 'The punishment of transportation cannot safely be abandoned,' concluded the Committee. Imprisonment 'as usually practised' was 'not an efficient punishment' for it involved 'too little suffering'; whether the 'improved new system' would be any better was 'not yet known'.[1]

---

[1] Report, 3–7, Bishop Nixon, q. 2127 ff. and 5085, Bishop Willson, 5500 ff., Bourke, 4217, 4234, 4262, PP 1847 (449). Twenty-four witnesses favoured transportation; only six doubted its efficacy as a deterrent punishment. Col. Jebb, Surveyor-General of Prisons, refused to commit himself, except that punishment should be certain, and that the first part of this punishment should be inflicted in England. The final 'exile' might be a reward or punishment according to the circumstances of the individual (2112–3). Cf. *P. Debs.*, 3rd Ser., xciii, 28 ff., 138 ff., 305 ff., 3, 4 and 10 June 1847.

For all that, the situation had changed since the discussions in the 1830s. The government had built some new prisons. It had extended the use of the separate system. It had formed a new penal establishment at Gibraltar and had extended that at Bermuda. These helped to meet the Van Diemen's Land crisis in 1846, and made it possible next year to try yet another new system, based on 'exile'. This plan, long mooted among penal reformers, envisaged transporting convicts only after 'reformatory' prison discipline at home. The prospect of such 'emigration' could be held out as an incentive to good conduct, and it would get rid of 'a considerable portion of the convict class'; but that they thought it still 'penal' was shown by the number of applications for a free pardon to return.[1]

From the colonial point of view such men might be welcome if labour was scarce; if they were not, Van Diemen's Land at least was still a penal colony which could be compelled to take them. But colonial approval would be the more forthcoming, it was hoped, because the men were expected to be 'reformed', after a term of imprisonment under the 'separate' system. From Millbank, Wakefield, Preston, the juvenile establishment at Parkhurst and the new 'model' prison opened at Pentonville in 1842, this was steadily extended after the 1843 circular on prison construction, and the appointment next year of Colonel Joshua Jebb as Surveyor-General of Prisons. The new 'prison palace' at Reading in 1845, Portland in 1848, the remodelled Dartmoor in 1850, prisons in the colonies on which the Inspectors regularly and enthusiastically reported, without ever having seen them or their sites, 'under the misapprehension that English models will at once and without any material changes, adapt themselves to colonial exigencies, and that every deviation from these models is an error', as Stephen remarked –all these and other 'massive granite monuments' testified to Jebb's 'misplaced architectural ingenuity' and the spread of the new prison discipline.[2] Surely as the result of silent and solitary meditation on past sins, reading the Bible, religious tracts and sermons, or perhaps Bishop Watson's *Apology*, or Porteous' *Evidences*, or Jones on the Trinity, or Leslie's *Short Method with the Deists*, the convict would emerge a new man, even if in time it appeared that mental deterioration was as likely

[1] Prison Inspectors to Sir George Grey, 13 Dec. 1846, HO 45/1393; Gairdner's minute on Fitz Roy to Gladstone, 6 Nov. 1846, CO 201/369.
[2] Circular on the uniform construction of prisons, 1843, HO 45/436; Webb, *Prisons*, 128–31, 177–8, 182, 187; Stephen's minute on Prison Inspectors' Report on Bermuda, 24 Sept. 1846, CO 37/115; Grey to Fitz Roy, 13 March 1848; Barry, 211. Cf. Joshua Jebb, *Modern Prisons, their Construction and Ventilation* (1844), Field, *op. cit.*; Chesterton, *Revelations*; Clay, *op. cit.*

as reform. Pentonville was 'the portal to a penal colony', declared the Home Secretary, Sir James Graham, when that great institution was opened in 1842; if the prisoner there was 'moulded for a better frame of mind', he would be sent out with a ticket-of-leave, though if his heart remained 'hardened', he would be transported as an 'abject convict'.[1]

By then the first 'exiles' had gone. They were not 'Pentonvillains', but juveniles from Parkhurst. South Africa, New South Wales and South Australia refused to take them and they were not appreciated in New Zealand; but they were welcome in Western Australia, and Van Diemen's Land had to have them despite the Governor's complaints.[2]

By 1844, there were adults who had served their time in 'separate confinement' in Pentonville, and who were ready to be sent abroad; but Stanley was not sure how far the 'very deep apparent impression, partly religious and partly prudential, of the evils of their former course of life, ... induced by much instruction and long solitude, would survive a free intercourse with the Convict society in Van Diemen's Land'. Though some were sent there, aware of the lack of employment Stanley decided to send some to the mainland instead. They would be 'exiles', not convicts. They would have conditional pardons so their despatch involved no breach of faith. Indeed since La Trobe had favoured the sending of juveniles to Port Phillip, and a memorial urging the introduction of Indian coolies into New South Wales had lamented an 'inevitable ruin' threatened by a 'scarcity of labour', Stanley, when refusing that request, might hope that the exiles would be favourably received; but, in any case, he said, the sending of five hundred annually was 'so momentous an object of National policy that we can acknowledge no conflicting motive as of sufficient importance to supersede it'; if they were not wanted in the existing Australian colonies, a 'separate settlement' for them would have to be found.[3]

At first this did not seem necessary. Gipps agreed they would be an

[1] Webb, 158, 183–5; Graham, *P. Debs.*, 23 May 1843, lxix, 842. Cf. Penitentiary and Prison Book, iii, HO 21/9, 102–7.
[2] Instructions to governors, their replies, 1842–3, and the decision to discontinue to New Zealand, March 1846, HO 45/239; *South Australian*, 3 and 21 Feb. 1843, 7 Jan. 1845; Grey to Stanley, 20 April 1843, 8 Feb. 1845, CO 13/32 and 44; Stanley to Gipps, 26 May and 7 June 1842; Gipps to Stanley, 16 Jan. 1844, encl. mins., NSW Legs. Council, 18 Nov. and 21 Dec. 1843; Hutt to Stanley, 1 Sept. 1845, and report on juveniles, 19 Feb. 1847, HO 45/619 and 1838; Phillips to Stephen, 31 July 1845, encl. Prison Inspectors' Report, CO 280/187, and above, p. 286. Cf. Graham to Visitors of Parkhurst, PP 1843 (171), xlii, 447.
[3] Stanley to Wilmot, 15 May and 19 June 1844; Stephen's minute on Phillipps to Stephen, 5 July 1844, CO 280/175; Stanley to Gipps, 27 July 1844; La Trobe to Deas Thomson, 22 Nov. 1842, encl. Gipps to Stanley, 16 Jan. 1843; Gipps to Stanley, 5 May 1843, and Stephen's minute, CO 201/333; Stanley to Gipps, 29 Sept. 1843.

advantage to Port Phillip. La Trobe welcomed them, and despite some protests in Melbourne, 175 exiles in the *Sir George Seymour* were quickly snapped up in March 1845 at Geelong and Portland, where employers were so short of labour that they had even been paying to bring ex-convicts across Bass Strait.[1] This was most gratifying; but soon the adverse reports about those who had been sent to Van Diemen's Land, together with the other stories coming from the island, compelled the government, in September 1845, to think about a new colony again.[2]

Such an idea had a long history. John Dunmore Lang and Sir Richard Bourke had mooted it in 1838; Russell had considered it in 1839; Franklin in 1841, Maconochie in 1844 and the Prison Inspectors in 1845 had suggested it again. Stephen, who doubted the practicability 'of sending . . . even reformed prisoners to Port Phillip or any existing colony', and found the accumulation of convicts in Van Diemen's Land 'so alarming that a fresh safety valve must be opened without delay', was an enthusiastic supporter. Though Stanley did not think it 'a complete or certain remedy', it was, he thought, 'the only measure I can devise (short of the cessation of transportation altogether) which appears to have a reasonable chance of being effectual'. The Treasury was 'not very favourably disposed', and Peel agreed only 'in deference to the judgment of those who know the evils requiring remedy'; but Graham was 'decidedly favourable to the experiment', and 'even if less sanguine than I am with regard to its probable success, in the present circumstances I would heartily recommend that it be tried'.[3]

At first Stephen thought that New South Wales might object, though it could perhaps be placated by removing to the new settlement any emancipists who might be unemployed, and all the convicts who still remained in the colony, including those at the Hyde Park Barracks; but in November he noted that reports of the demand for exiles at Port Phillip showed 'a very important change regarding the introduction of pardoned . . . convicts and it also shows that at the present moment the

---

[1] Gipps to La Trobe, 7 Dec. 1844, La Trobe to Gipps, 25 Dec., PLV, H 7266 and 6955; *Port Phillip Patriot*, 18 and 26 Dec. 1844; Gipps to Stanley, 19 Feb. 1845, with minutes by Stanley and Hope, CO 201/356, 9 April and 2 July 1845, encl. La Trobe to Deas Thomson 27 March and 14 June; Stanley to Gipps, 20 June 1845.

[2] Hampton's reports, 1 March, 7 May and 9 Aug. 1845, Boyd to the Rev. W. Russell, 29 April, PP 1846 (36).

[3] *Transportation Report*, PP 1837, Lang's evid., 4045 ff.; Bourke to Russell, 26 Oct. 1838, *Papers*, PP 1839 (582); Russell, mem. on Transportation, 1839, PRO 30/22/3; Maconochie to Stephen, 21 Sept. 1844, CO 280/178; Inspectors of Prisons report, encl. in Phillipps to Stephen, 31 May 1845, CO 280/187; Stanley's mem. to Cabinet, 27 Sept. 1845, with mins. by Stephen, Peel, Graham and Treasury, CO 206/62, 272 ff.

proposed North Australia plan would be popular . . . so far as employers of labour are concerned'. He hoped that this would make the convicts more attractive in the south too. 'The avidity for cheap manual labour is a passion, or a propensity, of capitalists, on which an almost boundless reliance may be placed,' he wrote. 'My strong impression is that the effect of the proposed colony of North Australia will be to make Emancipists and exiles more valued in the other colonies.' These might well oppose the arrival of 'hordes' of pardoned convicts; but if they knew the 'annual swarm' were being sent elsewhere, and could be disposed of, they 'would covet the presence of as many as could profitably be employed, feeling at ease about the introduction not being followed by an invasion from multitudes of their associates'.[1]

Stephen had long been interested in colonizing the north 'to complete the greatness of the Australian nation', and to anticipate any foreign power controlling its coastline. A penal settlement there, he had argued in 1842, would not only impose a punishment 'more formidable' than transportation to Van Diemen's Land, but would 'clear the way' for other settlers; this would then complete 'the colonization . . . of New Holland . . . one of those vast schemes of national policy into which Great Britain has been drawn by the current of events, and . . . which must be regarded as one of the most impressive movements of Divine Providence in the government of this world'. Without convicts or government expenditure, he thought a naval station like Port Essington would fail; since this was in difficulties at this moment an alternative project was attractive.[2]

The proposal was postponed by the Corn Law crisis at the end of 1845, but Gladstone, Stanley's successor at the Colonial Office, took it up again the following year. Transportation, he insisted, was 'an indispensable part and adjunct of the penal code'; the new colony was necessary unless the United Kingdom were 'to be deprived of the only effective secondary punishment, in reliance on which the punishment of death was discontinued', and it would 'promote . . . the development of the resources of New South Wales' by providing a 'depot of Labour' available to meet its wants and finding employment for the capital accumulated there'. He admitted that without the 'urgent difficulties' and 'vast accumulation of freed peoples' in Van Diemen's Land it could

[1] Minutes, 6 Sept. 1845, on Gipps to Stanley, 28 Nov. 1844 and 2 July 1845, CO 201/350 and 358; mem. to Hope, n.d. (? Sept. 1845), HO 45/960.
[2] Minutes on Bremer to Stanley, 2 Jan. 1842, and Trevelyan to Stephen, 17 June 1840, CO 201/329 and 303; Gipps to Stanley, 11 Aug. 1843; Stanley to Gipps, 14 March 1844; cf. D. Howard, 'English Activities on the North East Coast of Australia' (thesis for Ph.D., Univ. of London).

not be vindicated; but as it was, it was needed both for those pardoned there, and for 'exiles' from England. Gladstone hoped there would be no complaints from New South Wales, but in any case the government 'cannot surrender the interests of the Empire . . . Having practically relieved New South Wales at no small inconvenience to ourselves from the burden (as soon as it became a burden) of receiving convicts from this country', Britain was 'acquitted of any obligations' there.[1]

But when all seemed settled, second thoughts arose. At this moment, though the exiles were still unwelcome in Van Diemen's Land, Port Phillip was so ready to take them that the Prison Inspectors seemed to think their problem solved. Build a depot there, and there would be 'ready employment' for two thousand, they declared. Stephen correctly foresaw what was more likely, that the 'labour market would become stagnant' and that they might 'hereafter be in great need of a new colony'. To the Inspectors' plea that exiles did not deserve to face the 'hardships' of the north, he rather tartly rejoined that it was 'no great hardship to ask from criminals what multitudes of their fellow country-men solicit for in vain'.[2] Then the Poor Law Commissioners and Emigration Commissioners refused to send female migrants because the settlement would be too tough for them, and the Prison Inspectors refused to send the convicts' wives lest this would make the men's punishment too lenient; this meant that the settlers would all be men from Van Diemen's Land, 'without restraint', with 'all their vices', and without 'women to humanize them'. 'Turn where you will on this subjection of transportation and objections spring up in multitudes,' noted Stephen. This one was serious. 'Unless a certain assurance can be obtained for sending there a sufficient number of women, it ought to be abandoned,' he minuted. In July 1846, it was.[3]

Gladstone had been determined 'to try fairly and fully the present system of transportation' and to see it properly managed in Van Diemen's Land, so as to decide 'whether the system . . . can be worked with beneficial results . . . or other expedients decided on for the dis-posing of transportable offenders'; but for this, a 'breathing time' was

---

[1] To Fitz Roy, 7 May 1846, CO 395/1, and *Corr.*, PP 1847 (788); *P. Debs.*, 3 March 1846, lxxxiv, 482.
[2] Gipps to Stanley, 11 Feb. 1846, encl. La Trobe to Deas Thomson, 30 Jan.; Wilmot to Stanley, 23 Feb. 1846, with Stephen's minute; Phillipps to Stephen, 29 May and 2 June 1846, encl. mem. from Prison Inspectors, with minutes by Stephen and Lyttleton, CO 201/370; Stephen to Phillipps, 23 June, CO 202/52.
[3] Phillipps to Stephen, 22 June 1846, encl. report from Poor Law Commissioners, and Stephen's minute, CO 201/370; Grey to Fitz Roy, 15 Nov. 1846, *Corr.*, PP 1847 (788); Grey, *Colonial Policy*, ii, 66.

indispensable, to 'enable transportation in the future and to tranquillize the minds of the colonists . . . whose co-operation is necessary.' So as well as thinking of new settlements, he also turned to existing colonies to help him gain this respite.[1]

Should 'the absolute exclusion of transported convicts' continue? he asked Fitz Roy in April; might not a 'modified and carefully regulated introduction of Convict Labourers into New South Wales or some part of it' be desirable? Free labour there was falling below the demand. The convicts would be employed upon a 'system different from that of former times' which had proved objectionable. They would be so 'thinly dispersed' among the population as to be 'scarcely perceptible'. Perhaps some could be introduced under indentures; others might be employed on public works for which not enough free labourers were available. Upon this 'difficult but important and interesting subject' the Governor was to direct his 'reflections and inquiries'. Meanwhile Gladstone asked if English convicts might not be employed on harbour works in the Ionian Islands or in Table Bay, in preparing land for settlers in Natal or 'on any portion' of a railway proposed in Canada from Halifax to Quebec. But everywhere he found the colonies 'increasingly reluctant to accept what was formerly the boon of convict labour'. In Corfu, they would cost too much, he was told, apart from the objections of an 'independent government' to employing 'foreign convicts'. In Nova Scotia, the project would be 'distasteful to every class in the community'; in New Brunswick it would 'occasion very great jealousy and alarm'. Unfortunately, he concluded, 'the circle of space within which we can deposit Convicts becomes progressively narrower, while we much need it being greatly widened'.[2]

By this time, as well as looking for these possible outlets, Gladstone had taken other steps to relieve the pressure on Van Diemen's Land. He had persuaded the Treasury to ease the colony's financial burdens. He had recalled the Lieutenant-Governor, in the hope that his successor, with the aid of a new Controller-General, would be a more efficient administrator than his predecessor; but when Peel's ministry fell in July, he handed over his responsibilities to another Secretary of State,

[1] Gladstone's mem. on transportation, 23 April 1846, Gladstone Papers, BM, Add. MSS. 44735, 191-5; Gladstone to Graham, ib., 218.
[2] Gladstone to Fitz Roy, 30 April 1846; Gladstone to Maitland (Cape), 27 April, 17 June 1846, PP 1849 (217); Gladstone to Falkland (Nova Scotia), 3 Feb. 1846, CO 18/33; Falkland to Gladstone, 1 May, CO 217/192; Gladstone to Colebrook (New Brunswick), 3 Feb., Colebrook to Gladstone, 28 April, CO 188/94; Seaton (Corfu) to Gladstone, 22 June, HO 45/916; mem. on retirement. 2 July, Gladstone Papers, BM, Add. MSS. 44735, 264-79

the third Earl Grey. Grey agreed about the 'breathing time'; but he wanted it so that he could work out a different long-term policy, for 'any expectation of recurring to the former system . . . was altogether illusory'. He cancelled the North Australia project, but he also assured Sir William Denison, the new Lieutenant-Governor of Van Diemen's Land, that Gladstone's decision to suspend transportation there for two years would stand. This done, he was ready to plan a new departure.[1]

Like his cousin, Sir George Grey, formerly Under-Secretary for the Colonies and now at the Home Office, and like Lord John Russell, the Prime Minister, Grey, as Lord Howick, had been closely concerned with transportation in the 1830s, when he had come to dislike the system as it was then conducted. But he had shuddered at the 'enormous expense' of building prisons at home, and he had forecast that simply abolishing assignment would bring too many men in the colonial penal gangs, if no other provision were made for them; so to meet these difficulties he was sympathetic to an 'exile' system which would combine some punishment in England with some restraint in the colonies. Because of their labour shortage he thought the latter were 'well adapted for the reception of reclaimed offenders', and reformation, begun in prison at home, could there be economically and effectively completed.[2]

Such were substantially still his views, though before deciding his new policy he made inquiries in various continental countries about how they dealt with their major criminals. He opposed long terms of imprisonment at home and did not want to add 'four thousand yearly to the overcrowded jails', a view which the Prison Inspectors heartily agreed with. They wanted to get rid of as many as they could of the 'depraved and corrupting' convicts who could only with difficulty be dealt with in England. But if they were dispersed throughout the colonies, Grey argued, the benefit of their labour would outweigh the other disadvantages of having them; moreover, they would be accompanied by an equal number of free emigrants, and if well-behaved would have their wives and families sent out after them. The Australian colonies had special advantages as their destination, for they were difficult to return from, and they had a system of control in working order; so in future 'separate confinement' in prison would be followed by 'associated labour' in the dockyards; then would come 'assisted exile' to the colonies, where the men would be 'restrained', with a

[1] Grey to Denison, 30 Sept. 1846.
[2] Grey's mems., 20 April 1838, Russell Papers, PRO 30/22/3, 23 Nov. 1838, Grey Papers, Durham.

ticket-of-leave to prevent their 'congregation' in towns, and to make sure that the punishment was not 'lightly regarded'.[1] The colonies would not be asked to pay for the emigrants being sent, lest there should arise 'a clamour against the whole system . . . which would probably . . . end in its being abandoned'; since Britain was sending out 'great numbers . . . for its own convenience', it could 'justly be called upon to pay for the cost of any measure for mitigating the moral evils thus inflicted'. Sir George Grey was nervous that sending the wives might 'make transportation seem a boon'; however, he took the risk.[2] The whole scheme implied that 'deserving' men would be sent as a reward for good behaviour and sending wives would be a further stimulus to reform, which Russell thought would outweigh the evils of propagating a 'lascivious and burglarious race'. 'The transportation of male convicts to Van Diemen's Land as hitherto carried on' would be abandoned, though this did not mean, as many both at home and in the colony believed, that no more criminals would be sent out.[3]

On 5 March 1847, Grey outlined his proposals to the House of Lords, 'very badly' according to his Journal. Since 1843 he said, so many had been transported that Van Diemen's Land had been almost ruined. In future, the convict would have to undergo 'separate' imprisonment and then labour on the public works in England; only after that would he be sent to Australia, where there was a great demand for his labour. This was 'not part of his punishment . . . but a security against his again falling into crime'. He would receive a conditional pardon, and would have payment for his passage deducted from his earnings. Grey aroused opposition because he insisted he was 'virtually abolishing transportation'; but this he was not doing, except 'as hitherto carried on'.[4]

To work the scheme, the Home Office would have to co-operate; so would the Irish government, and so would a number of the colonies; but when explaining his plans to them Grey was little more successful

[1] Despatches from various European countries, in reply to queries made by Palmerston, for Grey, on penal policy, CO 323/236–8; Grey's Cabinet Minute, 19 Aug. 1846, ML C941; Grey, ii, 1–20; Prison Inspectors to Sir George Grey, 13 Dec. 1846, HO 45/1393.
[2] Stephen to Phillipps, 16 Nov. 1846, Phillipps to Stephen, 24 Dec., encl. mem. from Emigration Commissioners, with Grey's minute, CO 201/370, 262 ff.; Sir George Grey to Grey, 15 and 20 Jan. 1847, CO 201/387 and 280/217; Grey to Sir George Grey, 5 Feb., HO 45/311; Fitz Roy to Gladstone, 1 Sept. 1846; Grey to Fitz Roy, 24 March 1847, with encls.
[3] Russell to Grey, 5 May 1847, Grey Papers, 119–2; Grey to Denison, 5 Feb. 1847; cabinet minute, *loc. cit.*
[4] Grey's Journal, Grey Papers, Durham, C 3/13; Grey, ii, 15 ff.; *P. Debs.*, xc, 898 ff., Grey, Stanley, Denman, Duke of Richmond; in House of Commons, Sir James Graham, Lord Mahon, 4 June 1847, *ib.*, xciii, 325 and 354.

than when he tried to explain them to Parliament. The Prison Inspectors never paid much heed to colonial opinion, and neither the Irish nor the colonies appreciated the significance of the 'reformatory discipline' which was to precede the 'exile'. The Irish government continued to transport men who had not been 'reformed'; the colonies refused to believe that the 'exiles' were not just convicts under another name – though perhaps in this they were right.

'Her Majesty's Government have decided upon altogether abandoning the system of transportation to Van Diemen's Land,' Stephen, at Grey's direction, told the Treasury, in justifying temporary expenditure on the convicts then in the colony; he added that after the present overcrowding of the island had eased, the financial concessions he was asking for would 'tend to render Van Diemen's Land far more available than it otherwise would be for the reception of Convicts when their punishment is at an end'. Grey, when trying to explain his policy to Denison, personally added to the draft despatch the statement 'that it was not the intention' of the government to resume transportation there after the two years for which it had been suspended had expired. As Sir George Grey told the House of Commons that it was essential 'never to resume' transportation, and Lord John Russell dilated on the need to make colonies 'not merely the seats of malefactors . . . but communities fitted to set an example of virtue and happiness', who can blame the Tasmanians for misinterpreting the new policy in the direction of their own wishes, and believing that convicts would come to the colony no more, especially when the Lieutenant-Governor himself understood it in the same sense? In the light of all these declarations, the statement that there would be exiles instead tended to be overlooked.[1]

In his reply, in July 1847, Denison opposed what he understood as the decision to stop transportation. He reported that the demand for labour was picking up, and that cheap convict labour was still needed to develop the colony; without it, wages would rise, making many farms unprofitable, and so increasing the 'independence' of the labourer that 'drunkenness and debauchery' already 'prevalent to a degree hardly conceivable in England' would 'spread like a moral pestilence over the land'. But he admitted that the misinterpretation of Grey's despatch about not resuming transportation had been received with 'rejoicing' in the colony; inquiries he had made from the magistrates, public meetings and petitions had combined to convince him that 'the feelings

---

[1] Stephen's minute on Wilmot to Gladstone, 2 Sept. 1846, Stephen to the Treasury, 15 Feb. 1847, CO 280/196; Grey to Denison, 5 Feb. 1847; *P. Debs.*, 3, 4, 10 June 1847; xciii, 36 ff., 138 ff., 305 ff.; Denison to Grey, 10 July and 20 Aug. 1847.

of a large portion of the community are so fully enlisted in opposition to the convict system here that any attempt to revive it *in any form* would be looked on as a breach of faith', and would cause 'feelings of hostility' which would be 'embarrassing to government'. He added that he had told the Legislative Council that the British government had 'acted in accordance with the expressed wishes of a large proportion of the free inhabitants of the Colony'.[1] Grey was less perturbed by the misunderstanding than he should have been. 'The penal system known as transportation will not be renewed,' he wrote in April 1848. 'The diffusion of men, instead of concentrating them in Penal and Probation Gangs, totally changes its character.' But convicts would arrive, all the same.[2]

The mistrust aroused in this way increased as a result of the difficulty Grey had in disposing of the exiles, whose labour he quite wrongly expected many colonies to welcome. For this belief he did not have very much justification, unless the wish were father to the thought, but at least when he first announced his policy, he seemed to have time to look for people who would take them. Most of the future exiles had still to undergo their separate confinement and penal labour at home, and would not be ready for a year or more; in the meantime, Port Phillip was raising Grey's hopes by taking the few who were available. There, many agreed with Edward Curr when he declared that 'he did not choose to be ruined for virtue's sake'. After all, in 1846 a fifth of the population were former convicts, so there was no point in being superior and refusing more. Three shiploads sailed in 1847 with 828 men, and reports on their conduct and disposal were 'very satisfactory'.[3]

Opinion in Sydney was divided, but there seemed some hope there too. A committee of the New South Wales Legislative Council, appointed in response to Gladstone's inquiry, in its report in October 1846, stressed the advantages of transportation 'to our boundless interior which seems to have been created the vast solitude that it is and to have been assigned by Providence to the British nation as the fittest scene for the reformation of her criminals'. If transportation were revived, 'how many millions . . . might be saved? and withal how largely might the sum of human misery and crime be reduced? . . . How many souls that may otherwise perish might be turned to salvation? It seems to your Committee . . . that an amount of saving might accrue which

[1] Denison to Grey, *ib.*, and 30 Aug. 1847, encl. address to Legs. Council, CO 280/211. Author's italics.
[2] Minutes on Denison to Grey, 20 Aug.; Grey to Denison, 27 April 1848.
[3] *Port Phillip Patriot*, 8, 11 and 21 Jan. 1847; Census 1846; Eliot's minute on Fitz Roy to Grey, 21 Dec. 1847, CO 201/386; cf. CO 201/387 for correspondence with Home Office.

would go far towards the extinction of the National Debt, or enable Great Britain to organize a system of national education and immigration that would ultimately reduce to a merely nominal amount the crime and pauperism which are now . . . the main cause of the intestine disorders with which she is troubled'. Certainly the despatch of this report was accompanied and followed by petitions hostile to it, which moved Stephen to minute, in April 1847, 'If it is necessary to write anything . . . the answer should be, "there is no intention whatever of renewing the practice of transporting Convicts to New South Wales" '; but Grey, anxious to find outlets for his exiles, disagreed, and hoped for the best.[1]

While the Lords' Committee on the Criminal Law was at this moment receiving evidence favourable to transportation, a committee on Colonisation from Ireland was being told of the labour shortage in Australia, which made the colonists willing to receive 'convicts' or 'anyone'. Edward Macarthur pointed out, as he had already written privately, that the shortage created 'competition among employers' and 'tended to promote democracy', and both were regrettable. Although Eliot, one of the Emigration Commissioners, warned of the 'quick variations in the state of the labour market', Mrs. Chisholm stressed that 'the want of labour' was 'so irresistible' that unless it was procured from Ireland (which it was not) 'the colonists would have to have recourse . . . to the systematic introduction of Expirees from Van Diemen's Land and Norfolk Island'.[2]

With these opinions to back him, in September 1847 Grey told Fitz Roy that if the Council agreed with its committee, he would arrange for convicts who had 'undergone some portion of their punishment' to be sent to New South Wales with tickets-of-leave. This would be of 'great advantage to themselves, the Mother Country and the Colony'. Their families would be sent out 'whenever their conduct should be such as to entitle them to the indulgence', and an equal number of free emigrants would be sent at the cost of the British Treasury 'still further to guard against the social evils which have heretofore resulted from . . . transportation'; this would also help to make 'the system of secondary punishment in this Country subservient to the object of increasing the supply of labour in the Colony'.[3]

[1] NSW Legs. Council, *V & P*, 30 Oct. 1846; Fitz Roy to Gladstone, 6 Nov. 1846, and Stephen's minute, CO 201/369; Fitz Roy to Grey, 9 Jan., 1 and 24 Feb. 1847.
[2] *Colonisation from Ireland Report*, PP 1847 (737), evid., James Coghill, 3564-5, W. Verner, 3838, R. Therry, 3106, Caroline Chisholm, 4110; *ib.*, 1847-8 (200), evid., Eliot, 529-30, Edward Macarthur, 3025; *Criminal Law Report*, n. 1, p. 312.
[3] Grey to Fitz Roy, 3 Sept. 1847.

Just as Grey was writing this despatch, the Council met and repudi-
ated its Committee's report; but when it received these new proposals,
it had second thoughts. There had been no migrants for three years;
'under the exigencies of the labour market', the scheme was attractive.
So the Council agreed to accept the exiles, on the condition that an
equal number of free emigrants, and the men's wives and families were
sent with them. Fitz Roy wrote strongly in favour, and told Grey, in
April 1848, that this 'will be received as a boon by a large majority of
the people of this Colony, when the want of a sufficient supply of labour
is becoming daily more apparent'.[1]

Grey received this answer in August just after he had sent out a
circular despatch asking various colonies if they would take some of the
reformed prisoners whose preparatory discipline was then coming to an
end. But he naturally had not expected their replies immediately and
this conditional acceptance from New South Wales reached him at an
inopportune moment. The Parliamentary session was ending. The
financial depression of 1847–8 had not cleared. Although Grey had
approved renewing the policy of assisting free migration to Australia, he
felt he could not at once obtain the money to pay for it.[2] 'It will probably
be impossible to take advantage of the opening offered by the willingness of the Council now to receive Convicts, since this could not be
done without incurring a charge of breach of faith, unless the promised
free emigrants were also furnished', he minuted; so his first decision
was to write saying that no convicts would be sent 'unless the Colony
would receive them without the proposed advantage', on the terms on
which they were being offered to other colonies. Unfortunately he had
second thoughts, and he personally drafted a despatch, which was sent
in September, explaining that he would send out convicts *without
migrants*, while waiting for further advice from New South Wales; three
months later he informed Fitz Roy that an Order-in-Council permitting
convicts to be sent to New South Wales had been made, and that a
shipload was being sent out in the *Hashemy*.[3]

The result was trouble. Although during the first half of 1849 Grey's
minutes were extraordinarily optimistic, protests and petitions against
this 'breach of faith' were immediate and violent. In the past two years,
before the *Hashemy* arrived on 8 June 1849, the labour situation had

[1] Coghlan, i, 341–3 and 368; Fitz Roy to Grey, 25 Sept. 1847, 10 April 1848.
[2] Grey to the Governors of W. Australia, N. Zealand, the Cape, Ceylon, Mauritius, 7 Aug.
1848, *HRA*, xxvi, 590; Grey to Fitz Roy, 30 Aug. and 18 Dec. 1847, 8 July 1848.
[3] Minute on Fitz Roy to Grey, 10 April 1848, CO 201/396; Grey to Fitz Roy (signed by
Sir George Grey), 8 Sept. 1848; Grey to Fitz Roy, 4 Dec.

changed again, as Eliot had forecast it might. The revival of immigration had brought nearly 30,000 from the United Kingdom to the colony, in addition to many who had crossed from Van Diemen's Land. Of the total population, which had risen by nearly twenty per cent since 1847, nearly a third were free assisted immigrants; with the ex-convicts they made up a half of it, and like the rank and file of colonial born had little desire for competition in the labour market. Many of the middle and upper classes with less economic axe to grind did not want to revive the convict taint on the colony. Some squatters might still want convict labour if they could get it, but shepherds 'beyond the boundaries' had doubled in number since 1841; though 'mechanics' were very scarce, few convicts were skilled tradesmen and many employers were thinking of more immigrants rather than convicts to relieve their difficulties. Grey's changes of front, and the appearance he gave of breaking his part of a bargain, combined with resentment against this further example of English interference in local affairs, aided the opponents of his scheme.[1]

Although within a week of the *Hashemy*'s arrival, seventy-two per cent of its 'passengers' had obtained employment, and the rest were soon sent off to Moreton Bay, even prompter was a mass meeting on Circular Quay, Sydney, on 11 June 1849, where, despite pouring rain, a huge crowd collected to demonstrate against what Robert Lowe called the 'grossest outrage that has ever been perpetrated on any community' when 'the stately presence of their city, the beautiful waters of their harbour, were again polluted with . . . a ship freighted not with the comforts of life, not with the luxuries of civilized nations, not with the commodities of commerce . . . but with the moral degradation of a community – the picked and selected criminals of Great Britain'.[2]

Before the news of this demonstration reached London, reports of other protests had stimulated Grey to ask Parliament to grant £30,000 for free emigration. Merivale thought this would encourage New South Wales to take the convicts, but it was too late. The newly elected Legislative Council had protested against them in June, and Fitz Roy now recommended that no more be sent. Five ships, *Hashemy, Randolph, Mount Stewart Elphinstone, Havering* and *Adelaide*, had sailed, with 1,405 prisoners; even though they had all found work somewhere in the colony, it could be pacified only by stopping sending convicts and

---

[1] Grey's minutes on Fitz Roy to Grey, CO 201/411 and 412; Coghlan, i, 341 ff. and 363 ff.; Ralph Mansfield, *Analytical View of the Census of 1848*; G. C. Mundy, *Our Antipodes* (1855), 463 ff.
[2] Clark, *Sources*, 247; Fitz Roy to Grey, 1 May, 1 and 30 June 1849; cf. A. P. Martin, *Life of Lord Sherbrooke* (London, 1893), i, 380.

sending free migrants immediately instead. Grey agreed, though he still hoped that the Council might reverse its decision next year; but though he may have been right in thinking that 'the apprehensions of the Colonists were not a little visionary', his fear 'that even the worst of our convicts would find they had something to learn from the speakers at public meetings in despising truth and decency' was somewhat exaggerated, and to the extent it was true, it was the product of his own stubbornness. One outlet for exiles was closed, though since he hedged his decision with the reservation about again finding out the views of the colonists, he kept the controversy brewing for another year, and effectively prevented himself earning any goodwill.[1]

Nor by this time was Port Phillip any better. The labour shortage there had eased. Since 1844, 1,727 'Pentonvillains' had arrived at Melbourne, Geelong and Portland, and over two thousand men had crossed Bass Strait. In March 1849, La Trobe reported that 'the time had gone by' when exiles could readily gain employment. In the past three years they had not been so carefully selected as at first. Though some jobs were available in Geelong and the Western District, opposition in Melbourne was growing. Not all the men from the *Joseph Somes*, in September 1847, or the *Marion* in January 1848, found work easily, and in June the *Anna Maria* had to be diverted to Geelong. Early in 1849, the arrival of the *Eden* caused protest meetings, and of the 198 who disembarked from her, seventy-one left the depots in Geelong and Portland disengaged; in May the *Hashemy* and in August the *Randolph* almost provoked riots and had to be sent to Sydney without unloading their 'passengers'. What Stephen had once feared had now come to pass. The demand for the exiles' services had 'subsided'. They were 'viewed in . . . a virtuous and patriotic light', and all the resentment of the people of Port Phillip was roused 'against the desecration of their country'.[2]

Momentarily Grey had hopes in Moreton Bay, for in 1850 squatters there seemed willing to accept convicts and had quickly hired the men from the *Mount Stewart Elphinstone*, which Fitz Roy had sent from Sydney. When he heard this, Grey authorized the despatch of the *Bangalore*, with three hundred men; but this possible outlet was

[1] Treasury to the Colonial Office, 9 May 1849, CO 201/421; Fitz Roy to Grey, 21 March 1849, with minutes by Eliot and Grey, CO 201/412; Grey to Fitz Roy, 16 Nov. 1849; Fitz Roy to Grey, 8 Oct. 1850.
[2] Fitz Roy to Grey, 21 March 1849, encl. La Trobe to Deas Thomson, 7 March; La Trobe to Grey, 16 Feb., 14 Aug. and 8 Dec. 1849, CO 201/419; La Trobe to Deas Thomson, 17 May 1849, Fitz Roy to Grey, 12 and 27 June, 20 Nov., CO 201/414 and 417; Return of expirees and ticket-holders, Port Phillip, NSW Legs. Council, *V & P*, 1849, i, 901; Stephen to Hope, 1845, HO 45/960. Cf. Scott, *Vic. Hist. Mag.*, i.

quickly closed too, and this ship was the only one to go there directly. Though Grey remarked that he would 'learn with satisfaction that the Legislature had approved Convicts again being sent to the Northern part of the Colony', in fact he learned that it had resolved that 'no more convicts ought, under any conditions, be sent to any part of this colony'.[1] They might give 'a vast impetus' to the progress of the district, commented the *Moreton Bay Courier*, in January 1851, but there would be consequences which 'generations to come may have deep cause to deplore'. During the year opposition increased. Eliot argued that it would be regarded as a 'virtual breach of faith' to separate Moreton Bay from New South Wales, and then to send convicts there; but though Grey disagreed, and favoured such a move, his resignation, and increasing opposition from Moreton Bay itself, led to the idea being abandoned, and the excitement in New South Wales died down.[2]

In South Africa, opposition was even more violent. There, in 1841 and 1842, the Governor, Sir George Napier, had objected to receiving juveniles, and Stephen had agreed with him. 'The measure of sending boys from Parkhurst to any British colony except those who have hitherto been places of transportation, and except also, perhaps, Western Australia, can never be taken unless the Government are resolved to act in opposition to local feeling,' he wrote. 'The two great objections which will be raised in the colonies are first, a vague apprehension of danger and secondly a strong sense of indignity. That the Colony would be better without the boys is probably true on the whole, but there is no doubt that the Government have the right to send them. The practical question is, *whether the right be exercised?*' For the moment, it was not.[3]

To Gladstone's query about adult convicts in 1846, the Governor had replied that there were public works on which they could be 'beneficially employed', and which would have to be indefinitely postponed without financial help from Britain; so they would be acceptable if, as in Bermuda, they would be sent back to England when set free. But apart from the question of the convicts returning to the mother country, the British government would not pay for them. 'Highly

---

[1] Fitz Roy to Grey, 30 June, 17 Nov., 23 Dec. 1849, with minutes, 8 Oct. 1850; E. S. Hall to Grey, 1 Aug. 1849, PP 1850 (40).
[2] *Moreton Bay Courier*, 11 Jan. 1851; Grey to Fitz Roy, 10 April 1851; Fitz Roy to Grey, 31 July 1851, with minutes by Eliot and Grey; cf. Grey to Fitz Roy, 7 Dec. 1851; Grey, ii, 55. For petitions, Fitz Roy to Grey, 29 Jan., 26 Feb., 17 May, 5 Nov., 17 Dec. 1851.
[3] Napier to Stanley, 23 Oct. 1841, 2 July 1842, PP 1849 (217); Stephen's minute, and Stephen to Phillipps, 27 Sept. 1842, CO 48/220, 42; Stanley to Napier, 14 Nov. 1842, PP 1847 (742).

important as it is to find employment for Convicts,' wrote Stephen, 'I
do not believe that to get three hundred disposed of is a consideration
important enough to vindicate a plunge into an expense... of this magnitude, opening as it would a door for the admission of countless claims of
the same kind from almost every other quarter.' When he had to consider the matter, Grey agreed. It was 'not a favourable time for entering
on such undertakings', though he hoped it might be possible to do
something later.[1]

Two years later, in May 1848, Maitland's successor, Sir Harry Smith,
recommended that six hundred convicts be sent out to build a break-
water in Table Bay. Barracks would be necessary for them, but the
project would be a 'relief to the Treasury'; it could be paid for by a
loan, if Britain would guarantee it. Grey refused again. 'The guarantee
must rest on the Colonial, not the British Treasury; for there are many
other Colonial works for which similar assistance might be applied for,'
he wrote. Unlike Gladstone, he did not want to have convicts employed
on public works outside the United Kingdom; he wanted the colony to
take 'exiles'.[2]

This proposal, made in August 1848, at once evoked strong protests,
which became most violent when it was learned that he was sending the
Neptune with Irish political prisoners immediately, without waiting for
a reply to his despatch. 'Disperse them over the colony,' he told the
Governor. 'I trust they will be no encumbrance to you.' When he heard
of the uproar they were causing, he took a high line. The men were
reformed, he wrote the following March. They were not ordinary
criminals, but political offenders. 'Considering the efforts and sacrifices
made by the people of Great Britain for the defence of the colony, it is
reasonable to expect that when the true nature of the measures now in
contemplation are understood, the inhabitants will no longer feel unwilling to take their share in a policy which places it within their power,
without injury to the Cape, to render an important service to the mother
country . . . I trust it will not upon reflection appear unjust that the
Colony should be called upon to concur in an arrangement which is the
best for the Empire at large'.[3]

[1] Maitland to Gladstone, 10 Sept., encl. report of Legs. Council, 28 Aug., with minutes by
Stephen and Grey, CO 48/263, 182 ff.; Gladstone to Sir Henry Pottinger (Natal), 17 June
1846; Pottinger to Grey, 10 March 1847, encl. Col. Sec. (Natal) to Sec. to Governor of Cape,
17 Dec. 1846, CO 179/2.
[2] Smith to Grey, 8 May 1848, Grey's minute, CO 48/285; circular despatch, 7 Aug.,
HRA, xxvi, 590.
[3] Grey to Smith, 21 Dec. 1848, PP 1850 (1138); Smith to Grey, 19 Dec. 1848, 5 and 20 Jan.
1849, CO 48/288, 294; Grey to Smith, 19, 23 March 1849, PP 1849 (217).

Next month, in April, he yielded as far as the general issue was concerned, for after all the August proposal had explicitly sought colonial approval; but the Irish already despatched could 'not be treated contrary to the promises made to them'. Grey had heard of a plot hatched at New York to try and seize Irish prisoners at Bermuda and therefore had not wanted to send more there; the Cape seemed to be the best alternative. Though the arrangement was 'not free from inconvenience', Britain had 'a perfect right to send convicts' there without waiting for a reply to the previous proposal. 'This country has just paid more than £1,000,000 for the protection of the Colony and has a right to expect from it in return an assistance it can give . . . From its climate and the demand which exists for labour, there is reason to believe that this colony will afford very good prospects for men of good conduct.'[1]

The inhabitants of the Cape were not convinced, and became almost hysterical in their rage. Eliot feared 'some combination against their employment', and the 'threatening state of feeling' aroused all the more anxiety at the Colonial Office because of the 'excitement' also raised in other colonies; but Grey was afraid that if the convicts were removed, 'it would be a stimulus to the spirit of resistance elsewhere, which would be most dangerous'. He thought it best to wait to see the reception of his 'April despatch', explaining that the Irish were a special case.[2]

But the excitement only became greater. In June, the Governor reported the formation of an Anti-Convict Association. Next month, all the unofficial members of the Legislative Council resigned; those who replaced them had their houses damaged, could get no repairs done, no supplies and no credit from the banks. Supplies were refused to ships.[3] And so, after consulting Russell, who thought that, though the colonists were 'much in the wrong', the British government, which meant the Colonial Secretary, was wrong too, Grey gave way. He had not conceived it possible, he wrote, 'that even if the inhabitants of the Cape should entertain a fixed objection to ordinary convicts', they would have objected to two or three hundred men of 'this peculiar description' in 'that vast territory'; he thought they would have had 'more general regard for the interests of the British Empire', to which they were

[1] Grey to Smith, 18 April 1849, Smith to Grey, 24 May, Grey to Smith in reply, CO 48/294 and 296; Waddington to Merivale, 29 July, 1 Sept., 4 Dec. 1848, minutes thereon, Merivale to Waddington, 14 Sept., CO 37/125; Eliot (Bermuda) to Grey, 1 Nov. 1848, Grey to Eliot, 14 Dec., CO 37/123.

[2] Minutes by Eliot, Hawes and Grey on Smith to Grey, 20 Jan., 29 June and 24 July 1849, CO 48/294, 296, 297; private letter, Grey to Smith, 7 Aug. 1849, CO 48/298.

[3] Smith to Grey, 2 Aug., 17 and 30 Sept., 18 Oct. 1849, CO 48/298 and 299; Bell and Morrell, 312. Cf. P. Debs., cviii, 1373–99; Times, 19 Feb., 29 March, 15 Sept. 1849.

indebted for military assistance, and more 'humanity towards the unfortunate', but apparently he was wrong! In a climax of moral indignation, he told Smith, 'I shall forbear to express my opinion on the extraordinary proceedings of the inhabitants of the Cape . . . because I am unwilling to use terms which would alone adequately describe what I think'; but after reciting the whole story of the controversy in a 'brief review' of inordinate length, he ordered the *Neptune* to be sent on to Van Diemen's Land, whence it sailed on 19 March 1850, six months after it had arrived in Table Bay. He remained convinced of his own rectitude. In 1851 he told Russell that he was 'sorry you think that faith had not been kept with the Cape in the matter'; of this 'very serious charge, I cannot admit the justice'; but high-minded, stubborn men can be the cause of much political tumult.[1]

As in Van Diemen's Land, this trouble caused constitutional difficulties. The quarrel undermined the colonists' trust in Great Britain; it encouraged violent agitation. Stephen, now retired, told Grey that he thought the colonists had been 'hasty, passionate and extravagant' and had resorted to 'tumultuous methods of self-defence'; but it could be said that they had 'no other means of escape' from 'serious grievances', and Great Britain (that is, Grey) had 'injudiciously provoked' them by an error of judgment and 'what must now be considered as having been an indefensible aggression'. In May, Smith reported that although 'the anti-convict agitation was allayed', it would be 'misleading . . . to represent that the results of the strong feeling have ceased . . . Some years must elapse . . . before the colonists will approach political questions with calmness'. As W. P. Morrell has put it, 'Those Irish convicts had indeed led Lord Grey into a maze of difficulties. Instead of an agreed constitution, there was a whole series of unreconciled differences.'[2]

To Grey's inquiries in August 1848, the Governor of Ceylon had also said 'no'. The demand for labour in the island was decreasing, he reported, but he added that he would oppose the introduction of convicts, 'even if the prosperity of the colony were more certain and the means of controlling them more complete'. Opinion in Mauritius was hostile too. Economic difficulties were backed by questions of language, climate, 'facilities of procuring ardent spirits', and the hostile feelings of the French. The measure 'would arouse public discontent and expose Englishmen to the observation of the French population'. In New

[1] Grey to Smith, draft 30 Nov. 1849, CO 48/297, despatched 5 Dec.; Russell to Grey, 20 Nov. 1849, Grey to Russell, 4 June 1851, Grey Papers, 119–4, 120–4. Cf. John Mitchel's description, chs. xi–xiv.
[2] Stephen to Grey, 3 Oct. 1849, CO 48/297; Smith to Grey, 17 May 1850, CO 48/306; Morrell, 282; Corr. on Responsible Government at the Cape, PP 1850 (1137), xxxviii.

Zealand, Governor Grey strongly opposed the suggestion. The men would have 'an irresistible temptation' to get into the interior with the native population and cohabit with their women. This objection was 'deemed conclusive'. This practically left only Van Diemen's Land, whence many colonists were protesting too, following the misunderstanding there and the belief that Grey had misled them. 'If only the other colonies could be induced to take their share' all might yet be well, Eliot had commented; but they would not be so induced.[1]

The Canadians might have taken some, if Grey had been willing to pay for them; but he always argued as if they were a boon, not a burden. In 1846, Gladstone had offered a bribe when they had rejected his first request. He thought it 'very important to examine with the utmost care any opening that appears to present even a possibility of employing these unhappy persons in any part of the world'; so he explained that it was not a question whether employing convicts on public works would be 'abstractedly unpalatable' or not, but if the British government decided to incur expense on railway construction in British North America, 'which they would not otherwise contemplate', *provided* 'they could combine with that expenditure the certainty of finding occupation for a certain portion of the convict class', was there 'reason to believe such an offer would be well received'? Perhaps the officer surveying possible routes for the railways might 'bear in mind' the possibility of employing convict labour 'with reference to any particulars . . . to which it might have a relation'.[2] 'No irrational prejudices . . . should be allowed to oppose themselves to the great benefits which the proposed measure of affording Convict labour in carrying out the great work of the construction of a railroad from here to Quebec must necessarily confer on these colonies,' declared Sir John Hervey, when he replaced Colebrooke in New Brunswick. The colonial labour force was quite inadequate for such a work. He could keep the convict gangs separate from the free labourers and 'so obviate any cause of jealousy', and he could give public opinion 'a proper direction'. But by this time Grey had replaced Gladstone. Such convicts would not have been 'exiles', and they would have to be removed when the work was finished. Railway building was expensive. Grey did not approve of England paying

[1] Torrington to Grey, 9 Oct. 1848, CO 54/251; cf. Torrington's earlier report of labour shortage, 3 June 1847, CO 54/236; Gomm (Mauritius) to Grey, 1 Feb. 1849, encl. art. from *Le Mauricien*, and 8 June, CO 167/309; Sir George Grey (N.Z.) to Grey, 8 May 1849, with Eliot's minute, CO 209/71; Eliot's minute on Denison to Grey, 17 Nov. 1848, CO 280/232.
[2] Gladstone to Falkland and Colebrooke, 18 May 1846, CO 18/33; Stephen to Sir F. French (Ordnance), 30 May, CO 217/192.

for colonial works – even strategic ones. The railway boom at home had burst, and the government was facing financial stringency. He decided to let the matter drop.[1]

Agitation for building the railway and for British financial assistance for it continued, but with no mention of convict labour until 1851, when Joseph Howe, sent to England from Nova Scotia to secure help from the British government, thought he knew how to win Grey's support for proposals whose financial terms aroused his dislike. He suggested employing convicts after their good conduct on probation. A corps of five hundred could in due course settle on 'wild lands' and provide cheap labour and ultimately settlers for the colony. He did not believe the other North American colonies would object. But the New Brunswickers did object. Their Assembly viewed the scheme 'with unqualified disapprobation'; in any case they preferred a line from St. John, not from Halifax.[2]

In the West Indies, Grey would not allow Britain to pay for convict labour employed on colonial works either, even though, as in the case of harbour improvements at Bridgetown in the Barbados, and like the Canadian railway, they would benefit the mother country too. If the colony had to pay, local labour would be cheaper, reported the Governor; so the suggestion Grey made in 1850 was turned down.[3]

At Bermuda, convicts had been working in the dockyard since 1824; but Grey regarded this as only the second (or penal labour) stage of their punishment, as at Portsmouth in England, and from the naval establishment they were to be selected to go further afield as exiles. In 1842 the Governor had proposed allowing well-behaved ex-prisoners to settle on the island, as 'a premium for good conduct'; but though Stanley agreed, and it would have relieved the labour shortage there, the Legislative Council was willing only to employ convicts on colonial works, under special regulations to preserve the colony 'free from moral taint'; it refused to allow ex-convicts to settle just as four years before it had refused to receive juveniles.[4]

[1] Hervey to Grey, 30 Sept. 1846, CO 217/193, minutes by Rogers and Grey.
[2] Colebrooke to Grey, 30 March, 28 May, 13 Dec. 1847, CO (Index) 714/18570; Sir Edward Head to Grey, 31 March 1848, 26 April 1850, PP 1851 (313); Canada, Railroads, 1849–51, CO 42/580; Howe to Grey, 16 Jan. 1851, CO 217/207, 174 ff.; Hawes to Howe, 10 March 1851, PP 1851 (1344), xxxvi, 237; Head to Grey, 6 April 1851, CO 188/144, 159–60. Cf. J. A. Roy, *Joseph Howe* (Toronto, 1935), 146–163; Joseph Howe, *Speeches and Published Letters* (ed. W. Annand, 1858), ii, 75; *Halifax Colonist*, 24 April 1851.
[3] Colebrooke (Barbados) to Grey, 6 Feb., 7 Sept. 1850, and Grey's minutes, CO 28/172 and 174; Grey to Colebrooke, 13 March, CO 59/37.
[4] Bermuda, Index, i, CO 714/18477; Phillips to Stephen, 27 Jan. 1842, CO 37/107; Stanley to Reid, 31 Jan., CO 38/22; Reid to Stanley, 29 March, CO 37/107; Reid to Glenelg,

In 1846 the Admiralty agreed to an extra three hundred being sent to the dockyards there; during the next two years the establishment grew rapidly and Eliot greatly improved its management.[1] He assured Grey there was work for two thousand men for twelve years, 'double the present force', and he urged that the fortifications be 'pressed on', since in the years preceding the Clayton-Bulwer Treaty of 1850, it seemed to him that the United States wanted to make 'the Gulf of Mexico a *mare clausum*'; but the policy announced in 1847 was unpopular, for the prisoners, whether English or Irish, looked forward as a reward for good conduct to being discharged at home and not sent on to Australia, and so did those at Gibraltar.[2]

There, the penal establishment founded in 1842 had been extremely successful, largely, according to the Governor, Sir Robert Wilson, because Stanley had agreed to the prisoners being recommended for pardon and return to England, and this was an invaluable stimulus to good conduct and hard work. He had five hundred in 1845 and a hulk for an extra three hundred arrived in March 1847; but though he reported in September that he could employ two hundred and fifty more, Grey was unwilling to send them, and provide lodgings for them there, if they were going to be sent back to England.[3] Stephen the previous year had been more enthusiastic. He noticed that the practice at Gibraltar had shown that transportation could be made 'a reformatory and economical mode of punishment', by good superintendence, military discipline, ceaseless occupation, short sentences and a hope of pardon, plus 'zealous religious instruction and encouraging praise', with punishment, when necessary, by withdrawing 'indulgences'; he thought that something might be learnt from this in Van Diemen's Land, and perhaps convicts might be profitably employed in England on 'public works of magnitude', such as harbours of refuge. But this was no good at all and the Prison Inspectors turned down the idea at once. It was too expensive and the men might escape; besides both they and Grey

---

30 Oct. 1838, CO 37/99. On the establishment generally, Reid to Stanley, 11, 17 and 27 Oct. 1845, to Gladstone, 30 Jan. 1846, Eliot to Grey, 6 Jan. 1847, CO 37/110, 113 and 116.
[1] Bermuda Blue Book for 1844, CO 41/39; Phillipps to Stephen, 22 and 27 June 1846, with minutes by Stephen and Gladstone, CO 37/115; Reid to Gladstone, 9 July, to Grey, 17 Aug. 1846, CO 37/114; Waddington to Merivale, 29 July 1848, with minute by Grey, CO 37/122; Eliot to Grey, 12 April, 15 May, 19 July and 28 Aug. 1847, with Grey's minutes, CO 37/116 and 117.
[2] Phillipps, to Stephen, 23 June 1847, with Grey's minute, to Eliot, 9 July, Eliot's reply, 19 July, CO 37/119; Le Marchant to Hawes, 18 Oct., *ib.*; Wilson (Gib.) to Grey, 27 July 1847, CO 91/182.
[3] Wilson to Stanley, 9 Aug. 1843, 17 May 1845, CO 91/164 and 172; Wilson to Gladstone, 6 June 1846, CO 91/176, to Grey, 17 March, 26 Sept. 1847, CO 91/182.

wanted the men released in the colonies at the end of their sentences, not in England.[1]

So the upshot of all these inquiries was that the colonies would not employ British convicts on public works unless Britain would pay for them, which she refused to do; none, except Western Australia, was willing to receive Grey's 'exiles'. In September 1849 Under-Secretary Eliot thought that 'recent events' might force yet another 'revised system of secondary punishment . . . upon our consideration'; Grey strongly opposed such a suggestion, but in fact he had already substantially changed his policy.[2]

[1] Wilson to Gladstone, with Stephen's minute, 14 Feb. 1846, CO 91/176; Prison Inspectors, mem. on Harbours of Refuge, 23 April 1846, HO 45/1847; Phillipps to Stephen, 23 June, 9 July 1847, CO 37/119.
[2] Minutes by Eliot and Grey on Waddington to Merivale, 30 Sept. 1849, CO 201/421.

15

The End of Transportation

> I know not whether Laws be right,
> Or whether Laws be wrong;
> All that we know who lie in gaol
> Is that the wall is strong;
> And that each day is like a year
> A year whose days are long.
> OSCAR WILDE: *The Ballad of Reading Gaol*

The scornful rejection by so many colonies of the beneficent offers of
exiles after 1846 had compelled the British government to send nearly
all of them to Van Diemen's Land. There, it did not have to persuade a
colonial assembly to consent to receive them; but it did have to modify
the arrangements of the probation system to make it easier for the
colonial government to cope with the convicts on the island. There were
26,000 there in 1846, of whom more than 10,000 were on government
hands – 3,000 under punishment, 5,000 still in the probation gangs and
2,000 unemployed pass-holders. The transportation of males was then
suspended for two years, and the British government agreed to pay both
for part of the cost of the Police and Gaols and for the convicts employed
on public works, undertaken, as Grey told the Treasury, not for the
benefit of the colony, 'but for the convenience of the convict department'. He wanted to avoid quarrels arising from pin-pricking charges,
like Coroners' fees, which the Treasury was always anxious to impose
on it. 'It is of great importance to Great Britain to be rid of her criminals' and to keep Van Diemen's Land 'available as a place for their
reception', despite 'the desire of the inhabitants that it should cease to
be so used', he wrote. 'The charges are not heavy in amount, but are of a
kind peculiarly calculated to create irritation.' But the Treasury always
believed that a pinch-penny policy was the acme of statesmanship, and

it refused, for example, to pay rewards for the recapture of absconders.[1]

After reducing the financial burden, Grey looked forward to improved administration reducing the colonial opposition; he hoped that Wilmot's successor, Sir William Denison, an engineer officer who had had experience in dealing with convicts at Woolwich and Bermuda, and the new Controller-General, Dr. Hampton, would be able to prepare the way for the exiles whom he planned to send after the two years' 'breathing time' had elapsed. Eventually he had to send more to Van Diemen's Land than he had originally hoped, but Denison's reforms and the economic recovery in the colony did enable it to receive them, albeit unwillingly, in 1848 when they had completed the preliminary stages of the punishment foreshadowed the year before.

By then, this had been slightly modified; but if Russell 'quite approved' the changes, they no more endeared Grey's policy to the colonists than did his explanation that they had misunderstood it in the first place. They now learned that he had never intended to stop transportation for good and all, and that criminals, however they might be described, and whatever 'reformatory' discipline they might have undergone, were going to be sent to Van Diemen's Land again; in fact, in order to increase the government's control over them, they would have tickets-of-leave, not conditional pardons, so that technically they would still be convicts after all. Grey insisted that even so they would be reformed characters, which was doubtful, and that since they would be dispersed in private employment, they would not cause a revival of the evils of the probation gangs, which was true. They would provide cheap labour which would benefit the colonial economy; they would be accompanied by free migrants; they would not be very numerous. The colonists really had nothing to complain about, Grey thought; but many complained all the same. The Legislative Council viewed these plans 'with extreme regret', and local opposition grew as it became apparent that in fact nearly all Britain's 'exiles' were coming to Van Diemen's Land and migrants, apart from the convicts' families, were not.[2]

Certainly Denison was pleased. He insisted that 'the welfare of the colonies depends on the supply of labour'; a shortage had 'bad effects . . . on the morals of the community' and 'the only sure supply was the

[1] Grey to Denison, 30 Sept. 1846; minute on Wilmot to Gladstone, 2 Sept. 1846, Stephen to Treasury, 15 Feb. 1847, CO 280/196; Grey's minute on Trevelyan to Stephen, 15 Sept., 1847, Hawes to Trevelyan, 13 Oct., Trevelyan to Hawes, 12 Nov., CO 280/218; Grey's minute on Trevelyan to Merivale, 6 Nov. 1849, Merivale to Trevelyan, 30 Nov., Trevelyan to Merivale, 29 Dec., CO 280/250.
[2] Russell to Grey, 24 April 1848, Grey Papers, 119–3; Grey to Denison, 27 April 1848; Legs. Council, Mins., 14 Oct. 1848; return of emigrants, quoted Clark, *Documents*, 215.

annual deportation of convicts'. He calculated that between January 1847 and June 1849 the working population would have decreased by 4,825 had not 6,119 convicts either emerged from the gangs or landed in the colony, and this suggested to him that Van Diemen's Land needed 1,500 convicts every year, a figure he later raised to 2,000. 'We have ample means of controlling that number,' he declared, for with the help of the 'zeal and energy' of the Controller-General, he had extended the task-work system which had proved so successful in Bermuda, improved the supervision and discipline of the men, reorganized Port Arthur and begun the building of a 'model' penitentiary there.[1]

Grey was deeply gratified, and when he received the Controller's report, written in June 1848, he even wondered whether he could not send out 'the small residue of unmanageables who were an encumbrance to this country'. Meanwhile it had occurred to him that the 'exiles' now being sent with tickets-of-leave could be asked to repay their passage money, as well as behaving well, before being granted a conditional pardon. Russell thought this idea 'a very good one', but juveniles

LABOUR IN VAN DIEMEN'S LAND

1845 – 1853

| | Convicts Arriving | | Unemployed | |
	Male	Female	Passholders	Emigration
1845	2,263	607	3,268	
1846	786	340	2,025	
1847	645	624	1,194	3,908
1848	925	509	1,091	3,799
1849	982	865	618	3,617
1850	2,581	825	883	4,612
1851	1,496	658	38	7,463
1852	1,774	797		
1853	1,095	385		

should be exempt from the charge, though like the adults, they should go out with tickets-of-leave.[2] The Government should place all

[1] Denison to Grey, 10 July 1847, 1 Nov. 1848, 27 Sept. 1849; W. Denison, *Varieties of Vice-Regal Life* (London, 1870), i, 26 and 32; Hampton's reports, encl. Denison to Grey, 5 Dec. 1847, 27 June 1848, 5 Feb. 1849; statistical returns, encl. 20 Jan., 27 Sept. 1849.
[2] Grey's minute on Denison to Grey, 27 June 1848, CO 280/228; Waddington to Merivale, 25 May, 28 July, 25 Sept. 1848, with Grey's minutes, CO 280/235; Russell to Grey, 24 March, Grey Papers, 119–3; Waddington to Merivale, 30 Jan. 1849, with minutes, CO 201/421.

prisoners 'in circumstances favourable to their reform'. This was 'the main object for which this power . . . is retained over them,' Grey told Denison. They should be dispersed 'in the district where they may most easily find employment, at a distance from those temptations to which in a considerable town they must be exposed'. This control would be all the more necessary if Denison was right in having no 'very sanguine expectations' of the separate system 'producing a real and permanent reformation'.[1]

Whatever its effects might have been, Irish prisoners were not even subjected to it, and in 1848, owing to the increase in crime after the famine, the Irish authorities were at their wits' end. Between 1843 and 1846 the average number sentenced to transportation was 673 each year; in the twelve months to August 1848, it was 2,698; of all those so sentenced, 3,495 were in gaol, though the convict prisons had accommodation for only 1,863, and little provision for reformatory discipline. Grey told the Irish government that 'the success of the present transportation plan depends on the efficiency of reformatory punishment in the United Kingdom'; without it 'the colonies suffer by the introduction of large numbers of criminals whose evil propensities are not subdued, and this country suffers by making a transportation sentence . . . a reward instead of a punishment'. The Lord-Lieutenant, perhaps more realistically, argued that treatment in the colony was more important than prison training in Ireland, the Irish Chief Secretary insisted that Irish convicts had not the 'moral turpitude' of English, and Sir George Grey told the House of Commons he did not know why some of them had been sentenced to transportation at all.[2] But they had, and Denison complained of their 'inaptitude', 'want of intelligence' and a 'demeanour' showing the lack of 'moral and industrial training'. To correct these failings, Grey authorized him to send some of his prisoners to gangs in Van Diemen's Land, instead of giving them tickets-of-leave, even though this involved a further modification of the great reformatory scheme; hence, when in September 1850, Denison repeated his complaints of the convicts' misconduct, Eliot could comment, very truly, that the evils he reported had arisen 'not because the

[1] Grey's minutes on Denison to Grey, 5 and 13 Sept. 1848, CO 280/231; cf. ib., 13 August 1849; Waddington to Merivale, 25 April 1849, CO 201/421.

[2] Redington to Sir George Grey, 16 Feb. 1847, to Waddington, 27 June 1849, HO 45/1343 and 2957; Waddington to Merivale, 19 Sept. 1848, encl. Redington to Cornewall-Lewis, 12 Sept., with minutes, Grey to Denison, 2 Oct., Merivale to Waddington, 4 Oct., Waddington to Merivale, 10 Oct., Cornewall-Lewis to Merivale, 21 Oct., with minutes by Merivale and Grey, CO 280/235; Redington to Waddington, 27 June 1849, CO 280/250; Sir George Grey, 14 Feb. 1850, P. Debs., cviii, 788.

scheme of penal discipline contemplated by Her Majesty's Government is not sound', but because 'it is not carried out', just as the previously planned probation system had not been carried out because there had been no proper reformatory training in the gangs – if such a thing was possible.[1]

Grey's original plans for Norfolk Island were not carried out either. Mounting criticism of the incompetence of the Commandant, Major Childs, had caused Wilmot, in May 1846, to send a Commissioner to inquire into affairs there. His investigations had revealed a deplorable state of affairs. The 'old hands' were not kept separate from new arrivals. Schools and religious observances were neglected. The bakehouse was dilapidated, the water impure, rations the 'subject of general complaint'. The lumber-yard, where the convicts messed, and its buildings were 'filthy, the accommodation and general arrangements defective and wretched in the extreme'. There was inadequate superintendence and no inspection at night. 'Very heavy irons' were 'ordinary practice' even for men awaiting trial, and those who had *not* been sentenced to chains. The 'gag' was widely used. Yet orders were often flouted and 'instances of gross insubordination allowed to pass unnoticed'.[2]

All this indicated that Childs was 'totally unfitted' for his situation, and Wilmot decided to replace him; but before he could do so, a number of convicts rioted and killed some of their guards. The new Commandant, John Price, a former Hobart magistrate, restored order, but only by resorting to great severity, declaring that no system was possible except one based on 'the strictest discipline and coercion'. To Stephen, the Commissioner's report demonstrated 'the utter absurdity of maintaining Norfolk Island as a receptacle for convicts'. Grey thought 'the case so monstrous . . . that my own decided opinion is that without waiting for further inquiry and without a day's delay we ought to take immediate measures for breaking up the establishment altogether'; unfortunately, when Russell was told of this, he suggested that Denison should have discretion 'to modify the execution of his instructions'

[1] Redington to Waddington, 8 Sept. 1850, 22 Nov. 1851, Irish Chief Sec.'s Convict Letter Book 'A', 1849–52, vii, 6–16, nos. 133, 383, and cf. *ib.*, 18 Sept. 1848; Denison to Grey, 28 Sept. 1848, 31 Jan. 1849, with Grey's minutes, CO 280/231 and 242; *ib.*, 27 Sept. and 1 Oct. 1849; minutes on Waddington to Merivale, 28 May 1849, CO 280/250; Grey to Denison, 12 May 1849; Denison to Grey, 9 and 12 Sept. 1850, with Eliot's minutes, CO 280/263.

[2] See above, p. 309. Wilmot to Gladstone, 6 July 1846, encl. Report from Stewart to the Controller-General, 20 June 1846; Ullathorne, *Bishop Willson*, 57–61; Cullen, 'Bishop Willson', *Australasian Catholic Record*, xxvii, 226, and 'Bishop Willson and Norfolk Island', *Tas. Hist. Assoc.*, ii, 5 ff.; West, ii, 296–8; the Rev. T. B. Naylor to Stanley, CO 280/240. Fielding Browne's report, Col. Sec.'s Corr., 20/43/1220, Tas Arch.

because of the difficulty of disposing of the prisoners on the island; once this discretion was given, the determination that henceforth 'no convicts must be sent to Norfolk Island' was easily modified as well.[1]

Denison wanted it for colonial convict discipline. Stephen's resignation removed one of its principal critics from the Colonial Office. Though it was 'open to great objections', Grey came to argue that many of its evils in the past were due to 'adventitious causes'; he told Hampton to inspect the place, to try to improve the supervision, to introduce task-work and the separate system. Hampton favoured keeping it. The 'suspension' during 1847 had allowed the numbers on Norfolk Island to be reduced from nearly two thousand to about seven hundred and this alone improved its conditions. Grey still thought 'the establishment . . . ought to be got rid of', but only about sixty men would be sent there directly each year and it was needed for the 'doubly convicted'. He concluded that since retaining it was 'recommended after a personal inspection by an Officer of such extensive experience as Dr. Hampton', it should not 'at present be dispensed with'.[2]

The former chaplain, the Reverend T. Rogers, denounced Hampton's report as a 'deceptive document'. Certainly Hampton was only on the island for eight days. An opportunist and self-seeker little moved by any finer feeling, he was unlikely to criticize too harshly an establishment which his superior, Denison, wanted maintained; for all that he was probably right in his claim that Price had greatly improved its administration. It was unfortunate, thought Grey, that this had been effected only 'by extreme though doubtless necessary severity'; but 'the existence of some place of severe punishment' was necessary for convict discipline. 'The distance and isolation of Norfolk Island' seemed 'to exercise a powerful influence over offenders; the growing agitation in all the colonies against receiving convicts added to the case for the 'permanent retention' of Norfolk Island as a penal settlement. Price had increased the prisoners' rations, put up new buildings and extended the schools. On the basis of this report, Eliot minuted that 'the character of the station . . . seems to have undergone a complete transformation'. Unfortunately this was not true; but in November 1849, both Jebb and

[1] Wilmot to Gladstone, 8 July 1846; La Trobe to Grey, 30 Nov. 1846, encl. Burgess' report on the outbreak, 30 Oct. Price's report, 7 Dec. 1846, encl. in La Trobe to Grey, 8 Jan. 1847, and Stephen's minute, CO 280/205; Grey's minute on Naylor to Stanley, 8 July, 1846; Russell to Grey, 30 Sept., CO 280/240; Grey to Denison, 30 Sept. and 7 Nov. 1846; cf. West, ii, 297; Barry, 154 ff.; Ed. Rev., lx (1847), 245.

[2] Denison to Grey, 20 Aug. 1847, and minutes thereon, CO 280/211; Grey to Denison, 4 May 1848; Denison to Grey 15 March 1848, and minutes thereon, CO 280/226; Grey to Denison, 22 Dec. 1848.

the Home Office agreed that it should be retained, a decision which momentarily seemed justified when Bishop Willson reported at the same time 'a marvellous change since my former visit'.[1]

During these years, Van Diemen's Land continued to receive back prisoners after their term of 'ultra punishment' expired, but any British convicts who were still in New South Wales, and were sent to Norfolk Island for punishment, went back to Sydney; others in New South Wales who could not properly receive their tickets or conditional pardons were to be kept on Cockatoo Island in Port Jackson; not even females or invalids were to be sent down to Van Diemen's Land. These decisions avoided what Eliot in London admitted was 'in every other respect except economy' a 'course of doubtful policy', and which Denison had joined with the colonists in strongly opposing. In the end keeping them in New South Wales did not add much to British expenditure, for the home government merely paid the colony for keeping them; the convict department there, formerly so extensive, was broken up, except for the hospital and a small clerical staff to watch the movements of the ticket-holders.[2]

In 1850 Denison reported himself 'well satisfied' with the condition of his convict establishment. He hoped that the system might change the men's habits of conduct; he was sure that it benefited the 'moral condition' of the colony by keeping down wages. However, he thought the system would have to be modified to neutralize the opposition it was meeting. He urged that men be sent to carry out public works for which Britain should pay, 'for one of the great causes of the outcry against transportation in 1844-5 was the injudicious attempt of the Home Government to obtain from the colony payment for the labour of the convicts'; in due course they would earn a ticket-of-leave and seek private employment, but even then their right to change their masters should be restricted.[3]

These suggestions involved abandoning the principle, adopted in 1847, that prisoners should be kept at home during the 'penal' part of their sentence; but prison accommodation in Britain was still inadequate,

[1] Minutes on Denison to Grey, 15 March 1848, 5 Feb. 1849, CO 280/226 and 254; Merivale to Cornewall-Lewis, 5 Nov. 1849, Jebb to Waddington, 16 Nov., Cornewall-Lewis to Merivale, 12 and 21 Nov., Corr., PP 1850 (1153); Willson's report on Norfolk Island, Oct. 1849, encl. in Denison to Grey, 31 Jan. 1850, minutes on report, CO 280/259; Denison to Grey, 27 July 1850; Cullen, 229-230; Rogers, Review; Barry, John Price, 39.

[2] West, op. cit., i, 285; Grey to Fitz Roy, 4 May 1847; Eliot's minute on Denison to Grey, 31 Dec. 1847; Fitz Roy to Grey, 28 Oct. 1847, 5 April 1848, with encls.; Denison, minute no. 882, 30 Oct. 1847, Col. Sec.'s Corr., Denison, xxxi, Tas. Arch.; Grey to Fitz Roy, 23 Dec. 1848, to Denison, 22 Dec.

[3] Denison to Grey, 8 and 31 Jan., 2 May 1850; ib., 30 May, private, Grey Papers, 82-10.

and some gangs were needed in the colony for punishment and for those like the Irish who had had no reformatory discipline. 'Exiles' might be 'readily assimilated', but was exile alone sufficient punishment? Grey began to think of the reformatory effects of the old assignment system, as well as its evils, which he had denounced so vehemently in 1838 and again in 1847. Under a good master it was 'the best system'. To restore its best features and to 'disperse' the men, he told Denison in May 1850 to release prisoners to 'approved' employers in country districts. They should be paid wages, but they should repay their passage money to the Government in return for the Crown 'forbearing' to demand 'compulsory labour'. The men were to sign on for a year, so as not to be able to change their master, but they should have the prospect of progressing towards freedom by good conduct. As for public works, they should be expanded, and paid for from the land revenue; labour for them would come from those who could not find private employment, the Irish who had had little penal discipline at home, and those guilty of misconduct.[1]

These instructions marked another step away from Grey's earlier ideas; but would they make transportation appear 'manifestly conducive to the interests of the colonists', as Denison wanted, especially when Grey agreed that convicts be embarked 'early', as a 'temporary measure' until Dartmoor was ready? Grey admitted that colonial interests should be considered. In October he and Jebb agreed to supply more penal labour for public works by sending a small class of convicts intermediate between those with tickets-of-leave and the very worst criminals going to Norfolk Island; but when he sent another shipload of 'untreated' Irish for the public works gangs in February 1851, he seemed to be thinking primarily of the mother country. Denison could readily find work for them, though they would 'doubtless be complained of', he wrote; whether 'manifestly conducive to the interests of the colonists' no longer mattered.[2] But Denison had become alarmed by the arrival of 1,749 men between July and December 1850. He tightened up his control over ticket-holders by forbidding them to leave their masters for a period proportionate to their sentences, and triumphantly told Deas Thomson, in Sydney, 'I have succeeded in getting back the assignment system in a modified form.' But this removed the convicts' incentive

---

[1] Minutes and mem. by Eliot and Hawes on Denison to Grey, 27 Sept. 1849, CO 280/254; Grey to Denison, 24 May 1850.

[2] Minutes on Denison to Grey, 2 May 1850; Grey to Denison, 25 July; Jebb to Waddington, encl. in Waddington to Merivale, 8 July, 24 October 1850, CO 280/271; Merivale to Waddington, Grey to Denison, 7 Nov.; Waddington to Merivale, with Grey's minute, 6 Feb. 1851, CO 280/284.

to work hard and behave well in order to earn a conditional pardon quickly, so Grey refused to sanction it. He too thought it had 'virtually re-established the system of assignment', and since its defects had become apparent to him again he was not pleased.[1]

But however Grey's plans were changed, they did not appeal to the colonists. Opposition in Van Diemen's Land became increasingly vocal, despite Denison's improved supervision, the alleged advantage of convict labour, the reduction of the probation gangs to about a thousand and the fall in the number of unemployed pass-holders from 3,073 in October 1846 to 1,091 in December 1848. After the Legislative Council had condemned Grey's 'exile' policy in October 1848, its keener opponents formed an Anti-Transportation League at Launceston in January 1849, and another at Hobart three months later. Their members promised not to employ the new arrivals, but Grey was not to be moved. 'No one is more sensible than I am of the moral evils introduced into the colony by the former practice and no one is more anxious to mitigate them,' he wrote. But the colony had 'from a pecuniary point of view gained largely'; it had been 'established as a penal settlement', and the free inhabitants who 'had gone there of their own choice therefore could not represent its penal character as an intolerable grievance', a sentiment he repeated in the House of Lords next year.[2]

'Intolerable grievance' or not, the convicts remained more than a third of the population, and with the expirees, more than half; their conduct, naturally enough, was always open to criticism, and their 'moral evil' was 'contagious'. How are 'the children to escape from a measure of contamination . . . from . . . convict servants?' demanded the Quaker, G. W. Walker. In 1846, of the 240 persons convicted of serious crime, 126 were convicts and 92 ex-convicts; only twenty-two had always been free. In a population of 70,164, this showed a crime rate of about one in three hundred, certainly less than ten years before, and much less than the rate of one in 160 in 1844-5, but double that of England.[3]

Among a small, random sample taken from all those who arrived between 1841 and 1853, on the average about one-third of the English

---

[1] Denison to Grey, 3, 4 and 13 Dec. 1850, with Grey's minutes, CO 280/266 and 267; Denison to Deas Thomson, 12 Dec., Deas Thomson papers, ii, ML A1531-2; Grey to Denison, 4 Aug. 1851.
[2] VDL Legs. Council, *V & P*, 14 Oct. 1848; Ward, *Earl Grey*, 197-8; Denison to Grey, 5 Feb. 1849; Grey to Denison, 22 April 1849; *P. Debs.*, 1850, cix, 871.
[3] G. W. Walker to F. Cotton, 29 June 1847, *Hist. MSS. Tas.*, 146; Return of persons tried, Legs. Council Papers, 1848, No. 13; Statistical Returns, encl. Denison to Grey, 20 Jan. 1849.

and one-half the Irish either had a clean sheet or were convicted of only one offence by the magistrates. Of the offences committed, insubordination and neglect were together the most common, followed by absence without leave and drunkenness; but illegal possession and theft made up seven per cent, or about a thousand cases a year, and sexual offences totalled more than four hundred a year. As the convict population averaged about 25,000, this meant that between five and six per cent every year committed a crime, apart from a breach of discipline; if this did not turn the island into a Sodom or Gomorrah, as some critics implied, it was a grievance which opponents could readily seize on; and doubtless much was not detected. As a tribute to Maconochie's régime at Norfolk Island two of the best groups were those sent from there in the *Maitland* and *Duke of Richmond* in 1844, and the number with 'good' records shows that the hopes for reform in the antipodes were not entirely misplaced; but though most misconduct was petty, and the great majority of the convicts were quite law-abiding, there were enough who were not to arouse justified discontent.[1]

Grey could not attract the free migrants he wanted to counteract their influence. Apart from the convicts' families, only 773 arrived in three years from 1848, against nine times as many convicts; as Denison told the Legislative Council, free labourers would not stay 'as long as higher wages and greater advantages are held out to them in New South Wales', so, complained the colony's London agent, Van Diemen's Land seemed to be 'rapidly drawing towards that consummation of misfortune when the only people left will be the free employer, chained to the soil on which he has expended his all, and the convict passholder'.[2]

Denison did not much mind. He was sure convicts were needed to keep down wages, and this was all important for the colony's prosperity; but the refusal of free people to go out certainly made it harder for the ex-criminal to reform himself in a respectable society, and Grey's inability to keep his promise to send migrants provided another grievance. The arrival of the *Neptune*, in April 1850, bore witness to the success of the Cape in resisting transportation; in August the Launceston Anti-Transportation Association decided to seek help from the mainland,

[1] L. Robson, 'Male Convicts 1841–1853', *Tas. Hist. Assoc.*, ix, 50–4; Return of Convict Pass-holders, with offences, 1 Sept. 1845, encl. in Controller's Report, 23 Jan. 1846, CO 280/199. These figures suggest almost the same result as Dr. Robson's, when allowing for more limited period covered; cf. convict record books, Tas. Arch., *passim*.
[2] *Returns*, PP 1851 (681); Jackson to Hawes, 13 March 1849, quoting Denison, Bell and Morrell, *Documents*, 306.

and asked the people of the other Australian colonies, 'communities allied by blood, language and commerce' and 'liable to the same wrongs . . . to exert your influence to the intent that transportation to Van Diemen's Land may forever cease'.[1]

This appeal came at an opportune moment. In 1849, as in 1845, New South Wales tried to protect itself against pardoned convicts arriving from Van Diemen's Land. On both occasions, the policy was vetoed and New South Welshmen came to believe that the real reason for this disallowance was a determination to use the mainland colonies as 'the waste-butts of Tasmania's convict superfluities'. At this moment, Grey was still hoping to open Moreton Bay to transported convicts and he had asked the New South Wales Legislative Council to reconsider the convict question. On 16 September 1850, to put pressure on the Council, at a monster meeting in Old Barrack Square, Sydney, it was decided to form a New South Wales Association for Preventing the Revival of Transportation. Four days later the Launceston Circular arrived and was published in the *Herald*, so when the Association published a formal statement of its aims, these included co-operating 'with the colonists of Van Diemen's Land in their efforts to secure the cessation of transportation there.[2] So prodded, the New South Wales Council voted against having any convicts in any part of the colony under any conditions, and amid a flurry of petitioning to the Queen, the Launceston Association called an intercolonial conference to meet in Melbourne in January 1851. Though the New South Wales Association and the South Australians were at first lukewarm, the Victorian Anti-Transportation Association formed with the Tasmanians an Australian League, whose members bound themselves by a 'Solemn Engagement' to fight against this 'menace'; they vowed to 'represent to the British government and the British Parliament and to the British public that . . . it is a great moral obligation on the part of our parent State not to eject her criminals into other societies . . . but to manage and retain them within herself . . . If the colonists are compelled to own that their name and fame may be dishonoured to relieve the gaols of Great Britain . . . we are at a loss to imagine what advantages conferred by the sovereignty of Great Britain can compensate for the stigma of its brand.' In March, delegates went to Sydney, where the New South Wales Association was now ready to welcome them; by the end of the year, the League had extended to South Australia and New Zealand, and had nominated a

[1] Denison to Grey, 4 and 13 Dec. 1850; West, i, 296 ff.; Ward, 198–9.
[2] Gipps to Stanley, 20 Oct. 1845; Ward, 201 ff.; New South Wales Vagrancy Act, 13 Vic., no. 6; *S.M.H.*, 4 Jan. 1851; see above, pp. 324–6.

distinguished board to represent it in London, including Molesworth and Robert Lowe.[1]

Its supporters expected instant success, but the British government did not take its pretensions very seriously. Denison told Grey that its progress had been grossly exaggerated in an 'artificial press campaign'; 'little regard' was paid to it, and its effect was 'beneath contempt'. He had declared at the end of 1850 that 'the amount of evil arising from the non-employment leagues will be very limited and will be felt principally by the few rash enough to join them'. He continued to insist that convicts were both needed and wanted, leading Eliot to comment that 'there is something almost amusing in the account of this eager scramble for convicts in a community where some persons so loudly denounce their introduction', and Grey to suggest that 'the best way of dealing with the anti-transportation league would be to send no convicts for ten years', if only there was anything else to do with them. Even after he had come to the conclusion that transportation should be stopped, Eliot found it remarkable 'that if the state of the convict colonies be so bad, that one never meets anybody returned from them who does not admit that life and property were more secure there than in England . . . No one can have had any intercourse with persons who have resided there . . . without being aware how grossly inaccurate are the imputations alluded to'.[2]

Though Fitz Roy was more concerned by the agitation, public opinion was by no means unanimous, especially in Van Diemen's Land. There the abolitionists, led by the historian-journalist-clergyman, John West, and their allied fighters for self-government in the Legislative Council, had powerful support in the press and were skilful propagandists; but West's *History*, for all its manifold virtues, should not be regarded as the last word on a cause which the author had so much at heart, and which had not been won when the book was written. In Hobart particularly, the League's meetings were stormy. Its subscribers continued to employ convicts; even if the working classes bitterly opposed them, and employers might dislike them on principle, the latter feared 'the ruin that might ensure' if transportation stopped and wages rose; Denison expected that the gold discoveries, by attracting free men to the diggings and increasing the demand for food, would intensify the shortage of

---

[1] West, i, 305–7.
[2] Denison to Grey, 13, 21, 23 and 27 Dec., 1850; Denison to Grey, Private, 16 June, 10 July, 3 Sept., 18 Oct. 1851, Grey Papers, 82–10; minutes on Cooper to Denison, 22 April 1851, CO 280/300, and Denison to Grey, 1 Oct. and 18 Nov. 1851, CO 280/279 and 280; Ward, 212–3.

labour and the need for convicts.[1] In October 1851, Grey assured the Governor that Parliament still favoured transportation, and he showed no signs of changing his mind or his policy, though the previous January, Russell had confided to him that the establishment of a partially elected Legislative Council might make it difficult to keep on sending convicts to the colony. In October the anti-transportationists won every elective seat in the new Council. Agitation was having its effect. 'I am well aware of the great benefits we have derived from convict Labour and expenditure, and that we shall and do feel, in a pecuniary point, the change to free labour', confided Frederick Stieglitz to the pro-transportationist Leake; 'but depend upon it there shall be *peace* in these Colonies till transportation is entirely done away with'. Though a 'moderate man' he supported the anti-transportationist party.[2]

Grey firmly believed that punishment by separate confinement, penal labour and then transportation, as he had worked it out, was the best possible method of dealing with criminals. In September 1850, he sent out a circular despatch to all colonial governors describing it with pride and urging them to adopt it for their own felons. In the case of Great Britain, he was sure that it benefited *both* the mother country and the colonies, though as a judge in his own cause he possibly exaggerated the benefits which the latter gained from a policy so useful to the former. Though Fitz Roy thought that there were 'few English criminals who would not regard a free passage to the gold-fields via Hobart town as a great boon', Grey insisted that the gold discoveries did not affect 'the propriety of sending convicts to Van Diemen's Land'. Stubborn, confident in his integrity, his good intentions and his wisdom, despite his sympathy with colonial local self-government, Grey paid too little heed to colonial opinion, even though he tried to find out what that opinion was. 'His unpopularity arises in great degree from his public spirit,' wrote Henry Taylor, one of the under-secretaries at the Colonial Office. He was 'not a very convertible person', and took 'little account of the judgment of parties and individuals . . . when opposed to public interests', though in this case Denison was concerned to play down

---

[1] Fitz Roy to Grey, 31 July 1851; Townsley, 121–2; Denison to Grey, 21 Aug. 1851, Papers re Gold Discoveries, PP 1852 (1508), xxxiv, 81; cf. Denison to Leake, 16 Dec. 1851, *Hist. MSS. Tas.*, 76–7, and to Deas Thomson, 13 Oct. and 10 Dec., Deas Thomson papers, *loc. cit.*
[2] Grey to Denison, private, 18 Oct. 1851, Grey Papers, 82–10; Denison to Grey, private, 9 Oct. 1851, 24 March 1852, *ib.*; despatches, 16 Jan. 1852, encl. Hampton's report, and 9 Feb. 1852; Russell to Grey, 23 Jan. 1851, Grey Papers; Stieglitz to Leake, 18 Sept. 1851, *Tas. Hist. MSS.*, 79.

rather than to stress the intensity of local feeling.[1] This heedlessness was the cause of much trouble, but it was not the only cause. The successful disposal of the convicts in the colonies demanded a relation between the demand for their labour and its supply; the colonial demand was less than Grey hoped, and after 1847 the supply was far larger than he had expected, owing to the effects of the Irish famine. This he can hardly be blamed for not foreseeing; but like his ministerial colleagues, he failed to adapt his prejudices and his policy to the new circumstances.

By this time opposition in England had grown. A Select Committee on prison discipline in 1850 looked forward to the time when 'separate' imprisonment would become universal and would replace transportation; though in 1851 the House of Commons showed its lack of interest in the question by being counted out, the propaganda of the Anti-Transportation League was not without effect. After Robert Lowe returned home, the *Times* changed sides. It had welcomed Grey's policy in 1847 and condemned the selfishness of the Cape in 1849; but in 1852 it forecast a 'disastrous separation' arising 'from the infatuated perseverance in the present system', and argued that transportation was a 'frightful inducement to the commission of crime'.[2]

By then, too, the government had built more prisons. A Select Committee in 1847 had not confirmed the worst of the allegations which the *Times* had made about the hulks, but its report was so critical of their defects, that Sir George Grey, 'anxious to remedy the flagrant evils', determined to speed up their replacement. Temporarily this made overseas receptacles all the more necessary, especially since he refused to allow greater use of local prisons, which, he said, were needed for debtors, men awaiting trial and men sentenced by magistrates. In 1850 he told Parliament that there were still two thousand men in the hulks in Great Britain and Ireland. Including them, Parkhurst, Portland dockyard, Bermuda, Gibraltar and all the prisons in the United Kingdom there was room for only 12,900, while nearly 5,000 were sentenced to transportation every year; if those sent to Australia were to be kept at home, accommodation would have to be nearly doubled. But next year Dartmoor opened. A new gaol replaced the hulks at Portsmouth. With the end of the Irish famine, crime there fell back to its normal level. The number of convicts sent to Van Diemen's Land fell by one-third. All

---

[1] Minutes on Denison to Grey, 14 July and 21 Aug. 1851, CO 280/277 and 281; Circular despatch, 28 Sept. 1850, *Corr.*, PP 1852 (1517); Fitz Roy to Grey, 19 June 1851; Grey to Denison, 24 Jan. 1852; Henry Taylor, *Autobiography* (1885), i, 128, 203.

[2] *Prison Discipline* Report, PP 1850 (632); *P. Debs.*, 9 and 20 May 1851, cxvi, 743 ff. and 1168 ff.; *Times*, 6 March 1847, 15 Sept. 1849, 17 Aug., 1 and 6 Oct. 1852.

prisoners sentenced to transportation could be given the required probationary discipline before being sent out; 'for the first time' there were vacancies in the government prisons.[1]

In 1851, Jebb insisted that 'the hearts of many sink at the prospect of transportation', but in 1852 (was it the gold discoveries?) he was thinking of alternatives to it. More than a thousand criminals were unconditionally released from the hulks every year, he reported; it should be possible for other well-conducted prisoners to receive their conditional pardons in England after serving a suitable portion of their sentences, instead of being sent overseas. Longer prison terms at home might be substituted for transportation, for between 1842 and 1850, while nearly 30,000 men were sentenced to seven or ten years' transportation, fewer than five thousand were sentenced to more than twelve months in gaol. The new prison buildings made it possible to keep 16,000 convicts at home. Transportation cost £100 per man for the whole term of his sentence, but the *net* cost of home imprisonment, including buildings, was only £15 a year in England and £10 in Ireland; this was less than the cost of transportation for less than seven years.[2] Even so, 'the privilege of shooting so much moral rubbish upon other and distant premises is cheaply bought at such a rate', thought that percipient visitor to Australasia, Colonel Mundy, feeling indifferent to the views of the other colonists in those 'premises', who should have known what they were going to when they emigrated there. Three Metropolitan Police superintendents were nervous that 'trained thieves, hardened by repeated punishment . . . if retained in this country would greatly endanger the security of life and property', while 'transportation permanently rids us of a vast number of incorrigible criminals'. The prospect 'of retaining our convicts in England is perfectly terrible,' declared the Evangelical Tory and Factory reformer, Lord Shaftesbury.[3] At that moment there were about 80,000 convicts and exconvicts in the Australian colonies, or about ninety per cent of those who had been transported and were still alive; without transportation

---

[1] *Hulks Report*, PP 1847 (831); Hulks, annual reports; *Times*, 29 Jan. 1847; Voules to Sir George Grey, Oct. 1848, HO 45/1401; Jebb to Waddington, 19 March 1850, HO 12/1484, with Grey's minutes; *P. Debs.*, 1850, cix, 858 ff., cxii, 1246 ff.; Eliot's mem., 24 Jan. 1850, Grey Papers, Transportation; Jebb, annual report, Convict Prisons, 1850, PP 1851 (1419). A new prison for women was opened at Brixton in 1853.

[2] Jebb, *Prisons Reports*, 1850, 1851, 1852, PP; Jebb to Walpole, 1 Nov. 1852, Grey Papers, Transportation. For the new prisons, see above, p. 313. The last of the hulk establishments, at Woolwich, was broken up in 1853.

[3] G. C. Mundy, *Our Antipodes*, 485; mem. by Metropolitan Police, 1 March 1853, HO 45/4759; Shaftesbury to Adderley, 14 Nov. 1851, quoted, W. S. Childe-Pemberton, *The Life of Lord Norton* (London, 1909), 94.

these would have been living in the British Isles, but, said Jebb, 'the real ground for apprehension about discharged convicts' arose not from the fifteen hundred freed from 'reformatory institutions', who might have been transported instead, but from the seventy-five thousand released from the ordinary prisons. Perhaps he was mindful, too, of better economic conditions and the greater demand for labour at home; at all events, he insisted that release there was not unduly dangerous, that 'removal had ceased to deter', and that imprisonment was a practicable and not too expensive an alternative.[1]

On 14 December, Grey's Tory successor at the Colonial Office, Sir John Pakington, told Denison that England should not force the colonists 'into a furious opposition . . . extinguishing all loyalty and affection for the mother-country'; acting in response to 'proof of a growing public feeling . . . not manifested in Van Diemen's Land alone but in all the adjacent colonies', despite the advantages of transportation, the government had decided 'to comply with a wish so generally and forcibly expressed'. Its decision was influenced by 'the denunciations of the Press at home' and 'by the effects of the discovery of gold', but the fact remained that no more convicts would be sent to Van Diemen's Land.[2]

Aberdeen's coalition ministry which took office later that month confirmed this policy. The new Colonial Secretary, the Duke of Newcastle, told Denison in February 1853 that there were 'no insuperable obstacles to finding room in the existing prisons, aided by other establishments abroad, for the number of persons likely to come on the hands of the government'; he added, privately, the reasons for his decision – the strong feelings of part of the Van Diemen's Land population, the 'unanimous wish of the two neighbouring colonies', the growing feeling in Britain, 'the enormously increased expenditure caused by the high price of provisions and the rise of freights', the reduced 'deterring influence' since the gold discoveries, and 'the general rule that a Colonial Governor finds himself less embarrassed by an absolute though sudden change than where the discretion . . . of preparing for it exposes him to charges of unfairness and . . . undue exercise of his powers'. All these explanations played their part in the government's decision, but Palmerston, the new Home Secretary, implied that the colonial objections, whether these were 'well-founded or not', had been paramount. 'We had conceded to those Colonies the

[1] Jebb to Walpole, 1 Nov. 1852, to Grey, 9 Dec., Grey Papers; Jebb, *Report on Penal Servitude Act*, PP 1854-5 (2004).
[2] Pakington to Denison, 14 Dec. 1852.

principle and right of self-government, and that cession being made, we must . . . submit to its consequences,' he said. The colonies' refusal to receive criminals would 'compel us to alter the system which we had hitherto pursued'.[1]

On 27 November 1852 the last convict ship sailed for Hobart. On 29 December 1853, the order-in-council making Van Diemen's Land a penal colony was revoked. During the year, Parliament substituted sentences of four years' penal servitude for seven years' transportation and made proportionate changes up to fourteen years. Only the longest terms were retained. Whereas in 1853, 1,864 were sentenced to transportation, and 504 to penal servitude, in 1855 only 325 were sentenced to be transported and 2,048 to penal servitude. This, Jebb assured Grey in 1856, was 'a more certain and deterring punishment, independent of the wishes of any colony, efficacious and economical'.[2]

Grey thought the decision a blunder, and moved a resolution in the House of Lords condemning it. Great Britain should not yield to every colonial demand; it would be better 'to part with the colonies' than to retain them with the burden of protection and defence but 'no substantial authority over them'. Stanley (now Lord Derby) disagreed. Colonial opinion had been aroused by the 'gang system', not owing to its intrinsic defects, but because of the colony's economic collapse in 1844 soon after it had been introduced. The 'disposal of convicts' involved a 'choice of evils'; the 'worst choice' was 'to run one's head against a stone wall' by sending convicts 'to colonies which positively will not receive them'. Newcastle insisted that Great Britain had no right to force the continuance of the system on the colonies, and the House negatived Grey's motion by 54 to 37.[3]

To the end, transportation caused colonial conflicts. It embittered the struggle for self-government by intensifying the opposition of the Legislative Council to Denison throughout 1852, and by creating a dispute between the Lieutenant-Governor and his principal officials, Henry Chapman, the Colonial Secretary, and Adam Turnbull, the Clerk of the Executive Council and a nominated official member of the Legislature, both of whom had come to support the abolitionists. After

---

[1] Newcastle to Denison, 7 Feb. 1853; ib., priv., 22 Feb. Ne C. 9555, Newcastle MSS., Univ. of Nottingham (I owe this reference to Professor J. M. Ward); Palmerston, 18 Feb. 1853, P. Debs., cxxiv, 536, and minute on Jebb to Waddington, 22 Feb. 1853, HO 12/3015.
[2] Penal Servitude Act, 16 and 17 Vic. c.99, cf. 20 and 21 Vic. c.3; E. Ruggles-Brise, English Prison System (1921); E. du Cane, Punishment and Prevention of Crime (1885); Jebb to Grey, 11 July 1856, Grey Papers, 119–4; evid. Jebb, Transportation report, PP 1856 (296).
[3] Grey, Journal, 25 Feb. and 5 March 1853, Grey Papers, C3/17: House of Lords, 10 May P. Debs., cxxvii, 22–61; Times, 11 May.

self-government had been conceded, the old Legislative Council, during its dying days, insisted on inquiring into alleged corruption in the still Imperially controlled convict department and so aroused another controversy, this time with Denison's successor. The transported Irish rebels of 1848, who were constantly protesting against the restrictions which the Government very naturally placed on their movements, were another cause of criticism until 1854, when all had escaped or been pardoned.[1]

Transportation now ceased to Norfolk Island too. Price's administration had turned that place once more into a hell for its seven hundred prisoners, and there seems little doubt that Rogers' earlier charges were justified. Convicts perforce were still employed as constables, and on their word Price completely relied. For petty breaches of discipline he would extend sentences, order hard labour in chains, heavy floggings, or confinement in what were nominally solitary cells, but were in fact cramped, stinking, airless and crowded, on near starvation rations. The rattling of irons, the swish of the lash, the execrations of the victims of the martinet's tortures of the 'gag', or the 'frame' to which the victim was bound, with his head projecting without support for hours, became everyday sounds on the island. By 1851 Denison had begun to suspect the state of affairs there and in 1852, when Hampton and Bishop Willson visited the place again, they reported that it was only too terrible. Willson found 'gloom, sullen despondence and despair'; one Sunday, of 270 in church, there were only fifty-two without chains. In his defence, Price pointed out that he was dealing with the very worst of the convicts, which was true, but Hampton concluded that he was maintaining order only by a 'mere application of brute force by his subordinates'; he did not seem to distinguish between a crime and a mere breach of the regulations. Frightful excesses on the island were the inevitable result of a harsh, merciless system, dependent on espionage, carried out in a place far from inspection by superiors, and conducted by a man whose behaviour in many ways suggests paranoia. Price was 'one of those human tigers who if they cannot obtain some uniform to cover their crimes are apt to get hanged for them, or come to a violent end,' wrote George Ives later; and the environment and isolation of Norfolk Island offered him plenty of opportunities to indulge the cruelty of his nature. Denison now recommended that the settlement be abandoned, and the 'ultra' station be transferred to Port Arthur. This time there was no argument for delay. On the day after he was told

[1] Townsley, 111–121, 147–165; Mitchel, ch. 14–24; *Journal*, W. Smith O'Brien Papers, vol. 449, No. 3400, Nat. Lib. Dub.; Kiernan, *Irish Exiles*.

transportation to Tasmania was to cease he was ordered to prepare to evacuate Norfolk Island; the removal of the convicts, begun in 1854, on 7 May 1856 was complete.[1]

In the end, the Anti-Transportation League carried the day; but they also carried their colony to economic depression which lasted for a generation until the mining discoveries of the 1870s. If Grey's argument that transportation was desirable for the British criminal seems unproved, Denison's insistence that it was necessary for colonial prosperity was better founded. As the commissariat expenditure which had reached almost £300,000 a year between 1844 and 1847, and was still almost £200,000, declined to nothing, the economy lost its major stimulus, and since agricultural technique was backward, cheap labour and an assured market were all the more necessary to make farming pay. 'Every day will prove . . . more clearly the correctness of the views which I have taken . . . The press on the labour market here is very great,' wrote Denison in 1853. A steady exodus to the goldfields accompanied a decline in investment in the colony. A population which had risen from 24,500 in 1830 to over 70,000 in 1851 rose by only forty per cent in the next twenty years while that on the mainland quadrupled.[2]

However, Western Australians were willing to risk moral corruption for the economic advantages of transportation. In the 1840s, the colony was depressed. When the British government raised the price of land to £1 an acre it stopped its sale and so extinguished the immigration fund. Confronted with a lack of labour and no market, in 1846 some landowners and merchants began to think that a penal settlement might possibly make good these deficiencies. At first the Pentonville Commissioners did not want to send any of their reformed prisoners there; they hoped the men would 'lose themselves in a larger colony', and Grey agreed; but by August 1848, circumstances had so changed that he had become less particular. Any outlet was better than none. He included Western Australia in his circular inquiry about the reception of 'exiles', and its favourable reply was the more welcome because it was unique. On 1 May 1849 an order-in-council made the colony a place to which convicts could be sent.[3] Before news of this reached Perth, the

[1] Bishop Willson, encl. in Denison to Pakington, 15 Dec. 1852; Cullen, 231; Cash, 157 ff.; Rogers, op. cit.; Price to Denison, encl. in Denison to Grey, 12 June 1852; Hampton's report, encl. ib., 14 June; cf. Denison, i, 384, Warung, Convict Days, 53, Barry, John Price, 64 and passim, Ives, 167.

[2] Hartwell, 102, 137; Denison, i, 212.

[3] Hutt to Stanley, 26 Jan. 1846; Perth Gazette, 2 Jan. 1847; Pentonville Commissioners to Grey, 21 Nov. 1846, Grey to the Commissioners, 5 Dec., HO 45/960; Grey to Fitzgerald, 3 Aug. 1848; Fitzgerald to Grey, 24 Oct. 1848; Waddington to Merivale, 13 and 19 March 1849, CO 18/52; Grey to Fitzgerald, 1 and 2 June.

Governor had made a further request, this time for a 'regular penal settlement'. This was not what the Secretary of State had intended, but his appetite was whetted. 'Ask Sir George Grey if a very limited number of convicts might not, with advantage, be sent out', he minuted. As a general rule they should only be removed after they had undergone 'penal labour', when they could receive tickets-of-leave, but 'it might assist in meeting the difficulty now experienced in disposing of the Irish convicts, and at the same time afford the means of raising Western Australia from her present difficulties, if a very limited number of convicts were sent out to be employed there on public works'. When the Home Office agreed, Grey promised to send with them military pensioners and their families for the security of the colony and free women to equalize the sexes. In March 1850 the first batch of seventy-five convicts sailed. Their arrival in June brought a response to which Grey, despite his high ideals and strong sense of responsibility, was strangely unaccustomed – addresses thanking him for his help to the colony.[1]

As in Sydney and Hobart many years ago, the newcomers had at first to be put up in rented lodgings. Sheds and stores were hired from the harbour-master, but even when repaired they were not very secure and the men were able to come and go much as they pleased; fortunately they were well-chosen men and few went very far. By the end of 1852 they were more securely housed. The arrival of more than a thousand free migrants and nearly 1,500 convicts stimulated the economy and provided a market for local produce. The British Treasury agreed, if a little reluctantly, to follow the precedent belatedly accepted in Van Diemen's Land in 1846 and to pay two-thirds of the cost of the local police. The military pensioners on each ship were kept on as a guard until their successors arrived on the next. Everything seemed reasonably satisfactory.[2]

Before being transported the convicts served their penitentiary term and their 'penal labour' in England. They were selected for transportation on the basis of their good behaviour. When they arrived, they were placed for a time in close confinement again, either at Fremantle or later at Perth, and employed on public works, though before the local gaols

[1] Fitzgerald to Grey, 3 March, 16 July 1849, with minutes by Eliot and Grey; Merivale to Waddington, 6 June, 30 July, 24 Nov. 1849, Waddington to Merivale, 10 Aug., CO 18/52; Grey to Fitzgerald, 22 Oct., 9 Dec. 1849, 5 Jan. 1850; Fitzgerald to Grey, 15 and 17 July 1850; Bell and Morrell, *Documents*, 314–5.

[2] Hasluck, 33 ff.; Battye, 207 ff.; Newcastle to Fitzgerald, 12 Dec. 1853. The police payment was reduced to 60 per cent in 1855, following allegations of colonial extravagance (Sir George Grey to Fitzgerald, 26 Jan.).

were finished they were sent out in parties to work on the roads or to build country depots. Before long they received their tickets-of-leave. The time this took depended on the length of their sentence, how long they had served in England, their behaviour, and after 1857 on a system of marks which they could earn; but at first they were often eligible soon after they landed. At the end of 1852, 845 out of 1,469 who had arrived were working for private employers, who were thus relieved of difficulties which the attraction of the Victorian goldfields would otherwise have caused them. The ticket-holders were confined to a certain district and were closely supervised, but they were paid wages, could acquire property, and though subject to summary magisterial jurisdiction, they did not suffer from the brutal discipline which had so disfigured the history of the penal colonies in the east, and they were protected from ill-treatment by the Board of Visiting Magistrates.[1]

The local government wanted men for the public works. The gaol at Perth was not finished until 1856 and that at Fremantle until 1857; the stores and jetties there took even longer. However, in 1858, since it was found that the emancipists and ticket-holders were too well-behaved to fill the new Perth gaol, it was decided to use it as a depot for prisoners who could be employed in the town. 'This will infuse new life into it,' commented the *Perth Gazette*, 'not only by the execution of the many necessary Public works required, but also in a mercantile point of view by creating a large additional expenditure'. So local malefactors were moved to Fremantle and transports resided at Perth. 'An era of building' began for the capital, and a new Government House, Pensioners' Barracks, Town Hall and Market Place testified to the convicts' labours.[2]

Free migrants accompanied the convicts and during the 1850s the population tripled. The year after he retired in 1855 Governor Fitzgerald had been able to assure a House of Lords committee that the convicts had saved the colony. Its chief grievance was that there were not enough of them. The Act of 1853 substituting penal servitude for transportation for those who would be sentenced for less than fourteen years, and their release on 'licence' in England, made it impossible to find the thousand a year that the Legislative Council would have liked. Instead of the average of 2,649 transportation sentences a year between 1850 and 1852, there were only 298 a year between 1854 and 1856. Only 224 men sailed in 1859 and about 300 a year in 1860 and 1861. Then the regulation requiring the men to have served half their sentence at home

[1] Battye, 234 ff.
[2] Hasluck, 53 ff.

before being sent out was suspended and the average annual number more than doubled. Fewer were eligible for tickets-of-leave, and the greater numbers on government hands enabled Governor Hampton to carry out an extensive road-building programme.[1]

Hampton had arrived in 1862. After three voyages as a Surgeon-Superintendent he had been Controller-General in Van Diemen's Land from 1846 to 1855. There he had at first seemed an efficient officer, but had departed under suspicion of corruption. In Western Australia, he quarrelled with his Controller-General, who resigned in 1866, and then, as if to confirm the suspicions of his conduct in Tasmania, he appointed his son to this well-paid post, and gave him a lodging allowance, even though he continued to reside at Government House. Probably influenced by his former experience, he adopted greater severity towards the convicts, though he certainly had more in government service and perhaps their earlier despatch meant they were less reformed than before. Bread and water diet, dark cells, chain gangs and more flogging followed. Attempts to escape tripled. Accusations of tyranny and inefficiency multiplied. When Hampton abolished the Board of Visiting Magistrates in March 1867, disaster seemed imminent, but in May a new Controller arrived from England. At once he inquired into the recent special punishments. He reduced the chain-gangs and soon restored the establishment to its former efficiency; but by this time the British government had announced that transportation was to cease.[2]

Although it was suggested in 1853 and again in 1856, no female convicts were sent to Western Australia; but in eighteen years, thirty-seven ships with 9,635 male prisoners arrived at the fairly steady rate of two shiploads a year (between 550 and 600 men), though more came in 1851, 1853 and 1862, and fewer from 1859 to 1861. When they came they were badly needed and they brought results which 'without them Western Australia could only have achieved after years of struggling'. They provided a market for local food producers. In eighteen years, imports exceeded exports by £1,000,000, which roughly represented the British commissariat expenditure. As ticket-of-leave holders only about one in three were convicted of offences; and of these about forty

---

[1] P. Debs., 1857, cxliv, 352, cxlv, 137; Transportation Report, PP 1856 (244, 296 and 355), evid. Fitzgerald and cf. Eliot and Grey; HL, SC on Substitution of other Punishment for Transportation, PP 1856 (404); Battye, 234 ff., 246 ff. In 1854–6, 7,002 convicts were granted 'licences' for release in the UK; of these 1,144 were revoked because of misbehaviour or a further offence.

Townsley, 148 ff.; Battye, 253 ff.; F. K. Crowley, Australia's Western Third (1960), 34 ff.

per cent were drunkenness or absconding and less than one-fifth were serious.[1]

The colonial objections to transportation to Western Australia were the same as in the east. It was said to lower the moral tone of the colony. It certainly increased the surplus of males in the community and retarded the advance to greater self-government. The eastern colonies kept up a constant protest, although the substitution in 1863 of 'conditional releases' *within* Western Australia for conditional pardons permitting convicts to leave it should have met their more justifiable objections. The decision to stop it came from the British government when it was still popular enough in Parliament and in the colony. In 1856, Select Committees of both Houses of the British Parliament had supported transportation. Judges and police both favoured it. It was still thought 'more effectual and deterring, better adapted for the reformation of the convict, and more beneficial to this country' than any other punishment. The government and its officials were less enthusiastic. Jebb found that home imprisonment cost less than had been expected and that transportation had become the more expensive punishment. By 1861 it seemed that Great Britain was no longer gaining an advantage from it. The convict establishment in Western Australia was expensive. By then a new prison at Chatham had replaced the hulks in the Thames. In 1862 those at Bermuda were broken up. The English gaols were not full. Both the War Office and the Admiralty wanted to employ convict labour. At the same time louder protests were coming from Victoria and New South Wales against the continued transportation to Western Australia.[2]

Although Grey's Royal Commission on Transportation in 1863 recommended that it be used more extensively again, the government paid greater heed to the Committee on Prison Discipline, which in the same year recommended more repressive conditions for prisoners. In 1865 it persuaded Parliament to pass another Prisons Act which gave the Home Office greater power to impose them, and it announced that after 1867 transportation would cease. It had come to accept the view that a more severe, deterrent punishment was needed, and that transportation was no good for this; the arguments for 'reforming' the prisoners so staunchly advocated by Maconochie and taken up by M. D. Hill were pushed on one side, and a 'massive machine for the promotion

[1] Battye, 256 and app. iv; Hasluck, 37, 138–9, 146–7.
[2] *Transportation Reports*, 1856; HL, S.C. 1856, evid. Jebb, 1223; *P. Debs.*, cliv and clv; *Transportation Report*, PP 1861 (286), evid. Eliot, 500 ff., and app. I, nos. 4, 10 and 11; Newcastle to Kennedy, 15 March 1861; Johnson, *Hulks*, 172, cf. M. Kerr, *Hist. Stud.*, vi, 40 ff.

of misery' extinguished the lights lit by many of the previous generation of reformers.[1] Relics of Grey's ideas remained. Separate 'reformatory' confinement, followed by penal prison labour, with the men divided into five classes, with varying privileges, increasing as one was 'promoted' for 'good conduct', and then by release with a ticket-of-leave or on licence, remained the basis of punishment for serious crimes for a generation, but the regimen was terribly hard. Not until the report of a departmental committee in 1894-5 was the system seriously criticized; even then successive governments were very slow to carry out its recommendations.[2] On 12 October 1867, the last convict ship sailed for Western Australia. It carried, among others, sixty Fenians to complete the tally of political prisoners sent to Australia; it marked the end of an important aspect of Australian history and of the penal practice of the United Kingdom.[3]

Economically it had greatly helped Australian development. It had provided a labour force, which if less efficient than free workers was far better than no workers at all. It made private investment more profitable and caused very substantial government expenditure in the colonies. Socially it did no great harm. Though the crime rate was higher in Australia than in England, colonial morals were not destroyed. If it increased the disproportion between the sexes, this was something which corrected itself in due course. Homosexuality was largely confined to the penal settlements. Perhaps its greatest evil was to encourage brutality which an allegedly civilized community should deplore; but the early nineteenth century was a brutal age, in which pain and suffering were regarded as normal and inevitable if distressing in all walks of life.

For the United Kingdom, transportation at first had seemed a merciful means of getting rid of part of its criminal population; but as crime became a more serious social problem, penal reformers came to stress the need for a severe deterrent punishment. Here transportation failed, partly because it was misunderstood at home, partly because it is hopeless to rely solely on deterrence to get rid of crime. Because of this

---

[1] *Transportation Report*, PP 1863 (3190); mems. re transportation, *ib.*, (505); House of Lords, *Prison Discipline Report*, PP (499); *P. Debs.*, clxxvii, 137; Cardwell to Hampton, 12 May and 25 July 1865; 28 and 29 Vic. c.126; S. and B. Webb, *Prisons*, 187 ff.; Barry, 227-8; *Times*, 10 Oct. 1855; C. B. Adderley, *Punishment is not Education—A review of a charge . . .* (1856); M. D. Hill, *Letter to C. B. Adderley on his review . . .* (1856) and *Suggestions for the Repression of Crime . . .* (1857).

[2] A. Griffiths, *Fifty Years of Public Service* (1904), 175-6; E. Ruggles-Brise, 28 ff.; M. Davitt, *Leaves from a Prison Diary* (1885), 217 ff.; S. and B. Webb, 220 ff.

[3] The last six 'Imperial' convicts in Western Australia were pardoned in 1906 at the instigation of Alfred Deakin who was then Prime Minister.

failure, government opinion slowly turned against it. If it was in many cases successful in reforming the criminal, at least to the extent of removing him to an environment where he was more likely to be able to live honestly, this was thought less important because of the stress penal reformers placed on a narrow, evangelical religious training, and the fact that so many 'practical' men were indifferent to reform, even if they felt it desirable to pay lip-service to its need. In fact, transportation and assignment was the most effective reformatory punishment that was widely adopted before 1850; but at that time few accepted the principle that the aim of punishment and prison discipline should be reformation rather than the infliction of suffering, and most men would have agreed with Sir James F. Stephen that the 'criminal law is mainly a system of licensed revenge'.

When the need for reformatory training was admitted, as for example by Stanley and Grey, the means adopted for carrying it out were ill-chosen, owing partly to ignorance but still more to a passion for economy. This originally, and accidentally, had assisted reformation by encouraging assignment and the granting of tickets-of-leave, which had dispersed the men and with all their shortcomings provided a way for the criminal to 'work his way back' to normal society; but when assignment was forbidden, economy meant mal-administration. This had always been a defect. Authority was delegated and scattered; in the process, many who were unfitted wielded great power, which they flagrantly misused. This justified the charge that transportation was a lottery; and if this is true of all punishment and not only of assignment, it was not less true in this case, and from the abuses of the system can be marshalled a weighty indictment of it. Here lies the greatest of the difficulties in assessing the transportation system. By what standard can it be judged? Were its shortcomings greater than those to be found in other contemporary punishments, or even in those in force in the United Kingdom in the second, and allegedly more enlightened half of the nineteenth century? How far can the horrors of Norfolk Island be offset by the good training gained in assigned service for an enlightened master? How many convicts worked for enlightened masters? How many for brutes? How many for the more common, rather casual and indifferent? With all these imponderables, while the science of punishment is still hardly existent, and rational treatment of criminals is always disturbed by excited emotional reactions, one can only take refuge in a rather sceptical agnosticism. As a penal system, transportation had both virtues and defects, but when considering its effects on the colonies, one should not forget, as the Australian is apt to do, the important part it played in the evolution of 'secondary punishment' in the United Kingdom. For years it offered what seemed the only alternative to the death penalty, so frequently imposed until about 1830, and although finally abandoned as insufficiently deterrent, it provided an essential means of punishment at a time when the unreformed gaols made long terms of imprisonment virtually impossible.

CONVICT TRANSPORTATION

APPENDIX: The numbers transported

Unfortunately the exact number of convicts who arrived in Australia will never be definitely known, for although many records were kept, they are contradictory and not always accurate. The figures available include returns in the Governor's despatches (CO 201 and 280), returns made to Parliament in 1798, 1810, 1812, 1819 and 1838, later returns in the Van Diemen's Land Controller-General's reports, the colonial Blue Books and to other parliamentary inquiries, the lists prepared by the Home Office (HO 11, for British convicts only), indents, assignments, musters, surgeons' reports, logs, etc. All differ slightly, according to whether they refer to the numbers who embarked, sailed or arrived, and to years of departure or arrival. Sometimes discrepancies appear reconcilable only on the assumption of miscounting, but especially in the early years, some prisoners who embarked were relanded before sailing, without any apparent record being made. C. Bateson, in *Convict Ships* (Glasgow, 1959), compiled valuable and comprehensive tables, but I do not agree with his figures in every instance, and he was not concerned with those convicts who did not come from the United Kingdom. In the list that follows, I have disregarded transfers from one penal colony to another and I have placed the greatest (though by no means exclusive) reliance on the convict indents; but there are still occasions when I have had to guess which is the more likely of contradictory figures, and the grand total may be at least a hundred or so out, even assuming no errors in transcription or arithmetic. However, the casual compiling of the records is shown by the statement of J. T. Campbell, after mustering the prisoners in the *Providence*, in 1811.

'A muster of the convicts per the Ship Providence, Alex^r Barclay Mas^r., (from Cork) having been taken on board ship in Sydney Cove on Thursday the 4th of July 1811, by J. T. Campbell, Secretary, and Wm. Broughton, Acting Commissary, it then appeared that there were two male convicts on board, whose names do not appear in these indents, but who represented themselves in the following manner – namely –
1. "James Nowlan, tried in the County of Kildare on the 14th July 1809" – sentence unknown to him.
2. "Michael Glennan Sawyer aged 25 years, tried in the City of

Dublin"—does not recollect the time of his trial—says he received no sentence, but admits that he had been formerly under sentence for life.

It is here to be remarked that there is the name of James Nowlan mentioned in these Indents, but he is a different person from the above, being stated to have been tried in the City of Dublin in July 1810 and to have received Sentence of Transportation for seven years—and this latter Nowlan has not arrived. The officers of the Providence state that he never came on board, being permitted to enlist in the [?] CO—— of Cork.

'John Sheeheen mentioned in these Indents has arrived but no particulars of his Age, Place or Time of Trial or Sentence being annexed, these particulars are supplied by himself, namely that He is "36 years of age and a labourer that He was tried in the County of Cork on the 29th of Augt 1810 and received sentence of Transportation for seven years"—

'Elenor Doyle a Convict of Providence under similar circumstances . . .

'It is also to be observed that in these indents the name of Hugh McEver [?] aged 34 years tried in Drogheda in March 1810 sentenced 14 years transportation and Anne O'Donnel . . . had each of them a stroke of the Pen drawn along their name . . . and close by the name of the former was written "—? Sent to Cork Jail", and by the latter "sent to Cork Jail . . ."

'NB James Plunkett . . . was not put on board—as vouched by Capt. Barclay.'

No indent was ever sent from Ireland for the *Friendship* (1800) and that for the *Ann* (1801) was not sent until 1819 (*HRA* I, x, 203-4). Both Macquarie, for example on 24 August 1820 (*ib.*, 334) and Arthur, 10 Feb. 1825 (*HRA*, III, iv, 236) complained of faulty indents, as did Darling and Bourke later (5 April and 30 Dec. 1828, 4 Dec. 1829 and 30 Oct. 1834, *HRA* I, xiv, 116 and 565, xv, 155 and xvii, 564).

CONVICTS TRANSPORTED TO AUSTRALIA

Year of Ships' Arrival	Convicts sailed in ships arriving in year specified				Deaths		Convicts arrived from UK				Convicts from other colonies	Remarks
	From GB		From Ireland				in NSW		in VDL			
	M	F	M	F	M	F	M	F	M	F		
1788	568	191			20	3	548	188				First Fleet
1789	–											
1790	953	304			261	16	692	288				Includes Second Fleet
1791	1,736	150	133	22	173	3	1,696	169				Third Fleet
1792	645	135			30	14	610	121				5 escaped from *Pitt*
1793		17	235	70	1		233	87		–		1 executed
1794	24	60					24	60				
1795	1						1					
1796		132	168	70	10	1	158	200				7 convicts died of wounds in mutiny in *Marquis Cornwallis*
1797	203		151	45	30	2	324	43			1	2 males and 66 females sailed in *Lady Shore*, seized by crew
1798	296	96			9	2	287	94			2	
1799	297				94		203					Heavy death-roll in *Hills-borough*

Year of Ships' Arrival	Convicts sailed in ships arriving in year specified				Deaths		Convicts arrived from UK				Convicts from other colonies	Remarks
	From GB		From Ireland				in NSW		in VDL.			
	M	F	M	F	M	F	M	F	M	F		
1800	300	53	304	26	71	3	533	76			16	Includes *Royal Admiral* with heavy death-roll and Irish rebel ships *Minerva* and *Friendship*
1801	382	191	152	24	41	8	493	207				Heavy death-roll in *Hercules* and *Atlas*, Irish rebel ships
1802	251		484	54	106	2	629	52				
1803	578	130	127	37	28	5	383	162	294			*Calcutta* arr. Port Phillip in 1803, moved to VDL, 1804
1804	201	139			1	3	200	136				
1805												
1806	259	48	130	156	9	2	380	202			2	
1807	193	109	11		3	3	204	106				
1808	200	99			3	1	197	98				
1809		141	139	60	5	1	134	200				
1810	399	122			10	1	389	121			2	
1811	200		140	139	3	1	337	138			3	

Year of Ships' Arrival	Convicts sailed in ships arriving in year specified				Deaths		Convicts arrived from UK				Convicts from other colonies to both NSW and VDL	Remarks
	From GB		From Ireland				in NSW		in VDL			
	M	F	M	F	M	F	M	F	M	F		
1812	400	126			2	1	199	125	199		2	US privateer captured *Emu* with 49 females
1813	401		147	54	10		538	54				
1814	706	239	219	98	86	5	839	332			11	Sickness in *General Hewitt* and *Surry*
1815	700	110	214	69	11	8	903	171			9	From 1814 increasing numbers sent out
1816	732	102	370	84	8	4	1,094	182				
1817	1,501	103	320	89	25	3	1,796	189			17	12 shot in *Chapman*. Increasing numbers sent
1818	2,333	227	689	101	29	6	2,845	292	148	60		421 sent to VDL immediately on arrival in Sydney
1819	1,864		842		22		2,372		312		12	Irish Insurrection Act
1820	3,003	268	640	78	13		2,283	296	1,347	50	9	

Year of Ships' Arrival	Convicts sailed in ships arriving in year specified				Deaths		Convicts arrived from UK				Convicts from other colonies to both NSW and VDL	Remarks
	From GB		From Ireland				in NSW		in VDL			
	M	F	M	F	M	F	M	F	M	F		
1821	2,083	103	484	80	14	–	1,528	130	1,023	53	1	Fewer transported 1821–6; Bermuda establishment opened, 1823
1822	1,461	108	852	–	22	1	1,522	62	769	45		
1823	1,579	222	837	97	29	3	1,464	199	923	117	5	
1824	1,368	90	320	109	10	–	1,006	147	672	50	1	
1825	1,342	390	905	113	17	2	1,544	366	686	135		
1826	1,162	100	902	100	14	1	1,558	100	492	99	15	2 escaped
1827	2,225	562	745	161	24	12	2,103	501	843	210	–	
1828	2,625	271	755	274	40	5	2,330	371	1,010	169	11	
1829	2,942	501	1,177	177	45	7	3,151	492	925	179	14	
1830	4,036	363	698	319	47	8	2,766	444	1,921	230	13	Fewer to NSW, following Darling's protests
1831	3,307	549	908	300	36	10	2,300	504	1,879	335	41	
1832	3,054	249	936	283	35	5	2,720	381	1,235	146	20	Amphitrite wrecked, 101 females drowned
1833	5,067	730	813	261	67	24	3,479	636	2,334	331	23	More transported; 'severity' policy

Year of Ships' Arrival	Convicts sailed in ships arriving in year specified				Deaths		Convicts arrived from UK				Convicts from other colonies to both NSW and VDL	Remarks
	From GB		From Ireland				in NSW*		in VDL			
	M	F	M	F	M	F	M	F	M	F		
1834	3,275	435	790	175	40	3	2,658	456	1,367	151	42	George III sunk, 139 males drowned
1835	4,151	477	1,298	151	35	1	3,364	183	1,911	299	27	Neva wrecked, 145 females drowned
1836	4,065	596	970	397	45	10	3,083	668	1,907	315	89	
1837	3,533	350	749	301	61	5	2,815	533	1,406	113	75	20 more males died from scurvy after disembarking from Lord Lyndoch
1838	3,494	456	1,076	162	47	4	2,595	333	1,928	281	73	
1839	2,301	616	376	418	22	6	1,529	727	1,126	301	58	[1] 617 to Norfolk Is.
1840	2,552	397	555	250	31	3	1,992[1]	461	1,084	183	191[2]	[2] includes 141 rebels from Canada
1841	2,324	540	356	269	21	6			2,659	803	38	Waterloo wrecked at Cape; 143 drowned and 3 remained behind
1842	4,085	395	760	288	43	5			4,656	678	8	
1843	2,484	346	563	337	29	24			3,023	654	46	Gibraltar penal establishment opened 1842

*Including Norfolk Island

Year of Ships' Arrival	Convicts sailed in ships arriving in year specified				Deaths		Convicts arrived from UK				Convicts from other colonies to VDL	Remarks
	From GB		From Ireland				in NSW*		in VDL			
	M	F	M	F	M	F	M	F	M	F		
1844	3,337	531	480	120	20	10	650[3]		3,147	641	63	[3] 629 to Norfolk Is., 21 to Port Phillip
1845	2,823	340	200	269	7	2	955[4]		2,061	607	73	[4] 729 to Norfolk Is., 226 to Port Phillip
1846	1,047	340	719	–	28	7	884[5]		854	333	36	[5] 593 to Norfolk Is., 291 to Port Phillip
1847	912	339	–	454	7	7	536[6]		369	676	22	[6] To Port Phillip
1848	979	511	–	144	2	7	455[7]		717[8]	821	92	[7] To Port Phillip; [8] includes 462 from Gibraltar and Bermuda
1849	1,401	317	1,132	566	37	16	1,523[9]		969	867	45	[9] 198 to Port Phillip, 225 to Moreton Bay
1850	1,484	397	883	440	35	12	292[10]		2,040	825	32	[10] To Moreton Bay; WA received 173 English convicts
1851	550	402	898	261	7	4			1,441	659	39	Also 802 to WA
1852	1,450	420	324	384	20	8			1,754	796	22	Also 491 to WA
1853	592	219	590	168	10	4			1,072	383	20	Also 521 British and 583 Irish to WA, which received a further 7,065 convicts between 1854 and 1868

* Including Norfolk Island

SELECT BIBLIOGRAPHY

MANUSCRIPTS, GREAT BRITAIN AND IRELAND

(1) PRO, London:

CO — Despatches to and from various colonies: 201 and 202, NSW; 280 and 408, VDL; 395, North Australia; 18 and 397, Western Australia; 37, 38 and 41, Bermuda; 28 and 29, Barbados; 48 and 49, Cape Colony; 54, Ceylon; 65, Corsica; 91, Gibraltar; 167, Mauritius; 179, Natal; 188, New Brunswick; 217 and 218, Nova Scotia; 318, West Indies; 854, Circular. Also, 323 and 324, General Correspondence; 325, miscellaneous; 206, NSW, miscellaneous; 207, Spt. of Convicts, Entry Books; 284, VDL miscellaneous; Bigge Appendix, 201/118–21, 130, 140–2.

HO — 6, judges' recommendations; 7, on proposed Gambia settlement; 8 and 9, hulk lists; 10, convict papers; 11, transportation registers; 12 and 13, letters on criminal matters; 16, Old Bailey Sessions; 26 and 27, criminal registers; 28 and 29, correspondence with Admiralty; 30 and 35, correspondence with CO; 45, letters and papers; 48, Law Officers' correspondence; 84, criminal law amendment; 100 and 123, Ireland.

BT — 5, minutes.

WO — 17/241 re NSW Corps.

Adm. — 101 surgeons' journals.

Hatton Papers — 30/45/1.

Chatham Papers — 30/8/128, 169, 311, 363.

Russell Papers — 30/22/1–3, 5–7.

(2) British Museum, Add. MSS.:

Bentham Papers — 33546.

Gladstone
Papers   44364, 44735.
Liverpool
Papers   38195, 38223-5.
Newcastle
Papers   33053.
Peel   40195-9, 40315, 40331-2, 40448-9, 40451-2,
Papers   40467, 40571.
Place
Papers   27825-8.
Wellesley's
Irish Corr. 37298-37302.

(3) Public Register Office, Edinburgh:
    Books of Adjournal of the High Court of Judiciary.
    Reports of Criminal Proceedings, 1818-21.

(4) State Paper Office, Dublin:
    Chief Secretary's Letter Books, ser. A; Convict Office Letter
    Books, vii; Convict Papers, 1830-51; Convict Petitions; Con-
    vict Reference Books.
    Official Papers, 508, 560, 569; Rebellion Papers, 620; State of
    the Country Papers, 1796-1831, vi.

(5) County Archives:
    Armagh, County Museum:
    Blacker Autobiography.
    Bedford:
    Gaol and House of Correction Books; Charles Cartwright
    letters; Criminal Statistics (R. Roberts); Olney, Turvey and
    Harrold Assoc. for prosecuting criminals, minute books;
    Whitbread Papers.
    Essex:
    County Sessions Books; Game Law Returns; Indictments;
    Process Books.
    Hertfordshire:
    Sessions Record Books, 8 and 9.
    Lancashire:
    Calendar of Prisoners; Gaol Reports; Order Books; Quarter
    Sessions Minute Books; Transportation Contracts; T. Holden
    Correspondence.

Somerset:
Gaol Registers, Ilchester Gaol, Felon's Register and Description Book; Transportation Contracts.
Warwick:
Quarter Sessions, 1829–31.
Wiltshire:
Fisherton Gaol Book, Statistics of Crime.

(6) Other depositories, England and Ireland:
Belfast, PRO, John Martin, Diary.
Bodleian Library, Clarendon Papers, Irish dep.
Durham University, Grey Papers, Journal and Letters.
National Library, Dublin: W. S. O'Brien Papers; Richmond Papers; Wellesley Papers; Black Rock Assoc. for prosecuting felons, minutes.
Royal Commonwealth Soc., London, Arthur Papers.
West Ham Parish Records, Soc. for Prosecuting Felons, Minute Book.

Manuscripts, Australia

(1) National Library, Canberra:
Lachlan Macquarie, Letters to his brother Charles.
Irish Political Prisoners, Letters.
Van Diemen's Land Co., Annual Reports.

(2) Mitchell Library, Sydney:
(a) Official:
Bench Books: Cawdor and Stonequarry Creek, Dungog, Invermein, Port Stephens; Windsor Police Office, Letter Book.
Col. Sec's. Papers, espec. Carter's Barracks, Convicts, Moreton Bay, Newcastle, Norfolk Island, Police, Port Macquarie, Principal Supt. Convicts; Indents, Petitions, Register of Pardons.
Executive Council, Minutes.
Governors' Minutes and Memorandums.
NSW, Miscellaneous Papers, A664, A668, A2146.
Tasmanian Papers.
(b) Private:
Arthur Papers, A1962, A2161–95, A2214, D292.
Backhouse and Walker, Reports, B706–7.

Berry Papers, 4, 5, 11, 12, 15.
Bingle Papers, A128–30, A1825.
Bonwick Transcripts, Bigge Appendix.
Bourke Papers, 6–14, A1733–41.
Bowman Papers, A1684.
Brisbane Letter Book, A1559.
Duncan Campbell, Letter Books, A3225–30.
W. Campbell Papers, A3587.
T. Cook, an Exile's Lamentations, A1711.
E. J. Eyre, Autobiography, A1806.
Forbes Papers, Mem. on transportation A747, A1381, A1819.
Grey, Cabinet Minutes on transportation, C941.
Hanks, APA, B1165–7.
Hassall Corr., A1677.
Hawdon, Letters, A1329.
Hobler, Diary, C422–8.
P. G. King Papers, Norfolk Island, A1687, C187.
T. J. Lempriere, Diary.
Lang Papers, 1, 6 and 9. A2221, 2226, and 2229.
Macarthur Papers, 1, 4, 15 and 32, A2897, 2900, 2911, 2928.
Marsden Papers, 1 and 7, A1992, 1998.
Parramatta Female Factory Papers, A1813.
Parry Journal, A631 and A p 6.
Proctor, Landsman's Log, B1126.
Riley Papers, A106–111.
Sharpe Papers, A1502 and Journal, B217–8.
E. Deas Thomson Papers, A1531.

(3) Oxley Library, Brisbane:
    Book of Trials, Moreton Bay, 1835–6.
    Medical Records, Moreton Bay, 1829–34.
    Register of Convicts.
    Spicer Journal.

(4) Public Library, Victoria:
    Gipps–La Trobe Corr.
    Police Magistrates' Corr.
    Lonsdale, Letter Book.

(5) Royal Society, Hobart:
    Boyes Diary.

(6) State Archives, Tasmania:
Col. Sec.'s Corr., CSO, 1, 5, 14, 22, 42 (Muster-Master), 43 (Macquarie Harbour), 49 and 76.
Convicts, Principal Supt., Indents, Registers, Conduct Registers, espec. CON 14, 15, 22, 31, 32, 33, 40, 41, 85, 103.
Executive Council, Minute Books.
Governor's Letter Books and Mem., Go 52, 54, 61.
Immigration Papers.
Legislative Council, V & P.
Van Diemen's Land Co., Letter Books.

PARLIAMENTARY PAPERS

1 REPORTS

Year	No. of Paper	Short title, vol. and page
1776		SC on Transportation, CJ, xl, 959.
1778		SC on Hulks, CJ, xxxvi, 926.
1779		SC on Felons, CJ, xxxvii, 306.
1784		SC on Penitentiary Act, CJ, xxxix, 1040.
1785		SC on Transportation, CJ, xl, 954 and 1161.
1798		SC on Finance, 28th report, reprinted, PP 1810 (348) iv, 375.
1808	239	SC on Irish Prisons, ix, 351.
1809	265	*ib.*, vii, 577.
1810–11	199 & 207	SC on Penitentiary Houses, iii, 567 and 691.
1812	306	„ „ „ „ ii, 363.
	341	SC on Transportation, ii, 573.
1813–4	157	SC on State of the Gaols of the City of London, iv, 249.
1813–4	264	Irish Prisons, xiii, 213.
1814–5	37	Mr. A. Graham on Convicts on the Hulks, xi, 207.
	152	SC on King's Bench, Fleet and Marshalsea Prisons, iv, 533.
	473	SC on Mendicity in Metropolis, iii, 231.
1816	431	SC on Gaols, viii, 297.
	479	Disturbances in Ireland, ix, 569.
	510	SC on Police in the Metropolis, v, 1.
	667	SC on Mendicity, v, 391.

Year	No. of Paper	Short title, vol. and page
1817	233 & 484	SC on Police, vii, 1 and 321.
1818	423	*ib.*, 3rd Report, viii, 1.
1819	80	SC on Millbank Penitentiary, xvii, 333.
	579	SC on Gaols, vii, 1.
	585	SC on Criminal Law relating to Capital Punishment, viii, 1.
1822	440	SC on Police of Metropolis, iv, 93.
	448	Commissioner Bigge on the State of the Colony of NSW, xx, 539.
1823	33	*ib.*, on Judicial Establishments of NSW and VDL, x, 515.
	136	*ib.*, on State of Agriculture and Trade in NSW, x, 607.
	260	SC on Game Laws, iv, 107.
	311	Inspector-General of Prisons, on State of the Gaols in Ireland, xvi, 687.
	533	SC on Millbank Penitentiary, v, 403.
	561	SC on the Labouring Poor in Ireland, vi, 331.
1824	205 & 444	SC on Criminal Law, iv, 39 and 349.
	372	SC on Disturbances in Ireland, viii, 1.
1825	129	SC on State of Ireland, viii, 1.
	20 & 200	SC on Districts of Ireland under Insurrection Act, vii, 501.
1826	404	SC on Emigration, iv, 1.
1826–7	237 & 550	,, ,, ,, v, 2 and 223.
	534	SC on Criminal Commitments, vi, 5.
1828	477	Governor Macquarie's Report to Bathurst, xxi, 538.
	533	SC on Police, vi, 1.
	545	SC on Criminal Commitments, vi, 419.
1830	589, 654 & 665	SC on the Poor in Ireland, vii, 173, 451 and 649.
	667	SC on State of Poor in Ireland as exemplified by the Criminal Returns, vii, 1.
1830–1	64	Commissioners Enquiring into Colonial Receipts and Expenditure – NSW, iv, 67.

Year	No. of Paper	Short title, vol. and page
1831	276	SC on Secondary Punishments, vii, 519.
1831-2	547	„ „ „ „ vii, 559.
	677	SC on Disturbed Counties of Ireland, xvi, 1.
1834	593	W. Crawford on Penitentiaries in USA, xlvi, 349.
1835	438-41	HL, SC on the State of the Gaols, xi and xii.
1836	35-42 & 369	Report by Commissioners enquiring into the Condition of the Poorer Classes in Ireland, xxx-xxxiv.
	117	Inspectors, Scottish Prisons, xxxv, 359.
1837	79	Commissioners on Criminal Law (Juveniles), xxxi, 1.
	80	On Proposed Juvenile Prisons at Parkhurst, xlvi, 257.
	451	SC on Metropolitan Police Offences, xii, 509.
	518	SC on Transportation, xix, 1.
1837-8	669	ib., xxii, 1.
	121	Maconochie on Prison Discipline in VDL, xl, 237.
1839	169	Royal Commission on Constabulary, xix, 1.
	486	HL, SC on Ireland, xi and xii.
1843	457	On Prison Discipline, xxv and xxvi.
1845	605-6, 616, 657 672-3	Commissioners inquiring into Occupation of Land in Ireland (Devon Commission), xix-xxii.
1846	463	SC on Game Laws, ix, 1.
1847	149	Supt. of Hulks at Woolwich, xliii, 63.
	447 & 534	SC on Criminal Laws, Juvenile Offenders and Transportation, vii, 1 and 637.
	737	HL, SC on Colonisation from Ireland, vi, 563.
	831	Inquiry into the Hulks at Woolwich, xviii, 1.
1847-8	415 & 593	HL, SC on Colonisation from Ireland, xvii, 1.
1849	86	ib., xi, 485.
1850	632	SC on Prison Discipline, xvii, 1.
	1173	Prison Inspectors, xviii, 1.
	1176	Col. Jebb on Prisons, xxix, 151.
1851	1409 & 1419	Jebb on Convict Prisons, xxviii, 1 and 213.

Year	No. of Paper	Short title, vol. and page
1852	438	SC on Irish Outrages, xiv, 1.
	515	SC on Criminal and Destitute Juveniles, vii, 1.
	1524	Jebb on Convict Prisons, xxiv, 193.
1852–3	1572 & 1659	*ib.*, li, 1 and 247.
1854–5	2004	Jebb. on Substitution of Penal Servitude for Transportation, xxxiii, 729.
1856	244, 296 & 355	SC on Transportation, xvii, 1.
	404	HL, SC on Act substituting other punishments for transportation, xvii, 561.
	1986	Jebb on Convict Prisons, xxv, 33.
1857–8	2414	Jebb on Penal Servitude and transportation, xxix, 285.
1861	286	SC on Transportation, xiii, 505.
1863	499	HL, SC on Gaols and Prison Discipline, ix, 1.
	3190	Royal Commission on Penal Servitude, xxi, 1.

2 CORRESPONDENCE, RETURNS, ETC.

(*a*) Despatches, correspondence and papers re Transportation, Secondary Punishment and Convict Discipline: 1837–8 (309) 42: 15; 1839 (76 and 582) 34: 551 and 38: 741; 1841 (81 and 412) 17: 1 and 349; 1843 (158 and 159) 42: 353 and 451; 1845 (659) 37: 329; 1846 (36 and 402) 29:291; 1847 (785, 800 and 811) 48: 93; 1847–8 (941) 52: 7; 1849 (1022 and 1121) 43: 63; 1850 (1153 and 1285) 45: 11; 1851 (1361 and 1418) 45: 1; 1852 (1517) 46: 183.

(*b*) Correspondence re Convicts at the Cape: 1847 (742) 48: 80; 1849 (217) 43: 1; 1850 (1138 and 104) 38: 223 and 387.

(*c*) Other memorials, etc., on transportation: 1847 (169, 692 and 741) 39: 281 and 453, and 38: 539; 1851 (130 and 280) 45: 437 and 527; 1863 (505) 38: 1.

(*d*) Corr. on emigration: 1839 (536) 39: 371; 1840 (113) 33: 19; 1842 (301) 31: 1.

(*e*) Corr. on recall of Sir J. Eardley Wilmot, 1847 (262 and 400) 38: 513.

(*f*) Returns of criminal commitments, convictions, etc.: 1809 (265) 7: 577; 1810 (47 and 52) 14: 549; 1812 (45) 10: 217; 1813–14 (7–10, 163, 264, 336) 13: 99 ff.; 1814–5 (163) 11: 293; 1816 (269) 8: 365; 1818 (66) 16: 3; 1819 (59) 17: 305; 1821 (400) 21: 481 (620) 22: 159; 1822

(433, 489, 552) 14: 783; 1824 (250 and 174) 22: 153; 1829 (256) 22: 427; 1831–2 (282 and 375) 33: 1; 1833 (45) 29: 47; 1835 (34 and 535) 45: 15 and 345; 1837 (109) 46: 147; and annually thereafter, but see 1840 (252) 33: 355; 1851 (572) 46: 17.

(g) Game Law Returns, 1819 (75) 17: 65; 1820 (216) 12: 253; 1826 (387) 24: 511; 1826–7 (425) 20: 517; 1830–1 (375) 33: 1; 1846 (712) 34: 561.

(h) Reports on hulks, twice yearly from 1816, Millbank Penitentiary, annually from 1817, Irish Prisons from 1823, English and Scottish prisons from 1836, Parkhurst from 1839 and Pentonville from 1843.

(i) Other papers, 1814–5 (37, 170, 326, 331–2, 355) 11: 207; 1816 (366) 8: 295; 1818 (334) 16: 189; 1821 (439) 21: 465 and (557) 14: 199; 1852 (1508) 34: 1.

PUBLISHED RECORDS

Calendars: Home Office Papers, 1760–74; SP, Colonial, and America and West Indies.
HMC, 13th Report, Fortescue MSS. at Dropmore.
Great Britain: Commons Journals, Parl. Debates, Parl. Register.
Hist. MSS. of Tasmania, Reports, 1–5 (Hobart 1964).
Historical Records of Australia.
Historical Records of New South Wales.
Ireland: Commons Journals, Parl. Register.
Maryland, Archives (Maryland Hist. Assoc., Baltimore).
Middlesex, County Records (ed. J. C. Jeaffreson, 1886–92).
NSW, *Acts and Ordinances*, 1827–1844 (ed. T. Callaghan, Sydney, 1844), Legislative Council, V & P.
Old Bailey, Sessions Reports.
VDL, Legislative Council, V & P.

CONTEMPORARY MAGAZINES AND NEWSPAPERS

Magazines, etc.: *Annual Register, Blackwoods, Colonial Mag.* (1840), *Edinburgh Mag., Edinburgh Review, Gentleman's Mag., London Review* (1829), *Quarterly Review, Westminster Review.*
English Newspapers: *Times, Chelmsford Gazette, Colchester Gazette, Hunts., Beds. and Peterborough Gazette and Cambridge and Hertfordshire Independent Press; Hunts., Beds. and Cambridge Weekly Journal, Liverpool Mercury, Manchester Guardian, Morning Chronicle, Salisbury and Wiltshire Herald, Salisbury and Winchester Journal, Taunton Courier.*

Irish: *Belfast News Letter, Cork Advertiser, Dublin Evening Post, Freeman's Journal, Limerick Chronicle, Saunders' News Letter, Southern Reporter.*

NSW: *Australian, Colonist, Monitor, Sydney Gazette, Sydney Herald* (*Sydney Morning Herald* from Aug. 1842).

Port Phillip: *Port Phillip Patriot, Port Phillip Gazette.*

South Australia: *South Australian Register.*

VDL: *Colonial Times, Cornwall Chronicle, Hobart Town Advertiser, Hobart Town Courier, Launceston Advertiser, Murray's Review, Tasmanian, True Colonist.*

SELECT LIST – BOOKS, ARTICLES AND THESES
(Published London, unless otherwise stated. Some
titles have been shortened)

A Barrister, *Old Bailey Experience – Criminal Jurisprudence . . . and an
Essay on Penal Discipline* (1833)

ADDERLEY, C. P., *Transportation not necessary* (1851), *Punishment is
not Education* (1856)

A former Police Officer, *Adventures of Ikey Solomons* (1829)

A late resident (E. EAGAR), *Letters to Sir Robert Peel on the Advantages
of NSW and VDL as Penal Settlements* (1824)

ALLISON, W. R., *Remarks on Transportation* (Launceston, 1847)

ANDERSON, JOSEPH, *Recollections of a Peninsula Veteran* (1913)

ANLEY, CHARLOTTE, *Prisoners of Australia* (1841)

ANON, *Observations on the Expediency of erecting Provincial Penitentiaries in Ireland* (1821) (Halliday Pamphlets, Roy. Irish Acad.,
Dublin)

ANON (? GEORGE BARRINGTON), *Voyage to Botany Bay* (*c.* 1795),
Voyage to New South Wales (Dublin and NY., 1801)

An unpaid magistrate (R. THERRY), *Observations on the 'Hole and
Corner' Petition* (Sydney, 1834)

ARMITAGE, G., *History of the Bow Street Runners, 1729–1829* (1932)

ARTHUR, GEORGE, *Observations upon Secondary Punishment* (Hobart
Town, 1833); (ed.) *Defence of Transportation in reply to the remarks
of the Bishop of Dublin* (London and Hobart, 1835)

A Student of Politics, *Proposals for Preventing the Frequent Execution
and Exportation of Convicts* (1754)

ATKINS, BARBARA, 'Australia's Place in the Swing to the East – an
Addendum', *Hist. Stud.*, viii (1958)

ATKINS, THOMAS, *Wanderings of a Clerical Ulysses* (1859)

ATKINSON, JAMES, *Account of the State of Agriculture and Grazing In
New South Wales* (1826)

ATKINSON, JOSEPH B., *Penal Settlements and their Evils* (1847)

BACKHOUSE, JAMES, *Narrative of a visit to the Australian Colonies*
(1843)

BAR, C. L. VON, *History of Continental Criminal Law* (Eng. trans., 1916)

BARNARD, J., Tasmanian Statistics 1844–53, (Roy. Soc. of Tas.,
Proceedings, iii (1855)

BARNARD, MARJORIE, *Macquarie's World* (MUP, 1949)

BARNES, HARRY E., *Evolution of Penology in Pennsylvania* (Indianapolis, 1927), *History of Penal Reformatory and Correctional Institutions of New Jersey* (Trenton, N.J., 1918)

BARRY, JOHN V., *Alexander Maconachie of Norfolk Island* (MUP, 1958) *Life and Death of John Price* (Melbourne, 1964)

BASSETT, MARNIE, *The Hentys—an Australian Colonial Tapestry* (OUP, 1954)

BATESON, CHARLES, *Convict Ships* (Glasgow, 1959)

BATTYE, J. S., *Western Australia: A history, from its discovery to the Inauguration of the Commonwealth* (OUP., 1924)

BEAUMONT, GUSTAVE DE, and TOCQUEVILLE, ALEXIS DE, *On the Penitentiary System in the United States and its application in France* (trans. F. Lieber, Philadelphia, 1833)

BECCARIA, C., *Essay on Crimes and Punishments* (Eng. trans., 1767)

BELL, K. N., and MORRELL, W. P., *Select Documents on British Colonial Policy, 1830–1860* (1928)

BENNET, HENRY G., *Letter to Viscount Sidmouth* . . . (1819), *Letter to Earl Bathurst* . . . (1820)

BENNETT, J. M., 'Establishment of Jury Trial in N.S.W.', *Sydney Law Review*, 1961.

BENTHAM, JEREMY, *View of the Hard Labour Bill* (1778), *Principles of Penal Law* (1789), *Panopticon on the Inspection House* (1791), *Emancipate your Colonies* (1793), *Panopticon versus New South Wales* (1802), *Plea for a Constitution* (1803), *Works* (ed. J. Bowring, Edinburgh, 1838–42)

BEST, WILLIAM, *Substance of a charge delivered to the Grand Jury of Wiltshire at the Summer Assize, 1827* (1827)

BETTS, T., *Account of the Colony of Van Diemen's Land* (Calcutta, 1830)

BINGLE, JOHN, *Letter to Secretary of State for the Colonies* (Sydney, 1832)

BIRKENHEAD, EARL OF (ed.), *Adventures of Ralph Rashleigh* . . . (1929)

BISCHOFF, J., *Sketch of the History of VDL* (1832)

BLACKSTONE, W., *Commentaries on the Laws of England* (1765–9)

BLAND, WILLIAM, *Letters to Charles Buller, Jr., M.P., from the APA* (Sydney, 1849)

BLANE, GILBERT, *Select Dissertations on* . . . *Medical Science* (1822)

BLOSSEVILLE, E., *Histoire des Colonies Pénales de l'Angleterre dans l'Australie* (Paris, 1831)

BOYES, R. D., *First Years at Port Phillip* (Melbourne, 1935)

BRETON, WILLIAM H., *Excursions in NSW, Western Australia and VDL, 1830–3* (1833)

BRITTANICUS, *An address to the Magistrates and People of Great Britain on the punishment of Transportation and Imprisonment* (1819)

BRITTON, A., *History of New South Wales from the Records* (Sydney, 1894)

BROWN, PHILIP L. (ed.), *Narrative of George Russell* (OUP, 1935)

BROWNING, COLIN A., *The Convict Ship* (1844), *England's Exiles* (1842)

BUNBURY, T., *Reminiscences of a Veteran* (1861)

BURDON, J. A., *The Archives of British Honduras* (1931)

BURN, DAVID, *Visit to Port Arthur* (1842)

BURTON, WILLIAM W., 'State of Society and Crime in N.S.W.', *Col. Mag.*, i, 1840

BUTLER, J. D., 'British Convicts shipped to the American Colonies', *AHR*, ii (1896)

BYRNES, J. V., 'Andrew Thompson, the Outcast Goat' (M.A. thesis, Univ. of Sydney, 1961), 'Andrew Thompson', *JRAHS*, xlvii (1962)

Cambridge History of the British Empire (CUP), ii (1940) and vii a (1933)

CAMPBELL, ENID, 'Prerogative Rule in NSW, 1788–1823', *JRAHS*, l (1964)

CASH, MARTIN, *The Bushranger of Van Diemen's Land—a personal Narrative* (Hobart, 1870)

CHESTERTON, G. L., *Revelations of Prison Life* (1856)

CLARK, C. M. H., *A History of Australia, i, From earliest times to the Age of Macquarie* (MUP, 1962), *Select Documents in Australian History, 1788–1850* (Sydney, 1950), *Sources of Australian History* (World's Classics, 1957)

CLAY, W. L., *The Prison Chaplain—a memoir of the Rev. John Clay* (1861)

COBLEY, JOHN, *The Convicts, 1788–1792* (Sydney, 1965).

COGHLAN, T. A., *Labour and Industry in Australia* (Oxford 1918)

COLLINS, DAVID, *Account of the English Colony in New South Wale* (1798–1802)

COLQUHOUN, PATRICK, *Treatise on the Police of the Metropolis* (1795, 4th and 5th edns., 1797, 7th edn., 1806)

COLSON, A. M., 'Revolt of the Hampshire Agricultural Labourers' (M.A. thesis, Univ. of London, 1937)

CRAVES, W. F., 'The Compulsion of Subjects to Leave the Realm', *LQR*, vi (1890)

CROSS, A. L., 'English Criminal Law and Benefit of Clergy', *AHR*, xxii (1916)

CROWLEY, K., 'Master and Servant in early Australia' (M.A. thesis, Univ. of Melbourne, 1949)

CULLEN, J. H., *Young Ireland in Exile* (Dublin, 1928), 'Bishop Willson and Norfolk Island', *Tas. Hist. Assoc.*, ii (1952)

CUNNINGHAM, PETER, *Two Years in New South Wales* (2nd ed., 1827)

DALLAS, K. M., 'First Settlement in Australia', *Tas. Hist. Assoc.*, iii (1953), 'Transportation and Colonial Income', *Hist. Stud.*, iii (1949)

DALRYMPLE, ALEXANDER, *A Serious Admonition to the Public on the Intended Thief Colony at Botany Bay* (1786; reprinted, ed. G. Mackaness, Australian Hist. Monographs, No. 7, Sydney, 1953)

DARVALL, F. O., *Popular Disturbances and Public Order in Regency England* (OUP, 1934)

DAWSON, W. R. (ed.), *The Banks Letters. A Calendar of the Manuscript Correspondence of Sir Joseph Banks* (London, 1958)

DOUGLAS, D. C. (ed.), *English Historical Documents* (Eyre & Spottiswoode): vol. viii, 1660–1714, ed. A. Browning (1953); vol. ix, American Colonial Documents to 1776, ed. Merrill Jensen (1955); vol. x, 1714–1783, ed. D. B. Horn and M. Ransome (1957); vol. xi, 1783–1832, ed. A. Aspinall and E. Anthony-Smith (1960)

DUCHARMÉ, LEON, *Journal d'un Exile Politique aux Terres Australes* (Montreal, 1845; trans., ed. Mackaness, 1945)

EDEN, F. M., *State of the Poor* (1797)

EDEN, WILLIAM, *Principles of Penal Law* (1771)

ELDERSHAW, PETER, *Guide to the Public Records of Tasmania*, 3 vols. (Hobart, 1957–65).

ELLIS, MALCOLM H., *Lachlan Macquarie, His Life, Adventures and Times* (Sydney, 1947), *John Macarthur* (Sydney, 1955)

Encyclopaedia of the Laws of Scotland, art. 'Criminal Law'.

FIELD, JOHN, *Prison Discipline* (1848)

FIELDING, HENRY, *Inquiry into the Causes of the late Increase of Robbers* (1751)

FIELDING, JOHN, *Account of the Origin and Effects of a Plan of Police* (1753), *Plan for Preventing Robberies within twenty miles of London* (1755), *Extracts from such of the Penal Laws as particularly relate to the Peace and Good Order of the Metropolis* (1768)

FITZHARDINGE, L. F., 'Some First Fleet Reviews', *Hist. Stud.*, ix (1959)

FLETCHER, BRIAN H., 'Development of Small Scale Farming in N.S.W., 1788–1803' (M.A. thesis, Univ. of Sydney, 1962)

FORD, EDWARD, *Life and Work of William Redfern* (Sydney, 1952), *Medical Practice in Early Sydney* (Sydney, 1955).

FOSTER, T. C., *Letters on the Condition of the People of Ireland* (1846)

FROST, JOHN, *Horrors of Convict Life* (Preston, 1856)

FRY, H. P., *Letter to the Householders of Hobartown on effects of Transportation* (1847), *System of Penal Discipline* (1850)

FRY, K., and CRESSWELL, R. E. (ed.), *Memoirs of the Life of Elizabeth Fry with extracts from her Journal and Letters* (1847)

GARDINER, LYNDSAY, 'Eden-Monaro' (M.A. thesis, Camberra Univ. College, 1953)

GASH, NORMAN, *Mr. Secretary Peel* (Longmans, 1961)

GATES, WILLIAM, *Recollections of Life in Van Diemen's Land* (Lockport, 1850)

GEORGE, M. DOROTHY, *London Life in the Eighteenth Century* (LSE reprint, 1951); 'Combination Laws', *Economic Journal*, Supplement, 1927; 'Combination Laws', *Economic Hist. Review*, vi (1935–6)

GILCHRIST, A., *John Dunmore Lang, chiefly autobiographical* (Sydney, 1952)

GOLEBY, ALISON V., 'General Character of the Penal Administration at Moreton Bay, 1824–39' (B.A. thesis, Univ. of Queensland, 1949)

GORDON, DOUGLAS, 'Sickness and Death at the Moreton Bay Convict Settlement', *Medical Journal of Aust.*, Sept. 1963

GREENWOOD, GORDON, *Early American Australian Relations* (MUP 1944)

GREENWOOD, G. and J. LAVERTY, *Brisbane 1859–1959, a History of Local Government* (Brisbane, 1959)

GREY, HENRY (Earl), *Colonial Policy of Lord John Russell's Administration* (1852)

GRIFFITHS, A., *Memorials of Millbank* (1875)

GULLAND, J. A., 'History of the Criminal Law Reforms of the Period of Peel's Home Secretaryship 1822–7' (M.A. thesis, Univ. of London, 1930)

GURNEY, J. J., *Notes on Visits to Some Prisons* (1819)

HAKLUYT, RICHARD (ed. Janet Hampden)–*Voyages and Documents* (World's Classics, 1958)

HANWAY, JONAS, *Defects of Police* (1775)

HARLOW, V. T., *Founding of the Second British Empire, 1763–93* (Longmans, 1952)

HARLOW, V. T., and MADDEN, F., *British Colonial Developments, 1774–1834–Select Documents* (OUP, 1953)

HARRIS, ALEXANDER, *Settlers and Convicts* (1847)

HARRISON, F.–'When the Convicts Came', *Virginia Mag. of Hist. and Biog.*, xxx (1922)

HARTWELL, R. M., *Economic Development of Van Diemen's Land, 1820–1850* (MUP, 1954)

HASLEM, JOHN, *Convict Ships–narrative of a voyage to N.S.W. in 1816* . . . (1819)

HASLUCK, ALEXANDRA, *Unwilling Emigrants* (MUP, 1959)

HENDERSON, JOHN, *Observations on the Colonies of NSW and VDL* (Calcutta, 1832)

HILL, MICHAEL DAVENPORT, *Suggestions for Repression of Crime* . . . (1857)

HOLDSWORTH, WILLIAM S., *History of English Law*, vi, ix, x, xi, xiii (1932, 1938, 1952); 'Reform of the Criminal Law', *LQR*, lvi, 208; 'Judicial Attitude to Criminal Reform', *ib.*, lxv, 195

HOLFORD, GEORGE, *Account of the General Penitentiary at Millbank* . . . (1828), *Short Vindication of the General Penitentiary at Millbank* . . . (1822), *Statements and Observations concerning the Hulks* . . . (1826), *Substance of the Speech* . . . *on* . . . *Transportation* (1815), *Thoughts on the Criminal Prisons* . . . (1821)

HOOPER, F., 'Point Puer' (thesis for M.Ed., Univ. of Melbourne, 1954)

HOWARD, JOHN, *State of the Prisons* . . . (1777, 1780, 1784), *Account of the Principal Lazarettos in Europe* (1791)

HUME, DAVID, *Commentaries on the Laws of Scotland respecting Crimes* (1800)

HUNTER, JOHN, *Governor Hunter's Remarks on the Causes of the Colonial Expense of* . . . *N.S.W.* (1802)

HUTCHINSON, R. C., 'Mrs. Hutchinson and the Female Factories of Early Australia', *Tas. Hist. Assoc.*, xi (1963)

INGLETON, GEOFFREY C., *True Patriots All* (Sydney, 1952)

INNES, FREDERICK M., *Secondary Punishments* (1841)

IVES, GEORGE, *History of Penal Methods* (1914)

JERNEGAN, M. W., *The Laboring and Dependent Classes in Colonial America* (Social Service Monographs, No. 17, Univ. of Chicago Press, 1931)

JOHNSON, W. B., *English Prison Hulks* (1957)

JONES, B. M., *Henry Fielding, Novelist and Magistrate* (1933)

KENNAN, G., *Siberia and the Exile System* (N.Y., 1891)

KERR, M., 'British Parliament and Transportation in the eighteen-fifties', *Hist. Stud.*, vi (1953)

KIERNAN, T. J., *Irish Exiles in Australia* (Dublin 1954), *Transportation from Ireland to Sydney: 1791–1816* (Canberra, 1954)

KING, HAZEL, 'Sir Richard Bourke', *JRAHS*, xlix (1963–4); 'Police Organisation and Administration in the Middle District of New South Wales, 1825–51' (M.A. thesis, Univ. of Sydney, 1956)

KINGSMILL, JOSEPH, *Commonsense View of the Treatment of Criminals . . .* (1850)

LACKLAND, JACOB, *Common-Sense* (Launceston, 1847)

LAMBERT, R. S., *Prince of Pickpockets – a Study of George Barrington* (Faber, 1930)

LANG, JOHN DUNMORE, *Transportation and Colonisation* (1837)

LEMPRIERE, T. J., *Penal Settlement of Van Diemen's Land* (Launceston, Tas., 1954)

LEVY, M. C., *Governor George Arthur, a Colonial Benevolent Despot* (Melbourne, 1953)

LEWIS, GEORGE C., *On Local Disturbances in Ireland* (1836)

LOCKER-LAMPSON, G., *Consideration of the State of Ireland in the nineteenth century* (1907)

LOVELESS, GEORGE, *Victims of Whiggery* (1837)

MACARTHUR, JAMES, *New South Wales, its Present State and Future Prospects* (1837)

MACARTHUR-ONSLOW, S., *Some Early Records of the Macarthurs of Camden* (Sydney, 1914)

MCCORMAC, E. I., *White Servitude in Maryland, 1634–1820* (Johns Hopkins Univ. Press, 1904)

MCCULLOCH, S. C., 'Attempted Penal Reforms at Norfolk Island', *Hist. Stud.*, vii (1957)

MCENCROE, J., 'Norfolk Island, Past and Present, in Six letters on the Penal Administration of four successive Commandants, 1842', *Aust. Catholic Record*, xxxvi (1959)

MACKANESS, GEORGE, *Admiral Arthur Phillip* (Sydney, 1937), *Sir Joseph Banks* (Sydney, 1936), (ed.) *Some Proposals for Establishing Colonies in the South Seas* (Hist. Monog. 6, Sydney, 1943)

MCKAY, ANNE, 'Assignment System of Convict Labour in Van Diemen's Land, 1824–42' (M.A. thesis, Univ. of Tas., 1954)

MACONOCHIE, ALEXANDER, 'Criminal Statistics of Norfolk Island', *Jnl. of Stat. Soc.*, viii (1845); *General Views regarding the Social*

System of Convict Management (Hobart, 1839); Mark System of Prison Discipline (1855); Norfolk Island (1847); Thoughts on Convict Management (Hobart, 1838)

MACQUARIE, LACHLAN, Letter to ... Viscount Sidmouth in Refutation of Statements made by ... Henry Grey Bennet, M.P. ... (1821)

MACQUEEN, POTTER, Australia as she is and as she may be (1840)

MADGWICK, R. B., Immigration into Eastern Australia 1788–1851 (Longmans, 1937)

MANDEVILLE, B., Enquiry into the Causes of the Frequent Executions at Tyburn ... to which is added a Discourse on Transportation ... (1725)

MANNING, H. T., 'Colonial Policy of Whig Ministers, 1830–7', Can. Hist. Rev., xxiii (1952)

MANSFIELD, R., Analytical View of the Census (Sydney, 1841)

MARTIN, A. M., Statistics of the Colonies of the British Empire (1839)

MAYHEW, HENRY, London Labour and London Poor (1851)

MAYHEW, H., and BINNEY, C., Criminal Prisons of London (1862)

MELBOURNE, A. C. V., Early Constitutional History of Australia – New South Wales, 1788–1856 (OUP, 1934)

MELLISH, —, 'Convict Recollections of N.S.W.', London Mag., ii (1825)

MELVILLE, HENRY, History of VDL from the year 1824 to 1835 ... (Hobart, 1835, reprint, ed. Mackaness, Sydney, 1959), Present State of Australasia ... with remarks on Prison Discipline (1851)

MELVILLE, R. L., Life and Work of Sir John Fielding (1934)

MEREDITH, GEORGE, Correspondence between the Local Government of Van Diemen's Land and George Meredith, Esq. (Hobart, 1836)

MERIVALE, HERMAN, Colonisation and Colonies, lectures at the University of Oxford, 1839–41 (LSE reprint, 1928)

MILL, JAMES, Arts.: Government, Jurisprudence, Prisons, Colonies, Prison Discipline, Encyclopaedia Britannica (5th edn., 1820)

MILLER, E. MORRIS, Pressmen and Governors (Sydney, 1952)

MILLER, LINUS B., Notes of an Exile to VDL ... (Freedonia, N.Y., 1846)

MIREHOURSE, J., Crime and its Causes with Observations on Sir John Eardley-Wilmot's Bill (1840)

MITCHEL, JOHN, Jail Journal (Dublin, n.d.)

MONTAGU, JOHN, Statistical Returns of Van Diemen's Land, 1824–36 (Hobart 1836)

MORRELL, W. P., British Colonial Policy in the Age of Peel and Russell (1930)

MORRIS, J. R., 'Early Convict History of Maria Island', *Tas. Hist. Assoc.*, xi (1964)

MORRIS, RICHARD B., *Government and Labour in Early America* (Columbia Univ. Press, N.Y., 1946)

MORTLOCK, J. F., *Experiences of a Convict* (1865, reprinted, ed. G. Wilkes and A. G. Mitchell, SUP, 1965)

MUDIE, JAMES, *Felonry of New South Wales* (1837), *Vindication of his Conduct* (Sydney, 1834)

NEILD, J. C., *State of the Prisons* (1812) (reprinted from *Gentleman's Mag.*, 1804)

New South Wales from the Records, i, 1783-89, ed. G. Barton; ii, 1789-94, ed. A. Britton (Sydney, 1889 and 1894)

NICOL, JOHN, *Life and Adventures of John Nicol Mariner* (1822)

NUTTING, HELEN, 'The Most Wholesome Law–the Habeas Corpus Act of 1679', *AHR*, lxv (1960)

O'BRIEN, ERIS, *Foundation of Australia* (2nd ed., Sydney, 1950)

OLDHAM, TREVOR, 'The Administration of the System of the Transportation of British Convicts, 1763-1793' (Ph.D. thesis, Univ. of London, 1933; copy in Aust. National Library, Canberra)

PARKER, H. W., *Van Diemen's Land, its Rise, Progress and Present State* (1834)

PAUL, GEORGE O., *Considerations on Defects of prisons* (1784)

PAYNE, H. S., 'Statistical Study of Female Convicts in Tasmania, 1843-1853', *Tas. Hist. Assoc.*, ix (1961)

PHILLIPS, MARION, *A Colonial Autocracy* (London, 1909)

PHILLIPSON, C., *Three Criminal Law Reformers: Beccaria, Bentham, Romilly* (Dent, 1923)

PIKE, DOUGLAS, *Paradise of Dissent* (Adelaide, 1957)

POCOCK, Z. P., *Transportation and Convict Discipline* . . . (1847)

PRETYMAN, E. R., 'Macquarie Harbour Penal Settlement and its first Missionaries', *Tas. Hist. Assoc.*, i (1952)

PRIEUR, FRANÇOIS X., *Notes of a Convict of 1838* (Sydney, 1949)

QUENNELL, PETER (ed.), *London's Underworld* (1950), *Mayhew's Characters* (1951)

RADZINOWICZ, L., *History of English Criminal Law* (CUP, 1948-56)

RADZINOWICZ, L., and TURNER (ed.)–*Modern Approach to Criminal Law* (English Studies in Criminal Science, 1945)

RAYNER, J. L., and CROOK, G. T., *Complete Newgate Calendar* (Navarre Soc., 1926)

REESE, TREVOR, 'Origins of Colonial America and N.S.W.', *Australian Journal of Politics and History*, vii, (1961)

REID, THOMAS, *Two Voyages to NSW and VDL* (1822)

ROBSON, L. L., 'Origin and Character of Convicts transported to NSW and VDL, 1787–1852' (Ph.D. thesis, ANU, 1963); 'Origin of Women Convicts . . .', *Hist. Stud.*, xi (1963); 'Male Convicts transported to VDL, 1841–53', *Tas. Hist. Assoc.*, ix (1961); *The Convict Settlers of Australia* (MUP 1965)

RODERICK, COLIN, *John Knatchbull, from Quarter-deck to Gallows* (Sydney, 1963); *ib.* (ed.), *Adventures of Ralph Rashleigh, a penal exile in Australia* (Sydney, 1955)

ROE, MICHAEL, 'Administration of P. G. King' (M.A. thesis, Univ. of Melbourne, 1953); 'Australia's Place in the Swing to the East', 1788–1810, *Hist. Stud.*, viii (1958); 'Colonial Society in Embryo', *ib.*, vii (1956)

ROGERS, T., *Correspondence relating to the Dismissal of the Rev. T. Rogers from his Chaplaincy at Norfolk Island and Review of Dr. Hampton's First Report* (Launceston, 1849)

ROMILLY, SAMUEL, *Speeches of Sir Samuel Romilly . . .* (1820), *Memoirs of the Life of Sir Samuel Romilly . . .* (3rd edn., 1842)

ROSS, JAMES, *VDL Annual and Hobart Town Almanack*, including an Essay on Prison Discipline (Hobart, 1833); *ib*, including a Letter to Archbishop Whately (Hobart, 1835)

RUDÉ, GEORGE, 'Study of Popular Disturbances', *Hist. Stud.*, x (1963); 'Captain Swing and VDL', *Tas. Hist. Assoc.*, xii (1964)

SCOTT, ERNEST, 'Resistance to Transportation in Victoria', *Vic. Hist. Mag.*, i (1911); 'Canadian and U.S. Transported Prisoners of 1839', *JRAHS*, xxi (1936)

SCROPE, G. POULETT, *How is Ireland to be Governed? An address to the new administration of Lord Melbourne in 1834* (1846)

SHAW, A. G. L., 'Missing Land Grants in New South Wales', *Hist. Stud.*, v (1952); 'The Origins of the Probation System', *ib.*, vi (1953); 'Transportation from Ireland', review art., *ib.*, vii (1955); 'Sir John Eardley Wilmot in Tasmania', *Tas. Hist. Soc.*, xi (1965)

SIMPSON, H. B., 'Penal Servitude, its Past and Future', *LQR*, xv (1899)

SMITH, A. E., *Colonists in Bondage, White Servitude and Convict Labor in America*, 1607–1776 (Univ. of North Carolina Press, 1947); 'The Transportation of Convicts to the American Colonies in the Seventeenth Century', *AHR*, xxxix (1954)

SMITH, SYDNEY, *Works* (1878), ii

Society for the Improvement of Prison Discipline, *Reports*, 1822 ff.

STEPHEN, JAMES F., *History of the Criminal Law* (3 vols., 1883)

SYME, J., *Nine Years in Van Diemen's Land* (Dundee, 1848)

TAYLOR, E. R. G., *The Original Writings and Correspondence of the two Richard Hakluyts* (Hakluyt Soc., 1935)

TENCH, WATKIN, *Narrative of the Expedition to Botany Bay* (1789), *Complete Account of the Settlement at Port Jackson* (1793), (ed. L. Fitzhardinge) *Sydney's First Four Years* (Sydney, 1961–a reprint of the above)

THERRY, ROGER, *Reminiscences of Thirty Years Residence . . .* (1863)

TOWNSLEY, W. A., *Struggle for self-government in Tasmania* (Hobart, 1951)

TRUSLER, JOHN, *London Adviser and Guide* (1790)

ULLATHORNE, W., *Horrors of Transportation* (1837), *Memoir of Bishop Willson* (1887)

VAUX, JAMES HARDY, *Memoirs* (1819; ed. N. McLachlan, 1964)

WAKEFIELD, E., *Account of Ireland, Statistical and Political* (Dublin, 1812)

WAKEFIELD, EDWARD GIBBON, *Facts relating to the Punishment of Death in the Metropolis* (1831)

WALSH, G. P., 'English Colony in NSW, 1803', *New Zealand Geographer*, xviii (1962)

WARD, JOHN M., *British Policy in the South Pacific* (Sydney, 1948), *Earl Grey and the Australian Colonies–1846–57* (Melbourne 1958)

WARD, R., and MACNAB, K., 'Nature and Nurture in the First Generation of Native Born Australians', *Hist. Stud.*, x (1962)

WARUNG, PRICE (ASTLEY, WILLIAM), *Tales of the Convict System* (Sydney, 1892), *Tales of the Early Days* (Melbourne, 1894), *Tales of the Old Regime* (Melbourne, 1897), *Tales of the Isle of Death* (Melbourne, 1898), *Convict Days* (Sydney, 1960)

WATLING, T., *Letters from an Exile at Botany Bay* (1794, reprinted, ed. George Mackaness, Sydney, 1945)

WAUGH, D., *Three Years Practical Experience of a Settler in New South Wales . . .* (1838)

WEBB, RICHARD, *Charge to Limerick Grand Jury* (1831, Halliday Pamphlets, Roy. Irish Acad., 1509)

WEBB, SIDNEY and BEATRICE, *English Prisons under Local Government*, with Preface by George Bernard Shaw (1922); *Statutory Authorities for Special Purposes* (1922)

WENTWORTH, W. C., *A Statistical Account of the British Settlements in Australasia* (3rd edn., London, 1824)

WEST, JOHN, *History of Tasmania* (Launceston, 1852)

WESTERN, C. C., *Remarks on Prison Discipline* (1821)

WHATELY, RICHARD, *Thoughts on Secondary Punishment in a Letter to Earl Grey* (1832), *Remarks on Transportation* (1834)

WILMOT, JOHN EARDLEY, *Letter to the Magistrates on the Increase of Crime* (1827)

WILSON, JAMES M., *Statistics of Crime in Ireland, 1842–56* (Dublin, 1857)

WILSON, T. B., Narrative of a Voyage round the World (1835)

WOOD, G. A., 'Convicts', *JRAHS*, viii (1922)

WRAXALL, SIR NATHANIEL, *A Short Review of the Political State of Great Britain* (8th edn., 1787)

YOUNG, GEORGE, *Young of Formosa* (1928)

YOUNG, L. G., 'New South Wales under the Administration of Governor Bourke, 1831–7' (M.A. thesis, Univ. of Sydney, 1951)

Index